Mushrooms of the Gulf Coast States

NUMBER SEVENTY

The Corrie Herring Hooks Series

Mushrooms of the Gulf Coast States

A Field Guide to
Texas, Louisiana,
Mississippi,
Alabama, and
Florida

ALAN E. BESSETTE
ARLEEN R. BESSETTE
DAVID P. LEWIS

UNIVERSITY OF TEXAS PRESS
Austin

Publisher's Notice
Although this book includes information regarding the edibility of various mushrooms, it is *not* intended to function as a manual for the safe consumption of wild mushrooms. Readers interested in consuming wild fungi should consult other sources of information, especially experienced mycophagists, mycologists, or literary sources, before eating any wild mushroom. Neither the authors nor the publisher is responsible for any misidentifications, adverse reactions, or allergic responses that may occur from the consumption of wild mushrooms.

Requests for permission to reproduce material from this work should be sent to:
Permissions
University of Texas Press
P.O. Box 7819
Austin, TX 78713-7819
utpress.utexas.edu/rp-form

Library of Congress Cataloging-in-Publication Data

Names: Bessette, Alan, author. | Bessette, Arleen R., author. | Lewis, David P., 1946– author.
Title: Mushrooms of the Gulf Coast States : a field guide to Texas, Louisiana, Mississippi, Alabama, and Florida / Alan E. Bessette, Arleen R. Bessette, and David P. Lewis.
Description: First edition. | Austin : University of Texas Press, 2019. | Includes bibliographical references and index.
Identifiers: LCCN 2018032179 | ISBN 978-1-4773-1815-7 (pbk. : alk. paper) | ISBN 978-1-4773-1816-4 (library e-book) | ISBN 978-1-4773-1817-1 (nonlibrary e-book)
Subjects: LCSH: Mushrooms—Gulf States. | Mushrooms—Texas. | Mushrooms—Louisiana. | Mushrooms—Mississippi. | Mushrooms—Alabama. | Mushrooms—Florida.
Classification: LCC QK605.5.G85 B47 2019 | DDC 579.6—dc23
LC record available at https://lccn.loc.gov/2018032179

doi:10.7560/318157

Page ii: Lucas Dulaney with Amanitas
Page v: Robert S. Williams, 1939–2014

Robert S. Williams
1939–2014

This book is dedicated to Robert S. Williams, in appreciation for his forty years of study and documentation of fungi—particularly those of Florida and the Gulf States. Working independently, he self-published "*Lactarius* on the Gulf Coastal Plain," keys to the genera *Gymnopilus*, *Entoloma*, and *Hygrophorus*, and a key to Florida boletes. At the time of his death, he was in the process of writing "A Field Guide to the Mushrooms of Southwest Florida."
A long-standing member of the Gulf States Mycological Society and a lifetime member of the North American Mycological Association, Robert generously shared his enthusiasm and knowledge with all of us lucky enough to have known him.

Contents

Preface

THE GULF COAST STATES OF TEXAS, Louisiana, Mississippi, Alabama, and Florida comprise bioregions that support an almost unimaginable amount of mycological diversity. Starting in the western mountains of Texas, this area encompasses hill country, plains, and lake regions. It reaches down and across to the sandy oak and pine woods and the maritime forests of the Gulf Coastal Plain and barrier islands, to the swamps and marshlands of the Atlantic Coastal Plain. With an estimated eight to ten thousand mushroom species occurring in Texas alone (and just over 1,300 species collected and documented at the date of this printing), it is impossible to imagine, much less describe, every species, variety, or fungal form that may be encountered in this area.

Mycologically, the Gulf Coast States are basically uncharted. There are only three books exclusively dedicated to any of its five states: *Mushrooms of Mississippi: And Other Fungi and Protists* (2000), by Dr. George H. Dukes Jr.; *Common Florida Mushrooms* (2000), by Dr. James W. Kimbrough; and *Texas Mushrooms: A Field Guide* ([1992] 2013), by Susan Metzler, Van Metzler, and Dr. Orson K. Miller Jr. (scientific advisor). It can be a

notoriously difficult area to collect fungi in. Most of it is humid and subtropical (except for the southwestern tip of Florida, which boasts a tropical designation), and it is filled with the hindrances that thrive in such a simultaneously lush and harsh climate: snakes and other reptiles; stinging, biting, and blood-sucking insects and arthropods; intrusive mammals, such as wild hogs; high temperatures; and often unexpected and violent storms. Fungi fruit, mature, and decay in days, making correct timing imperative. A profusion of plants can make access to some areas frustrating, while commercial and residential development makes access to others impossible.

The present book is by no means a complete account of the mycoflora found in this geographically, biologically, and socially complex area. Our primary objective is to provide a current, comprehensive guide for some of the more commonly collected mushrooms of the Gulf Coast States, as well as a reference for some of the more unusual or less often encountered fungi found here. We hope to give our readers a base from which to begin exploring the mycological uniqueness of this most beautiful area. What will you discover?

Acknowledgments

THIS BOOK IS VERY MUCH LIKE THE FUNGI described within it: it is the fertile culmination of our relationship with a vast network of friends and colleagues. Ideas, knowledge, hypotheses, imagery, and more were all shared across distance and time, making possible something the three of us could not have accomplished alone. Thanks to all the individuals named below for being a part of the process. If we have failed to mention anybody, the fault is entirely ours and we offer our apologies.

Jason Bolin, Hal Burdsall, Todd Elliott, Roy Halling, Emma Harrower, Mike Hopping, Otto Miettinen, Greg Mueller, Alija Mujic, Bill Neill, Ron Petersen, John Plischke III, Jack Rogers, Bill Roody, Leif Ryvarden, Matt Schink, Matt Smith, and Rod Tulloss shared their technical knowledge and mycological expertise, assisted with mycological notes and species identification, or reviewed portions of the manuscript and offered valuable suggestions for its improvement.

Sarah Prentice, of the University of Florida Marston Science Library, Gainesville, Florida, provided access to numerous publications that improved the accuracy and thoroughness of our species descriptions. Penny Clark and Charlotte Holliman, of the Lamar University Special Collections, Beaumont, Texas, made available the use of the late William Cibula's and Dan Guravich's mushroom slide collections.

For assisting with specimen collecting, sharing their "secret spots," and contributing to the expanding knowledge of Gulf States fungi, heartfelt appreciation goes to: Jamie Bolin, Jason Bolin, David Borland, Bart Buyck, Jay Justice, Laurel Kaminsky, Juan Luis Mata, Rob Miller, Clark Ovrebo, and all the visiting and residential mycologists and members—past and present—of both the Gulf States Mycological Society and the Texas Mycological Society. Thanks also to Jamie Bolin for graciously agreeing to model the cowl knitted with mushroom dyed wool, and to Robert and Lucas Dulaney for allowing us to use the picture of Lucas as our frontispiece.

For being in the right place at the perfect moment and documenting it with their outstanding photography, we thank: Jason Bolin, Eric Bush, Jimmy Craine, Neil Dollinger, Tim Geho, Rosanne Healy, Mike Hopping, Jesús

Garcia Jiménez, Laurel Kaminsky, Renée Lebeuf, Joe Liggio, Taylor Lockwood, Jim Murray, Beatriz Ortiz-Santana, Sarah Prentice, Bill Roody, Mary Smiley, Matt Smith, Walt Sturgeon, Christian Schwarz, and Tom Taroni for the use of their images.

Special gratitude to Rosemary Williams who shared and allowed the use of extensive field notes, mushroom descriptions, and photographs of her husband, the late Robert S. Williams. Thanks also to Patricia Lewis for her help in collecting specimens, editing parts of the manuscript, testing the edibility of many species, and providing support and encouragement throughout the writing of this book.

Matt Smith gifted us with his precious time by reviewing the manuscript. His insightful questions, valuable suggestions, and shared knowledge and experience enabled us to add a level of depth and breadth to this book that would have been impossible without his input.

It goes without saying that this work would not have been possible without the support and guidance of our editor, Casey Kittrell, and all the staff at the University of Texas Press. Thanks again for taking on another of our fungal fantasies and turning it into a reality.

Mushrooms of the Gulf Coast States

Introduction

Geographic Area Covered by This Book

This book describes and illustrates macrofungi found in the Gulf Coast States, from Texas across to, and including, Florida. It is also a useful resource and reference guide for the north central and northeast portions of Mexico, for the Atlantic Coastal Plain of Georgia, South Carolina, North Carolina, and Virginia, and adjacent geographic areas as indicated on the map below.

Why Collect and Study Wild Mushrooms?

When you ask people why they collect and study wild mushrooms, you are likely to get a variety of answers. By far, the most popular response is collecting wild mushrooms to eat. Outdoor enthusiasts appreciate their beauty and diversity, while others enjoy photographing them. Mushrooms are used to make

jewelry, paper, and paint and to dye wool, silk, and other fibers. In recent years, there has also been a growing interest in ethnomycology: the study of human-fungal interactions, which includes researching not only the importance of fungi as food but also their medicinal qualities, their historical use in religious rituals, and their exciting new uses in biotechnology. Perhaps the most important reason to be involved in the world of mycology is to increase our knowledge and appreciation of the vital role fungi play in the very health and well-being of our planet.

Mushroom Structure and Function

Mushrooms belong to the Kingdom Fungi. Until about 1960, they were classified as plants. However, plants and fungi have some significant differences that separate them. Two notable differences are that fungi have chitin in their cell walls while plants do not, and

Geographic area covered by this book

fungi lack chlorophyll and cannot produce food for themselves. They obtain nutrients by external digestion and absorption. One group, the decomposers (**saprotrophs**), extract what they need from dead and decaying matter. Another group (**parasites**) attacks living plants, animals, or other fungi to supply their needs. A third group of fungi establishes a mutually beneficial relationship with living trees or other vascular plants. Called a **mycorrhizal** relationship, the participating partners obtain a portion of the nutrients and water that they need from each other.

A mushroom is a **fruitbody** that arises from a larger fungal organism, much like an apple is the fruitbody of an apple tree. The fungal organism, called the **mycelium**, is a vast network of fine filaments called **hyphae** that are interconnected and interwoven. It is usually concealed in the soil or within decaying wood or in other fungal substrates, such as mulch, leaves, or dung. When conditions are correct—proper temperature, moisture, nutrients, pH, daylight length, and so on—this living network gives rise to a fruitbody, the mushroom, that produces microscopic reproductive structures known as **spores**. If carefully done, picking a mushroom has no more of a negative ecological impact than picking a piece of fruit from a tree.

From a strict or narrow perspective, a mushroom is a fleshy fruitbody that has a cap, stalk, and gills. However, when broadly applied, mushrooms include fungi with many different shapes, sizes, fertile surfaces, and support structures. These are arranged in sections as described and illustrated in the "Color Key to the Major Groups of Fungi" (p. 8). The **fertile surface**, or specific portion of a mushroom on which spores are produced, may take the form of gills, tubes, spines, branches, or other surfaces.

In a mycorrhizal relationship, fungal mycelium is united with the root system of trees and other vascular plants in a partnership that provides otherwise inaccessible moisture and nutrients. The fungal partner in a mycorrhizal relationship increases the host plant's ability to obtain water and nutrients, including nitrogen, phosphorus, and potassium. In turn, the host plant gives the fungus carbohydrates, vitamins, and other nutrients essential for its growth. Because of this partnership, the growth of the host plant is accelerated. Additionally, plants in a mycorrhizal relationship tend to resist diseases much better than those without a fungal partner. Some mushrooms form mycorrhiza only with conifers, others only with hardwood trees, while others may have more than one mycorrhizal partner.

Two major types of mycorrhizal relationships are commonly found in association with trees and other vascular plants: **endomycorrhizae** and **ectomycorrhizae**. In an endomycorrhizal relationship, the fungal partner forms highly branched processes called **arbuscules** between the cell wall and the plasma membrane of the host plant root cells. In an ectomycorrhizal relationship, the hyphae of the fungal partner surround the lateral roots of the plant partner and form an extensive layer called a fungal sheath or mantle. The hyphae form what is called a **Hartig net** by entering the first few layers of the root and growing between—but not penetrating—the outer cortical cells. Most of the mycorrhizal mushrooms described in this book form ectomycorrhizal relationships. The vast majority of endomycorrhizal fungi are microscopic and, with rare exceptions, do not form a visible fruitbody.

Fungal mycelium in soil is widespread, allowing the formation of complex, diffuse mycorrhizal networks. For instance, two or more plants of the same or different species may be linked by the continuous mycelium of one or more fungal species. This integration of multiple fungal and plant species allows interaction, feedback, and adaptation which influences the growth, health, behavior, and survival of the species linked together in this way. Evidence now suggests that plants and fungi in these mycorrhizal networks communicate by biochemical signaling (Babikova et al. 2013), and the biodiversity and overall health of our forests are directly related to this mutually beneficial relationship.

Collecting and Documenting Wild Mushrooms

Recommended equipment for collecting mushrooms is neither expensive nor complicated. The basic items include a basket or rigid-sided container for carrying your specimens; a sturdy knife for digging, cutting, and cleaning; and waxed paper, brown paper lunch bags, or waxed paper sandwich bags for wrapping the mushrooms. We also find the following to be very useful: insect repellant, a walking stick, a compass or GPS tracker, cell phone, camera, trail maps, a whistle (voices do not carry well in forests), a pen or pencil and paper for taking field notes (or phone recorder), water, and a snack (unless bears are a possibility).

Dress appropriately for local weather conditions and the terrain where you will be collecting. Carry an awareness of possible encounters with wildlife and various arthropods: wild boars, snakes, alligators, ticks, chiggers, fire ants, spiders, and scorpions are common in some areas of the Gulf Coast States. Be mindful and use care when collecting. A walking stick is often useful to push and move aside brush and branches and to remove spiderwebs from your path before walking

face-first into them. Whenever possible, collect with a friend or, at the very least, be sure to tell someone where you are going.

Collecting methods vary depending on whether you are collecting for identification purposes or collecting for the table. When gathering known mushrooms for eating, see appendix C, "Mushrooms for the Table" (p. 571). When gathering unknown mushrooms for identification, it is important to collect entire specimens in various stages of development. This includes parts of the mushroom that may be partially buried. Carefully dig up specimens using a sturdy knife. Do not pull them up or cut them off at the base.

Once collected, it is important to keep your mushrooms in good condition to make sure key identifying features are not lost or damaged. Wrapping collections of a single species together in waxed paper or in brown paper sandwich bags is the most commonly recommended technique. This prevents different species from becoming mixed together, minimizes the loss of—or damage to—key features, and keeps specimens fresher by allowing moisture to escape and slowing down decay. Plastic wrap or plastic bags, on

Cowl knitted using mushroom-dyed wool

the other hand, speed up decay by retaining moisture. Do not collect every mushroom you find. Leave a few specimens in the field to help ensure continued spore dispersal.

Be aware of regulations and possible restrictions about collecting in state parks, national parks, on state lands, in conservation areas, and in other posted areas. Do not collect on private property without first obtaining permission. Finally, and maybe most importantly, collect gently. Disturb the substrate and the habitat as little as possible. In this way, you minimize damage to the mycelium and help ensure continued fungal growth, while leaving the area unspoiled for others to enjoy.

Take notes about *where* the mushrooms were growing (the substrate, location, and nearby tree species), *when* you collected them (month and date), and *how* they were growing (solitary, scattered, or in groups or clusters). You might want to taste and smell the mushroom you collected and add your observations to your notes. The taste, odor, and color of a mushroom's flesh are important features used in identifying specimens. If you choose to taste a mushroom, *be advised that some mushrooms taste hot and peppery and may irritate, burn, or numb your mouth if they are chewed for an extended period. However, you cannot be poisoned, and there is no significant risk, if you do not swallow the tissue.* To safely taste a mushroom (even poisonous ones), place a small piece onto the tip of your tongue, chew it with your front teeth for a few seconds, and then spit it out. If the taste is mild (not bitter or peppery), wait a minute and then chew a second small piece for fifteen to thirty seconds and again spit it out. Some mushrooms develop bitter or acrid tastes slowly, or the taste may be subtle. Wrap your field notes with your collections for future reference.

Taking one or more photographs of a mushroom in its natural habitat is also an excellent way to document its features. Specimens may undergo color changes and appear quite different several hours after being collected. Placing mushrooms in an air-conditioned environment or in the refrigerator may significantly alter their appearance. A documentary photograph showing various growth stages of a mushroom, as well as all its parts—including cap, entire stalk with its intact base, a cut specimen showing the cap and stalk flesh, gills or pore surface, and the presence or absence of any staining reactions—provides valuable information that greatly helps with identification, especially when identifying specimens several hours after they were collected.

Making a Spore Print

Sometimes prominent macroscopic field characteristics are not enough to identify wild mushrooms. Spore prints often bridge the gap between macroscopic and microscopic features and therefore can be an essential step in the identification process. Formed when mushroom spores drop undisturbed onto a surface, they are most helpful when working with boletes or gilled mushrooms and are sometimes useful when studying polypores, coral mushrooms, or other fungi.

Spore prints are simple to make. Cut the cap from the stalk, place it gill- or pore-side down on a piece of clean white paper, cover it with a cup or bowl to protect it from drafts, and leave it undisturbed for several hours or overnight. If you wish to save your specimen for further study or depositing into an herbarium, do not cut the stalk from the cap. Instead, cut an "X" in a stiff piece of paper,

 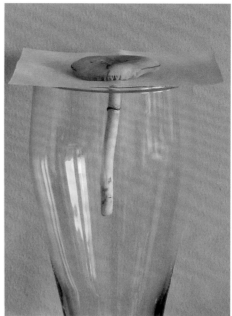

Making a spore print

insert the mushroom stalk through it so the fertile surface rests just above the paper, and suspend this over a glass that is tall enough to accommodate the length of the stalk (see photo). Dark spore prints on white paper are easy to see, while white or pale colored spore prints may require holding the paper at an angle to a bright light source. Clear glass is a useful alternative to paper: the spore deposit left on the glass can be held against light and dark backgrounds to determine its color. Aluminum foil, clear plastic, and half-white/half-black paper are also good choices. Wrapping mushroom caps in a piece of white paper while collecting in the field often provides a ready-made spore print to work with once you get home.

Notes on the Descriptions of Illustrated Species

With few exceptions, each fully described species consists of the following components:

Scientific name: The Latin binomial, or scientific name, is provided for each species. Some of the species names included in this book are currently based on European collections and, following future molecular analysis, may eventually be given new species names. The names we use may not be the same names found in other field guides because of recent taxonomic changes. We use currently accepted names based on those listed in either Index Fungorum (www.indexfungorum.org) and/or MycoBank (www.mycobank.org/).

Every mushroom species name consists of two parts. The first part is the genus, the first letter of which is always capitalized. The second part is the epithet, or species name, with all letters in lower case. Immediately following the scientific name is the author citation, which indicates the name of the individual(s) credited for first describing or subsequently renaming the mushroom. The author citation may be simple. For example, the entry "*Agaricus alachuanus* Murrill" indicates that this species was described and named by William Murrill. When the original author's name is enclosed in parentheses and followed by the name of one or more additional authors, it indicates who later reclassified the species. For example, "*Gymnopus biformis* (Peck) Halling" was originally described by Charles Peck as *Marasmius biformis* and later transferred to the genus *Gymnopus* by Roy Halling.

Synonyms: Former names assigned to a species are listed here. We also include the author citations for these names. Whenever synonyms are provided (including within the text), each is preceded by an equal sign. Not all synonyms, including some of the basionyms (original names), are provided for every species. In some cases, there are too many to list (sometimes more than twenty former names!) and/or some synonyms are not commonly used, or they are not included in other current reference guides.

Common name: One or more common names are listed when available. Resources for these names include other field guides and internet sites.

Macroscopic features: Information about the appearance of the mushroom, including size, shape, color, and staining reactions, is described here. Additional information including the odor and taste of the flesh is also included.

Spore print: Color shade and ranges are included in this section. Vital information for using portions of the keys to boletes and gilled mushrooms require this information.

Microscopic features: Although the descriptions in this book emphasize macroscopic features, we have provided microscopic information, including spore size, shapes, surface features, and color, for those who own or have access to a microscope. Additional microscopic information for structures such as asci, cystidia, paraphyses, and setae is included when it is useful for the identification of specific species.

Occurrence: The habit, substrate, habitat, and fruiting periods are described here. Mushrooms may appear outside of the stated fruiting period because of unusual weather conditions, incomplete understanding of particular species, the effects of climate change, or (as our friend Bill Yule often states) "mushrooms misbehaving."

Edibility: Species known to be edible are listed as such. Those described as poisonous, not recommended, or edibility unknown *should not be eaten.*

Remarks: This section includes brief discussion of similar species, the meaning of specific epithets, macrochemical test reactions when useful or diagnostic, and personal observations and comments by the authors.

How to Use This Book

This book is a guide designed to help readers identify more than one thousand fungi that occur in this region, more than 650 of which are fully described and illustrated. Although identifying mushrooms is sometimes possible by comparison to photographs, we highly recommend using the "Color Key to the Major Groups of Fungi" and the additional secondary keys when provided in the material on specific groups.

Mushroom species in this book are sorted into major groups based on the similarities of their macroscopic features and are arranged alphabetically. The color key contains eighteen major groups, each accompanied by a brief description of the key characteristics of the species included in it.

Mushroom identification may be easy, but sometimes it can be a difficult or seemingly impossible task. Microscopic examination may be required for positive identification of some species. The mushroom you are attempting to identify may not be included in this book, it may be too young or too old to be identifiable, or it may be an undescribed species. If you know a species and wish to read about it, consult the index. If the mushroom you wish to identify is unknown, follow the steps described in the Mushroom Identification Procedure below.

Mushroom Identification Procedure

1. Using the color key, determine which major group best describes your unknown mushroom. In some cases, the mushroom you are attempting to identify may actually be illustrated in the color key.

2. Go to the section of the book that deals with the major group appropriate for your mushroom, read the descriptions and examine the color illustrations provided in the group you have selected, and determine which spe-

cies most closely matches your unknown specimen.

Because boletes, gilled mushrooms, and polypores are such large groups, secondary keys are provided to help narrow down identification choices.

3. The secondary keys are dichotomous and consist of paired couplets. Carefully read each couplet *completely* and choose which one most closely describes your unknown mushroom. Proceed through the key until an individual species or group of species is identified.

4. If an individual species is identified, locate the description and color illustration that matches it; read the description and examine the color illustration. In some cases, the mushroom you are attempting to identify may not be the one fully described and illustrated. Instead, it may be one of the species partially described in the "Remarks" section. Partially described species may be illustrated in the color key; if not, additional resources may be required for positive identification.

5. If the couplet identifies a group of species, read each of the descriptions, examine the color illustrations, and determine which choice most closely matches your unknown specimen. Again, be sure to read the "Remarks" section of each description.

6. If the key choices do not result in a positive match, reread the key. If you remain unsuccessful, return to the color key and read the information provided for possible similar groups. If still unsuccessful, your unknown mushroom may not be included in this book.

Color Key to the Major Groups of Fungi

Bird's Nest Fungi (p. 21)

The small cup- to vase-shaped fruitbodies of these fungi contain numerous tiny egg-like sacs of spores called peridioles. Bird's Nest Fungi grow on woodchips, mulch, branches, leaves, dung, and other organic matter.

Crucibulum laeve
p. 22

Cyathus stercoreus
p. 23

Boletes (p. 24)

These fleshy mushrooms have a cap, stalk, and sponge-like undersurface consisting of vertically arranged tubes, each terminating in a pore. The tube layer is often easily separated from the cap tissue. They typically grow on the ground, rarely on wood. If you cannot identify your unknown mushroom in this section, try comparing it to species of *Albatrellus* in the Polypores group.

Boletinellus rompelii
p. 38

Boletus aurantiosplendens
p. 41

Boletus longicurvipes
p. 73

Boletus mahogonicolor
p. 86

Boletus ochraceoluteus
p. 49

Butyriboletus roseopurpureus p. 86

Caloboletus inedulis
p. 62

Gyroporus cyanescens
p. 69

Gyroporus purpurinus
pp. 32, 68

Leccinellum crocipodium
p. 82

Leccinellum griseum
p. 82

Phylloporus rhodoxanthus
p. 85

Pulveroboletus auriflammeus p. 87

Suillus granulatus
p. 96

Tylopilus appalachiensis
p. 109

Tylopilus rhoadsiae
p. 111

Carbon, Crust, Cushion, and Parchment Fungi (p. 128)

The fungi in this group have extremely variable shapes that do not match the descriptions provided for the other major groups. Many are round to cushion-shaped or thin and spreading crust-like growths. Others are erect and club-shaped to antler-like or highly irregular in form. Some are brightly colored, soft, and gelatinous while others are blackish, hard, and carbonaceous. Others are leathery or like parchment. Some have small, projecting, shelf-like caps, and one is vase- to bowl-shaped with a short stalk. The fertile surfaces of some species are roughened like sandpaper, while others may be rough and cracked, wrinkled, warted, toothed, or smooth. Although many grow on wood, some occur on other substrates. If you are unable to find a match here, try the Polypores group.

Apiosporina morbosa p. 146

Cymatoderma caperatum p. 131

Diatrype stigma p. 138

Hymenochaetopsis olivacea p. 129

Hymenochaetopsis tabacina p. 129

Hypoxylon ferrugineum p. 135

Hypoxylon fragiforme p. 135

Kretzschmaria deusta p. 132

Rhizina undulata p. 150

Stereum complicatum p. 140

Trichoderma chlorosporum complex p. 144

Xylaria allantoidea p. 146

Xylaria liquidambar p. 147

Xylaria oxyacanthae p. 147

Chanterelles and Similar Fungi (p. 151)

The fruitbodies of these fungi typically have a cap and stalk and are sometimes funnel-shaped. The undersurface of the cap has blunt, gill-like ridges that are often forked and cross-veined or nearly smooth. They usually grow on the ground.

Cantharellus cinnabarinus p. 153

Cantharellus tabernensis p. 155

Cantharellus tenuithrix p. 157

Cantharellus velutinus p. 153

Craterellus odoratus p. 154

Turbinellus floccosus p. 160

Corals and Cauliflowers (p. 161)

Fruitbodies in this group are of three types: bundles of erect, worm-like, unbranched appendages that are often fused at their bases; erect coral-like, repeatedly branched appendages; or a rounded, lettuce- or cauliflower-like cluster of fused branches. Members of this group usually grow on the ground, sometimes at the base of trees, or occasionally on wood.

Clavaria zollingeri p. 162

Clavulina cinerea p. 165

Clavulina floridana p. 165

Clavulinopsis aurantio-cinnabarina p. 163

Clavulinopsis fusiformis p. 163

Ramaria botrytis p. 170

Ramaria fumigata p. 170

Sparassis americana p. 172

Cordyceps, Tolypocladium, and Similar Fungi (p. 174)

Members of this group are parasitic species on larvae, pupae, adult arthropods, or hypogeous fungi. They often have a head and stalk, and their fertile surfaces are usually roughened like sandpaper. Some without a head produce copious powdery asexual spores. Some species cover their hosts with mycelium, causing them to appear mummified.

Akanthomyces aculeatus p. 175

Cordyceps militaris p. 175

Cordyceps olivascens p. 175

Gibellula leiopus p. 175

Ophiocordyceps dipterigena p. 175

Tolypocladium ophioglossoides p. 177

Cup Fungi (p. 178)

Fruitbodies in this group resemble small cups or saucers and have thin, brittle flesh. Some have stalks, and others are stalkless. They grow on the ground, on wood, or sometimes on other substrates.

Caloscypha fulgens p. 179

Helvella macropus p. 183

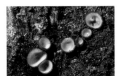

Humaria hemisphaerica p. 184

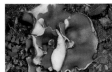

Peziza varia p. 182

Phillipsia domingensis p. 183

Sarcoscypha austriaca p. 183

Scutellinia erinaceus p. 184

Sphaerosporella brunnea p. 182

Urnula craterium p. 181

Wolfina aurantiopsis p. 181

Earth Tongues and Earth Clubs (p. 185)

Species in this group resemble erect tongues, clubs with rounded to oval heads, spatulas, spindles, or cylinders. Although they may occur in groups, their stalk bases are not fused, and they are typically unbranched. Their fertile surfaces may be smooth or wrinkled but are not roughened like sandpaper. They grow on the ground, on wood, or on decaying leaves.

Clavariadelphus americanus p. 186

Clavariadelphus truncatus p. 186

Leotia atrovirens p. 187

Leotia lubrica p. 187

Microglossum rufum p. 189

Underwoodia columnaris p. 186

Fiber Fans (p. 190)

These fan- or vase-shaped fruitbodies are leathery to fibrous-tough, sometimes with split or torn margins. They are typically some shade of brown or gray, with or without a whitish margin. Their fertile undersurfaces may be smooth or wrinkled and warted, but they lack pores (use a hand lens). They grow on the ground.

Thelephora anthocephala p. 191

Thelephora terrestris p. 191

Thelephora terrestris f. *concrescens* p. 191

Thelephora vialis p. 192

14

MUSHROOMS OF THE GULF COAST STATES

Gilled Mushrooms (p. 193)

The undersurface of the cap of the species in this group has blade-like, thin gills that radiate from a stalk or, on stalkless species, from the point of attachment to the cap margin. Species in this group grow on a variety of substrates. A few species with gill-like undersurfaces may also be found in the Boletes, Chanterelles and Similar Fungi, and Polypores groups.

Agaricus pocillator
p. 202

Amanita muscaria var.
flavivolvata p. 224

Amanita russuloides
p. 222

Amanita spreta
p. 212

Conocybe tenera
p. 248

Crepidotus mollis
p. 266

Entoloma quadratum
p. 274

Gliophorus laetus
p. 278

Gymnopilus sapineus
p. 284

Gymnopus dryophilus (A)
p. 287

Gymnopus luxurians
p. 285

Gymnopus subnudus
p. 285

Hebeloma sinapizans
p. 290

Hygrocybe cuspidata
p. 295

Hygrophorus hypothejus
p. 267

Hymenopellis incognita
p. 300

Lacrymaria lacrymabunda p. 383

Lactarius subpurpureus p. 324

Lactifluus deceptivus p. 336

Lactifluus petersenii p. 318

Megacollybia rodmanii p. 372

Mycena pura p. 376

Pluteus pellitus p. 396

Psathyrella delineata p. 260

Psathyrella pennata p. 389

Pseudoarmillariella ectypoides p. 277

Russula crustosa p. 410

Russula decolorans pp. 402, 403

Russula mariae pp. 401, 412

Tapinella panuoides p. 416

Tricholoma floridanum p. 423

Tricholoma niveipes p. 422

Tricholoma subluteum p. 419

Tricholoma sulphurescens p. 420

Hypomyces and Other Parasitic Fungi (p. 430)

Members of this group are parasitic species that cover and disfigure many types of fungi, especially gilled mushrooms, boletes, and polypores. They form a thin layer on their host organisms that may be roughened like sandpaper or sometimes powdery or moldy.

Hypomyces lactifluorum p. 433

Mycogone rosea p. 432

Jelly Fungi (p. 434)

These are distinctly gelatinous species that are soft or rubbery, or sometimes leathery to fibrous-tough. Most are cushion-shaped to brain-like, and a few are erect and spike- to antler-like or irregular. They often grow on wood but sometimes envelop or encrust plant stems, leaves, cones, and other organic debris.

Dacrymyces chrysospermus p. 444

Sebacina incrustans p. 441

Morels, False Morels, and Similar Fungi (p. 445)

The fruitbodies of this group have a distinct cap or sponge-like head and a conspicuous stalk. Caps or heads may be conic to bell-shaped, with pits and ridges, or brain-like, saddle-shaped, or irregularly lobed. Mature stalks are hollow or multichambered. They grow on the ground or on well-decayed wood.

Helvella crispa complex p. 446

Morchella punctipes p. 447

Polypores (p. 450)

These are hard and woody, tough and leathery, or sometimes firm and flexible fruitbodies with pores on their undersurfaces. They are often kidney-shaped to semicircular or fan-shaped but may also be circular, irregular, or, rarely, highly distorted. They vary in size from rather small to very large. Some polypores occur singly while others form large clusters.

The tube layer is not easily separated from the cap tissue. Pores are sometimes minute and often require a hand lens to see. Species in this group may be stalkless or centrally to laterally stalked. They usually grow on wood but sometimes on the ground. If you are unable to find a match here, try the Carbon, Crust, Cushion, and Parchment group or the Boletes group.

Albatrellus confluens
p. 455

Coltricia cinnamomea
p. 495

Coltricia perennis
p. 495

Daedaleopsis septentrionalis p. 462

Fistulina hepatica
p. 501

Ganoderma applanatum
p. 473

Ganoderma lobatoideum
p. 472

Ganoderma zonatum (A)
p. 473

Gloeophyllum striatum
p. 475

Hexagonia hydnoides
p. 477

Inonotus quercustris
p. 481

Laetiporus cincinnatus
p. 486

Pseudoinonotus dryadeus
p. 502

Pycnoporus sanguineus
p. 507

Puffballs, Earthballs, Earthstars, and Similar Fungi (p. 514)

The fruitbodies of species in this group are rounded, oval, pear- to turban-shaped or star-shaped. They are mostly stalkless but sometimes have a short stalk or stalk-like base. The interior spore mass is usually white when young and immature. As it matures, the spore mass becomes yellow, greenish, orange, purple, brown, or black and powdery. They grow on the ground, underground, or on wood. If you cannot identify your unknown mushroom in this section, try comparing it to the species listed in the Truffles and Other Hypogeous Fungi group.

Calostoma lutescens
p. 517

Calostoma ravenelii
p. 517

Geastrum saccatum
p. 524

Geastrum triplex
p. 524

Rhopalogaster
transversarius p. 531

Scleroderma floridanum
p. 534

Scleroderma meridionale
p. 533

Tulostoma brumale
p. 528

Stinkhorns (p. 536)

Species in this group have fruitbodies that are egg-shaped when young and become erect and phallic with a head and stalk, or pear-shaped to nearly round with or without a stalk, or squid-like with arched, tapered arms. Parts of the fruitbody are usually coated with a foul-smelling, slimy spore mass that often attracts a variety of arthropods. They grow on the ground, mulch, woodchips, or on decaying wood.

Blumenavia angolensis
p. 538

Clathrus crispus
p. 539

Lysurus periphragmoides
(A) p. 539

Phallus ravenelii
p. 545

Tooth Fungi (p. 546)

These are fleshy, leathery, or tough fungi with downward-oriented, uniformly shaped teeth or soft spines. Some species have a cap and stalk, others are fan-shaped to shelf- or icicle-like. They grow on the ground or on wood.

Hericium americanum
p. 549

Hericium corralloides
p. 549

Hydnellum concrescens
p. 553

Hydnellum scrobiculatum
p. 553

Hydnum rufescens
complex p. 550

Sarcodon scabrosus
p. 557

Truffles and Other Hypogeous Fungi (p. 560)

Because they are mostly underground fungi, these are not commonly collected. Most of the species in this group must be excavated, although species of Rhizopogon are sometimes found partially buried or completely aboveground. They are nearly round or lobed, and their smooth or roughened to warted outer rind-like surface is often thickened. Although they sometimes resemble puffballs or earthballs, their interior is usually chambered, marbled, or somewhat hollow. If you cannot identify your unknown mushroom in this section, try comparing it to the species listed in the Puffballs, Earthballs, Earthstars, and Similar Fungi group.

Elaphomyces species
complex p. 561

Tuber lyonii
p. 564

Species Descriptions and Illustrations

Bird's Nest Fungi

Small cup- to vase-shaped fruitbodies that contain numerous tiny egg-like sacs of spores called peridioles. Bird's Nest Fungi grow on woodchips, mulch, branches, leaves, dung, and other organic matter.

Crucibulum laeve (Huds.) Kambly

= *Crucibulum vulgare* Tul. & C. Tul.

COMMON NAMES: Common Bird's Nest, White-egg Bird's Nest.

MACROSCOPIC FEATURES: **Fruitbody** consisting of a cup and egg-like peridioles. **Cup** somewhat cylindric and tapered downward, 6–10 mm wide at the top, 6–10 mm high, protected when young by a white, membrane-like lid, and covered overall by yellowish-orange fibers that open at maturity; **interior** smooth, whitish; **exterior** hairy to finely velvety, yellowish orange, becoming paler yellow in age. **Peridioles** 1.5–2 mm wide, lens-shaped, whitish, each attached on the underside by a tiny, coiled cord.

MICROSCOPIC FEATURES: Spores 8–10 × 4–5.5 µm, elliptic, smooth, hyaline.

OCCURRENCE: Scattered to gregarious on twigs, fallen branches, woodchips, garden mulch, and other organic debris; year-round.

EDIBILITY: Inedible.

REMARKS: *Cyathus* species are similar Bird's Nest Fungi, but they have grayish-brown to gray or blackish peridioles. The Cannon Fungus, *Sphaerobolus stellatus* (not illustrated), has a tiny yellow-orange spore case, 1.5–3 mm wide, that splits open at maturity, forming 4–9 star-shaped to tooth-like rays and exposing a single peridiole which is forcibly ejected in response to moisture and light. It grows on decaying wood, sawdust, compost, and dung.

Crucibulum laeve

Cyathus striatus (Huds.) Willd.

COMMON NAME: Splash Cups.
MACROSCOPIC FEATURES: **Fruitbody** consisting of a cup and egg-like peridioles. **Cup** cone-shaped, 6–10 mm high, covered by a white, protective, membranous lid when young; **interior** vertically lined, smooth, shiny, gray to grayish white; **exterior** shaggy-hairy to wooly, faintly to distinctly fluted, reddish brown to chocolate brown or grayish brown. **Peridioles** 1.5–3 mm in diameter, flattened and often vaguely triangular, gray, each attached on the underside by a tiny, coiled cord.
MICROSCOPIC FEATURES: Spores 15–20 × 8–12 μm, elliptic, smooth, hyaline.

OCCURRENCE: Scattered or in dense groups on twigs, bark, woodchips, logs, and other woody debris; year-round.
EDIBILITY: Inedible.
REMARKS: *Hypocrea latizonata* (not illustrated) is a parasitic fungus that often forms a distinctive white band around the outside of the cups. *Cyathus stercoreus* (p. 9) has dark gray to black peridioles, a shaggy-hairy cup exterior, and the interior of its cup is not vertically lined. *Cyathus olla* (not illustrated) has grayish-brown peridioles, a smooth to minutely hairy cup exterior, and the interior of its cup is not vertically lined.

Cyathus striatus

Boletes

Fleshy mushrooms with a cap, stalk, and a sponge-like undersurface consisting of vertically arranged tubes, each terminating in a pore. The tube layer is often easily separated from the cap tissue. They typically grow on the ground, rarely on wood. If you cannot identify your unknown mushroom in this section, try comparing it to species of *Albatrellus* in the Polypores group.

Key to the Boletes

1a. Stalk with a ring, a ring zone, or resinous dots, smears, or both 2

1b. Stalk lacking a ring, a ring zone, or resinous dots and smears. 3

2a. Stalk lacking resinous dots and smears; cap margin fringed with cottony pieces of white, grayish, or tan partial veil; flesh white, quickly staining orange to orange red, then slowly blackish:
    Strobilomyces confusus
    Strobilomyces dryophilus

2b. Stalk with resinous dots and smears, at least on mature specimens, or, if lacking, a ring zone is present; flesh not staining, orange to orange red, then slowly blackish:
    Suillus brevipes
    Suillus cothurnatus
    Suillus decipens
    Suillus granulatus
    Suillus hirtellus
    Suillus salmonicolor
    Suillus tomentosus

3a. Stalk covered with conspicuous, pointed, white, brown, purple-brown, or black scabers:
    Leccinellum albellum
    Leccinellum crocipodium
    Leccinellum griseum
    Leccinum chalybaeum
    Leccinum roseoscabrum
    Leccinum rubropunctum
    Leccinum rugosiceps
    Sutorius eximius

3b. Stalk not as above; sometimes reticulate, coated with tiny punctae, or smooth. . . .4

4a. Pore surface markedly elongated with gill-like ridges and cross-walls or gill-like, strongly decurrent:
    Boletinellus merulioides
    Boletinellus proximus
    Boletinellus rompelii
    Phylloporus boletinoides
    Phylloporus leucomycelinus
    Phylloporus rhodoxanthus

4b. Pore surface not as above; pores round, angular, irregular, or somewhat elongated but not gill-like 5

5a. Stalk with fine to coarse reticulation. . . .6

5b. Stalk lacking reticulation 8

6a. Pore surface some shade of orange or red:
    Boletus carminiporus
    Boletus flammans
    Butyriboletus floridanus
    Butyriboletus frostii
    Lanmaoa borealis

6b. Pore surface white, creamy white, yellow, or pinkish brown to olive brown 7

7a. Pore surface white to creamy white at first, becoming grayish pink then pinkish brown at maturity:
    Austroboletus subflavidus
    Fistulinella jamaicensis
    Tylopilus appalachiensis
    Tylopilus balloui
    Tylopilus felleus
    Tylopilus ferrugineus
    Tylopilus griseocarneus
    Tylopilus indecisus
    Tylopilus minor
    Tylopilus plumbeoviolaceus
    Tylopilus rhoadsiae
    Tylopilus rubrobrunneus
    Tylopilus tabacinus
    Tylopilus variobrunneus
    Tylopilus violatinctus
    Veloporphyrellus conicus

7b. Pore surface white to creamy white,
　　 yellow, or olive brown, lacking pinkish
　　 tones:
　　　　 Alessioporus rubriflavus
　　　　 Aureoboletus russellii
　　　　 Boletus albisulphureus
　　　　 Boletus aurantiosplendens
　　　　 Boletus aureissimus var. *aureissimus*
　　　　 Boletus auripes
　　　　 Boletus luridellus
　　　　 Boletus nobilis
　　　　 Boletus oliveisporus
　　　　 Boletus pallidus
　　　　 Boletus pseudopinophilus
　　　　 Boletus sensibilis
　　　　 Boletus separans
　　　　 Boletus subtomentosus
　　　　 Boletus variipes
　　　　 Buchwaldoboletus lignicola
　　　　 Butyriboletus roseopurpureus
　　　　 Caloboletus inedulis
　　　　 Ceriomyces aureissimus var. *castaneus*
　　　　 Heimioporus betula
　　　　 Neoboletus pseudosulphureus
　　　　 Pulchroboletus rubricitrinus
　　　　 Pulveroboletus auriflammeus
　　　　 Retiboletus griseus var. *fuscus*
　　　　 Retiboletus griseus var. *griseus*
　　　　 Retiboletus ornatipes
　　　　 Xanthoconium affine
　　　　 Xerocomus hemixanthus
　　　　 Xerocomus hortonii
　　　　 Xerocomus illudens/*Xerocomus tenax*
　　　　 complex
　　　　 Xerocomus sclerotiorum

8a. Pore surface white to creamy white at
　　 first, becoming grayish pink then pinkish
　　 brown at maturity:
　　　　 Austroboletus gracilis
　　　　 Fistulinella jamaicensis
　　　　 Tylopilus alboater
　　　　 Tylopilus appalachiensis

　　　　 Tylopilus badiceps
　　　　 Tylopilus ferrugineus
　　　　 Tylopilus indecisus
　　　　 Tylopilus peralbidus
　　　　 Tylopilus plumbeoviolaceus
　　　　 Tylopilus rhodoconius
　　　　 Tylopilus rubrobrunneus
　　　　 Tylopilus sordidus
　　　　 Tylopilus violatinctus
　　　　 Tylopilus williamsii
　　　　 Veloporphyrellus conicus

8b. Pore surface differently colored, or if
　　 white, not pinkish brown at maturity . . . 9

9a. Pore surface staining greenish or blue to
　　 blackish blue when bruised, sometimes
　　 slowly. 10

9b. Pore surface not staining greenish or blue
　　 to blackish blue when bruised 11

10a. Cap some shade of pink or red:
　　　　 Baorangia bicolor complex
　　　　 Boletellus ananas
　　　　 Boletus fairchildianus
　　　　 Boletus miniato-olivaceus
　　　　 Boletus roseolateritius
　　　　 Boletus rufomaculatus
　　　　 Boletus sensibilis
　　　　 Hortiboletus campestris
　　　　 Hortiboletus rubellus
　　　　 Lanmaoa borealis
　　　　 Lanmaoa roseocrispans
　　　　 Pulchroboletus rubricitrinus
　　　　 Suillellus subluridus
　　　　 Suillellus subvelutipes
　　　　 Xerocomus sclerotiorum

10b. Cap whitish, buff, yellow, orange, or
　　 some shade of brown:
　　　　 Boletellus chrysenteroides
　　　　 Boletinellus merulioides
　　　　 Boletinellus rompelii
　　　　 Boletus fairchildianus
　　　　 Boletus lewisii

Boletus mahogonicolor
Boletus ochraceoluteus
Boletus oliveisporus
Boletus pallidus
Boletus patrioticus
Boletus roseolateritius
Boletus subgraveolens
Boletus subtomentosus
Buchwaldoboletus lignicola
Buchwaldoboletus sphaerocephalus
Cyanoboletus pulverulentus
Gyroporus cyanescens
Imleria badia
Lanmaoa roseocrispans
Neoboletus pseudosulphureus
Pulveroboletus ravenelii
Suillellus hypocarycinus
Suillellus pictiformis
Xerocomus hortonii
Xerocomus hypoxanthus
Xerocomus illudens/Xerocomus tenax
complex
Xerocomus pseudoboletinus

11a. Stalk stuffed with soft pith, developing
cavities or becoming hollow in age:
Gyroporus castaneus
Gyroporus phaeocyanescens
Gyroporus purpurinus
Gyroporus subalbellus
Gyroporus unbrinisquamosus

11b. Stalk solid, not stuffed with pith and not
hollow in age 12

12a. Cap white, whitish to straw, yellow, or
pink to rose and fading to pinkish tan:
Boletus flavissimus
Harrya chromapes
Pulveroboletus curtisii
Xanthoconium stramineum

12b. Cap differently colored, often some
shade of brown but sometimes orange to
brownish orange or red:
Aureoboletus auriporus
Aureoboletus gentilis
Aureoboletus innixus
Aureoboletus russellii
Boletus abruptibulbus
Boletus longicurvipes
Boletus longiniveipes
Boletus roodyi
Boletus weberi
Hemileccinum subglabripes
Suillus brevipes
Xanthoconium affine
Xerocomus hortonii
Xerocomus illudens/Xerocomus tenax
complex
Xerocomus morrisii

Alessioporus rubriflavus J. L. Frank, A. R. Bessette & A. E. Bessette

MACROSCOPIC FEATURES: **Cap** 5–14(21) cm wide, convex, eventually becoming broadly convex to nearly flat, with a sterile margin when young; surface viscid or dry, slightly velvety, sometimes finely cracked in age, dark wine red on very young buttons, soon developing a yellow ground color covered with streaks and splashes of various shades of wine red, red brown, and ocher which sometimes persist well into maturity, becoming olive to brownish over the disc in age, bruising greenish blue to bluish black; **flesh** firm, bright yellow, quickly staining dark blue when exposed; odor mildly unpleasant or not distinctive; taste unpleasant, sour, or sometimes astringent. **Pore surface** initially yellow, soon becoming pale orange yellow then olive brown, deeply depressed at the stalk when mature, quickly bruising blue, then slowly reddish brown; tubes 8–25 mm deep. **Stalk** enlarged downward, ventricose to clavate, typically with a pinched base, solid; surface dry, conspicuously reticulate over at least the upper half, finely velvety below, bright yellow near the apex or nearly overall, with dark wine-red to red-brown streaks and splashes below, especially near the base, quickly bruising blue, then slowly brownish; reticulation yellow toward the apex, yellow brown below, darkening when handled; mycelium whitish; **flesh** bright yellow, quickly staining blue when exposed, usually dark wine red near the base.

SPORE PRINT: Olive brown.

MICROSCOPIC FEATURES: Spores 13–19 × 4–6 μm, subellipsoid to subfusiform, smooth, pale brownish yellow.

OCCURRENCE: Solitary, scattered, or in groups on the ground in mixed oak and pine woods; summer–fall.

EDIBILITY: Edible.

REMARKS: *Rubriflavus* means "red and yellow," a reference to the colors of the fruitbody. Red portions of the cap cuticle immediately stain amber with KOH, and the flesh immediately stains orange with KOH. *Boletus flavissimus* (not illustrated), described from Florida, has a bright yellow cap, lacks red coloration in all stages of development, does not stain when bruised, and its stalk lacks reticulation. *Neoboletus pseudosulphureus* (p. 83) has a bright yellow cap that becomes duller yellow to tawny at maturity and typically develops brown to brownish-red tints, especially over the disc, in age. It has a yellow stalk that sometimes develops reddish tints, especially near the base, and usually lacks reticulation or is sometimes reticulate on the upper portion. It has smaller spores that measure 10–16 × 4–6 μm.

Alessioporus rubriflavus

Aureoboletus auriporus (Peck) Pouzar

= *Boletus auriporus* Peck

COMMON NAMES: Acidic Golden-pored Bolete, Golden-pored Bolete.

MACROSCOPIC FEATURES: **Cap** 2–8 cm wide, convex, becoming broadly convex to nearly flat, with a sterile margin; surface coated with tiny appressed fibrils, smooth or sometimes bumpy, moist and viscid when fresh, becoming dull when dry, color highly variable, pale pink, ochraceous, beige, or pale pinkish brown to vinaceous brown, fading in age or when dry; cuticle tastes acidic; **flesh** white to pale yellow, except under the cap surface where it is vinaceous, not staining blue when cut or bruised, occasionally staining pinkish; odor somewhat pungent or not distinctive; taste acidic or not distinctive. **Pore surface** brilliant golden yellow when young, becoming dull golden yellow to greenish yellow, and finally brownish yellow in age; usually slowly staining dull brick red when bruised, or sometimes unchanging; tubes 6–15 mm deep. **Stalk** slightly enlarged downward or nearly equal, typically narrowing abruptly at the base; surface viscid when fresh, pale yellow at the apex, streaked and flushed pale pinkish brown downward, with copious white mycelium at the base; **flesh** colored like the cap flesh.

SPORE PRINT: Olive brown.

MICROSCOPIC FEATURES: Spores 11–16 × 4–6 µm, fusiform-elliptic, smooth, pale brown.

OCCURRENCE: Solitary, scattered, or in groups under oaks; late spring–fall.

EDIBILITY: Edible.

REMARKS: *Auriporus* means "golden pores." An additional photograph illustrating the highly variable cap coloration of this species occurs in the "Color Key to the Major Groups of Fungi" (p. 8). Although *Aureoboletus gentilis* (not illustrated) has been described and illustrated in some American field guides, it may not occur in North America, or *Aureoboletus auriporus* may be a synonym of *Aureoboletus gentilis*. Molecular analysis of European and American collections is needed to resolve this issue. *Aureoboletus innixus* (p. 30) is similar but has a darker brown cap that is dry, the cap surface does not taste acidic, and the flesh has an odor that resembles witch hazel. It often grows in clusters fused at the stalk bases.

Aureoboletus auriporus

Aureoboletus innixus (Frost)
Halling, A. R. Bessette & A. E. Bessette

= *Boletus innixus* Frost
= *Boletus caespitosus* Peck
= *Pulveroboletus innixus* (Frost) Singer

COMMON NAME: Clustered Brown Bolete.
MACROSCOPIC FEATURES: **Cap** 3–7.5 cm wide, convex when young, becoming broadly convex to nearly flat, with a sterile margin; surface dry, slightly velvety, often cracked in age, dull reddish brown to dull cinnamon or yellow brown, often purplish or reddish near the margin; **flesh** white to pale yellow, sometimes tinged vinaceous beneath the cuticle; odor pungent; taste not distinctive. **Pore surface** bright yellow when young, becoming dull yellow in age, unchanging when bruised; tubes 3–10 mm deep. **Stalk** stout, solid, often club-shaped to swollen in the mid-portion, with a tapered base; surface dry or slightly viscid near the base, smooth or finely fibrillose, yellowish streaked with brown, staining brownish when handled, often with yellow basal mycelium; **flesh** colored like the cap flesh.
SPORE PRINT: Olive brown.
MICROSCOPIC FEATURES: Spores 8–11 × 3–5 μm, elliptic, smooth, pale brown.
OCCURRENCE: Solitary, scattered, or often in clusters in hardwoods, especially with oak; late spring–fall.
EDIBILITY: Edible.
REMARKS: *Innixus* means "reclining," referring to its habit of often leaning, especially when in tight clusters. The cap surface stains mahogany red to reddish brown with the application of KOH, develops a green flash, then stains dull orange red with NH4OH, and is pale olive with FeSO4. The flesh stains pale dull pinkish orange with KOH or NH4OH and pale gray with FeSO4. *Aureoboletus auriporus* (p. 29) has a viscid cap that easily peels, an acidic tasting cuticle, and flesh that lacks a distinctive odor.

Aureoboletus innixus

Aureoboletus russellii (Frost)
G. Wu & Zhu L. Yang

= *Boletellus russellii* (Frost) E. -J. Gilbert
= *Frostiella russellii* (Frost) Murrill

COMMON NAME: Russell's Bolete.

MACROSCOPIC FEATURES: **Cap** 3–13 cm wide, initially rounded to convex, becoming broadly convex in age; margin even and strongly incurved; surface dry, velvety, becoming cracked or forming scale-like patches in age, yellow brown to reddish brown, cinnamon brown, or olive gray; **flesh** pale yellow to yellow, usually brownish around larval tunnels, not staining blue when cut or bruised but may slowly stain brown; odor and taste not distinctive. **Pore surface** yellow to greenish yellow, not staining blue when bruised but may become a brighter yellow when cut or rubbed, usually somewhat depressed around the stalk in age; tubes up to 2 cm deep. **Stalk** equal or enlarging slightly downward, solid, typically curved at the base; surface dry, frequently viscid at the base when moist, reddish brown to pinkish tan, deeply grooved and ridged for most or all of its length, the ridges branched or torn to create a honeycomb or shaggy bark effect that resembles coarse reticulation; **flesh** colored like the cap flesh.

SPORE PRINT: Dark olive to olive brown.

MICROSCOPIC FEATURES: Spores 15–20 × 7–11 µm, elliptic, longitudinally striate with deep grooves or wrinkled with a cleft in the wall at the apex, pale brown.

OCCURRENCE: Solitary to scattered with oak or pine; summer–fall.

EDIBILITY: Edible.

REMARKS: *Russellii* refers to the American botanist John Lewis Russell, who made the first collection of this species; mycologist Charles Christopher Frost named this bolete in 1878 to honor his friend. The cap surface of *Aureoboletus russellii* stains reddish with NH4OH and olive gray with FeSO4. The flesh stains reddish with KOH and blackish blue with FeSO4. *Heimioporus betula* (p. 72) has a glabrous, shiny, red to orange cap and pitted spores.

Aureoboletus russellii

Austroboletus gracilis (Peck) Wolfe

= *Tylopilus gracilis* (Peck) Henn.
= *Porphyrellus gracilis* (Peck) Singer

COMMON NAME: Graceful Bolete.
MACROSCOPIC FEATURES: **Cap** 3–10 cm wide, convex to broadly convex; surface dry, finely velvety when young, sometimes cracked in age, maroon to reddish brown or cinnamon, sometimes tawny to yellow brown; **flesh** white or tinged pink, unchanging when cut or bruised; odor not distinctive; taste slightly acidic or not distinctive. **Pore surface** white when young, becoming pinkish to pinkish brown or tinged with burgundy when mature, darkening or staining brownish when bruised; tubes 1–2 cm deep. **Stalk** long and slender in proportion to the cap diameter, solid, enlarged downward or nearly equal, often curved; surface dry, colored like the cap or paler, with elevated, anastomosing rib-like lines that sometimes form an obscure, narrow reticulation overall or at least on the upper half, with white basal mycelium; **flesh** colored like the cap flesh.

SPORE PRINT: Pinkish brown to reddish brown.
MICROSCOPIC FEATURES: Spores 10–17 × 5–8 μm, narrowly ovoid to subelliptic, pitted, pale brown.
OCCURRENCE: Solitary, scattered, or in groups on the ground or on decaying wood in conifer and hardwood forests; late spring–fall.
EDIBILITY: Edible.
REMARKS: *Gracilis* means "slender." *Gyroporus castaneus* (p. 68) and *Gyroporus purpurinus* (pp. 9, 68) are similar but differ by having a white pore surface that does not become pinkish brown at maturity, hollow stalks, yellow spore prints, and smooth spores.

Austroboletus gracilis

Austroboletus subflavidus
(Murrill) Wolfe

= *Tylopilus subflavidus* Murrill
= *Porphyrellus subflavidus* (Murrill) Singer

COMMON NAME: White Coarsely-ribbed Bolete.

MACROSCOPIC FEATURES: **Cap** 3–10 cm wide, convex, becoming nearly flat, usually slightly depressed in age; surface dry, finely velvety, soon becoming cracked, white at first, turning buff or very pale yellowish to grayish yellow in age, sometimes with a pale ochraceous-salmon tinge; **flesh** white, not staining when cut or bruised; odor somewhat fruity; taste bitter. **Pore surface** white to grayish, sometimes with clear droplets when young and fresh, becoming pinkish to pinkish brown at maturity, unchanging when bruised; tubes 1–2 cm deep. **Stalk** nearly equal or tapered downward, rarely enlarged at the base, solid; surface dry, colored like the cap, with thick, raised, coarsely ribbed reticulation giving it a pitted appearance; **flesh** yellow in the base, white above.

SPORE PRINT: Reddish brown.

MICROSCOPIC FEATURES: Spores 15–20 × 6–9 µm, fusoid, minutely pitted, pale brown.

OCCURRENCE: Scattered or in groups with oak and pine; late spring-fall.

EDIBILITY: Inedible because of the bitter taste.

REMARKS: *Subflavidus* means "nearly yellow." *Tylopilus rhoadsiae* (p. 111) has a clavate stalk with a pinched base, prominent white or brown reticulation that is not coarsely ribbed, thick, raised, or pitted-looking, and it has smaller, smooth spores that measure 11–13.5 × 3.5–4.5 µm.

Austroboletus subflavidus

Baorangia bicolor complex (Kuntze) G. Wu, Halling & Zhu L. Yang

= *Baorangia rubelloides* G. Wu, Halling & Zhu L. Yang
= *Boletus bicolor* Peck
= *Boletus rubellus* subsp. *bicolor* (Kuntze) Singer
= *Boletus bicolor* var. *subreticulatus* A. H. Sm. & Thiers

COMMON NAMES: Red and Yellow Bolete, Two-toned Bolete.

MACROSCOPIC FEATURES: **Cap** 5–12.5 cm wide, convex when young, becoming nearly flat; margin initially incurved; surface dry, somewhat velvety, usually developing cracks in dry weather or when mature, dark red to rose red, fading to pale brownish orange yellow or tan in age; **flesh** yellow, unchanging or slowly and weakly staining blue when cut; odor and taste not distinctive. **Pore surface** bright yellow when young and fresh, becoming olive yellow in age, bruising blue quickly; tubes 3–10 mm deep. **Stalk** nearly equal, sometimes enlarged downward, solid; surface dry, smooth, rarely reticulate on the upper portion, yellow at the apex, red or rosy red on the lower two-thirds or more, unchanging or slowly staining blue when bruised or cut; **flesh** typically bright golden yellow that is a deeper yellow than the cap flesh, unchanging or erratically staining blue. SPORE PRINT: Olive brown.

MICROSCOPIC FEATURES: Spores 8–12 × 3.5–5 µm, oblong to slightly ventricose, smooth, pale brown.

OCCURRENCE: Solitary, scattered, or in groups associated with oaks; summer–fall.

EDIBILITY: Edible.

REMARKS: *Bicolor* means "having two colors." The name *Boletus bicolor* has been assigned to more than one species. In 1807, Italian botanist Giuseppe Raddi named an Italian bolete *Boletus bicolor*. In 1870, Charles Peck named a second, and different, bolete from Sand Lake, New York, *Boletus bicolor*. Then, in 1909, George Massee named a third bolete species from Singapore, *Boletus bicolor*. The genus Baorangia was erected, in part, to minimize the confusion created by Peck's and Massee's invalid use of the name following Raddi's original assignment of *Boletus bicolor*. The *Baorangia bicolor* complex is easily confused with a few similar species. *Boletus sensibilis* (p. 57) quickly bruises blue on all parts and has flesh that smells sweetly of fenugreek or curry. *Boletus rufomaculatus* (p. 56) has a mottled brick-red to brownish-red cap with a sterile margin, stalk flesh that is a paler yellow, and grows associated with beech. *Lanmaoa borealis* (not illustrated), previously thought to be only a northern species, has a red cap, yellow flesh that slowly stains blue at the stalk apex, orange-red to red pores that stain greenish blue, and a red stalk that may be reticulate at the apex.

Baorangia bicolor complex

Boletellus ananas (M. A. Curtis) Murrill

= *Boletus ananas* M. A. Curtis

COMMON NAME: Pineapple Bolete.
MACROSCOPIC FEATURES: **Cap** 3–10 cm wide, initially obtuse, becoming convex to broadly convex; surface dry, coated with coarse and overlapping purplish-red to dark red scales that become dull pinkish tan to dingy yellow in age and finally extend beyond the cap margin; **flesh** whitish on exposure, quickly becoming yellowish then blue, and finally bluish gray; odor and taste not distinctive. **Pore surface** yellow when young, occasionally tinged reddish brown in maturity, bruising blue; initially covered by a whitish partial veil that usually leaves remnants on the cap margin; tubes 9–16 mm deep. **Stalk** enlarged downward or nearly equal, dry, glabrous to slightly fibrillose, white to pale tan, at times with a reddish zone near the apex, usually lacking a ring; **flesh** colored like and staining like the cap flesh.

SPORE PRINT: Dark rusty brown to dark brown.
MICROSCOPIC FEATURES: Spores 15–24 × 7–11 μm, fusoid, with conspicuously longitudinally ridged thin wings that are spirally arranged, often having an indistinct apical pore, pale brown.
OCCURRENCE: Scattered or in groups, often on the bases of trees or on the ground with oak and pine; primarily spring–fall, year-round during mild winters.
EDIBILITY: Edible.
REMARKS: *Ananas* is the genus in which the pineapple is classified. *Suillellus pictiformis* (not illustrated) is a similar rare species, known only from Florida. Its cap has appressed to erect, shaggy, medium brown to dark brown scales and becomes cracked in age exposing yellow flesh. Its stalk is sheathed with shaggy to fibrillose, medium brown to dark brown scales, and its greenish-yellow to olive-yellow pore surface stains blue when bruised.

Boletellus ananas

Boletellus chrysenteroides (Snell) Snell

= *Boletus chrysenteroides* Snell

MACROSCOPIC FEATURES: **Cap** 3–6 cm wide, convex, becoming broadly convex; surface dry, initially dark brown and velvety, becoming bay-brown to chestnut brown and often cracked in age, exposed flesh lacking reddish tints; **flesh** whitish to pale yellow, staining blue when exposed, often slowly; odor and taste not distinctive. **Pore surface** pale yellow, becoming yellow to greenish yellow, quickly staining blue when cut or bruised; tubes 1.2–1.8 cm deep. **Stalk** equal or enlarged slightly downward, solid, dry, reddish brown to blackish brown, often yellowish at the apex, not reticulate, usually with punctae that may simulate a net-like pattern, staining blue, then slowly reddish when bruised; **flesh** colored and staining like the cap flesh.

SPORE PRINT: Olive brown to dark brown.

MICROSCOPIC FEATURES: Spores 10–16 × 5–8 μm, narrowly ovate to nearly oblong, longitudinally striate, yellowish to brownish.

OCCURRENCE: Solitary or in groups on decaying logs and stumps, at the base of standing trunks, or sometimes on the ground in hardwood or mixed oak and pine woods, especially associated with oak; summer–fall.

EDIBILITY: Edible

REMARKS: This small, dark bolete is unusual in that it most often grows on decaying wood rather than soil.

Boletellus chrysenteroides

Boletinellus merulioides
(Schwein.) Murrill

= *Gyrodon merulioides* (Schwein.) Singer

COMMON NAME: Ash Tree Bolete.

MACROSCOPIC FEATURES: **Cap** 4–12.5 cm wide, initially convex with an incurved margin, becoming depressed at the center to nearly funnel-shaped in age, often kidney-shaped; surface slightly velvety when young, slightly viscid and shiny when moist, smooth, yellow brown to olive brown or reddish brown; **flesh** thick in the center, thinning toward the margin, yellow, unchanging or sometimes staining bluish when exposed, usually reddish brown around larval tunnels; odor musty, unpleasant, or not distinctive; taste pungent, described as resembling raw potatoes, or not distinctive. **Pore surface** decurrent and not easily separated from the cap flesh; pores elongated and radially arranged with gill-like ridges and cross-walls, yellow to dull golden yellow or olive, usually slowly bruising greenish blue; tubes 3–6 mm deep. **Stalk** short, solid, eccentric to nearly lateral or sometimes central, often curved and pinched at the base; surface dry, colored like the pore surface on the upper portion, brownish to blackish at the base, sometimes mottled with reddish brown,

bruising reddish brown; **flesh** colored like the cap except at the base where it is usually reddish brown, sometimes staining bluish when exposed.

SPORE PRINT: Olive brown.

MICROSCOPIC FEATURES: Spores 7–11 × 6–7.5 μm, broadly elliptical to nearly globose, smooth, pale yellow in water mounts, ochraceous in KOH.

OCCURRENCE: Solitary or in groups on the ground or sometimes on wood, near or under ash trees; summer–fall.

EDIBILITY: Edible.

REMARKS: Although the Ash Tree Bolete occurs with ash trees, it is not mycorrhizal with them. It has evolved a relationship with a parasitic aphid that is sheltered in sclerotia which are produced by this bolete. The sclerotia surround and protect the aphid, and the aphid provides honeydew nutrients to the bolete. For more information about this bolete and this interesting relationship, refer to Brundrett and Kendrick (1987). *Boletinellus proximus* (not illustrated), known only from Florida, has a dark brown to purplish-brown cap that fades to brown or cinnamon buff in age, pale brown flesh that does not stain when exposed, a yellow to yellow-brown or olive-brown decurrent pore surface, angular to irregular, often elongated, and radially arranged pores, and an eccentric to central stalk that is yellow or colored like the cap. Its spores measure 7–10 × 5–7 μm, and it grows on the ground or on decaying wood in wet woodlands. *Boletinellus rompelii* = *Gyrodon rompelii* (p. 38) is like the above species, but it has a pinkish-red to rusty-red zone near the base of the stalk, and its flesh and pore surface stain blue when bruised.

Boletinellus merulioides

Boletinellus rompelii (Pat. & Rick) Watling

= *Gyrodon rompelii* (Pat. & Rick) Singer

MACROSCOPIC FEATURES: **Cap** 5–20 cm wide, convex to cushion-shaped, becoming broadly convex to nearly plane and depressed in age; margin even, often wavy or conspicuously lobed, inrolled to incurved and remaining so well into maturity; surface dry, subtomentose to fibrillose, sometimes nearly glabrous, grayish brown to yellowish brown or pinkish brown; **flesh** yellow to pale yellow, staining blue when exposed; odor and taste not distinctive. **Pore surface** decurrent, yellow at first, becoming dull yellow in age, bluing when bruised, pores radially arranged and elongated to nearly gill-like, 1–3 mm wide; tubes 3–10 mm deep. **Stalk** eccentric, nearly equal or tapered in either direction, solid; surface dry, pale yellow to yellow on the upper portion, with a pinkish-red to red zone near the base that becomes rusty red to reddish brown in age; **flesh** colored and staining like the cap flesh.

SPORE PRINT: Pale olive brown.

MICROSCOPIC FEATURES: Spores 7–10 × 6–7.5 µm, ellipsoid, smooth, dull yellow.

OCCURRENCE: Solitary, scattered, or in groups on the ground under hardwoods; summer–early winter.

EDIBILITY: Edible.

REMARKS: The pinkish-red to red zone near the stalk base is distinctive. An additional color illustration is shown in the "Color Key to the Major Groups of Fungi" (p. 9). The flesh stains pale green with $FeSO_4$ and ochraceous with NH_4OH. Compare with *Boletinellus merulioides* (p. 37), which lacks the pinkish-red to red zone near its stalk base.

Boletinellus rompelii

Boletus abruptibulbus Roody, Both & B. Ortiz

COMMON NAME: Abruptly Bulbous Sand Bolete.

MACROSCOPIC FEATURES: **Cap** 3–8 cm wide, convex, becoming broadly convex, with a narrow sterile margin; surface shiny, glabrous, dry to subviscid when wet, occasionally appressed-fibrillose, often developing tiny cracks in age, reddish brown or dark brown at first, becoming cinnamon brown in age; **flesh** white to very pale yellow, unchanging; odor and taste not distinctive. **Pore surface** narrowly depressed around the stalk, pores angular to nearly gill-like near the stalk, pale yellow when young, becoming pale golden yellow then yellowish olive to greenish olive in age; tubes 3–8 mm deep. **Stalk** nearly equal on the upper portion, strongly bulbous to abruptly bulbous below, solid, with a prominent rooting stalk (pseudorhiza) covered in sand; surface dry, pallid or yellowish at the apex, gradually darker and becoming colored like the cap toward the base, not reticulate, with white basal mycelium; **flesh** yellow, unchanging when exposed.

SPORE PRINT: Olive brown.

MICROSCOPIC FEATURES: Spores 13.5–19.8 (-22.5) × 5–7.2 µm, smooth, fusoid, grayish yellow in KOH, dextrinoid in Melzer's reagent.

OCCURRENCE: Solitary or in scattered groups in coastal oak and pine woods; winter–spring.

EDIBILITY: Edible.

REMARKS: The epithet *abruptibulbus* means having an abruptly bulbous base, a reference to the stalk base of this unique bolete. The cap surface and bulbous base of dried material immediately stain dark red with the application of NH4OH, then slowly fade. *Aureoboletus auriporus* (p. 29) is somewhat similar but differs by being shiny and viscid, with a brilliant yellow pore surface, smaller spores, and no strongly developed pseudorhiza.

Boletus abruptibulbus

Boletus albisulphureus (Murrill) Murrill

= *Gyroporus albisulphureus* Murrill

COMMON NAME: Chalk-white Bolete.

MACROSCOPIC FEATURES: **Cap** 4–12 cm wide, obtuse when young, becoming broadly convex in age; surface dry, glabrous, sometimes finely cracked in age, milk white to grayish white, occasionally with yellowish or brownish tinges, especially near the margin; **flesh** white, unchanging; odor somewhat pungent and medicinal or not distinctive; taste not distinctive. **Pore surface** white to buff initially, becoming yellow, then finally dingy olive yellow in age, attached to subdecurrent, unchanging when bruised; tubes 5–15 mm deep. **Stalk** nearly equal or enlarged downward, occasionally abruptly narrowed at the base, solid; surface dry, milk white to whitish, yellowish at the apex, with white to yellowish reticulation on the upper portion; **flesh** colored like the cap flesh.

SPORE PRINT: Olive brown.

MICROSCOPIC FEATURES: Spores 11–15 × 3.5–4.5 µm, subfusiform, smooth, hyaline to pale yellowish, some dextrinoid in Melzer's.

OCCURRENCE: Solitary, scattered, or in groups with oaks; summer–early winter.

EDIBILITY: Edible.

REMARKS: The epithet *albisulphureus* means "white and yellow." *Xanthoconium stramineum* (p. 121) is very similar but lacks reticulation on the stalk. *Tylopilus rhoadsiae* (p. 111) has a white cap and stalk which often have pinkish or pinkish-tan tinges, prominent white to brown reticulation, a white pore surface that becomes dull pinkish in age, and bitter tasting flesh.

Boletus albisulphureus

Boletus aureissimus var. aureissimus (Murrill) Murrill

= *Boletus auripes* var. *aureissimus* (Murrill) Singer
= *Ceriomyces aureissimus* Murrill

MACROSCOPIC FEATURES: **Cap** 4–14 cm wide, obtuse when young, becoming broadly convex to nearly flat; surface dry, glabrous, honey yellow to bright yellow or yellow ocher, often duller when mature; **flesh** yellow, unchanging; odor and taste not distinctive. **Pore surface** pale yellow to yellow, becoming olive yellow at maturity, often depressed around the stalk in age, unchanging when bruised; tubes 1–2.5 cm deep. **Stalk** often bulbous to clavate when young, becoming nearly equal in age, solid; surface dry, yellow to bright yellow, usually with fine yellow reticulation on the upper portion, or sometimes not reticulate; **flesh** yellow, unchanging.
SPORE PRINT: Yellow brown to olive brown.
MICROSCOPIC FEATURES: Spores 10–14 × 3–5 µm, ellipsoid-cylindric to subfusoid, smooth, yellowish.
OCCURRENCE: Solitary, scattered, or in groups with oak; summer–fall.
EDIBILITY: Edible.

REMARKS: The epithet *aureissimus* means "golden yellow." *Ceriomyces aureissimus* var. *castaneus* (not illustrated) is nearly identical but differs by having a velvety, purplish-brown cap surface, grows associated with Laurel Oak (*Quercus laurifolia*), and is known only from Florida. *Boletus auripes* (p. 42) has a yellow-brown to chestnut- or grayish-brown cap, and a golden-yellow stalk with yellow reticulation. *Retiboletus ornatipes* (p. 91) has a darker yellow or gray cap, much coarser and more prominent reticulation, and bitter tasting flesh. The Showy Orange Bolete, *Boletus aurantiosplendens* (p. 9) has a darker orange to brownish-orange or brownish-yellow cap, a yellow to apricot or orange stalk with tawny to reddish-brown streaks over the mid-portion, obscure to distinct reticulation, and yellow flesh that darkens or becomes bright orange when exposed, and grows associated with beech, oak, hickory, and pine. *Boletus ochraceoluteus* (p. 49) has a 2–7 cm wide, ochraceous-yellow to orange-ocher cap, bright yellow flesh that stains reddish then bluish green, a bright yellow pore surface, and grows in mixed oak and pine woods during summer and fall. The cap surface stains bluish green with NH4OH.

Boletus aureissimus var. *aureissimus*

Boletus auripes Peck

MACROSCOPIC FEATURES: **Cap** 4–13 cm wide, obtuse when young, becoming broadly convex to nearly flat when mature; surface dry, finely velvety to nearly glabrous, yellowish brown to chestnut or grayish brown, paler in age; **flesh** bright yellow, color intensifies when rubbed or bruised, not staining blue when exposed; odor and taste not distinctive. **Pore surface** pale yellow to yellow, becoming olive yellow in age, not bluing when bruised, often depressed around the stalk in age; tubes 1–2.5 cm deep. **Stalk** often bulbous to clavate when young, becoming clavate to nearly equal in age, solid; surface dry, golden yellow, with yellow reticulation at least on the upper portion; **flesh** colored like the cap flesh.

SPORE PRINT: Yellow brown to olive brown.
MICROSCOPIC FEATURES: Spores 10–14 × 3–5 µm, ellipsoid-cylindric to subfusoid, smooth, yellowish.
OCCURRENCE: Solitary, scattered, or in groups in hardwood forests, especially with oak and beech, sometimes in grassy areas where oak is present; summer–fall.
EDIBILITY: Edible.
REMARKS: *Auripes* means "golden yellow foot." *Boletus aureissimus* var. *aureissimus* (p. 41) is very similar but has a honey-yellow to bright yellow or yellow-ocher cap and finer reticulation on the stalk. *Ceriomyces aureissimus* var. *castaneus* (not illustrated) differs by having a velvety purplish-brown cap.

Boletus auripes

Boletus carminiporus A. E. Bessette, Both & Dunaway

MACROSCOPIC FEATURES: **Cap** 3–14 cm wide, convex, becoming broadly convex to nearly flat; margin sterile, initially incurved to inrolled, becoming decurved in age; surface dry to slightly viscid, glabrous or nearly so, dull red when young, becoming pinkish red to orange red, then fading to reddish orange to dull golden orange in age; **flesh** whitish to pale yellow, turning darker yellow when exposed or in age, unchanging; odor and taste not distinctive. **Pore surface** yellow when very young, becoming dark red to brownish red, then fading to dull red or orange red at maturity, bruising bluish green then dull olive, depressed around the stalk in age; tubes 3–12 mm deep, yellow, staining bluish green when cut or bruised. **Stalk** enlarged downward to a pinched base, rarely tapered downward or equal, solid; surface dry, distinctly reticulate overall or on the upper portion, rose pink at first, becoming dark red at the apex and paler red below, staining brownish red or slowly olive green to olive yellow when handled or bruised, without reddish hairs at the base; **flesh** pale yellow to yellow, darker than in the cap, not staining when exposed, becoming dull red around larval tunnels.

SPORE PRINT: Olive brown.

MICROSCOPIC FEATURES: Spores 8–11 × 3–4 μm, subfusoid, smooth, ochraceous.

OCCURRENCE: Solitary, scattered, in groups with mixed hardwoods, especially with beech, hickory, and oak, or in mixed oak and pine forests; summer–fall.

EDIBILITY: Unknown.

REMARKS: *Carminiporus* means "carmine-red pores." *Boletus flammans* (not illustrated) is very similar but differs by having yellowish flesh that quickly stains blue when exposed, growing associated with conifers, especially spruce, hemlock, and pine, and having larger spores that measure 10–16 × 4–5 μm. *Suillellus subluridus* (not illustrated) lacks reticulation on the stalk.

Boletus carminiporus

Boletus lewisii (Singer ex Both)
A. E. Bessette, Roody & A. R. Bessette

= *Pulveroboletus lewisii* Singer ex Both

MACROSCOPIC FEATURES: **Cap** 2.5–6 cm wide, with a sterile margin; surface dry to slightly viscid, subtomentose, dull reddish brown to purplish brown or umber brown; **flesh** whitish to pale yellow, reddish under the cuticle, slowly and erratically staining blue near the tubes when exposed; odor not distinctive; taste slightly acrid or not distinctive. **Pore surface** yellow when young, becoming dull yellow in age, slowly and weakly bruising blue then brownish; pores irregular to elongated, slightly depressed at the stalk in age; tubes 4–9 mm deep. **Stalk** nearly equal or tapered downward, ventricose at the base, flared at the apex, dry, solid, covered overall with brownish punctae, ground color yellow from the apex downward to the mid-portion, cinnamon brown to reddish brown downward to the base, basal mycelium white; **flesh** whitish to pale yellow, often with reddish stains at the base.

SPORE PRINT: Dark brownish olive.
MICROSCOPIC FEATURES: Spores 7–10 × 3.5–4.5 μm, ellipsoid to subfusoid, smooth, honey brown.
OCCURRENCE: Solitary, scattered, or in groups in mixed oak and pine woods; known only from Texas and Mississippi; summer–fall.
EDIBILITY: Unknown.
REMARKS: This bolete is named in honor of Texas mycologist, and co-author of this book, David P. Lewis, who first collected it.

Boletus lewisii

Boletus longiniveipes A. R. Bessette, A. E. Bessette, J. L. Frank, L. Kudzma & J. A. Bolin nom. prov.

COMMON NAME: Long-legged White Foot.

MACROSCOPIC FEATURES: **Cap** 4–16 cm wide, pulvinate to convex-depressed, becoming broadly convex to nearly plane; margin incurved when young, even; surface viscid when fresh, shiny when dry, glabrous to fasciculate-tomentose, pinkish brown to reddish tan, retaining its color well into maturity, fading as it dries; **flesh** whitish to pale yellow, reddish under the cuticle, slowly staining pinkish red then brownish when exposed or bruised, not bluing; odor and taste not distinctive. **Pore surface** yellow at first, becoming dull olive, and finally dark olive in age, staining dull reddish brown when bruised, not bluing, depressed around the stalk; pores angular, 1–2 per mm; tubes 1–2.6 cm deep. **Stalk** solid, nearly equal or slightly enlarged in either direction, with a pinched base, typically curved near the base; surface dry, longitu-dinally striate, lacking reticulation, finely punctate nearly overall, concolorous with the cap, with a conspicuous white basal mycelium covering up to 3 cm of the base of the stalk; **flesh** colored and staining like the cap flesh.

SPORE PRINT: Olive-brown.

MICROSCOPIC FEATURES: Spores 12–17 × 7–8 μm, thin-walled and fragile, oblong-elliptical, brownish.

OCCURRENCE: Solitary or scattered on the ground, under pine, or in mixed oak and pine woods; known only from Florida and coastal southeastern Georgia; summer–winter.

EDIBILITY: Edible.

REMARKS: The uniform coloration, elegant stature with its long, slender stalk, and the very prominent "white foot" makes this beautiful mushroom unmistakable. The cap surface stains dark maroon to reddish brown with KOH, very dark olive with NH4OH, and is negative with FeSO4; the flesh exhibits an olive flash then becomes dark amber with KOH, stains very pale blue with NH4OH, and stains faintly grayish olive with FeSO4.

Boletus longiniveipes

Boletus luridellus (Murrill) Murrill

= *Boletus subsensibilis* (Murrill) Murrill
= *Ceriomyces subsensibilis* Murrill

MACROSCOPIC FEATURES: **Cap** 4–12 cm wide, pulvinate when young, becoming broadly convex to nearly flat, with a sterile margin; surface dry, sometimes cracked, velvety to nearly glabrous, initially yellow-brown to amber brown, reddish brown, or streaked dull brown over a yellow ground color, becoming ochraceous tawny to hazel when mature; **flesh** yellow, quickly staining blue when cut; odor and taste not distinctive. **Pore surface** yellow when young, becoming greenish yellow to olive yellow in age, depressed around the stalk at maturity, quickly staining blue when bruised; tubes 8–16 mm deep. **Stalk** nearly equal or tapered in either direction, at times swollen near the middle, solid; surface dry, yellow near the apex or overall, occasionally brownish red on the lower portion or overall, with brown reticulation on the upper portion that is sometimes yellow at the apex, often with brownish punctae and dark red streaks at the base, quickly staining blue when bruised; **flesh** yellow except red at the base, quickly staining blue when exposed.

SPORE PRINT: Olive brown.

MICROSCOPIC FEATURES: Spores 12–17 × 4–6 µm, fusoid, smooth, pale yellow-brown.

OCCURRENCE: Scattered or in groups in grassy areas or in oak and pine woods; summer–fall.

EDIBILITY: Edible.

REMARKS: *Luridellus* means "dirty brownish." This bolete can be difficult to identify due to its variable cap and stalk color combinations. The brown cap, quickly blue staining yellow flesh and pore surface, brown stalk reticulation, and its association with oak and pine are key identification features.

Boletus luridellus

Boletus miniato-olivaceus Frost

COMMON NAME: Red and Olive Velvet-cap.

MACROSCOPIC FEATURES: **Cap** 5–15 cm wide, convex, becoming broadly convex to nearly flat; margin incurved at first, even or sterile; surface dry, velvety, red to rosy red when young, becoming pale rose-pink with olive tones, finally turning rosy tan to olive yellow with rosy tints when mature, often staining dark blue when bruised; **flesh** dull white to pale yellow, reddish under the cuticle, slowly staining blue when exposed; odor and taste not distinctive. **Pore surface** yellow at first, becoming dingy yellow to olive yellow, sometimes developing reddish tints in age, depressed at the stalk at maturity, quickly staining blue, then slowly turning brownish when bruised; tubes 6–16 mm deep. **Stalk** nearly equal or tapered in either direction, solid, often with a pinched base; surface dry, somewhat roughened with delicate, reddish punctae, sometimes longitudinally striate, with reddish tints over a yellow ground color, may be reticulate on the upper portion, often staining dark blue when bruised, basal mycelium yellowish; **flesh** yellow, usually darker than the cap flesh, reddish to brownish around larval tunnels, sometimes slowly staining blue.

SPORE PRINT: Olive-brown.

MICROSCOPIC FEATURES: Spores 10–15(18) × 4–6(7) μm, fusoid to subellipsoid, smooth, ochraceous.

OCCURRENCE: Solitary, scattered, or in groups in conifer, hardwood, or mixed woodlands, often with hemlock, birch, oak, or beech; summer–fall.

EDIBILITY: Reported to be poisonous, causing gastrointestinal distress.

REMARKS: *Miniato-olivaceus* means "colored with red and olive," a reference to the colors of the cap. Ongoing molecular analysis indicates that this species may belong in genus *Pulchroboletus*. The cap surface stains olive yellow, then rapidly olive green to olive bronze with KOH, and grayish olive with FeSO4. The flesh stains pale orange with KOH, pale yellowish with FeSO4, and is negative with NH4OH. *Boletus sensibilis* (p. 57) is very similar, but its cap does not develop olive tones in age. Its flesh has a distinctive odor that has been variously described as fruity, like maple syrup, fenugreek, curry, or licorice. Additionally, it has smaller spores that measure 10–13 × 3.5–4.5 μm.

Boletus miniato-olivaceus

Boletus nobilis Peck

COMMON NAME: Noble Bolete.

MACROSCOPIC FEATURES: **Cap** 7–20 cm wide, convex, becoming broadly convex to nearly plane; surface dry, smooth, glabrous, yellowish brown or reddish brown at first, finally becoming ochraceous to olive ochraceous or reddish ochraceous; **flesh** white, becoming yellowish near the tubes, unchanging; odor and taste not distinctive. **Pore surface** white at first, becoming yellow to pale ochraceous or brownish yellow, usually slightly depressed around the stalk in age; tubes 8–25 mm deep. **Stalk** nearly equal, sometimes swollen near the middle to slightly enlarged near the base, solid; surface dry, white to pale brownish orange-yellow, finely reticulate near the apex or on the upper half, glabrous below, rarely glabrous overall; reticulation white; **flesh** colored like the cap flesh.

SPORE PRINT: Dull ocher brown to dull rusty brown.

MICROSCOPIC FEATURES: Spores 11–16 × 4–5 μm, subfusiform, smooth, pale olivaceous.

OCCURRENCE: Solitary, scattered, or in groups with hardwoods, especially oak and beech; summer–fall.

EDIBILITY: Edible.

REMARKS: *Nobilis* means "noble or grand." *Boletus variipes* (p. 61) has a darker cap and more prominent white to brown reticulation that usually covers most of the stalk.

Boletus nobilis

Boletus ochraceoluteus A. E. Bessette, Both & A. R. Bessette

MACROSCOPIC FEATURES: **Cap** 2–7 cm wide, convex, becoming broadly convex to nearly plane in age; margin incurved, with a narrow band of sterile tissue when young, becoming even at maturity; surface dry to slightly viscid, somewhat velvety when young, becoming glabrous at maturity, finely cracked in age, ochraceous yellow to orange ocher or pale pinkish cinnamon with yellow on the margin at first, becoming dull brownish yellow in age; **flesh** pale to bright yellow, staining reddish and then bluish green within five minutes after being exposed; odor and taste not distinctive. **Pore surface** attached to subdecurrent, bright yellow when young, becoming dull yellow in age, slowly staining blue when bruised; tubes 8–13 mm deep. **Stalk** nearly equal or tapered in either direction, solid; surface dry, pale yellow with reddish tints or stains near the apex or almost overall, sometimes slowly staining blue, pruinose, with scant whitish to pale yellow basal mycelium; **flesh** yellow, staining reddish and then slowly bluish green when exposed.

SPORE PRINT: Olive brown to yellowish brown.

MICROSCOPIC FEATURES: Spores 10–14 × 4.5–6 μm, subfusiform to subellipsoid, smooth, brownish yellow.

OCCURRENCE: Scattered or in groups with oaks or in mixed oak and pine woods; summer–early winter.

EDIBILITY: Unknown.

REMARKS: *Ochraceoluteus* means "ochraceous and yellow," referring to the range of cap colors. The cap surface stains bluish green with NH4OH and exhibits an orange flash that soon becomes reddish brown with KOH. *Xerocomus hypoxanthus* (p. 123) has flesh that does not stain reddish, its stalk lacks reddish tints and is usually bright yellow at the base, and its cap surface stains blue to greenish blue with the application of NH4OH or KOH. *Xerocomus hemixanthus* (not illustrated) has a dark brown to reddish-brown cap and an arcuate-decurrent yellow pore surface that extends down on the stalk and forms a brown partial reticulum over a creamy buff ground color. It grows on the trunk bases of Eastern Hophornbeam or sometimes on Sweetgum, Swamp Maple, or American Hornbeam. Also compare with the *Xerocomus illudens/Xerocomus tenax* complex (p. 124), which has partial or complete reticulation on its stalk, and its stalk base is almost woody.

Boletus ochraceoluteus

Boletus oliveisporus (Murrill) Murrill

= *Ceriomyces oliveisporus* Murrill

MACROSCOPIC FEATURES: **Cap** 5–18 cm wide, convex, becoming broadly convex to nearly flat, with a sterile margin; surface dry, slightly velvety, usually finely cracked in age, reddish orange overall, may be paler yellow orange near the margin when young, becoming dark fulvous tinged with bay-brown or cinnamon brown to dull brown, and somewhat shiny in age, rapidly staining blue-black when bruised; **flesh** yellow, staining blue when cut, sometimes slowly; odor and taste not distinctive. **Pore surface** yellow to greenish yellow, becoming olive-yellow then olive-brown and depressed around the stalk in age, rapidly staining blue when bruised; tubes 5–20 mm deep. **Stalk** tapered in either direction or nearly equal, solid; surface dry, covered with distinct brown punctae nearly overall, sometimes nearly glabrous, at first yellow with reddish tinges, becoming olive-brown from the base upward as it matures, rapidly staining blue-black when bruised, reticulate on the upper portion or lacking reticulation entirely, conspicuously longitudinally striate; **flesh** colored and staining like the cap flesh, reddish brown at the very base and around larval tunnels.

SPORE PRINT: Olive-brown.

MICROSCOPIC FEATURES: Spores 11–17 × 4–6 μm, fusoid, smooth, ochraceous.

OCCURRENCE: Solitary, scattered, or in groups on the ground or on stumps under pines, sometimes in mixed oak and pine woods; summer–fall.

EDIBILITY: Unknown.

REMARKS: *Oliveisporus* means "olive-colored spores." All parts of this bolete instantly stain dark blue when handled or bruised. The Mahogany Bolete, *Boletus mahogonicolor* (pp. 9, 50), currently known only from Mississippi, has a silky and shiny, mahogany to reddish-brown or rose-brown cap that stains blue along the margin when bruised, very shallow tubes, 2–8 mm deep, and smaller spores that measure 10–13 × 3.5–4 μm. *Cyanoboletus pulverulentus* (p. 67) has a smaller, darker brown cap, raised longitudinal ridges on the stalk, and a cap surface that displays a green flash with NH_4OH. *Suillellus subvelutipes* (p. 95) has a red to orange pore surface.

Boletus oliveisporus

Boletus pallidus Frost

COMMON NAME: Pallid Bolete.

MACROSCOPIC FEATURES: **Cap** 4.5–15 cm wide, convex with an incurved margin, becoming broadly convex to nearly flat and sometimes slightly depressed in age; surface dry, smooth, glabrous or nearly so, often cracked in age, whitish to buff or pale brownish when young, becoming dingy brown with rose tints; **flesh** thick, whitish or pale yellow, sometimes slowly staining bluish or pinkish when cut; odor not distinctive; taste slightly bitter or not distinctive. **Pore surface** whitish to pale yellow when young, becoming yellow to greenish yellow, rapidly staining greenish blue then grayish brown when bruised; pores minute; tubes 1–2 cm deep. **Stalk** enlarged downward or nearly equal, solid; surface dry, smooth, sometimes slightly reticulate at the apex, whit-ish when young, usually developing brownish streaks especially towards the base, at times yellow at the apex, with occasional reddish flushes near the base in age, occasionally stains slightly blue when bruised, often with a white basal mycelium; **flesh** colored and staining like the cap flesh.

SPORE PRINT: Olive to olive brown.

MICROSCOPIC FEATURES: Spores 9–15 × 3–5 μm, narrowly oval to subfusoid, smooth, pale brown.

OCCURRENCE: Solitary, scattered, in groups, or caespitose in hardwood forests or in mixed woods under oaks; summer–fall

EDIBILITY: Edible.

REMARKS: *Pallidus* means "pallid." Its flesh stains pale rusty orange with the application of KOH, blue-green with NH4OH, and bluish green to grayish with FeSO4.

Boletus pallidus

Boletus patrioticus T. J. Baroni, A. E. Bessette & Roody

COMMON NAME: Patriotic Bolete.
MACROSCOPIC FEATURES: **Cap** 3–13 cm wide, convex at first, becoming broadly convex to nearly flat; margin sterile, initially incurved, becoming decurved in age; surface dry, somewhat velvety, olive when very young, soon pinkish to brick-red or dark red, often brownish red toward the margin, usually with olive to tarnished brass tints; **flesh** white to pale yellowish, pinkish red to purplish red under the cuticle or extending throughout the cap flesh, slowly staining blue beneath the reddish area when exposed; odor not distinctive; taste tart to acidic. **Pore surface** pale yellow when young, becoming olive-yellow at maturity, depressed around the stalk in age, staining blue when bruised; tubes 3–15 mm deep. **Stalk** typically enlarged downward, at times tapered downward or nearly equal, base often pinched, solid; surface dry, pruinose to scurfy, color variable, usually rosy red on the upper portion or nearly overall, olive toward the base, frequently a mixture of these colors over a yellow ground color, not reticulate, basal mycelium whitish to pale yellow; **flesh** whitish to pale yellow, becoming dingy yellow to brownish towards the base, staining bluish to greenish, sometimes rosy red when exposed.
SPORE PRINT: Olive brown.
MICROSCOPIC FEATURES: Spores 10–13 × 4–5.5 μm, subfusiform, smooth, deep golden brown.
OCCURRENCE: Solitary, scattered, or in groups, often in grassy areas or mixed woods with oak present; spring–fall.
EDIBILITY: Edible.
REMARKS: *Patrioticus* means "patriotic," and refers to the red, white, and blue colors displayed by the exposed flesh. The cap surface stains olive brown with KOH, olive amber with NH4OH, and olive gray with FeSO4.

Boletus patrioticus

Boletus pseudopinophilus J. L. Frank, A. E. Bessette, A. R. Bessette & J. Craine nom. prov.

= *Boletus edulis* f. *pinicola* (Vittad.) Vassilkov
= *Boletus pinicola* (Vittad.) A. Venturi

COMMON NAME: Pine-loving King Bolete.
MACROSCOPIC FEATURES: **Cap** 5–15 cm wide, initially convex, becoming broadly convex to nearly flat; margin sterile or nearly even, initially incurved; surface dry, usually wrinkled or shallowly pitted, reddish brown to dark rusty brown; **flesh** whitish, pinkish brown under the cuticle, unchanging when cut or exposed; odor spicy or not distinctive; taste not distinctive. **Pore surface** whitish when young, becoming yellow to olive yellow or brownish yellow when mature, bruising rusty brown, depressed around the stalk at maturity; tubes 8–25 mm deep. **Stalk** enlarged downward, occasionally bulbous, solid; surface dry, white to pale yellow near the apex, pale brown to brown below, darkening when handled or bruised, reticulate overall or at least on the upper two-thirds, reticulum whitish near the apex, becoming brownish below, darkening when handled; **flesh** colored like the cap flesh.

SPORE PRINT: Dark olive to olive brown.
MICROSCOPIC FEATURES: Spores 15–20 × 4–6 μm, fusoid to cylindrical, smooth, yellowish.
OCCURRENCE: Solitary, scattered, or in groups with conifers, especially pine, sometimes buried in duff; spring–fall.
EDIBILITY: Edible
REMARKS: *Pseudopinophilus* means "false *pinophilus*," a reference to *Boletus pinophilus* Pilát & Dermek, which is a European species and does not occur in North America.

Boletus pseudopinophilus

Boletus roodyi B. Ortiz, D. P. Lewis & Both

COMMON NAME: Roody's Bolete.
MACROSCOPIC FEATURES: **Cap** 5–16 cm wide, convex when young, becoming nearly flat or sometimes slightly depressed in the center; surface dry, smooth and glabrous to faintly velvety, sometimes cracked in age, with a faint whitish pruina when young, pinkish purple-red to blood-red or dark red overall, margin incurved at first, becoming decurved, sterile; **flesh** very pale yellow to nearly white, with a very narrow red line under the cap surface, unchanging when exposed or sometimes developing reddish stains; odor not distinctive; taste slightly astringent or not distinctive. **Pore surface** attached to narrowly depressed, bright yellow to pale golden yellow at first, becoming greenish yellow to greenish olivaceous in age, unchanging when bruised; tubes 5–10 mm deep. **Stalk** equal down to a narrowed base; surface dry, glabrous to finely pruinose, pale golden yellow near the apex, paler yellow downward toward the base, irregularly streaked, mottled, or flecked on the lower half, or sometimes only at the base, with red that is colored like the cap, not reticulate, basal mycelium white; **flesh** whitish to very pale yellow, golden yellow in larval tunnels, sometimes red in the base, unchanging when cut or exposed.
SPORE PRINT: Olive-brown.
MICROSCOPIC FEATURES: Spores 9.5–16.2 × 3.6–4.5 μm, fusoid, smooth, with grayish-yellow or greenish-yellow contents in KOH; dextrinoid or with pale grayish-blue contents in Melzer's.
OCCURRENCE: Solitary, scattered, or gregarious with hardwoods or in mixed oak and pine woods, usually associated with various species of oak; summer–fall.
EDIBILITY: Edible.
REMARKS: This bolete was named in honor of American mycologist William C. Roody. Ongoing molecular analysis indicates that this species may belong in genus *Pulchroboletus*. The cap surface develops a slate-blue flash that quickly changes to yellow-ocher with KOH or NH4OH. KOH stains the flesh pale bluish. When dried, the flesh odor is pleasant and sweet, with a vanilla-like scent. The *Baorangia bicolor* complex (p. 34) has flesh that slowly stains blue when exposed.

Boletus roodyi

Boletus roseolateritius A. E. Bessette, Both & Dunaway

COMMON NAME: Rosy Brick-red Bolete.

MACROSCOPIC FEATURES: **Cap** 4–15.5 cm wide, convex when young, becoming nearly flat in age; margin sterile, incurved and remaining so well into maturity; surface dry, somewhat velvety with a grayish bloom when young, almost glabrous at maturity, whitish along the margin, dark reddish salmon or burnt orange elsewhere, becoming rosy brick-red to reddish brown, finally fading to brownish orange with yellow tints and becoming dull dingy yellow in age, instantly staining dark blue when bruised; **flesh** pale lemon yellow, quickly staining blue when exposed, then fading to pale lemon yellow; odor and taste not distinctive. **Pore surface** orange red when young, becoming dull orange and finally orange yellow when mature, instantly staining blue when bruised; tubes 5–12 mm deep. **Stalk** equal or tapered in either direction, sometimes with a pinched base, solid; surface dry, with faint longitudinal striations, not reticulate, pale lemon yellow, quickly staining blue, then slowly rusty brown when handled or bruised, and developing rusty brown stains in age; **flesh** colored and staining like the cap flesh.

SPORE PRINT: Olive-brown.

MICROSCOPIC FEATURES: Spores 8.5–11 × 3.5–4.5(-5.5) µm, narrowly ellipsoid to subfusoid, smooth, pale ochraceous.

EDIBILITY: Unknown.

OCCURRENCE: Solitary, scattered, or in groups on river bottomland with beech, oak, and hickory; known only from McComb, Mississippi; summer. Its distribution range has yet to be established.

REMARKS: *Roseolateritius* means "rosy brick-red." The cap surface stains black with FeSO4 and is negative with KOH or NH4OH. *Boletus fairchildianus* (not illustrated) is similar but differs by having a darker red pore surface, a cap that stains olive with NH4OH and deep maroon or orange-yellow to brown with KOH, and much larger spores that measure 13–19 × 5–8 µm.

Boletus roseolateritius

Boletus rufomaculatus Both

MACROSCOPIC FEATURES: **Cap** 6.5–14 cm wide, rounded when young, becoming broadly convex to nearly flat; margin sterile and initially incurved; surface dry or subviscid, covered with tiny matted fibers, color dull rusty brown to ocher brown, rusty brown at the margin, becoming reddish, pale brown, or honey yellow, and finally dotted, splashed, and mottled with brick-red to brownish red in age; **flesh** pale yellow, slowly staining blue when cut or exposed, especially above the tube layer, sometimes staining blue only weakly and erratically; odor and taste not distinctive. **Pore surface** pale yellow when young, becoming darker yellow and finally yellowish olive, sometimes with rusty spots or reddish tints in age, shallowly depressed around the stalk at maturity, bruising blue; tubes 6–14 mm deep. **Stalk** equal or somewhat swollen in the middle and tapered at both ends, solid; surface dry, nearly glabrous, somewhat ribbed to pseudoreticulate, golden yellow near the apex, pale yellow below, dotted or mottled with burgundy red on the lower half or sometimes nearly overall, bruising blue, with white basal mycelium; **flesh** colored and staining like the cap flesh.

SPORE PRINT: Dark olive.

MICROSCOPIC FEATURES: Spores 10–13 × 3–4.5 μm, subfusiform, smooth, yellowish in Melzer's.

OCCURRENCE: Solitary, scattered, or in groups associated with beech in mixed woods; late spring–fall.

EDIBILITY: Edible.

REMARKS: *Rufomaculatus* means "spotted reddish," referring to the reddish spots and splashes on the mottled cap. The *Baorangia bicolor* complex (p. 34) has a glabrous dark red to apple-red cap with a margin that is even at all stages of development, a glabrous stalk that is red or rosy red on the lower two-thirds or more, darker golden yellow stalk flesh, and is associated with oaks.

Boletus rufomaculatus

Boletus sensibilis Peck

= *Boletus miniato-olivaceus* var. *sensibilis*
(Peck) Peck
= *Boletus sensibilis* var. *subviscidus* A. H. Sm.
& Thiers

COMMON NAME: Sensitive Bolete.
MACROSCOPIC FEATURES: **Cap** 5–16 cm wide,
convex at first, becoming broadly convex
to nearly flat; margin even; surface velvety
when young, dry, becoming nearly smooth at
maturity, pale to dark brick-red, dull rose or
sometimes dingy cinnamon in age, quickly
bruising blue; **flesh** pale yellow, staining
blue when exposed; odor faintly fruity or
sweet like maple syrup, fenugreek, curry, or
licorice; taste not distinctive. **Pore surface**
yellow at first, becoming browner or dull in
age, immediately staining blue when bruised;
tubes 8–12 mm deep. **Stalk** equal or slightly
enlarged downward, solid, dry, mostly yellow but often tinged pink or red on the lower
portion or near the base, sometimes finely
reticulate at the apex, quickly staining blue
when bruised or handled; **flesh** bright yellow,
more so than the cap flesh, quickly staining
blue when exposed.
SPORE PRINT: Olive brown
MICROSCOPIC FEATURES: Spores 10–13 ×
3.5–4.5 µm, suboblong to slightly ventricose,
smooth, pale brown; hymenial cystidia fusoid-
ventricose with an elongated neck.
OCCURRENCE: Scattered or in groups, usually
in hardwood forests; summer–fall.
EDIBILITY: Edible.
REMARKS: *Sensibilis* means "sensitive," referring to the fact that all parts of this bolete
instantly stain blue when handled or bruised.
The cap surface stains yellow with KOH or
NH_4OH and greenish gray with $FeSO_4$.
Boletus miniato-olivaceus (p. 47) has a cap that
develops olive tones in age, flesh without a
distinctive odor, and larger spores that measure 10–15(18) × 4–6(7) µm.

Boletus sensibilis

Boletus separans Peck

= *Boletus pseudoseparans* Grand & A. H. Sm.
= *Xanthoconium separans* (Peck) Halling &
    Both

COMMON NAME: Lilac Bolete.

MACROSCOPIC FEATURES: **Cap** 5–15 cm wide,
convex when young, becoming broadly
convex in age; margin even; surface dry,
somewhat velvety or smooth, usually pitted,
wrinkled, or lumpy and uneven; color ranges
from creamy white tinged with lilac to pinkish
brown, lilac brown, reddish brown, or at times
dark purple, usually paler near the margin,
becoming yellowish brown to nearly bronze
in age; **flesh** white, unchanging; odor not distinctive; taste sweet and nutty or not distinctive. **Pore surface** initially white, becoming
yellowish to ocher brown in age, unchanging
when bruised; tubes 1–3 cm deep. **Stalk** equal
or enlarged downward, solid; surface dry,
colored like the cap or paler, usually with lilac
tones in the mid-portion, sometimes purplish
overall, with a fine white reticulum over most
of its length or at least over the upper half;
flesh colored like the cap flesh.

SPORE PRINT: Brownish ocher to pale reddish
brown.

MICROSCOPIC FEATURES: Spores 12–16 ×
3.5–5 μm, narrowly subfusiform, smooth, pale
brown.

OCCURRENCE: Solitary, scattered, or in clusters
in mixed woods, oak woods, or sometimes
with pine; summer–winter.

EDIBILITY: Edible.

REMARKS: *Separans* means "separating," referring to the tube layer that sometimes pulls
away from the stalk as the cap expands. Lilac
areas of the cap and stalk stain aquamarine to
deep blue with NH4OH.

Boletus separans

Boletus subgraveolens A. H. Sm. & Thiers

MACROSCOPIC FEATURES: **Cap** 4–15 cm wide, initially convex, then broadly convex to flat in age, with an even margin that is incurved at first; surface dry or slightly viscid, smooth, becoming cracked in hot, dry weather, colored dull yellow brown or sometimes mottled with darker or paler shades of yellow or brown, typically stains dark blue then darker brown when fresh; **flesh** whitish yellow to pale yellow, staining blue when exposed; odor pungent and disagreeable; taste not distinctive. **Pore surface** brownish yellow when very young, soon becoming bright yellow-brown and then paler in age, depressed near the stalk, bruising dark blue then slowly brown; tubes 6–13 mm deep. **Stalk** tapered downward, usually pinched or noticeably pointed at the base, solid; surface dry, bright yellow at the apex, dull pale yellow and pruinose below, with a dark vinaceous-red to maroon base, developing yellowish-brown tints from the base upward in age or when handled, sometimes bruising bluish; **flesh** pale yellow to orange yellow with pinkish tints on the upper portion, dark vinaceous red to maroon or reddish cinnamon near the base, staining blue when exposed.

SPORE PRINT: Olive-brown.

MICROSCOPIC FEATURES: Spores 9–13 × 3.5–4.5 μm, subfusiform, smooth, yellowish brown.

OCCURRENCE: Solitary, scattered, or in groups with hardwoods, especially aspen and oak; summer–early winter.

EDIBILITY: Unknown.

REMARKS: *Subgraveolens* means "somewhat strong-smelling." Dried specimens of this bolete have a distinctly unpleasant smell. The cap surface displays a blue flash then slowly stains vinaceous with NH4OH.

Boletus subgraveolens

Boletus subtomentosus L.

= *Ceriomyces subtomentosus* (L.) Murrill
= *Xerocomus subtomentosus* (L.) Quél.

COMMON NAMES: Brown and Yellow Bolete, Suede Bolete, Yellow-cracked Bolete.

MACROSCOPIC FEATURES: **Cap** 5–18 cm wide, convex, becoming broadly convex in age; margin sterile, somewhat incurved at first; surface dry, covered with fine hairs, often cracked in age, olive brown to yellow brown; **flesh** whitish, unchanging or slightly staining blue when exposed; odor and taste not distinctive. **Pore surface** yellow at first, becoming dull yellow in age, staining slightly and slowly greenish then brownish when bruised; tubes 1–2.5 cm deep. **Stalk** nearly equal or tapered slightly downward, solid; surface dry, scurfy, sometimes with raised longitudinal lines that may form a net-like pattern near the apex, predominantly yellow with reddish-brown streaks, staining brownish to reddish brown when handled or in age, basal mycelium yellowish; **flesh** colored and staining like the cap flesh.

SPORE PRINT: Olive brown.

MICROSCOPIC FEATURES: Spores 10–15 × 3–5 μm, subfusoid to oblong, smooth, yellow.

OCCURRENCE: Solitary or scattered under hardwoods or conifers; summer–early winter.

EDIBILITY: Edible.

REMARKS: *Subtomentosus* means "somewhat coated with fine hairs," a reference to the surface of the cap. The cap surface instantly stains reddish brown with NH4OH.

Boletus subtomentosus

Boletus variipes Peck

= *Boletus variipes* var. *variipes* Peck
= *Boletus variipes* var. *fagicola* A. H. Sm. &
  Thiers

COMMON NAME: Variable-stalk Bolete.
MACROSCOPIC FEATURES: **Cap** 6–20 cm wide,
convex, becoming broadly convex to nearly
flat, with an even margin; surface dry, somewhat velvety to nearly smooth, color varying
from creamy tan to yellowish tan, grayish
brown to yellow brown or dark brown, usually cracked in age; **flesh** white, not staining
when exposed; odor and taste not distinctive.
Pore surface white at first, then yellowish
to yellowish olive in age, not staining when
bruised; tubes 1–3 cm deep. **Stalk** equal or
enlarged downward, solid; surface dry, whitish
to yellow brown or grayish brown, typically
reticulate, sometimes less obviously so, reticulation white or brown; **flesh** colored like the
cap flesh.

SPORE PRINT: Olive brown.
MICROSCOPIC FEATURES: Spores 12–18 × 4–6
µm, subfusoid, smooth, yellow.
OCCURRENCE: Scattered or in groups associated with hardwoods, especially oak, beech,
or aspen, sometimes with conifers, especially
pine; spring–fall.
EDIBILITY: Edible.
REMARKS: *Variipes* means "variable foot," referring to the color, shape, and amount of reticulation on its stalk. *Tylopilus felleus* (p. 105)
has bitter tasting flesh and a pore surface that
becomes pinkish brown as the spores mature.
Boletus nobilis (p. 48) has a taller stature, a
paler, often somewhat pitted cap, a white to
pale ocher stalk that is sometimes streaked
with pale brown, and white reticulation that
is delicate and normally limited to the upper
portion of the stalk.

Boletus variipes

Boletus weberi Singer

MACROSCOPIC FEATURES: **Cap** 4–7 cm wide, convex, becoming broadly convex to flat when mature; surface dry, cracked and scaly with pale yellow flesh showing in the cracks, brownish olive initially, becoming olive brown, sometimes with reddish tints; margin even, incurved, becoming decurved in age; **flesh** pale yellow, unchanging; odor not distinctive; taste tart, somewhat lemony. **Pore surface** dull red when young, becoming dull orange red, and finally reddish orange, depressed around the stalk in age, sometimes slowly staining brown when bruised; tubes 3–6 mm deep. **Stalk** enlarged downward, with a conspicuously pinched base, solid; surface dry, fibrillose-punctate, and pinkish red to dull purplish red over a pale yellow ground color on the upper portion, somewhat scaly-punctate, olive to brownish olive or olive brown over a yellow ground color on the lower portion, with tiny dark brown punctae overall, not reticulate; **flesh** pale yellow, becoming olive-yellow to dull mustard yellow at the base, with red or brown stains around larval tunnels.

SPORE PRINT: Olive brown.

MICROSCOPIC FEATURES: Spores 10–13 × 4–6 μm, narrowly ellipsoid to subfusoid, smooth, pale ochraceous.

OCCURRENCE: Solitary, scattered, or in groups with longleaf pine, often with bluejack oak nearby; late spring–summer.

EDIBILITY: Unknown.

REMARKS: *Weberi* refers to George F. Weber (1894–1976), a professor of plant pathology at the University of Florida at Gainesville, for whom it was named. Its dry, cracked, and scaly brownish cap, reddish pores, reddish and somewhat scaly stalk, and tart-tasting flesh, which is unchanging when exposed, are key features of this unusual bolete. The cap surface stains reddish brown with NH_4OH and is negative with $FeSO_4$. The flesh quickly stains greenish blue with NH_4OH and is negative with $FeSO_4$. *Caloboletus inedulis* (p. 9) has yellow pores that bruise blue and bitter-tasting flesh. Other similar red-pored boletes have flesh or pore surfaces that stain blue when cut or bruised.

Boletus weberi

Buchwaldoboletus hemichrysus
(Berk. & M. A. Curtis) Pilát

= *Boletus hemichrysus* Berk. & M. A. Curtis
= *Pulveroboletus hemichrysus* (Berk. & M. A. Curtis) Singer

COMMON NAME: Half Yellow Powdery Bolete.
MACROSCOPIC FEATURES: **Cap** 3–8 cm wide, obtuse to convex, becoming broadly convex at maturity; margin even, incurved at first and remaining so well into maturity; surface dry, floccose-scaly to somewhat velvety, often cracked in age, usually coated with powder, bright yellow to golden yellow; **flesh** yellow, staining blue, sometimes slowly, or unchanging; odor not distinctive; taste slightly acidic or not distinctive. **Pore surface** yellow when very young, soon becoming reddish brown, attached to subdecurrent, staining dark blue when bruised; tubes up to 1 cm deep. **Stalk** nearly equal or tapered in either direction, often with a narrowed base, solid; surface dry, color variable like the cap with reddish or reddish-brown tints or reddish brown overall, often with yellowish basal mycelium; **flesh** colored like the cap flesh.

SPORE PRINT: Olive-brown.
MICROSCOPIC FEATURES: Spores 6–9 × 2.5–4 µm, ellipsoid to subfusoid, smooth, yellowish.
OCCURRENCE: Solitary or scattered on pinewood, often at the base of trunks or on the ground attached to buried roots; late spring–early winter.
EDIBILITY: Edible.
REMARKS: *Hemichrysus* means "half yellow." The cap surface stains dark amber with KOH or NH4OH and yellow brown to gold with FeSO4. Its flesh stains olive to olive gray with a darker ring with KOH, olive yellow then soon fades with NH4OH, and slowly pale gray with FeSO4. *Buchwaldoboletus lignicola* (p. 64) has a scaly or velvety and suede-like yellowish-brown to reddish-brown cap and a yellow to golden-yellow pore surface. *Buchwaldoboletus sphaerocephalus* (not illustrated) has a sulphur-yellow cap when young that becomes pale yellow to whitish in age, a yellow pore surface that becomes dull yellow to brownish yellow, and a yellow stalk that lacks any reddish or brown tones.

Buchwaldoboletus hemichrysus

Buchwaldoboletus lignicola
(Kallenb.) Pilát

= *Boletus lignicola* Kallenb.
= *Pulveroboletus lignicola* (Kallenb.) E. A. Dick & Snell

MACROSCOPIC FEATURES: **Cap** 2.5–12 cm wide, convex when young, becoming broadly convex; margin sterile and wavy, inrolled when young and remaining so well into maturity; surface dry, velvety and suede-like, at times becoming finely cracked in age, reddish brown to yellow brown or rusty golden yellow, often darker brown at the margin, sometimes staining darker brown when bruised; **flesh** firm, pale yellow, quickly or slowly staining blue when cut; odor sweet, somewhat minty or citrus-like; taste weakly acidic or not distinctive. **Pore surface** initially yellow, becoming golden yellow to brownish yellow when mature, subdecurrent, staining dark greenish blue to blackish blue, then fading to reddish brown when bruised; tubes 3–12 mm deep. **Stalk** equal or tapered in either direction, typically narrowed at the base, often eccentric, solid; surface dry, somewhat velvety, golden mustard yellow at the apex and reddish brown to yellow brown below, staining darker brown when bruised, often with a fine reddish reticulum at the apex, basal mycelium yellow; **flesh** rusty toward the base, colored and staining like the cap flesh.

SPORE PRINT: Olive brown.

MICROSCOPIC FEATURES: Spores 6–10 × 3–4 μm, ellipsoid, smooth, yellowish.

OCCURRENCE: Solitary or scattered with pines, usually at the base of the tree or on stumps or roots, in pine or mixed oak and pine woods; late spring–early winter.

EDIBILITY: Unknown.

REMARKS: *Lignicola* means "growing on wood." The cap surface immediately stains intense black with NH4OH and is negative with FeSO4. *Phaeolus schweinitzii* (p. 498) is a polypore that often fruits with this bolete. Evidence suggests that *Buchwaldoboletus lignicola* is parasitic on *Phaeolus schweinitzii* (Nuhn, et al. 2013). *Buchwaldoboletus hemichrysus* (p. 63) is similar, but it has a brighter yellow to golden yellow, very powdery cap and a reddish-brown pore surface. *Buchwaldoboletus sphaerocephalus* (not illustrated) has a sulphur-yellow cap when young that becomes pale yellow to whitish in age, a yellow pore surface that becomes dull yellow to brownish yellow, and a yellow stalk that lacks any reddish or brown tones.

Buchwaldoboletus lignicola

Butyriboletus floridanus (Singer)
G. Wu, Kuan Zhao & Zhu L. Yang

= *Boletus floridanus* (Singer) Murrill
= *Boletus frostii* ssp. *floridanus* Singer
= *Exsudoporus floridanus* (Singer) Vizzini,
   Simonini & Gelardi
= *Suillellus floridanus* (Singer) Murrill

MACROSCOPIC FEATURES: **Cap** 4–15 cm wide, convex, becoming broadly convex to nearly flat; margin incurved at first; surface dry, somewhat velvety, pinkish red, rose red, purplish red, or brownish red, typically yellowish or whitish along the margin; **flesh** pale to bright yellow, quickly staining dark blue when exposed; odor and taste not distinctive. **Pore surface** color variable, ranging from reddish orange to pinkish red, at times with yellowish tints, or yellow overall with reddish tints, usually beaded with yellow droplets when young and fresh, often depressed around the stalk in age; tubes 6–12 mm deep. **Stalk** often bulbous when young, typically becoming club-shaped or at times nearly equal in age, solid; surface dry, yellow at the apex and red below, sometimes red overall, with conspicuous longitudinally elongated red reticulation over at least the upper half; **flesh** pale to bright yellow, quickly staining dark blue when exposed.
SPORE PRINT: Olive brown.
MICROSCOPIC FEATURES: Spores 13–18 × 4–5 μm, ellipsoid to fusoid, smooth, pale yellow-brown.
OCCURRENCE: Scattered or in groups with oaks or pines; summer–winter.
EDIBILITY: Edible.
REMARKS: *Floridanus* means "Florida," referring to where the type collection was found. The cap surface stains olive-black with the application of NH4OH. *Butyriboletus frostii* (p. 66) has much coarser raised reticulation and is darker red overall.

Butyriboletus floridanus

Butyriboletus frostii (J. L. Russell) Vizzini, Simonini & Gelardi

= *Boletus frostii* J. L. Russell
= *Exsudoporus frostii* (J. L. Russell) Vizzini, Simonini & Gelardi

COMMON NAME: Frost's Bolete.

MACROSCOPIC FEATURES: **Cap** 5–15 cm wide, rounded to convex when young, becoming broadly convex to nearly flat; margin initially incurved; surface smooth, shiny, dry, tacky when moist, deep blood red to candy apple red, sometimes developing yellowish areas in age, often with a narrow yellow band at the margin; **flesh** pale yellow to dull white, quickly staining blackish blue when cut; odor not distinctive; taste sour, acidic. **Pore surface** initially dark red, becoming paler in age, often exuding golden droplets of moisture when young, depressed around the stalk in age, instantly bruising blackish blue; pores minute; tubes 6–15 mm deep. **Stalk** enlarged downward or nearly equal, often curved at the base, solid; surface dry, dark red to pinkish red, white to yellowish at the base, staining blackish blue when bruised; covered over the entire length with coarse and deep reticulation which may be red, yellow, or a combination of both; **flesh** colored and bruising like the cap flesh.

SPORE PRINT: Olive brown.

MICROSCOPIC FEATURES: Spores 11–17 × 4–5 µm, elliptical, smooth, pale brown.

OCCURRENCE: Solitary, scattered, or in groups in hardwood forests or mixed woods, especially with oak; summer–fall.

EDIBILITY: Edible.

REMARKS: The epithet *frostii* honors Charles C. Frost (1805–1880), a mycologist from Vermont who first described several North American species of boletes. *Butyriboletus floridanus* (p. 65), while similar, differs by having a lighter red cap and less prominent reticulation on its stalk.

Butyriboletus frostii

Cyanoboletus pulverulentus (Opat.) Gelardi, Vizzini & Simonini

= *Boletus pulverulentus* Opat.

MACROSCOPIC FEATURES: **Cap** 4–12.5 cm wide, convex, becoming broadly convex to nearly flat; margin even; surface dry, initially somewhat dusty or powdery and slightly velvety, becoming glabrous and usually somewhat shiny in age, dark yellow brown to blackish brown or dark cinnamon brown, often developing reddish tints, instantly staining blackish blue when handled or bruised; **flesh** yellow, quickly staining blue when cut or exposed; odor and taste not distinctive. **Pore surface** yellow at first, becoming golden yellow to brownish yellow in age, instantly staining dark blue then dull brown when bruised; tubes 6–12 mm deep. **Stalk** nearly equal, at times enlarged downward, solid; surface dry, pruinose at the apex, yellow above and darker orange yellow downward, usually reddish brown and pruinose toward the base, often with raised longitudinal ridges, not reticulate, quickly staining dark blue then slowly dull brown when handled or bruised; **flesh** yellow, reddish brown in the base, instantly staining blue when exposed.

SPORE PRINT: Dark olive to olive-brown.

MICROSCOPIC FEATURES: Spores 11–15 × 4–6 μm, fusoid to elliptical, smooth, yellowish.

OCCURRENCE: Scattered or in groups with conifers or hardwoods; summer–fall.

EDIBILITY: Edible.

REMARKS: *Pulverulentus* means "dusty or powdery," referring to the cap, which often appears to be lightly coated with a layer of dust or powder. The cap surface displays a green flash with NH4OH. *Boletus oliveisporus* (p. 50) differs by typically being larger, and its fulvous to cinnamon-brown cap does not show a green flash reaction with NH4OH.

Cyanoboletus pulverulentus

Gyroporus castaneus (Bull.) Quél.

= *Boletus castaneus* Bull.

COMMON NAME: Chestnut Bolete.

MACROSCOPIC FEATURES: **Cap** 3–10 cm wide, convex to broadly convex when young, becoming nearly flat, sometimes slightly depressed; margin often split and flaring in age; surface velvety to nearly smooth, dry, yellow brown to orange brown or reddish brown; **flesh** brittle, white, unchanging; odor faintly pungent or not distinctive; taste not distinctive. **Pore surface** whitish to buff or yellowish, unchanging, depressed at the stalk in age; tubes 5–8 mm deep. **Stalk** nearly equal, often swollen in the middle or below, at times constricted at the apex and base, brittle, stuffed with a soft pith, developing several cavities or becoming hollow in age; surface dry, uneven, colored like the cap or sometimes slightly paler toward the apex; **flesh** firm, brittle, white.

SPORE PRINT: Pale yellow.

MICROSCOPIC FEATURES: Spores 8–13 × 5–6 μm, elliptical to ovoid, smooth, hyaline.

OCCURRENCE: Solitary, scattered, or in groups, usually associated with hardwoods, especially oak, but also in conifer woods; summer–winter.

EDIBILITY: Edible.

REMARKS: *Castaneus* refers to *Castanea*, the genus name for chestnut trees. It describes the chestnut-brown color of the cap and stalk of this common bolete. The cap surface stains amber orange with NH_4OH and is negative with $FeSO_4$. The cap and stalk of the Red Gyroporus, *Gyroporus purpurinus* (p. 9), are vinaceous to burgundy colored. *Austroboletus gracilis* (p. 32) is similar in color but differs by having a pore surface that is pinkish brown at maturity, a more slender solid stalk, softer flesh, and spores that are pinkish brown and pitted.

Gyroporus castaneus

Gyroporus phaeocyanescens Singer & M. H. Ivory

MACROSCOPIC FEATURES: **Cap** 4–12 cm wide, convex when young, becoming broadly convex to nearly flat; margin incurved when young, even; surface dry, coated with a thick, matted covering of hairs when young, becoming appressed-fibrillose to fibrillose-scaly in age, fulvous to yellow brown or grayish brown; **flesh** whitish, with a dark brown zone beneath the cuticle, staining indigo blue when exposed, sometimes erratically, finally fading to creamy buff; odor and taste not distinctive. **Pore surface** whitish at first, becoming pale yellow and somewhat darker in age, depressed or free near the stalk when mature, unchanging when bruised; tubes 5–15 mm deep. **Stalk** enlarged downward or nearly equal, solid, becoming hollow and brittle when mature; surface dry, coated with tiny fibrils, buff to pale straw yellow, darkening with age or when handled, especially near the base; **flesh** colored like and staining like the cap flesh.

SPORE PRINT: Pale yellow.

MICROSCOPIC FEATURES: Spores 9–15 × 5–7 μm, ellipsoid, smooth, pale yellow.

OCCURRENCE: Scattered or in groups with oaks; summer–fall.

EDIBILITY: Unknown.

REMARKS: *Phaeocyanescens* means "dark blue" and refers to the indigo-blue staining of the exposed flesh. This staining reaction sometimes does not occur in waterlogged specimens. The cap surface stains amber to orange-brown with KOH, reddish brown with NH4OH, and is negative with FeSO4. The flesh stains bright yellow with KOH, yellow with NH4OH, and pale yellow with FeSO4. *Gyroporus cyanescens* (p. 9) has a tan to brown cap and stains greenish blue to dark blue on all parts. *Gyroporus umbrinisquamosus* (not illustrated) has a yellow-ocher cap with conspicuous yellow-brown fibrillose scales, white, non-staining, mild tasting flesh, a white to pale yellowish pore surface, a stalk that is strongly enlarged downward, has pinkish tints on the upper part, and is pale yellow brown below.

Gyroporus phaeocyanescens

Gyroporus subalbellus Murrill

= *Suillus subalbellus* (Murrill) Sacc. & Trotter

MACROSCOPIC FEATURES: **Cap** 2.5–12 cm wide, convex at first, becoming nearly flat and frequently shallowly depressed in age; margin even; surface dry, nearly smooth, color ranging from apricot buff to pinkish buff or pinkish cinnamon to orange cinnamon, sometimes pale yellow to whitish, darkening to brownish in age or when handled; **flesh** white, unchanging; odor and taste not distinctive. **Pore surface** whitish initially, becoming pale yellow then dull yellow when mature, at times deeply depressed around the stalk, unchanging or slowly staining pinkish cinnamon when bruised or in age; tubes 3–8 mm deep. **Stalk** usually enlarged downward to a swollen or sometimes a tapered base, hollow or chambered and brittle in age; surface dry, smooth, whitish at first, soon becoming flushed pinkish to salmon-orange, especially toward the base, often staining cinnamon to brownish or olivaceous; **flesh** colored like the cap flesh.
SPORE PRINT: Yellowish buff.
MICROSCOPIC FEATURES: Spores 8–14 × 4–6 μm, ellipsoid to ovoid, smooth, hyaline.
OCCURRENCE: Scattered or in groups in oak and pine woods; summer–fall.
EDIBILITY: Edible.
REMARKS: *Subalbellus* means "somewhat whitish," referring to the colors of this pale bolete. *Tylopilus peralbidus* (p. 109) has similar colors, but its flesh is bitter tasting, its stalk is solid, and rather than yellowish-buff, it has a pinkish-brown spore print.

Gyroporus subalbellus

Harrya chromapes (Frost) Halling, Nuhn, Osm. & Manfr. Binder

= *Boletus chromapes* Frost
= *Leccinum chromapes* (Frost) Singer
= *Tylopilus chromapes* (Frost) A. H. Sm. & Thiers

COMMON NAMES: Chrome-footed Bolete, Yellowfoot Bolete.

MACROSCOPIC FEATURES: **Cap** 3–15 cm wide, convex at first, becoming broadly convex to nearly flat, sometimes slightly depressed in age; surface dry or slightly viscid when moist, pink to rose-colored initially, fading pinkish tan to dingy brown in age; **flesh** white, unchanging; odor not distinctive; taste slightly lemony or not distinctive. **Pore surface** white at first, becoming pinkish to dingy pinkish tan in age, unchanging; tubes 8–14 mm deep, colored like the cap flesh or paler. **Stalk** equal or tapered in either direction, often crooked at the base, solid; surface dry, white to pinkish, covered with scabers that are pink to reddish or sometimes whitish, with a bright chrome yellow base; **flesh** white, becoming chrome yellow at the base.

SPORE PRINT: Pinkish brown to reddish brown.

MICROSCOPIC FEATURES: Spores 11–17 × 4–5.5 µm, nearly oblong to narrowly oval, smooth, hyaline to pale brown.

OCCURRENCE: Solitary or in small groups with hardwoods and conifers; summer–fall.

EDIBILITY: Edible.

REMARKS: *Chromapes* means "chrome yellow foot," referring to this bolete's distinctive bright chrome yellow stalk base. *Harrya* honors American mycologist Harry D. Thiers (1919–2000). It is a small genus with only two species known worldwide to date. *Harrya chromapes* is the only species reported to occur in eastern North America.

Harrya chromapes

Heimioporus betula (Schwein.) E. Horak

= *Austroboletus betula* (Schwein.) E. Horak
= *Frostiella betula* (Schwein.) Murrill
= *Heimiella betula* (Schwein.) Watling

COMMON NAME: Shaggy-stalked Bolete.

MACROSCOPIC FEATURES: **Cap** 3–9 cm wide, rounded to convex and remaining so well into maturity; surface glabrous, viscid and shiny when moist; margin sterile; bright to dark red, orange or a blend of red and orange, or orange and yellow, often yellow at the margin; **flesh** soft, pale yellow, occasionally tinged orange beneath the cap surface, unchanging; odor not distinctive; taste sour or acidic. **Pore surface** bright to pale yellow or greenish yellow, unchanging, depressed around the stalk; tubes 1–1.5 cm deep. **Stalk** thin, slender, often curved near the base, solid and firm; surface dry, coarsely reticulate-shaggy, yellow when young, becoming reddish to yellow, with a massive pad of cottony, white mycelium at the base, reticulation yellow or sometimes reddish, raised; **flesh** colored like the cap flesh.

SPORE PRINT: Olive brown.

MICROSCOPIC FEATURES: Spores 15–19 × 6–10 µm, narrowly elliptical, ornamented with a loose reticulum and scattered minute pits, typically with a distinct apical pore, pale brown.

OCCURRENCE: Solitary or scattered in mixed hardwood and pine woodlands; summer–fall.

EDIBILITY: Edible.

REMARKS: *Betula* refers to the genus of birch trees (*Betula*), many of which bear shaggy bark. *Aureoboletus russellii* (p. 31) is not as colorful and has a dry, scaly cap.

Heimioporus betula

Hemileccinum subglabripes (Peck)
Šutara

= *Boletus subglabripes* Peck
= *Leccinum subglabripes* (Peck) Singer

COMMON NAME: Smoothish-stemmed
Boletus.

MACROSCOPIC FEATURES: **Cap** 4.5–12 cm
wide, convex when young, becoming broadly
convex or nearly flat in age, sometimes with
a broad umbo; margin even; surface smooth
to slightly wrinkled, ranging from chestnut-
brown, ocher, cinnamon, reddish brown to
bay-brown; cuticle tastes very tart; **flesh**
pale yellow to yellow, unchanging or rarely
staining slightly blue; odor not distinctive;
taste slightly acidic or not distinctive. **Pore
surface** yellow to bright yellow when fresh,
becoming duller or slightly greenish yellow
in age, unchanging; tubes 5–16 mm deep.
Stalk nearly equal, solid, sometimes rather
stout; surface dry, minutely scurfy with a thin
coating of tiny yellow scabers, yellow with
occasional reddish or reddish-brown tinges,
especially on the lower portion; **flesh** colored
like the cap flesh and often reddish in the base.

SPORE PRINT: Olive-brown.

MICROSCOPIC FEATURES: Spores $11-17(21)$
$\times 3-5(7)$ µm, narrowly fusoid, smooth, pale
brown.

OCCURRENCE: Solitary or scattered with hardwoods, especially birch and oak, occasionally
with conifers; summer–fall.

EDIBILITY: Edible.

REMARKS: *Subglabripes* means "nearly smooth
foot," referring to its stalk. The cap surface
stains pale amber, and the cap flesh stains pale
gray with the addition of NH4OH. *Xerocomus
hortonii* (p. 122) is very similar but differs
by having a conspicuously pitted cap and a
smooth or sometimes pruinose or reticulated
stalk. *Boletus longicurvipes* (p. 9) has a viscid,
yellow-orange to brownish-orange or ochraceous cap, yellow pores that do not stain blue
when bruised, and a long, curved, punctate
stalk. The cap surface stains cherry red to reddish orange with NH4OH and bright cherry
red with KOH. It grows on the ground with
oaks or in mixed oak and pine woods from
late spring to fall.

Hemileccinum subglabripes

Hortiboletus campestris (A. H. Sm. & Thiers) Biketova & Wasser

= *Boletus campestris* A. H. Sm. & Thiers

MACROSCOPIC FEATURES: **Cap** 2–5 cm wide, convex, becoming broadly convex in age; surface dry, somewhat velvety, usually becoming conspicuously cracked, especially toward the margin in age, rose red at first, becoming pinkish red with a hint of yellow visible in the cracks when mature; **flesh** pale yellow to yellow, bruising greenish blue when cut; odor and taste not distinctive. **Pore surface** initially yellow, becoming greenish yellow to olive yellow, usually depressed around the stalk in age, staining greenish blue when bruised; pores circular to angular, 1–2 per mm; tubes 4–8 mm deep. **Stalk** nearly equal, solid; surface dry, pruinose, pale yellow near the apex, deeper yellow downward toward the base, usually reddish pruinose, especially toward the base, not reticulate, basal mycelium yellow; **flesh** bright yellow throughout, staining greenish blue when exposed.

SPORE PRINT: Olive-brown.

MICROSCOPIC FEATURES: Spores 11–15 × 4.5–7 µm, elliptical to subfusoid, smooth, yellow ocher.

OCCURRENCE: Scattered or in groups in lawns and grassy places in parks, open woodlands, and roadsides; summer–fall.

EDIBILITY: Reportedly edible.

REMARKS: *Campestris* means "growing in fields." It is one of several small, confusing boletes that are red-capped, have yellow pores, and quickly bruise blue. *Hortiboletus rubellus* (p. 75) has a stalk covered with dull reddish-orange punctae from the base up toward a yellow apex, stalk flesh that is reddish orange in the base and yellow in the upper portion, and smaller spores that measure 10–13 × 4–5 µm.

Hortiboletus campestris

Hortiboletus rubellus (Krombh.) Simonini, Vizzini & Gelardi

= *Boletus fraternus* Peck
= *Boletus rubellus* Krombh.
= *Xerocomellus rubellus* (Krombh.) Šutara
= *Xerocomus rubellus* (Krombh.) Quél.

MACROSCOPIC FEATURES: **Cap** 2–8 cm wide, convex, becoming nearly plane in age; margin even; surface dry, somewhat velvety, often finely cracked in age, dark red, fading to brick-red or olivaceous brown; **flesh** pale yellow, slowly staining bluish green upon exposure; odor and taste not distinctive. **Pore surface** yellow, staining bluish green when bruised, typically depressed at the stalk when mature; tubes 6–10 mm deep. **Stalk** nearly equal, enlarged or tapered downward, often with a narrowed base, solid; surface dry, yellow at the apex, pruinose to punctate with dull reddish-orange dots and points, darkening to brown where handled; **flesh** yellow on the upper portion, reddish orange below, or at least near the base.

SPORE PRINT: Olive brown.
MICROSCOPIC FEATURES: Spores 10–13 × 4–5 µm, ellipsoid, smooth, pale brown.
OCCURRENCE: Solitary, scattered, or in groups in grassy areas, parks, gardens, flowerbeds, disturbed roadsides, along paths, or in hardwood and mixed woods, especially under oak and beech; summer–fall.
EDIBILITY: Unknown.
REMARKS: *Rubellus* means "reddish," a reference to the colors of its cap and stalk. Historically, there has been much confusion about the identification of this bolete and separating it from very similar species. *Hortiboletus campestris* (p. 74) is very similar, but its stalk flesh is bright yellow throughout, and it has somewhat larger spores that measure 11–15 × 4.5–7 µm. Its cap surface stains amber with KOH and dark green to blackish green with FeSO4. Its flesh stains orange with KOH and dull orange with FeSO4.

Hortiboletus rubellus

Imleria badia (Fr.) Vizzini

= *Boletus badius* (Fr.) Fr.
= *Xerocomus badius* (Fr.) E. -J. Gilbert

COMMON NAME: Bay Bolete.
MACROSCOPIC FEATURES: **Cap** 4–9 cm wide, convex at first, becoming nearly flat in age, occasionally depressed in the center; margin even, upturned when mature; surface dry or slightly viscid, smooth to somewhat velvety, ranging from chestnut brown to reddish brown or yellow brown, sometimes with olive tones; **flesh** white, usually staining bluish near the tubes when cut or exposed; odor and taste not distinctive. **Pore surface** pale yellow to greenish yellow, staining greenish blue to grayish blue when bruised; tubes 8–15 mm deep. **Stalk** equal or enlarged downward, solid; dry, smooth to somewhat pruinose, colored like the cap, not reticulate, with white basal mycelium; **flesh** colored and staining like the cap flesh.

SPORE PRINT: Olive-brown.
MICROSCOPIC FEATURES: Spores 10–14 × 4–5 μm, elliptical to fusiform, smooth, yellow.
OCCURRENCE: Solitary or scattered with pines or other conifers; summer–fall.
EDIBILITY: Edible.
REMARKS: *Badia* means "bay-brown," referring to the chestnut-brown or reddish-brown cap color. The cap surface stains green to blue with NH4OH, blackish with KOH, and bluish green with FeSO4. *Xanthoconium affine* (p. 120) has a dark brown to chestnut-brown or ocher-brown cap and an unchanging pore surface that is initially white then yellowish to dingy yellow brown in age.

Imleria badia

Lanmaoa roseocrispans A. E. Bessette, A. R. Bessette, Nuhn & Halling

MACROSCOPIC FEATURES: **Cap** 6–16 cm wide, pulvinate, distinctly folded and lobed when young, becoming broadly convex in age; margin strongly incurved, undulating, pinched and lobed when young, remaining so well into maturity, with a narrow band of sterile tissue; surface dry, somewhat velvety, with irregular pits and depressions, sometimes cracked in age, color variable, brick-red or rosy red over a yellow ground color when young, becoming yellow orange or mustard yellow with dull pinkish or rosy tones within the folds, with burgundy-red or brownish-red splashes on portions of mature specimens, slowly bruising greenish blue to grayish blue, especially along the margin; **flesh** thick, firm, pale yellow to yellow, becoming darker yellow when exposed or bruised, sometimes slowly staining grayish blue; odor and taste not distinctive. **Pore surface** yellow at first, becoming olive-yellow to olive-brown in age, dull brownish red around marginal folds, rapidly staining greenish blue to grayish blue when bruised, conspicuously depressed around the stalk in age; tubes 4–13 mm deep. **Stalk** strongly tapered downward, ventricose or with a pinched base, solid; surface scurfy-punctate nearly overall, sometimes smooth at the apex, often longitudinally striate, dull burgundy red to brownish red over a yellow ground color, darker at the base, typically yellow at the apex, staining greenish blue to grayish blue when bruised or handled, typically with pale yellow basal mycelium; **flesh** colored and staining like the cap flesh, usually orange-yellow to orange near the base.

SPORE PRINT: Olive brown.

MICROSCOPIC FEATURES: Spores 11–17 × 3–5 µm, subellipsoid to subfusoid, smooth, hyaline to pale brownish yellow.

OCCURRENCE: Solitary, scattered, or in groups or clusters in grassy areas with oaks; late summer–fall.

EDIBILITY: Unknown.

REMARKS: *Roseocrispans* means "rosy pink folds," referring to the coloration between the folds of the cap. Known only from Dunnellon, Florida, its distribution limits have yet to be established. This bolete is extremely robust, hefty, and dense. The strongly tapered stalk with a ventricose or pinched base and the remarkably folded and lobed cap margin with dull pinkish or rosy tones within the folds are its most distinguishing features. The cap surface quickly stains pale gray with NH4OH. The *Baorangia bicolor* complex (p. 34), while somewhat similar, is much less robust, hefty, and dense. It has a darker red cap with an even margin that is not distinctly folded and lobed, a red stalk that is not tapered downward, and smaller spores that measure 8–12 × 3.5–5 µm.

Lanmaoa roseocrispans

Leccinellum albellum (Peck) Bresinsky & Manfr. Binder

= *Leccinum albellum* (Peck) Singer

MACROSCOPIC FEATURES: **Cap** 2–6 cm wide, rounded to convex when young, becoming broadly convex in age; margin even; surface dry to moist, smooth or somewhat velvety, often distinctly pitted in age, sometimes cracked when mature, color varies from whitish to pale tan, pale gray to pinkish gray, or pinkish brown to medium brown, sometimes tinged with yellow; **flesh** white, unchanging; odor and taste not distinctive. **Pore surface** whitish to pale tan or pale gray, unchanging, depressed around the stalk at maturity; tubes 2–10 mm deep. **Stalk** equal to enlarged downward, solid; surface dry, whitish to pale olive-buff, with tiny white scabers that become grayish or brownish in age; **flesh** white, unchanging.

SPORE PRINT: Brown to olive brown.
MICROSCOPIC FEATURES: Spores 14–22 × 4–6 μm, cylindric to subfusiform, smooth, pale yellow.
OCCURRENCE: Scattered or in groups with hardwoods, especially oak; summer–fall.
EDIBILITY: Edible.
REMARKS: *Albellum* means "whitish," but specimens with brown, gray, and/or whitish colored caps can be found growing alongside each other. The cap surface stains olive with KOH or NH4OH and dark bluish gray with FeSO4. The flesh stains pale yellow with KOH or NH4OH and gray with FeSO4.

Leccinellum albellum

Leccinum chalybaeum Singer

MACROSCOPIC FEATURES: **Cap** 4–9 cm wide, obtuse when young, becoming convex to broadly convex; margin even; surface viscid, somewhat shiny when dry, smooth to slightly velvety, sometimes finely cracked when mature, initially buff to pinkish buff, becoming dingy yellow brown in age, occasionally with grayish-green to bluish-gray tints, especially near the margin; **flesh** stains pinkish then slowly pinkish brown to purplish gray to blackish when cut or exposed. **Pore surface** whitish to beige, typically staining dingy olive to brown when bruised, deeply depressed around the stalk in age; tubes up to 1.6 cm deep. **Stalk** typically short and thick, equal or enlarged downward, solid, extremely firm, almost woody; surface dry, whitish, covered with dingy white scabers that darken to brown in age; **flesh** colored and staining like the cap flesh.

SPORE PRINT: Olive-brown.

MICROSCOPIC FEATURES: Spores 16–18 × 5–6 µm, fusoid, smooth, brownish; caulocystidia fusoid to fusoid-ampullaceous.

OCCURRENCE: Scattered or in groups under oak or in mixed woods with oak and pine; summer–fall.

EDIBILITY: Edible.

REMARKS: *Chalybaeum* means "steel-gray," referring to the cap's staining reaction. The cap flesh stains yellow with KOH, slowly pale greenish blue with NH_4OH, and greenish blue with $FeSO_4$.

Leccinum chalybaeum

Leccinum roseoscabrum Singer & R. Williams

MACROSCOPIC FEATURES: **Cap** 2–7 cm wide, rounded to convex when young, becoming broadly convex; margin sterile; surface dry to slightly viscid, smooth to somewhat wrinkled or with shallow pits, dark brown to chestnut-brown, fading in age, often with paler spots; **flesh** firm, white, unchanging; odor not distinctive; taste slightly bitter or not distinctive. **Pore surface** initially white to whitish, becoming yellowish or grayish with a dull orange tint, usually depressed around the stalk in age, staining brownish when bruised; tubes up to 13 mm deep. **Stalk** enlarged downward, often curved, at times swollen near the middle, frequently with a pinched base, solid; surface dry, white on the upper portion, pinkish below, sometimes green or yellow at the base, with coarse rosy pink scabers that become brown or dark brown in age or when bruised or handled, with sparse white basal mycelium; **flesh** colored and staining like the cap flesh.

SPORE PRINT: Yellowish brown.
MICROSCOPIC FEATURES: Spores 12–18 × 3.5–6 μm, fusoid to cylindric, smooth, pale ochraceous brown.
OCCURRENCE: Scattered or in groups with hardwoods, especially oak; summer–early winter.
EDIBILITY: Edible.
REMARKS: *Roseoscabrum* means "rosy pink scabers." The cap surface stains brown with KOH and is negative with both $FeSO_4$ and NH_4OH. The flesh stains blue-green with $FeSO_4$, pale orange with NH_4OH, and is negative with KOH.

Leccinum roseoscabrum

Leccinum rubropunctum (Peck) Singer

= *Boletus rubropunctus* Peck

COMMON NAME: Ashtray Bolete.

MACROSCOPIC FEATURES: **Cap** 2–9 cm wide, convex when young, becoming broadly convex in age; margin even; surface distinctly furrowed or wrinkled, sometimes smooth, dry to slightly viscid, bald, bay-red to chestnut red or reddish brown; **flesh** yellowish, unchanging; odor like a dirty ashtray or stale cigarette butts; taste unpleasant. **Pore surface** bright golden yellow when young and fresh, becoming dull yellow to brownish yellow in age, unchanging, depressed around the stalk when mature; tubes 9–15 mm deep. **Stalk** tapered downward, often curved at the base, solid; surface dry, punctate with reddish dots and points on a yellow ground color, basal mycelium pale yellow; **flesh** colored like the cap flesh.

SPORE PRINT: Olive brown.

MICROSCOPIC FEATURES: Spores 15–21 × 5–6 μm, fusiform, smooth, pale brown.

OCCURRENCE: Solitary, scattered, or in groups with conifers or hardwoods; summer–winter.

EDIBILITY: Edible.

REMARKS: Molecular data does not support placement of this species in *Leccinum* or *Boletus*. Additional research is needed to determine where it taxonomically belongs. It is unusual in that it forms sclerotia in the soil. The cap surface stains amber with KOH or NH4OH and pale olive with FeSO4. The flesh stains pale orange with KOH, grayish olive with FeSO4, and displays a blue-green flash that quickly disappears with NH4OH. *Hemileccinum subglabripes* (p. 73) is similar, but the pale yellow flesh lacks the distinctive odor of this mushroom, the stalk is yellow with a thinner coating of yellow to red punctae and has smaller spores that measure 11–17 × 3–5 μm.

Leccinum rubropunctum

Leccinum rugosiceps (Peck) Singer

= *Boletus rugosiceps* Peck
= *Krombholzia rugosiceps* (Peck) Singer
= *Krombholziella rugosiceps* (Peck) Šutara

COMMON NAME: Wrinkled Leccinum.
MACROSCOPIC FEATURES: **Cap** 5–15 cm wide, convex when young, becoming broadly convex in age; margin sterile; surface dry, distinctly wrinkled, shallowly pitted when mature, orange-yellow when young, becoming yellow brown in age, sometimes dark tobacco brown on the disc, usually cracked in age, exposing pale yellow flesh; **flesh** white or pale yellow, slowly and sometimes faintly bruising reddish or burgundy when cut or exposed, staining most visible at the juncture of the cap and stalk; odor not distinctive; taste somewhat astringent or not distinctive. **Pore surface** dull to dingy yellowish, sometimes becoming ochraceous to dingy olive brown in age, unchanging or slowly bruising ochraceous or, rarely, very slowly staining blue green, deeply depressed around the stalk in age; tubes 8–14 mm deep. **Stalk** equal or tapered at the apex or base, solid; surface dry, pale yel-low to brownish with pale brown scabers that darken in age, unchanging; **flesh** colored and staining like the cap flesh.
SPORE PRINT: Olive brown.
MICROSCOPIC FEATURES: Spores 15–21 × 5–6 μm, fusiform, smooth, pale brown.
OCCURRENCE: Solitary or in groups with oaks, especially pin oak; summer–fall.
EDIBILITY: Edible.
REMARKS: *Rugosiceps* means "coarsely wrinkled cap." The cap surface stains orange-red with KOH, reddish or negative with NH4OH, and negative with FeSO4. *Leccinellum crocipo-dium* (p. 9) has a darker cap, a stalk that is often swollen in the middle or near the base, darker scabers, and flesh that stains pinkish gray to dull reddish or pale fuscous when cut or exposed. *Leccinellum griseum* (p. 9) has a distinctly wrinkled to pitted, or sometimes smooth, cap that is dull brown to blackish brown when young and typically develops olive-green tones as it ages. It has a whitish to grayish or grayish-brown pore surface, dark brown to blackish-brown scabers on a whitish stalk, and grows on the ground under oaks during summer and fall.

Leccinum rugosiceps

Neoboletus pseudosulphureus
(Kallenb.) W. Klofac

= *Boletus pseudosulphureus* Kallenb.
= *Boletus pseudosulphureus* var. *pallidus*
  Grund & K. A. Harrison

MACROSCOPIC FEATURES: **Cap** 4–20 cm wide, rounded when young, becoming broadly convex in age; margin even; surface dry, initially covered with tiny matted fibrils, becoming nearly glabrous in age, dull or shiny at maturity, bright yellow at first, becoming duller yellow to tawny, usually developing brown to brownish-red tints, especially over the disc, quickly staining bluish to bluish black when bruised; **flesh** bright yellow to greenish yellow, quickly staining blue when cut or exposed; odor not distinctive; taste acidic, astringent, or not distinctive. **Pore surface** bright yellow at first, becoming greenish yellow then brownish yellow when mature, quickly staining blue then slowly brownish when bruised, depressed around the stalk in age; tubes 8–12 mm deep. **Stalk** enlarged downward, solid; surface dry, bright yellow to yellow, quickly staining blue then slowly brownish when bruised, sometimes with reddish tints, especially near the base, usually not reticulate but at times with reticulation on the upper portion; **flesh** yellow, dark red at the base, quickly staining blue at the base or overall when cut or exposed.

SPORE PRINT: Olive-brown.

MICROSCOPIC FEATURES: Spores 10–16 × 4–6 μm, fusoid to ellipsoid-fusoid, smooth, brownish yellow.

OCCURRENCE: Solitary, scattered, or in groups with hardwoods, especially oak, or in mixed oak and pine woods or occasionally with pine; summer–winter.

EDIBILITY: Unknown.

REMARKS: *Pseudosulphureus* means "resembling *Boletus sulphureus* Fr.," an older name for *Buchwaldoboletus sphaerocephalus* (not illustrated). The cap surface stains orange to reddish with KOH, grayish to grayish olive with $FeSO_4$, and is negative with NH_4OH.

Neoboletus pseudosulphureus

Phylloporus boletinoides A. H. Sm. & Thiers

MACROSCOPIC FEATURES: **Cap** 2–10 cm wide, broadly convex at first, becoming nearly flat, occasionally shallowly depressed in age; margin sterile, strongly incurved and remaining so into maturity; surface dry, somewhat velvety to minutely scaly when young, becoming nearly smooth in age, cinnamon to dark pinkish brown, fading to dull yellow-brown; **flesh** white to whitish, slowly staining bluish gray to gray when cut or exposed; odor not distinctive; taste slightly acidic or not distinctive. **Pore surface** strongly decurrent, strongly radially arranged and gill-like with numerous crossveins, pale olive-buff at first, becoming dark olive-buff in age, at times with a bluish-green tinge near the margin, occasionally slowly staining bluish green to dark blue when bruised, typically not noticeably staining blue at all; tubes 3–5 mm deep. **Stalk** tapered downward or nearly equal, solid or hollow in the base; surface dry, smooth, pale yellow at the apex, pale cinnamon below, having a sparse layer of white basal mycelium; **flesh** colored and staining like the cap flesh or sometimes darker cinnamon toward the base.
SPORE PRINT: Olive brown.
MICROSCOPIC FEATURES: Spores 11–16 × 5–6.5 μm, subcylindric to narrowly oval, smooth, pale brown.
OCCURRENCE: Solitary or scattered in mixed oak and pine woods; summer–early winter.
EDIBILITY: Unknown.
REMARKS: *Boletinoides* means "having radially arranged and elongated pores," which this mushroom most decidedly has. The cap surface stains reddish to red-brown with NH4OH and is negative with FeSO4. *Phylloporus leucomycelinus* (p. 85) and *Phylloporus rhodoxanthus* (p. 9) have redder caps and yellow to golden-yellow pore surfaces.

Phylloporus boletinoides

Phylloporus leucomycelinus Singer

= *Phylloporus rhodoxanthus* ssp.
  albomycelinus Snell & Dick

COMMON NAME: Gilled Bolete.

MACROSCOPIC FEATURES: **Cap** 4–8 cm wide, rounded to convex when young, becoming nearly flat and at times slightly depressed in age; margin incurved at first, usually sterile; surface dry, slightly velvety, sometimes becoming finely cracked in age, dark red, reddish brown to chestnut, fading and paler over the disc in age; **flesh** whitish to pale yellow; odor and taste not distinctive. **Pore surface** yellow to golden yellow, strongly lamellate and decurrent, sometimes forked and crossveined, strongly radially arranged and gill-like, sometimes poroid, widely spaced, easily separable from the cap, usually unchanging but sometimes slowly staining bluish green to dark blue when bruised; tubes 8–16 mm deep. **Stalk** equal or pinched at the base, firm, solid, dry, usually having conspicuous ribs near the apex, yellow with reddish tints, covered overall with reddish-brown punctae, with a white to whitish basal mycelium; **flesh** colored like the cap flesh.

SPORE PRINT: Yellowish ochraceous.

MICROSCOPIC FEATURES: Spores 8–14 × 3–5 μm, ellipsoid to fusoid, smooth, pale yellowish.

OCCURRENCE: Scattered or in groups with hardwoods, especially beech and oak; summer–fall.

EDIBILITY: Edible.

REMARKS: *Leucomycelinus* means "having white mycelium," which is one of the most distinctive field characteristics of this mushroom. *Phylloporus rhodoxanthus* (p. 9) is nearly identical but differs by having yellow basal mycelium.

Phylloporus leucomycelinus

Pulchroboletus rubricitrinus (Murrill)
A. Farid & A. R. Franck

= *Boletus rubricitrinus* (Murrill) Murrill
= *Ceriomyces rubricitrinus* Murrill

MACROSCOPIC FEATURES: **Cap** 3–15 cm wide, convex when young, becoming nearly flat and sometimes slightly depressed in age; margin initially incurved, sterile; surface dry, glabrous to somewhat velvety, color variable, ranging from dull rose red to dull brick-red or reddish brown to tawny cinnamon when young and fresh, fading to tawny olive or dull brown when mature, sometimes with yellow tints, typically bruising blue black, cuticle tart or acidic tasting; **flesh** pale yellow to yellow, instantly staining blue when cut or exposed; odor not distinctive; taste slightly tart to acidic. **Pore surface** initially yellow, becoming dull yellow to olive-yellow, depressed around the stalk in age, staining blue when bruised; tubes 8–20 mm deep. **Stalk** equal or tapered in either direction, sometimes swollen near the base, solid; surface dry, yellow, usually with dull reddish to red-brown streaks and dots, especially toward the base, quickly staining blue green to blue black when handled or bruised, not reticulate or weakly so, only at the very apex, usually longitudinal striate nearly overall; **flesh** colored and staining like the cap flesh.

SPORE PRINT: Olive brown.

MICROSCOPIC FEATURES: Spores 13–19 × 5–8 µm, fusoid to subfusoid-ellipsoid, smooth, yellowish.

OCCURRENCE: Solitary, scattered, or in groups in oak or mixed oak and pine woods; spring–early winter.

EDIBILITY: Edible.

REMARKS: *Rubricitrinus* means "red and lemon yellow," referring to the prominent colors of this bolete. *Boletus fairchildianus* (not illustrated) is an uncommon and very similar bolete that has a dark red pore surface and is redder on the stalk. It was originally collected at the Fairchild Tropical Botanic Garden, Miami, Florida in 1942. *Butyriboletus roseopurpureus* (p. 9) has a pinkish-purple to dark purplish-red cap, pale yellow flesh that instantly stains dark blue when exposed, and tastes very sour, like lemon. Its pore surface is yellow and instantly stains blue when bruised, and its stalk is yellow overall or sometimes has burgundy red areas near the base and is reticulate nearly overall, or at least over the upper two-thirds. The Mahogany Bolete, *Boletus mahogonicolor* (p. 9), currently known only from Mississippi, has a mahogany to reddish-brown cap, shorter tubes 2–8 mm deep, and much smaller spores that measure 10–13 × 3.5–4 µm.

Pulchroboletus rubricitrinus

Pulveroboletus curtisii (Berk.) Singer

= *Boletus curtisii* Berk.

MACROSCOPIC FEATURES: **Cap** 3–9.5 cm wide, rounded to convex, becoming broadly convex to nearly flat; margin incurved when young, sterile; surface viscid and glutinous when fresh, bald, bright yellow to orange yellow, sometimes with brownish tints or whitish areas in age; **flesh** whitish, unchanging; odor and taste not distinctive. **Pore surface** whitish to buff or pale yellow when young, becoming duller and darker in age, frequently depressed around the stalk when mature, unchanging; tubes 6–12 mm deep. **Stalk** nearly equal, solid or hollow; surface viscid to glutinous when fresh, slightly scurfy near the apex, nearly smooth below, pale yellow to yellow, base sheathed with cottony white mycelium; **flesh** colored like the cap flesh.

SPORE PRINT: Olive brown.

MICROSCOPIC FEATURES: Spores 9.5–17 × 4–6 μm, elliptical to subventricose, smooth, yellowish.

OCCURRENCE: Solitary, scattered, or in groups in conifer or mixed woods, often with pines; summer–fall.

EDIBILITY: Unknown.

REMARKS: *Curtisii* refers to the British mycologist, Moses Ashley Curtis (1808–1872), after whom it is named. *Pulveroboletus auriflammeus* (p. 9) is generally smaller and has a brownish-orange to golden-yellow or chrome-yellow cap and stalk, a yellow to yellow-orange pore surface that does not stain blue, and reticulation at least on the upper portion of mature stalks.

Pulveroboletus curtisii

Pulveroboletus ravenelii (Berk. & M. A. Curtis) Murrill

= *Boletus ravenelii* Berk. & M. A. Curtis
= *Suillus ravenelii* (Berk. & M. A. Curtis) Kuntze

COMMON NAMES: Ravenel's Bolete, Powdery Sulphur Bolete.

MACROSCOPIC FEATURES: **Cap** 2.5–10 cm wide, convex, becoming broadly convex to nearly flat; margin incurved at first, usually fringed with partial veil remnants; surface dry and powdery to matted and tacky or glabrous when moist, bright yellow, soon becoming reddish orange to reddish brown on the disc; **flesh** thick, white to yellow, staining pale blue then brownish when cut or injured; odor somewhat like hickory leaves or not distinctive; taste acidic. **Pore surface** bright yellow, becoming greenish yellow to greenish olive, bruising greenish blue, covered at first with a bright yellow, cottony partial veil; tubes 5–8 mm deep. **Stalk** nearly equal, solid; surface dry, floccose to appressed-fibrillose from the base up to a delicate cottony ring near the apex, smooth above the ring, bright yellow; ring fragile, sometimes integrated with the floccose surface of the stalk and inconspicuous; **flesh** colored and staining like the cap flesh.

SPORE PRINT: Olive brown to olive gray.

MICROSCOPIC FEATURES: Spores 8–10.5 × 4–5 μm, ellipsoidal to oval, smooth, pale brown.

OCCURRENCE: Solitary, scattered, or in groups in conifer woods, especially under pine or hemlock and rhododendron; summer–fall.

EDIBILITY: Edible.

REMARKS: *Ravenelii* honors American botanist-mycologist Henry William Ravenel (1814–1887). This bolete is easy to recognize when young by the powdery coating on the fruitbody and the delicate cottony ring that usually remains on the upper stalk, at least initially, after the partial veil ruptures.

Pulveroboletus ravenelii

Retiboletus griseus var. *fuscus* Hongo

MACROSCOPIC FEATURES: **Cap** 4–9.5 cm wide, convex, becoming broadly convex to nearly flat; margin sterile; **surface** dry to slightly tacky, finely tomentose, dark brown to fuscous when young, becoming grayish brown to olive brown; **flesh** whitish to yellowish, sometimes slightly bluing or staining reddish when exposed; odor and taste not distinctive. **Pore surface** whitish at first, becoming dull grayish buff to grayish tan in age, staining brownish when bruised; tubes 4–12 mm deep. **Stalk** nearly equal down to a tapered, often curved, and somewhat rooting base where red droplets may be present, solid; surface dry, colored like the cap or pinkish gray, paler near the apex, sometimes with yellowish tints downward, covered nearly overall with conspicuous dark brown reticulation, basal mycelium white; **flesh** whitish to yellowish, typically slowly staining dark red where bruised.

SPORE PRINT: Pinkish brown to olive brown.

MICROSCOPIC FEATURES: Spores 11–17 × 4–6 μm, fusoid to oblong, smooth, pale brown.

OCCURRENCE: Solitary, scattered, or in groups on the ground under pines or in mixed oak and pine woods; summer–early winter.

EDIBILITY: Edible.

REMARKS: This bolete has been reported from Florida, Massachusetts, North Carolina, Virginia, and Japan. *Retiboletus griseus* var. *griseus* (p. 90) is very similar but has a somewhat paler cap, whitish flesh that does not stain red, and smaller spores that measure 9–13 × 3–5 μm.

Retiboletus griseus var. *fuscus*

Retiboletus griseus var. *griseus*
(Frost) Manfr. Binder & Bresinsky

= *Boletus griseus* Frost
= *Boletus griseus* ssp. *pinicaribaeae* Singer
= *Boletus griseus* var. *griseus* Frost
= *Xerocomus griseus* (Frost) Singer

COMMON NAME: Gray Bolete.

MACROSCOPIC FEATURES: **Cap** 5–14 cm wide, convex, becoming broadly convex to nearly flat, sometimes slightly depressed; margin even; surface dry, appressed-fibrillose, with grayish fibrils, often scaly in age, pale to dark gray or brownish gray when young, sometimes developing ocher tints in age; **flesh** whitish with dark yellow brown around larval tunnels, unchanging or slowly staining brownish when cut or bruised; odor and taste not distinctive. **Pore surface** whitish to grayish or dingy gray brown, becoming pinkish brown in age, not yellow at any stage, unchanging or staining brownish or gray when bruised; tubes 8–20 mm deep. **Stalk** nearly equal or tapered downward, often curved near the base, solid; surface whitish or grayish when young, developing yellow tones from the base upwards as it matures, sometimes with reddish stains, covered overall with a coarse, pale to yellowish reticulum that becomes brownish to blackish in age; **flesh** white with deep yellow at the base.

SPORE PRINT: Olive brown.

MICROSCOPIC FEATURES: Spores 9–13 × 3–5 μm, fusoid to oblong, smooth, pale brown.

OCCURRENCE: Solitary or scattered in mixed hardwoods, especially under oak; summer–fall.

EDIBILITY: Edible.

REMARKS: *Griseus* means "grayish," referring to the cap color of this bolete. *Retiboletus griseus* var. *fuscus* (p. 89) is a variety of *Retiboletus griseus* that is currently known from Florida, Massachusetts, North Carolina, Virginia, and Japan. It has a darker gray cap, whitish to yellowish flesh that slowly stains red when cut or bruised, grows under pines or in mixed oak and pine woods, and has larger spores that measure 11–17 × 4–6 μm.

Retiboletus griseus var. *griseus*

Retiboletus ornatipes (Peck) Manfr. Binder & Bresinsky

= *Boletus ornatipes* Peck

COMMON NAME: Ornate-stalked Bolete.
MACROSCOPIC FEATURES: **Cap** 4–20 cm wide, convex, becoming broadly convex to nearly flat or slightly depressed in the center; surface dull to somewhat powdery or slightly velvety, smooth, glabrous, and shiny when dry; color ranging from yellow, mustard yellow, olive yellow to yellow brown, or gray; **flesh** thick, yellow, unchanging; odor not distinctive; taste usually very bitter. **Pore surface** bright lemon yellow to deep rich yellow, becoming dingy brownish yellow in age, staining yellow orange to orange brown when bruised; tubes 4–15 mm deep. **Stalk** varying from nearly equal or swollen in the middle to tapered toward the base or sometimes with a swollen or club-shaped base, solid; surface dry, prominently and coarsely reticulate, usually over the entire length, yellow to somewhat brownish, staining darker when bruised or handled; **flesh** colored like the cap flesh, rarely staining bluish at the base.
SPORE PRINT: Olive brown to dark yellow brown.

MICROSCOPIC FEATURES: Spores 9–13 × 3–4 μm, oblong to slightly ventricose with an obtuse apex, smooth, pale brown.
OCCURRENCE: Solitary or in groups, often in caespitose clusters, in hardwoods or mixed woods, especially with oak or beech or sometimes under pine; late spring–fall.
EDIBILITY: Some collections are mild tasting and edible, but most collections are intensely bitter.
REMARKS: *Ornatipes* means "ornate foot," a reference to the coarsely reticulate stalk. The cap surface stains orangish to pale orange brown with KOH or NH4OH and is negative with FeSO4. Handling this bolete will stain fingers yellow. Gray-capped forms of *Retiboletus ornatipes* bear a strong resemblance to *Retiboletus griseus* (p. 90), which has mild tasting flesh and is typically yellow only on the lower portion of the stalk. Both species often appear in the same habitat at the same time. *Boletus aureissimus* var. *aureissimus* (p. 41) has a bright yellow to honey yellow or yellow-ocher cap, a yellow to bright yellow stalk with or without delicate reticulation on the upper portion, and mild-tasting flesh. *Pulveroboletus auriflammeus* (p. 9) is generally smaller and has a brownish-orange to golden-yellow or chrome-yellow cap and stalk, a yellow to yellow-orange pore surface that does not stain blue, and reticulation, at least on the upper portion of mature stalks.

Retiboletus ornatipes

Strobilomyces confusus Singer

MACROSCOPIC FEATURES: **Cap** 3–12 cm wide, convex, becoming nearly flat in age; margin fringed with cottony pieces of torn, grayish partial veil; surface dry, with a whitish to grayish ground color, covered with small, erect, often stiff and pointed, gray, purplish-gray, or blackish scales; **flesh** whitish, quickly staining orange red to orange, then black when cut or bruised; odor and taste not distinctive. **Pore surface** white when young, soon becoming gray, then finally black, bruising reddish orange or brick-red, then black; pores angular, covered with a cottony to wooly, grayish partial veil when young; tubes 1–1.8 cm deep. **Stalk** nearly equal or sometimes enlarged at the base, solid, with a ring or shaggy zone; surface dry, grayish, ridged or reticulate above the ring, shaggy to wooly below; **flesh** whitish, quickly staining reddish orange then slowly blackish when exposed.

SPORE PRINT: Blackish brown to black.

MICROSCOPIC FEATURES: Spores 10–12.5 × 9.5–10.5 µm, subglobose to short-elliptic, covered with irregular projections and short ridges that sometimes resemble a partial reticulum, grayish.

OCCURRENCE: Solitary, scattered, or in groups in mixed woods, often with oaks, sometimes with pines; summer–winter.

EDIBILITY: Edible.

REMARKS: *Strobilomyces dryophilus* (p. 93) has a dull grayish-pink to pinkish-tan cap that becomes darker brown in age, and its spores have a complete reticulum. The Old Man of the Woods or Pine Cone Bolete, *Strobilomyces strobilaceus* (not illustrated), is very similar but has a darker purplish-gray to blackish cap and stalk, and spores covered by a distinct reticulum.

Strobilomyces confusus

Strobilomyces dryophilus Cibula & N. S. Weber

MACROSCOPIC FEATURES: **Cap** 3–12 cm wide, convex, becoming broadly convex to nearly flat in age; margin fringed with cottony pieces of whitish to tan, torn partial veil; surface dry, with a whitish ground color, covered with coarse, wooly or cottony, appressed or erect, grayish-pink to pinkish-tan or pinkish-brown scales; **flesh** whitish, quickly staining orange to orange red, then slowly blackish when cut or bruised; odor and taste not distinctive. **Pore surface** white when young, soon becoming gray, and eventually black, staining reddish orange or brick-red then black when bruised, covered by a whitish to pale pinkish-tan, cottony to wooly partial veil when young; tubes 1–1.7 cm deep. **Stalk** nearly equal or sometimes enlarged at the base, solid, with a ring or shaggy zone; surface dry, pinkish tan to brownish, ridged or reticulate above the ring, shaggy to wooly below; **flesh** whitish, quickly staining orange to reddish orange, then slowly blackish when exposed.

SPORE PRINT: Blackish brown to black.

MICROSCOPIC FEATURES: Spores 9–12 × 7–9 μm, subglobose to short-ellipsoidal, covered by a distinct and complete reticulum, grayish.

OCCURRENCE: Solitary, scattered, or in groups under oaks; summer–winter.

EDIBILITY: Edible.

REMARKS: *Dryophilus* means "oak-loving," referring to its association with oak trees. The cap surface stains brown with NH4OH or FeSO4 and dark reddish brown with KOH. *Strobilomyces strobilaceus* (not illustrated) differs by having a darker purplish-gray to blackish cap and stalk. *Strobilomyces confusus* (p. 92) has a darker purplish-gray to blackish cap with smaller, more erect, stiff, and pointed scales, a darker stalk, and spores with irregular projections and short ridges that do not form a complete reticulum.

Strobilomyces dryophilus

Suillellus hypocarycinus (Singer) Murrill

= *Boletus hypocarycinus* Singer

MACROSCOPIC FEATURES: **Cap** 4–12 cm wide, rounded when young, becoming broadly convex in age; margin incurved when young, usually sterile; surface dry, somewhat velvety, brown to yellow brown, may have olive or cinnamon tones; **flesh** yellow, quickly staining blue when cut; odor and taste not distinctive. **Pore surface** red to orange red or dull orange, quickly staining blue when bruised, often somewhat depressed around the stalk in age; tubes 8–16 mm deep. **Stalk** slightly enlarged downward or nearly equal, solid; surface dry, whitish to yellowish, yellow at the apex, with carmine-red punctae on at least the lower portion, basal mycelium white; **flesh** yellow, rapidly staining blue when cut, lacking reticulation and reddish hairs at the base.

SPORE PRINT: Olive brown.

MICROSCOPIC FEATURES: Spores 8–12 × 3–4 µm, subfusoid to ellipsoid, smooth, brownish yellow.

OCCURRENCE: Solitary, scattered, or in groups on the ground, especially in river bottomlands, associated with oak and hickory; summer–fall.

EDIBILITY: Unknown.

REMARKS: The epithet *hypocarycinus* means "under hickory."

Suillellus hypocarycinus

Suillellus subvelutipes (Peck) Murrill

= *Boletus subvelutipes* Peck

COMMON NAME: Red-mouth Bolete.

MACROSCOPIC FEATURES: **Cap** 6–13 cm wide, initially convex, becoming broadly convex to nearly flat in age; margin even; surface dry, somewhat velvety to nearly smooth, sometimes becoming cracked in age, color ranging from cinnamon brown to yellow brown, reddish brown, or reddish orange to orange yellow, quickly staining dark bluish black when bruised; **flesh** bright yellow, quickly staining dark blue, then becoming whitish when exposed; odor not distinctive; taste slightly acidic or not distinctive. **Pore surface** varies from red, brownish red, dark maroon red, or red orange to orange when fresh, often with a yellow rim, becoming duller in age, quickly staining dark blue to blackish when bruised; tubes 8–26 mm deep. **Stalk** equal, solid; surface dry and scurfy, flushed red and yellow, usually yellow at the apex, quickly staining dark blue to blackish when handled or bruised, not reticulate, usually having short, stiff, dark red hairs at the base when mature, immature specimens having yellow hairs that become dark red in age; **flesh** colored and staining like the cap flesh.

SPORE PRINT: Dark olive brown.

MICROSCOPIC FEATURES: Spores 13–18 × 5–6.5 µm, fusoid-subventricose, smooth, pale brown.

OCCURRENCE: Solitary, scattered, or in groups, associated with hardwoods, especially oak, or sometimes under conifers; summer–fall.

EDIBILITY: Traditionally considered to be poisonous. However, we have had several recent reports of individuals who have eaten this bolete without ill effects. We have not personally consumed it and advise caution in experimenting with it.

REMARKS: *Subvelutipes* means "somewhat velvety foot," referring to the yellow or dark red hairs on the stalk base.

Suillellus subvelutipes

Suillus brevipes (Peck) Kuntze

= *Boletus brevipes* Peck
= *Rostkovites brevipes* (Peck) Murrill
= *Suillus brevipes* var. *subgracilis* A. H. Sm. &
   Thiers
= *Suillus pseudogranulatus* (Murrill) Murrill

COMMON NAMES: Short-stalked Suillus, Short-stemmed Slippery Jack.

MACROSCOPIC FEATURES: **Cap** 4–10 cm wide, hemispheric to nearly flat; surface viscid to glutinous, smooth, bald, often coated with adhering pine needles and debris, color light to dark brown or vinaceous brown to cinnamon brown or grayish brown, fading to cinnamon or tan when mature, sometimes mottled with paler areas or cream-colored nearly overall; **flesh** white, becoming yellowish, especially near the stalk apex in age; odor and taste not distinctive. **Pore surface** whitish to pale yellow at first, aging to yellow or dingy yellow, unchanging; tubes 3–10 mm deep. **Stalk** equal or enlarged at the base, base often pinched, solid; surface dry, glabrous, white to pale yellow, sometimes with brown stains near the base, may have inconspicuous resinous dots that become visible only in age; **flesh** white, unchanging.

SPORE PRINT: Cinnamon brown.

MICROSCOPIC FEATURES: Spores 7–10 × 2.5–3.5 µm, narrowly ellipsoidal, smooth, yellowish.

OCCURRENCE: Scattered, in groups, or in clusters with pines; summer–winter.

EDIBILITY: Edible.

REMARKS: *Brevipes* means "short foot," referring to its proportionally short stalk. Unlike most members of the genus *Suillus*, it lacks conspicuous resinous dots or sometimes has them on mature specimens. The Butterball or Granulated Slippery Jack, *Suillus granulatus* (p. 9), is similar, but it has a longer stalk with resinous dots and smears. Recent DNA data indicates that some Florida collections may be a unique species, *Suillus pseudogranulatus*.

Suillus brevipes

Suillus cothurnatus Singer

= *Boletus luteus* var. *cothurnatus* (Singer) Murrill

COMMON NAMES: Baggy-veiled Suillus, Booted Suillus.

MACROSCOPIC FEATURES: **Cap** 1.5–6 cm wide, obtuse to broadly convex, sometimes with a low umbo; margin usually with hanging whitish veil fragments; surface smooth, glabrous, viscid, color varying from yellow brown or olive brown to grayish brown or dark brown; **flesh** with orange-buff and pale yellow marbling; odor fragrant or not distinctive; taste not distinctive. **Pore surface** pale yellow to orange yellow, aging to brownish yellow, unchanging when bruised; pores irregular to radially elongated, initially covered by a thick, rubbery, baggy, glutinous, whitish to grayish partial veil that eventually tears and leaves a ring on the stalk; tubes up to 5 mm deep. **Stalk** equal or tapered downward, dry, solid, whitish to yellowish, brownish when mature, with brownish resinous dots on the upper portion or overall; ring median to superior, membranous, band-like, whitish to grayish, collapsed, the lower edge sometimes flaring; **flesh** colored like the cap flesh.

SPORE PRINT: Brown.

MICROSCOPIC FEATURES: Spores 8–10 × 2.5–3.5 μm, ellipsoid-oblong to subcylindric, smooth, honey-brown.

OCCURRENCE: Scattered or in groups with pines, sometimes on moss-covered trunks or stumps; year-round.

EDIBILITY: Edible.

REMARKS: *Cothurnatus* means "high boot," referring to the baggy partial veil that covers the pore surface and part of the stalk of young specimens. The cap surface stains brown with KOH and stains pinkish, then soon fades, with NH4OH. *Suillus salmonicolor* (not illustrated) is larger overall and has a more northern distribution. Its cap is more orange, its veil thicker, it often has salmon-orange flesh in the stalk base, and the cap surface stains purplish red then purplish black with both KOH and NH4OH.

Suillus cothurnatus

Suillus decipiens (Peck) Kuntze

= *Boletinus decipiens* Berk. & M. A. Curtis
= *Boletus decipiens* Peck

MACROSCOPIC FEATURES: **Cap** 4–9 cm wide, convex to nearly flat; margin strongly incurved and typically fringed with whitish, yellowish, or grayish fragments of veil tissue; surface dry, fibrillose, sometimes with small flattened scales, may be bald in places, color ranging from orange to dull yellow, tan, or pale reddish brown, staining grayish to blackish when bruised, sometimes slowly; **flesh** pale yellow to pinkish buff, unchanging or sometimes slowly reddening or darkening when exposed; odor and taste not distinctive. **Pore surface** orange yellow to yellow, aging to brownish yellow, bruising brownish, initially covered by a fibrillose, whitish, yellowish, or grayish partial veil that entirely disappears or leaves a thin, fragile ring zone on the upper portion of the stalk; pores angular to irregular, usually elongated and radially arranged; tubes up to 8 mm deep. **Stalk** usually enlarged downward, often curved at the base, solid; surface dry, cottony to somewhat velvety or fibrillose, orange to dull yellow, often bright yellow orange above the ring zone; **flesh** bright yellow, orange in the base, slowly darkening and developing reddish tints when exposed.

SPORE PRINT: Pale brown.

MICROSCOPIC FEATURES: Spores 9–12 × 3.5–4 μm, cylindrical to subellipsoidal, smooth, hyaline to pale ochraceous.

OCCURRENCE: Scattered or in groups in mixed oak and pine woods, sometimes in sphagnum mosses; summer–fall.

EDIBILITY: Edible.

REMARKS: *Decipiens* means "deceiving," referring to this bolete's close resemblance to other species. The cap surface stains pale gray to greenish gray with KOH, pinkish gray with NH_4OH, and slowly pale gray with $FeSO_4$. The flesh stains blue gray with KOH, pinkish to pale raspberry with NH_4OH, and slowly pale gray with $FeSO_4$. *Suillus hirtellus* (p. 99) differs by having appressed fibrils and scales on the cap and a stalk with prominent resinous dots and smears that lacks a ring or ring zone.

Suillus decipiens

Suillus hirtellus (Peck) Snell

= *Boletus hirtellus* Peck

MACROSCOPIC FEATURES: **Cap** 5–12 cm wide, convex to nearly flat; margin decorated with wooly tufts of sterile tissue that disappear in age; surface dry to slightly tacky, yellow, covered with scattered tufts of reddish, brownish, or grayish fibrils and scales, becoming bald in age, may bruise vinaceous brown; **flesh** yellow, unchanging or sometimes bruising weakly and erratically blue; odor and taste not distinctive. **Pore surface** initially pale yellow, sometimes with whitish to pinkish droplets when young, aging to dull yellow to olive yellow or dingy orange buff, unchanging or sometimes bruising vinaceous brown or, more rarely, bluish green; pores slightly elongated and radially arranged; tubes 3–8 mm deep. **Stalk** equal or enlarged downward, often curved, solid; surface dry, glabrous, pale yellow, with prominent yellowish resinous dots and smears that become brown or blackish brown in age, sometimes with reddish tints, especially towards the base, usually with white basal mycelium; **flesh** colored like the cap flesh.

SPORE PRINT: Ochraceous brown to dull cinnamon.

MICROSCOPIC FEATURES: Spores 7–11(-13) × 3–3.5 µm, nearly oblong, smooth, pale ochraceous.

OCCURRENCE: Scattered or in groups with conifers, especially pine; summer–winter.

EDIBILITY: Edible.

REMARKS: *Hirtellus* means "hairy or shaggy," referring to the appressed fibers and scales on the cap. The cap surface stains reddish brown with KOH, slowly pale grayish with $FeSO_4$, and is negative with NH_4OH. *Suillus decipiens* (p. 98) has a fibrillose cap, lacks resinous dots on its stalk, and has a fragile ring zone on the upper portion of the stalk.

Suillus hirtellus

Suillus tomentosus (Kauffman) Singer

= *Boletus tomentosus* Kauffman
= *Suillus tomentosus* var. *discolor* A. H. Sm.,
   Thiers & O. K. Miller

COMMON NAMES: Blue-staining Slippery Jack,
Poor Man's Slippery Jack.

MACROSCOPIC FEATURES: **Cap** 5–12 cm wide,
obtuse to nearly flat; margin even, becoming uplifted and wavy in age; surface dry,
fibrillose-scaly when young, becoming nearly
bald in age, yellow to orange yellow, scales and
fibers grayish, yellow ocher, dark olive yellow,
or reddish; **flesh** yellow, erratically and often
slowly bruising blue; odor and taste not distinctive. **Pore surface** initially brown to vinaceous brown or dingy cinnamon, sometimes
with yellowish droplets when young, aging
dingy yellow to olive yellow, bruising blue;
tubes 8–15 mm deep. **Stalk** equal or enlarged
downward, solid; surface dry or moist, yellow
to dull orange-yellow with darker orange to
brownish resinous dots and smears; **flesh** colored and staining like the cap flesh.

SPORE PRINT: Brown.

MICROSCOPIC FEATURES: Spores 7–12 ×
3–5 μm, fusoid to elongate-ovoid, smooth,
yellowish.

OCCURRENCE: Scattered or in groups with
conifers; summer–fall.

EDIBILITY: Edible.

REMARKS: *Tomentosus* means "covered with
matted hairs," referring to the cap surface of
young specimens. The blue staining reaction
of the pore surface distinguishes it from other
species of *Suillus*.

Suillus tomentosus

Sutorius eximius (Peck) Halling, Nuhn & Osmundson

= *Boletus eximius* Peck
= *Leccinum eximium* (Peck) Singer
= *Tylopilus eximius* (Peck) Singer

COMMON NAME: Lilac-brown Bolete.
MACROSCOPIC FEATURES: **Cap** 5–12 cm wide, hemispherical to nearly flat; surface dry, bald or finely velvety, purplish brown to grayish brown, usually with a whitish bloom when young; **flesh** whitish, grayish, reddish, or brownish lilac; odor slightly pungent or not distinctive; taste slightly bitter or not distinctive. **Pore surface** dark purple brown to brown when young, aging to reddish brown; tubes 9–22 mm deep. **Stalk** stout, equal or sometimes enlarged downward, solid; surface dry, pale purplish gray, densely covered with purple-brown scabers; **flesh** colored like the cap flesh.

SPORE PRINT: Pinkish brown.
MICROSCOPIC FEATURES: Spores 11–17 × 3.5–5 μm, narrowly subfusoid, smooth, hyaline to pale brown.
OCCURRENCE: Scattered or in groups with conifers or in mixed woods with oak; summer–fall.
EDIBILITY: Poisonous.
REMARKS: *Eximius* means "distinguished or excellent in size or beauty." This bolete might be confused with species of *Leccinum* because of the small scales on its stalk. *Leccinum* species are differentiated by yellow-brown spore prints. *Tylopilus plumbeoviolaceus* (p. 110) is similar but has a smooth stalk and intensely bitter-tasting flesh. *Tylopilus griseocarneus* (p. 106) is somewhat similar but has a reticulated stalk.

Sutorius eximius

Tylopilus alboater (Schwein.) Murrill

= *Boletus alboater* Schwein.
= *Porphyrellus alboater* (Schwein.) E. -J. Gilbert

COMMON NAME: Black Velvet Bolete.

MACROSCOPIC FEATURES: **Cap** 3–15 cm wide, convex to nearly flat; margin often sterile; surface dry, somewhat velvety, occasionally developing fine cracks in age, deep violet to dark grayish brown or nearly black, usually with a thin whitish bloom when young; **flesh** dense and firm, white or tinged gray, bruising pinkish to reddish gray, finally blackening; odor and taste not distinctive. **Pore surface** white or with a gray tinge when young, becoming dull pinkish brown, usually bruising reddish then slowly black; tubes 5–10 mm deep. **Stalk** equal or enlarged downward, solid; surface dry, colored like the cap or paler, especially near the apex, often covered with a thin whitish bloom, not reticulate or only slightly so at the apex; **flesh** colored and staining like the cap flesh.

SPORE PRINT: Pinkish brown.

MICROSCOPIC FEATURES: Spores 7–11 × 3.5–5 µm, narrowly oval, smooth, hyaline.

OCCURRENCE: Solitary to scattered with hardwoods, especially oak; late spring–fall.

EDIBILITY: Edible.

REMARKS: *Alboater* means "white and black." The cap surface stains amber orange with KOH and is negative with FeSO4 or NH4OH. Most species in the genus *Tylopilus*, including the very similar *Tylopilus williamsii* (p. 118), have bitter-tasting flesh, but *T. alboater* differs by having mild-tasting flesh. *Tylopilus griseocarneus* (p. 106) is somewhat similar but has a reticulated stalk.

Tylopilus alboater

Tylopilus badiceps (Peck) A. H. Sm. & Thiers

= *Boletus badiceps* Peck

COMMON NAME: Beveled-cap Bolete.

MACROSCOPIC FEATURES: **Cap** 4–8 cm wide, convex to broadly convex, sometimes depressed at the center in age; margin typically beveled to folded or obliquely truncate when mature; surface initially velvety and maroon, becoming purplish brown to dark reddish brown, then duller and smoother when mature; **flesh** white, sometimes slowly bruising pinkish to brown; odor sweet or not distinctive; taste not distinctive. **Pore surface** white, aging dingy white to brownish, not pinkish, usually bruising brownish; tubes 7–12 mm deep. **Stalk** equal or enlarged downward, solid; surface dry, colored like the cap but with decidedly more pronounced violaceous tones, or violaceous nearly overall, usually white at the apex and base, may have obscure narrow reticulation at the apex; **flesh** colored and staining like the cap flesh.

SPORE PRINT: Pinkish brown.

MICROSCOPIC FEATURES: Spores 8–11 × 3.5–4.5 μm, narrowly ellipsoidal, smooth, hyaline to yellowish.

OCCURRENCE: Solitary, scattered, or in groups with oaks; summer–fall.

EDIBILITY: Edible.

REMARKS: *Badiceps* means "reddish brown to maroon cap." The cap surface stains amber brown with NH4OH, while the stalk and white stalk base instantly stain blackish brown with NH4OH. *Tylopilus ferrugineus* (not illustrated) differs by having a reddish-brown cap, a stalk without violaceous tones, and a non-beveled cap margin. *Tylopilus indecisus* (p. 107) has an ochraceous-brown to pale brown or reddish-brown cap, a paler stalk without violaceous tones, and a non-beveled cap margin.

Tylopilus badiceps

Tylopilus balloui (Peck) Singer

= *Boletus balloui* Peck
= *Boletus balloui* var. *fuscatus* Corner
= *Gyrodon balloui* (Peck) Snell & Dick

COMMON NAME: Burnt Orange Bolete.
MACROSCOPIC FEATURES: **Cap** 5–12 cm wide,
convex, becoming nearly flat in age; margin
even, incurved at first; surface dry, bright
orange to bright orange red, fading to dull
orange, cinnamon, or tan in age; **flesh** white,
staining pinkish tan to violet brown when
exposed; odor not distinctive; taste mild or
bitter. **Pore surface** white to dingy white,
becoming tan or slightly pinkish in age, staining brown when bruised; tubes up to 8 mm
deep. **Stalk** equal or swollen on the lower portion, solid; surface smooth or scurfy, sometimes finely reticulate only at the apex, whitish
or tinged yellow to orange, staining brownish
when cut or bruised or in age; **flesh** colored
and staining like the cap flesh.

SPORE PRINT: Pale brown to reddish brown.
MICROSCOPIC FEATURES: Spores 5–11 × 3–5
μm, ellipsoidal, smooth, hyaline to pale
brown.
OCCURRENCE: Solitary, scattered, or in groups
on lawns under trees or in woods, especially
near oak, beech, and pine; summer–fall.
EDIBILITY: Edible.
REMARKS: Charles H. Peck named this species
in honor of American mycologist W. H. Ballou
(1857–1937), who made several collections
of this beautiful bolete. The epithet *balloui*
is incorrectly spelled as *ballouii* in most field
guides. *Tylopilus balloui* was transferred to
Rubinoboletus balloui (Peck) Heinem. and
Rammeloo, as listed in *Index Fungorum*. We
have not accepted this transfer based on the
conclusions reached by Osmundson and Halling (2010), which clearly indicate that this
taxon is more closely aligned with species of
Tylopilus rather than with *Rubinoboletus*.

Tylopilus balloui

Tylopilus felleus (Bull.) P. Karst.

= *Boletus felleus* Bull.
= *Boletus felleus* var. *minor* Coker & Beers
= *Tylopilus felleus* var. *uliginosus* A. H. Sm. & Thiers

COMMON NAME: Bitter Bolete.

MACROSCOPIC FEATURES: **Cap** 5–30 cm wide, rounded to nearly flat; surface dry, sometimes viscid when moist, bald, initially pinkish to reddish purple, developing shades of brown with or without purplish tints, finally becoming brown to tan when mature; **flesh** white, sometimes bruising reddish; odor not distinctive; taste very bitter and astringent. **Pore surface** initially white, aging to pinkish, vinaceous, or pinkish tan, usually bruising brown; tubes 1–2 cm deep. **Stalk** enlarged downward and often bulbous, solid; surface dry, brown almost overall, usually white at the apex and base, often developing olive or olive-brown stains when bruised or in age, with prominent reticulation over the upper third or more; **flesh** colored and staining like the cap flesh.

SPORE PRINT: Pinkish brown to reddish brown.

MICROSCOPIC FEATURES: Spores 11–17 × 3–5 μm, subfusoid, smooth, pale brown.

OCCURRENCE: Solitary or in groups on the ground or on decaying wood with conifers, especially pine, or in mixed woods; summer–fall.

EDIBILITY: Inedible for most people because of its extremely bitter taste.

REMARKS: *Felleus* is from the Latin word *fel*, meaning gall or bile, and refers to this bolete's bitter-tasting flesh. The Little Bitter Bolete, *Tylopilus minor* (p. 108) is similar but has a smaller stature, its stalk is nearly equal or only slightly enlarged downward with an abruptly narrowed base and more delicate reticulation, and it grows in association with oaks. The Variable Brown-net Bolete, *Tylopilus variobrunneus* (p. 116), has a greenish-brown to dark olive-brown or blackish-brown cap when young that becomes dull medium brown to chestnut brown when mature, dark brown reticulation that may be white at the stalk apex, and mild, or sometimes slightly bitter-tasting, flesh.

Tylopilus felleus

Tylopilus griseocarneus Wolfe & Halling

MACROSCOPIC FEATURES: **Cap** 4–11 cm wide, convex to nearly flat; surface dry, slightly velvety when young, sometimes developing cracks in age, color ranging from dull reddish brown to brown, dark olive brown, dark gray to brownish gray, or blackish; **flesh** grayish, bruising orangish to orange red and then black; odor and taste not distinctive. **Pore surface** initially black, aging to gray, staining grayish orange or a darker gray when mature; tubes 3–11 mm deep. **Stalk** equal or tapered in either direction, solid; surface dry, blackish brown to gray, sometimes paler at the apex, with prominent reticulation on the upper one-third or nearly overall, often darkly pruinose; **flesh** grayish, staining like the cap flesh.

SPORE PRINT: Pinkish to pinkish gray.
MICROSCOPIC FEATURES: Spores 8–14 × 3–5 μm, fusiform-ellipsoidal, smooth, hyaline.
OCCURRENCE: Scattered or in groups with oak or pine; summer–winter.
EDIBILITY: Reportedly poisonous.
REMARKS: *Griseocarneus* means "gray flesh." The cap surface stains vinaceous black with KOH. The cap flesh stains vinaceous pink with KOH and is negative with NH4OH or FeSO4. The stalk flesh stains reddish orange with KOH, gray blue with FeSO4, and is negative with NH4OH. *Tylopilus alboater* (p. 102) has white or whitish pores and lacks prominent reticulation on the stalk. *Sutorius eximius* (p. 101) is similar but lacks reticulation on its stalk. *Strobilomyces* species, have shaggy caps and margins with hanging partial veil remnants.

Tylopilus griseocarneus

Tylopilus indecisus (Peck) Murrill

= *Boletus indecisus* Peck

MACROSCOPIC FEATURES: **Cap** 5–17 cm wide, convex, becoming broadly convex to nearly plane in age; margin even; surface dry, somewhat velvety, ochraceous brown to pale brown or reddish brown; **flesh** white, unchanging or slowly staining pinkish or brownish when exposed; odor and taste not distinctive. **Pore surface** white, becoming pinkish or brownish with age, staining brown when bruised; tubes 6–12 mm deep. **Stalk** enlarged downward or nearly equal, solid; surface dry, whitish when young, becoming pale brown at maturity and staining brown when bruised, usually with fine reticulation at the apex; **flesh** colored and staining like the cap flesh.
SPORE PRINT: Pinkish brown.
MICROSCOPIC FEATURES: Spores 10–15 × 3–5 μm, narrowly subfusiform, smooth, pale brown.

OCCURRENCE: Scattered or in groups with oaks or pines; late spring–early winter.
EDIBILITY: Edible.
REMARKS: The cap surface stains dark blackish brown with NH4OH. *Tylopilus badiceps* (p. 103) is similar but has a dark brown to maroon cap with a beveled to folded margin and a darker stalk with pale to distinctly violaceous tones. *Tylopilus ferrugineus* (not illustrated) is also similar, but it has a darker reddish-brown cap and stalk. It has white, mild-tasting flesh that slowly stains pink and then brownish when exposed, a white to pinkish-buff pore surface that bruises brown, and it grows on the ground with oaks during summer and fall. The addition of a drop of NH4OH to the cap surface produces a dark violet to vinaceous flash that becomes reddish brown to blackish brown.

Tylopilus indecisus

Tylopilus minor Singer

= *Boletus minor* (Singer) Murrill

COMMON NAME: Little Bitter Bolete.
MACROSCOPIC FEATURES: **Cap** 3–8(15) cm
wide, pulvinate, becoming broadly convex
to nearly plane in age; margin even; surface
dry, glabrous to finely velvety, pale brown
to brown or sometimes dull whitish, often
with pinkish tones; **flesh** white, unchanging
when exposed; odor not distinctive; taste
bitter. **Pore surface** white at first, becoming
pale brownish pink and often depressed at
the stalk in age, not staining when bruised;
tubes 4–7(18) mm deep. **Stalk** nearly equal
or slightly enlarged downward, usually with
an abruptly narrowed base, solid; surface dry,
with pale to brownish reticulation near the
apex or extending to the mid-portion or sometimes lacking, white to whitish at first, becoming brownish to cinnamon, apex and base
whitish, basal mycelium white; **flesh** white.

SPORE PRINT: Pinkish brown.
MICROSCOPIC FEATURES: Spores 9–15 × 3–5
µm, fusoid, smooth, yellowish to hyaline.
OCCURRENCE: Solitary, scattered, or in groups
in hardwoods or in mixed woods with oak;
late spring–fall.
EDIBILITY: Inedible because of the bitter taste.
REMARKS: *Tylopilus felleus* (p. 105) is similar
but has a larger stature. Its stalk is enlarged
downward, often bulbous at the base, and has
prominent reticulation over the upper third
or more. It grows in association with conifers,
especially pines.

Tylopilus minor

Tylopilus peralbidus (Snell & Beardslee) Murrill

= *Boletus peralbidus* Snell & Beardslee

MACROSCOPIC FEATURES: **Cap** 4.5–13 cm wide, convex to nearly flat, often depressed over the disc when mature; surface dry, bald to somewhat velvety, developing fine cracks in age, initially white, becoming ochraceous tan to chamois, and finally brownish, bruising cinnamon to brown; **flesh** white, sometimes bruising pale pinkish brown or buff, usually slowly; odor bleach-like or unpleasant; taste bitter. **Pore surface** initially whitish, becoming buff or tinged pinkish in age, bruising brown; tubes 6–10 mm deep. **Stalk** equal or tapered in either direction, often with a pointed base, solid; surface dry, smooth, white to brownish or colored like the cap, bruising brown; **flesh** white, staining like the cap flesh.

SPORE PRINT: Pinkish brown.

MICROSCOPIC FEATURES: Spores 7–12 × 2.3–3.5 µm, cylindric or cylindric-subclavate, smooth, pale honey-yellow.

OCCURRENCE: Solitary, scattered, or in groups in lawns, along roads, or in oak or pine woods; spring–fall.

EDIBILITY: Unknown.

REMARKS: *Peralbidus* means "whitish throughout," referring to the prominent color of this bolete. The cap surface stains yellow with KOH, dark blue green with FeSO4, and is negative with NH4OH. The flesh immediately stains dark bluish gray with FeSO4 and pale yellow with KOH or NH4OH. *Tylopilus rhoadsiae* (p. 111) has pores that do not stain when bruised, and its stalk has prominent, coarse reticulation over the upper half or more. *Tylopilus rhodoconius* (p. 111) has whitish flesh with hyaline marbling and a brownish cap and stalk that bruise darker brown when handled. The Appalachian Yellow-brown Bolete, *Tylopilus appalachiensis* (p. 9) has a dry, somewhat velvety, chamois to brownish-yellow cap that typically becomes darker brown and sometimes cracked in age. It has white flesh that slowly stains pinkish then pale brown and tastes bitter. The pore surface is whitish at first, slowly becoming pinkish brown in age, and stains brown when bruised. The stalk is colored like the cap or paler and lacks reticulation or is reticulate only at the apex. It grows on the ground with hardwoods, especially oaks.

Tylopilus peralbidus

Tylopilus plumbeoviolaceus (Snell & Dick) Singer

= *Boletus plumbeoviolaceus* Snell & Dick

COMMON NAME: Violet-gray Bolete.
MACROSCOPIC FEATURES: **Cap** 4–15 cm wide, convex to broadly convex with a narrow sterile margin, becoming nearly plane in age; surface glabrous, smooth, shiny, at times becoming cracked, brownish to grayish brown or dull cinnamon, at times tinged with purplish areas, especially toward the margin, or entirely purple when young; **flesh** firm when fresh, white, not staining when cut or bruised; odor slightly pungent or not distinctive; taste very bitter.
Pore surface dull white when young, becoming very pale brownish to pinkish tan with age, not staining when bruised or just barely bruising very light pinkish brown, depressed at the stalk at maturity; tubes 4–18 mm deep. **Stalk** nearly equal or enlarged downward, solid; surface dry, purple with white mycelium at the base when young, at times becoming grayish purple or purplish brown, smooth and glabrous except for a narrow zone of reticulation at the apex; **flesh** colored like the cap flesh.
SPORE PRINT: Purplish brown.
MICROSCOPIC FEATURES: Spores 10–13 × 3–4 μm, ellipsoid, smooth, pale brown.
OCCURRENCE: Solitary or in small groups in hardwoods with oak; early summer to late fall.
EDIBILITY: Inedible due to the bitter taste.
REMARKS: *Plumbeoviolaceus* means "grayish violaceous," referring to the overall colors. *Tylopilus violatinctus* (p. 117) is similar, but it has a paler grayish-lilac to pinkish-lilac cap, a pale lilac stalk that is white at the apex, and smaller spores.

Tylopilus plumbeoviolaceus

Tylopilus rhoadsiae (Murrill) Murrill

= *Boletus rhoadsiae* (Murrill) Murrill
= *Gyroporus rhoadsiae* Murrill

COMMON NAME: Pale Bitter Bolete
MACROSCOPIC FEATURES: **Cap** 6–15 cm wide, convex to nearly flat; surface dry, bald to slightly velvety, white to whitish, tinged with buff, grayish buff, pinkish, or pinkish tan, may become tan, pinkish brown, or golden brown in age; **flesh** white, unchanging; odor not distinctive; taste bitter. **Pore surface** initially white, aging to dull pinkish, unchanging; tubes 9–20 mm deep. **Stalk** equal or enlarged above a pinched base, solid, with white basal mycelium; surface dry, white or colored like the cap, with prominent white or brown reticulation on the upper half or nearly overall; **flesh** colored like the cap flesh.

SPORE PRINT: Pinkish to brownish vinaceous.
MICROSCOPIC FEATURES: Spores 11–13.5 × 3.5–4.5 μm, oblong-elliptic, smooth, hyaline to pale yellow.
OCCURRENCE: Scattered or in groups with pines or oaks; summer–winter.
EDIBILITY: Inedible because of its bitter taste.
REMARKS: The epithet *rhoadsiae* honors Louise and Arthur S. Rhoads, who first collected this bolete in Putnam County, Florida. The cap surface stains pale yellow with KOH or NH_4OH and gray with $FeSO_4$. *Tylopilus peralbidus* (p. 109) is similar but lacks reticulation on its stalk. *Tylopilus rhodoconius* (p. 112) has a darker brown cap and stalk, which bruise brown, and white to creamy-white flesh with hyaline marbling.

Tylopilus rhoadsiae

Tylopilus rhodoconius T. J. Baroni, Both & A. E. Bessette

MACROSCOPIC FEATURES: **Cap** 4–14 cm wide, hemispheric at first, becoming broadly convex to nearly flat in age; margin sterile; surface dry, finely tomentose, developing fine cracks in age, initially pale ochraceous to brownish orange, becoming pale brown and finally darker brown, remaining paler toward the margin, bruising dark brown; **flesh** soft, white to pale creamy white with hyaline marbling, slowly staining pale pinkish, and finally a dingy pinkish flesh color when exposed; odor faintly of chlorine or not distinctive; taste mild or initially mild then very bitter. **Pore surface** whitish with a faint flush of pink when young, becoming white, then pinkish buff, and finally vinaceous fawn when mature, staining dull brown, then dark cinnamon brown to tobacco brown when bruised; pores nearly circular; tubes 6–10 mm deep. **Stalk** equal to strongly ventricose, tapered to a point at the base, often with a short, root-like projection; surface dry, solid, finely pruinose, white near the apex, yellow brown to reddish brown downward or colored like the cap, bruising dark cinnamon brown to tobacco brown when handled, with white basal mycelium; **flesh** colored and staining like the cap flesh.

SPORE PRINT: Pink to reddish gray.

MICROSCOPIC FEATURES: Spores 8.4–13 × 2–3.5 μm, cylindric, smooth, hyaline.

OCCURRENCE: Scattered or in groups on sandy soil with oak, pine, or in mixed oak, beech, and pine woods; summer–fall.

EDIBILITY: Unknown.

REMARKS: *Rhodoconius* refers to the pinkish to reddish-gray color of the accumulated spore deposit of this bolete. The cap surface slowly stains pale yellow brown with KOH or NH_4OH and bluish green to bluish gray with $FeSO_4$; the flesh stains olivaceous and then quickly fades to colorless with KOH and stains bluish green to bluish gray with $FeSO_4$. *Tylopilus peralbidus* (p. 109) is similar but differs by having a paler cap and stalk, not readily bruising brown when handled, and having slightly smaller spores.

Tylopilus rhodoconius

Tylopilus rubrobrunneus Mazzer & A. H. Sm.

COMMON NAME: Reddish-brown Bitter Bolete.
MACROSCOPIC FEATURES: **Cap** 8–30 cm wide, broadly convex to nearly flat, sometimes slightly depressed in age; margin initially incurved to inrolled; surface dry, bald, may develop cracks in age, dark to bright purple when young, becoming purple brown, dark reddish brown, dull brown, or cinnamon when mature; **flesh** white, unchanging or slowly bruising brown; odor not distinctive; taste very bitter. **Pore surface** initially whitish to very pale brownish, aging to dingy pinkish brown, bruising brown; tubes 8–20 mm deep. **Stalk** equal or enlarged downward, solid; surface dry, white to brown, developing olive or olive-brown stains from the base upward, bald or with fine apical reticulation; **flesh** white, staining like the cap flesh.
SPORE PRINT: Reddish brown to dull pinkish brown.

MICROSCOPIC FEATURES: Spores 10–14 × 3–4.5 µm, suboblong to nearly fusoid, smooth, pale brown.
OCCURRENCE: Scattered, in groups, or caespitose clusters in hardwood forests, especially with beech or oak, also in mixed oak and pine woods; summer–fall.
EDIBILITY: Inedible due to its bitter taste.
REMARKS: *Rubrobrunneus* means "reddish brown." The purple areas of the cap surface bleach pinkish brown with KOH or NH4OH and are negative with FeSO4. *Tylopilus violatinctus* (p. 117) is similar but has a pale purplish to grayish-violet or pale brown cap and does not develop olive-brown stains on the stalk. The stalk of *Tylopilus felleus* (p. 105) has more prominent reticulation. *Tylopilus plumbeoviolaceus* (p. 110) lacks olive stains on the stalk.

Tylopilus rubrobrunneus

Tylopilus sordidus (Frost) A. H. Sm. & Thiers

= *Boletus sordidus* Frost

= *Porphyrellus sordidus* (Frost) Snell MAC-
ROSCOPIC FEATURES: **Cap** 4.5–13 cm wide,
convex, becoming broadly convex to nearly
flat; margin sterile when young, becoming
even when mature; surface dry, glabrous to
somewhat velvety, becoming cracked in age,
gray brown to olive brown or dark brown,
often with dark greenish or bluish tints along
the margin; **flesh** whitish, staining blue green
when exposed, sometimes with reddish tints;
odor slightly pungent or not distinctive; taste
unpleasant or not distinctive. **Pore surface**
whitish to grayish buff when young, becoming pinkish brown then reddish brown to
yellow brown, staining dark blue to dark blue
green, then dark brownish red when bruised;
tubes 6–20 mm deep. **Stalk** slightly enlarged
downward or nearly equal, solid; surface dry,
minutely scurfy, brownish with much darker
longitudinal streaks, typically paler toward the
upper portion and whitish at the base, with
greenish or bluish-green tints near the apex;
flesh colored and staining like the cap flesh.
SPORE PRINT: Reddish brown.
MICROSCOPIC FEATURES: Spores 10–14 × 4–6
μm, subellipsoidal, smooth, pale brown.
OCCURRENCE: Solitary, scattered, or in groups
with hardwoods, especially oak, also under
various conifers; summer–fall.
EDIBILITY: Unknown.
REMARKS: *Sordidus* means "dirty or smoky,"
referring to the overall colors of this bolete.
When wrapped in waxed paper for several
minutes, the exposed flesh of this bolete stains
the paper a dark blue-green color.

Tylopilus sordidus

Tylopilus tabacinus (Peck) Singer

= *Tylopilus tabacinus* var. *amarus* Singer
= *Tylopilus tabacinus* var. *dubius* Singer

COMMON NAME: Tobacco-brown Tylopilus.
MACROSCOPIC FEATURES: **Cap** 4.5–18 cm
wide, obtuse when young, becoming broadly
convex to nearly flat; margin even and wavy;
surface dry, smooth, slightly velvety, becoming
finely cracked in age, yellow brown to orange
brown or tobacco brown; **flesh** white, usually
slowly staining purplish buff or pinkish buff
when exposed, often brown at maturity; odor
variously described as fruity, fishy, pungent, or
not distinctive; taste slightly bitter or not distinctive. **Pore surface** whitish or sometimes
brown at first, becoming brown to yellow-
brown with darker brown patches and stains,
usually depressed at the stalk in age; tubes
1–1.5 cm deep. **Stalk** enlarged to bulbous
when young, becoming nearly equal in age,
solid; surface dry, colored like the cap or paler,
usually lighter toward the apex, prominently
reticulate, at least over the upper portion,
usually glabrous on the lower portion; **flesh**
colored like the cap flesh or sometimes burgundy brown near the base, staining like the
cap flesh.
SPORE PRINT: Pinkish brown to reddish brown.
MICROSCOPIC FEATURES: Spores (10)12–
14(17) × 3.5–4.5 µm, fusoid to ellipsoidal,
smooth, hyaline to pale honey-yellow; pleurocystidia 45–60 × 6.5–12.5 µm, lanceolate
to narrowly fusoid-ventricose; cheilocystidia
absent.
OCCURRENCE: Scattered or in groups in woods
and at their edges or around trees in lawns,
usually with oak and pine; summer–fall.
EDIBILITY: Edible.
REMARKS: *Tabacinus* means "color of tobacco."
The cap surface stains rusty brown to dark
maroon with KOH, vinaceous with NH_4OH,
and pale olive-gray with $FeSO_4$. Specimens
with bitter tasting flesh were previously identified as var. *amarus*. *Tylopilus felleus* (p. 105)
is similar, but its pores are white when young
and become pinkish, vinaceous, or pinkish tan
in age, and it has very bitter tasting flesh.

Tylopilus tabacinus

Tylopilus variobrunneus Roody, A. R. Bessette & A. E. Bessette

COMMON NAME: Variable Brown-net Bolete.
MACROSCOPIC FEATURES: **Cap** 4–12 cm wide, convex, becoming broadly convex to nearly plane in age; margin incurved at first, with a narrow band of sterile tissue when young, becoming decurved and even at maturity; surface dry, somewhat velvety, dark olive brown to greenish brown or blackish brown when young, becoming dull brown to chestnut brown when mature; **flesh** dull white, slowly staining pinkish rose to brownish pink when exposed; odor not distinctive; taste slightly bitter or not distinctive. **Pore surface** whitish at first, becoming yellow brown to brownish pink, staining brown when bruised, sometimes slowly, depressed at the stalk in age; tubes 5–13 mm deep. **Stalk** enlarged downward or nearly equal, usually with a pinched base, solid; surface dry, dull white on the upper portion, becoming pale brown below, dark brown toward the base, with prominent reticulation over the upper two-thirds, or at least over the upper half; reticulation white near the apex, brown below; **flesh** concolorous with and staining like the cap flesh.
SPORE PRINT: Pinkish brown.
MICROSCOPIC FEATURES: Spores 9–13 × 3–4.5 μm, subfusiform to subelliptic, smooth, brownish.
OCCURRENCE: Scattered or in groups on the ground with oaks or in mixed oak and pine woods; summer–fall.
EDIBILITY: Edible, but sometimes with an unpleasant aftertaste.
REMARKS: *Variobrunneus* means "variable brown colors," a reference to the cap and stalk. *Tylopilus felleus* (p. 105) is similar, but it has very bitter-tasting flesh and a paler stalk. Compare with *Tylopilus badiceps* (p. 103), which has a beveled cap margin and mild-tasting flesh.

Tylopilus variobrunneus

Tylopilus violatinctus T. J. Baroni & Both

COMMON NAME: Pale Violet Bitter Bolete.

MACROSCOPIC FEATURES: **Cap** 7.5–14 cm wide, hemispheric, becoming broadly convex to nearly flat in age; margin sterile and strongly incurved at first; surface dry, somewhat velvety when young, becoming nearly glabrous when mature, sometimes cracked in age, grayish violet to bluish violet when young, becoming pale purplish, purplish pink, or tan to dull brown when mature, bruising rusty violet to dark violet; **flesh** white, unchanging or becoming very pale slate-colored when exposed; odor pungent or not distinctive; taste intensely bitter. **Pore surface** white to dull pink at first, becoming brownish, typically depressed at the stalk in age, unchanging; tubes up to 1.5 cm deep. **Stalk** enlarged downward or nearly equal, sometimes with a bulbous base, solid; surface dry, nearly glabrous, colored like the cap or paler at first, becoming brown with a white apex and base, sometimes staining dull yellow to yellow brown when bruised, occasionally with inconspicuous reticulation at the apex; **flesh** colored like the cap flesh.

SPORE PRINT: Reddish brown.

MICROSCOPIC FEATURES: Spores 7–10 × 3–4 μm, subfusiform, smooth, pale yellow.

OCCURRENCE: Solitary, scattered, or in groups under oak and pine, also with beech; late spring–fall.

EDIBILITY: Unknown.

REMARKS: *Violatinctus* means "tinged violet." The cap surface stains yellowish to brownish yellow with NH4OH, dingy pale yellowish to amber with KOH, and is negative with FeSO4. The flesh stains yellow, then quickly develops a blue ring around the yellow, with FeSO4. The Violet-gray Bolete, *Tylopilus plumbeoviolaceus* (p. 110) is similar but has a dark purple stalk. *Tylopilus rubrobrunneus* (p. 113) is typically more robust, has a purple-brown to vinaceous-brown cap that fades to pinkish cinnamon in age, and develops olive-brown stains on its stalk, especially when handled.

Tylopilus violatinctus

Tylopilus williamsii Singer & J. Garcia

MACROSCOPIC FEATURES: **Cap** 4–10 cm wide, hemispheric when young, becoming broadly convex to nearly flat in age; margin even, incurved at first; surface dry, somewhat velvety, often uneven in age, dark magenta to purple violet or brownish purple when young, fading to pinkish gray to pale yellow brown; **flesh** white, unchanging; odor not distinctive; taste bitter. **Pore surface** white at first, becoming pale pinkish at maturity, bruising yellowish to yellow brown; tubes 1–1.5 cm deep. **Stalk** nearly equal overall, solid; surface dry, glabrous, whitish to pale yellow or grayish, typically streaked with beige and grayish orange, slowly discoloring brown when handled, in age, or following refrigeration; **flesh** colored like the cap flesh.

SPORE PRINT: Pink.

MICROSCOPIC FEATURES: Spores 7.5–11 × 3.5–4.5 μm, fusoid to ellipsoid, smooth, hyaline to pale yellow.

OCCURRENCE: Scattered or in groups under oaks; summer–fall.

EDIBILITY: Inedible because of the bitter taste.

REMARKS: The epithet *williamsii* honors Florida mycologist Robert S. Williams (1939–2014), who first collected and described it. The cap surface stains orange yellow with KOH and orange with NH4OH. The flesh stains greenish with FeSO4. *Tylopilus plumbeoviolaceus* (p. 110) differs by having a violet or purple stalk that is sometimes reticulate at the apex. *Tylopilus violatinctus* (p. 117) has a paler and more lilac cap that bruises violet, a concolorous stalk with a white apex, and a base that typically stains yellowish when bruised.

Tylopilus williamsii

Veloporphyrellus conicus (Ravenel)
B. Ortiz, Yan C. Li & Zhu L. Yang

= *Fistulinella conica* var. *conica* (Ravenel)
Pegler & T. W. K. Young
= *Fistulinella conica* var. *reticulata* (Wolfe)
Singer
= *Mucilopilus conicus* (Ravenel) Wolfe
= *Tylopilus conicus* (Ravenel) Beardslee

COMMON NAME: Conical Shaggy-capped
Bolete.
MACROSCOPIC FEATURES: **Cap** 2.5–9.5 cm
wide, bluntly conical when young, becoming convex in age; surface dry, shaggy or scaly
when young, and often developing a network
of ridges and small depressions in age, pinkish
tan to golden yellow, yellow brown or salmon-tinged, with white flesh showing between the
scales or beneath the ridges; margin fringed
with thin flaps of membranous, sterile veil
tissue, at least when young; **flesh** white,
unchanging; odor fruity or not distinctive;
taste not distinctive. **Pore surface** white when
young, becoming grayish pink to pinkish
brown; tubes 8–14 mm deep. **Stalk** slender,
nearly equal, often curved, solid; surface dry,
smooth or minutely wrinkled, occasionally
reticulate, white or yellow, sometimes with
pinkish tones, especially toward the mid-portion; **flesh** colored like the cap flesh.
SPORE PRINT: Pinkish brown to reddish brown.
MICROSCOPIC FEATURES: Spores 14–21 ×
4–6 μm, elongate-fusoid, smooth, hyaline to
honey-yellow, pseudoamyloid in Melzer's.
OCCURRENCE: Solitary or scattered under pine
and in mixed woods, often in bottomlands
along streams; summer–fall.
EDIBILITY: Edible.
REMARKS: *Conica* means "cone-shaped," a
reference to the shape of the young cap.
Fistulinella jamaicensis (not illustrated) has a
1.5–4.5 cm wide cap that is rounded to convex
when young and becomes broadly convex
at maturity. The cap is glabrous to slightly
velvety, pink to brownish pink when young,
and becomes grayish to grayish brown with
amber-yellow spots in age. The flesh is white,
does not stain, and lacks a distinctive odor and
taste. Its pore surface is white at first, becomes
brownish pink, and is pinkish brown when
mature. The stalk is whitish above, yellow
below, and often has small brownish scales. Its
spores measure 8.5–14.5 × 4.5–6.5 μm, and it
grows in hardwood, wet areas during summer.

Veloporphyrellus conicus

Xanthoconium affine (Peck) Singer

= *Boletus affinis* Peck
= *Boletus affinis* var. *maculosus* Peck
= *Xanthoconium affine* var. *affine* (Peck)
    Singer
= *Xanthoconium affine* var. *maculosus* (Peck)
    Singer
= *Xanthoconium affine* var. *reticulatum* (A. H.
    Sm.) Wolfe

MACROSCOPIC FEATURES: **Cap** 4–11.5 cm
wide, convex to broadly convex, becoming
nearly flat in age; margin even; surface dry,
somewhat velvety, smooth or wrinkled, dark
brown to chestnut brown or ocher brown,
sometimes with white to pale yellow spots
or patches; **flesh** white, unchanging; odor
and taste not distinctive. **Pore surface** white
at first, becoming yellowish to dingy yellow
brown, bruising dull yellow to brownish,
depressed at the stalk in age; tubes 6–20 mm
deep. **Stalk** nearly equal or tapered in either
direction, solid; surface smooth or with sparse
to conspicuous brown reticulation, dry, whitish, often with brownish streaks on the middle
portion or base; **flesh** colored like the cap
flesh.

SPORE PRINT: Bright yellow brown to rusty
ochraceous.

MICROSCOPIC FEATURES: Spores $(9–)12–16 \times$
$3–5$ μm, narrowly ventricose to nearly cylindrical, smooth, yellowish.

OCCURRENCE: Usually in groups, sometimes in
caespitose clusters, or scattered in hardwoods,
especially with oak or beech, also under pines;
spring–fall.

EDIBILITY: Edible but see remarks below.

REMARKS: The cap surface stains reddish
brown with NH_4OH and is negative with
KOH or $FeSO_4$. The key identification features include the brown cap that sometimes
has pale yellow spots, white flesh that does not
stain when exposed, white to yellow-brown
pores, and a whitish stalk with brownish
streaks that may be reticulate or not reticulate.
Some collections of this bolete taste good,
while others are mediocre or unpleasant.

Xanthoconium affine

Xanthoconium stramineum
(Murrill) Singer

= *Boletus stramineus* (Murrill) Murrill

MACROSCOPIC FEATURES: **Cap** 4–9 cm wide, convex, becoming broadly convex to nearly flat; margin incurved at first, sterile; surface dry, glabrous and smooth when young, sometimes becoming cracked and uneven in age, white at first, becoming whitish to pale straw-colored or tinged brownish; **flesh** white, unchanging or slowly staining pinkish brown when exposed; odor variously described as slightly fruity, unpleasant, or not distinctive; taste somewhat bitter or not distinctive. **Pore surface** white to whitish at first, becoming buff to yellowish buff or pale yellow brown in age, unchanging; tubes 3–10 mm deep. **Stalk** enlarged downward or nearly equal, usually with a swollen base, solid; surface dry, glabrous, white to whitish, not staining when bruised; **flesh** white, staining like the cap flesh.

SPORE PRINT: Brownish yellow to yellowish rusty brown.

MICROSCOPIC FEATURES: Spores 10–15 × 2.5–4 µm, cylindrical, smooth, yellowish to hyaline.

OCCURRENCE: Solitary, scattered, or in groups on sandy soil or in grassy areas, under oak and pine; summer–fall.

EDIBILITY: Reported to be edible, but in our experience, it has a sour, bitter, and unpleasant taste.

REMARKS: *Stramineum* means "straw-colored," referring to the cap color. The cap stains bluish gray with $FeSO_4$, quickly salmon pink then fades on dark areas with KOH, and is negative with NH_4OH. *Boletus albisulphureus* (p. 40) is similar but has a reticulate stalk. *Gyroporus subalbellus* (p. 70) has a brittle stalk that becomes hollow when mature.

Xanthoconium stramineum

Xerocomus hortonii (A. H. Sm. & Thiers) Manfr. Binder & Besl

= *Boletus hortonii* A. H. Sm. & Thiers

COMMON NAMES: Corrugated Bolete, Horton's Bolete.

MACROSCOPIC FEATURES: **Cap** 4–10 cm wide, convex becoming broadly convex; surface dry or somewhat viscid, corrugated and deeply pitted, tan to reddish tan or ocher brown to reddish brown; **flesh** whitish to pale yellow, not staining when cut or bruised; odor and taste not distinctive. **Pore surface** yellow when young, becoming olive yellow, unchanging or rarely and slowly staining blue when bruised; tubes 5–10 mm deep. **Stalk** nearly equal or enlarged downward, solid; surface dry, smooth to lightly pruinose, at times with delicate reticulation on the upper half, pale yellow to tan, sometimes reddish at the base; **flesh** colored like the cap flesh.

SPORE PRINT: Olive brown.

MICROSCOPIC FEATURES: Spores 12–15 × 3.5–4.5 μm, somewhat boat-shaped, smooth, yellow.

OCCURRENCE: Solitary, scattered, or in groups in hardwoods or mixed woods, especially with oak and beech; summer–fall.

EDIBILITY: Edible.

REMARKS: The epithet *hortonii* honors American mycologist Charles Horton Peck (1833–1917). The cap surface develops a blue-green flash, then stains olive brown with NH4OH. *Hemileccinum subglabripes* (p. 73) has a relatively smooth cap and a scurfier stalk. *Leccinum rugosiceps* (p. 82) has a pitted to cracked cap, brownish scabers on its stalk, and flesh that stains dull reddish when exposed.

Xerocomus hortonii

Xerocomus hypoxanthus Singer

= *Boletus hypoxanthus* (Singer) Murrill

MACROSCOPIC FEATURES: **Cap** 2.5–7 cm wide, convex, becoming broadly convex to nearly flat; margin even or nearly so; surface dry, somewhat velvety to granular, often finely cracked in age, tawny brown to pale red brown or pale yellow brown to orange brown; **flesh** yellowish to yellow, staining slightly blue or not at all when exposed; odor and taste not distinctive. **Pore surface** yellow, staining bluish or greenish when bruised or sometimes unchanging, often depressed at the stalk in age; pores usually elongated near the stalk; tubes 6–12 mm deep. **Stalk** nearly equal, solid; surface dry, pale yellow to pale tawny with a yellow apex, and usually with a yellow base, often coated with tiny, brownish, powdery flakes over the mid-portion, basal mycelium yellow; **flesh** colored and staining like the cap flesh.

SPORE PRINT: Olive brown.

MICROSCOPIC FEATURES: Spores 8–14 × 4–5 μm, fusoid, smooth, yellowish.

OCCURRENCE: Solitary, scattered, or in groups on sandy soil or humus in hardwoods, especially with oak, or in mixed oak and pine woods or on decaying trunks of hardwoods or saw palmetto; summer–fall.

EDIBILITY: Unknown.

REMARKS: *Hypoxanthus* means "yellow beneath," referring to the color of its pores and stalk. The cap surface stains blue to green blue with NH_4OH or KOH. The flesh stains blue to bluish with NH_4OH. *Xerocomus hemixanthus* (not illustrated) is similar but has a dark brown to reddish-brown or chestnut-brown cap, reddish-brown raised ribs near the stalk apex, and a white to yellowish-white basal mycelium. Its cap surface stains dark reddish brown with KOH, tan with NH_4OH, and grows on the trunk bases of Eastern Hophornbeam or sometimes on Sweetgum or Swamp Maple. *Boletus ochraceoluteus* (p. 49) has flesh that stains reddish then bluish green, and the cap surface stains reddish brown with KOH or NH_4OH. *Xerocomus pseudoboletinus* (not illustrated) has a large, up to 18 cm wide, reddish-brown to ochraceous-tawny cracked cap, with yellow showing in the cracks of mature specimens, and yellow flesh that is unchanging or sometimes staining weakly green when exposed. The pores are yellow and stain blue when bruised. The pores are elongated near the stalk, which is pale yellow on the upper portion and brownish toward the base, sometimes with brownish longitudinal ribs.

Xerocomus hypoxanthus

Xerocomus illudens (Peck) Singer/ *Xerocomus tenax* complex (A. H. Sm. & Thiers) Nuhn & Halling

MACROSCOPIC FEATURES: **Cap** 3–10 cm wide, convex, becoming nearly flat, sometimes slightly depressed; margin even or slightly sterile, incurved at first, sometimes becoming uplifted, lobed, and irregular in age; surface dry, somewhat velvety, sometimes cracked in age, yellow brown to pinkish cinnamon or dull brick-red to reddish brown, sometimes with an olivaceous tint; **flesh** whitish to pale yellow, unchanging or slowly staining pinkish red when exposed; odor not distinctive; taste acidic or not distinctive. **Pore surface** bright yellow at first, becoming dingy yellow and depressed at the stalk when mature, usually slowly staining cinnamon red to reddish brown or sometimes slowly staining bluish then cinnamon red, rarely unchanging; pores large, angular to somewhat rounded, larger near the stalk; tubes 8–16 mm deep. **Stalk** tapered downward or sometimes nearly equal, solid, firm and almost woody at the base; surface dry, reticulate overall, or at least on the upper portion, or with raised longitudinal lines that may form a partial reticulum at the apex or nearly overall, whitish with pale rose to pinkish-cinnamon or yellowish tints, basal mycelium whitish or pale yellow; **flesh** colored like the cap flesh.

SPORE PRINT: Olive brown.

MICROSCOPIC FEATURES: Spores 9–14 × 4–6 µm, ellipsoidal to subfusoid, smooth, dull yellow to pale brown.

OCCURRENCE: Solitary, scattered, or in groups in hardwoods with oak, sometimes with pines; summer–fall.

EDIBILITY: Unknown.

REMARKS: *Illudens* means "to mimic or imitate," a reference to its similarity with other species. *Tenax* means "tenacious, tough, or firm," referring to the texture of its stalk or

Xerocomus illudens/Xerocomus tenax complex (A)

its tenacious hold on the substrate. In 1898, Charles Peck described *Boletus illudens*. When Smith and Thiers examined Peck's type collection, they discovered that it was a mixture of two species and so designated a lectotype for *Boletus illudens* Peck, which represented Peck's original description of it. In 1971, they described *Boletus tenax*, which is currently considered an illegitimate name because it had previously been assigned to a different species in 1777. Smith and Thiers described the stalk of *Boletus tenax* as having a distinct, wide-meshed, fine reticulum either overall or only over its upper half. They wrote in their description of *Boletus illudens* that its stalk was usually marked by coarse ridges and anastomosing lines but was not finely reticulate. The descriptions of *Boletus illudens* by other mycologists, including Both, Coker and Beers, Singer, and Snell and Dick, all report its stalk to be strongly reticulate. For many years, mycologists have struggled with this conflict-

ing information and the problem of how to differentiate *Xerocomus illudens* from *Boletus tenax*. Some authors have attempted to use macroscopic or microscopic features, or macrochemical testing, as a means for differentiating *Xerocomus illudens* from *Boletus tenax*, but the results have always been inconclusive due to the taxonomic uncertainty of specimens tested or examined. Recent phylogenetic analysis places *Boletus tenax* in the *Xerocomus* clade, therefore supporting the new combination *Xerocomus tenax* Nuhn & Halling (2015). It is possible that *Xerocomus illudens* and *Xerocomus tenax* are the same species or that two or more species are collectively represented by these two taxa. Until additional molecular analysis has been completed, we have elected to consider this a species complex.

Xerocomus illudens/Xerocomus tenax complex (B)

Xerocomus morrisii (Peck) M. Zang

= *Boletus morrisii* Peck

COMMON NAME: Red-speckled Bolete.

MACROSCOPIC FEATURES: **Cap** 3–9 cm wide, convex to broadly convex with a narrow, overlapping band of sterile tissue at the margin; surface dry, somewhat velvety at first, becoming glabrous in age, olive brown to reddish brown; often yellow to olive gold on the margin; **flesh** pale yellow, slowly staining reddish when exposed; odor and taste not distinctive. **Pore surface** yellow to orange yellow or tinged reddish near the stalk, becoming orange to brownish orange in age, deeply depressed at the stalk when mature; tubes 6–12 mm deep. **Stalk** nearly equal or enlarged downward, solid; surface yellow beneath a covering of reddish or reddish-brown punctae, basal mycelium yellow; **flesh** colored and staining like the cap flesh.

SPORE PRINT: Olive brown.

MICROSCOPIC FEATURES: Spores 10–16 × 4–6 µm, ellipsoidal to spindle-shaped, smooth, yellowish.

OCCURRENCE: Solitary or sometimes in small groups, often in sandy soil, with pines; summer–fall.

EDIBILITY: Reportedly edible.

REMARKS: This species was named for Boston mycologist and artist George Edward Morris (1853–1916), the collector of the type specimen. *Leccinum rubropunctum* (p. 81) differs in that its yellowish flesh does not stain when exposed, and it has an unpleasant odor reminiscent of stale cigarette butts or a dirty ashtray.

Xerocomus morrisii

Xerocomus sclerotiorum

A. E. Bessette, M. E. Smith, A. R. Bessette & H. Hitchcock nom. prov.

COMMON NAME: Whitey's Bolete.
MACROSCOPIC FEATURES: **Cap** 4–10 cm wide, hemispheric at first, becoming convex to broadly convex at maturity; margin sterile, bright yellow with the yellow often persistent, incurved at first; surface dry, dull or somewhat shiny, smooth or nearly so, pinkish red to rose red or purplish red, sometimes with olive tints, becoming dull rose pink to brownish pink or brownish orange in age, slowly staining blackish blue when bruised; **flesh** pale yellow, sometimes with a pinkish tinge under the cuticle, staining blue when exposed, sometimes weakly and erratically; odor not distinctive; taste acidic. **Pore surface** bright yellow at first, becoming dull yellow then brownish yellow to brown at maturity, staining blue then slowly dull brown when bruised, depressed near the stalk in age; tubes 6–15 mm deep. **Stalk** enlarged downward or nearly equal, solid; surface dry, yellow at the apex, red on the lower portion or sometimes nearly overall, with conspicuous red to reddish-brown punctae over a yellow ground color, becoming dark wine red to brownish red in age, staining dark blue then dull brown when handled or bruised, longitudinally striate, occasionally reticulate near the very apex, with white basal mycelium and yellowish rhizomorphs; **flesh** brighter and deeper yellow than the cap flesh, reddish brown around larval tunnels, staining blue green, sometimes slowly and erratically.
SPORE PRINT: Olive brown.
MICROSCOPIC FEATURES: Spores (12)14–16(18) × 4–6 µm, subfusoid to fusiform, smooth, hyaline to pale brownish yellow.
OCCURRENCE: Scattered or in groups on sandy soil or on pincushion moss in woods with mixed oaks; summer–fall.
EDIBILITY: Edible.
REMARKS: The term *sclerotiorum* refers to the hidden, irregularly shaped orange sclerotia that this bolete forms in leaf litter and soil. Ongoing molecular analysis indicates that this species may belong in genus *Pulchroboletus*. The common name honors Dr. Harold "Whitey" Hitchcock, who first collected it. All parts of this bolete stain orange with KOH. *Hortiboletus rubellus* (p. 75) has reddish-orange flesh in the lower portion of its stalk, tubes that do not form half-tubes when split lengthwise, and smaller spores. *Pulchroboletus rubricitrinus* (p. 86) has a similarly colored cap that lacks a bright yellow margin, has a more yellow longitudinally striate stalk streaked with red, and different macrochemical test reactions.

Xerocomus sclerotiorum

Carbon, Crust, Cushion, and Parchment Fungi

Fungi in this group have extremely variable shapes that do not match the descriptions provided for the other major groups. Many are round to cushion-shaped, or thin and spreading crust-like growths. Others are erect and club-shaped to antler-like or highly irregular in outline. Some are brightly colored, soft, and gelatinous, while others are blackish, hard, and carbonaceous. Others are leathery or like parchment. Some have small, projecting, shelf-like caps, and one is vase- to bowl-shaped with a short stalk. The fertile surfaces of some species are roughened like sandpaper, while others may be rough and cracked, wrinkled, warted, toothed, or smooth, but all lack pores (use a hand lens). Although many grow on wood, some occur on other substrates. If you are unable to find a match here, try the Polypores group.

Biscogniauxia atropunctata
(Schwein.) Pouzar

= *Diatrype atropunctata* (Schwein.) Berk.

= *Hypoxylon atropunctatum* (Schwein.) Cooke

COMMON NAME: Hypoxylon Canker of Oak.

MACROSCOPIC FEATURES: **Fruitbody** an applanate stroma, up to 50 cm or more long and 25 cm or more wide; **outer surface** thin, white, punctuated by black ostioles, becoming blackish overall in age; **interior** carbonaceous, with embedded perithecia.

MICROSCOPIC FEATURES: Spores 20–30 × 11.5–14.5 µm, elliptical with rounded ends, smooth, with a straight, spore-length germ slit, brown.

OCCURRENCE: On trunks and logs of oaks and other hardwoods; year-round.

EDIBILITY: Inedible.

REMARKS: *Atropunctata* means "having dark dots," a reference to the black ostioles that contrast with the white outer surface. The Brown-toothed Crust, *Hymenochaetopsis olivacea* = *Hydnochaete olivacea* (p. 10), is a resupinate, spreading crust up to 20 cm long and 10 cm wide, with dry, leathery, yellow-brown to reddish-brown jagged teeth. It grows year-round on the underside of fallen hardwood branches, especially oak. *Hymenochaetopsis tabacina* = *Hymenochaete tabacina* (p. 10) forms a thin spreading crust with small, shelf-like, concentrically zoned, stalkless caps that grow in overlapping clusters.

Biscogniauxia atropunctata

Byssomerulius incarnatus
(Schwein.) Gilb.

= *Merulius incarnatus* Schwein.
= *Phlebia incarnata* (Schwein.) Nakasone & Burds.

COMMON NAME: Coral-pink Merulius.
MACROSCOPIC FEATURES: **Fruitbody** consisting of stalkless caps, 3–8 cm long, 2–4 cm wide, semicircular to fan-shaped, somewhat leathery to cartilaginous; **upper surface** moist or dry, subglabrous to finely pubescent, coral pink when young and fresh, becoming salmon buff in age; **lower surface** poroid, consisting of a network of radiating branched folds, pinkish ocher to salmon buff; **flesh** 2–4 mm thick, spongy to leathery, whitish to buff.

SPORE PRINT: White.
MICROSCOPIC FEATURES: Spores 4–5 × 2–3 μm, elliptic, smooth, hyaline.
OCCURRENCE: In overlapping clusters on logs and stumps of hardwood trees, often intertwined with fruitbodies of *Stereum ostrea* (p. 140) or other *Stereum* species; summer–winter.
EDIBILITY: Unknown.
REMARKS: Recent reports suggest that it may be parasitic on *Stereum*. *Phlebia tremellosa* (p. 136) is a spreading, often coalescing crust with a hairy to wooly, white to pale yellow upper surface and a yellowish to brownish-orange or pinkish-orange lower surface.

Byssomerulius incarnatus

Cymatoderma caperatum
(Berk. & Mont.) D. A. Reid

= *Stereum caperatum* (Berk. & Mont.) Berk.
= *Thelephora caperata* Berk. & Mont.

COMMON NAME: Goblet Fungus.
MACROSCOPIC FEATURES: **Fruitbody** 2–10
cm wide, wrinkled to folded, vase- to bowl-
shaped, attached to wood by a short stalk;
upper (inner) surface conspicuously longitudinally ribbed, glabrous and shiny when
moist and fresh, color highly variable, a mixture of whitish to pinkish, lavender or purple,
and darkest toward the margin when fresh,
often brownish downward, becoming yellowish to whitish in age; margin divided into
slightly concave, somewhat zonate, rounded
or pointed teeth-like lobes with finely torn
edges; **lower (outer) surface** convex, undulating, uneven, glabrous, color variable, whitish, yellow, pinkish to lavender or purple, and
darkest toward the margin, often brownish
downward; **stalk** 1–3.5 cm long, 3–12 mm
thick, nearly equal down to an enlarged base,
solid, whitish with yellow or brownish tints;
flesh thin, papery to somewhat cartilaginous,
whitish.
SPORE PRINT: White.
MICROSCOPIC FEATURES: Spores 8–11 × 3–4
µm, subcylindric, smooth, hyaline.
OCCURRENCE: Solitary, scattered, or in groups
on decaying hardwood logs and branches;
summer–early winter.
EDIBILITY: Inedible.
REMARKS: *Cymatoderma* means "wavy skin."
Caperatum means "wrinkled or folded."
Another image of this species is shown in
the "Color Key to the Major Groups of
Fungi" (p. 8).

Cymatoderma caperatum (B)

Daldinia concentrica (Bolton) Ces. & De Not.

= *Hypoxylon concentricum* (Bolton) Grev.

COMMON NAMES: Carbon Balls, Crampballs.
MACROSCOPIC FEATURES: **Fruitbody** 2–5 cm wide, cushion-shaped to nearly round or irregular; **surface** furrowed, finely roughened, somewhat shiny, often with minute pores (use hand lens), reddish brown to black; **interior** fibrous or powdery and carbon-like, concentrically zoned when cut vertically, dark purplish brown alternating with darker or sometimes whitish zones, with perithecia embedded in a single layer near the surface.
MICROSCOPIC FEATURES: Spores 12–17 × 6–9 μm, irregularly elliptic with one side flattened, smooth, dark brown.
OCCURRENCE: Solitary or in clusters on decaying hardwood logs, stumps, and trees; year-round.

EDIBILITY: Inedible.
REMARKS: The origin of the name "Crampballs" dates to a time when a tea made from this fungus was believed to ease menstrual cramps. The concentrically zoned interior is the most significant identification feature. The Carbon Cushion, *Kretzschmaria deusta* = *Ustulina deusta* (p. 10), has a thick, spreading, crust-like fruitbody that forms irregularly shaped patches up to 40 cm long and 10 cm wide. The upper surface is grayish white, soft, and powdery at first and becomes hard, finely roughened, black, and resembles burnt wood when mature. It has irregularly elliptic, smooth, dark brown spores that measure 28–36 × 7–10 μm and have one side flattened. It grows on stumps and roots of hardwoods year-round. Recently *Daldinia childiae* has been proposed as a new name for this species.

Daldinia concentrica

Erastia salmonicolor (Berk. & M. A. Curtis) Niemelä & Kinnunen

= *Hapalopilus salmonicolor* (Berk. & M. A. Curtis) Pouzar
= *Poria rubens* Overh. & J. Lowe

MACROSCOPIC FEATURES: **Fruitbody** up to 15 cm or more wide, resupinate, annual, soft and waxy when fresh, resinous and hard when dry; margin cottony, light orange. **Pore surface** bright orange to pink when fresh, drying darker orange brown; **pores** angular, thin-walled, entire, 3–5 per mm. **Flesh** thin; odor and taste not distinctive.

SPORE PRINT: White.
MICROSCOPIC FEATURES: Spores 3.5–5.5 × 2–2.5 μm, oblong to short-cylindric, smooth, hyaline.
OCCURRENCE: On decaying conifer wood; summer–fall.
EDIBILITY: Inedible.
REMARKS: It causes a yellowish stringy sap rot in conifers. It is widespread in North America and also occurs in Cuba. Addition of KOH produces a dull red to purplish-red reaction.

Erastia salmonicolor

Glaziella aurantiaca (Berk. & M. A. Curtis) Cooke

= *Glaziella vesiculosa* Berk.
= *Xylaria aurantiaca* Berk. & M. A. Curtis

MACROSCOPIC FEATURES: **Fruitbody** up to 6 cm wide, bladder-like to convoluted or brain-like, hollow, often intricately folded, loosely attached to the substrate; margin incurved, wavy, and lobed; **upper surface** glabrous, smooth, bright orange, fading and becoming brownish in age; **lower surface** uneven, pale yellow, with a perforation that enters a cavity; **flesh** thin, tough, somewhat gelatinous.

MICROSCOPIC FEATURES: Spores very large, 200–415 × 200–380 μm, globose to subglobose or broadly ellipsoid, smooth, hyaline.

OCCURRENCE: Solitary on the ground or on very decayed wood; uncommon and primarily known from the tropical regions of south Florida; year-round.

EDIBILITY: Unknown.

REMARKS: The first specimen of *Glaziella aurantiaca* was collected in Cuba but was mistakenly described by Berkeley and Curtis as a species of *Xylaria*. A decade later, Berkeley erected the genus *Glaziella* for a specimen collected in Brazil. He named the fungus *Glaziella vesiculosa* and was apparently unaware that he and Curtis had previously described the fungus as *Glaziella aurantiaca*.

Glaziella aurantiaca

Hypoxylon rubiginosum (Pers.) Fr.

MACROSCOPIC FEATURES: Fruitbody highly variable in size and shape but often cushion-shaped; individual fruitbodies usually fusing and forming crust-like patches up to 10 cm or more in diameter; **exterior** hard, dry, conspicuously roughened and uneven, often furrowed, brick-red to reddish brown or purplish brown; **interior** a blackish layer of embedded perithecia.

MICROSCOPIC FEATURES: Spores 9–12 × 4–5.5 μm, irregularly elliptic with one side flattened and a straight, spore-length germ slit, ends narrowly rounded, smooth, dark brown.

OCCURRENCE: In groups or confluent patches on trunks, logs, and stumps of hardwoods; year-round.

EDIBILITY: Inedible.

REMARKS: The Red Cushion Hypoxylon, *Hypoxylon fragiforme* (p. 10), forms cushion-shaped or round fruitbodies that are 2–16 mm wide and have a hard, dry, conspicuously roughened exterior with raised dots. The fruitbodies are grayish white at first and become salmon pink then cinnamon to brick-red when mature, and finally blacken in age. It grows on a wide variety of hardwoods. *Hypoxylon ferrugineum* (p. 10) forms brick red to hazel crust-like patches on a variety of hardwood branches. Its spores measure 13.5–17 × 6.5–8.5 μm. *Annulohypoxylon cohaerens* = *Hypoxylon cohaerens* (not illustrated) has 1.5–8 mm wide, cushion-shaped to rounded, hard, blackish fruitbodies with nipple-like bumps and grows on beech logs and stumps. *Annulohypoxylon annulatum* (not illustrated) is very similar, but the nipple-like bumps are surrounded by small depressions, and it grows on oaks.

Hypoxylon rubiginosum

Phlebia tremellosa (Schrad.)
Nakasone & Burds.

= *Merulius tremellosus* Schrad.

COMMON NAME: Trembling Merulius.
MACROSCOPIC FEATURES: **Fruitbody** a spreading, often coalescing crust, sometimes with cap-like projections; **upper surface** appearing translucent and gelatinous, wrinkled, hairy to wooly, white to pale yellow; **lower surface** poroid, consisting of ridges and shallow pits, yellowish to brownish orange or pinkish orange; **flesh** thin, gelatinous to cartilaginous, nearly hyaline or with an orange tint; odor and taste not distinctive.

MICROSCOPIC FEATURES: Spores 3–4 × 0.5–1.5 µm, allantoid, smooth, hyaline.
OCCURRENCE: On logs, branches, or stumps of hardwoods, especially oak; summer–early winter.
EDIBILITY: Of no culinary value.
REMARKS: *Byssomerulius incarnatus* (p. 130) has coral-pink to salmon-buff caps that are often associated with *Stereum* species.

Phlebia tremellosa

Punctularia strigosozonata
(Schwein.) P. H. B. Talbot

= *Merulius strigosozonatus* Schwein.
= *Phlebia strigosozonata* (Schwein.) Lloyd
= *Stereum strigosozonatum* (Schwein.) G.
  Cunn.

MACROSCOPIC FEATURES: **Fruitbody** a nearly circular, stalkless, leathery to waxy, flattened to upturned cap, up to 4 cm wide and often spreading and laterally fused to form colonies up to 18 cm long; **upper surface** reddish brown, becoming grayish in age, coarsely hairy, with concentric furrows and multicolored band-like zones; **flesh** very thin, reddish brown to purplish black; **lower surface** smooth at first, becoming radially elongated and wrinkled to folded, often with wart-like knobs, dull reddish to reddish brown and darkening in age.

SPORE PRINT: White.
MICROSCOPIC FEATURES: Spores 6–8 × 3.5–4 μm, elliptic, smooth, hyaline.
OCCURRENCE: On logs and branches of hardwood trees, especially beech and oak; year-round.
EDIBILITY: Inedible.
REMARKS: *Strigosozonata* means "having coarse hairs in distinct zones."

Punctularia strigosozonata

Rhytisma americanum Hudler & Banik

COMMON NAME: Tar Spot of Maple.
MACROSCOPIC FEATURES: **Fruitbody** 5–12
mm wide, typically circular, a slightly raised
tar-like cushion on maple leaves; **surface**
dry, somewhat shiny or dull, black, marked
by a serpentine pattern of alternating shallow
ridges and depressions (use a hand lens).
MICROSCOPIC FEATURES: Spores 50–88 × 1.5–
2.5 µm, filiform, smooth, aseptate, hyaline.
OCCURRENCE: Solitary, scattered, or in groups,
sometimes coalescing on leaves of red or silver
maple; fall–winter.

EDIBILITY: Inedible.
REMARKS: *Rhytisma salicinum* (not illustrated)
is similar and occurs on leaves of Coastal Plain
Willow and Black Willow and has spores that
measure 60–90 × 1.5–3 µm. *Diatrype stigma*
(p. 10) forms a 1–2 mm thick, up to 20 cm
or more long, spreading crust that is highly
variable in size and shape. It has a shiny or
dull, finely roughened, minutely cracked
dark brown to black exterior with perithecia embedded just below the surface in a
single layer. It grows on decaying hardwood
branches and logs year-round.

Rhytisma americanum

Scorias spongiosa (Schwein.) Fr.

COMMON NAME: Honeydew Eater.

MACROSCOPIC FEATURES: **Fruitbody** up to 6 cm high and 15 cm or more wide. At first a loosely stranded or tangled cobwebby mat, cream to buff, adhering to leaves and twigs; this thickens into a brownish-yellow mass resembling a gelatinous sponge and producing asexual spores. Months later, the mass darkens to brown or black and generates sexual ascospores.

MICROSCOPIC FEATURES: Spores 12–15 × 2.5–3 μm, cylindric to elliptic, 3-septate, smooth, yellowish hyaline.

OCCURRENCE: With colonies of the Beech Blight Aphid, *Grylloprociphilus imbricator*, on leaves, twigs, and branches of American beech trees; asexual stage appears in late summer and persists through winter, sexual stage develops during spring.

EDIBILITY: Inedible.

REMARKS: This sooty mold feeds on the honeydew of Beech Blight Aphids. Unlike the aphids, it does not attack the tree.

Scorias spongiosa

Stereum ostrea (Blume & T. Nees) Fr.

COMMON NAME: False Turkey-tail.
MACROSCOPIC FEATURES: **Fruitbody** fan- to oystershell-shaped, up to 8 cm wide, thin, leathery, overlapping or sometimes laterally fused; **upper surface** covered with fine silky hairs, typically concentrically zoned with reddish-brown, gray, yellow, and orange bands, often whitish at the margin; **flesh** thin, leathery, tough, whitish to buff; **lower surface** smooth, reddish brown to reddish buff or buff.
SPORE PRINT: White.
MICROSCOPIC FEATURES: Spores $5-7.5 \times 2-3$ µm, cylindric, smooth, hyaline.
OCCURRENCE: In groups or dense clusters on decaying hardwood branches, logs, and stumps; year-round.
EDIBILITY: Inedible.
REMARKS: It is often misidentified as the Turkey-tail, *Trametes versicolor* (p. 510), a polypore with many tiny pores on its white undersurface (use a hand lens). *Stereum subtomentosum* (p. 142) is very similar, but its margin and pore surface stain yellow when injured. The Crowded Parchment, *Stereum complicatum* (p. 10) has a much smaller, typically concentrically zoned cap that is variously colored from orange to orange yellow, ochraceous gray, or reddish brown. Its lower surface sometimes exudes red juice when cut. It grows in groups or overlapping clusters, often laterally fused to form rows on twigs and branches of conifer and hardwood trees, especially oaks year-round. *Stereum hirsutum* (not illustrated) is similar but smaller, has a dense coating of stiff hairs on its upper surface, and its lower surface does not exude red juice when cut. The Goblet Fungus, *Cymatoderma caperatum* (p. 131), has a funnel-shaped cap with a strongly tooth-like and markedly incised margin, a stalk that is 5–20 mm long or sometimes rudimentary, and it grows year-round on decaying hardwoods.

Stereum ostrea

Stereum striatum (Fr.) Fr.

COMMON NAME: Silky Parchment.

MACROSCOPIC FEATURES: **Fruitbody** a spreading crust of fan- to shell-shaped caps that are often laterally fused; **cap** up to 1.5 cm wide, rounded, somewhat flattened, attached to the substrate at a central point; **upper surface** dry, shiny, pale gray to silvery or buff, with radiating silky fibers; **flesh** very thin and tough; **lower surface** smooth, buff to yellowish or brownish at first, becoming whitish in age.

SPORE PRINT: White.

MICROSCOPIC FEATURES: Spores 6–8.5 × 2–3.5 μm, cylindric, smooth, hyaline.

OCCURRENCE: In groups or clusters on decaying twigs and branches of hardwoods, especially American hornbeam; year-round.

EDIBILITY: Inedible.

REMARKS: *Podoscypha ravenelii* (not illustrated) has a 3–30 mm wide, cinnamon-buff to bay, often zonate and shiny, funnel-shaped cap that is sometimes split on one side and is smooth on its lower surface. It has a 5–10 mm long stalk and grows year-round on the ground, rarely on wood.

Stereum striatum

Stereum subtomentosum Pouzar

= *Stereum arcticum* (Fr.) Mussat

COMMON NAME: Yellowing Curtain Crust.

MACROSCOPIC FEATURES: **Fruitbody** 3–7 cm wide, fan- to oystershell-shaped, thin, leathery, overlapping or sometimes laterally fused in rows, with a narrow, stalk-like attachment; **upper surface** dry, appressed-fibrillose to nearly glabrous, concentrically zoned, ocher yellowish to yellow brown or grayish orange, often with a whitish bloom, sometimes covered with green algae when mature, staining yellow when injured, especially near the margin; margin whitish to pale yellow, thin, undulating; **flesh** thin, tough, yellowish; **lower surface** smooth to slightly roughened, often finely cracked when dry, yellowish to ochraceous, staining yellow when injured.

SPORE PRINT: White.

MICROSCOPIC FEATURES: Spores 5.5–6.5(-7.5) × 2–3 μm, elliptic-cylindric, smooth, hyaline, amyloid; clamp connections and cystidia lacking; basidia narrowly clavate, with four sterigmata.

OCCURRENCE: Scattered, in groups, or overlapping clusters on numerous species of hardwoods; year-round.

EDIBILITY: Inedible.

REMARKS: *Stereum ostrea* (p. 140) is very similar but does not stain yellow when injured. *Stereum hirsutum* (not illustrated) is similar but smaller, has a dense coating of stiff hairs on its upper surface, is broadly attached, and does not stain yellow when injured.

Stereum subtomentosum

Terana coerulea (Lam.) Kuntze

= *Pulcherricium coeruleum* (Lam.) Parmasto
= *Corticum coeruleum* (Lam.) Fr.

COMMON NAME: Velvet Blue Crust.
MACROSCOPIC FEATURES: **Fruitbody** a
rounded to irregular thin crust, up to 2 cm
wide, that becomes confluent and spreads to
form patches up to 16 cm or more in diameter; **surface** dry, velvety, dark blue to blackish
blue with a paler margin.
SPORE PRINT: White.
MICROSCOPIC FEATURES: Spores 6–10 × 4–5
μm, elliptic, smooth, hyaline.
OCCURRENCE: In fused clusters, usually on the
underside of decaying hardwoods, logs, and
branches, especially oaks; summer–winter.
EDIBILITY: Inedible.
REMARKS: It is easy to identify because of its
distinctive velvety surface and blue color.

Terana coerulea

Thuemenella cubispora (Ellis & Holw.) Boedijn

= *Chromocreopus cubispora* (Ellis & Holw.) Seaver
= *Hypocrea cubispora* Ellis & Holw.

MACROSCOPIC FEATURES: **Fruitbody** up to 1 cm wide, erumpent through bark, lobed or tuberculate, tending to coalesce into elongated or irregularly shaped compound cushions; margin rounded or sometimes elevated when raised with a short, stout stalk; **surface** bright lemon yellow at first, later becoming dull orange to brownish, eventually dotted with brown punctuations from an accumulation of spores at the ostioles of the embedded perithecia.

MICROSCOPIC FEATURES: Spores 6–8(10) × 4–6 μm, elliptic to cuboid or angular, smooth or finely wrinkled, with oil drops, uniseriate, yellowish to reddish brown.

OCCURRENCE: In clusters on dead wood and bark; summer–early winter.

EDIBILITY: Unknown.

REMARKS: Not commonly encountered. *Trichoderma sulphurea* = *Hypocrea sulphurea* (not illustrated) forms a spreading, yellow to orange fruitbody on barkless wood and typically grows in association with *Exidia* species. The Yellow Cushion Hypocrea, *Trichoderma chlorosporum* complex = *Hypocrea chlorospora* (p. 10), has a 1–3 mm wide, cushion-shaped to nearly round, pale yellow, soft fruitbody that develops green dots and is finally green to dark green at maturity. It has globose to elliptic spores that measure 4–6 × 3–4 μm, and it grows on decaying wood from summer to early winter.

Thuemenella cubispora

Trichoderma peltatum (Berk.) Samuels, Jaklitsch & Voglmayr

= *Hypocrea peltata* Berk.

MACROSCOPIC FEATURES: **Fruitbody** up to 8 cm in diameter, cushion-shaped to brain-like, often intricately folded, attached to the substrate at a central point; margin incurved, wavy, and lobed; **upper surface** fleshy or leathery, light tan; **lower surface** smooth except for shallow ridges that radiate from the point of attachment, pale tan; the point of attachment is rudimentary; **perithecia** numerous, crowded, immersed, and inconspicuous. **Flesh** leathery, whitish; odor and taste not recorded.

MICROSCOPIC FEATURES: Four large, 2-celled spores per ascus that break apart to form eight single-celled spores, 2–6.5 × 2–5 μm, subglobose, finely spinulose, hyaline.

OCCURRENCE: Solitary, in groups, or fused clusters, usually on hardwood logs, stumps, and branches, rarely on pines; year-round.

EDIBILITY: Unknown.

REMARKS: The cushion-shaped fruitbody with radial ridges on the lower surface is distinctive and resembles a parasitized gilled mushroom growing on wood. Because this species thrives at body temperature and has been found in a human lung, smelling and tasting are not recommended.

Trichoderma peltatum

Xylaria allantoidea (Berk.) Fr.

MACROSCOPIC FEATURES: **Fruitbody** cylindric-allantoid to clavate or irregular, typically with a pointed apex and a rudimentary stalk, rounded to somewhat flattened; **surface** smooth or nearly so, glabrous, tan to dull brown, becoming blackish and somewhat roughened with age. **Flesh** firm, flexible, white.

MICROSCOPIC FEATURES: Spores $(8.5-)10-12 \times (3-)3.5-4.5$ μm, ellipsoid-inequilateral, single-celled, with a conspicuous straight germ slit usually less than the full length of the spore, brown.

OCCURRENCE: Solitary, in groups, or clusters on decaying hardwood; year-round.

EDIBILITY: Inedible.

REMARKS: *Allantoidea* means "sausage-shaped," a reference to the teleomorph stage of this fungus. The anamorph stage of this species is shown in the "Color Key to the Major Groups of Fungi" (p. 10). It is a variable, undulating, and lobed pale grayish mass that is covered with a whitish to pale gray powder consisting of lacrimoid, truncate, hyaline conidia that measure $7-12 \times 4-5.5$ μm. Black Knot of Cherry, *Apiosporina morbosa* = *Dibotryon morbosum* (p. 10), consists of hard, black, carbonaceous, finely roughened fruitbodies that are spindle-shaped to clavate or irregularly elongated. They clasp or envelop branches and twigs of cherry and plum trees year-round.

Xylaria allantoidea teleomorph

Xylaria magnoliae J. D. Rogers

COMMON NAMES: Cone Flickers, Magnolia-cone Xylaria.

MACROSCOPIC FEATURES: **Fruitbody** 2.5–7.5 cm high, up to 2 mm thick, upright, slender, filamentous to spindle-shaped, sometimes branched, tough; **surface** covered with white asexual spores when immature, becoming black and roughened at maturity, and covered with sexual spores that are produced in embedded perithecia.

MICROSCOPIC FEATURES: Spores 11–17 × 3–6 μm, spindle-shaped or irregularly elliptic, smooth, yellowish.

OCCURRENCE: Several to many on decaying magnolia cones; spring–fall.

EDIBILITY: Inedible.

REMARKS: This fungus is easy to identify because of its exclusive association with magnolia cones. *Xylaria liquidambar* (p. 10) forms upright, slender, filamentous to spindle-shaped, white or black fruitbodies on the fallen fruits of Sweetgum (*Liquidambar styraciflua*). *Xylaria oxyacanthae* (p. 10) grows on hickory and pecan nut shells. *Xylaria persicaria* (not illustrated) grows on peach seeds. The Beechmast Candlesnuff, *Xylaria carpophila* (not illustrated), grows on fallen beech husks, usually under leaves.

Xylaria magnoliae

Xylaria polymorpha (Pers.) Grev.

COMMON NAME: Dead Man's Fingers.
MACROSCOPIC FEATURES: **Fruitbody** 2–9 cm high, 1–3 cm thick, irregularly clavate to spindle-shaped or sometimes flattened, unbranched; **surface** white or bluish and powdery on the upper portion and blackish below (asexual stage), becoming hard, black, wrinkled, and finely roughened, sometimes minutely cracked at maturity, with perithecia embedded just beneath the surface in a single layer (sexual stage); **stalk** rudimentary or absent; **interior** white, fibrous-tough.
MICROSCOPIC FEATURES: Spores 22–30 × 5–9 μm, spindle-shaped or irregularly elliptic with one side flattened, with a long straight germ slit that extends about ½ to ⅔ of the spore length, smooth, dark brown.
OCCURRENCE: Solitary, in groups, or densely clustered on decaying hardwood stumps or on the ground arising from buried wood; year-round.

EDIBILITY: Inedible.
REMARKS: *Polymorpha* means "many shapes." *Xylaria poitei* (not illustrated) is very similar but much larger, sometimes twice as large or more, and has smaller spores that measure 14–18 × 5.5–7.5 μm. *Xylaria longipes* (not illustrated) is also similar but has a long stalk and smaller spores that measure 13–15 × 5–7 μm. The Candle Snuff Fungus or Stag's Horn, *Xylaria hypoxylon* (not illustrated), forms slender fruitbodes up to 10 cm high that are often flattened and antler-like, whitish on the upper portion, black below, and eventually black overall. It may be scattered but usually grows in dense clusters on decaying hardwood branches, logs, and stumps and has spores that measure 12–15 × 4.5–6 μm.

Xylaria polymorpha

Xylobolus frustulatus (Pers.) P. Karst.

= *Stereum frustulatum* (Pers.) Fr.

COMMON NAME: Ceramic Parchment.
MACROSCOPIC FEATURES: **Fruitbody** up to
25 mm wide, a crust-like layer of numerous
many-sided plates resembling broken pieces
of dull ceramic tile that are aggregated into
irregular patches; **upper surface** pinkish
white to reddish brown when young, becoming tan to grayish tan in age. **Flesh** up to 1 mm
thick, very hard, whitish.
SPORE PRINT: White.

MICROSCOPIC FEATURES: Spores 3.5–5 × 2.5–3
µm, oval, smooth, hyaline.
OCCURRENCE: In clusters up to 16 cm wide
on barkless hardwood stumps and logs;
year-round.
EDIBILITY: Inedible.
REMARKS: *Frustulatus* means "full of crumbs," a
reference to the fragmented appearance of this
unusual fungus. *Laxitextum bicolor* (not illustrated) forms a spongy-pliant, crust-like, and
spreading patch of overlapping caps, with a
coffee-colored, felty upper surface and a white
lower surface.

Xylobolus frustulatus

Xylobolus subpileatus (Berk. & M. A. Curtis) Boidin

= *Stereum frustulatum* var. *subpileatum* (Berk. & M. A. Curtis) A. L. Welden

COMMON NAME: Bacon of the Woods.

MACROSCOPIC FEATURES: **Fruitbody** 1–6 cm broad, up to 1.5 mm thick, corky to very hard, drying rigid, resupinate to effused-reflexed, often laterally fused; **upper surface** typically undulating, somewhat zonate, sometimes concentrically sulcate, tomentose, grayish orange to pale brown at first, becoming reddish brown to dark cinnamon brown in age; margin even, whitish or brownish; **lower surface** smooth or slightly velvety, often deeply cracked in age, whitish to pale orange, light buff, or pinkish buff. **Flesh** pale orange; odor not distinctive.

SPORE PRINT: Unknown.

MICROSCOPIC FEATURES: Spores 4–5 × 3 µm, cylindric, smooth, hyaline.

OCCURRENCE: Perennial on logs and trunks of hardwoods, especially oak, often covering large areas.

EDIBILITY: Too tough to be of interest.

REMARKS: *Subpileatus* means "having partially developed caps." The contrasting pale lower surface and dark upper surface helps to identify this species. Fire Crust, *Rhizina undulata* (p. 10), has a 2–6 cm wide, crust-like or cushion-shaped fruitbody attached to burned ground, well-decayed wood, or forest debris by a mass of thin root-like filaments. The outer surface is smooth, reddish brown to dark brown or blackish with a paler creamy white margin. It has spindle-shaped, smooth spores that measure 22–40 × 8–11 µm.

Xylobolus subpileatus

Chanterelles and Similar Fungi

Fungi in this group typically have fruitbodies with a cap and stalk that are sometimes funnel-shaped. The undersurface of the cap has blunt, gill-like ridges that are often forked and crossveined or nearly smooth. They usually grow on the ground.

Cantharellus altipes Buyck & V. Hofst.

MACROSCOPIC FEATURES: **Cap** 1–5.5 cm broad, mostly irregularly lobed or folded towards the margin; surface smooth but cottony-felty when viewed with a hand lens, especially when dry, often becoming finely scaly or disrupted with age, usually a deep egg-yolk yellow to vivid clear yellow, sometimes with a greenish hue; **flesh** firm to tough, whitish, very slowly turning yellow, then rusty; odor of apricots; taste not distinctive. **Fertile surface** variable, sometimes with well-developed folds and appearing branched, sometimes also with much lower anastomosing veins, yellow to pale pinkish yellow but paler and almost cream-colored or even off-white when young in some specimens. **Stalk** 4.5–5 cm long, 4–7 mm thick, slender, cylindrical or slightly narrowing downwards; surface smooth to fibrous or almost finely scaly, colored like the cap or paler, nearly off-white at the base.

SPORE PRINT: Unknown.

MICROSCOPIC FEATURES: Spores 7.3–12 × 4.4–5.7 µm, somewhat kidney-shaped, smooth, hyaline.

OCCURRENCE: Solitary or in groups in upland mixed pine and hardwood forests; summer.

EDIBILITY: Edible.

REMARKS: Described from East Texas, this species is characterized by its rather long stalk in comparison to its cap diameter and its rather large spores. *Cantharellus iuventateviridis* (not illustrated) has a 1.2–4.7 cm broad cap that is convex at first and soon becomes depressed at the center or funnel-shaped. The cap surface is golden to grayish yellow, often with olive tints, and becomes olive yellow to brownish yellow in age; the margin is strongly inrolled at first, sometimes irregularly lobed, frequently crenate when young, pubescent, olive green at first, and olive yellow at maturity. The fertile surface is pale yellow to peachy yellow and has decurrent, well-differentiated gill folds or thick veins that regularly fork. The stalk surface has yellowish-brown tinges and is distinctly paler than the cap. It grows in wet or muddy places with water oaks and other hardwoods during summer.

Cantharellus altipes

Cantharellus coccolobae Buyck, P. A. Moreau & Courtec.

COMMON NAME: Sea Grapes Chanterelle.

MACROSCOPIC FEATURES: **Cap** 2–5.5 cm broad, convex, becoming flattened to slightly depressed at the disc; surface smooth to finely tomentose-fibrillose toward the margin, dull, with a greasy aspect when wet, salmon to dull red or reddish pink, slightly hygrophanous and fading rapidly to pale pink or pinkish orange; margin strongly incurved when young and often remaining so well into maturity, sometimes concentrically zoned, staining yellowish when bruised; **flesh** firm, white, reddish pink close to the cap surface, yellowing in the lower stalk half; odor fruity or not distinctive; taste mild at first, then slowly acrid on the tip of the tongue. **Fertile surface** decurrent, composed of thick veins, without well-developed gill-like folds, forked, lacking crossveins, sometimes with barely visible veins or nearly smooth, usually very pale pink when young, becoming salmon pink at maturity. **Stalk** 2–3.5 cm long, 5–8 mm thick, nearly equal with a more enlarged base; surface smooth, pale pink close to the gills, more orange to yellowish toward the base, distinctly yellowing upon handling or when cut, mostly in the lower half.

SPORE PRINT: Whitish.

MICROSCOPIC FEATURES: Spores 7.9–10 × 4.8–6 µm, ellipsoid, smooth, hyaline.

OCCURRENCE: Scattered, in groups, or clusters on the ground, associated with *Coccoloba* species, Sea Grapes. It has been collected from the Lesser Antilles, the Yucatán of Mexico, and from Naples, Florida southward.

EDIBILITY: Edible.

REMARKS: It is closely related to the Cinnabarred Chanterelle, *Cantharellus cinnabarinus* (p. 11), and *Cantharellus texensis* (p. 158), neither of which is associated with Sea Grapes. *Cantharellus velutinus* (p. 11) has a minutely fuzzy to scaly, peach- to pinkish-orange or orange-yellow cap, and its fertile surface is pale pinkish orange or yellowish, with decurrent, rounded gill-like ridges and crossveins. It has previously been misidentified as *Cantharellus persicinus* (not illustrated) in several American field guides.

Cantharellus coccolobae

Cantharellus lateritius (Berk.) Singer

= *Craterellus lateritius* Berk.

COMMON NAME: Smooth Chanterelle.
MACROSCOPIC FEATURES: **Cap** 3–12 cm wide, convex to nearly plane, sometimes with a low, broad umbo or slightly depressed, becoming funnel- or vase-shaped in age; surface dry, nearly smooth, yellow orange to yellow; margin thin, incurved when young, becoming uplifted and wavy in age, often crimped or lobed; **flesh** thick, firm, white; odor fragrant like apricots or not distinctive; taste not distinctive. **Fertile surface** decurrent, with forked, blunt, gill-like ridges and crossveins or sometimes nearly smooth, pale yellow to yellow or orange. **Stalk** 2–8 cm long, 7–20 mm thick, tapered downward, solid or hollow; surface moist or dry, glabrous, smooth, pale yellow to orange yellow.
SPORE PRINT: Pale pinkish yellow.

MICROSCOPIC FEATURES: Spores 7.5–12 × 4.5–6.5 μm, elliptic, smooth, hyaline.
OCCURRENCE: Scattered or in groups with hardwoods, especially oaks, often abundant in stream bottomland hardwood forests; summer–fall.
EDIBILITY: Edible.
REMARKS: Compare with *Omphalotus illudens* (p. 380), which has true gills with sharp edges and fruits in large clusters on decaying wood. The Fragrant Chanterelle, *Craterellus odoratus* = *Cantharellus odoratus* (p. 11), has a fruitbody up to 16 cm wide, consisting of a large orange cluster composed of several funnel-shaped, hollow caps. The odor of its flesh is variously described as fragrant, fruity, or resembling violets. Its multiple small, funnel-shaped caps arising from a common base and bright orange-yellow colors help distinguish this species.

Cantharellus lateritius

Cantharellus lewisii Buyck & V. Hofst.

MACROSCOPIC FEATURES: **Cap** 3–10 cm broad, convex to depressed; surface moist, covered with dark purplish-lilac to brownish flattened scales over a pale yellow to grayish-yellow or ocher ground color, usually dark purple lilac overall when very young; margin inrolled at first and remaining so well into maturity; **flesh** up to 4 mm thick, tough, whitish to dingy yellow, quickly yellowing then becoming rusty when exposed; odor fruity like apricots or not distinctive; taste not distinctive. **Fertile surface** consisting of decurrent gill-like folds that are strongly and transversely crossveined, lighter yellow than the cap. **Stalk** up to 6 cm long, 5–7 mm broad, nearly equal, solid; surface moist, glabrous, light yellowish.
SPORE PRINT: Off-white to pale cream.
MICROSCOPIC FEATURES: Spores 7.1–9 × 4.2–5.2 μm, ellipsoid or often somewhat kidney-shaped, smooth, hyaline.
OCCURRENCE: Scattered or in groups with hardwoods, especially oaks, often abundant in stream bottomland hardwood forests; summer–fall.

EDIBILITY: Edible.
REMARKS: *Cantharellus lewisii* honors American mycologist David Lewis. *Cantharellus tabernensis* (p. 11) has a smaller, 1–5 cm wide, lighter-colored cap with a yellowish-brown or darker brown disc that becomes orange yellow at maturity. It has a decurrent, vivid orange-yellow to yellow fertile surface composed of forked, blunt, gill-like ridges and crossveins, and it grows on the ground in well-drained, mixed pine and hardwood forests, usually near mature pines, during summer and fall; it has been reported from Louisiana and Mississippi. *Cantharellus quercophilus* (not illustrated) has a small, up to 3.5 cm wide, glabrous, pale brown to grayish-yellow or blond cap, sometimes with darker concentric zones that become funnel-shaped with an incurved margin. It has a cream to pale yellow fertile surface and grows in association with oak. It is only known from the type location near Caldwell, Texas.

Cantharellus lewisii

Cantharellus minor Peck

COMMON NAME: Small Chanterelle.
MACROSCOPIC FEATURES: **Cap** 1–3 cm wide,
convex, becoming shallowly depressed; margin incurved at first, wavy; surface glabrous,
egg-yolk yellow to orange yellow; **flesh** thin,
pale yellow; odor fragrant or not distinctive;
taste slightly acrid or not distinctive. **Fertile
surface** gill-like with blunt edges, decurrent,
subdistant, very narrow, sparingly branched,
not anastomosing, colored like the cap or
paler. **Stalk** 2–5 cm long, 2–7 mm thick,
subcylindric, becoming hollow in age; surface
glabrous, colored like the cap or paler.

SPORE PRINT: Light yellowish orange.
MICROSCOPIC FEATURES: Spores 7.5–10
× 4.5–6 µm, broadly ellipsoid to oblong,
smooth, hyaline.
OCCURRENCE: Scattered or in groups with
hardwoods, especially oaks, often in bottomland hardwood forests; spring–summer.
EDIBILITY: Edible.
REMARKS: The small cap diameter, thin stalk,
and bright yellow coloration are good field
identification features.

Cantharellus minor

Cantharellus tenuithrix Buyck & V. Hofst.

COMMON NAMES: Chanterelle, Golden Chanterelle.

MACROSCOPIC FEATURES: **Cap** 4–14 cm wide, convex at first, becoming nearly plane, sometimes with a depressed center, or funnel-shaped; margin inrolled at first, often lobed or wavy and uplifted in age; surface dry, smooth, glabrous, egg-yolk yellow to bright orange; **flesh** thick, firm, white, slowly staining rusty orange; odor fragrant like apricots or not distinctive; taste not distinctive. **Fertile surface** composed of decurrent gill-like ridges with blunt edges, with or without inconspicuous crossveins, pale yellow to yellow or pale orange. **Stalk** 1.5–3 cm long, 7–10 mm thick, nearly equal, solid; surface smooth, glabrous, whitish to pale yellow.

SPORE PRINT: Pale cream.

MICROSCOPIC FEATURES: Spores 6.9–9.8 × 3.5–4.8 µm, elliptical, sometimes constricted in middle, smooth, hyaline.

OCCURRENCE: Solitary, scattered, or in groups in or near woods, often in dryer habitats with pines; late spring–early winter.

EDIBILITY: Edible.

REMARKS: For many years, this mushroom has been called *Cantharellus cibarius* (not illustrated), which is a European species. Its overall larger and more robust size separates it from *Cantharellus altipes* (p. 152), which has a longer stalk in relation to a smaller-diameter cap. The Midwestern Yellow Chanterelle, *Cantharellus flavus* (not illustrated), is nearly identical, but it has larger spores that measure 7.5–11 × 4–6 µm.

Cantharellus tenuithrix

Cantharellus texensis Buyck & V. Hofst.

MACROSCOPIC FEATURES: **Cap** 1.5–4 cm broad, convex, becoming broadly convex to nearly plane then deeply depressed; surface moist, fibrillose-scaly on the disc, less so toward the margin, cinnabar red; **flesh** thin, white; odor not distinctive; taste slightly acrid. **Fertile surface** decurrent, with subdistant, forking, blunt, gill-like ridges with crossveins, colored like the cap or paler. **Stalk** 3.5–4 cm long, 3–6 mm broad, nearly equal, solid; surface moist or dry, glabrous, colored like the cap.
SPORE PRINT: White.

MICROSCOPIC FEATURES: Spores 8–9.5 × 4–4.5 μm, elliptic, smooth, hyaline.
OCCURRENCE: Scattered or in groups in mixed pine and hardwood forests; known only from the Big Thicket in eastern Texas; spring–fall.
EDIBILITY: Edible.
REMARKS: We suspect that it is more widespread because of the difficulty of distinguishing it from the Cinnabar-red Chanterelle, *Cantharellus cinnabarinus* (pp. 11, 153), which is very similar but has shorter spores that measure 7–8 × 5–5.5 μm.

Cantharellus texensis

Craterellus fallax A. H. Sm.

COMMON NAME: Black Trumpet.
MACROSCOPIC FEATURES: **Cap** 2–8 cm broad,
4–10 cm high, trumpet-shaped; margin flaring, entire to wavy or lobed, sometimes frayed
or deeply incised, sometimes ragged in age;
upper surface and interior of the trumpet
dry and unpolished, roughened or varying to
slightly scaly, blackish when wet but fading to
dingy grayish brown or wood brown, drying
dark brown to reddish brown; **flesh** very thin,
moderately brittle; odor faintly fragrant or not
distinctive; taste not distinctive. **Fertile surface** decurrent, smooth or with shallow, blunt,
vein-like ridges, gray to brown or blackish,
often with ocher-orange tints, bruising blackish. **Stalk** indistinct, a short extension below
the fertile surface, often hollow; surface dark
brown to blackish.

SPORE PRINT: Salmon buff.
MICROSCOPIC FEATURES: Spores 9–14 × 6–9
μm, broadly elliptic in face view, subelliptic in
profile, smooth, hyaline.
OCCURRENCE: Scattered or in groups on
the ground in conifer or hardwood forests;
summer–fall.
EDIBILITY: Edible.
REMARKS: It was originally described from
Michigan. *Craterellus cornucopioides* (not illustrated) is similar, but it has a white spore print.
Craterellus foetidus (not illustrated) is also
similar, but it grows in caespitose clusters; has
a very strong, fragrant odor; and has smaller
spores that measure 8.5–12 × 5–7 μm.

Craterellus fallax

Gomphus ludovicianus R. H. Petersen, Justice & D. P. Lewis

MACROSCOPIC FEATURES: **Cap** 4–18 cm wide, obconical and shallowly depressed when young, becoming funnel-shaped; margin incurved, even, wavy or lobed; surface coarsely scaly and roughened, deep grayish yellow to olive brown with some purplish hues, staining darker when bruised; **flesh** thick, grayish to pale purplish gray; odor and taste not distinctive. **Fertile surface** strongly decurrent, composed of radial ridges and anastomosing crossveins, purple gray. **Stalk** 3–10 cm long, 1.5–3 cm thick, nearly equal, solid; surface moist, glabrous, dull purplish gray with mottled whitish areas and conspicuous white basal mycelium.

SPORE PRINT: Unknown.

MICROSCOPIC FEATURES: Spores 12–17 × 4.5–7 μm, ellipsoid, ornamentation minutely rugulose, hardly definable, weakly cyanophilous, hyaline.

OCCURRENCE: Scattered or in groups in xeric mixed pine and hardwood forests; known only from central Louisiana and East Texas; fall–early winter.

EDIBILITY: Unknown.

REMARKS: It is closely related to *Gomphus crassipes* (not illustrated), known from the Atlas Mountains of North Africa, and is like the Pig's Ear, *Gomphus clavatus* (not illustrated), which has a more lobed fruiting body and more northern distribution. The Scaly Vase Chanterelle, *Turbinellus floccosus* = *Gomphus floccosus* (p. 11), has a 4–16 cm wide cap that is funnel- to vase-shaped. The upper surface is covered with numerous coarse, orange to reddish-orange scales. The creamy-white to pale yellow fertile surface is strongly decurrent, with forked, blunt, vein-like ridges and crossveins. It grows on the ground with conifers or in mixed woods during summer and fall.

Gomphus ludovicianus

Corals and Cauliflowers

Fruitbodies in this group are of three types: bundles of erect, worm-like, unbranched appendages that are often fused at their bases; erect coral-like, repeatedly branched appendages; or a rounded, lettuce- or cauliflower-like cluster of branches attached to a partially buried stalk-like base. Members of this group usually grow on the ground, sometimes at the base of trees, or occasionally on wood.

Artomyces pyxidatus (Pers.) Jülich

= *Clavicorona pyxidata* (Pers.) Doty

COMMON NAME: Crown-tipped Coral.
MACROSCOPIC FEATURES: **Fruitbody** up to
13 cm high and 10 cm wide, erect, coral-like,
repeatedly branched, arising from a short,
velvety, whitish to brownish, stalk-like base;
branches 2–5 mm thick, erect, crowded,
smooth, whitish to yellowish or tan; **branch
tips** have crown-like points (use a hand lens)
and are colored like the branches; **flesh** tough
or brittle, whitish; odor not distinctive; taste
somewhat peppery or not distinctive.
SPORE PRINT: White.
MICROSCOPIC FEATURES: Spores 4–5 × 2–3 μm,
elliptic, smooth, hyaline, amyloid.

OCCURRENCE: Solitary, scattered, or in groups
on decaying hardwoods; spring–fall.
EDIBILITY: Edible.
REMARKS: Crown-like branch tips and growth
on decaying wood are its important field
identification features. *Clavulina coralloides*
(p. 165) grows on soil, as does *Tremellodendron schweinitzii* (p. 173). The Magenta Coral,
Clavaria zollingeri (p. 11), has reddish-purple
branches that are darkest toward the tips. It
grows on the ground in mixed woods and has
spores that measure 5–7.5 × 3–4.5 μm. The
Violet-branched Coral, *Clavulina amethystina*
(not illustrated), has lilac-purple branches,
very brittle lilac-purple flesh that lacks a distinctive odor and taste, and larger spores that
measure 7–12 × 6–8 μm.

Artomyces pyxidatus

Clavaria fragilis Holmsk.

= *Clavaria cylindrica* Gray
= *Clavaria vermicularis* Sw.

COMMON NAME: White Worm Coral.
MACROSCOPIC FEATURES: **Fruitbody** consisting of erect branches, 3–12 cm high and 2–5 mm thick; **branches** tapered downward, worm-like to fusiform cylinders, typically unbranched, white overall or sometimes yellowish near the tips; **flesh** thin, brittle, white; odor and taste not distinctive.
SPORE PRINT: White.
MICROSCOPIC FEATURES: Spores 4–7 × 3–5 μm, elliptic, smooth, hyaline, inamyloid.
OCCURRENCE: In clusters on the ground in woodlands or sometimes in grassy areas; summer–early winter.

EDIBILITY: Edible.
REMARKS: *Fragilis* refers to the brittle flesh. The Spindle-shaped Yellow Coral, *Clavulinopsis fusiformis* (p. 11), forms dense clusters of erect, cylindric to worm-like, bright to dull yellow fruitbodies that grow on the ground in pastures and woodland. *Clavulinopsis aurantiocinnabarina* (p. 11) forms clusters of erect, cylindric to worm-like, reddish-orange to pale orange fruitbodies that are yellow to whitish near the base and grow on the ground in woodlands and grassy areas. *Clavulinopsis laeticolor* = *Clavaria pulchra* (not illustrated) has a deep golden-yellow fruitbody and spores that measure 6–7 × 4.5–5 μm.

Clavaria fragilis

Clavaria rubicundula Leathers

COMMON NAME: Smoky Worm Coral.

MACROSCOPIC FEATURES: **Fruitbody** consisting of erect, unforked branches, up to 12 cm high and 1.5–6 mm thick; **branches** cylindric to worm-like, apex rounded or somewhat pointed, hollow in age; surface smooth, pinkish buff to pale grayish pink; **flesh** whitish, brittle; odor weak, resembling tincture of iodine or not distinctive; taste not distinctive.

SPORE PRINT: White.

MICROSCOPIC FEATURES: Spores 5.5–8.5 × 3–4 μm, elliptic, smooth, hyaline, inamyloid.

OCCURRENCE: In dense clusters on the ground in hardwoods and mixed woods; late spring–fall.

EDIBILITY: Unknown.

REMARKS: *Rubicundula* means "reddish or ruddy." *Clavaria fragilis* (p. 163) is pure white. Other similar corals are repeatedly forked.

Clavaria rubicundula

Clavulina coralloides (L.) J. Schröt.

= *Clavulina cristata* (Holmsk.) J. Schröt.

COMMON NAME: Crested Coral.

MACROSCOPIC FEATURES: Fruitbody up to 9 cm high and 5 cm wide, extremely variable in shape, sparingly branched, except near the tips which are crested with numerous jagged and tooth-like or sometimes more blunt-tipped points; **branches** smooth to wrinkled or longitudinally grooved, white to yellowish or grayish ocher, sometimes blackened from the base upward when attacked by a parasitic fungus; **flesh** soft and fragile, white; odor and taste not distinctive.

SPORE PRINT: White.

MICROSCOPIC FEATURES: Spores 7–10 × 6–8 µm, subglobose, smooth, hyaline.

OCCURRENCE: Solitary, scattered, or in groups on the ground or among mosses in woodlands, especially in pinewoods; summer–fall.

EDIBILITY: Edible.

REMARKS: The Gray Coral, *Clavulina cinerea* (p. 11), is very similar, but its branch tips are pointed or blunt, not tooth-like and jagged. Both the Crested Coral and Gray Coral may be blackened from the base upward when attacked by *Helminthosphaeria clavariarum*, a parasitic fungus (see photo below). *Clavulina floridana* = *Clavaria floridana* (p. 11) has a 5–8 cm high, erect, sparingly branched fruitbody with acute tips. It has compressed or furrowed, pale grayish to pale brownish-gray branches with paler whitish to yellowish branch tips. The flesh is fragile, white, and lacks a distinctive odor or taste. The spores measure 7–8.5 × 5.8–7.5 µm and are sub-globose to very short ellipsoid, with a large central oil drop, hyaline, and inamyloid. The fruitbodies may be solitary or grow in groups on the ground or on decaying twigs and leaves in tropical hammocks during summer.

Clavulina coralloides

Ramaria concolor (Corner) R. H. Petersen

= *Ramaria concolor* var. *stricta* Corner

MACROSCOPIC FEATURES: **Fruitbody** 4–14 cm high, 4–10 cm wide, repeatedly branched, usually with a well-developed base up to 2 cm wide, with numerous white rhizomorphs; **branches** vertically oriented and elongated, often flattened, smooth, pale yellowish tan to pale cinnamon, sometimes with ocher tints; **branch tips** colored like the branches, not yellow; **flesh** whitish, becoming brownish when exposed, fairly tough; odor fragrant, sweet, or not distinctive; taste bitter.
SPORE PRINT: Rusty yellowish.

MICROSCOPIC FEATURES: Spores 7.5–10.5 × 3.5–5 µm, elliptic to cylindric, roughened, pale yellowish tan.
OCCURRENCE: Solitary, scattered, or in groups on well-decayed, downed conifer or hardwood logs; late spring–early winter.
EDIBILITY: Unknown.
REMARKS: Addition of $FeSO_4$ to the branches produces a green reaction. Addition of KOH to the branches produces an orangish to brownish reaction. *Ramaria stricta* (not illustrated) is nearly identical, but the branch tips are yellow, and the branches are dull yellowish buff to orange buff, becoming brownish with age, and bruising purplish brown.

Ramaria concolor

Ramaria conjunctipes (Coker) Corner

= *Clavaria conjunctipes* Coker

MACROSCOPIC FEATURES: **Fruitbody** up to 10 cm high, 3–7 cm wide, consisting of several to many repeatedly forked branches with slender bases that form a compound, stalk-like structure coated with white rhizomorphs and mycelium, often growing in a cluster with their bases touching each other but not fused together; **branches** rounded, smooth to somewhat pitted and wrinkled, pale salmon-orange to yellow-orange; **branch tips** bright lemon yellow, branches and branch tips fading to cinnamon buff in age; **flesh** flexible and firm, colored like the branches; odor sometimes described as fragrant or medicinal or not distinctive; taste not distinctive.

SPORE PRINT: Yellowish.

MICROSCOPIC FEATURES: Spores 7–8.5 × 4–5 μm, short-elliptic, smooth to very finely roughened, pale yellow.

OCCURRENCE: Solitary, scattered, or in groups on the ground, usually in leaf litter, hardwoods, or mixed conifer and hardwoods; summer–fall.

EDIBILITY: Unknown.

REMARKS: *Conjunctipes* means "joined together at the base." This species is easy to identify because of the slender bases that form a compound, stalk-like structure. The Straight-branched Coral, *Ramaria stricta* = *Clavaria stricta* (not illustrated), is very similar, but the erect and coral-like branches of its fruitbody arise from an indistinct or sometimes well-developed stalk base that is thickly whitish tomentose. It has elongated, upright and nearly parallel, repeatedly forked branches that are grayish orange to ocher orange near the base, pale yellow upward, and sometimes slowly stain purplish brown when bruised. The branch tips are yellow when young and darken in age. The odor of its flesh is variously described as fragrant, sweet, or anise-like, and it has a bitter or metallic taste. It grows on fallen branches, logs, and stumps of conifer or hardwoods from spring through early winter. The addition of $FeSO_4$ to the branches produces a green stain.

Ramaria conjunctipes

Ramaria formosa (Pers.) Quél.

= *Clavaria formosa* Pers.

COMMON NAME: Yellow-tipped Coral.

MACROSCOPIC FEATURES: **Fruitbody** up to 20 cm high, 5–15 cm wide, consisting of a cluster of branches arising from a common stalk; **branches** erect, crowded, rounded, repeatedly forked, smooth or wrinkled, coral pink to pale salmon, becoming brownish in age; **branch tips** typically forked and blunt, pale yellow, becoming brownish; **stalk** thick, pinkish or whitish; **flesh** fibrous or brittle, colored like the stalk; odor not distinctive; taste bitter.

SPORE PRINT: Pale brownish yellow.

MICROSCOPIC FEATURES: Spores 8–15 × 4–6 μm, elliptic, finely warted; hyaline.

OCCURRENCE: Solitary, scattered, or in groups on the ground under conifers or hardwoods; summer–fall.

EDIBILITY: Poisonous, causing gastrointestinal distress.

REMARKS: The addition of $FeSO_4$ to the branches produces a green stain. *Ramaria stricta* (not illustrated) also has yellowish branch tips but grows on wood. The fruitbody of *Ramaria conjunctipes* (p. 167) has yellow tips and salmon-orange to yellow-orange branches, which arise from slender bases that touch each other but are not fused.

Ramaria formosa

Ramaria murrillii (Coker) Corner

= *Clavaria murrillii* Coker

MACROSCOPIC FEATURES: **Fruitbody** up to 12 cm high, erect, slender, and coral-like, with numerous branches arising from a distinct, rounded, central stalk; **branches** rounded, tough, smooth, pinkish brown to pale rusty brown, darkening when bruised; **branch tips** pointed or blunt, whitish at first, becoming brown at maturity; **stalk** up to 6 cm long and 1 cm thick, nearly equal or enlarged downward, often twisted and sometimes divided, with a pointed and rooting base, tough, whitish tomentose over most of its lower portion, usually with whitish rhizomorphs that stain pinkish when bruised; **flesh** moderately thick, whitish, and sometimes staining pinkish, tough; odor not distinctive; taste bitter.

SPORE PRINT: Ochraceous.

MICROSCOPIC FEATURES: Spores 6.5–9.5 × 3.5–5.5 μm, narrowly elliptic to bottle-shaped, with conspicuous sharp spines, rusty ochraceous.

OCCURRENCE: Solitary, scattered, or in groups on the ground in hardwoods or mixed conifer and hardwoods, usually with oak; summer–fall.

EDIBILITY: Unknown.

REMARKS: The branches stain green with FeSO4. This mushroom was named in honor of American mycologist William Alphonso Murrill (1869–1957), who first collected it in 1904. *Ramaria grandis* (not illustrated) is larger and stouter, up to 18 cm high and 15 cm wide, with reddish-brown branches and white branch tips, white flesh that quickly stains lavender-brown when cut and tastes bitter to astringent. It has oblong spores that measure 10–12 × 6–7.5 μm, with long, sharp spines.

Ramaria murrillii

Ramaria subbotrytis (Coker) Corner

= *Clavaria subbotrytis* Coker

COMMON NAME: Rose Coral.

MACROSCOPIC FEATURES: **Fruitbody** up to 15 cm high, erect, and coral-like, with numerous branches arising from a distinct central stalk; **branches** rounded, fleshy to somewhat brittle; **surface** glabrous, rose coral to salmon pink at first, fading to creamy ochraceous at maturity; **branch tips** bluntly rounded, rose coral to salmon orange when young, becoming salmon pink to creamy ochraceous in age; **stalk** up to 3 cm long and 2 cm thick, nearly equal or somewhat enlarged downward, usually with a pointed base, concolorous with the branches or whitish; **flesh** thick, somewhat brittle, pinkish or white, often marbled with watery areas at the stalk base; odor and taste faintly reminiscent of sauerkraut or not distinctive.

SPORE PRINT: Yellowish.

MICROSCOPIC FEATURES: Spores 8–11 × 3–4 μm, elliptic, minutely roughened, yellowish.

OCCURRENCE: Solitary, scattered, or in groups on the ground in hardwoods and mixed conifer and hardwoods; summer–fall.

EDIBILITY: Edible.

REMARKS: *Ramaria botrytis* (p. 11) is very similar, but it has whitish to pale pink branches with strongly contrasting rosy-red to purplish branch tips and larger, minutely roughened, and faintly, longitudinally twisted-striate spores that measure 11–20 × 4–6 μm. *Ramaria fumigata* (p. 11) has a stout fruitbody up to 12 cm high, 5–8 cm wide, consisting of a few main branches that fork repeatedly and a large stalk-like base. Its branches and branch tips are lilac to violet when young and become dull grayish tan to smoky yellowish at maturity. The stalk is often bulbous, sometimes tapered downward or nearly equal, and lilac to violet except for a whitish base. It grows on the ground with hardwoods during summer and fall. The lilac to violet areas stain bright red with KOH, and the branches stain green with $FeSO_4$. In some field guides *Ramaria fumigata* is labeled *Ramaria fennica*. Some taxonomists believe that *Ramaria fennica* is a European species that may not occur in eastern North America and that the actual species that occurs here is *Ramaria fumigata*.

Ramaria subbotrytis

Ramariopsis kunzei (Fr.) Corner

= *Clavaria kunzei* Fr.

COMMON NAME: White Coral.

MACROSCOPIC FEATURES: **Fruitbody** up to 8 cm high; **branches** erect and coral-like, repeatedly forked, arising from a short stalk; **surface** smooth, white, usually developing a distinct pinkish to pale apricot tinge in age; **flesh** white, brittle to somewhat flexible; odor and taste not distinctive.

SPORE PRINT: White.

MICROSCOPIC FEATURES: Spores 3−5.5 × 2.5−4.5 µm, broadly elliptic to nearly round with minute spines, hyaline.

OCCURRENCE: Solitary or scattered on the ground in woods; summer–fall.

EDIBILITY: Edible with caution; see comments below.

REMARKS: *Ramariopsis kunzei* does not stain green with the application of FeSO4. *Scytinopogon angulisporus* = *Clavaria angulispora* (not illustrated) is similar, but its fruitbody is soft, flexible, and pure white, with slender stalks that repeatedly branch and terminate in short, flattened, pointed branches.

Ramariopsis kunzei

Sparassis americana R. H. Petersen

COMMON NAME: American Cauliflower Mushroom.

MACROSCOPIC FEATURES: **Fruitbody** 15–30 cm high and wide, a rounded, lettuce-like cluster of flattened branches attached to a common, partially buried stalk-like base that is 5–14 cm long, 2–5 cm thick, tough, dark brown to blackish; **branches** densely arranged, with leaf- to fan-like, curly, flexible lobes; **surface** smooth, azonate, whitish, cream to pale yellow, or tan; **flesh** thin, white; odor fragrant or not distinctive; taste not distinctive.

SPORE PRINT: White.

MICROSCOPIC FEATURES: Spores 5–7 × 3–4 μm, oval, smooth, hyaline.

OCCURRENCE: Solitary or in groups on the ground in conifer or mixed woods, sometimes on well-decayed conifer logs and stumps; summer–early winter.

EDIBILITY: Edible.

REMARKS: This species was previously identified as *Sparassis crispa*, but molecular studies have shown that *Sparassis crispa* is a European species that does not occur in North America. The edible Cauliflower Mushroom, *Sparassis spathulata* = *Sparassis herbstii* (not illustrated), differs by growing with hardwoods and having zoned, spoon-shaped, less flexible branches that are widest at the tips and taper downward.

Sparassis americana

Tremellodendron schweinitzii (Peck) G. F. Atk.

= *Tremellodendron pallidum* Burt

COMMON NAMES: False Coral Mushroom, Jellied False Coral.

MACROSCOPIC FEATURES: **Fruitbody** up to 10 cm high and 14 cm wide, very tough, coral-like, densely clustered and compact, consisting of numerous erect and forked branches that are broadly flattened to somewhat rounded; **branches** leathery to fibrous-tough, white to buff, fused together at their bases and sometimes on the upper portions; **flesh** very tough, whitish; odor not distinctive; taste slightly bitter to rancid or not distinctive.

SPORE PRINT: White.

MICROSCOPIC FEATURES: Spores 7.5–12 × 4–6.5 µm, ovoid to allantoid, smooth, hyaline.

OCCURRENCE: Solitary, scattered, or in groups on the ground in hardwoods; summer–fall.

EDIBILITY: Edible.

REMARKS: The very tough fruitbody, forked branches that are broadly flattened to rounded and frequently fused, very tough flesh, and growth on the ground are good field identification features. *Tremellodendropsis semivestita* = *Lachnocladium semivestitum* (not illustrated) is smaller, more delicate, has non-fused branches, and has larger, hyaline, subelliptic to amygdaliform spores that measure 12–18 × 6–7 µm. *Lentaria byssiseda* (not illustrated) has a fruitbody up to 6 cm high and 0.5–4.5 cm wide, with a short stalk and numerous branches that are repeatedly forked and have several slender, tapering tips. The branches are pale rosy pink to pinkish tan, stain brownish when bruised, and darken to pinkish brown at maturity. The branch tips are whitish and become pinkish brown to reddish brown or sometimes greenish in age. It grows on twigs, leaves, or decaying hardwood, sometimes on cones, during summer and fall. The White Green-algae Coral, *Multiclavula mucida* = *Clavaria mucida* (not illustrated), is a Basidiomycete lichen. It has a tiny, fusiform to cylindric or tine-like fruitbody that is up to 15 mm high, white to creamy white, tough and waxy, and grows on algae-covered, wet, decaying wood during summer and fall.

Tremellodendron schweinitzii

Cordyceps, Tolypocladium, and Similar Fungi

Members of this group are parasitic species on larvae, pupae, adult arthropods, or on hypogeous fungi. They often have a head and stalk, and their fertile surfaces are usually roughened like sandpaper. Some species cover their hosts with mycelium, causing them to appear mummified.

Ophiocordyceps melolonthae (Tul. & C. Tul.) G. H. Sung, J. M. Sung, Hywel-Jones & Spatafora

= *Cordyceps melolonthae* (Tul. & C. Tul.) Sacc.

COMMON NAME: Beetle Cordyceps.
MACROSCOPIC FEATURES: **Fruitbody** up to 10 cm high, 3–15 mm thick, with a head and stalk; **head** oval to fusiform, whitish to yellowish, finely roughened; **flesh** thin, whitish to pale yellow; **stalk** nearly equal or clavate to fusiform, smooth, yellowish.
MICROSCOPIC FEATURES: Spores 4–10 × 1–2.5 μm, elliptic, smooth, hyaline.
OCCURRENCE: Solitary or several attached to a buried beetle larva; spring–fall.
EDIBILITY: Unknown.
REMARKS: Compare with the Trooping Cordyceps, *Cordyceps militaris* (p. 12), which has an orange head and stalk and grows on pupae and larvae of moths and butterflies. *Cordyceps olivascens* (p. 12) has a cylindric, very light green to olive-buff fruitbody attached to buried or partially buried insects. *Akanthomyces aculeatus* (p. 12) covers the host adult moth with creamy-white to yellowish mycelium in the anamorph or asexual stage, resulting in what appears to be a mummified moth, sometimes fixing it to the substrate. *Gibellula leiopus* (p. 12) covers the host spider with white to yellowish mycelium in the anamorph or asexual stage, resulting in what appears to be a mummified spider. *Ophiocordyceps dipterigena* (p. 12) has a small fruitbody consisting of one or more orange-cinnamon to cinnamon-brown, hemispherical heads on a cylindrical stalk that is attached to buried or partially buried flies during summer and fall.

Ophiocordyceps melolonthae

Purpureocillium atypicola (Yasuda)
Spatafora, Hywel-Jones & Luangsa-ard

= *Isaria atypicola* Yasuda
= *Nomuraea atypicola* (Yasuda) Samson
= *Spicaria atypicola* (Yasuda) Petch

MACROSCOPIC FEATURES: **Fruitbody** up to
6 cm high, 2.5–5 mm wide, with a head and
stalk; **head** cylindrical to subfusiform, often
curved, dry, scurfy, grayish tan to light gray
purple; **flesh** firm, whitish; **stalk** rounded,
smooth, light brown.
MICROSCOPIC FEATURES: Spores 4.5–6 × 1.5–2
μm, cylindric, usually with two oil drops,
smooth, hyaline.
OCCURRENCE: Solitary or scattered on buried
decaying spiders in woodlands; summer–fall.
EDIBILITY: Unknown.
REMARKS: Observation of the dead host
requires very careful excavation.

Purpureocillium atypicola

Tolypocladium capitatum (Holmsk.) Quandt, Kepler & Spatafora

= *Cordyceps capitata* (Holmsk.) Link

COMMON NAMES: Head-like Elaphocordyceps, Round-headed Elaphocordyceps.

MACROSCOPIC FEATURES: **Head** 6–20 mm wide and tall, irregularly rounded, finely roughened like sandpaper, dark reddish brown to olive black; **flesh** white, thick, firm; odor and taste not distinctive; **stalk** 2–8 cm long, 5–16 mm thick, nearly equal overall, smooth to slightly ridged, fibrous, yellow to dull yellow, becoming olive brown in age.

MICROSCOPIC FEATURES: Spores 16–28 × 2.5–3.5 µm, cylindric to thread-like, smooth, hyaline, inamyloid.

OCCURRENCE: Solitary or in groups in woods, on buried, walnut-shaped, reddish-brown fruitbodies of *Elaphomyces* species (the rounded, thick-walled structures at the stalk bases shown in the photo); summer–fall.

EDIBILITY: Unknown.

REMARKS: This fungus is parasitic on its host and must be carefully excavated to retrieve the entire structure. The Adder's Tongue or Golden-thread Cordyceps, *Tolypocladium ophioglossoides* (p. 12), has a spindle-shaped to oval or club-shaped head and is connected to *Elaphomyces* species by thick strands of golden rhizomorphs.

Tolypocladium capitatum

Cup Fungi

Fruitbodies in this group resemble small cups or saucers and have thin, brittle flesh. Some have stalks and others are stalkless. They grow on the ground, on wood, or sometimes on other substrates.

Aleuria aurantia (Pers.) Fuckel

= *Peziza aurantia* Pers.

COMMON NAME: Orange Peel.

MACROSCOPIC FEATURES: **Fruitbody** 1–10 cm wide, cup- to saucer-shaped or somewhat variable; margin occasionally torn at maturity, stalkless; **inner surface** smooth, bright orange to yellow orange; **outer surface** pale orange, downy at first, becoming glabrous in age; **flesh** thin, brittle, pale orange; odor and taste not distinctive.

MICROSCOPIC FEATURES: Spores 17–24 × 9–11 μm, elliptic, coarsely warted and reticulate, usually with projecting spines at one or both ends, typically containing two oil drops, hyaline.

OCCURRENCE: Solitary, scattered, or in groups or clusters, often along roadsides, in waste areas and disturbed soil, in gardens, or under trees; year-round.

EDIBILITY: Edible but tasteless.

REMARKS: The Blue-staining Cup, *Caloscypha fulgens* (p. 12), has a 1–5 cm wide, irregularly cup-shaped fruitbody that is frequently split on one side. The inner surface of the cup is bright yellow orange to orange, and the outer surface is yellow and often stained dark bluish green, especially toward the margin.

Aleuria aurantia

Chlorociboria aeruginascens (Nyl.) Kanouse ex C. S. Ramamurthi, Korf & L. R. Batra

= *Chlorociboria aeruginascens* (Nyl.) Kanouse
= *Chlorosplenium aeruginascens* (Nyl.) P. Karst.

COMMON NAMES: Blue-stain Fungus, Green-stain Fungus.

MACROSCOPIC FEATURES: **Fruitbody** 3–8 mm wide, shallowly cup-shaped to nearly flat, often asymmetrical; **inner surface** smooth or wrinkled, blue green, sometimes with yellow tints; **lower surface** finely roughened, blue green; **flesh** thin; **stalk** 3–6 mm long, frequently eccentric, tapered downward, blue green.

MICROSCOPIC FEATURES: Spores 5–7(10) × 1–2.5 μm, elliptic to irregularly fusiform, with two oil drops, one at each end, smooth, hyaline.

OCCURRENCE: In groups or clusters on decaying hardwoods; spring–fall.

EDIBILITY: Unknown.

REMARKS: Pigments in the hyphal threads of this fungus stain wood blue green. *Chlorociboria aeruginosa* (not illustrated) is nearly identical, but its stalk is generally central, forming a very symmetrical cup, and it has larger spores that measure 8–15 × 2–4 μm.

Chlorociboria aeruginascens

Galiella rufa (Schwein.) Nannf. & Korf

= *Bulgaria rufa* Schwein.

COMMON NAME: Hairy Rubber Cup.
MACROSCOPIC FEATURES: **Fruitbody** up to 3 cm high, 1–3 cm wide, cup-shaped; **inner surface** smooth, orange to reddish orange or reddish brown; **outer surface** covered with a dense layer of matted wooly hairs, tough, brown to blackish brown; margin finely toothed; **flesh** rubbery-gelatinous.
MICROSCOPIC FEATURES: Spores 18–20 × 8–10 µm, elliptic with narrow ends, finely roughened, hyaline.
OCCURRENCE: In groups or clusters on decaying hardwoods; summer–fall.
EDIBILITY: Edible.

REMARKS: *Rufa* means "reddish orange," referring to the color of the inner surface. *Wolfina aurantiopsis* (p. 12) is similar, but it forms larger, shallow cups up to 7 cm wide, with a pale yellow to ochraceous inner surface and tough flesh that becomes corky on drying. It has much larger, broadly elliptic spores that measure 27–33 × 16–18 µm and grows on decaying wood, woodchips, or nearby soil during fall and early winter. The Devil's Urn, or Black Tulip, *Urnula craterium* (p. 12), has a blackish-brown to black, deeply cup-shaped fruitbody up to 11 cm high, with a distinct stalk up to 4 cm long that tapers downward. It has hyaline, smooth, broadly elliptic spores that measure 25–35 × 10–15 µm and grows in groups or clusters on decaying wood or on the ground attached to buried wood during late winter and spring.

Galiella rufa

Peziza phyllogena Cooke

= *Peziza badioconfusa* Korf

COMMON NAME: Common Brown Cup.

MACROSCOPIC FEATURES: **Fruitbody** 3–15 cm wide, cup-shaped, flattening with age, stalkless; **inner surface** smooth, brown, with hints of pink, purple, or olive; **outer surface** scurfy or granular, pale reddish brown to purple brown; **flesh** thin, brittle, brownish; odor and taste not distinctive.

MICROSCOPIC FEATURES: Spores 16–21 × 8–10 µm, elliptic, finely warted, with two oil drops, hyaline.

OCCURRENCE: Scattered or clustered on rich soil or decaying wood; spring–fall.

EDIBILITY: Reportedly edible.

REMARKS: The Recurved Cup, *Peziza varia* (p. 12), has a smooth, pale to dark yellow-brown or dark brown inner surface, a scurfy, white to gray-brown outer surface, and spores that measure 14.5–17.7 × 8–10.5 µm. Two other species, *Lamprospora ammophila* and *Sphaerosporella brunnea* are much smaller and quite prolific. The Sand-loving Cup, *Lamprospora ammophila* = *Peziza ammophila* (not illustrated), has a stalkless, cup-shaped, brown fruitbody up to 3 cm high and 4 cm wide that soon splits and becomes star-shaped. The cup margin is often lobed and split, and the fruitbody is often buried in sand with only the lobed, uppermost portion of the cup rim exposed. *Sphaerosporella brunnea* (p. 12) has a 2–6 mm wide, shallowly cup-shaped, reddish-brown to dark brown fruitbody with a raised margin. It has smooth, hyaline, round spores that measure 14–18 µm, with one large oil drop, and grows on sandy soil near water oaks, among mosses, or on burned ground from spring through late fall.

Peziza phyllogena

Sarcoscypha occidentalis (Schwein.) Sacc.

= *Peziza occidentalis* Schwein.

COMMON NAME: Stalked Scarlet Cup.
MACROSCOPIC FEATURES: **Fruitbody** up to 4.5 cm high, 5–16 mm wide, shallowly cup-shaped with a distinct stalk; **inner surface** smooth, shiny, bright red; **outer surface** smooth to finely roughened, pinkish red to pinkish orange; **flesh** very thin, brittle, whitish to pinkish; **stalk** 1–3 cm long, 1.5–3 mm thick, nearly equal, smooth, white.
MICROSCOPIC FEATURES: Spores 18–22 × 10–12 µm, elliptic, with several oil drops, smooth, hyaline.
OCCURRENCE: Scattered, in groups, or clusters on decaying hardwood branches; late winter–spring.
EDIBILITY: Unknown.
REMARKS: *Sarcoscypha austriaca* (p. 12) also has a bright red and shiny inner surface, a pinkish-red to pinkish-orange outer surface, and grows on branches in springtime and early summer. It is larger, up to 5 cm wide, and either has a short, thick stalk that is colored like the outer surface or is stalkless. *Phillipsia* species are brightly colored cup fungi, which are widely distributed in subtropical and tropical areas of the world. There are approximately 17 species in the genus. *Phillipsia domingensis* is the type species, and the genus name honors English botanist William Phillips (1822–1905). *Phillipsia* species (p. 12) are stalkless or have a short stalk and often have moderately thick flesh. They grow on decaying hardwoods and are occasionally collected along the Gulf Coast states during summer and fall. *Helvella macropus* (p. 12) has a smooth, gray to gray-brown cup, a somewhat hairy, rounded, gray to gray-brown stalk, and spores that measure 19–28 × 10–13 µm with one large and two smaller oil drops. It grows on the ground during summer and fall. The Ribbed-stalked Cup or Elfin Cup, *Helvella acetabulum* (not illustrated), has a brown, cup-shaped fruitbody up to 7 cm wide and a distinctive white stalk that is conspicuously ribbed and branched and extends over the outer surface. It has broadly elliptic spores that measure 16–20 × 11–14 µm and grows on the ground under hardwoods during spring and summer.

Sarcoscypha occidentalis

Scutellinia scutellata (L.) Lambotte

= *Peziza scutellata* L.

COMMON NAME: Eyelash Cup.

MACROSCOPIC FEATURES: **Fruitbody** a stalkless shallow cup, 3–20 mm wide; **inner surface** smooth, shiny, orange red to bright orange; **outer surface** orange; margin covered with long, stiff, brown hairs.

MICROSCOPIC FEATURES: Spores 16–21 × 10–14 µm, elliptic, finely roughened, sometimes with oil drops, hyaline.

OCCURRENCE: Scattered, in groups, or clusters on decaying wood or nearby soil; late spring–fall.

EDIBILITY: Unknown.

REMARKS: The Orange Eyelash Cup, *Scutellinia erinaceus* (p. 12), is very similar, but it has a pale orange-yellow to orange inner surface, a dull brownish-orange outer surface, and grows on wood from spring through fall. The Brown-haired White Cup, *Humaria hemisphaerica* (p. 12), has a 1–3 cm wide, cup-shaped fruitbody with a smooth, whitish to pale gray inner surface and a brownish yellow outer surface that is covered by a dense layer of brownish hairs, which project from the margin over part of the inner surface. It grows on soil, among mosses, and on decaying wood from summer through early winter. Molecular data indicates that this "species" may be a complex of several closely related taxa.

Scutellinia scutellata

Earth Tongues and Earth Clubs

The species in this group resemble erect tongues, clubs with rounded to oval heads, spatulas, spindles, or cylinders. Although they may occur in groups, their stalk bases are not fused, and they are typically unbranched. Their fertile surfaces may be smooth or wrinkled but are not roughened like sandpaper. They grow on the ground, on wood, or on decaying leaves.

Clavariadelphus ligula (Schaeff.) Donk

= *Clavaria ligula* Schaeff.

COMMON NAMES: Spoon-shaped Club, Strap-shaped Coral.

MACROSCOPIC FEATURES: **Fruitbody** 3–10 cm high, 6–20 mm wide, elongated and clavate or somewhat flattened and tongue-shaped, unbranched, smooth when young, becoming longitudinally wrinkled in age; apex rounded or blunt, dull yellow to pale orange yellow or pale brownish orange; **flesh** thick, firm to spongy, white; odor not distinctive; taste mild to slightly bitter or metallic; **stalk** poorly defined, sometimes whitish tomentose at the base.

SPORE PRINT: White to creamy white.

MICROSCOPIC FEATURES: Spores 10–18 × 3–6 μm, narrowly elliptic, with yellow oil drops, smooth, hyaline.

OCCURRENCE: Scattered, in groups, or clusters on humus or pine needles under conifers; summer–fall.

EDIBILITY: Unknown.

REMARKS: *Ligula* means "little tongue or spoon." *Clavariadelphus americanus* (p. 13) is similar but much larger, up to 30 cm high and 2–6 cm wide, and grows under oaks and pines. *Clavariadelphus pistillaris* (not illustrated) is nearly identical to *Clavariadelphus americanus* but grows exclusively with beech. *Clavariadelphus truncatus* (p. 13) is also similar but much larger, up to 15 cm high, 3–7 cm wide, and typically top-shaped to clavate, with a flattened apex that is sometimes slightly depressed. The Fluted-stalked Fungus, *Underwoodia columnaris* (p. 13), known only from Texas in the Gulf Coast States region, has an erect, column-like, cylindric to fusiform, deeply fluted fruitbody that tapers upward to a rounded tip and lacks a distinct cap and stalk. The interior is chambered, and the outer surface has longitudinal grooves or wrinkles, is cream to tan when young, and becomes pale brown in age. It typically grows in clusters with fused bases on the ground under hardwoods during summer and fall.

Clavariadelphus ligula

Leotia viscosa Fr.

COMMON NAMES: Green-headed Jelly Club, Green-capped Jelly Babies.

MACROSCOPIC FEATURES: **Fruitbody** consisting of a head and stalk; **head** 6–20 mm wide, irregularly rounded and flattened, smooth to distinctly furrowed or brain-like; margin distinctly inrolled, gelatinous, moist, dark green to blackish green; **stalk** 2–4 cm long, 6–10 mm thick, enlarged downward or nearly equal, smooth, slippery, pale yellow to orange yellow; **flesh** soft, gelatinous, greenish; odor and taste not distinctive.

MICROSCOPIC FEATURES: Spores 18–20 × 5–6 μm, narrowly elliptic to fusiform with rounded ends, straight or curved, multiseptate at maturity, smooth, hyaline.

OCCURRENCE: Scattered, in groups, or clusters on soil in woods, also on sand dunes or other sandy areas; year-round.

EDIBILITY: Unknown.

REMARKS: It often occurs on old sand dunes along the Gulf Coast during fall and winter. The Ochre Jelly Club, *Leotia lubrica* (p. 13), is very similar, but it has a yellow to orange-yellow head and stalk. *Leotia atrovirens* (p. 13) has a pea-green to bluish-green cap that darkens in age and a pale green to whitish stalk.

Leotia viscosa

Mitrula elegans Berk.

COMMON NAME: Swamp Beacon.

MACROSCOPIC FEATURES: **Fruitbody** up to 5 cm high, consisting of a head and stalk; **head** 5–20 mm long, 3–10 mm thick, pear- to spindle-shaped, elliptical or irregularly rounded, smooth to slightly wrinkled, shiny, translucent yellow to orange, becoming dull orange in age; **stalk** up to 4 cm long, 1–3 mm thick, slightly enlarged downward, shiny, smooth, whitish to pale translucent gray, sometimes with a pinkish tint; **flesh** somewhat gelatinous, yellowish; odor and taste not distinctive.

MICROSCOPIC FEATURES: Spores 11–18 × 1.5–3 µm, narrowly elliptic or slightly clavate, smooth, hyaline.

OCCURRENCE: Scattered or in groups in wet areas on decaying leaves and twigs in woodlands and bogs; spring–summer.

EDIBILITY: Unknown.

REMARKS: *Elegans* means "choice or elegant." *Mitrula lunulatospora* (not illustrated) is similar and occurs in the same habitats but has a pale pink head. It has allantoid to crescent- or boat-shaped spores that are 1-celled or 2-celled with a septum, smooth, hyaline, and measure 11–19 × 2–4 µm.

Mitrula elegans

Trichoglossum farlowii (Cooke)
E. J. Durand

= *Geoglossum farlowii* Cooke

COMMON NAME: Rough Black Earth Tongue.
MACROSCOPIC FEATURES: **Fruitbody** up to
8 cm high, consisting of a head and stalk;
head 1.2–3 cm high and 3–10 mm wide,
hollow, elliptic to oval or spindle-shaped,
often flattened with a longitudinal furrow,
dry, minutely velvety to spiny (use a hand
lens), blackish brown to black; **stalk** 2–6 cm
long, 2–5 mm thick, nearly equal, slightly
compressed, often curved, densely velvety,
blackish-brown to black; **flesh** thin, tough,
dark brown; odor and taste not distinctive.
MICROSCOPIC FEATURES: Spores 45–85 × 6–7
µm, needle-like to cylindric, 0–6-septate (but
mostly 3-septate), smooth, grayish or brownish; setae more than 150 µm long, pointed,
brown.

OCCURRENCE: Solitary, in groups, or clusters
on the ground, among mosses, or on well-
decayed wood; summer–early winter.
EDIBILITY: Unknown.
REMARKS: The Smooth Black Earth Tongue,
Geoglossum difforme (not illustrated), is nearly
identical but has a bald, shiny surface, spores
with 12–15 septa, and lacks setae. Several
Trichoglossum and *Geoglossum* species are
similar and require microscopic examination
of their spores and the presence or absence of
setae for positive identification. *Trichoglossum*
species have setae, whereas *Geoglossum* species
lack them. The Orange Earth Tongue, *Microglossum rufum* (p. 13), has a yellow-orange to
orange fruitbody with a fine scaly stalk and
grows on the ground, among mosses, or on
decaying wood during summer through early
winter.

Trichoglossum farlowii

Fiber Fans

These are fan- or vase-shaped fruitbodies that are leathery to fibrous-tough, sometimes with split or torn margins. They are typically some shade of brown or gray, with or without a whitish margin. Their fertile undersurfaces may be smooth or wrinkled and warted, and they lack pores (use a hand lens). They grow on the ground.

Thelephora terrestris Ehrh.

COMMON NAMES: Common Fiber Vase, Earth Fan.

MACROSCOPIC FEATURES: **Fruitbody** 2–5 cm high, up to 7 cm wide, partially erect and spreading, consisting of circular to fan-shaped, stalkless caps in overlapping clusters, often laterally fused and forming patches that are up to 30 cm or more in diameter; **upper surface** covered with short, stiff hairs that are matted and wooly or scaly, concentrically zoned, rusty brown to dark brown or grayish brown, becoming blackish brown in age; margin white or brown, wooly, coarsely torn, often with small, fan-shaped outgrowths; **lower surface** wrinkled and finely warted, pinkish brown to brown; **flesh** thin, leathery, brown; odor and taste not distinctive.

SPORE PRINT: Purple brown.

MICROSCOPIC FEATURES: Spores 8–12 × 6–9 μm, angularly oval to elliptic, nearly smooth to warted or spiny, purplish.

OCCURRENCE: Solitary or in overlapping clusters on the ground, sometimes attached to roots, seedlings, or mosses, in conifer or mixed conifer and hardwoods; year-round.

EDIBILITY: Inedible.

REMARKS: *Thelephora terrestris* f. *concrescens* (p. 13) is similar, but it forms overlapping clusters that envelop and clasp the stems and branches of woody plants, especially oak. *Thelephora anthocephala* (p. 13) has a coral-like fruitbody with numerous flattened brown branches and whitish tips, and the odor of its flesh is not distinctive. *Thelephora palmata* (not illustrated) has a coral-like fruitbody with numerous flattened, spoon- to fan-shaped, brown branches with whitish tips, and the odor of its flesh is intensely fetid and disagreeable.

Thelephora terrestris

Thelephora vialis Schwein.

COMMON NAME: Vase Thelephore.
MACROSCOPIC FEATURES: **Fruitbody** up to 10 cm high, 5–13 cm wide, erect, highly variable, typically a cluster of ascending lobe-like caps arising from a common central stalk; **cap** spoon- to funnel-shaped or fused and somewhat vase-shaped; **inner (upper) surface** striate or minutely scaly, whitish to yellowish; **outer (lower) surface** wrinkled, dingy yellow, becoming grayish brown; **flesh** thick, leathery, whitish to grayish; odor disagreeable or not distinctive; taste not distinctive; **stalk** erect, enlarged downward, solid, whitish to grayish, minutely pubescent.

SPORE PRINT: Brown.
MICROSCOPIC FEATURES: Spores 4.5–8 × 4.5–6.5 μm, angular, warted and minutely spiny, olive buff.
OCCURRENCE: Solitary, scattered, or in groups on the ground in hardwoods, especially with oak; summer–winter.
EDIBILITY: Inedible.
REMARKS: It is sometimes used to dye wool and silk.

Thelephora vialis

Gilled Mushrooms

In this group of fungi, the undersurface of the caps have knifeblade-like, thin gills that radiate from a stalk or, on stalk-less species, from the point of attachment to the cap margin. Species in this group grow on a variety of substrates. A few species with gill-like undersurfaces may also be found in the Boletes, Chanterelles and Similar Fungi, and Polypores groups.

Key to the Gilled Mushrooms

1a. Spore print not obtainable because the gills are convoluted and chambered; mushroom growing in sandy soil, especially sand dunes:
    Macowanites arenicola

1b. Spore print obtainable 2

2a. Spore print green to grayish green:
    Chlorophyllum molybdites

2b. Spore print some other color 3

3a. Spore print white, cream, yellow, ocher orange, grayish, or lilac 4

3b. Spore print some other color 12

4a. Mushroom with warts or patches on the cap or with a volva at the stalk base:
    Amanita abrupta
    Amanita albocreata
    Amanita amerifulva
    Amanita amerirubescens
    Amanita amerivirosa
    Amanita arkansana
    Amanita atkinsoniana
    Amanita brunnescens
    Amanita ceciliae
    Amanita cinereoconia
    Amanita cokeri
    Amanita cylindrispora
    Amanita daucipes
    Amanita farinosa
    Amanita flavoconia
    Amanita flavorubescens
    Amanita hesleri
    Amanita jacksonii
    Amanita lavendula
    Amanita longipes
    Amanita muscaria var. *guessowii*
    Amanita mutabilis
    Amanita onusta
    Amanita parcivolvata
    Amanita pelioma
    Amanita persicina
    Amanita polypyramis
    Amanita rhopalopus
    Amanita roseitincta
    Amanita spreta
    Amanita subcokeri
    Amanita thiersii
    Amanita vaginata group
    Amanita volvata group
    Amanita westii

4b. Mushroom lacking warts, patches, or a volva, but cap may have scales or other features 5

5a. Mushroom growing on the ground; gills exuding a milk-like latex when cut or bruised:
    Lactarius alachuanus
    Lactarius argillaceifolius
    Lactarius atroviridis
    Lactarius chelidonium var. *chelidonium*
    Lactarius chrysorrheus
    Lactarius croceus
    Lactarius delicatus
    Lactarius gerardii
    Lactarius hysginus
    Lactarius imperceptus
    Lactarius indigo var. *diminutivus*
    Lactarius indigo var. *indigo*
    Lactarius lignyotus var. *lignyotus*
    Lactarius maculatipes
    Lactarius paradoxus
    Lactarius peckii var. *peckii*
    Lactarius proximellus
    Lactarius psammicola
    Lactarius quietus
    Lactarius rimosellus
    Lactarius salmoneus var. *salmoneus*
    Lactarius speciosus
    Lactarius subisabellinus
    Lactarius subpalustris
    Lactarius subplinthogalus
    Lactarius subpurpureus

Lactarius subserifluus
Lactarius subvernalis var. *cokeri*
Lactarius tomentosomarginatus
Lactarius vietus
Lactarius xanthydrorheus
Lactarius yazooensis
Lactifluus allardii
Lactifluus corrugis
Lactifluus deceptivus
Lactifluus glaucescens
Lactifluus hygrophoroides
Lactifluus luteolus
Lactifluus piperatus
Lactifluus rugatus
Lactifluus volemus var. *flavus*
Lactifluus volemus var. *volemus*
Multifurca furcata

5b. Mushroom growing on the ground or on wood but not exuding a milk-like latex when cut or bruised. 6

6a. Mushroom growing on the ground; cap and stalk brittle and easily crumbled:
Russula atropurpurea
Russula ballouii
Russula compacta
Russula decolorans
Russula earlii
Russula eccentrica
Russula grata
Russula hixsonii
Russula parvovirescens
Russula perlactea
Russula subgraminicolor
Russula subsericeonitens
Russula variata
Russula virescens
Multifurca ochricompacta

6b. Mushroom growing on the ground or on wood, but cap and stalk not brittle and easily crumbled. 7

7a. Mushroom growing on the ground; cap and gills with a waxy consistency like soft candle wax when rubbed and crushed between thumb and fingers; cap usually brightly colored, often red, sometimes orange, yellow, or white:
Cuphophyllus pratensis
Cuphophyllus virgineus
Gliophorus laetus
Gliophorus perplexus
Gliophorus psittacinus
Gloioxanthomyces nitidus
Humidicutis marginata
Hygrocybe andersonii
Hygrocybe caespitosa
Hygrocybe cantharellus
Hygrocybe chamaeleon
Hygrocybe coccinea
Hygrocybe conica
Hygrocybe conicoides
Hygrocybe cuspidata
Hygrocybe flavescens
Hygrocybe miniata
Hygrocybe mississippiensis
Hygrocybe trinitensis
Hygrophorus hypothejus
Hygrophorus russula
Hygrophorus subsordidus
Porpolomopsis calyptriformis

7b. Mushroom growing on the ground or on wood; cap and gills not waxy when rubbed and crushed between thumb and fingers 8

8a. Mushroom stalkless or with a rudimentary or short lateral stalk:
Anthracophyllum lateritium
Lentinellus ursinus
Panellus stipticus
Pleurotus ostreatus
Pleurotus pulmonarius
Plicaturopsis crispa
Schizophyllum commune

8b. Mushroom with a conspicuous stalk that
　 is usually central 9

9a. Mushroom with a small stature; stalk
　 1–6 mm thick 10

9b. Mushroom with a larger stature; stalk
　 more than 6 mm thick 11

10a. Growing on wood:
　　 Collybia zonata
　　 Crinipellis scabella
　　 Cyptotrama asprata
　　 Gerronema chrysophylla
　　 Gerronema strombodes
　　 Gymnopus biformis
　　 Gymnopus dichrous
　　 Gymnopus subnudus
　　 Lentinus arcularius
　　 Lentinus crinitus
　　 Lentinus tricholoma
　　 Leucocoprinus birnbaumii
　　 Leucocoprinus longistriatus
　　 Marasmius rotula
　　 Micromphale brevipes
　　 Mycena epipterygia var. *lignicola*
　　 Mycena epipterygia var. *viscosa*
　　 Mycena galericulata
　　 Mycena haematopus
　　 Mycena inclinata
　　 Mycena semivestipes
　　 Mycetinis opacus
　　 Ripartitella brasiliensis
　　 Tetrapyrgos nigripes
　　 Xeromphalina campanella
　　 Xeromphalina kauffmanii
10b. Growing on the ground, on leaf litter,
　　 cones, nuts, or other mushrooms:
　　 Asterophora lycoperdoides
　　 Asterophora parasitica
　　 Baeospora myosura
　　 Crinipellis scabella
　　 Gymnopus biformis
　　 Gymnopus iocephalus

　　 Gymnopus spongiosus
　　 Gymnopus subnudus
　　 Lepiota phaeostictiformis
　　 Lepiota sanguiflua
　　 Leucocoprinus birnbaumii
　　 Leucocoprinus cepistipes
　　 Leucocoprinus fragilissimus
　　 Leucocoprinus ianthinus
　　 Leucocoprinus longistriatus
　　 Leucopaxillus gracillimus
　　 Marasmius capillaris
　　 Marasmius fulvoferrugineus
　　 Marasmius pulcherripes
　　 Marasmius siccus
　　 Mycena atkinsoniana
　　 Mycena clavicularis
　　 Mycena epipterygia var. *viscosa*
　　 Mycena galericulata
　　 Mycena leptocephala
　　 Mycena pura
　　 Mycetinis opacus
　　 Rugosomyces cyanellus
　　 Strobilurus conigenoides
　　 Tetrapyrgos nigripes

11a. Growing on wood:
　　 Armillaria mellea
　　 Callistosporium luteo-olivaceum
　　 Callistosporium purpureomarginatum
　　 Gymnopus dryophilus
　　 Gymnopus luxurians
　　 Lentinula raphanica
　　 Lentinus tigrinus
　　 Lepiota besseyi
　　 Leucoagaricus americanus
　　 Leucoagaricus meleagris
　　 Leucopaxillus laterarius
　　 Megacollybia texensis
　　 Neolentinus lepideus
　　 Omphalotus illudens
　　 Omphalotus subilludens
　　 Oudemansiella canarii
　　 Panus conchatus

Panus neostrigosus
Pleurotus pulmonarius
Pseudoarmillariella ectypoides
Tricholomopsis decora
Tricholomopsis formosa
Tricholomopsis rutilans

11b. Growing on the ground:

Armillaria gallica
Chlorophyllum hortense
Chlorophyllum subrhacodes
Clitocybe robusta
Cystoderma amianthinum
Desarmillaria tabescens
Gymnopus dryophilus
Hymenopellis furfuracea
Hymenopellis incognita
Laccaria amethystina
Laccaria bicolor
Laccaria laccata complex
Laccaria laccata var. pallidifolia
Laccaria ochropurpurea
Laccaria trichodermophora
Laccaria trullisata
Laccaria vinaceobrunnea
Lepiota besseyi
Lepista subconnexa
Leucoagaricus americanus
Leucoagaricus meleagris
Leucopaxillus albissimus complex
Leucopaxillus laterarius
Limacella illinita
Macrocybe titans
Macrolepiota procera
Marasmius nigrodiscus
Panus conchatus
Panus tephroleucus
Rhodocollybia maculata
Tricholoma caligatum
Tricholoma equestre
Tricholoma floridanum
Tricholoma inamoenum
Tricholoma intermedium

Tricholoma niveipes
Tricholoma odorum
Tricholoma portentosum
Tricholoma saponaceum
Tricholoma sejunctum
Tricholoma subluteum
Tricholoma subresplendens
Tricholoma sulphurescens
Tricholoma sulphureum
Tricholomopsis rutilans

12a. Spore print pink, salmon, pinkish buff to pinkish tan, or brownish pink. 13
12b. Spore print some shade of brown or black 14

13a. Growing on wood:

Phyllotopsis nidulans
Pluteus atromarginatus
Pluteus cervinus
Pluteus longistriatus
Pluteus magnus
Pluteus pellitus
Pluteus petasatus
Volvariella bombycina
Volvariella taylori

13b. Growing on the ground:

Clitocybe irina
Clitopilus prunulus
Entoloma abortivum
Entoloma farlowii
Entoloma incanum
Entoloma megacystidiosum
Entoloma murrayi
Entoloma quadratum
Entoloma strictius
Entoloma vernum
Lepista nuda
Lepista subconnexa
Rhodocollybia butyracea
Rhodocollybia maculata
Volvariella taylori

14a. Spore print rusty brown, yellowish
     brown, brown, or dark brown. 15
14b. Spore print dark purple brown to black . .
     17

15a. Growing on wood:
     Agaricus endoxanthus
     Agrocybe pediades
     Bolbitius reticulatus
     Bolbitius titubans
     Crepidotus applanatus
     Crepidotus mollis
     Cyclocybe aegerita
     Galerina marginata
     Gymnopilus armillatus
     Gymnopilus fulvosquamulosus
     Gymnopilus hispidus
     Gymnopilus lepidotus
     Gymnopilus liquiritiae
     Gymnopilus palmicola
     Gymnopilus penetrans
     Gymnopilus rufosquamulosus
     Gymnopilus sapineus
     Gymnopilus spectabilis
     Pholiota highlandensis
     Pholiota polychroa
     Pseudomerulius curtisii
     Simocybe centunculus
     Tapinella atrotomentosa
15b. Growing on the ground, on dung or
     manure, on compost, or among mosses. .
     16

16a. Partial veil web-like, leaving a fibrillose
     annular zone, or sometimes evanescent:
     Cortinarius albidus
     Cortinarius alboviolaceus
     Cortinarius argentatus
     Cortinarius atkinsonianus
     Cortinarius atrotomentosus
     Cortinarius aureifolius
     Cortinarius cinnamomeus
     Cortinarius corrugatus

     Cortinarius hesleri
     Cortinarius iodeoides
     Cortinarius iodes
     Cortinarius lewisii
     Cortinarius marylandensis
     Cortinarius obliquus
     Cortinarius sanguineus
     Cortinarius semisanguineus
     Cortinarius violaceus
     Pholiota highlandensis
16b. Partial veil not web-like, sometimes
     membranous and typically leaving a ring
     on the stalk, or partial veil absent:
     Agaricus alachuanus
     Agaricus auricolor
     Agaricus endoxanthus
     Agaricus gennadii
     Agaricus placomyces
     Agaricus pocillator
     Agaricus rhoadsii
     Agaricus subalachuanus
     Agrocybe pediades
     Agrocybe retigera
     Bolbitius titubans
     Conocybe apala
     Conocybe tenera
     Cortinarius caperatus
     Galerina calyptrata
     Galerina tibiicystis
     Hebeloma crustuliniforme
     Hebeloma sarcophyllum
     Hebeloma sinapizans
     Hebeloma syrjense
     Inocybe calospora
     Inocybe rimosa

17a. Mature gills liquifying and forming a
     black inky fluid:
     Coprinopsis lagopides
     Coprinopsis lagopus
     Coprinus americanus
     Coprinus comatus
     Coprinus sterquilinus

17b. Mature gills not liquifying 18

18a. Growing on wood:
       Coprinellus disseminatus
       Hypholoma capnoides
       Hypholoma lateritium
       Psathyrella delineata
       Psathyrella pennata
       Psathyrella rugocephala
18b. Growing on the ground, among mosses,
    on dung, or manure:
       Hypholoma ericaceum
       Hypholoma fasciculare
       Lacrymaria lacrymabunda
       Panaeolina foenisecii
       Panaeolus semiovatus
       Panaeolus solidipes
       Parasola plicatilis
       Psathyrella pennata
       Psilocybe cubensis

Agaricus alachuanus Murrill

MACROSCOPIC FEATURES: **Cap** 2–5.5 cm wide, convex, becoming broadly convex to nearly plane, sometimes slightly depressed over the center; surface dry, covered with tiny, imbricate purple scales over a whitish to buff ground color, with a dark purple-brown to nearly blackish disc; margin incurved at first and remaining so well into maturity, sterile, somewhat undulating. **Gills** free, up to 3 mm thick, moderately close, white becoming pinkish, then deep chocolate brown to grayish brown when mature. **Stalk** 4–5.8 cm long, 3.5–6 mm wide, nearly equal or slightly enlarged downward to a bulbous base; surface dry, slightly fibrillose, whitish, sometimes with dull orange to brownish streaks or tinges; ring superior to median, thin, delicate, whitish to brownish yellow. **Flesh** up to 3 mm thick, white; odor and taste not distinctive.
SPORE PRINT: Dark brown.

MICROSCOPIC FEATURES: Spores 4.5–6.8 × 3–4.5 µm, broadly ellipsoid to subglobose, lacking a germ pore, thick-walled, dark brown; cheilocystidia napiform to saccate.
OCCURRENCE: Scattered or in groups on the ground under oaks or in mixed oak and pine woods; summer–fall.
EDIBILITY: Unknown, but too small to be of culinary interest.
REMARKS: We have included the "cf." designator because of slight variations when compared to Murrill's description which may be due to genetic variability. *Agaricus subalachuanus* (not illustrated) is similar, but it has a 2–3.5 cm wide, white cap with rosy-buff scales, a darker disc, and an appendiculate margin. It has a 2–3.5 cm long and 2–5 mm thick, white stalk that is nearly equal, with a delicate, white median to superior ring. It has spores that measure 6–7 × 3–4 µm, lacks cheilocystidia, and grows in open fields and lawns during early summer.

Agaricus alachuanus

Agaricus endoxanthus Berk. & Broome

= *Agaricus rotalis* K. R. Petersen, Desjardin & Hemmes

MACROSCOPIC FEATURES: **Cap** 2.5–9.5 cm wide, convex to bell-shaped with a conspicuous umbo, becoming broadly convex and somewhat depressed at maturity; surface dark brown to blackish, becoming cracked and radially split from the margin to the disc, exposing white to pinkish flesh; margin often split in age; **flesh** 4–14 mm thick, white, staining brown; odor strongly phenolic; taste unpleasant. **Gills** free, moderately broad, whitish at first, becoming purple brown. **Stalk** 3.5–7(-12) cm long, 4–14 mm wide, tapered upwards with a truncate base, stuffed with white threads; surface whitish toward the apex, grayish brown to pale brown below; flesh whitish above, bright yellow toward the base; partial veil thick, white, leaving a large, persistent, white superior ring.

SPORE PRINT: Dark brown.
MICROSCOPIC FEATURES: Spores 4.2–6.5 × 3–5 µm, ellipsoid-ovoid, smooth, dark brown.
OCCURRENCE: Scattered or in groups on wood-chip mulch, in landscaped areas, or on the ground with subtropical plants; reported from extreme southeastern Georgia and Florida.
EDIBILITY: Unknown.
REMARKS: *Agaricus endoxanthus* is a tropical species that was originally described from Sri Lanka. It was also described from the Hawaiian Islands as *Agaricus rotalis*.

Agaricus endoxanthus

Agaricus placomyces Peck

COMMON NAME: Flat-cap Agaric.
MACROSCOPIC FEATURES: **Cap** 4.5–9 cm wide, convex, becoming broadly convex with a low broad umbo, sometimes flattened on the disc; surface dry, covered with tiny, grayish to grayish-brown scales over a white ground color; disc grayish brown. **Gills** free, crowded, white at first, turning pink and finally blackish brown in age. **Stalk** 4–10 cm long, 5–13 mm wide, enlarged downward to a bulbous or sometimes abruptly bulbous base; surface smooth, white, slowly staining brown when handled or in age; partial veil membranous, white, with cottony patches, leaving a superior to median, single-layered ring with cottony patches on the undersurface. **Flesh** white, base typically staining yellow when cut or rubbed; odor and taste not distinctive.
SPORE PRINT: Dark brown.

MICROSCOPIC FEATURES: Spores 4.5–6 × 3.5–4.5 μm, oval to elliptic, smooth, pale brown.
OCCURRENCE: Scattered or in groups on the ground in woods, especially hardwoods, in grassy areas with trees, or on sawdust piles; summer–fall.
EDIBILITY: Poisonous.
REMARKS: *Agaricus pocillator* (p. 14) is similar, but it has a double-layered ring and an abruptly bulbous stalk base. *Agaricus gennadii* complex = *Agaricus chlamydopus* (not illustrated) has a large, 5–16 cm wide cap with a strongly inrolled margin when young. The cap surface is soft and cottony, white to grayish or brownish, and may be glabrous or have tiny scales. The stalk is white, with a sheathing veil from the base up to a thin ring that eventually collapses. It has broadly ellipsoid, smooth, brown spores that measure 7–10 × 5.5–8 μm, grows on lawns, golf courses, and cemeteries during summer and fall, and is edible.

Agaricus placomyces

Agaricus rhoadsii Murrill

= *Agaricus weberianus* Murrill

MACROSCOPIC FEATURES: **Cap** up to 6.5 cm wide, truncate-conic to expanded; surface dry, fibrillose, purplish brown to reddish brown; margin white, sterile, widely projecting, appendiculate. **Gills** free, crowded, narrow, whitish to dull pink and finally purplish brown. **Stalk** up to 8 cm long, 6–10 mm wide, and tapering upward, bulbous; surface smooth, white; ring very large, membranous, apical, persistent and double, smooth and white above, decorated with yellowish-brown scales below. **Flesh** firm, white; odor not distinctive; taste unknown.

SPORE PRINT: Dark brown.

MICROSCOPIC FEATURES: Spores 5.3–7 × 3.5–5.5 µm, ellipsoid to broadly ellipsoid or ovoid, smooth, brown.

OCCURRENCE: Scattered or in groups on the ground with oaks; known only from Florida; late summer.

EDIBILITY: Unknown.

REMARKS: The brownish fibrillose cap and firm, milk-white flesh help to distinguish this species. It was named for A. S. Rhoads, a plant pathologist from Florida. *Agaricus auricolor* (not illustrated) has a yellow cap with a yellow-orange disc that becomes brownish overall in age. The stalk has a slightly bulbous base, is often deeply sunken into the soil, and has a thin, delicate ring with yellowish floccose patches on the underside. It has thin, yellowish flesh that stains darker yellow when bruised and has a strong odor and taste of almond extract. It grows singly or in groups in grassy areas or along grassy wooded borders and trails during summer and fall.

Agaricus rhoadsii

Agrocybe pediades (Fr.) Fayod

= *Agrocybe semiorbicularis* (Bull.) Fayod

COMMON NAME: Hemispheric Agrocybe.
MACROSCOPIC FEATURES: **Cap** 1–5 cm wide, hemispheric when young, becoming broadly convex in age; surface viscid to slightly glutinous or suede-like when fresh, becoming dry, shiny, and often cracked on the disc in age, ocher to rusty ocher at first, becoming ocher yellow to yellow or buff in age; margin incurved and remaining so well into maturity, even. **Gills** attached, close, broad, buff to pale brownish when young, becoming orange brown to pale rusty brown at maturity. **Stalk** 2–7 cm long, 1.5–12 mm thick, nearly equal or tapered downward, pale yellow to ochre or pale brown, finely fibrillose, typically slightly bulbous at the base, often with white rhizomorphs. **Flesh** thin, whitish; odor farinaceous; taste farinaceous or somewhat bitter to disagreeable.

SPORE PRINT: Dark brown.
MICROSCOPIC FEATURES: Spores 10–14 × 7–10 µm, elliptic, with a prominent germ pore, smooth, pale brown.
OCCURRENCE: Scattered or in dense groups on lawns or fields, on wood mulch, or sawdust mixed with manure; spring–fall.
EDIBILITY: Edible, but of poor quality.
REMARKS: Specimens gathered on sawdust mixed with manure tend to be much more robust than those collected on lawns.

Agrocybe pediades

Agrocybe retigera (Spreg.) Singer

MACROSCOPIC FEATURES: **Cap** 1.5–4 cm wide, convex, becoming nearly plane, occasionally umbonate; surface moist, finely wrinkled, breaking up into flat, scaly areas, dull white to pale yellow with light brownish shades when older. **Gills** ascending adnate to adnexed, close to subdistant, up to 5 mm wide, finely fimbriate to eroded, white when young, dull brownish when mature. **Stalk** 3–5.5 cm long, 3–5 mm wide, equal with a small bulbous base; surface dry, longitudinally striate, glabrous except for a cottony tomentum at the base, white, staining pale yellow to buff. **Flesh** 1–3 mm thick; odor farinaceous; taste farinaceous-bitter.

SPORE PRINT: Brown.

MICROSCOPIC FEATURES: Spores 13–18 × 7.5–9 μm, truncate, elliptic, smooth, apical pore present, brown.

OCCURRENCE: Scattered or in groups on lawns; summer.

EDIBILITY: Unknown.

REMARKS: This species is characterized by its whitish, finely wrinkled cap and growth on lawns. It has also been reported from South America. The Poplar Mushroom, *Cyclocybe aegerita* = *Agrocybe aegerita* (not illustrated), has a large, 5–15 cm wide, yellowish to pale reddish-brown or darker brown, sometimes wrinkled cap that may be cracked in age. It has a membranous ring on the stalk and typically fruits in clusters on living or dead hardwood trees, especially willows, maples, poplars, and box elders. It is sometimes cultivated as an edible species, and its spores measure 9–11 × 5–7 μm.

grocybe retigera

Amanita abrupta Peck

COMMON NAME: American Abrupt-bulbed
Lepidella.
MACROSCOPIC FEATURES: **Cap** 3.5–10 cm wide,
convex, becoming plane; surface covered with
sharp, conical to flattened warts which are
easily washed off, white with a slightly cream
or buff disc; margin appendiculate. **Gills** free,
close, 5–10 mm wide, white, drying yellowish
on the margin, covered by a white partial veil
when young. **Stalk** 4.5–9 cm long, 5–10 mm
wide, with an abruptly enlarged base; surface
fibrous, white, drying cream to yellowish; ring
apical, pendant, membranous, ample, upper
surface striate, white; volva consisting of tiny,
scattered, white floccose warts on top of the
basal bulb. **Flesh** thick at the disc, white; odor
and taste not distinctive.

SPORE PRINT: white.
MICROSCOPIC FEATURES: Spores 6–10 × 5–9
μm, globose to elliptic, smooth, amyloid.
OCCURRENCE: Common in mixed pine and
hardwood forests; late spring–fall.
EDIBILITY: Unknown.
REMARKS: It is distinguished by its abrupt
basal bulb, sharp conical warts, and overall
white color. It is one of the easier *Amanita* species to recognize.

Amanita abrupta

Amanita albocreata (G. F. Atk.) E. -J. Gilbert

= *Amanitopsis albocreata* G. F. Atk.

COMMON NAME: Ringless Panther.

MACROSCOPIC FEATURES: **Cap** 2.5–8 cm wide, convex, becoming broadly convex to nearly plane; margin striate to tuberculate-striate; surface viscid when moist, glabrous, white to pale yellow or white with a yellow or tan disc, not staining when bruised, with randomly distributed warts or patches that are easily removed. **Gills** free or narrowly adnexed, crowded, moderately broad, white, covered by a white partial veil when young; lamellulae truncate. **Stalk** 5–15 cm long, 5–13 mm thick, slightly tapered upward, solid or stuffed, with an abrupt, subglobose to ovoid basal bulb; surface dry, white, lacking a ring; volva sheathing the stalk base like a stocking, with a slightly free, collar-like margin. **Flesh** thin, white; odor and taste not distinctive.

SPORE PRINT: White.

MICROSCOPIC FEATURES: Spores 7–9.5 × 6–9 μm, globose to subglobose or broadly elliptic, hyaline, inamyloid; basidia 4-sterigmate.

OCCURRENCE: Solitary, scattered, or in groups on the ground in conifer or hardwoods or mixed oak and pine woods; late spring–fall.

EDIBILITY: Unknown, presumed toxic.

REMARKS: *Albocreata* means having a white volva that sheaths the stalk base like a stocking. The Small Funnel-veil Amanita, *Amanita multisquamosa* (not illustrated), is similar and has a white or whitish cap with a tan or brown disc, but it has a superior to median ring on the stalk that is sometimes funnel-shaped due to expansion of the cap. It occurs in mixed conifer and hardwood forests. *Amanita pubescens* (not illustrated) has a small, 3.5–5.3 cm wide, pale yellow cap with pale yellowish warts, white to pale yellow gills, a narrow, ringless stalk with a marginate basal bulb, and a dirty, white volva consisting of easily removed floccose to tomentose patches. It grows in open areas with nearby oaks during summer and fall.

Amanita albocreata

Amanita amerifulva Tulloss

COMMON NAME: American Orange-brown Ringless Amanita.

MACROSCOPIC FEATURES: **Cap** 4–10 cm wide, convex, becoming nearly plane, typically somewhat umbonate; surface moist and tacky, glabrous, reddish brown to tawny or brownish orange; margin striate. **Gills** free, close, 5–7 mm wide, whitish. **Stalk** 7–15.5 cm long, 5–15 mm wide, tapered upward, lacking a basal bulb, hollow; surface moist, glabrous, dingy brownish orange; ring absent; volva small, saccate, white, sometimes with orangish-brown tinges. **Flesh** 1–2 mm thick, whitish; odor not distinctive.

SPORE PRINT: White.

MICROSCOPIC FEATURES: Spores 8–14 × 6.8–12.5 μm, globose to subglobose, smooth, inamyloid.

OCCURRENCE: Scattered or in groups on the ground in mixed pine and hardwood forests; spring–late fall.

EDIBILITY: Edible, but not recommended because of possible confusion with other possibly poisonous species.

REMARKS: *Amerifulva* means "American and colored like a fox." It is distinguished by its tawny cap, lack of a ring, and its white, saccate volva. The Tawny Grisette, *Amanita fulva* (not illustrated), is a European species that does not occur in North America.

Amanita amerifulva

Amanita amerirubescens complex
Tulloss

COMMON NAME: Eastern American Blusher.
MACROSCOPIC FEATURES: **Cap** 3–20 cm wide, convex, becoming plane, slightly umbonate; surface moist, with pinkish to reddish floccose patches or sometimes glabrous, varying from white to rust brown or grayish orange with reddish stains; margin not striate or slightly striate. **Gills** free, close, up to 4 mm broad, finely fimbriate, white with reddish stains, covered by a white partial veil when young. **Stalk** 6–25 cm long, 7–40 mm wide, equal with a bulbous base, moist, apex pruinose, fibrillose below to the base, pale orange with reddish stains; ring apical, membranous, red on the upper surface; volva consisting of indistinct rings of floccose veil material. **Flesh** thick, white with reddish stains; odor and taste not distinctive.

SPORE PRINT: White.
MICROSCOPIC FEATURES: Spores 7–9.8 × 5.6–7.3 µm, subglobose to broadly ellipsoid, smooth, hyaline, amyloid.
OCCURRENCE: In mixed pine and hardwood forests; spring–fall.
EDIBILITY: Edible, but not recommended. It contains hemolytic compounds and must be cooked to detoxify them.
REMARKS: It is characterized by its medium size, grayish-orange cap, and reddish stains. Carefully compare it to *Amanita flavorubescens* (p. 219), which has a yellow cap, a yellow, fringed ring, yellowish volva material on its stalk base, and is considered toxic. The Blusher, *Amanita rubescens* (not illustrated), is a European species that does not occur in eastern North America.

Amanita amerirubescens complex

Amanita amerivirosa Tulloss

COMMON NAME: Four-spored Destroying Angel.

MACROSCOPIC FEATURES: **Cap** 8–15 cm wide, rounded-campanulate when young, becoming convex then broadly convex to nearly plane; surface dry, glabrous, matte to somewhat shiny, white, not staining when bruised, lacking warts or patches; margin incurved and remaining so well into maturity, not striate or sometimes weakly translucent-striate on mature specimens. **Gills** narrowly adnate to nearly free, crowded, white to creamy white, not staining when bruised, covered by a white partial veil when young; with several tiers of lamellulae. **Stalk** 12–20 cm long, 1–2 cm thick, narrowing upward, with a globose to subglobose basal bulb, solid; surface dry, white, with small white recurved fibers on the upper half, glabrous below; ring apical, membranous, delicate, white; volva saccate with a flaring upper portion that sometimes adheres to the stalk, white. **Flesh** thick at the disc, white; odor and taste not distinctive.

SPORE PRINT: White.

MICROSCOPIC FEATURES: Spores 9–12 × 8–11 µm, globose to subglobose, occasionally broadly ellipsoid, smooth, hyaline, amyloid; basidia 4-sterigmate.

OCCURRENCE: Solitary, scattered, or in groups on the ground with oaks or pines; late spring–early winter.

EDIBILITY: Deadly poisonous.

REMARKS: Addition of a drop of KOH to the cap cuticle produces a yellow reaction. It has been previously illustrated and described as *Amanita virosa* in many American field guides, but DNA sequencing has demonstrated that it is a European species that does not occur in North America. The Destroying Angel or Two-spored Destroying Angel, *Amanita bisporigera* (not illustrated), is very similar, but it has a smaller stature. The cap is 2.5–10 cm wide, and its stalk is 5.5–14 cm long. Except for the disc, which may be straw yellow, tan, pinkish, or lavender, all parts of this mushroom are pure white. The spores measure 7–10 × 6–9 µm, and the basidia are 2-sterigmate. It grows on the ground with pines or hardwoods, especially oaks, from late spring through early winter.

Amanita amerivirosa

Amanita atkinsoniana Coker

MACROSCOPIC FEATURES: **Cap** 4–13 cm wide, convex, becoming plane; surface covered with sharp, conical to flattened, brownish warts which are easily washed off, white with a slightly cream or buff disc; margin appendiculate. **Gills** adnexed to free, close, 5–9 mm wide, white to slightly creamy, covered by a white partial veil when young. **Stalk** 8–12 cm long, 1–2.8 cm wide, tapered slightly upward, basal bulb ventricose to turnip-shaped; surface covered with fibers that merge into a scaly volva, whitish to creamy white; ring apical, adhering to the stalk, floccose, striate, white, becoming dark reddish orange to reddish brown; volva consisting of a set of concentric curved scales, grayish orange to brownish orange, becoming more yellowish brown in age. **Flesh** thick at the disc, white; odor of chlorine; taste not distinctive.

SPORE PRINT: White.

MICROSCOPIC FEATURES: Spores 8.1–13 × 6.1–7.9 µm, elliptic, smooth, amyloid.

OCCURRENCE: Scattered or in groups under pines or in bottomland hardwood forests, fall–winter.

EDIBILITY: Unknown.

REMARKS: *Atkinsoniana* honors American mycologist George Francis Atkinson (1854–1918). The distinctive features of this mushroom are its brownish warts, whitish cap, and yellowish to brownish scales on the base of the stalk. It resembles *Amanita onusta* (p. 226), which has more grayish tones, larger warts, and is more deeply tapered into the ground.

Amanita atkinsoniana

Amanita brunnescens G. F. Atk.

COMMON NAME: Cleft-foot Amanita.

MACROSCOPIC FEATURES: **Cap** 3–12 cm wide, convex to plano-convex at first, becoming nearly plane at maturity; surface dry, with white mealy volval material, bronze to teak to brownish, with reddish stains; margin slightly striate. **Gills** free, close, 5–12 mm wide, white with reddish stains, covered by a white to whitish partial veil when young. **Stalk** 6–11 cm long, 6–20 mm wide, gradually enlarging downward to a marginate basal bulb that often splits and forms a distinct cleft; surface moist, glabrous, stuffed with pith, white with dark brownish to reddish stains; ring apical, becoming appressed to the stalk, white to dingy white; volva sparse, whitish, developing reddish stains. **Flesh** about 6 mm thick, white with reddish stains; odor earthy or not distinctive; taste not distinctive.

SPORE PRINT: White.

MICROSCOPIC FEATURES: Spores 8.6–9.1 × 7.1–8.6 µm, globose to subglobose, smooth, amyloid.

OCCURRENCE: Scattered or in groups with conifers or hardwoods or in mixed forests; spring–early winter.

EDIBILITY: Unknown.

REMARKS: The Hated Caesar, *Amanita spreta* (p. 14), has a brown or grayish-brown cap with a patch or two of white volva tissue. The white partial veil gives rise to a white, membranous, skirt-like ring. The volva is a white sac that often flares away from the base. *Amanita aestivalis* (not illustrated) has a white cap with reddish stains. *Amanita spissa* (not illustrated) has a 6.5–16 cm wide, brownish-gray to olive-brown cap that is covered with erect to flat, grayish-brown warts. It has a brownish-gray stalk with an enlarged base that does not stain reddish brown when bruised. It has white flesh with a fruity to slightly nauseous odor.

Amanita brunnescens

Amanita ceciliae complex
(Berk. & Broome) Bas

COMMON NAME: Cecilia's Ringless Amanita.
MACROSCOPIC FEATURES: **Cap** 5.5–12 cm
wide, convex, becoming plane; surface viscid,
glabrous, covered with brownish-gray warts,
yellowish brown to grayish brown; margin
striate. **Gills** free, close, about 3–8 mm wide,
white when young, becoming grayish in
age. **Stalk** 7–16 cm long, up to 2 cm wide,
enlarged downward, typically hollow and
spongy; surface glabrous, light gray with a
white apex; ring lacking; volva consisting of
broken grayish scales on the stalk base. **Flesh**
2–3 mm thick at the disc, white; odor and
taste not distinctive.

SPORE PRINT: White.
MICROSCOPIC FEATURES: Spores 9.6–11.7 ×
9.6–11.5 μm, globose, smooth, inamyloid.
OCCURRENCE: Scattered or in groups in mixed
pine and hardwood forests; spring–early
winter.
EDIBILITY: Unknown.
REMARKS: This species is characterized by its
grayish-brown cap with grayish warts and a
volva which breaks apart on the stalk. Dr. Rod
Tulloss has studied the complex and has several forms under consideration as new species.

Amanita ceciliae complex

Amanita cinereoconia G. F. Atk.

MACROSCOPIC FEATURES: **Cap** 3.5–7.5 cm wide, plano-convex at first, becoming nearly plane at maturity, depressed at disc; surface dry, whitish to brownish gray, covered with grayish, powdery to granular material, with some larger pyramidal warts on the disc; margin appendiculate. **Gills** adnexed, close, 4–10 mm wide, white to cream. **Stalk** 5–12 cm long, 4–13 mm wide, nearly equal down to an enlarged, bulbous, and pointed base; surface dry to moist, covered with fine, mealy to powdery material, white to grayish; ring usually lacking or sometimes apical and covered with whitish to grayish, fragile, floccose material; volva covered with grayish, floccose to powdery material. **Flesh** up to 3 mm thick at the disc, white; odor of old meat or chlorine; taste unpleasant or not distinctive.

SPORE PRINT: White.
MICROSCOPIC FEATURES: Spores 8–12 × 4.5–7 μm, elliptic, smooth, amyloid.
OCCURRENCE: Gregarious or scattered in mixed hardwood and pine forests; spring–fall.
EDIBILITY: Unknown.
REMARKS: The overall grayish, powdery volval material helps distinguish this species. *Amanita onusta* (p. 226) is similar but has more pronounced volval warts and a more rooting base.

Amanita cinereoconia

Amanita cylindrispora Beardslee

MACROSCOPIC FEATURES: **Cap** 4–8 cm wide, convex, becoming plane; surface dry to viscid when wet, glabrous, universal veil a large brown patch of easily removable material, fibrillose towards the margin, white with reddish-brown stains; margin even. **Gills** adnate, crowded, white, drying brown, covered by a white partial veil when young. **Stalk** 4–12 cm long, 5–15 mm wide, solid, with a large, ventricose, rooting, basal bulb that is often deeply buried in sand; surface glabrous to slightly fibrillose, white, becoming lavender gray with age; ring apical, fibrillose-scaly, delicate, white; volva consisting of remnants that sheath the basal bulb. **Flesh** thin, whitish; odor of chlorine or not distinctive; taste not distinctive.

SPORE PRINT: White.

MICROSCOPIC FEATURES: Spores 10.9–15 × 3.1–5.5 μm, cylindric to bacilliform, smooth, weakly amyloid.

OCCURRENCE: Found in mixed pine and hardwood forests; late spring–early winter.

EDIBILITY: Unknown.

REMARKS: It was originally described from Florida and has been found in the Big Thicket region of Texas several times. It is closely related to *Amanita peckiana* (not illustrated), which lacks the deeply rooting basal bulb and has more pinkish colors.

Amanita cylindrispora

Amanita daucipes (Sacc.) Lloyd

COMMON NAME: Carrot-foot Amanita.
MACROSCOPIC FEATURES: **Cap** 6–29 cm wide, convex, becoming plano-convex at maturity; surface dry, covered with fine, fawn-colored to orange-cinnamon particles; margin appendiculate with mealy particles. **Gills** free, close, 10–13 mm wide, yellow, covered by a whitish partial veil when young. **Stalk** 14.5–19 cm long, 1.0–3.3 cm wide, equal above a bulbous to turnip-shaped basal bulb; surface whitish and coated with pinkish-orange to orange-cinnamon, mealy particles; ring apical, pendant, underside covered with mealy particles, striate on the upper surface, white with some pinkish and cream colors; volva consisting of scattered, pinkish-orange to orange-cinnamon, mealy particles on the stalk base. **Flesh** 6–10 mm thick at the disc, white to pale yellow; odor of chlorine; taste not distinctive.

SPORE PRINT: White.
MICROSCOPIC FEATURES: Spores 9–11.7 × 5.2–7.5 μm, elliptic, smooth, amyloid.
OCCURRENCE: Solitary or scattered in mixed hardwood and pine forests; late spring–fall.
EDIBILITY: Unknown.
REMARKS: It is one of our most striking *Amanita* species. The pinkish-orange to orange-cinnamon colors and massive cap and stalk base are most distinctive. Compare with *Amanita roseitincta* (p. 231), which is smaller, has more floccose veil material, and has inamyloid spores.

Amanita daucipes

Amanita farinosa Schwein.

COMMON NAME: Powder-cap Amanita.

MACROSCOPIC FEATURES: **Cap** 2.5–6.5 cm wide, convex, becoming plane; surface dry, covered with brownish-gray, granulose material; margin sulcate-striate. **Gills** free, close to subdistant, about 1 mm wide, intervenose, white. **Stalk** 3–6.5 cm long, 3–9 mm wide, tapered toward the apex, with a small subglobose to oval basal bulb, powdery, whitish to grayish; ring absent; volva consisting of brownish-gray, pruinose remnants, usually only near the top of the bulb. **Flesh** thin, white; odor and taste not distinctive.

SPORE PRINT: White.

MICROSCOPIC FEATURES: Spores 6.3–9.5 × 4.5–8 μm, subglobose, smooth, inamyloid.

OCCURRENCE: Solitary or scattered in bottom-land hardwood forests or mixed oak and pine woodlands; spring–early winter.

EDIBILITY: Unknown.

REMARKS: This small and overlooked species is recognized by its dry, granulose, sulcate-striate cap, lack of a ring, and evanescent volva which is apparent as pruinose material on the stalk base. At first glance it may appear to be a *Russula* species.

Amanita farinosa

Amanita flavoconia G. F. Atk.

COMMON NAME: Yellow Patches.
MACROSCOPIC FEATURES: **Cap** 3–9 cm wide, convex, becoming plane; surface dry or viscid, mandarin orange to brownish yellow, covered with buttercup-yellow to reddish floccose warts which are easily washed off; margin non-striate or slightly striate. **Gills** free, close, about 6 mm wide, white, covered by a white to yellow partial veil when young. **Stalk** 6.5–10.5 cm long, 5–15 mm wide, with a slightly enlarged, ovoid basal bulb, glabrous to scaly, white to pale yellow or orange yellow; ring apical, membranous, white to light yellow or yellow; volva consisting of floccose patches, colored like the cap, easily removed. **Flesh** about 5 mm thick at the disc, white, yellow under the cuticle; odor not distinctive.
SPORE PRINT: White.
MICROSCOPIC FEATURES: Spores 6.6–8.6 × 4.5–6.5 µm, elliptic, smooth, amyloid.
OCCURRENCE: Solitary, scattered, or in groups in mixed pine and hardwood forests; spring–early winter.

EDIBILITY: Unknown.
REMARKS: *Amanita frostiana* (not illustrated) is similar, but it has globose, inamyloid spores and a moderately to strongly striate cap margin. *Amanita flavorubescens* (p. 219) has a pale yellowish cap with yellow warts and some reddish-brown stains. *Amanita amerirubescens* (p. 209) typically has a reddish-brown cap, sometimes with olive tints. The volvas of these species are pulverulent and, when removed from the ground, are usually left there. The Gulf Coast Lemon Amanita, *Amanita levistriata* (not illustrated), has a small, 2.3–6.6 cm wide cap that is ocher yellow over the disc and paler yellow to deep buff toward the faintly striate margin. The cap surface is covered with yellowish-olive, felted patches or fine powdery scales. It has a whitish to cream stalk with pale yellow tints on the lower portion, a skirt-like membranous ring, and an ovoid to turnip-shaped basal bulb. It has inamyloid, smooth, globose to subglobose spores that measure 6.5–11 × 5.5–9.5 µm and grows on the ground in hardwoods or mixed woods from late spring through fall.

Amanita flavoconia

Amanita flavorubescens G. F. Atk.

COMMON NAME: Yellow Blusher.
MACROSCOPIC FEATURES: **Cap** 4.5–10 cm wide, convex, becoming plane; surface viscid, glabrous, covered with yellow floccose warts which are easily washed off, pale brownish to pale yellow with reddish-brown stains; margin slightly striate. **Gills** free, close, about 5 mm wide, white with reddish stains, covered by a white partial veil when young. **Stalk** 5–12 cm long, 1–2 cm wide, equal with a slightly enlarged, ovoid basal bulb; surface fibrillose to pruinose, whitish with reddish-brown stains; ring apical, membranous, striate, white with a yellow fringe; volva consisting of pulverulent, yellowish floccose patches that are easily removed. **Flesh** about 4 mm thick at the disc, white, staining reddish brown when bruised; odor not distinctive.

SPORE PRINT: White.
MICROSCOPIC FEATURES: Spores 8.1–10.2 × 5.5–7 µm, elliptic, smooth, amyloid.
OCCURRENCE: Scattered or in groups in mixed pine and hardwood forests; spring–early winter.
EDIBILITY: Unknown.
REMARKS: *Flavorubescens* means "yellow and reddish." *Amanita flavoconia* (p. 218) has an orange to brownish-yellow cap with occasional yellow warts, a yellow to orangish stalk, and lacks reddish stains.

Amanita flavorubescens

Amanita hesleri Bas

COMMON NAME: Hesler's Amanita.
MACROSCOPIC FEATURES: **Cap** 5–11.5 cm
wide, convex, becoming plane; surface dry to
slightly viscid, white to dingy white, covered
with concentric, brown to grayish-brown
pyramidal warts; margin appendiculate. **Gills**
close to crowded, adnexed, 5–8.5 mm wide,
white. **Stalk** 6–14 cm long, 8–15 mm wide,
tapered upward from an enlarged, slightly
clavate base, solid; surface dry, covered with
fine, floccose to powdery material, white with
grayish brown at the base; ring absent; volva
consisting of obscure brownish concentric
rings. **Flesh** up to 6 mm thick at the disc,
white; odor of old socks or not distinctive;
taste not distinctive.

SPORE PRINT: White.
MICROSCOPIC FEATURES: Spores 9–12 × 5.5–
7.5 μm, elliptic, smooth, amyloid.
OCCURRENCE: Gregarious to scattered with
pines, in mixed conifer and hardwoods, and in
bottomland hardwood forests; spring–fall.
EDIBILITY: Unknown.
REMARKS: It was originally described from
Tennessee and North Carolina. The viscid,
concentric, brown to grayish-brown volva
warts help distinguish this species. It was
named for Lexemuel R. Hesler (1888–1977),
who did pioneering work in the Great Smoky
Mountains region.

Amanita hesleri

Amanita jacksonii Pomerl.

= *Amanita umbonata* Pomerl.

COMMON NAME: American Caesar's
Mushroom.

MACROSCOPIC FEATURES: **Cap** 7–14 cm wide,
convex, becoming nearly plane; surface viscid,
glabrous, disc reddish orange, more orange
yellow at the margin; margin sulcate-striate.
Gills free, close to crowded, 5–12 mm wide,
pale yellow, covered when young by a pale
yellowish-orange partial veil. **Stalk** 9–15 cm
long, 10–16 mm wide, tapered upward or
nearly equal, lacking a basal bulb, stuffed with
pith or hollow; surface creamy yellow to light
yellow, partially covered by yellowish-orange
scale-like patches or bands; ring apical, membranous, persistent, with a striate top, yellow;
volva egg-like, elongated, becoming saccate
in age, white. **Flesh** 7–8 mm thick at the disc,
yellow to orange under the cuticle; odor not
distinctive.

SPORE PRINT: White.

MICROSCOPIC FEATURES: Spores 7.6–11.1 ×
5.6–7 μm, broadly elliptic, smooth, inamyloid.

OCCURRENCE: Solitary, scattered, or in groups
on the ground in mixed pine and hardwood
forests; late spring–fall.

EDIBILITY: Edible, but be sure of your
identification.

REMARKS: *Jacksonii* honors Canadian amateur
mycologist and botanical illustrator Henry
Alexander Carmichael Jackson (1877–1961).
It is one of several very similar species currently being evaluated using molecular
analysis. It has been called *Amanita caesarea*,
which is a European species that is not found
in North America. *Amanita arkansana* (not
illustrated) is similar, but its cap is bright yellow over the disc and more amber yellow near
the striate margin. It grows on the ground in
mixed pine and hardwood forests during summer and fall. It is edible, but ensure the correct
identification.

Amanita jacksonii

Amanita lavendula complex (Coker) Tulloss, K. W. Hughes, Rodrig. Cayc. & Kudzma

= *Amanita citrina* f. *lavendula* (Coker) Veselý
= *Amanita citrina* var. *lavendula* (Coker) Sartory & Maire
= *Amanita mappa* var. *lavendula* Coker

COMMON NAME: Coker's Lavender Staining Amanita.

MACROSCOPIC FEATURES: **Cap** 5–12 cm wide, hemispherical to plano-convex, becoming plane; surface viscid, glabrous, often with some veil remnants, pale yellow to greenish yellow, sometimes with dull reddish-brown spots or streaks, especially over the disc; margin typically not striate. **Gills** slightly adnexed then free, close, about 6 mm wide, white, covered by a whitish to light yellow partial veil when young. **Stalk** 6–13 cm long, 6–20 mm wide, equal, with a marginate-depressed, bulbous base; surface fibrous to pruinose, light yellow above the ring, whitish below; ring apical, thin and fragile, collapsing against the stalk, light yellow; volva consisting of floccose patches on the margin of the basal bulb, usually coated with sand. **Flesh** up to 6 mm thick, white; odor resembling radishes or potatoes; taste unpleasant or not distinctive. The cap, stalk, and volva often display lavender tints when specimens are collected following freezing temperatures.

SPORE PRINT: White.

MICROSCOPIC FEATURES: Spores 5.5–8.1 × 5.5–7 μm, subglobose, smooth, amyloid.

OCCURRENCE: Scattered or in groups in mixed pine and hardwood forests; fall–winter.

EDIBILITY: Unknown.

REMARKS: The North American species *Amanita lavendula* was mistakenly named *Amanita citrina* = *Amanita mappa* (the Citron Amanita) in American field guides. *Amanita citrina* is a European species that does not occur in North America. We have designated *Amanita lavendula* as a complex because there are at least three North American species that are macroscopically nearly identical. Molecular analysis is required to separate them. The *Amanita russuloides* complex (p. 14) has a 2.5–12 cm wide, pale yellow cap with a few white warts that often wash off. The cap margin is weakly striate, a partial veil may be present or absent, and the stalk base has a small bulb that is usually topped by a roll of free tissue. *Amanita albocreata* (p. 207) has a whitish cap with a yellow or tan disc and scattered warts or patches. It lacks a ring and grows in mixed pine and hardwood forests during late spring through fall.

Amanita lavendula

Amanita longipes Bas ex Tulloss & D. T. Jenkins

COMMON NAME: Dog-legged Lepidella.
MACROSCOPIC FEATURES: **Cap** 2.5–8 cm wide, hemispheric at first, becoming broadly convex; surface dry, covered with a dense layer of fine powder, white overall or with a pale grayish-buff to pale grayish-brown disc; margin incurved when young, not striate, typically appendiculate. **Gills** attached to nearly free, close, whitish, covered at first by a white, fibrous-cottony partial veil. **Stalk** 5–15 cm long, 6–20 mm wide, enlarged downward and clavate, then tapered abruptly and radicating, often dog-legged or flattened or both; surface dry, scurfy to powdery, white, sometimes with reddish stains; ring absent; volva typically absent or consisting of sparse, whitish, floccose remnants. **Flesh** white; odor faintly resembling disinfectant or not distinctive; taste unpleasant or not distinctive.

SPORE PRINT: White.
MICROSCOPIC FEATURES: Spores 8–18 × 4–7 μm, elliptic, smooth, hyaline, amyloid.
OCCURRENCE: Solitary, scattered, or in groups on the ground in mixed woods, especially with oak and pine; summer–early winter.
EDIBILITY: Unknown.
REMARKS: *Longipes* means "having a long stalk." *Amanita rhoadsii* var. *rhoadsii* (not illustrated) has a 5–11 cm wide, white cap with an appendiculate margin, white gills, and a ringless, white stalk with a rooting, fusiform to somewhat turnip-shaped basal bulb. Its flesh has an odor of old ham or dirty socks, and its spores are strongly bacilliform, smooth, and amyloid. It grows in mixed pine and hardwood forests during summer and early fall.

Amanita longipes

Amanita muscaria var. *guessowii*
Veselý

= *Amanita muscaria* var. *formosa* Pers.

COMMON NAMES: Fly Agaric, Yellow-orange
Fly Agaric.

MACROSCOPIC FEATURES: **Cap** 5–20 cm wide,
convex, becoming nearly plane; surface pale
yellow to orange, darkest at the center, with
numerous cream-colored warts that darken
with age or may wash off; margin often weakly
striate at maturity. **Gills** free or narrowly
attached, crowded, white, covered by a thin,
white partial veil when young. **Stalk** 6–15
cm long, up to 3 cm thick, white to cream-
colored, with multiple partial or complete
rings of volva tissue on the lower portion; base
somewhat bulbous; ring superior, pendant,
often collapsing or falling off. **Flesh** white;
odor and taste not distinctive.

SPORE PRINT: White.

MICROSCOPIC FEATURES: Spores 9–12 × 6.5–8
μm, elliptic, smooth, hyaline, inamyloid.

OCCURRENCE: solitary or in groups on the
ground with conifers or hardwoods; summer–
early winter.

EDIBILITY: Poisonous.

REMARKS: *Amanita muscaria* var. *flavivolvata*
(p. 14) has a vivid red cap when young that
becomes orange-red to light yellow or cream
in age, and a whitish to yellowish median partial veil that leaves behind a ring with a ragged,
dull yellow to brownish margin. *Amanita*
persicina (p. 228) is also similar, but its cap is
pale orange to melon orange or orange red.
Amanita parcivolvata (p. 227) is smaller and
lacks a ring on its stalk.

Amanita muscaria var. guessowii

Amanita mutabilis Beardslee

MACROSCOPIC FEATURES: Cap 4.5–11 cm wide, plano-convex, becoming plane in age; surface moist to viscid, covered with a large, flat volval patch, glabrous, white to whitish; margin slightly appendiculate. **Gills** free, close, up to 11 mm wide, whitish, covered by a white partial veil when young. **Stalk** 6–11.5 cm long, 1–2 cm wide, tapered upward, with a globose to ovoid, marginate to submarginate basal bulb; surface dry, glabrous to fibrous, white, staining pinkish when bruised; ring subapical, pendant, white; volva with a free limb on the upper portion, white. **Flesh** 4–6 mm thick at the disc, white, quickly staining bright pink; odor variously described as oily, resembling anise, or musty; taste not distinctive.

SPORE PRINT: White.

MICROSCOPIC FEATURES: Spores 10–14.5 × 5.5–9 μm, elliptic, smooth, amyloid.

OCCURRENCE: Gregarious in sandy soil under pines and hardwoods, especially oaks; summer–early winter.

EDIBILITY: Unknown.

REMARKS: *Mutabilis* means "changing," a reference to the color change when its flesh is bruised. *Amanita bisporigera* (not illustrated) is similar, but it does not stain pink when bruised. *Amanita subsolitaria* (not illustrated) has a 5–8 cm wide, dull white cap that often becomes yellow in age and an appendiculate margin. It has subdistant, white gills that become yellow in age and a whitish, bulbous to fusiform, and slightly rooting stalk that stains golden yellow when bruised.

Amanita mutabilis

Amanita onusta (Howe) Sacc.

COMMON NAME: Gunpowder Lepidella.
MACROSCOPIC FEATURES: **Cap** 3–10.5 cm
wide, conical, becoming plano-convex with
a depressed disc; surface dry, covered with
small, fibrillose to granular, brownish-gray
warts over a whitish ground color; margin
appendiculate with a 1–2 mm wide band.
Gills adnexed, close to subdistant, 5–7 mm
wide, ivory yellow to cream-colored, covered by a whitish to creamy-gray partial veil
when young. **Stalk** 4–15 cm long, 8–18 mm
wide, nearly equal with an enlarged root-like,
radicating, and often bent basal bulb; surface
dry, scurfy, whitish, and often covered with
brownish-gray powder; ring delicate, whitish

to creamy gray, usually breaking up and leaving fragments on the stalk apex; volva consisting of concentric gray warts or recurved scales
on top of the basal bulb. **Flesh** about 4mm
thick at the disc, white with some brownish under the cuticle; odor of chlorine; taste
unpleasant or not distinctive.
SPORE PRINT: White.
MICROSCOPIC FEATURES: Spores 8–10 × 5–6
μm, short-elliptic, smooth, amyloid.
OCCURRENCE: Scattered or in groups on the
ground under hardwoods; spring–fall.
EDIBILITY: Unknown.
REMARKS: *Amanita cinereoconia* (p. 214) is
similar, but it has grayish, granular volval
material instead of well-formed warts.

Amanita onusta

Amanita parcivolvata (Peck)
E. -J. Gilbert

COMMON NAME: Ringless False Fly Agaric.
MACROSCOPIC FEATURES: **Cap** 3–12 cm wide, convex, becoming plane with a slight umbo; surface viscid when moist, scarlet to crimson, covered with small, pyramidal, floccose, pale yellow warts, becoming orange to yellow orange as it ages; margin strongly striate to tuberculate-striate. **Gills** free, close, 3–7 mm wide, white to cream. **Stalk** 6–10 cm long, 5–15 mm wide, nearly equal with a slightly enlarged basal bulb; surface moist or dry, glabrous to finely fibrous or furfuraceous, white to pale yellow; ring absent; volva consisting of powdery, yellow remnants on the stalk base that are sometimes arranged in concentric rings. **Flesh** white; odor and taste slightly unpleasant or not distinctive.

SPORE PRINT: White.
MICROSCOPIC FEATURES: Spores 9–14 × 6–8 µm, elliptic to cylindric, smooth, inamyloid.
OCCURRENCE: Solitary to gregarious in hardwood forests; summer–fall.
EDIBILITY: Unknown.
REMARKS: It is called the Ringless False Fly Agaric because it resembles a small version of *Amanita muscaria* var. *guessowii* (p. 224), which is larger and has a ring on its stalk.

Amanita parcivolvata

Amanita persicina (D. T. Jenkins) Tulloss & Geml

= *Amanita muscaria* var. *persicina*
    D. T. Jenkins

COMMON NAME: Peach-colored Fly Agaric.

MACROSCOPIC FEATURES: **Cap** 4–20 cm wide, convex to nearly flat, surface moist to viscid, pale orange to melon orange or orange red, darkest over the disc, with numerous yellow warts that become tan in age and may wash off; margin often weakly striate at maturity. **Gills** free or narrowly attached, crowded, cream-colored, sometimes with a pinkish tinge, covered with a thin, white partial veil when young. **Stalk** enlarged downward or nearly equal, 8–25 cm long, up to 3 cm thick, white, lower portion coated with scattered fragments of white volval tissue. **Flesh** white; odor and taste not distinctive.

SPORE PRINT: White.

MICROSCOPIC FEATURES: Spores 7–13 × 6–8.5 µm, elliptic, smooth, hyaline, inamyloid.

OCCURRENCE: Along roadways in grassy areas, near conifers, or in mixed woods; fall–winter.

EDIBILITY: Poisonous.

REMARKS: *Amanita muscaria* var. *guessowii* (p. 224) is very similar, but it has a pale yellow to orange cap.

Amanita persicina

Amanita polypyramis (Berk. & M. A. Curtis) Sacc.

MACROSCOPIC FEATURES: **Cap** 7.5–20 cm wide, convex, becoming plane; surface dry, white, covered at first with large pyramidal warts that are up to 3 mm high and 4 mm wide at the base, soon breaking up into powdery and mealy material; margin appendiculate. **Gills** free, close to crowded, very wide, whitish, becoming creamy white, covered by a white partial veil when young. **Stalk** 9–20 cm long, 2–7 cm wide, enlarged slightly downward to a subglobose to broadly clavate or submarginate basal bulb that elongates with age; surface dry, covered with floccose, mealy patches, white; ring apical, delicate, with floccose patches underneath, white, usually tearing and hanging from cap margin; volva consisting of floccose and pyramidal warts around the stalk base. **Flesh** thick, white; odor of chlorine; taste unpleasant or not distinctive.

SPORE PRINT: White.
MICROSCOPIC FEATURES: Spores 9–14 × 5–10 µm, elliptic, smooth, amyloid.
OCCURRENCE: Scattered or in groups on the ground under pines; late summer–fall.
EDIBILITY: Unknown.
REMARKS: *Polypyramis* means "many tiny pyramids," a reference to the abundant pyramidal warts on the cap and stalk base. The large size, mealy volval material, and overall white color make this an easy mushroom to identify. The cap is often nearly as large as a dinner plate. *Amanita chlorinosma* (not illustrated) is very similar and has an odor of chlorine, but it has smaller spores that measure 8–11 × 5–7 µm.

Amanita polypyramis

Amanita rhopalopus Bas

= *Amanita radicata* Peck
= *Amanita rhopalopus* f. *turbinata* Bas

COMMON NAME: American Club-footed
Lepidella.
MACROSCOPIC FEATURES: **Cap** 8–16 cm wide,
plano-convex, slightly depressed on the disc;
surface dry, cinnamon buff, with a heavy concentration of erect pyramidal warts that are
3–4 mm high with pointed tips that become
fewer and smaller toward the margin; margin
appendiculate. **Gills** free, close to crowded,
up to 15 mm wide, creamy buff, covered by
a rough, whitish to dingy whitish partial veil
when young. **Stalk** 9–21 cm long, 2–5.5 cm
wide, tapered upwards from a large, club- to
turnip-shaped basal bulb; surface dry, ragged-
scaly, dull whitish with some yellowish tints;
ring absent or sometimes apical, striate on the
upper surface, dingy whitish; volva consisting of a few wart-like scales on top of the bulb.
Flesh up to 10 mm thick, white with a yellowish tint; odor of chlorine; taste unpleasant or
not distinctive.
SPORE PRINT: White.
MICROSCOPIC FEATURES: Spores 8–11 × 5–7.5
μm, subglobose to short elliptic, smooth,
amyloid.
OCCURRENCE: Solitary, scattered, or in groups
on the ground in mixed hardwood and conifer
forests, often with beech, magnolia, oak, and
pine; summer–fall.
EDIBILITY: Unknown.
REMARKS: The large size, club- to turnip-
shaped basal bulb, and chlorine odor help
distinguish this species.

Amanita rhopalopus

Amanita roseitincta (Murrill) Murrill

= *Amanita komarekensis* D. T. Jenkins & Vinopal

COMMON NAME: Rose-tinted Amanita.

MACROSCOPIC FEATURES: **Cap** 3–7.5 cm wide, convex, becoming plano-convex with a slight umbo; surface dry to subviscid, covered with powdery to pruinose volval remnants, pale pinkish brown at first, fading to dark buff or creamy white in age; margin striate. **Gills** free, close to subdistant, 4–8 mm wide, white, covered by a pinkish-rose to salmon-colored partial veil when young. **Stalk** 10–14 cm long, 8–11 mm wide, with an enlarged ellipsoid to turnip-shaped basal bulb; surface pruinose at the apex, glabrous below, light pinkish cinnamon; ring apical, thin, pinkish rose to salmon-colored; volva pulverulent-floccose, tawny to hazel or with pale pinkish-brown to salmon tints. **Flesh** 5–8 mm thick at the disc, white with a reddish tint in the button stage; odor variously reported as fruity or resembling ham or clover; taste not distinctive.

SPORE PRINT: White.

MICROSCOPIC FEATURES: Spores 8–12 × 6–9 μm, elliptic, smooth, inamyloid.

OCCURRENCE: Solitary, scattered, or in groups on the ground in mixed pine and hardwood forests; spring–fall.

EDIBILITY: Unknown.

REMARKS: It was first described from Biloxi, Mississippi, in 1914 by Murrill. The salmon colors are striking but soon fade in bright sunlight. *Amanita daucipes* (p. 216) has similar coloration but is more massive, has a white partial veil, and has amyloid spores.

Amanita roseitincta

Amanita subcokeri Tulloss nom. prov.

COMMON NAME: False Coker's Lepidella.

MACROSCOPIC FEATURES: **Cap** 7–14 cm wide, convex, becoming broadly convex to nearly plane; surface dry, often shiny, white to cream, covered with white, cream, or grayish pyramidal warts and scales that darken to brown at their tips in age; margin decurved to incurved, non-striate, sometimes hung with partial veil fragments. **Gills** free to very narrowly attached, close to crowded, white to pale cream, covered by a white partial veil when young. **Stalk** 5.5–13 cm long, 1–2.5 cm wide, enlarged downward to a bulbous base, faintly longitudinally striate, fibrillose to satiny, white, becoming pale buff in age; bulb carrot- to spindle-shaped or dog-legged, often radicating, with coarse, recurved scales, white with reddish-brown stains; ring subapical to superior, persistent, sometimes double, strongly striate above, with white fibers that connect the underside to the stalk; volva con-sisting of indistinct rings of floccose material on the lower stalk or tips of the bulb scales. **Flesh** thick, white, unchanging, or slowly staining tan when cut or bruised; odor strong, like a combination of burnt sugar and cedar wood; taste unknown.

SPORE PRINT: White.

MICROSCOPIC FEATURES: Spores 8–14.3(-19) × 5.2–7.5(-10.9) μm, ellipsoid to elongate or cylindric, smooth, hyaline, amyloid.

OCCURRENCE: Scattered or in groups on the ground with conifers or hardwoods, especially pine and oak; late spring–fall.

EDIBILITY: Unknown.

REMARKS: Coker's Amanita, *Amanita cokeri* (not illustrated), is very similar, but the recurved scales are white and do not develop reddish-brown stains. The spores measure 9–14 × 6.4–9.3 μm. The names *Amanita cokeri* and *Amanita subcokeri* honor William Chambers Coker (1872–1953), a prominent North Carolina botanist and mycologist.

Amanita subcokeri

Amanita thiersii Bas

COMMON NAME: Thiers' Lepidella.

MACROSCOPIC FEATURES: **Cap** 3.5–21 cm wide, conical, becoming plane, sometimes with a slight umbo; surface moist, smooth or rough, with soft, felty volva material and large scales that are more pointed at the disc, white; margin appendiculate. **Gills** free, close, up to 10 mm broad, fimbriate, whitish, becoming cream in age. **Stalk** 8–21 cm long, 1–4 cm wide, slightly clavate at first but more equal with age; surface moist, covered with soft, felty, very sticky material arranged in somewhat concentric circles, white to cream; ring apical, tomentose on the bottom, barely adhering to the stalk, with cottony material under the ring on young specimens; volva broken up as fine, lace-like material from the base to the ring. **Flesh** 5–18 mm thick, white; odor strong and unpleasant; taste unpleasant or not distinctive.

SPORE PRINT: White.

MICROSCOPIC FEATURES: Spores 7.5–10.1 × 7–9 μm, globose to sublobose, smooth, hyaline, amyloid.

OCCURRENCE: On lawns and other grassy areas; summer–fall.

EDIBILITY: Unknown.

REMARKS: *Amanita thiersii* was named for Harry D. Thiers (1919–2000), who discovered it in College Station, Texas, and did pioneering work on Texas mushrooms in the 1950's. The habit of fruiting on lawns is an unusual feature for *Amanita* species. It is one of the more primitive species in this genus because it is not mycorrhizal and can decompose cellulose. The Nauseous Lepidella, *Amanita nauseosa* (not illustrated), occurs on lawns, but its 7.5–22 cm wide cap surface is covered with a yellowish-brown to orange-brown floccose layer that breaks up into concentric rings. It has white flesh with a strong odor that has been variously described as resembling an old mouse nest, stale urine, meaty, or disagreeable. It is also one of the few non-mycorrhizal *Amanita* species.

Amanita thiersii

Amanita vaginata complex (Bull.) Lam.

MACROSCOPIC FEATURES: **Cap** 4–9.5 cm, convex, becoming plane; surface glabrous, moist, grayish overall or grayish brown over the disc; margin strongly striate. **Gills** free, close, 4–5 mm broad, fimbriate, white to pale gray. **Stalk** 9.5–18 cm long, 5–11 mm broad, nearly equal, lacking a basal bulb, moist, finely fibrous, hollow, white; without a ring; volva saccate, very fragile, usually appressed to the stalk, white. **Flesh** 3–4 mm thick, white; odor and taste not distinctive.

SPORE PRINT: White.

MICROSCOPIC FEATURES: Spores 8.5–10 × 7.5–10.5 µm, globose, smooth, hyaline, inamyloid.

OCCURRENCE: On the ground with conifers, hardwoods, or in mixed woodlands; summer–early winter.

EDIBILITY: Unknown.

REMARKS: *Amanita vaginata* is a collective species concept in North America. The true *Amanita vaginata* is a European species, and the many forms found in North America are likely undescribed species.

Amanita vaginata

Amanita volvata complex (Peck) Lloyd

COMMON NAME: American Amidella.
MACROSCOPIC FEATURES: **Cap** 3.5–5.5 cm wide, convex to plano-convex; surface glabrous, moist, whitish, sometimes with a brownish disc; margin non-striate to faintly striate. **Gills** free, crowded, white. **Stalk** 4.5–7 cm long, 5–11 mm wide, tapered slightly toward the apex, stuffed, minutely floccose-scaly, white; without a ring; volva saccate, thick, membranous, lobed, white. **Flesh** thick, whitish; odor and taste not distinctive.

SPORE PRINT: White.
MICROSCOPIC FEATURES: Spores 6–14 × 4.5–9 µm, ellipsoid to elongate, smooth, amyloid.
OCCURRENCE: Solitary or in groups in damp soil in mixed conifer and hardwood forests or in hardwood river bottomlands; summer–fall.
EDIBILITY: Unknown.
REMARKS: *Amanita peckiana* (not illustrated) is similar, but it has a pinkish-white volva, and its cap typically has pinkish fibrils, squamules, and patches.

Amanita volvata

Amanita westii (Murrill) Murrill

MACROSCOPIC FEATURES: **Cap** 7.0–13.5 cm wide, convex to plano-convex, eventually plane; surface dry, covered with large, floccose pyramidal scales that are 2–4 mm high, up to 1 cm wide, denser at the disc, larger and less common towards the margin, pale reddish brown with white ground color showing in the cracks; margin appendiculate. **Gills** crowded to subdistant, adnate, up to 11 mm broad, initially white to pale grayish, becoming reddish brown to blackish purple brown when mature; edges fimbriate to almost crenate. **Stalk** 7–13 cm long, 1.5–2 cm wide, nearly equal above a subnapiform to broadly fusiform and slightly rooting bulb, dry, covered with floccose material, solid, grayish; ring apical, membranous and easily detached; volva consisting of felted patches on the lower stalk and bulb. **Flesh** up to 2 cm thick, white, quickly bruising reddish to pale reddish brown, eventually blackish; odor of anise; taste not distinctive.

SPORE PRINT: White.

MICROSCOPIC FEATURES: Spores 8.5–15.5 × 5.8–8.2 µm, elliptic, smooth, often constricted in the middle, hyaline, amyloid.

OCCURRENCE: Solitary to gregarious with post oak, hickory, and other hardwoods; summer–fall.

EDIBILITY: Unknown.

REMARKS: This rare species was originally described from Florida in 1945 and was not reported again until it was rediscovered in Eastern Texas in 1987. The large pyramidal warts and color change to red is similar to *Amanita amerirubescens* (p. 209). From a distance, it resembles a species of *Strobilomyces*. The Bruising Lepidella, *Amanita pelioma* (not illustrated), has a 4–9 cm wide, grayish-buff to creamy-buff or whitish cap with small, pyramidal or granular scales. It has creamy-buff to pale brown or cinnamon-brown gills, a pale grayish to grayish-olive stalk that stains bluish green to dark bluish green on the lower portion and base, and buff to brownish flesh with an odor of chlorine.

Amanita westii

Anthracophyllum lateritium (Berk. & M. A. Curtis) Singer

= *Plicatura lateritia* (Berk. & M. A. Curtis) Murrill

MACROSCOPIC FEATURES: **Cap** 5–25 mm wide, convex, shell- to kidney-shaped; surface dry, subtomentose to glabrous, radially wrinkled, pale reddish brown at first, becoming dark reddish brown to blackish with age; margin incurved at first, remaining so well into maturity, surpassing the gills. **Gills** strongly arched, subdistant to distant, narrow, pale rusty brown to dark reddish brown, becoming blackish in age. **Stalk** absent or rudimentary. **Flesh** thin, pale yellowish brown; odor and taste not distinctive.

SPORE PRINT: White.

MICROSCOPIC FEATURES: Spores 9.5–15 × 5.5–8 μm, oblong-ellipsoid to elongate-ellipsoid, with a tapered base, smooth, hyaline.

OCCURRENCE: In large groups or clusters on decaying hardwood trees, especially oaks; year-round.

EDIBILITY: Unknown, but hardly worthwhile.

REMARKS: The small, stalkless, and dark reddish-brown cap, gills that appear deep reddish, and tendency to grow in large clusters on hardwoods are the key identification features.

Anthracophyllum lateritium

Armillaria gallica Marxm. & Romagn.

COMMON NAME: Bulbous Honey Fungus.

MACROSCOPIC FEATURES: **Cap** 2–7 cm wide, convex at first, becoming broadly convex to nearly plane; surface dry or somewhat viscid, with erect whitish to yellowish or brownish hairs or fine brownish scales that sometimes wash off in the rain; margin often adorned with white partial veil remnants. **Gills** adnate to slightly decurrent, subdistant, whitish, usually staining pinkish to brownish when injured or in age, covered by a whitish partial veil when young. **Stalk** 4–10 cm long, 5–12 mm thick, enlarged downward to a swollen base that is often yellow, typically with a fragile, white or yellowish superior ring, sometimes longitudinally grayish striate or attached to black rhizomorphs. **Flesh** thin, whitish; odor sweet or not distinctive; taste sometimes bitter or not distinctive.

SPORE PRINT: White.

MICROSCOPIC FEATURES: Spores 7–9.5 × 4.5–6 µm, ellipsoid, smooth, hyaline, inamyloid.

OCCURRENCE: Solitary, scattered, or in small groups on the ground, attached to roots or sometimes at the base of hardwood trees or stumps, occasionally on conifers; late summer–winter.

EDIBILITY: Edible but sometimes bitter when not thoroughly cooked.

REMARKS: Solitary to scattered growth on the ground and a swollen, yellowish stalk base are good field identification features. It is a pathogen associated with Armillaria root disease. *Armillaria mellea* (p. 239) has a honey-yellow cap, grows in dense clusters on wood, and typically occurs during fall.

Armillaria gallica

Armillaria mellea (Vahl) P. Kumm.

COMMON NAMES: Honey Mushroom, Boot-lace Fungus.

MACROSCOPIC FEATURES: **Cap** 4–15 cm wide, convex with slight umbo at first, becoming nearly plane or somewhat depressed at the center; surface moist to viscid when wet, covered with erect scales radiating from the disc and denser at the center, honey yellow with a darker center or grayish orange to yellowish brown. **Gills** adnate-decurrent, close, up to 8 mm broad, white, developing reddish-brown stains with age, covered by a whitish to yellowish partial veil when young. **Stalk** 5–15 cm long, 6–15 mm wide, clavate to clavate-bulbous, often with a pinched base; surface moist, fibrillose, tomentose at the base, apex whitish, grayish yellow below; ring apical and becoming appressed on the upper stalk, cottony. **Flesh** up to 12 mm thick, white; odor and taste not distinctive.

SPORE PRINT: Pale cream.

MICROSCOPIC FEATURES: Spores 8.5–12 × 6–7 μm, broadly elliptic to oval, smooth, hyaline, inamyloid.

OCCURRENCE: In groups or large clusters on conifer or hardwood trunks or stumps; fall.

EDIBILITY: Edible and good but make certain it is cooked well.

REMARKS: It is a potent forest pathogen and is spread by black, "boot-lace" rhizomorphs that are often seen under the bark of decaying trees. *Desarmillaria tabescens* (p. 271) is similar but lacks a ring on its stalk. *Armillaria gallica* (p. 238) has a pinkish-brown to reddish-brown cap with erect yellowish or brownish hairs or fine scales that sometimes wash off in the rain. The margin is sometimes adorned with white remnants of the partial veil. The stalk is enlarged downward to a yellowish club-shaped base, which may have black rhizomorphs. It has a thin, fibrous partial veil that leaves a white or yellowish ring zone on the stalk. It grows in small groups on the ground, attached to buried roots or at the base of dead hardwoods during late summer through winter.

Armillaria mellea

Asterophora lycoperdoides (Bull.) Ditmar

COMMON NAME: Star-bearing Powder Cap.

MACROSCOPIC FEATURES: **Cap** 1–2 cm wide, rounded to convex; surface dry, cottony at first, becoming thickly covered with brown powder. **Gills** attached, thick and malformed, distant, often forked, white to pale gray or beige. **Stalk** 2–5 cm long, 3–10 mm thick, equal, smooth or silky, white to pale brownish, stuffed, becoming hollow in age, lacking a partial veil. **Flesh** thin, white; odor and taste farinaceous.

SPORE PRINT: White, sometimes difficult to obtain.

MICROSCOPIC FEATURES: Spores of two types—basidiospores (sexual spores) 5–6 × 3–4 μm, elliptic, smooth, hyaline, inamyloid; clamydospores (asexual spores) 13–20 × 10–20 μm excluding spines or warts, pale brown, inamyloid.

OCCURRENCE: In clusters on the caps of decaying mushrooms, especially *Russula* and *Lactarius* species; summer–fall.

EDIBILITY: Unknown.

REMARKS: The chlamydospores resemble microscopic stars. *Asterophora parasitica* (not illustrated) parasitizes the same hosts. It has darker brownish, less deformed gills and a cap that does not become powdery at maturity.

Asterophora lycoperdoides

Baeospora myosura (Fr.) Singer

COMMON NAME: Conifer-cone Baeospora.
MACROSCOPIC FEATURES: **Cap** 5–20 mm wide, convex; surface moist, smooth, cinnamon to pale tan. **Gills** attached, crowded, narrow, white. **Stalk** 1–5 cm long, 1–2 mm wide, minutely hairy on the upper portion, with longer hairs at the base, hollow, whitish to brownish. **Flesh** thin, white; odor and taste not distinctive.
SPORE PRINT: White.
MICROSCOPIC FEATURES: Spores 3–4.5 × 1–2.5 μm, elliptic, smooth, hyaline, amyloid.

OCCURRENCE: In groups on conifer cones, especially pines; summer–winter.
EDIBILITY: Unknown, hardly worthwhile.
REMARKS: The restricted habitat on conifer cones, small stature, and amyloid spores are good identification features. Other species, like *Gymnopilus penetrans* (p. 284) and *Gymnopilus sapineus* (pp. 14, 284), may also grow on conifer cones, but they have a yellow to orange-yellow cap and an orange-brown spore print.

Baeospora myosura

Bolbitius titubans (Bull.) Fr.

= *Bolbitius variicolor* G. F. Atk.
= *Bolbitius vitellinus* (Pers.) Fr.

COMMON NAME: Yellow Bolbitius.
MACROSCOPIC FEATURES: **Cap** 1–7 cm wide, conical at first, becoming nearly plane in age, often with a broad umbo; surface slimy, egg-yolk to greenish yellow when fresh, fading to grayish or pale tan and sometimes retaining a yellowish disc; margin conspicuously striate to the disc at maturity. **Gills** free or narrowly attached, whitish to pale yellow at first, becoming brown at maturity, sometimes gelatinous in wet weather. **Stalk** 3–12 cm long, up to 1 cm thick, equal, hollow and fragile, slightly viscid, scurfy, pale yellow. **Flesh** thin, yellowish; odor and taste not distinctive.

SPORE PRINT: Rusty brown.
MICROSCOPIC FEATURES: Spores 11–15 × 6–8 μm, elliptic, with an apical pore, smooth, brownish yellow.
OCCURRENCE: Solitary, scattered, or in groups on dung, grass, compost, or woodchips; spring–late fall.
EDIBILITY: Edible.
REMARKS: *Titubans* means "fragile and faltering," a reference to the stalk. The caps of similar species of *Conocybe* are not slimy. *Bolbitius reticulatus* (not illustrated) has a viscid to slimy, purple to lilac-gray, striate cap and grows on hardwood logs and woodchips.

Bolbitius titubans

Callistosporium luteo-olivaceum
(Berk. & M. A. Curtis) Singer

= *Callistosporium luteofuscum* Singer
= *Collybia luteo-olivacea* (Berk. & M. A. Curtis) Sacc.

MACROSCOPIC FEATURES: **Cap** 1.5–3 cm wide, convex to broadly convex, becoming plane to plano-convex; surface moist or dry, dull, glabrous, dark olive to olive brown or olive yellow when young, becoming more yellow as it matures. **Gills** adnate with a short decurrent tooth, close, narrow, pale yellow when young, becoming dark yellow, sometimes with reddish tints, drying deep vinaceous. **Stalk** 3.5–5 cm long, 2–4 mm wide, tapering toward the apex, hollow; surface moist, glabrous, and becoming obscurely fibrillose when older, colored like the gills, with a white tomentum at the base. **Flesh** thin, 2–3 mm, soft, colored like the cap or paler; odor not distinctive; taste disagreeable and bitter.

SPORE PRINT: White.
MICROSCOPIC FEATURES: Spores 3–4.5 × 2.5–3 µm, obscurely ovoid to ellipsoid, smooth, thin-walled, hyaline, often with reddish pigments in oil drops or near the wall.
OCCURRENCE: Scattered or in groups on well-decayed conifer logs and stumps, rarely on hardwoods; spring–fall.
EDIBILITY: Unknown.
REMARKS: *Callistosporium purpureomarginatum* (not illustrated) has a reddish-purple cap with a thin, violet to blackish band at the margin, reddish-purple marginate gills, and grows on decaying hardwoods, especially oak, during summer and fall. The cap surface produces a pinkish red reaction with KOH.

allistosporium luteo-olivaceum

Chlorophyllum hortense (Murrill) Vellinga

= *Chlorophyllum humei* (Murrill) Vellinga
= *Lepiota hortensis* Murrill
= *Lepiota humei* Murrill
= *Leucoagaricus hortensis* (Murrill) Pegler

MACROSCOPIC FEATURES: **Cap** 4–10 cm wide, ovoid when young, becoming broadly convex to nearly plane with a persistent umbo; surface dry, fibrillose to finely scaly, brownish yellow on the disc, becoming dingy cream-colored to light buff outward toward the margin; margin rounded, typically striate, eroded or split in age; scales somewhat concentrically arranged, whitish to light brown; **flesh** thin, soft, whitish, staining vinaceous brown on exposure; odor and taste not distinctive. **Gills** attached when young, becoming free at maturity, crowded, white; edges entire. **Stalk** 4–7 cm long, 3–6 mm thick, nearly equal down to a somewhat enlarged base, solid, hollow in age; surface dry, smooth, glabrous, and white above the ring, fibrillose and brownish below, staining dark vinaceous red then brown when bruised; partial veil submembranous, leaving a white ring with a brown double edge.

SPORE PRINT: White.

MICROSCOPIC FEATURES: 8–10 × 6–7 μm, ellipsoid, smooth, hyaline, dextrinoid.

OCCURRENCE: Scattered or in groups in gardens, lawns, on manure, and in open areas in mixed oak and pine woods; summer–early winter.

EDIBILITY: Unknown.

REMARKS: *Leucoagaricus meleagris* (p. 358) has a smaller cap, up to 5.5 cm wide, with a dark brown disc and a spindle-shaped stalk with a tapered base that is anchored by a branching mass of white to grayish mycelial strands. *Lepiota phaeostictiformis* (not illustrated) has a very small cap, 1–3 cm wide, with blackish scales and a blackish disc on a white ground color, a 1.5–3 mm thick stalk, and grows on decaying wood and leaf litter.

Chlorophyllum hortense

Chlorophyllum molybdites (G. Mey.) Massee

= *Lepiota molybdites* (G. Mey.) Sacc.

COMMON NAME: Green-spored Lepiota.

MACROSCOPIC FEATURES: **Cap** 7–30 cm wide, round at first, becoming convex to broadly convex, often with a broad umbo; surface dry, white, covered with large pinkish-brown to cinnamon patches when young that become scale-like in age, usually clustered toward the disc. **Gills** free, close, up to 13 mm broad, white, becoming greenish. **Stalk** up to 25 cm long, 1–2.5 cm wide, nearly equal or slightly larger at the base; surface glabrous to somewhat fibrillose, hollow, white turning grayish brown and staining dark reddish brown with age; ring apical, movable, ample, colored like the cap. **Flesh** 8–11 mm thick, soft, white, bruising brownish red; odor and taste not distinctive.

SPORE PRINT: Green to grayish green.

MICROSCOPIC FEATURES: Spores 9–13 × 6–9 μm, subovoid to elliptic, with an apical pore and thickened walls, smooth, hyaline, dextrinoid.

OCCURRENCE: Scattered, in groups, or fairy rings in grassy areas, especially irrigated areas; summer–early winter.

EDIBILITY: Poisonous, causing severe gastrointestinal upsets.

REMARKS: It is one of the most common summer mushrooms found on lawns in the Gulf Coast region and one of the most frequent causes of serious mushroom poisoning in eastern North America. Hospitalization is often required to prevent acute, life-threatening dehydration.

Chlorophyllum molybdites

Chlorophyllum subrhacodes (Murrill) Vellinga

= *Macrolepitota subrhacodes* (Murrill) Akers
= *Lepiota subrhacodes* Murrill

MACROSCOPIC FEATURES: **Cap** 7–10 cm wide, egg-shaped to nearly round at first, soon bell-shaped, then becoming nearly flat with an umbo at maturity; surface dry, prominently scaly with scales concentrated on the disc, with a white to cream ground color beneath the brown scales; **flesh** thick, whitish, staining orange to reddish when bruised or exposed, especially in the stalk base; odor and taste not distinctive. **Gills** free, close to crowded, white, becoming brownish in age. **Stalk** 6–13 cm long, 7–15 mm thick, slender, tapered upward from a bulbous base, hollow at maturity; surface dry, pale grayish with a pinkish tint, staining brownish when bruised; partial veil thick, white, leaving a prominent, movable, double-edged superior ring.

SPORE PRINT: White.
MICROSCOPIC FEATURES: Spores 7–11 × 5–6.3 µm, ovoid to almond-shaped, with a distinct germ pore, smooth, hyaline, dextrinoid.
OCCURRENCE: Solitary or scattered in woods, usually associated with oaks; summer–early winter.
EDIBILITY: Edible.
REMARKS: *Chlorophyllum molybdites* (p. 245) has gills that turn dull green when mature and a grayish-green spore print.

Chlorophyllum subrhacodes

Clitopilus prunulus (Scop.) P. Kumm.

COMMON NAMES: Sweetbread Mushroom, the Miller.

MACROSCOPIC FEATURES: **Cap** 3–12 cm wide, convex to nearly flat or sunken in the center; surface dry, felt-like, whitish to grayish, with an inrolled margin that becomes wavy and irregular in age. **Gills** decurrent, close, white, becoming pinkish with age. **Stalk** 2.5–7.5 cm long, 3–15 mm wide, often somewhat eccentric; surface dry, dull white to pale grayish. **Flesh** firm, white; odor and taste farinaceous.

SPORE PRINT: Salmon-pink.

MICROSCOPIC FEATURES: Spores 9–12 × 4–7 µm, elliptic with longitudinal ridges in profile, appearing angular in end view, hyaline, inamyloid.

OCCURRENCE: Solitary or in small groups in mixed forests; summer–fall.

EDIBILITY: Edible with caution.

REMARKS: The whitish to grayish cap, decurrent gills, farinaceous odor, and salmon spore print help distinguish this species.

Clitopilus prunulus

Conocybe apala (Fr.) Arnolds

= *Conocybe albipes* Hauskn.
= *Conocybe lactea* (J. E. Lange) Métrod

COMMON NAMES: White Dunce Cap, White Cone Head.

MACROSCOPIC FEATURES: Cap 1–3 cm wide, conical, becoming bell-shaped, often with a flaring edge when mature; surface dry, white to pale tan or slightly darker at the center; margin radially wrinkled or striate; **flesh** thin, white; odor and taste not distinctive. **Gills** nearly free, close, white at first, becoming brown at maturity. **Stalk** 4–10 cm long, 1–3 mm thick, slightly enlarged downward to a small basal bulb, hollow, extremely fragile, white.

SPORE PRINT: Reddish brown.

MICROSCOPIC FEATURES: Spores 10–14 × 6–9 μm, elliptic, with a truncated end and an apical pore, smooth, pale brown.

OCCURRENCE: In groups on lawns and other grassy areas; spring–late fall, sometimes year-round.

EDIBILITY: Edible, but not recommended due to possible confusion with deadly poisonous *Conocybe* species.

REMARKS: This mushroom is most commonly observed in the morning and often disappears by noon. It is particularly common in irrigated areas. *Conocybe tenera* (p. 14) has a reddish-brown to rusty or fulvous cap that fades to pale tawny or ochraceous and usually grows in woods or rich humus in gardens, lawns, fields, and fertilized areas.

Conocybe apala

Coprinellus disseminatus (Pers.) J. E. Lange

= *Coprinus disseminatus* (Pers.) Gray
= *Coprinus floridanus* Murrill

COMMON NAME: Fairy Inkcap.
MACROSCOPIC FEATURES: **Cap** 6–20 mm wide at maturity, egg-shaped at first, becoming bell-shaped or convex in age; surface dry, finely hairy or with shiny granules at first, later smooth with deep radial grooves and a scalloped margin; color variable from almost white with a yellowish-brown center to gray brown with a brown center. **Gills** free or attached, nearly distant, pale then black but not dissolving. **Stalk** 1.3–4 cm long, 1–2 mm thick, nearly equal, hollow, white or gray, smooth; base has downy or stiff white hairs; partial veil absent. **Flesh** very thin, whitish; odor and taste not distinctive.

SPORE PRINT: Black.
MICROSCOPIC FEATURES: Spores 7–10 × 4–5 μm, elliptic, with an apical pore, smooth; blackish.
OCCURRENCE: In clusters on decaying logs or stumps or at the base of living trees; year-round.
EDIBILITY: Edible, but insubstantial.
REMARKS: Most other species of Inky Caps have gills that dissolve when mature.

Coprinellus disseminatus

Coprinopsis lagopus (Fr.) Redhead, Vilgalys & Moncalvo

= Coprinus lagopus (Fr.) Fr.

COMMON NAME: Woolly-stalked Coprinus.
MACROSCOPIC FEATURES: **Cap** 1–5 cm wide, oval to elliptic at first, becoming convex to nearly plane at maturity; surface covered with a dense coating of erect to recurved, white to grayish white, cottony fibers or scales, which gradually disappear in age, white at first, becoming grayish then finally black, usually with a brown disc, often persisting, becoming shallowly fissured then deeply sulcate at maturity; margin often split and sometimes revolute in age; **flesh** grayish to black; odor and taste not distinctive. **Gills** attached at first, soon free, close, white at first, becoming gray then black as the mushroom deliquesces. **Stalk** 4–10 cm long, 1.5–4 mm wide, nearly equal or slightly enlarged downward, hollow at maturity; surface dry, floccose at first, becoming smooth in age, white.
SPORE PRINT: Violaceous black.
MICROSCOPIC FEATURES: Spores 10–13 × 6–7 μm, ellipsoid to almond-shaped, smooth, violaceous brown.
OCCURRENCE: Solitary, scattered, or in groups on woodchips, sawdust, or other woody debris; summer–fall.
EDIBILITY: Unknown.
REMARKS: *Coprinopsis lagopides* (not illustrated) is similar and usually found on burned soil, wood, or humus, has smaller subglobose to ovoid spores that measure 6–9 × 5–7 μm, and deliquesces more quickly.

Coprinopsis lagopus

Coprinus comatus (O. F. Müll.) Pers.

COMMON NAME: Shaggy Mane.
MACROSCOPIC FEATURES: **Cap** 4–10 cm wide, cylindrical at first, becoming widely conic to nearly plane in age; surface very shaggy-scaly, often with a yellowish-brown disc and scattered brownish scales, otherwise white; margin slowly dissolves away until the entire cap, including the gills, has deliquesced; **flesh** soft, fibrous, white; odor and taste not distinctive. **Gills** free, crowded, very narrow, white, becoming black and inky. **Stalk** 5–12.5 cm long, 10–20 mm wide, tall and straight with a slightly bulbous base, hollow; surface smooth with a ring of veil tissue on the lower portion, white.

SPORE PRINT: Black.
MICROSCOPIC FEATURES: Spores 10–14 × 6–8.5 µm, ellipsoid, truncate with an apical pore, smooth, purple brown.
OCCURRENCE: Scattered or in groups or clusters in grassy areas, on soil, and in woodchips; year-round.
EDIBILITY: Edible, but must be collected before it deliquesces.
REMARKS: *Coprinus sterquilinus* (not illustrated) is a smaller, white to whitish mushroom that grows on dung or manured soil; it has larger spores that measure 16–22 × 10–13 µm. Compare with *Coprinus americanus* (not illustrated), which has a silvery-gray cap when young and fresh and smaller spores that measure 7.5–9 × 5–6 µm.

Coprinus comatus

Cortinarius albidus Peck

= *Phlegmacium albidum* (Peck) M. M. Moser

MACROSCOPIC FEATURES: Cap 5–10 cm wide, convex, then expanded; surface glabrous, with a separable, viscid cuticle, white or whitish, shiny when dry; **flesh** thick, white; odor and taste not distinctive. **Gills** adnexed-emarginate, moderately wide, close, white at first, then pale brown to pinkish cinnamon; edges even. **Stalk** 5–8 cm long, 8–16 mm wide, solid; surface fibrillose from the cortina, with an oblique, marginate-depressed bulb, white, attached to white mycelium; cortina copious, white.

SPORE PRINT: Rusty brown.

MICROSCOPIC FEATURES: Spores 9–11 × 5–6.5 μm, elliptic, slightly roughened, brown.

OCCURRENCE: Scattered or in groups on the ground in hardwoods or mixed woods; late summer–early winter.

EDIBILITY: Unknown.

REMARKS: The white cap and stalk, viscid cuticle, and oblique, marginate-depressed bulb are good field identification characters.

Cortinarius albidus

Cortinarius alboviolaceus (Pers.) Fr.

= *Agaricus alboviolaceus* Pers.

COMMON NAME: Silvery-violet Cort.
MACROSCOPIC FEATURES: **Cap** 3–9.5 cm
wide, bell-shaped at first, becoming convex
to nearly flat in age, with a low, wide umbo;
surface dry, shiny, silky, coated with flattened,
silvery fibrils, pale violet to lilac buff; margin
incurved when young and remaining so long
into maturity; **flesh** pale violet; odor and
taste not distinctive. **Gills** attached, close,
wide, pale violet to grayish lilac when young,
becoming cinnamon brown in age; edges
sometimes eroded. **Stalk** 4–12 cm long, 5–10
mm wide above, up to 2 cm wide at or near
the clavate base, dry, stuffed, colored like the
cap; partial veil cortinate, white, leaving a thin,
fibrous annular zone, sheathed from the base
up to the annular zone by a silky, white veil.

SPORE PRINT: Rusty brown.
MICROSCOPIC FEATURES: Spores 6.5–10 × 4–6
µm, elliptic-oval to narrowly-elliptic, finely
roughened, pale brown.
OCCURRENCE: Solitary or in groups on the
ground with conifers or hardwoods; fall–early
winter.
EDIBILITY: Reported to be edible, but not
recommended.
REMARKS: *Cortinarius obliquus* (not illustrated)
has an abruptly bulbous base that is set at an
oblique angle to the stalk. *Cortinarius iodes*
(p. 261) has a viscid, lilac to purplish cap with
yellow spots and a viscid, white stalk. *Lepista
nuda* (p. 353) is similar in color, lacks a veil,
and has a pinkish-buff spore print.

Cortinarius alboviolaceus

Cortinarius argentatus (Pers.) Fr.

= *Agaricus argentatus* Pers.

MACROSCOPIC FEATURES: **Cap** 5–9 cm wide, bell-shaped then broadly convex; surface dry, silky, silver violet, with brown tints in age; **flesh** white to pale violet, unchanging when exposed; odor not distinctive or radish-like; taste not distinctive. **Gills** attached, close, initially purple, becoming rusty brown. **Stalk** 5–8 cm long, up to 1 cm thick at the apex, club-shaped with a fat basal bulb, pale violet, lacking a sheath below the ring zone; partial veil a whitish cortina that becomes rusty at maturity.

SPORE PRINT: Rusty brown.
MICROSCOPIC FEATURES: Spores 7–9.5 × 5–6 μm, elliptic, slightly roughened, pale brown.
OCCURRENCE: Solitary or in groups under hardwoods, especially oaks, or in mixed woods; summer–fall.
REMARKS: The stalk of *Cortinarius alboviolaceus* (p. 253) is sheathed from the base up to the annular zone by a silky, white veil. *Cortinarius obliquus* (not illustrated) has an abruptly bulbous base that is set at an oblique angle to the stalk.

Cortinarius argentatus

Cortinarius atkinsonianus Kauffman

MACROSCOPIC FEATURES: **Cap** 6–9 cm wide, convex then flattening; surface smooth, sticky, often yellow at first but developing a mottling of olive and/or tawny tones, eventually becoming reddish brown; **flesh** violet, fading by maturity; odor and taste not distinctive. **Gills** attached, initially violet, sometimes with greenish-yellow edges, soon turning rusty. **Stalk** 6–8 cm long, 12–18 mm thick at the apex, enlarging downward to a bulb that may be flattened or rimmed, violet but may show yellowish fibrils as well, colors unchanging when bruised; partial veil a greenish-yellow cortina.

SPORE PRINT: Rusty cinnamon.

MICROSCOPIC FEATURES: Spores 13–16 × 7–8.5 μm, almond-shaped to elliptic, rough, pale brown.

OCCURRENCE: Solitary or in groups among fallen leaves in hardwoods or mixed woods; fall.

EDIBILITY: Edible but not recommended due to possible confusion with other purplish *Cortinarius* species.

REMARKS: *Atkinsonianus* honors American botanist and mycologist George F. Atkinson (1854–1918).

Cortinarius atkinsonianus

Cortinarius atrotomentosus
Harrower

MACROSCOPIC FEATURES: Cap 2.6–9.1 cm wide, convex; surface dry, tomentose to fine scaly, dark violet to dark brown with age; **flesh** purple gray to reddish brown; odor and taste not distinctive. **Gills** adnexed, close to subdistant, dark violet. **Stalk** 7.5–13.1 cm long, 8–26 mm wide, ventricose; surface silky-glabrous, olive brown to brownish grey with age, basal mycelium lilac to grayish magenta.
SPORE PRINT: Rusty brown.

MICROSCOPIC FEATURES: Spores 9–14 × 6–8 μm, ellipsoid to amygdaloid, strongly verrucose, pale brown.
OCCURRENCE: To date, it is known only from the Apalachicola National Forest near Crawfordville, Florida, and from the Ordway-Swisher Biological Station, Hawthorne, Florida; late fall.
EDIBILITY: Unknown.
REMARKS: *Cortinaius violaceus* (p. 265) has smaller spores, the context is mauve rather than violet to grayish, and it occurs with conifers or hardwoods.

Cortinarius atrotomentosus

Cortinarius aureifolius Peck

= *Dermocybe aureifolia* (Peck) M. M. Moser

MACROSCOPIC FEATURES: **Cap** 1–4 cm wide, convex to bell-shaped at first, becoming nearly plane at maturity, often with a depressed center; surface dry, densely fibrillose-tomentose, sometimes scaly, especially on the disc, cinnamon brown or darker; **flesh** thin, yellowish brown or pallid; odor radish-like; taste not distinctive. **Gills** attached, subventricose, close, yellow then rusty cinnamon. **Stalk** 3–6 cm long, 3–6 mm wide, nearly equal, rather short, solid, surface fibrillose, yellow.

SPORE PRINT: Ochraceous cinnamon.

MICROSCOPIC FEATURES: Spores 10–12.5 × 4–6 μm, oblong, smooth, pale brown.

OCCURRENCE: In sandy areas with oaks and pines; late fall–winter.

EDIBILITY: Unknown.

REMARKS: This species resembles *Cortinarius cinnamoneus* (p. 259) in color, but its short stalk, longer spores, and different habitat easily distinguish it. Its general appearance is similar to some species of *Inocybe*.

Cortinarius aureifolius

Cortinarius caperatus (Pers.) Fr.

= *Rozites caperatus* (Pers.) P. Karst.

COMMON NAME: Gypsy.

MACROSCOPIC FEATURES: **Cap** 5–15 cm wide, egg-shaped, becoming broadly convex with a low umbo; surface moist or dry, usually slightly wrinkled, initially coated with a thin whitish bloom over a ground color of pale yellow to yellowish brown or orange brown, the whitish bloom persisting longest at the center of the cap; **flesh** white to yellowish; odor and taste not distinctive. **Gills** attached, close, pale yellow then rusty. **Stalk** 5–13 cm long, up to 2.5 cm thick, equal or enlarged downward, whitish to pale brown, scurfy above the ring; partial veil membranous, white, leaving a thick, white superior ring.

SPORE PRINT: Rusty brown.

MICROSCOPIC FEATURES: Spores 9–14 × 7–9 µm, almond-shaped, slightly roughened, pale brown.

OCCURRENCE: Scattered or in groups on the ground with conifers or hardwoods; summer–early winter.

EDIBILITY: Edible.

REMARKS: The membranous partial veil is unusual in this genus, as is the whitish bloom on the cap. Be certain of your identification before considering the Gypsy as food.

Cortinarius caperatus

Cortinarius cinnamomeus (L.) Fr.

= *Dermocybe cinnamomea* (L.) Wünsche

MACROSCOPIC FEATURES: **Cap** 1.5–6 cm wide, bell-shaped to convex, obtuse to subumbonate, the umbo often vanishing; surface silky or minutely and densely scaly from the innate or appressed, yellowish fibrils, shiny, yellowish cinnamon to yellowish tawny; **flesh** thin, pale greenish yellow or straw-yellow, rarely deep yellow; odor and taste not distinctive. **Gills** adnate, varying to adnexed-emarginate or scarcely subdecurrent, rather wide, close, yellow to greenish yellow or brownish yellow. **Stalk** 2.5–10 cm long, 3–10 mm wide, equal, often flexuous, stuffed, becoming hollow in age; surface fibrillose, yellow to greenish yellow when fresh, darker after handling, attached to a yellow mycelium; cortina fibrillose, greenish yellow.

SPORE PRINT: Rusty brown.
MICROSCOPIC FEATURES: Spores 6–7.5 × 4–4.5 µm, short, elliptic, smooth, pale brown.
OCCURRENCE: Found in pine uplands with scattered hardwoods; fall–winter.
EDIBILITY: Unknown.
REMARKS: *Cortinarius semisanguineus* (p. 264) is similar but has blood-red gills. *Cortinarius aureifolius* (p. 257) has a shorter stalk and longer spores.

ortinarius cinnamomeus

Cortinarius corrugatus Peck

COMMON NAMES: Wrinkled Cort, Corrugated Cort.

MACROSCOPIC FEATURES: **Cap** 3–10 cm wide, initially bell-shaped but becoming broadly convex, usually with a low umbo; surface sticky and radially wrinkled, color variable, yellowish brown with orange tints or dull orange brown to reddish brown; **flesh** white, staining yellowish when exposed; odor and taste not distinctive. **Gills** attached, close, pale lilac gray at first, then rusty. **Stalk** 5–12 cm long, up to 2 cm thick, whitish and often fibrillose or scurfy at the apex, tawny to pale brown below, nearly equal above a small bulb that is often ringed with slime; partial veil a cortina leaving little or no trace on the stalk.

SPORE PRINT: Rusty brown.

MICROSCOPIC FEATURES: Spores 10–15 × 7–10 µm, broadly elliptic, very rough-tuberculate, pale brown.

OCCURRENCE: Scattered or in groups in mixed pine and hardwood forests; summer–fall.

EDIBILITY: Unknown.

REMARKS: *Psathyrella delineata* (p. 15) has a reddish-brown to orange-brown cap that is conspicuously radially grooved and wrinkled. It has a white partial veil that does not leave a ring, its spores measure 6.5–9 × 4.5–5.5 µm, and it grows on decaying hardwoods. *Psathyrella rugocephala* (not illustrated) is very similar and also grows on decaying wood, but it has larger spores that measure 9–11 × 6–8 µm.

Cortinarius corrugatus

Cortinarius iodes Berk. & M. A. Curtis

= *Cortinarius heliotropicus* Peck

COMMON NAMES: Viscid Violet Cort, Spotted Cort.

MACROSCOPIC FEATURES: **Cap** 3–12 cm wide, convex, becoming plane with a depressed disc; surface viscid, smooth, dark lilac to purplish with yellow spots or streaks; **flesh** up to 3 mm thick, white to pale violet; odor radish-like; taste not distinctive. **Gills** adnate to subdecurrent, subdistant, moderately broad, purplish at first, becoming rusty brown. **Stalk** 4–12 cm long, 10–25 mm wide, somewhat clavate; surface viscid, smooth, white with purplish blotches; cortina a fibrillose zone near the apex.

SPORE PRINT: Rusty brown.

MICROSCOPIC FEATURES: Spores 9–10.6 × 6–7.1 µm, ellipsoid, roughened, thick-walled, pale brown.

OCCURRENCE: Scattered or in groups on the ground with hardwoods, usually in low, moist areas; fall.

EDIBILITY: Unknown.

REMARKS: The sticky cap surface is mild tasting. *Cortinarius iodeoides* (not illustrated) has smaller spores that measure 7–8 × 4–5 µm, and its sticky cap tastes bitter. Also compare with *Cortinarius alboviolaceus* (p. 253), which has a dry cap and clavate stalk base.

Cortinarius iodes

Cortinarius lewisii O. K. Miller

MACROSCOPIC FEATURES: **Cap** 2.5–7.5 cm wide, becoming widely convex to nearly plane at maturity, with a broad umbo when mature; surface dry, with tiny appressed squamules, bright orange yellow to yellow; margin incurved at first, yellow to apricot yellow; **flesh** firm, deep buff; odor musky to radish-like; taste not distinctive. **Gills** notched to narrowly attached, close, narrow, whitish at first, becoming yellowish, and finally rusty brown at maturity. **Stalk** 4–10 cm long, 3–12 mm wide, nearly equal or somewhat enlarged downward; surface dry, fibrillose, white to creamy white, with white basal mycelium; partial veil dense, white in the button stage but soon yellow, leaving a bright yellow ring near the apex that typically becomes one to several partial or complete, yellow, annular ring zones on mature specimens.

SPORE PRINT: Rusty brown.

MICROSCOPIC FEATURES: Spores 6–7.5 × 5–6 μm, subglobose to globose, warted, pale brown.

OCCURRENCE: Scattered or in groups in mixed pine and hardwood forests, usually near bay-gall communities; spring–fall.

EDIBILITY: Unknown.

REMARKS: The dry, minutely squamulose, yellowish cap and whitish stalk with yellow ring zones are good field identification characters. It was named for Texas mycologist and coauthor of this book David Lewis, who discovered it in the 1970s.

Cortinarius lewisii

Cortinarius marylandensis (Ammirati) Ammirati, Niskanen & Liimat.

= *Dermocybe marylandensis* Ammirati

MACROSCOPIC FEATURES: **Cap** 1–6 cm wide, bell-shaped, becoming broadly convex or flat with a low umbo; surface dry, silky smooth to finely hairy, orange red to brownish red; **flesh** yellowish or pinkish; odor and taste radish-like or not distinctive. **Gills** attached, subdistant, brownish red before turning rusty at maturity. **Stalk** 2–7 cm long, up to 1.5 cm thick, equal, colored like the cap, with a thin, fibrous ring zone; partial veil a red cortina; flesh colored like the cap flesh and reddening toward the base.

SPORE PRINT: Rusty brown.
MICROSCOPIC FEATURES: Spores 7.5–9 × 4–5 μm, elliptic, slightly roughened, pale brown.
OCCURRENCE: Scattered or in groups on the ground with hardwoods, sometimes common in hardwood bottomland forests; spring–fall.
EDIBILITY: Unknown.
REMARKS: The cap surface stains rose then purplish with the application of KOH. The very similar *Cortinarius sanguineus* (not illustrated) is associated with conifers, and its cap produces a red reaction with KOH. *Cortinarius hesleri* (not illustrated) has a bright reddish-orange cap, gills, and stalk, and slightly larger, coarsely ornamented spores that measure 7.5–10.2 × 4.8–6.6 μm.

Cortinarius marylandensis

Cortinarius semisanguineus (Fr.) Gillet

= *Cortinarius cinnamomeus* f. *semisanguineus* (Fr.) Sacc.
= *Dermocybe semisanguinea* (Fr.) M. M. Moser

COMMON NAME: Red-gilled Cort.

MACROSCOPIC FEATURES: **Cap** 1.5–7 cm wide, conical to bell-shaped, becoming convex to plane, with a low, broad umbo; surface moist or dry, appressed-fibrillose to fibrillose-scaly, sometimes rimose on the disc, yellow brown to cinnamon buff, darker over the disc in age; margin incurved at first; **flesh** solid, firm, whitish to yellowish; odor not distinctive; taste not distinctive or slightly bitter. **Gills** adnate to adnexed or emarginate, close to somewhat crowded, up to 9 mm broad, dull red to blood red or rusty brown. **Stalk** 2.5–8 cm long, 3–15 mm broad, more or less equal; surface appressed-fibrillose, pale yellow to dull yellow or colored like the cap, becoming olivaceous in age; cortina yellowish, evanescent.

SPORE PRINT: Rusty brown.

MICROSCOPIC FEATURES: Spores 5.5–12 × 4–6 μm, elliptic, roughened with small to moderate warts, pale brown.

OCCURRENCE: Scattered or in groups on the ground under pines; fall–winter.

EDIBILITY: Unknown.

REMARKS: It is commonly collected for dyeing silk and wool. *Cortinarius cinnamomeus* (p. 259) is similar, but it has yellow gills.

Cortinarius semisanguineus

Cortinarius violaceus (L.) Gray

= *Agaricus violaceus* L.

COMMON NAME: Violet Cort.

MACROSCOPIC FEATURES: **Cap** 5–12 cm broad, convex, becoming broadly convex to nearly plane, with or without a small umbo; surface dry, covered with fibers that form minute, erect tufts or scales, especially over the disc, dark violet to purple; margin incurved when young, expanded in age; **flesh** rather thick, dark violet to grayish; odor and taste not distinctive. **Gills** adnate, subdistant, broad, dark violet at first, becoming grayish cinnamon brown. **Stalk** 7–14 cm long, 1–2.5 cm thick, enlarged downward to a club-shaped base, solid; surface dry, covered with tiny, matted fibrils, dark violet to purplish; partial veil cortinate, violet, leaving a thin, fibrous annular zone.

SPORE PRINT: Rusty brown.

MICROSCOPIC FEATURES: Spores 12–17 × 8–10 μm, elliptic, roughened with warts, pale brown.

OCCURRENCE: Solitary or in groups under conifers; fall–winter.

EDIBILITY: Reportedly edible, but not recommended.

REMARKS: *Cortinarius atrotomentosus* (p. 256) is very similar, but it has mauve flesh, smaller spores, and grows with Live Oak rather than conifers.

Cortinarius violaceus

Crepidotus applanatus (Pers.) P. Kumm.

COMMON NAME: Flat Crep.

MACROSCOPIC FEATURES: **Cap** 1–4 cm broad, shell- or fan-shaped, relatively thin in profile; surface moist, smooth, sometimes finely hairy near the point of attachment, white when young, becoming pale brown when mature, hygrophanous; margin often striate. **Gills** attached, close or crowded, narrow, radiating from the attachment point, colored like the cap. **Stalk** absent. **Flesh** thin, watery brownish; odor and taste not distinctive.

SPORE PRINT: Brown.

MICROSCOPIC FEATURES: Spores 4–5.5 μm, globose, finely punctate, pale brown.

OCCURRENCE: In groups or overlapping clusters on decaying hardwood, rarely reported on conifers; summer–early winter.

EDIBILITY: Unknown.

REMARKS: *Applanatus* means "flattened horizontally," a reference to the shape of the fruitbody. The Jelly Crep, *Crepidotus mollis* (p. 14), is similar, but it has an ocher-brown to orange-brown or tan, clamshell-shaped cap that is covered with tiny, brownish scales.

Crepidotus applanatus

Cuphophyllus pratensis (Fr.) Bon

= *Hygrocybe pratensis* var. *pratensis* (Fr.)
   Murrill
= *Hygrophorus pratensis* (Fr.) Fr.

COMMON NAMES: Meadow Waxcap, Salmon
Waxcap.

MACROSCOPIC FEATURES: **Cap** 2–7 cm wide,
obtuse to convex when young, becoming
broadly convex, typically with a low, broad
umbo at maturity; surface smooth, moist then
dry, often cracked on the disc in age, reddish
orange to salmon orange or dull orange when
young, fading to pale orange to orange yellow
or pale tawny in age; margin incurved when
young; **flesh** thick, somewhat brittle, whitish to pale reddish cinnamon; odor and taste
not distinctive. **Gills** decurrent, subdistant
to distant, often with crossveins, salmon buff
to pale orange. **Stalk** 3–8 cm long, 5–20 mm
thick, tapered downward or nearly equal,
often curved; surface dry, smooth, whitish to
pale salmon buff.

SPORE PRINT: White.

MICROSCOPIC FEATURES: Spores 5–8 × 3–5 μm,
ellipsoid, subovoid, or subglobose, smooth,
hyaline, inamyloid.

OCCURRENCE: Solitary, scattered, or in groups
in grassy areas or on humus in woods;
year-round.

EDIBILITY: Edible.

REMARKS: *Pratensis* means "of meadows."
Humidicutis marginata = *Hygrophorus mar-
ginatus* (not illustrated) has a yellow orange
to orange or sometimes dull orange cap with
an olive disc, orange to brilliant orange non-
decurrent gills, a yellow to pale orange-yellow
stalk, and grows on the ground in conifer or
hardwoods from late spring through early
winter. The Late Fall Waxcap, or Herald of
Winter, *Hygrophorus hypothejus* (p. 14), has a
glutinous to viscid, olive-brown to red-brown
or yellow-brown cap that becomes dull yellow on the margin in age, white to pale yellow
decurrent gills, and a whitish to pale yellow
stalk. It grows on the ground with conifers
from fall to winter.

Cuphophyllus pratensis

Cuphophyllus virgineus (Wulfen) Kovalenko

= *Hygrocybe virginea* (Wulfen) P. D. Orton & Watling

COMMON NAME: Snowy Waxcap.
MACROSCOPIC FEATURES: Cap 1–7 cm wide, hemispheric at first, becoming nearly flat when mature, often with a low umbo or central depression; surface moist, white to cream or ivory, smooth, whitish; margin initially incurved, translucent-striate halfway to the center when fresh; **flesh** moderately thick, white; odor and taste not distinctive. **Gills** decurrent, subdistant, sometimes forked, white. **Stalk** 2–12 cm long, up to 1 cm thick, nearly equal or tapered downward, round or somewhat flattened; surface dry, smooth, white.

SPORE PRINT: White.
MICROSCOPIC FEATURES: Spores 6–9 × 4–6 µm, elliptic, smooth, hyaline, inamyloid.
OCCURRENCE: Scattered or in groups on the ground in grassy areas or woodlands; summer–early winter.
EDIBILITY: Edible.
REMARKS: The Dirty Southern Waxcap, *Hygrophorus subsordidus* (p. 299), has a larger cap that is white overall or sometimes pale yellow on the disc.

Cuphophyllus virgineus

Cyptotrama asprata (Berk.) Redhead & Ginns

= *Cyptotrama chrysopepla* (Berk. & M. A. Curtis) Singer
= *Lepiota asprata* (Berk.) Sacc.
= *Xerula asprata* (Berk.) Aberdeen
= *Xerulina asprata* (Berk.) Pegler

COMMON NAME: Golden Scruffy Collybia.
MACROSCOPIC FEATURES: **Cap** 5–25 mm wide, convex to broadly convex; surface dry, finely granular to scaly, often becoming wrinkled or furrowed in age, golden at first, becoming bright yellow, sometimes translucent-striate. **Gills** attached to slightly decurrent, distant, white. **Stalk** 1–5 cm long, 1.5–3 mm thick, solid, fairly tough, with scurfy golden granules over a paler yellow ground color. **Flesh** thin, yellowish; odor and taste not distinctive.
SPORE PRINT: White.
MICROSCOPIC FEATURES: Spores 8–12 × 6–7.5 μm, lemon-shaped to broadly oval, smooth, hyaline, inamyloid.
OCCURRENCE: Scattered or in groups on hardwood sticks or logs, especially oak; year-round.
EDIBILITY: Unknown.
REMARKS: *Asprata* means "roughened," a reference to the scurfy golden granules on the stalk.

Cyptotrama asprata

Cystoderma amianthinum (Scop.) Fayod

= *Lepiota amianthina* (Scop.) P. Karst.

COMMON NAMES: Corn Silk Cystoderma, Pungent Cystoderma.

MACROSCOPIC FEATURES: **Cap** 2–5 cm wide, broadly conical, becoming convex, often with a low umbo; surface dry, granular or nearly smooth, with or without radial wrinkles, sometimes finely cracked, yellow to reddish brown; margin hung with white, tooth-like fragments of partial veil. **Gills** attached, close or crowded, white to pale yellow. **Stalk** 3–7.5 cm long, 3–8 mm thick, equal or enlarged downward, dry, with a coarsely granular sheath on the lower portion, smooth above, apex white, colored like the cap below the partial veil; partial veil sparse, fibrous, sometimes forming a thin superior ring that soon disappears; with white basal mycelium. **Flesh** thin, white; odor variously described as resembling corn silk or geraniums or not distinctive; taste not distinctive.

SPORE PRINT: White.

MICROSCOPIC FEATURES: Spores 5–6 × 3–4 µm, elliptic, smooth, hyaline, amyloid.

OCCURRENCE: Solitary, scattered, or in groups among mosses or in needle duff under conifers; summer–early winter.

EDIBILITY: Unknown.

REMARKS: A yellow to reddish-brown cap with partial veil fragments on the margin, a sheathing stalk, white basal mycelium, and a pungent odor are the key identification features.

Cystoderma amianthinum

Desarmillaria tabescens (Scop.)
R. A. Koch & Amie

= *Armillaria tabescens* (Scop) Emel

COMMON NAME: Ringless Honey Mushroom.
MACROSCOPIC FEATURES: **Cap** 3–10 cm wide, convex to broadly convex with a very broad umbo; surface moist or dry, covered with orangish-brown to reddish-brown erect scales and darker tufts of fibers. **Gills** adnate to subdecurrent, subdistant, whitish at first, becoming pinkish brown. **Stalk** 7.5–20 cm long, 4–15 mm wide, tapering from the apex to the base, somewhat brittle; surface moist, fibrillose, whitish near the apex, yellow-ish to brownish below, sometimes with a grayish-green area near the base. **Flesh** up to 6 mm thick, colored like the cap but lighter; odor not distinctive; taste astringent or not distinctive.

SPORE PRINT: White.
MICROSCOPIC FEATURES: Spores 6–9 × 4.5–6 μm, broadly elliptical, smooth, hyaline, inamyloid.
OCCURRENCE: In dense groups or clusters on old stumps and from buried wood; fall–early winter.
EDIBILITY: Edible but be certain to cook it well. Specimens collected on or around pecan stumps may have an unpleasant taste.
REMARKS: It is considered a weak pathogen of trees but apparently less lethal than *Armillaria mellea*. *Armillaria mellea* (p. 239) is similar, but its stalk has a ring.

Desarmillaria tabescens

Entoloma abortivum (Berk. & M. A. Curtis) Donk

= *Clitopilus abortivus* (Berk. & M. A. Curtis) Sacc.
= *Pleuropus abortivus* (Berk. & M. A. Curtis) Murrill
= *Rhodophyllus abortivus* (Berk. & M. A. Curtis) Singer

COMMON NAME: Abortive Entoloma.
MACROSCOPIC FEATURES: **Cap** 5–10 cm broad, convex, sometimes with a low broad umbo or becoming slightly depressed at the disc; surface somewhat fibrous or smooth, pale gray to grayish brown; margin inrolled and often becoming irregular in age; **flesh** thick, white; odor and taste farinaceous. **Gills** typically decurrent, grayish at first, soon becoming pinkish. **Stalk** 2.5–10 cm long, 5–15 mm broad, usually enlarged at the base, solid; surface dry, scurfy, whitish to grayish, base usually coated with white mycelium.
SPORE PRINT: Salmon pink.
MICROSCOPIC FEATURES: Spores 8–10 × 4.5–6 μm, elliptic and angular, typically 6-sided, smooth, hyaline, inamyloid.

OCCURRENCE: Scattered or in groups on the ground, on humus or near rotting stumps in woods; summer–early winter.
EDIBILITY: Edible with caution.
REMARKS: The aborted form, which is whitish to pinkish and has a pinkish-marbled appearance in cross section, is thought to be a parasite of *Armillaria* species. Both forms are edible but care must be taken not to confuse them with other *Entoloma* species. *Entoloma megacystidiosum* (not illustrated) has a 2–7 cm wide, conic-umbonate to nearly plane white cap, white flesh that has a farinaceous odor and taste, white to vinaceous-buff or vinaceous-cinnamon gills with fimbriate edges, and a long, thin, white, somewhat twisted stalk. The spores are 5- to 8-sided, somewhat angular-nodulose, hyaline, and measure 10–14 × 7–9 μm. It has unusually large cheilocystidia and pleurocystidia that are fusoid, ventricose or obclavate, and often have a slender, tapering neck. It grows on the ground in mixed oak and pine woods during summer and fall.

Entoloma abortivum

Entoloma incanum (Fr.) Hesler

= *Leptonia incana* (Fr.) Gillet
= *Rhodophyllus incanus* (Fr.) E. Horak

COMMON NAMES: Green Entoloma, Green Leptonia.

MACROSCOPIC FEATURES: **Cap** 1–5 cm wide, convex with a central depression; surface dry, silky to smooth, olive yellow to green or blue green, darkest centrally, fading to yellowish brown in age; margin usually striate and often split when mature; **flesh** yellowish, bruising blue green; odor of mice cages; taste not distinctive. **Gills** attached, distant, whitish to pale green, becoming pinkish at maturity, bruising blue green. **Stalk** 2–7 cm long, up to 4 mm thick, equal and hollow; surface smooth, colored like the cap, bruising blue green; with white basal mycelium; partial veil and ring absent.

SPORE PRINT: Salmon pink.

MICROSCOPIC FEATURES: Spores 8.5–13 × 7–9.5 μm, elliptic and angular, 6– or 7-sided, hyaline, inamyloid.

OCCURRENCE: In groups or clusters on the ground in woodlands, grassy areas, roadsides, and disturbed soil; year-round.

EDIBILITY: Unknown, possibly poisonous.

REMARKS: The green color of the cap and stalk, the blue staining reaction, and the distinctive odor of mice cages make this mushroom easy to identify. *Entoloma farlowii* = *Rhodophyllus farlowii* (not illustrated) has a 1–3 cm wide, convex cap with a depressed disc. It has a moist cap surface that is glabrous, translucent-striate halfway to the disc, and rich orange yellow with darker orange striae. Its flesh is white to yellowish and lacks a distinctive odor. It has salmon-pink gills, a twisted stalk that is colored like the cap, and grows on the ground with mixed pine and hardwoods during summer.

Entoloma incanum

Entoloma murrayi (Berk. & M. A. Curtis) Sacc.

= *Entoloma cuspidatum* (Peck) Sacc.
= *Inocephalus murrayi* (Berk. & M. A. Curtis) Rutter & Watling
= *Nolanea murrayi* (Berk. & M. A. Curtis) Sacc.

COMMON NAME: Yellow Unicorn Entoloma.
MACROSCOPIC FEATURES: **Cap** 1–4 cm broad, conical to bell-shaped with a conspicuous, pointed umbo; surface moist or dry, silky, shiny, finely wrinkled, bright yellow at first, fading in age; margin slightly lobed, sometimes translucent-striate; **flesh** thin, pale yellow; odor and taste not distinctive. **Gills** narrowly adnate, becoming emarginate, often with a decurrent tooth, close to subdistant, pale yellow, finally with a pinkish tint, edges uneven. **Stalk** 5–12 cm long, 2–5 mm broad, equal, at times twisted, hollow; surface dry, silky-striate, colored like the cap.

SPORE PRINT: Salmon pink.
MICROSCOPIC FEATURES: Spores 9–12 × 8–12 µm, 4- or 5-sided, smooth, hyaline.
OCCURRENCE: Solitary, scattered, or in groups on the ground with conifers or hardwoods; spring–summer, occasionally in the fall.
EDIBILITY: Unknown.
REMARKS: The Salmon Unicorn Entoloma, *Entoloma quadratum* = *Entoloma salmoneum* (p. 14), has a salmon-orange cap and gills.

Entoloma murrayi

Entoloma strictius (Peck) Sacc.

= *Agaricus strictior* Peck
= *Rhodophyllus strictior* (Peck) Singer
= *Nolanea strictior* (Peck) Pomerl.

COMMON NAME: Straight-stalked Entoloma.
MACROSCOPIC FEATURES: **Cap** 2–7 cm broad, broadly conical to convex with a distinct umbo; surface moist or dry, glabrous, hygrophanous, striate, grayish brown when wet, paler when dry; **flesh** thin, brownish when wet, whitish or pallid when dry; odor and taste not distinctive. **Gills** adnexed or nearly free, medium broad, close, whitish at first, becoming pinkish. **Stalk** 5–10 cm long, 2–4 mm wide, straight, equal or slightly tapering upward, hollow; surface silky, fibrillose or sometimes glabrous, longitudinally twisted-striate, colored like the cap or a little paler, easily splitting longitudinally; basal mycelium white.
SPORE PRINT: Salmon pink.
MICROSCOPIC FEATURES: Spores 9.5–13 × 7.5–9 μm, ellipsoid, 5- or 6-sided, smooth, hyaline; lacking cheilocystidia and pleurocystidia.
OCCURRENCE: Solitary, scattered, or in groups in mixed pine and hardwood forests; spring–fall.
EDIBILITY: Unknown.
REMARKS: The Early Spring Entoloma, *Entoloma vernum* (not illustrated), is very similar, but its stalk is faintly longitudinally ridged, not longitudinally twisted-striate, it has slightly smaller spores that measure 8–11 × 7–8μm, and it fruits in early spring.

Entoloma strictius

Galerina marginata (Batsch) Kühner

= *Galerina autumnalis* (Peck) A. H. Sm. & Singer

COMMON NAME: Deadly Galerina.
MACROSCOPIC FEATURES: **Cap** 1–6.5 cm wide, convex, becoming broadly convex in age, sometimes with a low, broad umbo; surface smooth, sticky, translucent-striate at the margin when moist, brown, hygrophanous; **flesh** thin, brown, watery; odor not distinctive or slightly farinaceous; taste not distinctive. **Gills** attached or slightly decurrent, close, yellowish then pale rusty brown. **Stalk** 2–10 cm long, 3–8 mm thick, nearly equal or slightly enlarged at the base, hollow; surface dry, pale brown at the apex, darkening below, often fibrillose below the ring; base usually covered with white mycelium; partial veil thin, white, membranous, leaving a persistent superior or median ring.
SPORE PRINT: Rusty brown.
MICROSCOPIC FEATURES: Spores 8–11 × 5–6.5 μm, elliptic, roughened, pale brown.

OCCURRENCE: Solitary, in small groups or clusters on logs or stumps; spring–fall.
EDIBILITY: Deadly poisonous.
REMARKS: Not to be confused with species of *Armillaria* which have a white spore print and may grow simultaneously on the same log or stump. *Galerina calyptrata* (not illustrated) has a small, 5–13 mm broad, conical cap that becomes broadly conical at maturity. The cap surface is moist, glabrous, translucent-striate, very hygrophanous, rusty brown to light brown with yellowish-brown striae, and fades to grayish yellow. It has white fibers from the torn partial veil on the margin. The stalk is golden yellow toward the apex and light brown below. Its spores are 9–10 × 6–7 μm, calyptriform, smooth, pale brown, and it grows in low moss colonies, often on the sides of trees during winter and spring. *Galerina* is a large genus with more than two hundred species, many of which can only be positively identified using microscopic characteristics.

Galerina marginata

Gerronema strombodes (Berk. & Mont.) Singer

= *Chrysomphalina strombodes* (Berk. & Mont.) Clémencon
= *Omphalia strombodes* (Berk. & Mont.) Sacc.
= *Omphalina strombodes* (Berk. & Mont.) Murrill

MACROSCOPIC FEATURES: **Cap** 2–5 cm broad, convex with an umbilicate center, becoming somewhat funnel-shaped in age; surface slightly sticky or dry, greenish yellow to grayish brown with darker brownish radial fibers, fading to ocher or cream toward the margin, with a darker brown center; margin incurved at first, later expanding and often splitting in age; **flesh** thin, whitish to cream; odor not distinctive, taste somewhat bitter or not distinctive. **Gills** decurrent with some forking, close to subdistant, broad, white at first, becoming cream-colored to pale yellow at maturity. **Stalk** 2.5–6.5 cm long, up to 6 mm wide, nearly equal, hollow; surface dry, smooth or with longitudinal fibers, whitish to grayish brown.

SPORE PRINT: White.

MICROSCOPIC FEATURES: Spores 7–9 × 4–5.5 µm, elliptic, smooth, hyaline, inamyloid.

OCCURRENCE: In groups or clusters on decaying conifer or hardwood; summer.

EDIBILITY: Unknown.

REMARKS: The Golden-gilled Gerronema, *Gerronema chrysophylla* = *Chrysomphalina chrysophylla* (not illustrated), is similar but has bright yellow to orange-yellow gills, a yellowish spore print, and fruits on conifer wood. *Pseudoarmillariella ectypoides* = *Omphalina ectypoides* (p. 15) is also similar, but it has a minutely scaly, brownish-yellow to yellowish-brown cap, yellowish, strongly decurrent gills, a 3–9 mm thick stalk that is enlarged downward, amyloid spores, and it is restricted to conifer wood.

Gerronema strombodes

Gliophorus psittacinus (Schaeff.) Herink

= *Hygrocybe psittacina* (Schaeff.) P. Kumm.
= *Hygrophorus psittacinus* (Schaeff.) Fr.

COMMON NAMES: Parrot Waxcap, Parrot Mushroom.

MACROSCOPIC FEATURES: **Cap** 1–3 cm wide, broadly conical at first, becoming convex to nearly flat, sometimes with a broad umbo; surface viscid to glutinous when moist, smooth, with a translucent-striate margin when young, green at first but changing into some combination of blue green, olive green, orange, yellow, or rarely pink; **flesh** thin, colored like the cap; odor and taste not distinctive. **Gills** attached, nearly distant, waxy, yellowish, greenish, or reddish. **Stalk** 3–7 cm long, 2–5 mm thick, nearly equal; surface smooth, glutinous, usually green at least at the apex, with whitish, pale yellow, or pinkish shades below.

SPORE PRINT: White.

MICROSCOPIC FEATURES: Spores 6.5–10 × 4–6 μm, elliptic, smooth, hyaline, inamyloid.

OCCURRENCE: In groups or clusters in woods or grassy areas; summer–early winter.

EDIBILITY: Edible.

REMARKS: The Perplexing Waxcap, *Gliophorus perplexus* (not illustrated), is nearly identical, but its cap is orange-brown and lacks the green coloration when young. *Gliophorus laetus* (p. 14) has a glutinous to viscid convex cap that is often depressed at the center. The cap color is highly variable and ranges from shell pink to peach, cream, yellow, orange, gray, or a mixture of these colors. It has non-decurrent gills, a glutinous stalk that is colored like the cap, and grows among sphagnum mosses or in wet woodlands from summer through early winter.

Gliophorus psittacinus

Gloioxanthomyces nitidus (Berk. & M. A. Curtis) Lodge, Vizzini, Ercole & Boertm.

= *Hygrocybe nitida* (Berk. & M. A. Curtis) Murrill
= *Hygrophorus nitidus* Berk. & M. A. Curtis

MACROSCOPIC FEATURES: **Cap** 1–4 cm wide, broadly convex or nearly flat when young, disc very soon becoming depressed, deeply infundibuliform in age, sometimes perforating; surface smooth, glabrous, viscid, somewhat striate when moist, bright yellow to apricot yellow, fading to pale yellow or whitish in age; margin incurved and remaining so, well into maturity; **flesh** very thin, soft, fragile, yellowish to whitish; odor and taste not distinctive. **Gills** long-decurrent, subdistant to distant, yellow to pale yellow, often with darker yellow edges, intervenose. **Stalk** 3–8 cm long, 2–5 mm thick, nearly equal or enlarged toward the apex, hollow, smooth, viscid, colored and fading like the cap.

SPORE PRINT: White.
MICROSCOPIC FEATURES: Spores 6.5–9 × 4–6 μm, ellipsoid to subovoid, smooth, hyaline, inamyloid.
OCCURRENCE: Scattered or in groups on humus, wet soil, or among mosses with conifers or hardwoods or in bogs; late spring–early winter.
EDIBILITY: Unknown.
REMARKS: *Hygrocybe flavescens* (p. 296) has a slightly depressed, orange to yellow-orange or yellow cap with a somewhat striate margin when moist. It has attached, close to subdistant, yellow gills and grows on soil or humus in conifer or hardwoods from late spring through early winter.

Gloioxanthomyces nitidus

Gymnopilus armillatus Murrill

= *Flammula armillata*

MACROSCOPIC FEATURES: **Cap** 5–10 cm wide, convex, becoming broadly convex; surface moist or dry, smooth, minutely squamulose over the disc, glabrous toward the margin, yellow to orange yellow or ocher orange, darkest over the center; margin incurved and remaining so well into maturity, even, entire; **flesh** firm, pale yellow; odor not distinctive; taste very bitter. **Gills** sinuate with a decurrent tooth, close to crowded, broad, entire, pale yellow, becoming rusty brown in age. **Stalk** 8–10 cm long, 6–16 mm thick, enlarged downward or nearly equal, solid, fibrillose, longitudinally striate, pale yellow at the apex, darker below, yellow brown near the base, staining brownish in age or when handled; partial veil submembranous to fibrous, usually leaving a ring, pale yellow; ring superior, membranous, persistent, pale yellow then rusty brown.

SPORE PRINT: Rusty brown.

MICROSCOPIC FEATURES: Spores 8–10 × 4.5–6 μm, ellipsoid to ovoid, minutely warted, pale rusty brown, non-dextrinoid, lacking a germ pore.

OCCURRENCE: Scattered, in groups or clusters on the ground attached to buried wood, sometimes on roots of hardwoods, especially Sweetgum; summer–late fall.

EDIBILITY: Unknown.

REMARKS: *Gymnopilus spectabilis* (not illustrated) is very similar, but the gills are broadly attached, and the spores are dextrinoid.

Gymnopilus armillatus

Gymnopilus lepidotus Hesler

MACROSCOPIC FEATURES: **Cap:** 4–8 mm broad, convex to broadly convex; surface dry, fibrillose-scaly; scales tufted-erect, yellow; margin even; **flesh** thick, firm, pale yellow; odor not distinctive; taste promptly bitter. **Gills** attached, close, broad, edges fimbriate, with numerous lamellulae, orange. **Stalk** 2–4 cm long, 2–4 mm thick, equal or slightly enlarged at the apex, solid; surface pruinose near the apex, glabrous below, whitish; partial veil cobwebby, yellowish, usually disappearing by maturity.
SPORE PRINT: Rusty brown.

MICROSCOPIC FEATURES: Spores 5.5–7.5 × 4.5–5 μm, ellipsoid to ovoid, minutely warted, lacking a germ pore, light rusty brown.
OCCURRENCE: Scattered or in groups on decaying Sweetgum logs and stumps; known from Florida and Georgia; summer.
EDIBILITY: Unknown.
REMARKS: The small yellow cap with erect scales and growth on Sweetgum logs and stumps are good field identification features. *Gymnopilus hispidus* (not illustrated) has an umbilicate to infundibuliform cap, larger spores that measure 7.5–9 × 5.5–6μm, and also grows on wood.

Gymnopilus lepidotus

Gymnopilus liquiritiae (Persoon) Karst.

= *Flammula liquiritiae* (Pers. ex Fr.) Kumm.

MACROSCOPIC FEATURES: **Cap** 2–8 cm broad, convex then plane, sometimes subumbonate; surface moist or dry, not viscid, glabrous or nearly so, fulvous to ochraceous tawny or ochraceous orange to orange brown; margin even, weakly striate; **flesh** pale orange to tawny yellow; odor sometimes slightly fragrant or resembling raw potatoes or not distinctive; taste bitter. **Gills** attached to notched, seceding, close to crowded, at first ochraceous buff to pale orange yellow, becoming ochraceous orange to ochraceous tawny or orange, sometimes with reddish-brown spots, edges fimbriate. **Stalk** 3–7 cm long, 3–10 mm broad, tapered in either direction or nearly equal, hollow; surface dry, longitudinally fibrillose or subglabrous, whitish to dingy orange, with a whitish or yellowish apex; partial veil and ring absent.

SPORE PRINT: Rusty brown.

MICROSCOPIC FEATURES: Spores 7–10 × 4–6 µm, ellipsoid, minutely warted, lacking a germ pore, pale rusty brown, dextrinoid.

OCCURRENCE: Scattered or in groups on decaying conifer wood or sawdust, occasionally on decaying hardwoods; summer–early winter.

EDIBILITY: Unknown.

REMARKS: *Gymnopilus rufosquamulosus* (not illustrated), reported only from Texas, has a buff to tawny cap with small red to orange scales, pale yellowish flesh with a pleasant odor and a bitter taste, and a dingy yellowish-brown stalk with a superior ring. It also grows on wood and has spores that measure 7–9 × 4.5–5.5 µm.

Gymnopilus liquiritiae

Gymnopilus palmicola Murrill

= *Flammula palmicola* (Murrill) Murrill

MACROSCOPIC FEATURES: **Cap** 2–5 cm broad, convex to nearly plane, becoming depressed in age; surface dry, with soft cottony tufts or scales at first, becoming subglabrous at maturity, pale rusty brown to ochraceous; margin even; **flesh** thin, whitish to yellowish; odor not distinctive; taste bitter. **Gills** adnate, close, broad, yellowish at first, becoming rusty brown when mature. **Stalk** 3–5 cm long, 3–5 mm broad, nearly equal, solid; surface slightly fibrillose, yellowish or colored like the cap but paler; partial veil strongly developed, pale yellow, sometimes leaving a poorly developed ring.

SPORE PRINT: Rusty brown.

MICROSCOPIC FEATURES: Spores 7–10 × 5–7.5 μm, ellipsoid, coarsely warted, lacking a germ pore, pale rusty brown, dextrinoid.

OCCURRENCE: Solitary, scattered, or in groups on decaying logs or stumps of palms and living orchids; summer–winter, sometimes year-round.

EDIBILITY: Unknown.

REMARKS: *Gymnopilus fulvosquamulosus* (not illustrated) has a larger cap, 4–8 cm broad, with conspicuous fibrillose, tawny scales on a yellow-ocher to brighter yellow ground color. It fruits on decaying hardwoods and has spores that measure 7–10 × 5–6 μm. The addition of $FeSO_4$ to the flesh slowly stains olive.

Gymnopilus palmicola

Gymnopilus penetrans (Fr.) Murrill

= *Flammula penetrans* (Fr.) Quél.
= *Fulvidula penetrans* (Fr.) Singer

MACROSCOPIC FEATURES: **Cap** 2–5 cm broad,
bell-shaped to convex, becoming broadly
convex to nearly plane in age; surface moist
or dry, glabrous, yellow to golden yellow or
pale orange yellow, fading in age; margin even;
flesh white to whitish; odor not distinctive; taste bitter. **Gills** attached to sinuate,
close, pale yellow or yellowish white at first,
becoming rust-spotted in age. **Stalk** 2.5–6 cm
long, 3–7 mm broad, nearly equal or enlarged
downward; surface dry, glabrous or nearly so,
pale yellow to yellowish white, with a white
tomentum over the base; partial veil fibrillose,
white, not leaving a ring, sometimes leaving a
faint annular zone.

SPORE PRINT: Orange-brown.
MICROSCOPIC FEATURES: Spores 6.5–10 ×
4–5.5 μm, ellipsoid, lacking a germ pore,
warted, ochraceous, dextrinoid.
OCCURRENCE: Solitary, scattered, or in groups,
mostly on decaying conifer wood and cones;
summer–early winter.
EDIBILITY: Unknown.
REMARKS: *Gymnopilus sapineus* (p. 14) is very
similar but has a minutely scaly cap (use a
hand lens) that often becomes rimose in age,
a scanty yellowish partial veil, and flesh that
usually has a pungent odor.

Gymnopilus penetrans

Gymnopus biformis (Peck) Halling

= *Collybia biformis* (Peck) Singer
= *Marasmius biformis* Peck

MACROSCOPIC FEATURES: **Cap** 1–2.5 cm wide, convex to broadly convex, sometimes depressed on the disc; surface dry, hygrophanous, glabrous to somewhat fibrillose, sometimes wrinkled to shallowly furrowed on the margin, reddish brown, fading to pinkish brown in age; margin incurved and entire when young; **flesh** thin, whitish; odor and taste not distinctive. **Gills** adnate, often forming a collar around the stalk, close, moderately broad, whitish to grayish, becoming pale pinkish buff at maturity. **Stalk** 1.5–5 cm long, 1–4 mm thick, equal, tough; surface dry, white on the upper portion, tawny to vinaceous brown toward the base, covered with a dense layer of downy, whitish to tawny hairs.

SPORE PRINT: White to cream.
MICROSCOPIC FEATURES: Spores 6.4–8.6 × 3.2–4.4 µm, lacrimoid to obovoid, smooth, hyaline, inamyloid.
OCCURRENCE: Scattered or in groups on soil or pine straw with conifers or hardwoods; year-round.
EDIBILITY: Unknown.
REMARKS: *Gymnopus subnudus* (p. 14) is similar, but it has paler, more distant gills, bitter-tasting flesh, and typically fruits on sticks, leaves, and humus. *Gymnopus luxurians* (p. 14) has a larger, 2–8 cm wide cap, close to crowded, whitish to pinkish-buff gills, a 2–13 mm thick, twisted-striate stalk that is covered with fine white hairs that easily brush off, and is whitish toward the apex and brown below. It grows in dense clusters on decaying woodchips or in lawns on buried wood during summer and fall.

Gymnopus biformis

Gymnopus dichrous (Berk. & M. A. Curtis) Halling

= *Collybia dichrous* (Berk. & M. A. Curtis) Gilliam

MACROSCOPIC FEATURES: **Cap** 1–5 cm wide, convex, becoming nearly plane or with an uplifted margin; surface moist or dry, striate, often wrinkled, translucent toward the margin when wet, reddish brown or dark brown at the center and paler toward the margin, fading with age. **Gills** narrowly attached or free, close to subdistant, crossveined, whitish, sometimes with rusty spots. **Stalk** 1–5 cm long, 1–5 mm thick, nearly equal above a slightly bulbous base, dry, finely hairy, hollow, whitish at the apex and reddish brown below, with white hairs at the base; partial veil absent. **Flesh** thin, white; odor and taste not distinctive.

SPORE PRINT: White to cream.
MICROSCOPIC FEATURES: Spores 10–12 × 3–4.5 μm, lacrimoid to elliptic, smooth, hyaline, inamyloid.
OCCURRENCE: In groups or clusters on hardwood sticks, logs, and stumps; summer–fall.
EDIBILITY: Unknown.
REMARKS: *Gymnopus biformis* (p. 285) has closely spaced gills and grows on soil or pine straw with conifers or hardwoods year-round.

Gymnopus dichrous

Gymnopus dryophilus (Bull.) Murrill

= *Collybia dryophila* (Bull.) P. Kumm.

COMMON NAMES: Oak-loving Gymnopus, Oak-loving Collybia.

MACROSCOPIC FEATURES: **Cap** 1–7 cm wide, convex at first, becoming broadly convex to nearly plane in age; surface smooth, moist, silky, hygrophanous, dark reddish brown when young, soon fading to orange brown, tan, or yellowish tan, usually remaining darker over the disc; margin even, often uplifted in age. **Gills** attached to nearly free, crowded to close, whitish to pinkish buff or sometimes yellowish. **Stalk** 3–9 cm long, 2–8 mm thick, nearly equal or enlarged downward, sometimes bulbous, often with white rhizomorphs; surface dry, whitish near the apex, yellowish or darker toward the base. **Flesh** whitish to yellowish; odor and taste not distinctive.

SPORE PRINT: White to cream.

MICROSCOPIC FEATURES: Spores 5–7 × 3–3.5 µm, lacrimoid to elliptic, smooth, hyaline, inamyloid.

OCCURRENCE: Scattered in groups or clusters on the ground or on decaying wood in oak or pine woods; late spring–early winter.

EDIBILITY: Edible.

REMARKS: *Dryophilus* means "oak-loving." A second photograph of this mushroom is shown in the "Color Key to the Major Groups of Fungi" (p. 14). It is often parasitized by the Collybia Jelly, *Syzygospora mycetophila* (not illustrated). This parasite forms brain-like, cup-shaped, or irregular, pale yellow to brownish-yellow fruitbodies on the cap and stalk of its host. The Yellow-Cap Collybia, *Gymnopus subsulphureus*, is similar but has a pale to bright yellow cap and pinkish to yellow rhizomorphs.

Gymnopus dryophilus (B)

Gymnopus iocephalus (Berk. & M. A. Curtis) Halling

= *Collybia iocephala* (Berk. & M. A. Curtis) Singer
= *Marasmius iocephalus* (Berk. & M. A. Curtis) Penn.

COMMON NAME: Violet Gymnopus.

MACROSCOPIC FEATURES: **Cap** 1.2–4 cm wide, convex, becoming broadly convex to plane in age, sometimes shallowly depressed on the disc; surface moist or dry, wrinkled and striate to shallowly grooved nearly to the disc, color variable, violet, purple, vinaceous, fading to purplish lilac to pinkish lilac; margin inrolled at first, becoming uplifted and wavy in age; **flesh** purplish lilac to pinkish lilac; odor pungent and disagreeable; taste unpleasant. **Gills** attached to notched, subdistant to distant, reddish purple to violet. **Stalk** 2–7 cm long, 1.5–4 mm thick, enlarged downward or nearly equal, apex often expanded, dry, hollow, whitish or sometimes tinged pale pinkish lilac, minutely pubescent overall.

SPORE PRINT: White.

MICROSCOPIC FEATURES: Spores 6.5–9 × 3–4.5 μm, ovoid, smooth, hyaline, inamyloid.

OCCURRENCE: Scattered or in groups on leaf litter and humus, usually in hardwoods or mixed woods; summer–early winter.

EDIBILITY: Unknown.

REMARKS: The cap, gills, and stalk stain bright blue with the application of KOH.

Gymnopus iocephalus

Gymnopus spongiosus (Berk. & M. A. Curtis) Halling

= *Collybia spongiosa* (Berk. & M. A. Curtis) Singer
= *Marasmius spongiosus* Berk. & M. A. Curtis

COMMON NAME: Hairy-stalked Gymnopus.

MACROSCOPIC FEATURES: **Cap** 8–35 mm wide, convex with an inconspicuous umbo, expanding to nearly plane at maturity; surface dry, glabrous, becoming wrinkled on the margin in age, reddish brown, fading to grayish orange or buff, whitish along the margin; margin inrolled when young; **flesh** thin, white; odor and taste not distinctive. **Gills** attached to nearly free, close to crowded, narrow, white to creamy white. **Stalk** 2–6 cm long, up to 4 mm thick at the apex, wider below, equal to subclavate, sometimes twisted, pliant; base often spongy and thickened; surface whitish at the apex, reddish brown below, covered with tawny, long, soft, or stiff hairs which are often inconspicuous in wet weather.

SPORE PRINT: White.

MICROSCOPIC FEATURES: Spores 6.2–8.4 × 3.5–4.2 µm, lacrimoid to ellipsoid, smooth, hyaline, inamyloid.

OCCURRENCE: Solitary, scattered, in groups, or clusters on leaf and needle litter with conifers, hardwoods, or in mixed woods; summer–winter.

EDIBILITY: Unknown.

REMARKS: The stalk stains green with the application of KOH or NH4OH. The hairy, rusty-brown stalk and spongy base are good field identification features. *Gymnopus subnudus* = *Collybia subnuda* (p. 14) has a 1–3.5 cm wide, cinnamon-brown to pinkish-brown cap and subdistant to distant whitish gills. Its stalk is 1–5 mm thick, whitish above, brownish below, and sometimes nearly blackish at the base. It is subglabrous at the apex and coated with whitish to grayish hairs below. It grows on humus, leaf litter, dead twigs, or acorn involucres in hardwoods or mixed woods year-round.

Gymnopus spongiosus

Hebeloma crustuliniforme (Bull.) Quél.

= *Agaricus crustuliniformis* Bull.

COMMON NAME: Poison Pie.

MACROSCOPIC FEATURES: **Cap** 3–11 cm wide, convex, becoming nearly flat at maturity; surface smooth, viscid, creamy white to dirty yellow brown, darkest at the center; margin inrolled when young, uplifted and wavy in age; **flesh** white; odor like radish; taste bitter or unpleasant. **Gills** attached and notched, close to crowded, whitish at first, turning grayish brown, often dotted with liquid that dries as brown spots; edges fringed and white (use a hand lens). **Stalk** 3–13 cm long, up to 2 cm thick, equal or with a small bulb, hollow, scurfy at the apex, white to buff, staining brownish from the base upward when handled, often with white mycelium at the base; lacking a partial veil or ring zone, lacking an internal hanging tooth-like cone at the apex as it becomes hollow.

SPORE PRINT: Brown.

MICROSCOPIC FEATURES: Spores 9–13 × 5–7.5 μm, elliptic, slightly roughened, pale brown, dextrinoid.

OCCURRENCE: Scattered, in groups, or sometimes in arcs or fairy rings on the ground under hardwoods or conifers or in grassy areas near shrubs; summer–early winter.

EDIBILITY: Poisonous.

REMARKS: The poisonous Rough-stalked Hebeloma or Scaly-stalked Hebeloma, *Hebeloma sinapizans* (p. 14), is very similar, but it has a larger cap, a stouter stalk that becomes scaly on the upper portion, and an internal hanging tooth-like cone at the apex as it becomes hollow. *Hebeloma sarcophyllum* (not illustrated) has a white cap and stalk with gills that are white at first and become pinkish.

Hebeloma crustuliniforme

Hebeloma syrjense P. Karst.

COMMON NAME: Corpse Finder.

MACROSCOPIC FEATURES: **Cap** 2.5–5 cm wide, convex, becoming nearly flat at maturity; surface slimy-viscid, orange brown, fading to ocher brown; margin incurved at first; **flesh** compact, thick, whitish; odor not distinctive; taste unknown. **Gills** attached, close, fairly broad, whitish when young, becoming reddish brown to cinnamon at maturity; edges fringed (use a hand lens). **Stalk** 4–6.5 cm long, 3–6 mm thick, nearly equal, hollow at maturity; surface dry, scurfy near the apex and longitudinally striate below, sometimes with yellow-brown stains; lacking a partial veil or ring zone.

SPORE PRINT: Pale cinnamon.

MICROSCOPIC FEATURES: Spores 8–10.5 × 5–6 µm, elliptic, faintly roughened, pale brown.

OCCURRENCE: Solitary or in groups or clusters on the ground under hardwoods; summer–early winter.

EDIBILITY: Unknown.

REMARKS: The common name refers to its occurrence near decaying animal carcasses or human remains.

ebeloma syrjense

Hygrocybe andersonii Cibula & N. S. Weber

COMMON NAME: Clustered Dune Hygrocybe.
MACROSCOPIC FEATURES: **Cap** 1.3–3.3 cm wide, convex with a flattened to depressed disc; surface smooth to slightly scurfy, color variable from orange yellow, orange, or deep reddish orange to scarlet, becoming reddish brown to nearly black in age; disc often blackish; margin incurved at first; **flesh** thin, orange yellow to reddish orange; odor and taste not distinctive. **Gills** attached to sinuate or subdecurrent, subdistant, waxy, yellow orange to brownish orange or deep orange, becoming blackish in age. **Stalk** 2.5–5 cm long, 6–10 mm thick, cylindrical to flattened, solid or hollow; surface glabrous, smooth, often with longitudinal furrows, colored like the cap or paler on the upper portion, becoming yellowish orange to pale yellow at the base.

SPORE PRINT: White.
MICROSCOPIC FEATURES: Spores 16–19 × 3.8–5.6 µm, rod-shaped with a distinct projection, smooth, hyaline, inamyloid.
OCCURRENCE: In groups or clusters in tree-colonized sand dunes near the shrub Sandhill Rosemary (*Ceratiola ericoides*), in coastal areas, and barrier islands; fall–spring.
EDIBILITY: Unknown.
REMARKS: Its bright colors, clustered manner of growth, and association with Seaside Rosemary in tree-colonized sand dunes are good field identification features. The Clustered Waxcap, *Hygrocybe caespitosa* (not illustrated), has a honey yellow cap that is covered with tiny brown scales, and it grows in clusters on the ground in conifer or hardwoods from late spring to early winter.

Hygrocybe andersonii

Hygrocybe chamaeleon (Cibula)
D. P. Lewis & Ovrebo

= *Hygrophorus chamaeleon* Cibula

COMMON NAME: Chameleon Waxcap.
MACROSCOPIC FEATURES: **Cap** 1–4 cm wide, convex to flat, becoming depressed on the disc, at times funnel-shaped; surface moist, sometimes with tiny cracks or crevices, fibrillose to somewhat scaly over the disc, color variable, dark red to reddish brown at the margin when moist, drying to reddish brown to brownish orange; litter-covered caps are often pale yellow to olive green or grayish; **flesh** thin, hygrophanous, yellowish to reddish; odor and taste not distinctive. **Gills** adnate to decurrent, subdistant to distant, waxy, color variable, pale yellow, greenish yellow, reddish orange, or grayish; edges finely toothed. **Stalk** 3–6.5 cm long, 5–9 mm thick, rounded, hollow; surface dry or moist, glabrous, with a shiny luster, apex dark red to reddish orange, becoming yellowish below; base light yellow to cream.
SPORE PRINT: White.
MICROSCOPIC FEATURES: Spores highly variable in size, mostly 12–17 × 7–10 µm, others 6.5–8.5 × 4–5.5 µm, ellipsoid to oval, smooth, hyaline, inamyloid.

OCCURRENCE: In groups or clusters in leaf litter in low areas under magnolia and in mixed woods; summer–fall.
EDIBILITY: Unknown.
REMARKS: *Chamaeleon* means "able to change," a reference to the variable colors of the cap, gills, and stalk. The Mississippi Waxcap, *Hygrocybe mississippiensis* (not illustrated), has a very small, 5–10 mm wide, bright red cap, pale yellow to yellowish-pink adnexed gills with a decurrent tooth, and a thin stalk that is colored like the cap but paler at the apex and darker below. It has smooth, ellipsoid to subovate spores that measure 7.5–8.4 × 4.7–5.8 µm, and it grows on leaf litter, soil, or decaying stumps in mixed bottomland forests during summer and fall. *Hygrocybe trinitensis* (not illustrated) has a very small, 3–10 mm wide, scarlet cap with a depressed center. It is markedly translucent-striate and often has a narrow yellow zone around the margin. It has widely spaced, decurrent, coral-red gills and a scarlet stalk with a yellowish base. The spores are ellipsoid, smooth, and measure 6–11(13) × 3.5–6 µm. It grows in St. Augustine grass from spring through fall.

Hygrocybe chamaeleon

Hygrocybe coccinea (Schaeff.) P. Kumm.

= *Hygrophorus coccineus* (Schaeff.) Fr.

COMMON NAME: Scarlet Waxcap.

MACROSCOPIC FEATURES: **Cap** 2–7 cm wide, conical when young, becoming convex to nearly flat with an umbo at maturity; surface moist or dry, smooth, bright red when young, fading to orange red in age; **flesh** thin, fragile, red to reddish orange; odor and taste not distinctive. **Gills** adnate, close to subdistant, waxy, yellowish or reddish orange to creamy orange, often with a yellowish margin. **Stalk** 2–8 cm long, 2–10 mm thick, equal, hollow, frequently compressed; surface dry, smooth, yellow orange to orange red, paler yellow toward the base, which is often coated with white mycelium.

SPORE PRINT: White.

MICROSCOPIC FEATURES: Spores 7–11 × 4–5 μm, ellipsoid, smooth, hyaline, inamyloid.

OCCURRENCE: Solitary, scattered, or in groups on the ground with conifers or hardwoods; summer–fall.

EDIBILITY: Reported as edible.

REMARKS: The flesh slowly stains gray in $FeSO_4$. *Coccinea* comes from the Latin term *coccin*, which means "scarlet." Compare with *Hygrocybe conica* (p. 295), which is similar, but all parts slowly stain black in age or when bruised.

Hygrocybe coccinea

Hygrocybe conica (Schaeff.) P. Kumm.

= *Hygrophorus conicus* (Schaeff.) Fr.

COMMON NAME: Witch's Hat.
MACROSCOPIC FEATURES: **Cap** 2–9 cm wide, sharply conical to bell-shaped, usually with an umbo; surface smooth, slightly viscid when moist, otherwise dry, orange to dark orange red or red, paler near the margin, sometimes yellow overall, often with olive-green tints, slowly staining black when bruised or in age; **flesh** thin, fragile, colored like the cap, bruising black; odor and taste not distinctive. **Gills** free, close, waxy, light yellow to greenish orange, staining black in age or when bruised. **Stalk** 2–10 cm long, 3–10 mm thick, equal, hollow at maturity, rounded, striate or twisted-striate, yellow to yellow orange, pale yellow near the base, staining black when bruised or in age.
SPORE PRINT: White.

MICROSCOPIC FEATURES: Spores 8–10 × 5–5.6 µm, ellipsoid, smooth, hyaline, inamyloid.
OCCURRENCE: Solitary or scattered on the ground with conifers or hardwoods, also in open grassy areas; summer–early winter.
EDIBILITY: Often reported as poisonous.
REMARKS: The name *conica* refers to the cone-shaped cap. Compare with *Hygrocybe coccinea* (p. 294), which is similar but does not stain black. *Hygrocybe cuspidata* (p. 14) has a sharply conic, brilliant red to scarlet cap that becomes broadly conic and fades to orange red in age and does not stain black. The Dune Witch's Hat, *Hygrocybe conicoides* (not illustrated), occurs in coastal sand dunes from September through January. It slowly stains black overall and is often buried nearly up to its cap in sand. Its gills develop salmon-orange to reddish tones, and it has larger spores that measure 10–14 × 4–6 µm.

Hygrocybe conica

Hygrocybe flavescens (Kauffman) Singer

= *Hygrophorus flavescens* (Kauffman) A. H. Sm. & Hesler

COMMON NAME: Golden Orange Waxcap.

MACROSCOPIC FEATURES: **Cap** 2–7 cm wide, broadly convex to nearly flat or slightly depressed at the disc; surface viscid when fresh, becoming dry and shiny, glabrous, orange to yellow orange or yellow; margin somewhat striate when moist; **flesh** thin, waxy, yellowish; odor and taste not distinctive. **Gills** attached, close to subdistant, yellow. **Stalk** 4–7 cm long, 5–16 mm thick, nearly equal, often grooved and easily split, hollow in age; surface moist or viscid, colored like the gills near the apex, yellow or orange downward to a whitish base.

SPORE PRINT: White.

MICROSCOPIC FEATURES: Spores 6–10 × 4–6.5 μm, ellipsoid, smooth, hyaline, inamyloid.

OCCURRENCE: Scattered or in groups on soil and humus in conifer or hardwoods; late spring–early winter.

EDIBILITY: Unknown.

REMARKS: *Gloioxanthomyces nitidus* (p. 279) has a viscid, depressed to funnel-shaped, bright yellow cap, long-decurrent yellow gills, a bright yellow stalk, and grows on the ground or among mosses in bogs or woodlands from late spring through early winter. The Parrot Mushroom, *Gliophorus psittacinus* (p. 278), has a small, glutinous to viscid cap that is green when young and becomes variously colored with mixtures of yellow, orange, brown, or green as it matures. It has yellow to orange non-decurrent gills, a viscid stalk colored like the cap, and grows on the ground in grassy areas or woodlands year-round. The Perplexing Waxcap, *Gliophorus perplexus* (not illustrated), is nearly identical to *Gliophorus psittacinus*, but its cap is orange brown and lacks the green coloration when young. *Gliophorus laetus* (pp. 14, 278) has a glutinous to viscid convex cap that is often depressed at the center. The cap color is highly variable and ranges from shell pink to peach, cream, yellow, orange, gray, or a mixture of these colors. It has non-decurrent gills, a glutinous stalk that is colored like the cap, and grows among sphagnum mosses or in wet woodlands from summer through early winter.

Hygrocybe flavescens

Hygrocybe miniata (Fr.) P. Kumm.

= *Hygrophorus miniatus* (Fr.) Fr.

COMMON NAME: Fading Scarlet Waxcap.
MACROSCOPIC FEATURES: **Cap** 2–4 cm wide, convex, becoming broadly convex to nearly flat, with a depressed disc in age; surface smooth, brilliant scarlet when moist, fading to orange or yellow and becoming fibrillose-scurfy when dry; **flesh** thin, colored like the cap or paler; odor and taste not distinctive. **Gills** adnate to slightly decurrent, close to subdistant, waxy, colored like the cap when young, becoming paler orange to orange pink or yellow in age. **Stalk** 2.5–7 cm long, 3–6 mm thick, equal or compressed, stuffed; surface dry, smooth, colored like the cap when young, fading to orange yellow or yellow in age.
SPORE PRINT: White.
MICROSCOPIC FEATURES: Spores 6–8 × 4–6 μm, ellipsoid, often constricted in the middle and widened near the base, smooth, hyaline, inamyloid.
OCCURRENCE: Scattered or in groups on the ground, among mosses, or on decaying wood in hardwoods or mixed woods; summer–early winter.
EDIBILITY: Reported to be edible.
REMARKS: The name *miniata* refers to "the color of red lead or cinnabar red." *Hygrocybe cantharellus* (not illustrated) has a dry, finely scurfy, orange, scarlet, or orange-red cap and ivory, creamy-yellow, or orange-yellow gills that are typically strongly decurrent. The Pink Waxcap, *Porpolomopsis calyptriformis* = *Hygrocybe calyptriformis* (not illustrated), has a sharply conic to broadly convex, coral-red to salmon-pink cap with a sharply pointed umbo. *Hygrophorus russula* (p. 298) has a compact, squatty stature that resembles a *Russula* species. Its cap is streaked and spotted vinaceous pink to purplish red over a whitish ground color, and it grows on the ground with oaks from summer to early winter.

Hygrocybe miniata

Hygrophorus russula (Schaeff. ex Fr.) Kauffman

= *Tricholoma russula* (Schaeff. ex Fr.) Gillet

COMMON NAME: Russula-like Waxcap.
MACROSCOPIC FEATURES: **Cap** 5–12 cm wide, convex with a cottony inrolled margin at first, becoming nearly flat or centrally depressed; surface sticky or dry, minutely scaly or smooth, streaked or mottled with vinaceous pink to purplish red over a whitish ground color, sometimes bruising yellow near the margin; **flesh** firm, white or tinged pink, sometimes bruising yellow; odor not distinctive; taste bitter or not distinctive. **Gills** attached, becoming decurrent at maturity, close or crowded, spotted or flushed with purplish red in age. **Stalk** 3–8 cm long, up to 3.5 cm thick, nearly equal, solid; surface dry, powdery at the apex and smooth below, initially white, then colored like the cap.

SPORE PRINT: White.
MICROSCOPIC FEATURES: Spores 6–8 × 3–5 μm, elliptic, smooth, hyaline, inamyloid.
OCCURRENCE: Solitary, scattered, or in groups on the ground, usually under oaks; summer–early winter.
EDIBILITY: Edible, but sometimes bitter.
REMARKS: The compact, squatty stature of this mushroom resembles a species of *Russula*, but its flesh is waxy and does not easily crumble.

Hygrophorus russula

Hygrophorus subsordidus Murrill

COMMON NAME: Dirty Southern Waxcap.

MACROSCOPIC FEATURES: **Cap** 4–10 cm wide, convex to nearly plane, often with a depressed center; surface viscid, glabrous or somewhat finely cracked, white overall or sometimes pale yellow on the disc; margin even, undulating or lobed; **flesh** moderately thick, white; odor and taste not distinctive. **Gills** adnexed or adnate-subdecurrent, subdistant, sometimes forked, waxy, white, not staining when handled or bruised; edges even. **Stalk** 3–8 cm long, 1–2 cm thick, nearly equal or tapered downward; surface moist or dry, white, pruinose near the apex and fibrillose below.

SPORE PRINT: White.

MICROSCOPIC FEATURES: Spores 5.5–8 × 3–4 μm, oblong-cylindric, smooth, hyaline, inamyloid.

OCCURRENCE: Scattered or in groups on the ground in oak or pine woods or grassy areas where oaks are present; fall–winter.

EDIBILITY: Edible.

REMARKS: *Subsordidus* means "near *sordidus*," a reference to *Hygrophorus sordidus* (not illustrated), which is a more northern species. The Snowy Waxcap, *Cuphophyllus virgineus* (p. 268), has a 1–7 cm wide, moist, white to cream or ivory cap, white decurrent gills, a white stalk, and grows on the ground in grassy areas or woodlands from summer through early winter.

Hygrophorus subsordidus

Hymenopellis furfuracea (Peck) R. H. Petersen

= *Collybia radicata* var. *furfuracea* Peck
= *Oudemansiella furfuracea* (Peck) Zhu L. Yang, G. M. Muell, G. Kost & Rexer
= *Xerula furfuracea* (Peck) Redhead, Ginns & Shoemaker

COMMON NAME: Rooted Collybia.
MACROSCOPIC FEATURES: **Cap** 2–14 cm wide, convex to nearly flat, typically with a low, broad umbo; surface often wrinkled, especially around the umbo, or sometimes smooth, with a thick, rubbery cuticle, moist or dry, light brown to dark grayish brown; **flesh** white, not staining; odor and taste not distinctive. **Gills** attached to nearly free, subdistant, white. **Stalk** 7–30 cm long on the aboveground portion, 3–20 mm thick, enlarged downward, white beneath a covering of grayish to brownish scales or fibers; underground portion a long, tapered taproot up to 20 cm or more long.

SPORE PRINT: White.
MICROSCOPIC FEATURES: Spores 14–17 × 9.5–12 μm, broadly oval to elliptic, smooth, hyaline, inamyloid.
OCCURRENCE: Solitary, scattered, or in groups on the ground or on well-decayed wood in hardwoods or mixed woods; spring–fall.
EDIBILITY: Edible.
REMARKS: *Furfuracea* means "scurfy or flaky," a reference to the appearance of the aboveground portion of the stalk. The large, rubbery cap, whitish gills, and long, underground taproot are good field identification features. *Hymenopellis incognita* (p. 14) has a 2–7 cm wide cap that is brown to dark brown over the umbo and disc and brownish orange to yellowish brown outward. It has subdistant, yellowish-white gills and a 4–15 mm thick, grayish-orange to brownish-orange stalk that is enlarged downward to a radicating base. It grows in mixed hardwood forests during fall and early winter.

Hymenopellis furfuracea

Hypholoma ericaeum (Pers.) Kühner

= *Coprinarius ericaeus* Kumm.
= *Naematoloma ericaeum* (Pers.) A. H. Sm.
= *Psilocybe ericaea* Quélet
= *Stropharia subumbonatescens* Murrill

MACROSCOPIC FEATURES: **Cap** 1.2–6 cm broad, ovoid to ellipsoid in the button stage; surface glabrous except for fibrillose remains of the veil along the margin at first, viscid to subviscid when moist but soon dry, color variable, buffy brown to olive brown on the margin and tawny on the disc, hygrophanous and fading to pale pinkish buff to ochraceous buff or yellow ocher, sometimes deep orange yellow on the disc; margin appressed against the stalk, expanding to obtusely conic then nearly plane, with a small nipple-shaped umbo or a slightly depressed disc; **flesh** dull white to pale yellow; odor slightly radish-like; taste radish-like to astringent or not distinctive. **Gills** attached, subdistant, whitish to grayish, becoming deep purplish gray to almost black; edges whitish, becoming eroded. **Stalk** 4–13 cm long, 2.5–10 mm thick, nearly equal, solid; surface brown at first, becoming white near the apex and creamy white below, finally yellow in age, usually with a superior fibrillose zone and white basal mycelium.

SPORE PRINT: Purple-brown.

MICROSCOPIC FEATURES: Spores 11–13.5 × 6.5–8 μm, ellipsoid to subovoid, with an apical pore, thick-walled, smooth, brownish.

OCCURRENCE: Scattered or in groups in grassy wet areas near ponds, in sphagnum mosses, along roadsides, or in low moist areas in pine woodlands; fall–winter.

EDIBILITY: Unknown.

REMARKS: It is widely distributed along the Gulf Coast and has been reported as far north as Ohio. The Sphagnum-bog Galerina, *Galerina tibiicystis* (not illustrated), has a 2–3 cm wide, conical cap that becomes sharply umbonate. Its cap surface is moist, glabrous, translucent-striate, hygrophanous, yellow ocher to brownish yellow or golden brown, becoming lighter yellow as it dries. It has brownish-yellow, even or finely fimbriate gills, a dull yellow or brownish stalk, and grows partially to deeply embedded in sphagnum mosses during spring.

Hypholoma ericaeum

Hypholoma fasciculare (Huds.) P. Kumm.

= *Hypholoma subviride* (Berk. & M. A. Curtis) A. H. Sm.

COMMON NAME: Sulphur Tuft.
MACROSCOPIC FEATURES: **Cap** 2–8 cm wide, convex to nearly flat, often with an umbo; surface smooth, moist or dry, orange yellow to sulfur yellow or greenish yellow, with a darker orange to brownish-orange disc; margin occasionally rimmed with veil remnants; **flesh** pale yellow, bruising brownish; odor not distinctive; taste bitter. **Gills** attached, close, yellow to greenish yellow when young, becoming grayish then tinged pale purple brown at maturity. **Stalk** 5–12 cm long, 3–10 mm thick, nearly equal or tapered in either direction; surface fibrillose, pale yellow to yellow, becoming fulvous from the base upward; partial veil fibrous to cortinate, usually leaving a thin, superior ring zone.

SPORE PRINT: Purple brown.
MICROSCOPIC FEATURES: Spores 6.5–8 × 3.5–4 μm, elliptic, with an apical pore, smooth, pale purple brown.
OCCURRENCE: In clusters on conifer or hardwood logs and stumps or on the surrounding soil; spring–fall.
EDIBILITY: Poisonous.
REMARKS: *Fasciculare* means "bundles," a reference to the growth habit of this mushroom. Although *Hypholoma subviride* is considered a synonym of *Hypholoma fasciculare*, as listed above and in *Index Fungorum*, it is sometimes treated as a distinct species. It has a smaller cap, 1–3 cm wide, a thinner and shorter stalk, and virtually identical spores. The Brick Cap, *Hypholoma lateritium = Hypholoma sublateritium* (p. 303), has a brick-red cap with a paler margin and grows in clusters on hardwood stumps and logs.

Hypholoma fasciculare

Hypholoma lateritium (Schaeff.) P. Kumm.

= *Hypholoma sublateritium* (Fr.) Quél.

COMMON NAME: Brick Cap.
MACROSCOPIC FEATURES: **Cap** 2–10 cm wide, convex, becoming broadly convex to nearly flat; surface smooth with a few yellowish hairs, moist or dry, brick-red centrally, paler at the margin; **flesh** thick, dull yellow, not staining; odor not distinctive; taste sometimes bitter or not distinctive. **Gills** attached, close, pale yellow to greenish yellow at first, later tinged purple. **Stalk** 5–12 cm long, up to 1.5 cm thick, nearly equal, pale and smooth at the apex, dull brown and covered with reddish-brown fibers below the ring; partial veil a whitish cortina, leaving a thin ring.

SPORE PRINT: Dark purplish brown.
MICROSCOPIC FEATURES: Spores 6–7 × 3.5–4.5 μm, elliptic, with an apical pore, smooth, pale brown.
OCCURRENCE: In groups or clusters on hardwood logs; summer–early winter.
EDIBILITY: Edible.
REMARKS: *Hypholoma capnoides* (not illustrated) has a yellow-orange to reddish-orange or orange-cinnamon cap, typically with white veil remnants on the margin. It has a whitish, cortinate partial veil that leaves remnants on the cap margin and a thin annular zone and grows on decaying conifer wood during summer through early winter.

Hypholoma lateritium

Inocybe rimosa (Bull.) P. Kumm.

= *Inocybe fastigiata* (Schaeff.) Quél.

COMMON NAME: Straw-colored Fiber Head.
MACROSCOPIC FEATURES: **Cap** 2–9 cm wide, broadly conical when young, becoming broadly convex to nearly flat with a distinct conical umbo in age; surface slippery when wet, silky and shiny when dry, covered overall with radial fibers, golden or straw yellow to honey brown, often darker over the disc; margin incurved when young, whitish, becoming cracked and yellowish in age; **flesh** white; odor and taste not distinctive. **Gills** attached, close, whitish when young, becoming grayish then coffee brown at maturity. **Stalk** 4–9 cm long, 3–12 mm thick, nearly equal or slightly tapered downward; surface silky, fibrillose, longitudinally striate, whitish, developing yellowish tinges in age; partial veil and ring absent.

SPORE PRINT: Brown.
MICROSCOPIC FEATURES: Spores 9–15 × 5–8 μm, elliptic, smooth, pale brown.
OCCURRENCE: Solitary, scattered, or in groups on the ground and among mosses under conifers or hardwoods; summer–winter.
EDIBILITY: Poisonous.
REMARKS: *Rimosa* means "having cracks or fissures," a reference to the cap. *Inocybe calospora* (not illustrated) has a dry, brown, scaly cap with a pointed umbo, whitish to brown gills with white edges, a pale brown to reddish-brown, finely hairy stalk, grows in groups on the ground with hardwoods. It has subglobose spores with prominent spines; spores measure 9–13 × 8–11 μm.

Inocybe rimosa

Laccaria amethystina Cooke

= *Clitocybe amethystina* (Cooke) Peck
= *Collybia amethystina* (Cooke) Quél.

COMMON NAME: Amethyst Laccaria.
MACROSCOPIC FEATURES: **Cap** 0.5–5 cm wide, convex to flat or centrally depressed; surface moist or dry, strongly hygrophanous, often translucent-striate or striate, finely pruinose to fibrillose, occasionally becoming finely fibrillose-scaly, bright grayish purple when young and fresh, fading to pinkish purple then grayish to buff; margin inrolled at first; **flesh** thin, pale pinkish purple; odor and taste not distinctive. **Gills** attached to slightly decurrent, subdistant, dark grayish purple, fading to pinkish purple, retaining the purple color longer than the cap. **Stalk** 2–7.5 cm long, 1.5–8 mm thick, nearly equal or slightly bulbous at the base; surface dry, longitudinally striate, fibrillose, grayish purple when young, soon fading to pinkish purple or pale pinkish brown; basal mycelium violet at first, becoming white.
SPORE PRINT: White to very pale violet.
MICROSCOPIC FEATURES: Spores excluding ornamentation 7–10 × 6.5–10 μm, globose, spiny, hyaline; spines 1.5–3 μm long.
OCCURRENCE: Solitary, scattered, or in groups on the ground or among mosses in hardwoods or mixed woods, usually with oak or beech; summer–fall.
EDIBILITY: Unknown.
REMARKS: *Amethystina* means "violet," a reference to the colors of this mushroom. The Pink Mycena, *Mycena pura* (p. 15), is similar but smells and tastes like radish.

Laccaria amethystina

Laccaria laccata complex (Scop.) Cooke

= Clitocybe laccata (Scop.) P. Kumm.

COMMON NAME: Common Laccaria.
MACROSCOPIC FEATURES: **Cap** 1–6 cm wide, convex, becoming nearly plane, sometimes with a central depression or perforation, hollow in age; surface dry, finely scaly or smooth, orange brown to reddish brown, fading to buff; margin wavy and uplifted at maturity, typically not striate, often torn or split on older specimens; **flesh** thin, colored like the cap; odor and taste not distinctive. **Gills** attached or decurrent, close to subdistant, pinkish, sometimes tinged with purple. **Stalk** 1.5–10 cm long, 3–10 mm thick, nearly equal down to a slightly swollen base; surface fibrillose, sometimes longitudinally striate, colored like the cap; basal mycelium white.

SPORE PRINT: White.
MICROSCOPIC FEATURES: Spores excluding ornamentation 7–11 × 5–8.5 μm, subglobose to ellipsoid, hyaline, inamyloid; spines 1–2.3 μm long.
OCCURRENCE: Scattered or in groups on the ground with conifers or hardwoods; year-round.
EDIBILITY: Edible.
REMARKS: *Laccaria laccata* var. *pallidifolia* (not illustrated) has a glabrous to finely scaly cap, globose to subglobose spores that measure 6.4–13 × 6–11.5 μm, and 0.5–2 μm long spines. It grows on the ground with pines year-round. *Laccaria trichodermophora* (p. 308) has a larger cap, pale violet basal mycelium that fades to white, and smaller spores.

Laccaria laccata complex

Laccaria ochropurpurea (Berk.) Peck

= *Clitocybe ochropurpurea* (Peck) Sacc.

COMMON NAME: Purple-gilled Laccaria.
MACROSCOPIC FEATURES: **Cap** 5–13 cm wide, obtuse to convex, becoming nearly plane; surface smooth to very finely fibrous or slightly scaly, sometimes cracking in age, light violet brown or pinkish buff at first, fading to buff or whitish in age; margin incurved at first, not striate; **flesh** thick, violet buff; odor and taste not distinctive. **Gills** attached to somewhat decurrent, close to subdistant, thick and waxy, dark purple or violet to violet gray. **Stalk** 5–15 cm long, 1.5–3.5 cm thick, sometimes enlarged at the base; surface coarsely fibrous, usually with brownish to reddish-brown longitudinal striations or scales or both, ground color light violet brown or pinkish buff at first, fading to buff in age.

SPORE PRINT: White to pale violet.
MICROSCOPIC FEATURES: Spores excluding ornamentation 6.5–11 × 6.5–9.5 μm, globose to subglobose, spiny, hyaline, inamyloid; spines 1–1.5 μm long.
OCCURRENCE: Solitary, scattered, or in groups on the ground with conifers or in mixed woods, especially with oak and pine, sometimes in grassy areas or road cuts; summer–early winter.
EDIBILITY: Edible.
REMARKS: Compare with *Laccaria trullisata* (p. 309), which occurs in sand dunes or very sandy areas with sand covering much of the stalk. It has smooth to very finely roughened spores. Both *Laccaria ochropurpurea* and *L. trullisata* are easy to differentiate from other *Laccaria* species due to their larger size.

Laccaria ochropurpurea

Laccaria trichodermophora
G. M. Muell.

MACROSCOPIC FEATURES: **Cap** 1–7 cm wide, convex to plane, occasionally uplifted, often depressed at the center; surface moist or dry, strongly pruinose to fibrillose, becoming fibrillose-scaly to scaly, hygrophanous, brownish orange to reddish brown, fading to light brown or buff, typically darkest over the disc; margin incurved at first, not striate, becoming wavy, lobed, or eroded in age; **flesh** thin, pale pinkish to vinaceous pink; odor and taste not distinctive. **Gills** sinuate to adnate, often with a decurrent tooth, subdistant, vinaceous pink. **Stalk** 2–12 cm long, 2–11 mm thick, nearly equal down to a slightly enlarged base, hollow in age; surface dry, fibrillose, inconspicuously to moderately longitudinally striate, whitish to pale brown or reddish brown, sometimes paler at the apex and darker below; basal mycelium pale violet when fresh, soon fading to white.

SPORE PRINT: White.

MICROSCOPIC FEATURES: Spores excluding ornamentation 6–10.6 × 6–9.2 μm, subglobose to broadly ellipsoid, spiny, hyaline; spines 0.5–2 μm long.

OCCURRENCE: Scattered or in groups on the ground in conifer or mixed woods, usually with pines; fall–winter.

EDIBILITY: Edible.

REMARKS: The *Laccaria laccata* complex (p. 306) is similar, but it has a smaller cap, white basal mycelium, and larger spores. Other similar species, such as *Laccaria bicolor* (not illustrated), have a much more northern distribution.

Laccaria trichodermophora

Laccaria trullisata (Ellis) Peck

= *Clitocybe trullisata* Ellis

COMMON NAME: Sandy Laccaria.
MACROSCOPIC FEATURES: Cap 3.5–7.5 cm wide, convex to plane, sometimes depressed at the center; surface dry, fibrillose to finely scaly, grayish purple when very young, becoming red brown to brown or buff to pinkish buff; margin incurved, not striate; **flesh** thick, pale purple to pale purple gray; odor and taste not distinctive. **Gills** attached to somewhat decurrent, close to subdistant, thick and waxy, purple to dark violet gray, becoming dull reddish violet in age. **Stalk** 4–9 cm long, 1–2.5 cm thick, enlarged at the base; surface dry, fibrillose, longitudinally striate, brown to buff or pinkish buff, covered with sand on the lower portion or overall.

SPORE PRINT: White.
MICROSCOPIC FEATURES: Spores 14–21 × 5.5–8 μm, subfusiform to fusiform-ellipsoid, smooth to very finely roughened, hyaline.
OCCURRENCE: Scattered or in groups in sand or very sandy soil, especially in dunes, usually with pines; summer–winter.
EDIBILITY: Edible.
REMARKS: When growing in dunes, it is often buried up to the cap in sand. The elliptical, smooth spores separate this mushroom from all other *Laccaria* species.

Laccaria trullisata

Laccaria vinaceobrunnea G. M. Muell.

MACROSCOPIC FEATURES: **Cap** 7–25(-42) mm wide, obtuse to convex, becoming plane to uplifted, often depressed over the center; surface finely fibrillose to fibrillose-scaly, hygrophanous, purplish lilac when young, becoming dark vinaceous brown to reddish brown, then fading to orange brown, and finally buff in age; margin decurved to plane, entire or eroded, not striate or finely striate when wet; **flesh** thin, light brownish vinaceous; odor and taste not distinctive. **Gills** adnate to arcuate, subdistant to distant, thick, waxy, purple. **Stalk** 1–6(-10) cm long, 2–7 mm thick, nearly equal down to a slightly enlarged or somewhat clavate base, fibrillose, occasionally with recurved fibrils or finely striate, colored like the cap; basal mycelium violet.

SPORE PRINT: White.

MICROSCOPIC FEATURES: Spores excluding ornamentation 7–10.6 × 6.4–10 μm, subglobose to broadly ellipsoid, spiny, hyaline; spines 0.5–1.8 μm long. Cheilocystidia 31–95 × 5–11 μm abundant, filamentous to clavate, hyaline.

OCCURRENCE: Scattered or in groups in sandy soil under Live Oak; year-round.

EDIBILITY: Unknown.

REMARKS: *Vinaceobrunnea* means "vinaceous brown," a reference to the cap color. The small cap diameter, growth in sandy soil under Live Oak, subglobose to broadly ellipsoid spores, and abundant cheilocystidia are good identification features.

Laccaria vinaceobrunnea

Lactarius alachuanus Murrill

MACROSCOPIC FEATURES: **Cap** 5–7.5 cm wide, convex to nearly flat, often shallowly depressed, and sometimes with a slight umbo; surface azonate, glabrous, moist to viscid when fresh, pale pinkish cinnamon to pale yellowish cinnamon when young, becoming pinkish buff in age. **Gills** narrowly attached to slightly decurrent, moderately broad, close, sometimes forking, pinkish buff, slowly darkening when bruised. **Stalk** 2.5–7 cm long, 10–16 mm thick, nearly equal or tapered downward, often curved at the base, dry, solid, pinkish buff, with a white canescence, pinkish cinnamon when rubbed. **Flesh** moderately thick, firm, whitish; odor not distinctive or sometimes aromatic; taste slightly bitter, then moderately acrid. **Latex** white on exposure, unchanging, not staining the gills; taste slowly and moderately acrid.

SPORE PRINT: White to creamy white.

MICROSCOPIC FEATURES: Spores 7.5–9 × 6–7.5 μm, broadly ellipsoid, ornamented with warts and ridges that sometimes form a partial reticulum, prominences up to 1.5 μm high, hyaline, amyloid.

OCCURRENCE: Scattered or in groups on sandy soil and rotting wood in mixed oak and pine woods; fall–winter.

EDIBILITY: Unknown.

REMARKS: Large fruitings are very common in Central Florida following rainy periods. Considerable variation in cap color may be observed depending on moisture content. Compare with *Lactifluus allardii* (p. 340), which has a similarly colored cap and stalk, but its latex slowly becomes greenish olive then brownish and stains gills dull green to olive and, finally, dull brown.

Lactarius alachuanus

Lactarius argillaceifolius Hesler & A. H. Sm.

MACROSCOPIC FEATURES: **Cap** 4–18 cm wide, convex, becoming broadly convex with a depressed center; surface finely pubescent when young, becoming glabrous, slimy and sticky when wet, azonate, lilac brown when young, fading to lilac tan or pale lilac gray, and finally pale tan or pinkish buff at the center. **Gills** attached to slightly decurrent, broad, close, cream when young, developing pinkish tints near the margin, and finally flushed dull brownish orange in age, staining buff or olive brown to dark brown when bruised. **Stalk** 6–9 cm long, 1.5–3.5 cm thick, nearly equal or tapering downward, slimy or dry, whitish, spotted and stained brownish in age, not scrobiculate. **Flesh** firm, white to buff; odor not distinctive; taste mild to slowly slightly acrid. **Latex** creamy white on exposure, staining the gills grayish brown to dark brown or olive brown; taste mild to slowly slightly acrid.
SPORE PRINT: Pinkish buff.

MICROSCOPIC FEATURES: Spores 7–11 × 7–8 µm, subglobose to elliptic, ornamented with warts and ridges that sometimes form a partial reticulum, prominences up to 1 µm high, hyaline, amyloid.
OCCURRENCE: Scattered or in groups in hardwoods, especially with oak; July–October.
EDIBILITY: Unknown.
REMARKS: *Lactarius fumaecolor* (not illustrated) is very similar, but it has narrow gills that stain yellow-brown to dark brown where injured, white latex that tastes slowly acrid, and spores with prominences that do not form a reticulum. The Willow Milky, *Lactarius controversus* (not illustrated), has a pinkish to lavender or brownish cap, pale pink to pale vinaceous-brown gills, and white, unchanging latex that does not stain tissues and tastes slowly acrid. It grows under willow or poplar. *Lactarius albolutescens* (not illustrated) has an azonate, yellowish to pale tan or pale dull pinkish cap, pale grayish-pink to pale lavender gills, and white latex that soon changes to greenish yellow and tastes slowly acrid. It grows under mixed pines and hardwoods.

Lactarius argillaceifolius

Lactarius atroviridis Peck

MACROSCOPIC FEATURES: **Cap** 6–15 cm wide, broadly convex, becoming flat with a depressed center; surface dry, scurfy to minutely scaly, pitted, various shades of green, ranging from olive to dark grayish green, usually zoned with concentrically arranged dark green spots. **Gills** attached to slightly decurrent, close, cream to pinkish white, occasionally forked near the stalk, staining greenish gray to brownish; edges typically olive brown to greenish. **Stalk** 2–8 cm long, 1–3 cm thick, nearly equal, hollow, dry, colored and streaked like the cap, scrobiculate. **Flesh** whitish to pinkish brown, not staining; odor not distinctive; taste acrid. **Latex** white on exposure, very slowly turning greenish, staining gills dark grayish green to greenish brown; taste acrid.

SPORE PRINT: Cream to buff.

MICROSCOPIC FEATURES: Spores 7–10 × 6–9 μm, subglobose to elliptic, ornamented with warts and ridges that form a partial reticulum, prominences up to 0.5 μm high, hyaline, amyloid.

OCCURRENCE: Solitary to scattered in conifer or hardwoods; summer–fall.

EDIBILITY: Unknown.

REMARKS: The green colors of the cap and stalk and darker green spots are distinctive features.

Lactarius atroviridis

Lactarius chelidonium var. *chelidonium* Peck

COMMON NAME: Celandine Lactarius.
MACROSCOPIC FEATURES: **Cap** 5–8 cm wide, convex, becoming broadly convex to nearly flat, disc depressed, surface slightly viscid, glabrous, grayish green to grayish yellow or yellow brown, with bluish green tints in age, sometimes with a few narrow zones on the margin. **Gills** attached to slightly decurrent, narrow, close, forked and wavy near the stalk, grayish yellow. **Stalk** 2.5–4 cm long, 7–20 mm thick, nearly equal, dry, glabrous, hollow in age, colored like the cap. **Flesh** yellow at first, becoming blue overall, staining green where bruised; taste mild. **Latex** scant, yellow on exposure, changing to dingy brownish yellow, staining gills green; taste mild.

SPORE PRINT: Yellowish.
MICROSCOPIC FEATURES: Spores 8–10 × 6–7 µm, ellipsoid, ornamented with warts and ridges that form a partial reticulum, prominences up to 0.5 µm high, hyaline, amyloid.
OCCURRENCE: Scattered or in groups on sandy soil under pines; summer–fall.
EDIBILITY: Edible.
REMARKS: The cap of *Lactarius paradoxus* (p. 324) is zoned with bands of grayish blue, grayish purple, green, and blue; it stains green when bruised. It has scanty, dark vinaceous-brown latex on exposure that stains tissues green.

Lactarius chelidonium var. *chelidonium*

Lactarius chrysorrheus Fr.

COMMON NAME: Gold Drop Milk Cap.
MACROSCOPIC FEATURES: **Cap** 3–9 cm wide, convex, then soon slightly depressed over the disc, becoming broadly funnel-shaped in age; surface moist to lubricous or subviscid, soon dry with a whitish canescence, glabrous, azonate or with watery spots more or less arranged in zones, subhygrophanous, whitish to pale yellowish cinnamon with darker spots when young, fading to nearly whitish overall in age. **Gills** attached to short-decurrent, narrow, close, sometimes forked near the stalk, whitish to pale orange buff or slightly darker, usually not discoloring but sometimes spotting vinaceous or brown. **Stalk** 3–8 cm long, 1–2 cm thick, nearly equal, moist or dry, glabrous, hollow in age, whitish, sometimes flushed orange-buff in age, at times somewhat strigose at the base. **Flesh** thin, whitish, soon becomes yellow when cut; odor not distinctive; taste distinctly acrid, slowly at times. **Latex** copious, white on exposure, quickly changing to yellow, not staining tissues; taste acrid, slowly at times.

SPORE PRINT: Pale yellow.
MICROSCOPIC FEATURES: Spores 6–9 × 5.5–6.5 μm, broadly ellipsoid, ornamented with warts and ridges that sometimes form a partial reticulum, prominences up to 0.5 μm high, hyaline, amyloid.
OCCURRENCE: Solitary, scattered, or in groups in hardwoods and mixed woods, especially with oak; summer–fall.
EDIBILITY: Unknown.
REMARKS: *Lactarius moschatus* (not illustrated), reported only from Texas, is also similar, but it has a faintly zonate, pinkish-tan cap, watery to white latex that does not change color, and white to whitish flesh that tastes musky.

actarius chrysorrheus

Lactarius croceus Burl.

MACROSCOPIC FEATURES: **Cap** 5–10 cm wide, convex, becoming broadly convex to nearly flat with a depressed center; surface glabrous, slimy when wet, shiny when dry, bright orange to saffron yellow initially, fading to paler yellow orange or yellowish tan in age, azonate or sometimes distinctly zoned with darker orange bands. **Gills** attached to slightly decurrent, broad, close to subdistant, creamy buff to pale yellow tan, staining sulfur yellow where cut or bruised. **Stalk** 3–6 cm long, 1–2 cm thick, nearly equal, stuffed, becoming hollow, glabrous, at times velvety at the base, colored like the cap or paler, sometimes spotted brownish. **Flesh** thick, whitish, staining sulfur yellow before the latex changes color; odor not distinctive; taste bitter or acrid. **Latex** white on exposure, soon changing to sulfur yellow, staining gills and flesh sulfur yellow; taste bitter or acrid.

SPORE PRINT: Yellowish.

MICROSCOPIC FEATURES: Spores 7.5–10 × 5.5–7.5 μm, elliptic, ornamented with warts and ridges that form a partial reticulum, prominences up to 0.6 μm high, hyaline, weakly amyloid.

OCCURRENCE: Solitary or scattered in hardwoods, especially with oak; summer–fall.

EDIBILITY: Unknown.

REMARKS: The orange cap and white latex that changes to sulfur yellow are its distinctive features. *Croceus* means saffron-colored, a reference to the color of its cap and stalk.

Lactarius croceus

Lactarius delicatus Burl.

MACROSCOPIC FEATURES: **Cap** 6–12 cm wide, convex with a depressed disc, becoming funnel-shaped; surface slimy-viscid, glabrous, faintly zonate, pale orange yellow with yellowish salmon tints over the disc; margin inrolled and covered with coarse short hairs at first. **Gills** attached to subdecurrent, narrow, close, sometimes forked near the stalk, whitish, becoming pale buff to pale orange yellow. **Stalk** 1.5–5 cm long, 1.5–2.3 cm thick, nearly equal or tapered downward, viscid, glabrous, stuffed to hollow, scrobiculate, colored like the cap. **Flesh** firm, white; odor pungent or not distinctive. **Latex** scant, white on exposure, soon changing to sulphur yellow; taste acrid.

SPORE PRINT: Whitish with a yellowish-salmon tint.

MICROSCOPIC FEATURES: Spores 7–9.5 × 6–7 μm, broadly ellipsoid, ornamented with isolated warts and ridges that form a partial reticulum, prominences up to 0.5 μm high, hyaline, amyloid.

OCCURRENCE: Scattered or in groups in hardwoods, usually with oaks; summer–fall.

EDIBILITY: Unknown.

REMARKS: *Lactarius pseudodelicatus* (not illustrated), reported from Florida, is very similar; it has a creamy white spore deposit, white latex that is unchanging, and flesh with a distinct odor of lemon extract or disinfectant and a slightly acrid to acrid taste.

actarius delicatus

Lactarius gerardii Peck

COMMON NAME: Gerard's Milky.

MACROSCOPIC FEATURES: **Cap** 3–13 cm wide;
convex, becoming broadly convex to flat,
wrinkled, with a depressed center in age, with
or without an umbo; surface dry, slightly
sticky when wet, velvety when dry, azonate,
brown to yellow brown or tan. **Gills** attached
to decurrent, broad, subdistant to distant,
crossveined, whitish to cream. **Stalk** 3.5–8 cm
long, 8–20 mm thick, nearly equal or enlarged
downward, usually with an abruptly tapered
base, stuffed when young, becoming hollow in
age, dry, velvety, dark brown to yellow-brown,
paler and often plicate at the apex. **Flesh** firm,
thin, white, not staining; odor not distinctive;
taste mild, then slowly slightly acrid. **Latex**
white on exposure, unchanging, not staining;
taste mild, then slowly slightly acrid.

SPORE PRINT: White.

MICROSCOPIC FEATURES: Spores 7–10 × 7.5–9
μm, globose to subglobose or broadly ellipsoid, ornamented with warts and ridges that
form a reticulum, prominences up to 0.8 μm
high, hyaline, amyloid.

OCCURRENCE: Scattered or in groups under
hardwoods or conifers; summer–fall.

EDIBILITY: Edible.

REMARKS: The flesh stains yellow with KOH.
Lactarius gerardii var. *subrubescens* (not illustrated) is very similar, but its flesh stains vinaceous pink when exposed. *Lactifluus petersenii*
(p. 15) has a smoky yellowish-brown cap,
close gills, a nearly equal concolorous stalk,
and dingy brown to pinkish-brown latex on
exposure.

Lactarius gerardii

Lactarius imperceptus Beardslee & Burl.

MACROSCOPIC FEATURES: **Cap** 3–9 cm wide, broadly convex to nearly flat, usually slightly depressed on the disc with a small umbo at maturity, glabrous, azonate; surface dry to slightly sticky when wet, pale cinnamon to pinkish cinnamon or pale reddish brown, typically pitted and stained with darker pinkish cinnamon; margin sometimes striate in age. **Gills** attached to slightly decurrent, close, whitish to pinkish white, usually staining brownish, occasionally forked at the stalk. **Stalk** 3–9 cm long, 6–20 mm thick, tapered downward or nearly equal, solid, dry to moist, pinkish white, darkening in age, glabrous, with a whitish tomentose base. **Flesh** whitish, sometimes staining yellow when exposed; odor not distinctive; taste acrid, sometimes slowly. **Latex** white to creamy white on exposure, sometimes slowly darkening to yellow; taste bitter then acrid, or only acrid, sometimes slowly.
SPORE PRINT: White to pale cream.
MICROSCOPIC FEATURES: Spores 8–11 × 7–8.5 µm, broadly ellipsoid, ornamented with heavy bands that do not form a complete reticulum, prominences up to 1.5 µm high, hyaline, amyloid.

OCCURRENCE: Solitary, scattered, or in groups on the ground or in needle litter in conifer or hardwoods, especially with oaks or pines; summer–winter.
EDIBILITY: Unknown.
REMARKS: The flesh stains pale olive with FeSO4. The staining of the flesh and color change of the latex are variable features, especially if the fruiting bodies are soaked following heavy rainfall. *Lactarius subisabellinus* (not illustrated) has an azonate, pale pinkish-buff or buff cap, cream-colored or slightly darker gills that don't stain when bruised, and a whitish to buff stalk. It has mild-tasting flesh, white, unchanging latex that tastes mild, a whitish to pale yellow spore print, and grows on the ground, usually with oaks, during summer through early winter. *Lactarius fumosus* (not illustrated) has a pale dingy yellow-brown to smoky-tinged whitish cap, white, unchanging latex that stains tissues reddish, mild-tasting white flesh that slowly becomes faintly acrid, and a pinkish-buff spore print. *Lactarius eburneus* (not illustrated) has a dull yellow-buff to cinnamon-buff or pale reddish-brown cap, a white stalk, whitish to light buff gills, mild-tasting white flesh, scant white latex that stains gills reddish, and a white spore print.

Lactarius imperceptus

Lactarius indigo var. *diminutivus*
Hesler & A. H. Sm.

COMMON NAME: Diminutive Indigo Milk Cap.
MACROSCOPIC FEATURES: **Cap** 3–5 cm wide, convex to nearly flat, often depressed at the center, becoming broadly funnel-shaped in age; surface viscid to slimy, glabrous, somewhat zonate, dark blue when fresh, gray blue with a silvery sheen when dry, becoming gray green to olive green with age; margin sometimes striate, inrolled at first. **Gills** decurrent to long-decurrent, broad, close, with several tiers of lamellulae, colored like the cap, becoming green with age, staining indigo when bruised, aging slowly to gray green or olive. **Stalk** 1.5–2.5 cm long, 5–8 mm thick, tapered downward, solid, becoming hollow in age, colored like the cap. **Flesh** white, quickly changing to dark blue, then to green after thirty minutes; odor and taste not distinctive. **Latex** copious, deep indigo blue, unchanging, staining tissues dark indigo; taste mild.

SPORE PRINT: White.
MICROSCOPIC FEATURES: Spores 7–9 × 6–7.5 µm, subglobose to broadly ellipsoid, ornamented with lines and warts that form a broken to complete reticulum, prominences up to 0.5 µm high, hyaline, amyloid.
OCCURRENCE: Scattered or in groups on the ground among grasses and weeds, usually in pinewoods; summer–early winter.
EDIBILITY: Unknown.
REMARKS: *Lactarius indigo* var. *indigo* (p. 321) is a more robust species with a much larger cap and stalk, scant dark blue latex that slowly turns green; it grows in conifer or hardwoods.

Lactarius indigo var. *diminutivus*

Lactarius indigo var. *indigo*
(Schwein.) Fr.

COMMON NAMES: Indigo Milk Cap, Indigo Milky.

MACROSCOPIC FEATURES: **Cap** 5–15.5 cm wide, convex to convex-depressed, becoming broadly funnel-shaped; surface viscid, glabrous, zonate to nearly azonate, dark blue when fresh, fading to grayish blue to grayish with a silvery luster, often with dark green areas where bruised; margin inrolled at first. **Gills** attached or short-decurrent, broad, close, sometimes forked near the stalk, dark blue at first, becoming paler blue at maturity, developing yellowish tints in age, staining green when bruised. **Stalk** 2–8 cm long, 1–2.5 cm thick, nearly equal or tapered downward, hollow in age, viscid but soon dry, dark blue when young, paler blue in age, sometimes with a sheen, often scrobiculate. **Flesh** thick, firm, whitish, rapidly staining dark blue on exposure then slowly greenish; odor not distinctive; taste mild or, rarely, slightly bitter then slightly acrid. **Latex** scant, dark blue on exposure, slowly becoming dark green; taste mild.

SPORE PRINT: Creamy white.

MICROSCOPIC FEATURES: Spores 7–9 × 5.5–7.5 μm, broadly ellipsoid to subglobose, ornamented with ridges that form a partial to complete reticulum, prominences up to 0.5 μm high, hyaline, amyloid.

OCCURRENCE: Solitary, scattered, or in groups in conifer or hardwoods; summer–winter.

EDIBILITY: Edible.

REMARKS: *Lactarius indigo* var. *diminutivus* (p. 320) is similar but has a much smaller, viscid to slimy cap that is dark blue at first and soon becomes gray blue then gray green to olive green in age and copious, unchanging, dark blue latex.

Lactarius indigo var. indigo

Lactarius lignyotus var. *lignyotus* Fr.

COMMON NAME: Chocolate Milky.

MACROSCOPIC FEATURES: **Cap** 2–10 cm wide, convex with an incurved margin and a small, pointed umbo when young, becoming nearly flat or with a depressed disc and retaining the umbo; surface velvety, dry, usually wrinkled, azonate, blackish brown, slowly fading in age to dingy yellow brown; margin sulcate to plicate. **Gills** attached to somewhat decurrent, close to subdistant, white, slowly becoming pale ochraceous. **Stalk** 5–11 cm long, 5–13 mm thick, enlarged downward or nearly equal, solid, with distinct longitudinal ridges at the apex, dry, velvety, blackish brown to pale yellow brown with a white base. **Flesh** white, staining rosy pink to dull reddish when cut; odor not distinctive; taste mild or slightly bitter, not acrid. **Latex** copious, white on exposure, unchanging, staining gills reddish; taste mild to slightly bitter, not acrid.

SPORE PRINT: Bright ocher.

MICROSCOPIC FEATURES: Spores 9–11 × 9–10 μm, nearly globose, ornamented with warts and ridges that form a partial reticulum, prominences up to 1.5 μm high, hyaline, amyloid.

OCCURRENCE: Scattered or in groups on the ground and among mosses under conifers or hardwoods with oaks; summer–fall.

EDIBILITY: Unknown.

REMARKS: *Lactarius lignyotus* var. *canadensis* (not illustrated) has subdistant, white gills with dark brown edges at first that become distant and pale ochraceous tan in age. It has mild-tasting, white, unchanging latex that stains tissues reddish and dries vinaceous brown. *Lactarius texensis* (not illustrated) has a plicate and distinctly wrinkled, dark brown to nearly black cap, dark to pale tan gills with dark brown edges, a dark brown stalk, and mild-tasting, white latex.

Lactarius lignyotus var. *lignyotus*

Lactarius maculatipes Burl.

MACROSCOPIC FEATURES: **Cap** 5–9 cm wide, broadly convex, becoming nearly flat with a depressed center, often broadly funnel-shaped in age; surface glabrous, slimy and sticky when fresh, whitish to cream overall, becoming tawny on the disc in age, with pale yellow zones and spots which darken in age. **Gills** decurrent, narrow, crowded, sometimes forked, whitish, becoming pinkish buff, staining yellowish to pale ocher when cut or bruised. **Stalk** 3–8 cm long, 1–2.5 cm thick, tapered downward, slimy, colored like the cap, spotted and streaked with darker tan, staining yellow when bruised or in age, scrobiculate. **Flesh** white, slowly staining yellowish on exposure; odor not distinctive; taste slowly acrid. **Latex** white on exposure, unchanging, staining gills and flesh yellowish; taste slowly acrid.

SPORE PRINT: Pinkish buff to yellowish.

MICROSCOPIC FEATURES: Spores 6.5–8 × 6–7.5 µm, subglobose to broadly ellipsoid, ornamented with warts and ridges that sometimes form a partial reticulum, prominences up to 1 µm high, hyaline, amyloid.

OCCURRENCE: Scattered or in groups on the ground under oaks; summer–winter.

EDIBILITY: Unknown.

REMARKS: Compare with *Lactarius psammicola* f. *glaber* (not illustrated), which has a broadly funnel-shaped cap with alternating zones of light buff and pale tan to darker dull orange, and flesh and latex that tastes strongly burning, acrid.

actarius maculatipes

Lactarius paradoxus Beardslee & Burl.

COMMON NAME: Silver-blue Milky.
MACROSCOPIC FEATURES: **Cap** 5–8 cm
wide, broadly convex, becoming flat with
a depressed center, often funnel-shaped in
age; surface glabrous, slimy to sticky when
wet, with a silvery sheen when young, zoned
with bands of grayish blue, grayish purple,
green, and blue, staining green when bruised.
Gills attached to slightly decurrent, narrow
to broad, close, occasionally forked near the
stalk, pinkish orange, staining blue green
when bruised. **Stalk** 2–3 cm long, 1–1.5 cm
thick, nearly equal or tapered downward, hollow, dry, colored like the cap, staining green
when bruised or in age. **Flesh** thick, whitish
with greenish to bluish tints, slowly staining greenish when cut or bruised; odor not
distinctive; taste mild or slightly acrid. **Latex**
scant, dark vinaceous brown on exposure,
staining tissues green; taste mild or slightly
acrid.

SPORE PRINT: Cream to yellow.
MICROSCOPIC FEATURES: Spores 7–9 × 5.5–6.5
μm, broadly ellipsoid, ornamented with warts
and ridges that form a partial reticulum, prominences up to 1 μm high, hyaline, amyloid.
OCCURRENCE: Solitary, scattered, or in groups
on the ground or in grass under pines, oaks,
and palmetto palms; summer–winter.
EDIBILITY: Edible.
REMARKS: *Lactarius chelidonium* var. *chelidonium* (p. 314) is similar, but it has a grayish-
green cap with blue and yellow tints and
yellow latex. The Variegated Milky, *Lactarius
subpurpureus* (p. 15), has a reddish-pink to
vinaceous-pink cap that is spotted or zonate
and sometimes stained emerald green, a stalk
that is colored like the cap with darker red
scrobiculation, gills that are colored like the
cap, and scant wine-red latex.

Lactarius paradoxus

Lactarius peckii var. peckii Burl.

COMMON NAME: Peck's Milky.

MACROSCOPIC FEATURES: **Cap** 5–15.5 cm wide, broadly convex with a depressed center; surface dry, velvety when young then scurfy to nearly glabrous, color variable, typically dull brick-red or brownish red but also orange brown to orange red or dull reddish orange, often paler toward the margin, usually distinctly zoned with darker bay-red to orange-red bands, often fading in age; margin sometimes striate on young specimens. **Gills** decurrent, close, narrow, pale cinnamon buff at first, soon tinged pinkish cinnamon and darkening in age, staining rusty brown to reddish brown. **Stalk** 2–6 cm long, 1–2.5 cm thick, nearly equal, hollow in age, covered with a whitish bloom when young, colored like the cap but usually paler, often spotted reddish brown or dull orange in age, not scro-biculate. **Flesh** firm, pale vinaceous brown, not staining when cut; odor not distinctive; taste extremely acrid. **Latex** copious, white on exposure, unchanging, not staining tissues; taste extremely acrid.

SPORE PRINT: White.

MICROSCOPIC FEATURES: Spores 6–7.5 μm, globose to subglobose, ornamented with warts and ridges that form a partial to complete reticulum, prominences up to 0.8 μm high, hyaline, amyloid.

OCCURRENCE: Solitary, scattered, or in groups on the ground in oak woods; summer–fall.

EDIBILITY: Unknown.

REMARKS: It has gills which are among the darkest in the genus. *Lactarius peckii* var. *glaucescens* (not illustrated) is nearly identical except that the latex dries pale bluish green. *Lactarius peckii* var. *lactolutescens* (not illustrated) is also nearly identical, but it has very acrid white latex that quickly changes to ivory yellow on exposure and dries pale yellowish green.

Lactarius peckii var. *peckii*

Lactarius proximellus Beardslee & Burl.

MACROSCOPIC FEATURES: **Cap** 2.5–6 cm wide, broadly convex-umbilicate, then expanding to shallowly funnel-shaped; surface viscid when wet, whitish pruinose in the center, distinctly zonate, zones tawny to brownish orange with darker brownish-orange to cinnamon zones; margin uplifted at length and more or less fluted, sometimes striate. **Gills** attached to slightly decurrent, narrow to moderately broad, close, sometimes forked near the stalk, whitish at first, becoming pale brownish yellow. **Stalk** 1.3–2 cm long, 8–10 mm thick, nearly equal or enlarged slightly at the apex, pruinose when young, pale yellow, becoming pale bluish green where bruised. **Flesh** pale cream; odor not distinctive; taste very acrid. **Latex** scant, white on exposure, unchanging; taste very acrid.

SPORE PRINT: Very pale yellow.

MICROSCOPIC FEATURES: Spores 7.5–9 × 6–7.5 µm, broadly ellipsoid, ornamented with warts and ridges that form a partial reticulum, prominences up to 0.5 µm high, hyaline, amyloid.

OCCURRENCE: On sandy soil or in grassy areas under oaks or pines; summer–early winter.

EDIBILITY: Unknown.

REMARKS: The stocky stature, tawny to brownish-orange zonate cap, whitish to pale brownish-yellow gills, and scant acrid latex are its distinctive features. *Lactarius peckii* (p. 325) is similar, but it has darker pinkish-cinnamon gills and copious latex.

Lactarius proximellus

Lactarius psammicola f. *psammicola* A. H. Sm.

MACROSCOPIC FEATURES: **Cap** 4–14 cm wide, convex to broadly convex and deeply depressed, expanding to broadly vase-shaped; surface glutinous, coarsely fibrillose, the fibrils agglutinated, ochraceous buff to ochraceous orange, becoming dingy yellow brown in age, with conspicuous light buff zones, especially when young; margin inrolled and coarsely strigose at first, becoming appressed-fibrillose in age. **Gills** decurrent, narrow, close, sometimes forked near the stalk, whitish to light buff at first, becoming darker and sordid ochraceous in age, sometimes staining pinkish lilac. **Stalk** 1–3 cm long, 1–2 cm thick, tapered downward, dry, stuffed or hollow, whitish to grayish, often scrobiculate. **Flesh** thick, dingy buff, sometimes staining pinkish lilac; odor not distinctive; taste acrid. **Latex** copious, white on exposure, slowly changing to pale dingy pinkish lilac or not changing or staining this color; taste very acrid.

SPORE PRINT: Yellowish.

MICROSCOPIC FEATURES: Spores 7.5–9 × 6–7.5 μm, ellipsoid, ornamented with warts and ridges that sometimes form a partial reticulum, prominences up to 0.5 μm high, hyaline, amyloid.

OCCURRENCE: In hardwoods or mixed woods, usually with oak present; summer–early winter.

EDIBILITY: Unknown.

REMARKS: The flesh stains pale dull bluish gray with $FeSO_4$. *Lactarius psammicola* f. *glaber* (not illustrated) is very similar, but it has a glabrous, viscid cap with light buff to pale tan and dull orange zones and whitish flesh with a slightly fragrant odor.

Lactarius psammicola f. *psammicola*

Lactarius quietus (Fr.) Fr.

= *Lactarius quietus* var. *incanus* Hesler &
    A. H. Sm.

MACROSCOPIC FEATURES: **Cap** 3–11 cm
wide, broadly convex, becoming flat with a
depressed center in age; surface coated with a
layer of tiny, whitish, silky fibrils when young,
soon glabrous or with scattered small bumps,
moist or dry, at times with water spots, typically zonate, dark purplish brown or purplish
gray when young, becoming dark red brown at
the center in age, with a paler pinkish-brown
to pinkish-buff margin; margin slightly translucent-striate when mature. **Gills** attached to
slightly decurrent, narrow, often forked, close,
white to whitish with pink tints, becoming
cinnamon, staining orange cinnamon in age.
Stalk 4–14 cm long, 5–10 mm thick, equal
or slightly enlarged at the base, solid, becoming hollow, dry, covered with a layer of tiny,
whitish, silky fibrils when young, colored like
the cap and darkening progressively toward
the apex as it matures. **Flesh** pale pinkish buff;
odor sweet, fragrant, often like burnt sugar, or,
rarely, not distinctive; taste mild then slowly
weakly acrid. **Latex** white on exposure in
young specimens, soon watery as specimens
mature; taste mild then slowly, weakly acrid.

SPORE PRINT: Pinkish buff.

MICROSCOPIC FEATURES: Spores 6.5–9 × 5–7.5
µm, elliptic, ornamented with warts and
ridges that sometimes form a partial reticulum, prominences up to 0.6 µm high, hyaline,
amyloid.

OCCURRENCE: Scattered or in groups under
oaks; summer–early winter.

EDIBILITY: Unknown.

REMARKS: The flesh in the stalk base stains
grayish with $FeSO_4$. The typically zonate
brownish cap and fragrant, slowly, weakly
acrid-tasting flesh are good identification
features. *Lactarius helvus* (not illustrated) has
an orange-brown to pale cinnamon-brown cap
and stalk, creamy-white gills that become pale
pinkish cinnamon, flesh variously described as
fragrant like maple sugar or resembling chicory or fenugreek, and watery latex. *Lactarius
hysginus* (not illustrated) has a sticky to slimy
reddish-brown cap with a pinkish-cinnamon
margin, whitish gills when young that become
orange yellow at maturity, a scrobiculate stalk
that is colored like the cap, acrid flesh, and a
yellowish spore print. It grows on the ground
with conifers during summer and fall.

Lactarius quietus

Lactarius rimosellus Peck

= *Lactarius obnubiloides* Thiers.

MACROSCOPIC FEATURES: **Cap** 2–8 cm wide, convex, becoming depressed and typically papillate or umbonate at maturity; surface dry, azonate, somewhat wrinkled, becoming rimulose-areolate, especially toward the margin, dull ferruginous to rusty brown at first, soon becoming dull vinaceous pink to pinkish cinnamon, fading to pale vinaceous cinnamon in age. **Gills** decurrent, narrow, close, sometimes forked near the stalk, whitish then somewhat yellowish or ochraceous, finally colored like the cap. **Stalk** 3–8 cm long, 3–10 mm thick, nearly equal overall, sometimes with a pinched base, dry, hollow in age, nearly glabrous, colored like the cap or paler. **Flesh** thin, brittle, colored like the cap or paler; odor fragrant, often sweet; taste mild or sometimes disagreeable. **Latex** white to whey-like or watery on exposure, unchanging, not staining tissues; taste mild.

SPORE PRINT: Whitish to yellowish.
MICROSCOPIC FEATURES: Spores 7–10 × 6.5–8 μm, ellipsoid, ornamented with isolated warts that are occasionally connected by fine lines or bands that do not form a reticulum, prominences up to 1 μm high, hyaline, amyloid.
OCCURRENCE: Scattered or in groups on the ground, among mosses, on decaying logs and stumps, in deep pine needle humus, or under conifers; summer–winter.
EDIBILITY: Unknown.
REMARKS: *Rimosellus* means "finely cracked," a reference to the cap surface. *Lactarius neotabidus* (not illustrated) has a 1–4.5 cm wide, azonate, rusty to cinnamon-red or apricot-orange cap that is convex to somewhat funnel-shaped, with a slight umbo, and a translucent-striate margin. It has a rusty-red stalk with reddish-tan hairs, white to watery-white, mild-tasting latex, and grows with mosses in wet areas.

Lactarius rimosellus

Lactarius salmoneus var. *salmoneus*
Peck

= *Lactarius salmoneus* var. *curtisii* (Coker)
   Hesler & A. H. Sm.

MACROSCOPIC FEATURES: **Cap** 2.5–8 cm wide, convex, becoming nearly flat and depressed at the center; surface dry, somewhat velvety, azonate, white at first, becoming orange nearly overall as the white layer wears away, staining orange when bruised, sometimes staining bluish green. **Gills** attached to decurrent, narrow, close to subdistant, typically not forked, light orange at first, becoming paler orange to ochraceous buff in age, staining dark orange or green when bruised. **Stalk** short, 1.2–2.5 cm long, 6–13 mm thick, tapered downward, dry, glabrous, hollow in age, white at first, becoming light orange overall as the white layer wears away or sometimes retaining white areas, usually not scrobiculate, sometimes staining green. **Flesh** moderately thick, firm, light orange, staining darker orange especially near the gills when exposed; odor slightly fragrant or not distinctive; taste slightly peppery or mild. **Latex** scant, dark orange on exposure, staining gills dark orange; taste slightly peppery or mild.

SPORE PRINT: Creamy white.

MICROSCOPIC FEATURES: Spores 7.5–9 × 5–6 μm, ellipsoid, ornamented with warts and ridges that form a partial reticulum, prominences up to 0.4 μm high, hyaline, amyloid.

OCCURRENCE: Solitary, scattered, or in groups on the ground or in wet areas under pine or in mixed oak and pine woods; summer–fall.

EDIBILITY: Unknown.

REMARKS: *Salmoneus* is a reference to the orange colors of all parts of this mushroom.

Lactarius salmoneus var. *salmoneus*

Lactarius speciosus Burl.

MACROSCOPIC FEATURES: **Cap** 3–10 cm wide, broadly convex, becoming nearly flat with a depressed center in age, often broadly funnel-shaped; surface sticky when young, becoming dry, covered with a thin layer of fibrils, pale cinnamon or orange brown, conspicuously zonate with bands of pinkish tan and cinnamon brown; margin inrolled and bearded with coarse hairs when young, expanded to uplifted and glabrous in age. **Gills** attached to slightly decurrent, close, cream to pinkish buff, staining dull lilac when cut or bruised. **Stalk** 3–5 cm long, 1–2.5 cm thick, equal, hollow, dry, whitish to buff, often scrobiculate with reddish-brown and yellowish spots and streaks. **Flesh** thick, firm, whitish; odor not distinctive; taste mild to slightly bitter or acrid. **Latex** white on exposure, unchanging, staining the gills and flesh dull lilac; taste mild to slightly bitter or acrid.

SPORE PRINT: White.

MICROSCOPIC FEATURES: Spores 10–13.5 × 9–11 μm, broadly ellipsoid, ornamented with warts and ridges that form a partial reticulum, prominences up to 2 μm high, hyaline, amyloid.

OCCURRENCE: Scattered or in groups in hardwoods and mixed woods; summer–early winter.

EDIBILITY: Unknown.

REMARKS: The zonate, pale cinnamon to orange-brown cap, inrolled and bearded margin on young specimens, and white latex that stains gills dull lilac when cut are good field identification features.

Lactarius speciosus

Lactarius subpalustris Hesler & A. H. Sm.

MACROSCOPIC FEATURES: **Cap** 10–20 cm wide, broadly convex to nearly flat with a depressed center; surface slimy to viscid, glabrous, azonate to obscurely zonate, dingy pinkish gray with ochraceous tones, with orange-olive to dingy yellow-brown spots and often developing a dingy gray cast overall in age. **Gills** decurrent, broad, close to subdistant, creamy buff at first, becoming pinkish buff to cinnamon buff in age, readily staining lilac where injured. **Stalk** 5–10 cm long, 1.5–2.5 cm thick, viscid but soon dry, firm, hollow in age, glabrous, colored like the cap but paler, typically scrobiculate. **Flesh** thick, watery buff, soon staining bright lilac; odor not distinctive; taste mild. **Latex** whey-like, pale dingy buff on exposure, unchanging, staining tissues lilac; taste mild to somewhat bitter.

SPORE PRINT: Pinkish buff.
MICROSCOPIC FEATURES: Spores 8–11 × 7–9 μm, subglobose to broadly ellipsoid, ornamented with bands and warts that do not form a reticulum, prominences up to 2 μm high, hyaline, amyloid.
OCCURRENCE: Scattered or in groups in moist areas or lowlands, usually in mixed conifer and hardwoods; summer–fall.
EDIBILITY: Unknown.
REMARKS: *Subpalustris* refers to "marshes, swamps, fens, and boggy areas," where this mushroom often grows. The flesh and latex stain purple with FeSO4. *Lactarius maculatus* (not illustrated) is similar, but it has a concentrically spotted and zonate, dull grayish-lilac to brownish-gray cap, whitish gills, a scrobiculate stalk that is colored like the cap, and white latex that stains tissues dull lilac and tastes weakly to distinctly acrid.

Lactarius subpalustris

Lactarius subplinthogalus Coker

= *Lactarius marylandicus* A. H. Sm. & Hesler

MACROSCOPIC FEATURES: **Cap** 3–5 cm wide, nearly plane, becoming broadly funnel-shaped in age; surface nearly glabrous when young, becoming finely wrinkled in age, whitish when young, becoming yellowish buff to pale tan, and finally brownish yellow in age; margin uplifted and conspicuously scalloped or pleated. **Gills** attached to slightly decurrent, broad, distant, colored like the cap, staining rosy salmon when cut and bruised. **Stalk** 3–8 cm long, 7–15 mm thick, equal or tapered slightly downward, solid, becoming hollow, glabrous, dry, cream with orangish or orange-brown stains in age. **Flesh** whitish, staining rosy salmon when cut or bruised; odor not distinctive; taste acrid. **Latex** white on exposure, unchanging, staining gills and flesh rosy salmon; taste acrid.

SPORE PRINT: Pinkish buff to cinnamon buff.
MICROSCOPIC FEATURES: Spores 7.5–9.5 × 7–8 µm, subglobose to broadly ellipsoid, ornamented with warts and ridges that do not form a reticulum, prominences up to 2.5 µm high, hyaline, amyloid.
OCCURRENCE: Solitary to scattered under oak or in oak and pine woods; summer–fall.
EDIBILITY: Unknown.
REMARKS: Compare with *Lactarius subvernalis* var. *cokeri* (p. 335), which also has white, unchanging latex that stains gills and flesh pinkish to pinkish orange, but the gills are crowded.

Lactarius subplinthogalus

Lactarius subserifluus Longyear

MACROSCOPIC FEATURES: **Cap** 2–7 cm wide, convex-depressed, becoming funnel-shaped in age, usually umbonate or papillate; surface dry, glabrous, orange brown, becoming paler in age; margin often finely scalloped to wavy in age. **Gills** decurrent, narrow or broad, subdistant, yellowish, soon stained vinaceous cinnamon, and orange cinnamon overall or tinted vinaceous in age. **Stalk** 5–12 cm long, 3–7 mm thick, nearly equal, moist, hard, glabrous, orange cinnamon on the upper portion, dark rusty brown below; base with orange-cinnamon hairs. **Flesh** thin; odor not distinctive; taste mild or faintly acrid. **Latex** watery on exposure, unchanging, staining the gills vinaceous cinnamon; taste mild.

SPORE PRINT: Pinkish buff.

MICROSCOPIC FEATURES: Spores 6–7.5 × 6–7 μm, globose to subglobose, ornamented with warts and ridges that form a partial reticulum, prominences up to 1.5 μm high, hyaline, amyloid.

OCCURRENCE: Solitary to scattered or rarely in groups under oak and hickory; summer–fall.

EDIBILITY: Unknown.

REMARKS: Its distinguishing features include the orange-brown cap, orange-cinnamon to rusty brown stalk with orange-brown hairs at the base, yellowish subdistant decurrent gills that are soon stained vinaceous cinnamon, and the small spores.

Lactarius subserifluus

Lactarius subvernalis var. *cokeri*
(A. H. Sm. & Hesler) Hesler & A. H. Sm.

= *Lactarius cokeri* A. H. Sm. & Hesler

MACROSCOPIC FEATURES: **Cap** 2–6 cm
wide, broadly convex to flat, and shallowly
depressed when mature, with or without an
umbo; surface dry, unpolished to powdery,
glabrous and finely wrinkled in age, azonate
to faintly zonate at the margin, whitish when
young, becoming buff-tinged to pale smoky
brownish; margin lobed or wavy, sometimes
arcuate. **Gills** broadly attached to short-
decurrent, crowded, narrow, forking near the
stalk, whitish to pinkish buff, spotting pinkish where injured. **Stalk** 5–7 cm long, 8–15
mm thick, equal to slightly enlarged at the
base, stuffed or hollow, dry, white, covered
by whitish bloom when young, pallid when
the bloom is removed, staining pinkish where
bruised. **Flesh** fairly thick, white, staining
onionskin brown when cut; odor not distinctive; taste acrid. **Latex** white, unchanging,
staining gills and flesh pinkish where cut; taste
acrid.

SPORE PRINT: Yellow.

MICROSCOPIC FEATURES: Spores 7–9 μm,
globose to subglobose, ornamented with a
complete reticulum of coarse and fine ridges,
prominences 0.6–1.5 μm high, hyaline,
amyloid.

OCCURRENCE: Scattered or in groups under
hardwoods; summer–fall.

EDIBILITY: Unknown.

REMARKS: *Lactarius subvernalis* var. *subvernalis*
(not illustrated), reported only from the Sam
Houston National Forest, Texas, is similar, but
it has a pale tan to pinkish-tan or yellowish
cap that becomes darker yellow over the disk
and latex that is milk white on exposure and
changes to yellow ocher.

Lactarius subvernalis var. *cokeri*

Lactarius tomentosomarginatus
Hesler & A. H. Sm.

MACROSCOPIC FEATURES: **Cap** 4–9 cm wide, convex-depressed, becoming vase-shaped; surface dry, appressed-fibrillose to silky, white at first, becoming flushed dull grayish pink, and finally pale dingy orange brown; margin incurved and long remaining arched, lacking a cottony roll on all stages. **Gills** decurrent, narrow, crowded, often forked, especially near the stalk, white when young, becoming pinkish buff then cinnamon buff, and darkening to dull brown in age. **Stalk** 3–5 cm long, 1.3–3 cm thick, nearly equal or narrowed downward, dry, solid, firm, somewhat velvety, white. **Flesh** thick, hard, white, slowly darkening to more or less pinkish buff where cut; odor not distinctive; taste acrid. **Latex** scant, white on exposure, unchanging, staining tissues cinnamon buff; taste acrid.
SPORE PRINT: Whitish.
MICROSCOPIC FEATURES: Spores 9–11 × 7–8.5 µm, ellipsoid, ornamented with isolated warts and indistinct lines that do not form a reticulum, prominences up to 0.7 µm high, hyaline, amyloid.
OCCURRENCE: Solitary, scattered, or in groups in hardwoods or mixed woods, usually with oak; summer–fall.

EDIBILITY: Unknown.
REMARKS: The flesh stains vinaceous cinnamon with FeSO4. The Deceptive Milky, *Lactifluus deceptivus* (p. 15), is similar and has a strongly acrid taste, but it has a larger cap and stalk, a conspicuous cottony inrolled margin on young specimens, and larger spore prominences that measure up to 1.5 µm high. *Lactarius angustifolius* (not illustrated) has a velvety, azonate, white cap, crowded tan to yellowish gills, abundant, extremely acrid, white latex that stains the gills dull yellow buff, and grows with hardwoods. *Lactarius caerule-itinctus* (not illustrated) has a deeply funnel-shaped, azonate, white to whitish cap, and close, often forked, white gills that stain pale brown when bruised. It has a finely pubescent to nearly glabrous stalk that is milk white tinged pale blue and becomes more intensely blue after being picked. The flesh is white and tastes slowly and distinctly acrid. It has copious, whitish, unchanging latex that stains tissues pale brown. It grows on the ground in mixed woods during late summer and fall. *Lactarius echinatus* (not illustrated) has an ivory-yellow cap that sometimes becomes pale olive gray in age, yellowish to pale tan gills, a white to yellowish stalk, white flesh that changes to brownish lavender when cut, and white latex that tastes acrid and disagreeable.

Lactarius tomentosomarginatus

Lactarius vietus (Fr.) Fr.

= *Lactarius parvus* Peck
= *Lactarius trivialis* var. *gracilis* Peck
= *Lactarius varius* Peck

MACROSCOPIC FEATURES: **Cap** 1–8 cm wide, broadly convex, becoming flat in age with a depressed center; surface dry, slightly sticky when wet, glabrous, moist, azonate, dark vinaceous brown to reddish brown when young, fading to pale grayish brown or pale lilac gray in age; margin wavy and sometimes finely scalloped or pleated in age. **Gills** attached to slightly decurrent, broad, close, pinkish white to cream, soon staining dingy brown when bruised. **Stalk** 3–6 cm long, 8–18 mm thick, equal, fragile, dry or moist, pale pinkish brown overall. **Flesh** whitish to pinkish buff; odor not distinctive; taste acrid. **Latex** white on exposure, changing to or drying olive gray, staining gills gray to olive gray or grayish brown; taste acrid.

SPORE PRINT: White to cream.

MICROSCOPIC FEATURES: Spores 7.5–9 × 6–7.5 μm, ellipsoid to broadly ellipsoid, ornamented with warts and ridges that sometimes form a partial reticulum, prominences up to 0.4 μm high, hyaline, amyloid.

OCCURRENCE: Scattered or in groups or clusters on decaying conifer or hardwoods or sometimes on the ground; summer–fall.

EDIBILITY: Unknown.

REMARKS: The flesh slowly stains grayish with $FeSO_4$. The dark brown cap that fades to pinkish brown or lilac gray, acrid, white latex that changes to olive gray, pinkish-buff gills that soon stain dingy brown when bruised, and its typical growth habit on wood are its distinctive features. *Lactarius cinereus* var. *fagetorum* (not illustrated) has an azonate, gray to olivaceous-gray or olive-buff cap with lilac tinges, crowded, white to creamy-white gills that stain brownish in age, and acrid, white latex that does not stain tissues. It grows under hardwoods, especially beech.

Lactarius vietus

Lactarius xanthydrorheus Singer

MACROSCOPIC FEATURES: **Cap** 9–25 mm wide, broadly convex to nearly flat, and sometimes shallowly depressed at maturity; surface dry, subglabrous, papillate, conspicuously rugose-venose over the disc, dingy yellowish olive or more brownish, especially on the disc; margin arcuate, sometimes short-sulcate. **Gills** arcuate-decurrent, narrow, subdistant, cream-colored, unchanging and not staining when bruised. **Stalk** 11–22 mm long, 2–4 mm thick, nearly equal, dry, subglabrous, solid at first, becoming hollow in age, colored like the gills, with whitish basal mycelium. **Flesh** fragile, white, not changing when cut; odor not distinctive; taste mild. **Latex** watery on exposure, instantly changing to yellow, not staining tissues; taste mild.

SPORE PRINT: Whitish.
MICROSCOPIC FEATURES: Spores 7.5–9 × 6–7.5 µm, ellipsoid to broadly ellipsoid, ornamented with spines and ridges that form a partial reticulum, prominences up to 1.5 µm high, hyaline, amyloid.
OCCURRENCE: Scattered or in groups under hardwoods, especially oak; summer–fall.
EDIBILITY: Unknown.
REMARKS: The small stature, papillate and coarsely wrinkled vein-like cap, and mild-tasting flesh are the distinctive identification features of this uncommon milk mushroom.

Lactarius xanthydrorheus

Lactarius yazooensis Hesler & A. H. Sm.

MACROSCOPIC FEATURES: **Cap** 5–15.5 cm wide, convex, becoming broadly convex with a depressed center then broadly funnel-shaped; surface viscid when wet, glabrous, buff to pale yellow, and conspicuously zonate, darker zones orange ochraceous to rusty orange or dull orange red, gradually becoming paler and more ochraceous, with alternating cinnamon-buff and paler zones on mature specimens; margin inrolled and minutely pubescent at first. **Gills** attached, becoming decurrent, moderately broad, crowded, pallid to pale vinaceous cinnamon at first, becoming vinaceous cinnamon to dull vinaceous or light pinkish brown, slowly staining brownish. **Stalk** 2–6 cm long, 1–2.5 cm thick, nearly equal, dry, glabrous, whitish to pallid or somewhat discolored in age. **Flesh** firm, pallid, unchanging when cut; odor not distinctive; taste excruciatingly acrid. **Latex** copious, milk white on exposure, unchanging, not staining tissues; taste exceedingly acrid.

SPORE PRINT: Buff to yellowish.
MICROSCOPIC FEATURES: Spores 7–9 × 6–7.5 µm, subglobose to broadly ellipsoid, ornamented with warts and ridges that do not form a complete reticulum, prominences up to 1.5 µm high, hyaline, amyloid.
OCCURRENCE: Scattered or in groups in grassy areas under hardwoods, especially oaks; summer–fall.
EDIBILITY: Unknown.
REMARKS: The conspicuously zonate cap, excruciatingly acrid-tasting flesh, and color change of the gills from pallid to dull vinaceous or light pinkish brown are its distinguishing features.

Lactarius yazooensis

Lactifluus allardii (Coker) De Crop

= *Lactarius allardii* Coker

MACROSCOPIC FEATURES: **Cap** 6–15.5 cm
wide, convex, becoming broadly convex with
a depressed center; surface dry, somewhat velvety to nearly glabrous, azonate, whitish when
very young or when covered by fallen leaves,
soon pale pinkish cinnamon to pinkish buff,
often with grayish-red tints then becoming
pale cinnamon to orange brown, and finally
dull brick-red in age, typically streaked and
spotted white, especially on the margin. **Gills**
attached to decurrent, close to subdistant
at first, becoming nearly distant at maturity,
white to ivory yellow. **Stalk** 2–5 cm long,
1–3 cm thick, tapered downward to nearly
equal, hollow, dry, glabrous, colored like the
cap or paler. **Flesh** firm, compact, white,
slowly staining pinkish then olivaceous when
exposed; odor pungent in age or not distinctive; taste acrid. **Latex** white on exposure,
slowly becoming greenish olive then brownish, staining gills dull green to olive then
slowly dull brown; taste acrid.

SPORE PRINT: White to creamy white.
MICROSCOPIC FEATURES: Spores 8–11 × 5–8
µm, ellipsoid to subglobose, ornamented with
warts and ridges that do not form a reticulum, prominences up to 0.2 µm high, hyaline,
amyloid.
OCCURRENCE: Scattered or in groups in hardwoods and mixed woods; summer–fall.
EDIBILITY: Unknown.
REMARKS: Its flesh rapidly stains vinaceous
red with the application of FeSO4. *Lactarius
similis* (not illustrated), reported only from
Mississippi, is very similar, but it has a smaller,
pale vinaceous-cinnamon cap that often fades
to pale yellow and mild-tasting latex. Also
compare with *Lactarius alachuanus* (p. 311),
which has white latex that does not stain gills.

Lactifluus allardii

Lactifluus corrugis (Peck) Kuntze

= *Lactarius corrugis* Peck

COMMON NAME: Corrugated-cap Milky.
MACROSCOPIC FEATURES: **Cap** 4–20 cm wide; convex, becoming broadly convex to nearly flat with a depressed center in age; surface velvety, dry, azonate, distinctly wrinkled to finely corrugated, reddish brown to vinaceous brown, paler and sometimes orange brown on the margin, often with a whitish bloom, especially when young. **Gills** attached, close, occasionally forked, pale cinnamon to pale golden brown, staining darker brown when bruised. **Stalk** 5–11 cm long, 1.5–3 cm thick, equal, solid, dry, velvety, pale grayish cinnamon to pale pinkish cinnamon, sometimes with a whitish bloom. **Flesh** whitish, staining brown; odor slightly or strongly fishy in mature mushrooms, often not distinctive in young specimens; taste mild. **Latex** copious, white on exposure, unchanging, staining gills and flesh tawny brown; taste mild.

SPORE PRINT: White.
MICROSCOPIC FEATURES: Spores 9–12 × 8.5–12 μm, subglobose, ornamented with warts and ridges that form a partial reticulum, prominences up to 0.8 μm high, hyaline, amyloid.
OCCURRENCE: Solitary to scattered in hardwoods and mixed woods, usually with oak present; summer–fall.
EDIBILITY: Edible.
REMARKS: *Lactifluus volemus* var. *volemus* (p. 348) is very similar but has a less wrinkled, dark orange-brown to cinnamon-brown cap that is paler orange brown toward the margin. *Lactifluus volemus* var. *flavus* (p. 347) is also similar, but it has a yellow to orange-yellow cap and a cream to pale yellow stalk.

Lactifluus corrugis

Lactifluus glaucescens (Crossl.) Verbeken

= *Lactarius glaucescens* Crossl.
= *Lactarius piperatus* var. *glaucescens* (Crossl.) Hesler & A. H. Sm.

MACROSCOPIC FEATURES: **Cap** 4–12 cm wide, convex, becoming nearly flat with a depressed center; surface dry, dull to somewhat shiny, glabrous, sometimes rimose-areolate in dry weather, white to pale cream when young, becoming dingy yellow brown in age, especially over the center. **Gills** subdecurrent to decurrent, broad, crowded, often forked, whitish to dull cream, very slowly staining brown when bruised. **Stalk** 3–9 cm long, 1–3 cm thick, tapered downward or sometimes nearly equal, dry, solid, glabrous, white to pale cream. **Flesh** thick, hard, pale cream, unchanging or very slowly staining pale bluish green when cut; odor faintly pungent or not distinctive; taste acrid. **Latex** white to whitish on exposure, not staining tissues, drying pale bluish green; taste very acrid.

SPORE PRINT: White to yellowish.

MICROSCOPIC FEATURES: Spores 6.5–9 × 5–7 μm, broadly ellipsoid, ornamented with warts and fine lines that do not form a reticulum, prominences up to 0.2 μm high, hyaline, amyloid.

OCCURRENCE: Solitary, scattered, or in groups in hardwoods, especially oak; summer–winter.

EDIBILITY: Poisonous, according to the late Florida mycologist Robert Williams.

REMARKS: The latex stains yellow to orange with KOH. *Lactifluus piperatus* (p. 345) is very similar, but it has white latex that does not dry bluish green.

Lactifluus glaucescens

Lactifluus hygrophoroides (Berk. & M. A. Curtis) Kuntze

= *Lactarius hygrophoroides* Berk. & M. A. Curtis

COMMON NAME: Hygrophorus Milky.
MACROSCOPIC FEATURES: **Cap** 3–10 cm wide, broadly convex, becoming nearly flat with a depressed center in age, sometimes broadly funnel-shaped; surface dry, glabrous to slightly velvety, sometimes slightly wrinkled toward the margin in age, dull orange to orange brown or dull orange cinnamon. **Gills** attached to slightly decurrent, broad, distant at maturity, crossveined, white to cream or yellowish buff. **Stalk** 3–5 cm long, 5–15 mm thick, nearly equal, solid, dry, pale orange brown to orange yellow. **Flesh** white; odor not distinctive; taste mild. **Latex** white on exposure, unchanging, not staining gills or flesh; taste mild.

SPORE PRINT: White.
MICROSCOPIC FEATURES: Spores 7.5–10.5 × 6–7.5 µm, elliptic, ornamented with warts and ridges, prominences up to 0.4 µm high, hyaline, amyloid.
OCCURRENCE: Solitary, scattered, or in groups in hardwoods; summer–early winter.
EDIBILITY: Edible.
REMARKS: *Lactifluus rugatus* (p. 346) is very similar, but it has conspicuous concentric wrinkles near the cap margin, white flesh that stains vinaceous to dull red with $FeSO_4$, and grows in hardwoods, especially oak.

Lactifluus hygrophoroides

Lactifluus luteolus (Peck) Verbeken

= *Lactarius luteolus* Peck

COMMON NAME: Buff Fishy Milky.
MACROSCOPIC FEATURES: **Cap** 2.5–8 cm
wide, convex to nearly flat, often shallowly
depressed in age; surface dry, slightly velvety,
azonate, whitish to buff with a white bloom,
becoming brownish in age. **Gills** attached
to slightly decurrent, close, white becoming cream, staining yellow brown to brown.
Stalk 2.5–6 cm long, 6–20 mm thick, tapered
downward or nearly equal, solid to stuffed,
dry, slightly velvety, whitish to buff, staining
brown. **Flesh** white, staining brown; odor not
distinctive in young specimens, soon becoming fishy or unpleasant and resembling spoiled
crab; taste mild. **Latex** copious, sticky, watery
white to white on exposure, unchanging,
staining gills brown; taste mild.

SPORE PRINT: White to cream.
MICROSCOPIC FEATURES: Spores 7–9 × 5.5–7
µm, elliptic, ornamented with warts and
ridges that sometimes form a partial reticulum, prominences up to 0.8 µm high, hyaline,
amyloid.
OCCURRENCE: Solitary, scattered, or in groups
on the ground in hardwoods or mixed woods,
usually with oak present; summer–early
winter.
EDIBILITY: Edible.
REMARKS: Its distinctive features are the
slightly velvety, whitish cap, copious sticky
latex that stains tissues brown, and the strong
fishy to spoiled crab-like odor of the flesh of
mature specimens.

Lactifluus luteolus

Lactifluus piperatus (L.) Roussel

= *Lactarius piperatus* (L.) Pers.

COMMON NAMES: Peppery Milky, Peppery White Milk Cap.

MACROSCOPIC FEATURES: Cap 3–15.5 cm wide, convex, becoming nearly flat to depressed, and finally funnel-shaped; surface dry, azonate, glabrous or sometimes uneven to finely wrinkled, white when young, becoming creamy white with ochraceous to dingy tan stains in age. **Gills** attached to decurrent, narrow, very crowded, often forked one or more times, white at first, becoming pale cream at maturity, usually not staining but sometimes staining yellowish when bruised. **Stalk** 2–8 cm long, 1–2.5 cm thick, nearly equal, dry, firm, solid, pruinose, white. **Flesh** white, unchanging when cut, not staining or sometimes slowly staining yellowish; odor not distinctive; taste quickly and strongly acrid. **Latex** white on exposure, unchanging, not staining tissues or sometimes slowly staining the gills yellowish and drying yellow; taste quickly and strongly acrid.

SPORE PRINT: White.

MICROSCOPIC FEATURES: Spores 4.5–7 × 5–5.5 μm, ellipsoid, ornamented with fine lines and isolated particles that do not form a reticulum, prominences up to 0.2 μm high, hyaline, amyloid.

OCCURRENCE: Solitary, scattered, or in groups on the ground under conifers or hardwoods.

EDIBILITY: Edible.

REMARKS: *Lactifluus glaucescens* (p. 342) is very similar, but its white to whitish latex dries bluish green. *Lactarius subvellereus* var. *subdistans* (not illustrated) is similar and has a white cap and stalk, white gills that are subdistant to distant and become yellowish in age. They sometimes have hyaline droplets, and stain brownish to pinkish where injured. Its latex is white on exposure, dries creamy yellow, and has a strongly acrid taste.

actifluus piperatus

Lactifluus rugatus (Kühner & Romagn.) Verbeken

= *Lactarius hygrophoroides* var. *rugatus* Hesler
  & A. H. Sm.
= *Lactarius rugatus* Kühner & Romagn.

MACROSCOPIC FEATURES: **Cap** 4.5–8 cm wide,
convex to flat, becoming cup-shaped with a
depressed center; surface dull and velvety,
with concentric wrinkles near the margin, dry,
rusty orange brown, darker toward the center,
azonate; margin incurved and lobed. **Gills**
subdecurrent, distant, thick and rigid, with
3–4 tiers of lamellulae, narrow, cream-colored
to pale golden color in age, not staining or
only weakly staining brown when bruised.
Stalk 3.5–6 cm long, 1–1.6 cm thick, nearly
equal, stuffed, tomentose, dry, orange cream
to vinaceous cinnamon. **Flesh** thick, rigid;
odor not distinctive; taste mild. **Latex** white
to watery, abundant, unchanging; taste mild.

SPORE PRINT: White.

MICROSCOPIC FEATURES: Spores 7.5–9 × 6–7.5
μm, ellipsoid, ornamented with isolated warts
and ridges that do not form a complete reticulum, prominences up to 0.5 μm high, hyaline,
amyloid.

OCCURRENCE: Solitary or scattered in hardwoods; summer–fall.

EDIBILITY: Unknown.

REMARKS: Its flesh stains dull brownish red to
rose color with FeSO4. *Lactifluus hygrophoroides* (p. 343) is similar but does not have the
concentric wrinkles near the margin and has
white flesh that does not stain vinaceous to
dull red with FeSO4.

Lactifluus rugatus

Lactifluus volemus var. *flavus* (Fr.) Kuntze

= *Lactarius volemus* var. *flavus* Hesler & A. H. Sm.

MACROSCOPIC FEATURES: **Cap** 2–9 cm wide, convex and somewhat flattened, becoming depressed with an uplifted margin; surface dry, velvety, azonate, ivory yellow to orange yellow, brownish where bruised. **Gills** attached, whitish to cream, close, narrow to somewhat broad, forked near the stalk, staining brown from the latex. **Stalk** 3–10 cm long, 4–16 mm thick, nearly equal, solid, dry, velvety, cream to pale yellow. **Flesh** firm, whitish to ivory, staining brownish from the latex; odor strong and fishy or not distinctive; taste mild. **Latex** white, unchanging, staining all parts brown; taste mild.

SPORE PRINT: White.
MICROSCOPIC FEATURES: Spores 6.5–9 × 6–8 μm, globose to subglobose, ornamented with broad to narrow bands forming a partial to complete reticulum, prominences 0.2–0.5 μm high, hyaline, amyloid.
OCCURRENCE: Scattered or in groups in hardwoods or mixed woods; summer–early winter.
EDIBILITY: Edible.
REMARKS: *Lactifluus volemus* var. *volemus* (p. 348) is nearly identical but has a dark orange-brown to cinnamon-brown cap and a dull orange to pale orange-brown stalk.

Lactifluus volemus var. *flavus*

Lactifluus volemus var. *volemus* (Fr.) Kuntze

= *Lactarius volemus* (Fr.) Fr.

COMMON NAMES: Apricot Milk Cap, Bradley, Voluminous-latex Milky, Weeping Milk Cap.

MACROSCOPIC FEATURES: **Cap** 5–10 cm wide, broadly convex, becoming nearly flat with a depressed center, then broadly funnel-shaped in age; surface dry, pruinose to velvety when young, becoming glabrous to finely wrinkled at maturity, dark orange brown to cinnamon brown at the center, paler orange brown toward the margin, fading in age to pale orange brown then honey yellow. **Gills** attached to slightly decurrent, broad, close, often forked, whitish to cream, slowly bruising tawny brown. **Stalk** 5–11.5 cm long, 5–20 mm thick, nearly equal or tapered at the base, solid, sometimes hollow in age, nearly glabrous, pale orange brown to dull orange. **Flesh** thick, brittle, white, staining brownish when cut or bruised; odor not distinctive in very young specimens, soon becoming fishy as the mushrooms mature; taste mild. **Latex** copious, white on exposure, becoming creamy white then brownish or grayish, and staining gills and flesh tawny brown; taste mild.

SPORE PRINT: White.

MICROSCOPIC FEATURES: Spores 7.5–10 × 7.5–9 μm, globose to subglobose, ornamented with warts and ridges that form a complete reticulum, prominences up to 1 μm high, hyaline, amyloid.

OCCURRENCE: Solitary, scattered, or in groups in hardwoods or mixed woods; summer–fall.

EDIBILITY: Edible.

REMARKS: The flesh instantly stains dark blue-green with $FeSO_4$. The latex stains fingers and clothing brown. *Lactifluus volemus* var. *flavus* (p. 347) is nearly identical, but it has a yellow to orange-yellow cap and a cream to pale yellow stalk.

Lactifluus volemus var. *volemus*

Lentinellus ursinus (Fr.) Kühner

= *Panellus ursinus* (Fr.) Murrill

COMMON NAME: Bear Lentinus.

MACROSCOPIC FEATURES: **Cap** 2.5–10 cm wide, semicircular, convex to nearly flat; surface glabrous or finely velvety to fuzzy, at least at the center, dark brown, becoming paler brown toward the margin; **flesh** thin, whitish to pale brown; odor fruity or not distinctive; taste acrid or bitter. **Gills** attached, close to subdistant, color variable but typically pinkish to brownish; edges ragged to coarsely toothed. **Stalk** absent or rudimentary.

SPORE PRINT: White.

MICROSCOPIC FEATURES: Spores 3–4.5 × 2–3.5 µm, subglobose to oval, with minute amyloid spines, hyaline.

OCCURRENCE: In groups or clusters on decaying hardwoods, especially oak, maple, and beech; late spring–early winter.

EDIBILITY: Inedible.

REMARKS: The fuzzy cap, coarsely toothed gill edges, lack of a stalk, growth on decaying hardwoods, and acrid taste are good field identification features.

ntinellus ursinus

Lentinula raphanica (Murrill)
Mata & R. H. Petersen

= *Armillaria raphanica* Murrill

MACROSCOPIC FEATURES: **Cap** 2–7.5 cm wide, convex, becoming broadly convex to nearly plane in age; surface moist or dry, smooth, appressed-fibrillose when young, often becoming wrinkled at maturity, especially on the disc, dark reddish brown at first, becoming pale reddish brown to dull ocher or dingy yellow in age; margin entire, with a sterile band of tissue, often adorned with torn patches of partial veil, especially when young; **flesh** rubbery, whitish; odor of garlic or radish or sometimes not distinctive; taste resembling garlic. **Gills** attached, very crowded, white, staining reddish then brown when bruised; edges finely scalloped or toothed. **Stalk** 2–8 cm long, 3–10 mm thick, slightly enlarged downward or nearly equal, often curved near the base; surface dry, conspicuously scaly, white to yellowish or ocher; partial veil white, tearing and remaining attached to the cap margin, typically not forming a ring.

SPORE PRINT: White.
MICROSCOPIC FEATURES: Spores 4.5–6 × 2–3 μm, elliptic, smooth, hyaline.
OCCURRENCE: Scattered or in dense groups on decaying wood, especially hardwood; summer–early winter.
EDIBILITY: Unknown.
REMARKS: *Raphanica* means "radish," a reference to the odor and taste of this mushroom. *Lentinus tricholoma* = *Polyporus tricholoma* (not illustrated) has a 1–4 cm wide, flat to centrally depressed cap that is glabrous or coated with scattered hairs. Its margin is adorned with conspicuous projecting cilia up to 4 mm long that agglutinate or disappear when mature. It has an ochraceous to pale brown pore surface and very small pores, (5)7–9 per mm. Its stalk is pale to dark brown and it grows on decaying hardwood. *Lentinus arcularius* = *Polyporus arcularius* (p. 488) is very similar to *Lentinus tricholoma*, but it has larger pores, 1–2 per mm.

Lentinula raphanica

Lentinus crinitus (L.) Fr.

= *Panus crinitus* (L.) Singer

MACROSCOPIC FEATURES: Cap 2.5–7.5 cm wide, convex with a depressed center, often funnel-shaped; margin incurved at first, becoming somewhat elevated and wavy at maturity, usually adorned with loose, projecting hairs; surface dry, with dense, long, pale yellowish brown to dark reddish brown radiating hairs, silky and shiny at the center; **flesh** thin, tough and leathery, white to buff; odor and taste not distinctive. **Gills** deeply decurrent, close to crowded, whitish to cream; edges finely toothed. **Stalk** 2–4 cm long, 2–6 mm thick, nearly equal or tapered in either direction, solid; surface dry, scurfy, colored like the cap but usually paler, especially toward the apex.
SPORE PRINT: White.
MICROSCOPIC FEATURES: Spores 5.5–8 × 1.8–3 μm, elliptic, smooth, hyaline, inamyloid.
OCCURRENCE: Scattered, in groups, or clusters on decaying hardwoods; year-round.
EDIBILITY: Inedible.

REMARKS: *Crinitus* means "having long hairs," a reference to the cap surface. *Lentinus tigrinus* (not illustrated) is similar, but its cap surface is dark grayish brown at first and soon becomes light cinnamon to buff, with numerous dark brown scales that are especially dense on the disc. The stalk surface is dark grayish brown at first and soon becomes light cinnamon to buff. It has slightly larger spores and grows singly, in groups, or clusters on hardwood logs, stumps, or dead roots year-round. The Zoned Crinipellis, *Collybia zonata* = *Crinipellis zonata* (not illustrated), has a 1.2–4 cm broad, convex to nearly flat cap with a small depression at the center. It has a dry surface, coated with orangish to orange-brown hairs that are stiff and radially arranged over a creamy-white ground color, and typically appears zoned. The stalk is tough, brown, decorated like the cap, and is attached to decaying hardwood, especially twigs, during summer. *Crinipellis scabella* = *Crinipellis stipitaria* (not illustrated) is smaller and grows on grass roots, plant stems, woody debris, and tree bark.

ntinus crinitus

Lepiota besseyi H. V. Sm. & N. S. Weber

MACROSCOPIC FEATURES: **Cap** 2.5–9 cm wide, truncate-ovoid to rounded-conic in the button stage, expanding to convex then nearly flat in age; margin incurved when young, sometimes faintly striate in age; surface dry, remaining intact over the disc longer than elsewhere, soon breaking up into small concentric scales away from the disc; scales and disc dull reddish brown to cinnamon brown or darker brown over a white to pale buff ground color; **flesh** up to 4 mm thick, soft, white to pale buff, staining orange to red then slowly reddish brown; odor fragrant; taste acidic. **Gills** free, close, white to pale buff, quickly staining orange to red then slowly reddish brown. **Stalk** 3.5–10.5 cm long, 4.5–11 mm thick, slightly enlarged to somewhat bulbous, tapered upward, white and glabrous or somewhat fibrillose above the ring, with irregular dull reddish-brown to darker brown patches and bands over a white to pale buff ground color below the ring, staining orange to red then brown when bruised or in age, with many white rhizomorphs at the base; partial veil membranous, leaving a ring or sometimes veil fragments on the cap margin; ring superior or median, flaring at first then collapsing against the stalk or sometimes evanescent, upper surface white, lower surface scaly and reddish brown to dark brown.

SPORE PRINT: Dark creamy buff.
MICROSCOPIC FEATURES: Spores 9–11 × 7–8 μm, broadly ovate to broadly ellipsoid, smooth, hyaline, dextrinoid; pleurocystidia and cheilocystidia abundant, 35–90 × 9–25 μm, ventricose to broadly fusoid or clavate.
OCCURRENCE: Scattered, in groups, or clusters on woodchips; summer–early winter.
EDIBILITY: Unknown.
REMARKS: This species is named for E. A. Bessey (1877–1957), the former University of Michigan botanist, who collected it in Hawaii. *Lepiota sanguiflua* (not illustrated) has a whitish cap with a very dark brown to blackish disc and small, concentrically arranged, concolorous scales that extend nearly to the margin. It has pale yellow gills, white flesh that stains yellow then reddish or brownish when bruised, and a minutely scurfy, whitish stalk that is only slightly enlarged downward and sometimes has a thin, band-like ring on the upper portion. Red juice is released from the cut stalk of fresh specimens. Its spores measure 7.5–10.5 × 5.5–7.5 μm, and it grows on the ground or in piles of leaves with hardwoods, especially oak, during summer and fall. *Leucoagaricus americanus* (p. 355) has a glabrous stalk and larger spores that measure 8–14 × 5–10 μm.

Lepiota besseyi

Lepista nuda (Bull.) Cooke

= *Clitocybe nuda* (Bull.) Bigelow & A. H. Sm.

COMMON NAME: Blewit.
MACROSCOPIC FEATURES: **Cap** 4–20 cm wide, convex, becoming broadly convex to nearly plane; margin inrolled at first, becoming uplifted and wavy at maturity; surface tacky when moist, smooth or with small central cracks, dirty pinkish to lilac gray or violet, fading toward tan; **flesh** thick, soft, lavender or tan to whitish; odor fragrant or not distinctive; taste bitter or not distinctive. **Gills** adnexed, crowded, violet at first, becoming buff or tan. **Stalk** 3–10 cm long, 1–3 cm thick, equal or with a bulbous base; surface dry, slightly hairy or flaky, off-white to lavender, bruising dark lavender and aging to tan; partial veil absent.
SPORE PRINT: Pinkish.
MICROSCOPIC FEATURES: Spores 5.5–8 × 3.5–5 μm, elliptic, smooth or roughened, hyaline, inamyloid.

OCCURRENCE: Solitary, scattered, or in groups on the ground in lawns, landscaped areas, compost piles, and rich woodlands; summer–early winter.
EDIBILITY: Edible.
REMARKS: Potentially toxic species of *Cortinarius* are similar but easily differentiated by their spore prints, which are brown. *Rugosomyces cyanellus* = *Calocybe cyanella* (not illustrated) has a 2–4.5 cm wide, convex to broadly convex, dusky violet-blue cap that is often depressed at the center and a sterile margin. It has whitish slightly decurrent gills that develop yellowish to pale brownish stains, a 2–5 mm wide, bluish-gray to grayish stalk that is darker at the apex and paler below, and white flesh with a farinaceous odor. The spore print is white, and it grows on leaf litter in hardwood or mixed conifer and hardwood forests. It has ellipsoid spores that measure 4–5 × 2.5–3.3 μm.

Lepista nuda

Lepista subconnexa (Murrill) Harmaja

= *Clitocybe subconnexa* Murrill

MACROSCOPIC FEATURES: **Cap:** 2.5–9 cm broad, convex, becoming nearly plane with age; surface smooth, satiny white at first, buff to pale brownish when old, especially on the disc; margin incurved at first, wavy when expanded; **flesh** white or tinged pinkish, brittle; odor fragrant or not distinctive; taste mild when young, becoming bitter or astringent when mature. **Gills** attached to short-decurrent, often separable from the cap flesh, close to crowded, sometimes forked, narrow, whitish to pale pinkish buff. **Stalk** 3–10 cm long, 5–20 mm wide, nearly equal or slightly tapered upward, dry, dull, silky, tomentose at the base, grayish buff, hollow with age; flesh colored like the cap flesh.

SPORE PRINT: Pale pinkish buff.
MICROSCOPIC FEATURES: Spores 4.5–6 × 3–3.5 μm, elliptic, minutely warted, hyaline.
OCCURRENCE: Densely caespitose on the ground in hardwoods and mixed woods; summer–early winter.
EDIBILITY: Edible when young and fresh, unappealing when older.
REMARKS: *Clitocybe irina* (not illustrated) is edible, grows in more loosely scattered groups, often in fairy rings, has a fragrant odor, and has larger spores that measure 7–10 × 4–5 μm. *Clitocybe robusta* (not illustrated), edibility unknown, is typically larger, develops a skunk-like odor in age, and has a pale yellow spore print. *Leucopaxillus albissimus* complex (p. 361) is white at first, becomes yellow brown on the disc as it ages, and has amyloid spores.

Lepista subconnexa

Leucoagaricus americanus (Peck) Vellinga

= *Agaricus americanus* Peck
= *Lepiota americana* (Peck) Sacc.

COMMON NAME: Reddening Lepiota.

MACROSCOPIC FEATURES: **Cap** 3–15 cm wide, narrowly convex at first, becoming convex then nearly plane in age, typically with a low, broad, central umbo; surface dry, dull reddish brown overall when young, breaking up into concentric rings of dull reddish-brown scales on a white ground color at maturity; white ground color bruises yellow then slowly reddish brown; margin incurved at first, uplifted at maturity, finely striate; **flesh** thin, soft, fragile, white, bruising like the cap; odor and taste not distinctive. **Gills** free, close, white, bruising like the cap and flesh. **Stalk** 5–14 cm long, 6–22 mm thick, spindle-shaped or enlarged downward, hollow in age; surface dry, glabrous, white, bruising yellow then dull reddish, and aging dull reddish; cut flesh often yellow to orange, especially at the base; partial veil white, leaving a double-edged, white superior ring.

SPORE PRINT: White.

MICROSCOPIC FEATURES: Spores 8–14 × 5–10 µm, elliptic with a thick-walled pore, smooth, hyaline, dextrinoid.

OCCURRENCE: Scattered or in clusters near stumps, on woodchips, compost piles, gardens, and grassy areas; summer–early winter.

EDIBILITY: Edible.

REMARKS: *Lepiota besseyi* (p. 352) is similar and stains reddish when bruised, but its cap has smaller scales, its stalk has small reddish-brown scales, at least on the lower half, and it is not enlarged in the middle. It grows on lawns and woodchips.

Leucoagaricus americanus

Leucoagaricus meleagris (Gray) Singer

= *Lepiota meleagris* (Gray) Sacc.
= *Leucocoprinus meleagris* (Gray) Locq.

MACROSCOPIC FEATURES: **Cap** 2–5.5 cm wide, ovate to hemispherical when young, becoming broadly convex at maturity, often with a low, broad umbo; surface moist or dry, dark brown to cinnamon brown or occasionally pinkish brown over the disc, with small, often concentrically arranged, dark brown scales scattered over a whitish ground color; margin incurved at first, striate, often split on older specimens; **flesh** white, staining orange red to dull red then slowly dull brown when bruised; odor and taste not distinctive. **Gills** free, close to crowded, white to yellowish, often stained pinkish brown to reddish brown on older specimens, sometimes with reddish drops adhering on young, fresh specimens. **Stalk** 4–8 cm long, 4–12 mm thick, enlarged downward and spindle-shaped with a tapered base, anchored by a mass of whitish mycelial strands, whitish on the upper portion, coated with tiny dark brown scales near the base;

partial veil membranous, whitish, delicate, leaving a whitish to brownish, immovable ring near the center of the stalk.

SPORE PRINT: White.

MICROSCOPIC FEATURES: Spores 8–12 × 5.5–8.5 μm, broadly elliptic to ovate, smooth, hyaline, dextrinoid.

OCCURRENCE: In groups or clusters or sometimes solitary, on compost piles, leaf litter, or decaying woodchips; year-round.

EDIBILITY: Unknown.

REMARKS: *Lepiota sanguiflua* (not illustrated) has a whitish cap with a very dark brown to blackish disc and small, concentrically arranged, concolorous scales that extend nearly to the margin. It has pale yellow gills, white flesh that stains yellow then reddish or brownish when bruised, and a minutely scurfy, whitish stalk that is enlarged slightly downward to a bulbous base and sometimes has a thin, band-like ring on the upper portion. Red juice is released from the cut stalk of fresh specimens. It grows on the ground or in piles of leaves with hardwoods, especially oak, during summer and fall.

Leucoagaricus meleagris

Leucocoprinus birnbaumii (Corda) Singer

= *Lepiota lutea* (Bolton) Mattir.

COMMON NAME: Yellow Houseplant Mushroom.

MACROSCOPIC FEATURES: **Cap** 2–6 cm wide, bell-shaped to broadly conic, typically with an umbo; surface dry, powdery or with tiny scales, bright to pale yellow, becoming pale yellow to whitish or tan in age; margin distinctly striate to the disc; **flesh** very thin, whitish to pale yellow; odor and taste not distinctive. **Gills** free, crowded, whitish to pale yellow; edges fimbriate. **Stalk** 4–11.5 cm long, 1.5–6 mm thick, enlarged downward or sometimes nearly equal; surface dry, smooth or powdery, colored like the cap; partial veil fibrous-cottony, bright yellow, leaving a movable persistent or evanescent ring.

SPORE PRINT: White.

MICROSCOPIC FEATURES: Spores 8–13 × 5–8 µm, elliptic, smooth, thick-walled, hyaline, dextrinoid.

OCCURRENCE: Scattered or in groups or clusters on rich soils, among woodchips used for landscaping, among pine needles, in greenhouses, and on soil in potted plants; year-round.

EDIBILITY: Poisonous.

REMARKS: Compare with *Leucocoprinus fragilissimus* (p. 359), which has a very narrow and extremely fragile stalk that measures 1–3 mm thick.

Leucocoprinus birnbaumii

Leucocoprinus cepistipes
(Sowerby) Pat.

= *Lepiota cepistipes* (Sowerby) P. Kumm.

COMMON NAME: Onion-stalk Lepiota.
MACROSCOPIC FEATURES: **Cap** 2–7 cm wide, ovoid at first, becoming bell-shaped to broadly convex with an umbo; surface dry, granular to scaly, usually smooth on the disc, white to whitish overall or with a pinkish-tan to grayish-brown disc, sometimes yellowish in age; margin with deep radial grooves, sometimes splitting; **flesh** thin, fragile, white; odor not distinctive; taste bitter or not distinctive. **Gills** free, crowded, white, becoming dingy white in age; edges floccose. **Stalk** 4–12 cm long, 3–6 mm thick, slightly enlarged downward or nearly equal, often with a swollen base, hollow at maturity; surface dry, white or tinted pinkish, typically bruising yellowish, coated with powdery white scales, at least on the lower half, smooth above the ring; partial veil white, leaving a white superior ring.

SPORE PRINT: White.
MICROSCOPIC FEATURES: Spores 7–10 × 6–8 μm, broadly elliptic, with an apical pore, smooth, hyaline, weakly dextrinoid.
OCCURRENCE: Scattered or in groups on wood mulch, straw, organic compost, lawns, rich soil, greenhouses, and flowerpots; summer–early winter.
EDIBILITY: Unknown.
REMARKS: *Cepistipes* means "onion-stalk." *Leucocoprinus ianthinus = Leucocoprinus lilacinogranulosus* (not illustrated) has a deeply sulcate cap margin, a dull purple to purplish-brown disc, and is covered with dull purple to purplish-brown scales at maturity.

Leucocoprinus cepistipes

Leucocoprinus fragilissimus
(Ravenel ex Berk. & M. A. Curtis) Pat.

= *Lepiota fragilissima* (Ravenel ex Berk. &
   M. A. Curtis) Morgan

COMMON NAME: Fragile Leucocoprinus.
MACROSCOPIC FEATURES: **Cap** 1–4.5 cm wide,
ovate to bell-shaped when young, becoming
broadly convex with a small umbo; surface
translucent-striate to sulcate from the margin
to the disc, tawny to ocher brown on the
umbo, pale bright yellow over the remainder
or pale yellowish white on the margin, fading
in age; **flesh** very thin, whitish; odor and taste
not distinctive. **Gills** attached to nearly free,
narrow, white. **Stalk** 4–16 cm long, 1–3 mm
thick, enlarged downward, extremely fragile,
pale grayish yellow, darkening in age, coated
with tiny yellowish scales; partial veil whitish
to pale yellow, leaving a superior ring.

SPORE PRINT: White.
MICROSCOPIC FEATURES: Spores 9–13 × 7–8
μm, elliptic, with an apical pore, smooth, hyaline, dextrinoid.
OCCURRENCE: Solitary or scattered on
the ground with conifers or hardwoods;
summer–fall.
EDIBILITY: Unknown.
REMARKS: *Fragilissimus* means "fragile," a reference to the very thin and delicate stalk. Compare with *Leucocoprinus birnbaumii* (p. 357),
which has a thicker, sturdier stalk.

Leucocoprinus fragilissimus

Leucocoprinus longistriatus (Peck)
H. V. Sm. & N. S. Weber

= *Lepiota longistriata* Peck

MACROSCOPIC FEATURES: **Cap** 2.5–6 cm wide, convex to nearly plane, with a low, broad umbo; surface striate from the margin to the disc, appressed-fibrillose at the center, becoming fibrillose-scaly over the remainder to the margin, whitish or very pale gray, brownish on the umbo; **flesh** thin, whitish; odor and taste not distinctive. **Gills** free, close, narrow, white. **Stalk** 4–7.5 cm long, 2–6 mm thick, tapered upward from an enlarged base, hollow at maturity; surface smooth, white; partial veil whitish, leaving a delicate ring that often disappears by maturity.

SPORE PRINT: White.
MICROSCOPIC FEATURES: Spores 6–9 × 4.5–5 μm, elliptic, smooth, hyaline, inamyloid.
OCCURRENCE: Scattered or in groups on the ground in woodlands, grassy areas, gardens, or on woodchips; summer–fall.
EDIBILITY: Unknown.
REMARKS: *Longistriatus* means "having long lines or grooves." Compare with *Chlorophyllum hortense* (p. 244), which has flesh that stains vinaceous brown on exposure and larger, ellipsoid spores.

Leucocoprinus longistriatus

Leucopaxillus albissimus complex
(Peck) Singer

= *Agaricus albissimus* Peck

COMMON NAME: White Leucopax.
MACROSCOPIC FEATURES: **Cap** 3–12 cm wide, convex when young, becoming broadly convex or shallowly depressed in age; surface dry, glabrous or finely velvety, white overall at first, becoming buff to pale yellow brown over the disc in age, sometimes remaining white overall; margin incurved and remaining so well into maturity, finely ribbed or smooth; **flesh** thick, white, unchanging when exposed; odor aromatic and sweet or not distinctive; taste farinaceous-bitter. **Gills** attached to decurrent, close to crowded, white. **Stalk** 3–7 cm long, 7–15 mm thick, enlarged downward, often with a swollen base or nearly equal, solid; surface glabrous or sometimes weakly fibrous-scaly, especially at the apex, whitish, with copious white basal mycelium and trapped debris.

SPORE PRINT: White.
MICROSCOPIC FEATURES: Spores 5–8.5 × 4–5.5 μm, ellipsoid to ovoid, with sparse strongly amyloid warts, hyaline.
OCCURRENCE: Scattered or in groups or fairy rings on humus or needles in conifer or mixed woodlands; summer–early winter.
EDIBILITY: Unknown.
REMARKS: We have chosen to treat this as a complex because in their monograph on the genus *Leucopaxillus*, Singer and Smith (1943) list at least a dozen forms and varieties of this species. Eventually some of these forms and varieties may be treated as distinct species, but that will only occur following molecular analysis. *Leucopaxillus laterarius* (p. 363) is similar, but the cap disc has a pinkish tinge, and it grows on leaves and debris of hardwoods or sometimes on well-decayed hardwood stumps.

eucopaxillus albissimus

Leucopaxillus gracillimus Singer & A. H. Sm.

= *Clitocybe rappiana* Murrill

MACROSCOPIC FEATURES: **Cap** 2–6 cm wide, broadly convex to almost flat, usually with an umbo, sometimes depressed on the disc; surface moist or dry, glabrous, smooth or finely cracked, pinkish red to coral red, darkest on the umbo, becoming dull brownish red in age; margin incurved at first, becoming uplifted, lobed or wavy and split or eroded in age; **flesh** thin, white; odor and taste not distinctive. **Gills** decurrent, extremely close, very narrow, white. **Stalk** 2.5–6 cm long, 2–6 mm thick, nearly equal, often bent or curved at the base; surface glabrous, smooth, white; basal mycelium white, with trapped debris.

SPORE PRINT: White.
MICROSCOPIC FEATURES: Spores 3–5.5 × 2.2–4 μm, short ellipsoid to globose, with strongly amyloid warts, hyaline.
OCCURRENCE: Scattered or in groups on the ground among leaves with hardwoods, especially oak and hickory, or in mixed woods; summer–early winter.
EDIBILITY: Unknown.
REMARKS: This species has been reported from several countries and territories, including Brazil, Puerto Rico, and St. John US Virgin Islands. Although fairly common in the tropics, it is uncommon in the Gulf Coast states. It has also been found in southeastern Georgia.

Leucopaxillus gracillimus

Leucopaxillus laterarius (Peck) Singer & A. H. Sm.

= *Agaricus laterarius* Peck

MACROSCOPIC FEATURES: **Cap** 4–12(-20) cm wide, obtuse, becoming broadly convex to nearly plane or slightly depressed; surface dry, unpolished, appressed-fibrillose, sometimes finely cracked or scurfy on the disc in age, white overall or with a pinkish to pale pinkish-brown or yellowish flush at the center; margin inrolled at first, frequently striate or shallowly grooved; **flesh** thick, firm, white; odor farinaceous and sometimes rather disagreeable; taste astringent to very bitter. **Gills** attached to subdecurrent, crowded, narrow, white, becoming pale cream in age. **Stalk** 4–11 cm long, 6–20 mm thick, nearly equal to clavate, solid; surface bald to minutely pubescent, smooth, white overall; basal mycelium white, with trapped debris.

SPORE PRINT: White.
MICROSCOPIC FEATURES: Spores 3.5–5.5 × 3.5–4.7 μm, globose to subglobose or short ellipsoid, with strongly amyloid warts, hyaline.
OCCURRENCE: Solitary, scattered, or in groups on leaves and debris of hardwoods or sometimes on well-decayed hardwood stumps.
EDIBILITY: Unknown.
REMARKS: *Leucopaxillus albissimus* (p. 361) is similar, but it grows on humus or needles in conifer or mixed woods and has larger, ellipsoid spores.

Leucopaxillus laterarius

Limacella illinita (Fr.) Maire

= *Agaricus illinitus* Fr.

MACROSCOPIC FEATURES: **Cap** 2–7 cm wide, convex, becoming nearly plane in age; surface white to creamy white or grayish brown, coated with hyaline slime when fresh; margin incurved and remaining so well into maturity; **flesh** white; odor and taste not distinctive. **Gills** free or nearly so, close, white. **Stalk** 5–10 cm long, 3–10 mm thick, solid; surface slimy, whitish, staining brownish where bruised, lacking a ring or sometimes with a sparse fibrillose ring zone.

SPORE PRINT: White.

MICROSCOPIC FEATURES: Spores 4–6.5 μm, globose to broadly elliptic, smooth, hyaline, inamyloid.

OCCURRENCE: Scattered or in groups in various habitats, including woods, fields, wooded lawns, and sand dunes; summer–early winter.

EDIBILITY: Unknown.

REMARKS: *Illinita* means "smeared," a reference to the covering of slime. The slime layer is a universal veil that does not leave a volva.

Limacella illinita

Macowanites arenicola S. L. Mill. & D. Mitch.

COMMON NAME: Sandy Mac.

MACROSCOPIC FEATURES: **Cap** 2–5 cm wide, convex to broadly convex, at times with a slight central depression; surface smooth, tacky or dry, usually with adhering granules of sand, whitish to cream or pale grayish yellow, occasionally with pinkish tones or blotches; margin incurved at first and remaining so well into maturity; **flesh** thin, watery white to grayish; odor reminiscent of old yogurt; taste not distinctive. **Gills** convoluted and chambered, pale to light yellow or ochraceous. **Stalk** 1.5–3 cm long, 5–12 mm thick, cylindrical or slightly tapered toward the base, solid at first, becoming chambered with age; surface with low, longitudinal ribs or nearly smooth; whitish or tinged grayish.

SPORE PRINT: Not obtainable.

MICROSCOPIC FEATURES: Spores 8.8–10.4 × 6.5–7.2 μm, broadly elliptic to elliptic, with low warts and connecting lines that form a partial reticulum, hyaline, amyloid.

OCCURRENCE: Scattered or in groups in sandy soil, especially on old dunes that are colonized with oak and pine; winter–spring.

EDIBILITY: Unknown.

REMARKS: This mushroom looks like, and is closely related to, species of *Russula*. The cap often barely rises above the sand surface or remains buried and is overlooked except for a slight hump in the sand. Unlike normal gilled mushrooms, the Sandy Mac does not forcibly discharge its spores; instead, the spores are passively released as the gill chambers disintegrate or when the spores are dispersed by various arthropods.

Macowanites arenicola

Macrocybe titans (H. E. Bigelow & Kimbr.) Pegler, Lodge & Nakasone

= *Tricholoma titans* H. E. Bigelow & Kimbr.

COMMON NAME: Giant Gilled Mushroom.

MACROSCOPIC FEATURES: **Cap** 8–80 cm wide, convex, becoming nearly plane in age, sometimes depressed on the disc; surface dry or moist, often with watery spots or small scales over the center, glabrous elsewhere, buff near the margin, darker on the disc, darkening in age; margin incurved and remaining so well into maturity, often conspicuously undulating and sometimes upturned; **flesh** thick, firm, white; odor variously described as resembling cyanide or green pecans; taste musty to disagreeable or not distinctive. **Gills** attached and strongly sinuate, crowded, grayish buff to pale grayish yellow, sometimes with brownish stains. **Stalk** 7.5–30 cm long, 3–12 cm thick,

clavate to bulbous, often with a tapered base, solid, tough; surface dry, whitish to buff, darkening when bruised, coated with scattered or concentrically arranged dark brown scales.

SPORE PRINT: White to creamy white.

MICROSCOPIC FEATURES: Spores 5.5–8 × 4–5.5 μm, broadly ellipsoid to ovoid, smooth, hyaline, inamyloid.

OCCURRENCE: Usually in dense clusters, sometimes solitary or in groups on the ground in grassy areas, woodlands, or disturbed areas; summer–early winter.

EDIBILITY: Edible.

REMARKS: It is a tropical and subtropical species that is expanding its range. In addition to being found along the Gulf Coast, it has been reported as far north as Durham, North Carolina. It is the largest gilled mushroom in North America.

Macrocybe titans

Macrolepiota procera (Scop.) Singer

= *Lepiota procera* (Scop.) Gray

COMMON NAME: Parasol.

MACROSCOPIC FEATURES: **Cap** 7–25 cm wide, egg-shaped when young, becoming bell-shaped then broadly convex to nearly flat with an umbo in age; surface dry, reddish brown and nearly sooth when young, soon breaking up into coarse reddish-brown scales and patches with white flesh showing between, fading to dull pale brown in age; margin incurved at first, often wrinkled on mature specimens; **flesh** thick, white, sometimes slightly tinged reddish; odor and taste not distinctive. **Gills** free, close, white at first, darkening in age; edges somewhat wooly. **Stalk** 15–30 cm long, 8–13 mm thick, enlarged downward to a bulbous base; surface dry, coated with tiny brownish scales on a white ground color; partial veil white, leaving a persistent, thick-edged, movable superior ring.

SPORE PRINT: White.

MICROSCOPIC FEATURES: Spores 15–20 × 10–13 µm, broadly elliptic, with a large apical pore, smooth, hyaline, dextrinoid.

OCCURRENCE: Solitary, scattered, or in groups on the ground in woodlands or grassy areas; summer–early winter.

EDIBILITY: Edible with caution due to possible confusion with the poisonous *Chlorophyllum molybdites*.

REMARKS: *Procera* means "lofty," a reference to the tall stature of this mushroom. *Chlorophyllum subrhacodes* (p. 246) is smaller overall and has much smaller spores. *Chlorophyllum molybdites* (p. 245) has gills that turn dull green when mature, a grayish-green spore print, and is poisonous.

Macrolepiota procera

Marasmius fulvoferrugineus Gilliam

MACROSCOPIC FEATURES: Cap 1.5–4.5 cm
wide, cushion- to bell-shaped at first, becoming convex, often with a small umbo; surface
dry, dull, slightly velvety, strongly plicate to
sulcate, tawny brown to rusty brown, usually
darkest on the disc; margin deeply pleated;
flesh thin, tough, brownish; odor and taste
mildly farinaceous or not distinctive. **Gills**
attached and notched, sometimes nearly
free, distant, yellowish white. **Stalk** 2.5–6.5
cm long, up to 1.5 mm thick, slender, round,
cartilaginous, hollow at maturity; surface
smooth, shiny, pinkish near the apex, brown
to blackish brown on the lower portion, with a
tuft of white basal mycelium.
SPORE PRINT: White.
MICROSCOPIC FEATURES: Spores 15–18 × 3–4.5
µm, oblanceolate, curved-clavate or fusoid-
clavate, smooth, hyaline.

OCCURRENCE: Scattered or in groups on decaying leaves and humus in woods; late spring–
early winter.
EDIBILITY: Unknown.
REMARKS: It is often confused with *Marasmius
siccus* (p. 371), which has a smaller, orange cap
and slightly larger spores that measure 15–22
× 3–5 µm. *Marasmius pulcherripes* (not illustrated) has a 5–20 mm wide cap that is convex
to bell-shaped at first and becomes broadly
convex at maturity, often with a tiny umbo.
The cap surface is pleated, glabrous or nearly
so, pink to pinkish brown, and fades in age
while retaining a darker disc. It has subdistant,
white to pinkish gills and a very thin, wiry,
reddish-brown stalk with a blackish base and
white basal mycelium. It grows on litter under
conifers or hardwoods from summer through
early winter.

Marasmius fulvoferrugineus

Marasmius nigrodiscus (Peck) Halling

= *Collybia nigrodisca* Peck
= *Gymnopus tenuifolius* Murrill

COMMON NAME: Black-eyed Marasmius.
MACROSCOPIC FEATURES: **Cap** 3–10 cm wide, convex to nearly flat with a low, broad umbo; surface glabrous, smooth or finely wrinkled, dry, cream to pale tan or yellow brown, darker on the disc; margin incurved at first and remaining so well into maturity, often with short striations; **flesh** thin, whitish; odor of bitter almonds or not distinctive; taste bitter or not distinctive. **Gills** attached and notched or sinuate, close to subdistant, white to dull pale yellow. **Stalk** 5–10 cm long, 6–10 mm thick, nearly equal or tapered upward, sometimes twisted; surface dry, whitish or colored like the cap, longitudinally striate.

SPORE PRINT: White to pale buff.
MICROSCOPIC FEATURES: Spores 7–9 × 3–5 μm, elliptic to lacrimoid, smooth, hyaline.
OCCURRENCE: Scattered or in groups or clusters on the ground with conifers, hardwoods, or in mixed woods; summer–fall.
EDIBILITY: Reportedly edible.
REMARKS: *Nigrodiscus* means "having a dark center," a reference to its cap. It is unusually large for a species of *Marasmius*.

Marasmius nigrodiscus

Marasmius rotula (Scop.) Fr.

COMMON NAME: Pinwheel Marasmius.
MACROSCOPIC FEATURES: **Cap** 3–20 mm wide, convex with a small depression at the center, prominently sulcate; surface dry, white to yellowish or rarely pale orange, typically with a dark center; **flesh**, thin, white to pale yellow; odor not distinctive; taste slightly bitter or not distinctive. **Gills** attached to a collarium, which may be either free from the stalk or collapsed on the upper portion of it, distant to subdistant, white to pale yellow. **Stalk** 1.5–8.5 cm long, 0.3–1 mm thick, wiry, sometimes with a tiny basal bulb and rhizomorphs; surface yellowish white to brownish at the apex, reddish brown to blackish brown overall at maturity.
SPORE PRINT: White.
MICROSCOPIC FEATURES: Spores 6–9.5 × 3–4.5 μm, somewhat lacrimoid, smooth, hyaline.
OCCURRENCE: In groups or clusters on decaying wood; year-round.

EDIBILITY: Inedible.
REMARKS: *Rotula* means "little pinwheel." *Marasmius capillaris* (not illustrated) is very similar, but it grows on oak leaves and does not grow in clusters. *Mycetinis opacus* (not illustrated) has a 3–15 mm wide, pale brown to whitish cap and a 0.5–1.5 mm thick stalk that is pale brown and darkest toward the base. Pale brown rhizomorphs often erupt from the substrate, like flyaway hairs, a short distance away from the mushroom. It grows in loose groups on dead twigs or leaves of rhododendron, hemlock, oak, or other substrates from summer through early winter. The Horse-hair Fungus, *Micromphale brevipes* = *Marasmius brevipes* (not illustrated) has a 2–11 mm wide, sulcate-striate, brown to dark reddish-brown cap and distant, ochraceous-salmon to light brown gills. It has a 1–4 mm long, less than 0.5 mm wide stalk that is dark reddish brown to blackish. The fruitbodies occur on black rhizomorphs suspended on hardwood twigs.

Marasmius rotula

Marasmius siccus (Schwein.) Fr.

COMMON NAME: Orange Pinwheel Marasmius.
MACROSCOPIC FEATURES: **Cap** 3–25 mm wide, cushion- to bell-shaped at first, becoming convex, depressed or umbonate on the disc; surface somewhat roughened, strongly plicate to sulcate when mature, pale orange to reddish orange or brownish orange, often darkest on the disc; **flesh** thin, white; odor and taste not distinctive. **Gills** sinuate or free, distant, white to pale yellow; lamellulae absent or few. **Stalk** 2–7 cm long, 0.2–1 mm thick, nearly equal, cartilaginous, hollow, dark yellow to reddish brown at first, darkening from the base upward as it ages; rhizomorphs absent.

SPORE PRINT: White.
MICROSCOPIC FEATURES: Spores 15–22 × 3–5 μm, club- to spindle-shaped, often curved, smooth, hyaline.
OCCURRENCE: Scattered or in groups on decaying leaves, twigs, and conifer needles; late spring–early winter.
EDIBILITY: Unknown.
REMARKS: *Marasmius fulvoferrugineus* (p. 368) has a larger, tawny-brown to rusty-brown cap and slightly smaller spores that measure 15–18 × 3–4.5 μm.

arasmius siccus

Megacollybia texensis R. H. Petersen & D. P. Lewis

MACROSCOPIC FEATURES: **Cap** 4–8.5 cm broad, plane to slightly depressed, and then occasionally with a small, shallow umbo; surface smooth, delicately radially streaked, sometimes almost invisibly so, medium gray brown to pallid gray tan; margin incurved at first, becoming plane or somewhat uplifted at maturity, often ragged to lacerate, thin, not striate; **flesh** thin; odor and taste not distinctive. **Gills** adnate with a small to considerable decurrent tooth, subdistant, up to 12 mm broad, white to off-white; edges often deeply eroded. **Stalk** 5–14.5 cm long, 3–8 mm thick, equal to gradually enlarged downward to an often abruptly expanded base; surface delicately lined to minutely silky, slightly twisted, pale dull light brown downward where handled to nearly concolorous with the cap; the expanded base often extends as a stout pseudorhiza.

SPORE PRINT: White.

MICROSCOPIC FEATURES: Spores 6.5–10 × 5–7.5 μm, ellipsoid to ovate, smooth, thin walled, hyaline, inamyloid.

OCCURRENCE: In mixed pine and hardwood forests; known from Texas and Louisiana; summer–fall.

EDIBILITY: Unknown.

REMARKS: It was previously thought to be *Megacollybia platyphylla* (not illustrated), but recent DNA research has shown it to be a different species. It was also determined that *Megacollybia platyphylla* does not occur in North America but only in Europe and Russia. The Platterful Mushroom, *Megacollybia rodmanii* (p. 15), is a more northern species that is morphologically indistinguishable, and both species require molecular analysis for positive identification.

Megacollybia texensis

Multifurca furcata (Coker) Buyck & V. Hofst.

= *Lactarius furcatus* Coker

MACROSCOPIC FEATURES: **Cap** 6–10 cm wide, convex to broadly convex, becoming funnel-shaped at maturity; surface somewhat viscid, tomentose, azonate, pale ochraceous. **Gills** decurrent, narrow, crowded, repeatedly forked, ochraceous with a tint of salmon. **Stalk** 2–3 cm long, 1–1.5 cm thick, solid, firm, tough, surface viscid, light yellowish with small ochraceous spots. **Flesh** thin, white, with dull ochraceous zones; odor not distinctive; taste acrid. **Latex** white on exposure, slowly changing to bluish green; taste moderately acrid.

SPORE PRINT: Pinkish ochraceous.

MICROSCOPIC FEATURES: Spores 3.5–5.5 × 3.5–4 μm, ellipsoid to subglobose, ornamented with a few bands and occasional fine lines that do not form a complete reticulum; prominences only up to 0.2 μm high, hyaline, amyloid.

OCCURRENCE: Solitary, scattered, or in groups under hardwoods or mixed woods; summer–fall.

EDIBILITY: Unknown.

REMARKS: The crowded, decurrent, repeatedly forked, ochraceous gills and the acrid, white latex that slowly changes to bluish green are good identification features.

Multifurca furcata

Multifurca ochricompacta (Bills & Miller) Buyck & V. Hofst.

= *Russula ochricompacta* Bills & Miller

MACROSCOPIC FEATURES: **Cap** 6–15 cm broad, broadly convex with a depressed center; surface dry, dull, chalk-like, minutely rugulose, coarsely areolate or even lacerate, sometimes with small irregular mounds near the margin, white to cream-colored, pinkish buff, creamy buff, or apricot buff; margin inrolled at first and remaining so well into maturity; **flesh** hard, brittle, up to 15 mm thick, white with concentric grayish zones; odor strong, of lemon oil; taste bitter. **Gills** adnate to subdecurrent, close to subdistant, 3–5 mm broad, forking mostly towards the margin, initially white, becoming buff yellow to yellow ocher, not exuding latex when cut or injured. **Stalk** 2–10 cm long, 2–2.5 cm broad, equal or expanded at the apex, tapered to the base; surface dry, dull, densely pruinose or short pubescent near the apex, the pubescence almost forming a reticulate pattern at times, often scrobiculate, nearly concolorous with the cap; base white-strigose.

SPORE PRINT: Ochraceous to vivid orange.

MICROSCOPIC FEATURES: Spores 4.8–5.8 × 3.9–4.6 μm, subglobose to broadly obovate or obovate, hyaline; ornamentation amyloid, up to 0.3 μm high, often appearing almost smooth, with a fine reticulation of interconnecting ridges.

OCCURRENCE: Scattered or in groups in mixed oak and pine woods, beech slope forests, and streams, bottomland hardwood forests; summer.

EDIBILITY: Unknown.

REMARKS: It was originally described from Virginia. The whitish cap and stalk, ochraceous to vivid orange spore print, and strong odor of lemon help to distinguish this species. The genus *Multifurca* was created to accommodate those species of *Russula* and *Lactarius* that have the following characteristics: forking gills, concentrically zoned caps, scrobiculate stalks, and small spores with low ornamentation.

Multifurca ochricompacta

Mycena epipterygia var. *viscosa*
(Secr. ex Maire) Ricken

MACROSCOPIC FEATURES: **Cap** 8–10 mm wide, ovoid to obtusely conic at first, becoming broadly conic to bell-shaped at maturity; surface moist to slightly viscid, often with a whitish powdery coating when young, yellowish gray to greenish gray, becoming brownish in age, sometimes with dull reddish-brown spots or streaks; **flesh** thin, brownish; odor strongly farinaceous to pumpkin-like; taste strongly rancid-farinaceous and very unpleasant. **Gills** attached, subdistant, yellowish to greenish yellow or sometimes whitish, often developing reddish-brown spots; edges pale. **Stalk** 3–8 cm long, 0.75–3 mm thick, glabrous, smooth; surface lemon yellow to greenish yellow, becoming reddish near the base, distinctly white-pruinose when young.
SPORE PRINT: White.

MICROSCOPIC FEATURES: Spores 8–11 × 5–8 μm, lacrimoid to elliptic, smooth, hyaline, amyloid.
OCCURRENCE: Scattered, in groups, or clusters on or near conifer wood, often at the base of standing trees; summer–early winter.
EDIBILITY: Inedible.
REMARKS: *Mycena epipterygia* var. *lignicola* (not illustrated) is similar, but it has a greenish-yellow to yellow cap with a paler margin, a greenish-yellow to yellow stalk, white gills that do not develop reddish-brown spots, and it grows on decaying conifer wood. *Mycena clavicularis* (not illustrated) has a 5–20 mm wide, gray or bluish-gray cap that slowly fades to sordid yellowish or whitish in age. It has subdistant, whitish gills that soon become pale gray. The stalk is 2–5 cm long, 1–1.5 mm thick, bluish black to fuscous when young, and fades to grayish in age. It grows on pine needles during winter.

Mycena epipterygia var. *viscosa*

Mycena haematopus (Pers.) P. Kumm.

COMMON NAME: Bleeding Mycena.

MACROSCOPIC FEATURES: **Cap** 1–4 cm wide, oval at first, becoming bell-shaped to convex, typically with an umbo; surface pruinose when young and dry, smooth and shiny when moist, striate, reddish brown or grayish brown to pinkish beige, paler toward the margin; margin serrate and extending beyond the gills; **flesh** thin, fragile, watery, reddish brown, exuding blood-like reddish-brown juice when injured; odor not distinctive; taste bitter or not distinctive. **Gills** attached to sinuate, close to subdistant, pinkish white to pale vinaceous. **Stalk** 4–10 cm long, 1.5–4.5 mm thick, nearly equal, pruinose or glabrous, hollow, fragile, colored like cap or darker, exuding a reddish-brown juice when broken.

SPORE PRINT: White.

MICROSCOPIC FEATURES: Spores 8–11 × 5–7 μm, oval to elliptic with a small apiculus, smooth, hyaline, amyloid.

OCCURRENCE: Usually in clusters on decaying hardwood; spring–early winter.

EDIBILITY: Unknown.

REMARKS: It is often infected with *Spinellus fusiger* (not illustrated), a parasitic mold that forms long, projecting hairs on the cap. *Mycena atkinsoniana* (not illustrated) has a reddish-brown cap with yellow toward the margin, yellowish gills with maroon edges, and it grows on the fallen leaves of oaks and beech. The Pink Mycena, *Mycena pura* (p. 15), has a 2–7.5 cm wide, convex to nearly flat cap with a translucent-striate margin. It has a pinkish to pale reddish, purplish, or grayish-lilac cap surface, and whitish to purplish flesh with an odor and taste strongly of radish. The stalk is colored like the cap, and it grows on humus in conifers or hardwoods during spring to late fall.

Mycena haematopus

Mycena inclinata (Fr.) Quél.

MACROSCOPIC FEATURES: **Cap** 1–6 cm wide, broadly conical with a broad umbo, striate to shallowly sulcate; surface viscid or dry, smooth, brownish on the disc and paler toward the margin, fading to whitish in age; margin finely serrate when young and sometimes split in age; **flesh** thin, whitish; odor farinaceous and unpleasant; taste farinaceous. **Gills** attached, close or subdistant, whitish to yellowish. **Stalk** 5–10 cm long, 1.5–4 mm thick, equal, hollow, smooth, whitish near the apex, yellowish in the mid-portion, and reddish brown below.

SPORE PRINT: White.

MICROSCOPIC FEATURES: Spores 7–10 × 5–7 µm, broadly ellipsoid, smooth, hyaline, amyloid.

OCCURRENCE: In groups or clusters on decaying hardwood; spring–early winter.

EDIBILITY: Unknown.

REMARKS: *Mycena galericulata* (not illustrated) has a brownish cap with a darker umbo, lacks the serrated margin, and its lower stalk lacks reddish tints. The odor and taste of its flesh is mildly farinaceous or not distinctive. It grows in clusters on or near hardwoods.

Mycena inclinata

Mycena semivestipes (Peck) A. H. Sm.

= *Omphalia semivestipes* Peck

MACROSCOPIC FEATURES: **Cap** 1–3.5 cm wide, convex to broadly convex; surface smooth, viscid when fresh, dark brown, fading to brown or grayish with a darker center; margin striate; **flesh** thin, whitish or brownish; odor bleach-like; taste bitter or unpleasant. **Gills** attached or slightly decurrent, close, white, sometimes with a pinkish tinge. **Stalk** 2–6 cm long, 1–3 mm thick, equal, tough, whitish at the apex, brown to dark brown below, covered with tiny soft hairs near the base.

SPORE PRINT: White.

MICROSCOPIC FEATURES: Spores 4–5 × 2–3 μm, ellipsoid, smooth, hyaline, amyloid.

OCCURRENCE: In clusters on decaying hardwood trunks, logs, or stumps; spring–early winter.

EDIBILITY: Unknown.

REMARKS: *Semivestipes* means "having a partially decorated stalk," a reference to the soft hairs on the stalk base. *Mycena leptocephala* (not illustrated) has a similarly colored cap but more distant gills, and it grows on conifer litter.

Mycena semivestipes

Neolentinus lepideus (Fr.) Redhead & Ginns

COMMON NAMES: Scaly Lentinus, Train Wrecker.

MACROSCOPIC FEATURES: **Cap** 5–20 cm wide, convex to nearly flat; surface slightly viscid or dry, whitish to buff, with darker brownish scales; margin incurved at first, sometimes beaded with droplets when fresh; **flesh** tough, white to yellowish; odor somewhat pungent or fragrant; taste not distinctive. **Gills** attached and notched or slightly decurrent, close to subdistant; edges nearly even when young, becoming serrate, whitish to buff, bruising brownish. **Stalk** 3–15 cm long, 1–3 cm thick, tapered downward and abruptly narrowed at the base, solid; surface nearly glabrous above the ring, scurfy to scaly below, whitish to brownish; partial veil whitish, leaving a persistent superior ring.

SPORE PRINT: White.

MICROSCOPIC FEATURES: Spores 9–12 × 4–5 µm, subcylindric, smooth, hyaline, inamyloid.

OCCURRENCE: Solitary or scattered on decaying wood, especially pine, also on railroad ties and fence posts; spring–early winter.

EDIBILITY: Edible.

REMARKS: *Lepideus* means "scaly," referring to the cap and stalk. *Lentinus tigrinus* (not illustrated) has a smaller, dark grayish-brown cap when young, and its surface breaks up into many small, dark scales, especially over the disc.

Neolentinus lepideus

Omphalotus illudens (Schwein.) Bresinsky & Besl.

= *Clitocybe illudens* (Schwein.) Sacc.

COMMON NAME: Jack O'Lantern.

MACROSCOPIC FEATURES: **Cap** 7–20 cm wide, convex, becoming broadly convex to nearly flat, sometimes depressed on the disc but retaining a small umbo; surface dry, smooth, bright orange, stained reddish brown in age; margin incurved and wavy; **flesh** thick, firm, pale orange; odor unpleasant or not distinctive; taste not distinctive. **Gills** decurrent, close, bright orange to yellow orange. **Stalk** 5–20 cm long, 1–2 cm thick, equal or tapered downward, solid, surface dry, smooth, yellow orange.

SPORE PRINT: Creamy white to pale yellow.

MICROSCOPIC FEATURES: Spores 3–5 μm, globose, smooth, hyaline, inamyloid.

OCCURRENCE: Clustered at the base of hardwood trees and stumps, especially oak; late spring–early winter.

EDIBILITY: Poisonous.

REMARKS: The gills of fresh Jack O' Lanterns often glow green in the dark. The cap stains green with the application of KOH or NH4OH. It is often mistaken for the smaller, edible *Cantharellus tenuithrix* (p. 157), which does not grow on wood, has a yellower cap, low, forking, gill-like ridges, and doesn't grow in dense clusters. *Omphalotus subilludens* (p. 381) has a smaller, dull orange to orange-brown cap and much larger, 5.5–8.5 × 3.7–5.3 μm, ellipsoid spores.

Omphalotus illudens

Omphalotus subilludens (Murrill) Bigelow

= *Clitocybe subilludens* Murrill
= *Monodelphus subilludens* Murrill

COMMON NAME: Southern Jack O'Lantern.
MACROSCOPIC FEATURES: **Cap** 5–12(15) cm wide, convex to subexpanded, often centrally depressed to funnel-shaped; surface dry, innately fibrillose, smooth to slightly wrinkled, dull orange to orange brown, often with darker vinaceous-brown spots and streaks; margin even, undulate or lobed, sometimes darker orange brown to reddish brown; **flesh** up to 1 cm thick, firm, yellowish, unchanging when cut; odor unpleasant or not distinctive; taste slightly astringent. **Gills** deeply decurrent, close to subdistant, medium-broad, orange yellow. **Stalk** 3–8 cm long, 1.5–4 cm thick, eccentric or central, tapered downward and sometimes enlarged near the base, solid, colored like the cap or paler, basal mycelium scant, whitish.

SPORE PRINT: Pale yellow.
MICROSCOPIC FEATURES: Spores 5.5–8.5 × 3.7–5.3 µm, ellipsoid, smooth, hyaline, inamyloid.
OCCURRENCE: In groups or clusters on decaying conifer or hardwood stumps, on saw palmetto trunks, and sometimes on the ground attached to buried wood; summer–early winter.
EDIBILITY: Unknown.
REMARKS: The cap and flesh stain green with the application of KOH or NH4OH. The addition of FeSO4 stains the cap vinaceous and the flesh grayish. Cuticle hyphal incrustations are yellowish brown in Melzer's and green in KOH mounts. *Omphalotus illudens* (p. 380) has a larger, bright orange cap and much smaller, round spores that measure 3–5 µm.

Omphalotus subilludens

Oudemansiella canarii (Jungh.) Höhn.

MACROSCOPIC FEATURES: **Cap** 2–7 cm wide, convex at first, becoming broadly convex to nearly plane; surface viscid, grayish brown at first, becoming pale grayish brown over the disc and sordid white toward the margin, radially wrinkled and sometimes cracked, especially on the disc, with scattered, dark grayish-brown, cottony, scale-like tufts that may easily wash off; margin weakly translucent-striate to shallowly sulcate, typically hung with white veil remnants, especially when young; **flesh** soft, white; odor and taste not distinctive. **Gills** attached with a decurrent tooth, close, white, with 3–4 ranks of lamellulae. **Stalk** 3–7 cm long, 6–15 mm thick, nearly equal down to an abruptly enlarged base, curved or conspicuously bent on the lower portion, solid; surface white on the upper portion and base, grayish to brownish in the mid-portion.

SPORE PRINT: White.

MICROSCOPIC FEATURES: Spores 19–25 × 18–23 μm, globose to subglobose, thick-walled, smooth, hyaline; pileipellis a disarticulating trichodermium with rod-shaped terminal cells.

OCCURRENCE: Solitary, scattered, or in groups on trunks and large branches of hardwoods, especially oak; summer–fall.

EDIBILITY: Edible.

REMARKS: This is a tropical species that occurs along the Gulf Coast and northward into Georgia. *Oudemansiella cubensis* (not illustrated) is a similar tropical species that may also occur in the Gulf Coast Region. Its pileipellis is a trichodermium of erect and entangled hyphae, and it has smaller spores that measure 15–17 × 14–16 μm.

Oudemansiella canarii

Panaeolina foenisecii (Pers.) Maire

= *Panaeolus foenisecii* (Pers.) J. Schröt.

COMMON NAME: Lawnmower's Mushroom.
MACROSCOPIC FEATURES: **Cap** 0.5–3 cm wide, bell-shaped, then convex; surface dry, smooth, reddish brown or grayish brown, fading to grayish tan or showing bands of grayish tan as the cap dries; margin slightly striate when fresh. **Gills** attached, close, brown, darkening with age, gill faces may be mottled with paler edges. **Stalk** 2.5–10 cm long, up to 3 mm thick, equal, smooth, white to pinkish brown; partial veil absent. **Flesh** pale brown, not staining when bruised; odor and taste not distinctive.
SPORE PRINT: Dark brown to purplish brown.
MICROSCOPIC FEATURES: Spores 11–18 × 6–9 μm, elliptic, roughened, with an apical pore, pale purplish brown.
OCCURRENCE: Scattered or in groups in grassy areas; year-round.

EDIBILITY: Weakly hallucinogenic.
REMARKS: The Velvety Psathyrella or Weeping Widow, *Lacrymaria lacrymabunda* = *Psathyrella velutina* (p. 15), has a 2–12 cm wide, dry, yellowish-brown to orange-brown or reddish-brown cap covered with hairs that sometimes aggregate into small scales or disappear in age. The cap is darkest over the disk, sometimes radially wrinkled, and the margin is often hung with partial veil remnants. The gills are pale brown at first and become mottled dark brown with whitish edges when mature. A fragile ring zone is sometimes present on the upper portion of the stalk. It has a blackish-brown spore print, warted spores that measure 8–12 × 5–8 μm, and grows in grassy areas, along roadsides, or near hardwoods during summer through early winter. Also compare with *Conocybe apala* (p. 248) and *Agrocybe pediades* (p. 204), both of which have brown spore prints.

Panaeolina foenisecii

Panaeolus solidipes (Peck) Sacc.

= *Anellaria sepulchralis* (Berk.) Singer
= *Panaeolus sepulchralis* (Berk.) Sacc.

MACROSCOPIC FEATURES: **Cap** 4–10 cm wide, convex, becoming broadly convex; surface dry, smooth to wrinkled, often rimose-areolate in dry weather or in age, white to light gray or yellowish buff; margin incurved at first and often remaining so well into maturity; **flesh** moderately thick, whitish; odor and taste not distinctive. **Gills** attached, close, moderately broad, pale gray at first, becoming mottled with black, and finally black overall at maturity; edges white. **Stalk** 6–18 cm long, 5–15 mm thick, solid; surface dry, longitudinally twisted-striate, sometimes with moisture droplets at the apex when fresh, white to grayish white; partial veil and ring absent.

SPORE PRINT: Black.

MICROSCOPIC FEATURES: Spores 14–21 × 9–14 µm, ellipsoid, truncate, with an apical pore, smooth, blackish.

OCCURRENCE: Scattered, in groups, or clusters on dung or manure; year-round.

EDIBILITY: Edible, but not recommended.

REMARKS: *Panaeolus semiovatus* (not illustrated) is very similar and also grows on dung or manure, but it has a superior to median ring or ring zone on its stalk.

Panaeolus solidipes

Panellus stipticus (Bull.) P. Karst.

COMMON NAME: Luminescent Panellus.
MACROSCOPIC FEATURES: **Cap** 5–30 mm wide, semicircular to kidney-shaped; surface minutely scaly to hairy or fuzzy, dingy white to pale brown; **flesh** thin, flexible, tough, whitish to pale brown; odor not distinctive; taste acrid. **Gills** attached to decurrent, close to crowded, pinkish to pale brown. **Stalk** 3–10 mm long, 2–5 mm thick, lateral, hairy, whitish to pale brown.

SPORE PRINT: White.
MICROSCOPIC FEATURES: Spores 3–6 × 2–3 μm, oblong to allantoid, smooth, hyaline, amyloid.
OCCURRENCE: In groups or clusters on decaying hardwood logs, sticks, and stumps; year-round.
EDIBILITY: Inedible.
REMARKS: When viewed in total darkness for several minutes, fresh specimens will produce a whitish or greenish glow.

Panellus stipticus

Panus neostrigosus Drechsler-Santos & Wartchow

= *Lentinus strigosus* Fr.
= *Lentinus rudis* (Fr.) Henn.
= *Panus rudis* Fr.

COMMON NAMES: Hairy Panus, Ruddy Panus.
MACROSCOPIC FEATURES: **Cap** 2–10 cm wide, fan- to kidney-shaped or broadly funnel-shaped; surface dry, densely hairy, purplish when young, becoming reddish brown to pinkish tan; margin inrolled or incurved and sometimes lobed. **Gills** decurrent, close or crowded, narrow, purplish at first, becoming whitish to pale tan. **Stalk** rudimentary or up to 1–4 cm long and 1 cm thick, eccentric to lateral, densely hairy, solid, dry, colored like the cap or paler. **Flesh** tough, white; odor not distinctive; taste slightly bitter or not distinctive.

SPORE PRINT: White.
MICROSCOPIC FEATURES: Spores 4.5–7 × 2–4 µm, elliptic, smooth, hyaline, inamyloid.
OCCURRENCE: Solitary, in groups, or clusters on decaying hardwood logs and stumps; year-round.
EDIBILITY: Inedible.
REMARKS: *Panus conchatus* = *Lentinus torulosus* (not illustrated) has a similarly colored cap that may be smooth, cracked, or scaly but not hairy. It also has decurrent gills and a velvety to fuzzy stalk. It grows on wood or on the ground from buried roots.

Panus neostrigosus

Panus tephroleucus (Mont.) T. W. May & A. E. Wood

= *Lentinus tephroleucus* Mont.
= *Panus siparius* (Berk. & M. A. Curtis) Singer

MACROSCOPIC FEATURES: **Cap** 6–40 mm wide, convex, deeply umbilicate to funnel-shaped; surface dry, scaly toward the margin, dark purple at first, becoming paler purple to lilac then fading reddish brown to grayish brown and sometimes yellowish; disc typically glabrous and often finely striate; margin inrolled on young specimens, expanding and becoming nearly plane at maturity; **flesh** very thin, leathery, creamy white; odor and taste not distinctive. **Gills** deeply decurrent, close to subdistant, creamy white; edges entire. **Stalk** 2–10 cm long, 2–12 mm thick, nearly equal or enlarged at either end, central or eccentric, solid; surface dry, uniformly velvety to distinctly hairy, colored like the cap or darker.

SPORE PRINT: White.
MICROSCOPIC FEATURES: Spores 6–8 × 2.5–4 µm, oblong-cylindric to lacrimoid, smooth, hyaline, inamyloid.
OCCURRENCE: Solitary, scattered, or in groups on the ground arising from a sclerotium or decaying wood; spring–fall.
EDIBILITY: Inedible.
REMARKS: The small, umbilicate to funnel-shaped cap, deeply decurrent gills, and velvety to hairy, darkly colored stalk are good field identification features.

anus tephroleucus

Parasola plicatilis (Curtis) Redhead, Vilgalys & Hopple

= *Coprinus plicatilis* (Curtis) Fr.

COMMON NAMES: Japanese Umbrella Inky, Pleated Inky Cap.

MACROSCOPIC FEATURES: **Cap** 1–3.5 cm wide, oval to conical, becoming bell-shaped to nearly flat, sometimes upturned; surface deeply sulcate from the disc to the margin, yellowish brown at first, becoming gray and often retaining a yellowish-brown disc; **flesh** very thin, fragile, whitish to grayish; odor and taste not distinctive. **Gills** free, subdistant, grayish at first, becoming black at maturity. **Stalk** 5–9 cm long, 1–3 mm thick, nearly equal down to a slightly swollen base, fragile, hollow; surface dry, smooth, white.

SPORE PRINT: Black.

MICROSCOPIC FEATURES: Spores 10–14 × 7–10 μm, angular-ovoid to lemon-shaped, with a conspicuous germ pore, smooth, blackish.

OCCURRENCE: Solitary, scattered, or in groups in grassy areas; spring–late fall.

EDIBILITY: Reportedly edible.

REMARKS: Although the gills of this mushroom become black when mature, they do not form an inky fluid like some other similar inky caps.

Parasola plicatilis

Pholiota highlandensis (Peck) Quadr. & Lunghini

= *Pholiota carbonaria* (Fr.) Singer

COMMON NAMES: Burnsite Pholiota, Charred Pholiota.

MACROSCOPIC FEATURES: **Cap** 2–6 cm wide, hemispherical at first, becoming convex to nearly flat or slightly depressed, with or without a small umbo; surface viscid to glutinous when moist, shiny when dry, smooth, yellowish brown to reddish brown, sometimes with an olive tint; margin incurved and remaining so well into maturity; **flesh** thin, yellowish to brownish; odor not distinctive; taste astringent or not distinctive. **Gills** attached, close to crowded, white to yellowish at first, becoming grayish brown at maturity; edges finely toothed. **Stalk** 2–5 cm long, 5–10 mm thick, cylindrical, solid when young, becoming hollow in age; surface moist or dry, fibrillose-scaly, pale yellow, covered with yellowish-brown scales; partial veil web-like, yellowish, leaving a fibrillose, superior annular zone.

SPORE PRINT: Dark brown.

MICROSCOPIC FEATURES: Spores 6–8 × 4–5 μm, elliptic to oval, with a distinct apiculus and germ pore, smooth, grayish yellow.

OCCURRENCE: Scattered, in groups, or clusters on charred ground, campfire pits, or charred wood; year-round.

EDIBILITY: Unknown.

REMARKS: The Charcoal Psathyrella, *Psathyrella pennata* = *Psathyrella carbonicola* (p. 15), has a dark brown cap, gills, and stalk and also grows on charred soil or wood. Some species of *Gymnopilus* are similar and produce brown spore prints, but their spores are warted and lack a germ pore.

Pholiota highlandensis

Pholiota polychroa (Berk.) A. H. Sm. & H. J. Brodie

COMMON NAME: Variable Pholiota.

MACROSCOPIC FEATURES: **Cap** 1.5–10 cm wide, obtuse to convex, becoming broadly convex to nearly flat, often with a low umbo; surface glutinous to viscid, with delicate vinaceous scales when young, especially along the margin, becoming glabrous, color variable, greenish to blue green or dark olive, usually with olivaceous or purplish tones, often with dull orange to yellow hues, especially on the disc; margin usually adorned with hanging triangular flaps of veil tissue; **flesh** soft, whitish to greenish; odor and taste not distinctive. **Gills** attached or somewhat decurrent, close to crowded, pale cream to lilaceous at first, becoming grayish to brown or dark purplish brown with an olivaceous tone; edges whitish. **Stalk** 2–7.5 cm long, 3–8 mm thick, nearly equal or tapered downward, solid or hollow; surface fibrillose-scaly from the base upward to a thin, evanescent ring, somewhat longitudinally striate and yellowish to pale blue green above the ring, reddish brown below, at times with a mat of tawny hairs at the base; partial veil leaving a thin superior ring or annular zone.

SPORE PRINT: Purplish brown to brown.

MICROSCOPIC FEATURES: Spores 6–8 × 3–4.5 μm, oblong to elliptic or bean-shaped, with a minute apical pore, smooth, brownish.

OCCURRENCE: Usually in groups or clusters on decaying hardwood, rarely on conifers; spring–early winter.

EDIBILITY: Unknown.

REMARKS: *Polychroa* means "having many colors," a fitting name for this highly variable mushroom.

Pholiota polychroa

Phyllotopsis nidulans (Pers.) Singer

= *Panus nidulans* (Pers.) Pilát

COMMON NAME: Orange Mock Oyster.

MACROSCOPIC FEATURES: **Cap** 2.5–9 cm wide, semicircular to fan-shaped, broadly convex; surface dry, densely fuzzy, orange to yellowish orange, developing brownish tones in age, sometimes with a whitish bloom when young; margin inrolled at first, becoming incurved and remaining so well into maturity; **flesh** soft, pale orange; odor unpleasant and often compared to rotting cabbage; taste unpleasant or not distinctive. **Gills** attached, close to crowded, orange to yellowish orange. **Stalk** rudimentary, lateral, colored like the cap, or absent.

SPORE PRINT: Pale pink.

MICROSCOPIC FEATURES: Spores 6–8 × 3–4 µm, allantoid, smooth, hyaline, inamyloid.

OCCURRENCE: Solitary, in groups, or clusters on conifers or hardwoods; year-round.

EDIBILITY: Inedible.

REMARKS: The combination of a fuzzy orange cap, a rudimentary stalk, unpleasant odor, and pink spore print makes this mushroom easy to identify.

Phyllotopsis nidulans

Pleurotus ostreatus complex (Jacq.)
P. Kumm.

COMMON NAME: Oyster Mushroom.
MACROSCOPIC FEATURES: **Cap** 4–18 cm wide,
convex, oystershell- to fan-shaped; surface
moist or dry, smooth, color variable, white to
creamy white, buff, tan, or brown; **flesh** thick,
firm, white; odor anise-like, fragrant, fruity,
or not distinctive; taste not distinctive. **Gills**
decurrent, close to subdistant, white, creamy
white, or grayish white. **Stalk** lateral, rudimentary or absent, up to 3.5 cm long and thick
when present, usually tapered downward,
solid; surface dry, white to dingy white, often
coated, at least near the base, with downy
white hairs.

SPORE PRINT: Whitish to grayish or lilac.
MICROSCOPIC FEATURES: Spores 7–12 ×
3–5 μm, cylindric, smooth, hyaline, inamyloid.
OCCURRENCE: In groups or clusters on decaying hardwood logs, stumps, or trunks, sometimes on conifers; fall–winter.
EDIBILITY: Edible.
REMARKS: *Ostreatus* means "oyster," referring
to the shape of the cap. *Pleurotus pulmonarius*
(not illustrated) is very similar and begins
fruiting on hardwoods during summer. It has a
more developed stalk, paler cap, and often has
short striations on the cap margin.

Pleurotus ostreatus

Pluteus atromarginatus (Konrad) Kühner

= *Pluteus cervinus* subsp. *atromarginatus* Konrad
= *Pluteus cervinus* var. *atromarginatus* Singer

COMMON NAME: Black-edged Pluteus.
MACROSCOPIC FEATURES: **Cap** 3–10 cm broad, obtuse to convex, finally plane or with a low umbo; surface blackish brown, streaked from appressed black fibrils, at times squamulose; **flesh** cottony and soft, white; odor and taste not distinctive. **Gills** free, close, 7–10 mm broad, white at first, becoming pinkish; edges dark brown to black. **Stalk** 5–10 cm long, 4–12 mm thick, nearly equal; surface coated with dark fibers but paler than the cap.

SPORE PRINT: Dull pink.
MICROSCOPIC FEATURES: Spores 6.5–8 × 4.5–5 µm, elliptic, smooth, hyaline.
OCCURRENCE: Solitary, scattered, or in groups on decaying hardwood logs; fall–winter.
EDIBILITY: Edible.
REMARKS: *Pluteus cervinus* (p. 394) is similar but has a paler cap, and its gill edges are not dark brown to black.

Pluteus atromarginatus

Pluteus cervinus (Schaeff.) P. Kumm.

= *Pluteus atricapillus* (Batsch) Fayod

COMMON NAMES: Fawn Mushroom, Deer Mushroom.

MACROSCOPIC FEATURES: **Cap** 3–12 cm wide, convex, becoming broadly convex to nearly flat in age; surface often wrinkled when young, becoming nearly smooth or streaked with tiny fibers, with various shades of brown, most often dull brown to grayish brown; margin even, entire; **flesh** thick, soft, white; odor and taste radish-like or not distinctive. **Gills** free, close to crowded, white when young, becoming pale pink to salmon in age. **Stalk** 5–10 cm long, 6–20 mm thick, nearly equal or enlarged downward, solid; surface dry, white, often with dull brown to grayish fibers.

SPORE PRINT: Salmon or brownish pink.

MICROSCOPIC FEATURES: Spores 5.5–7 × 4–6 μm, elliptic, smooth, hyaline.

OCCURRENCE: Solitary or in groups on decaying conifers or hardwoods, often on the ground coming up from buried wood or on sawdust piles; spring–early winter.

EDIBILITY: Edible.

REMARKS: *Cervinus* means "pertaining to the color of deer," a reference to the cap colors. Some authors recognize specimens with a blackish-brown cap and thicker stalk as a distinct species called *Pluteus magnus* (not illustrated). *Pluteus atromarginatus* (p. 393) is similar, but it has a darker cap, and its gill edges are dark brown to black.

Pluteus cervinus

Pluteus longistriatus (Peck) Peck

= *Agaricus longistriatus* Peck

COMMON NAME: Pleated Pluteus.

MACROSCOPIC FEATURES: **Cap** 1–5 cm wide, convex at first, becoming nearly flat at maturity, with or without a central depression or umbo; surface dry, slightly scaly over the center and radially striate, then furrowed from the margin to the disc as it ages, grayish brown; **flesh** thin, white; odor and taste not distinctive. **Gills** free, close, white at first, becoming pinkish at maturity. **Stalk** 2–8 cm long, 1.5–3 mm thick, nearly equal, solid; surface longitudinally striate, white, smooth to slightly scurfy.

SPORE PRINT: Salmon pink.

MICROSCOPIC FEATURES: Spores 6–7.5 × 5–5.5 μm, subglobose, smooth, hyaline.

OCCURRENCE: Scattered or in groups on decaying hardwood debris; summer–late fall.

EDIBILITY: Edible.

REMARKS: *Longistriatus* means "having long furrows," a reference to the markings on the cap.

Pluteus longistriatus

Pluteus petasatus (Fr.) Gillet

= *Agaricus petasatus* Fr.

MACROSCOPIC FEATURES: **Cap** 4–10 cm wide, bell-shaped or convex at first, becoming broadly convex at maturity, sometimes with a low, obtuse umbo; surface smooth at first, soon becoming finely cracked on the disc and forming tiny brownish fibers and scales over the center or nearly overall, whitish to buff or brownish, darkest on the disc and paler toward the margin; margin often conspicuously split; **flesh** thin, white; odor somewhat radish-like; taste not distinctive. **Gills** free, close, white at first, becoming pink to dull pink. **Stalk** 4–10 cm long, 6–12 mm thick, nearly equal or enlarged downward, solid; surface smooth or longitudinally striate, white, becoming brownish at the base.

SPORE PRINT: Dull pink.

MICROSCOPIC FEATURES: Spores 6–7.5 × 4.5–5 µm, elliptic, smooth, hyaline.

OCCURRENCE: In groups or clusters on wood mulch, sawdust, or decaying wood, especially stumps; year-round.

EDIBILITY: Edible.

REMARKS: *Pluteus pellitus* (p. 15) is very similar, but it has a smooth white cap, with or without an umbo, and is sometimes brownish on the disc.

Pluteus petasatus

Pseudomerulius curtisii (Berk.) Redhead & Ginns

= *Meiorganum curtisii* (Berk.) Singer, J. Garcia
    & L. D. Gomez

= *Paxillus curtisii* Berk.

MACROSCOPIC FEATURES: **Cap** 2–5 cm wide, fan- or shell-shaped; surface dry, fuzzy or smooth, brownish yellow to olive yellow, sometimes with reddish-brown stains; margin inrolled at first; **flesh** tough, yellowish; odor pungent and unpleasantly sweet or not distinctive; taste bitter or not distinctive. **Gills** radiating from a narrowed point of attachment, close, thick, crinkled, freely forking and fusing, with crossveins present, not easily peelable from the cap as a layer, yellow orange, staining darker orange. **Stalk** rudimentary or absent.

SPORE PRINT: Olive yellow to yellowish brown.
MICROSCOPIC FEATURES: Spores 3–3.5 × 1.5–2 μm, broadly elliptic, smooth, pale yellow, dextrinoid.
OCCURRENCE: Solitary, in groups, or clusters on decaying conifer logs and stumps; summer–early winter.
EDIBILITY: Unknown.
REMARKS: The species was named in honor of the American botanist Moses Ashley Curtis (1808–1872).

Pseudomerulius curtisii

Psilocybe cubensis (Earle) Singer

= *Stropharia cyanescens* Murrill

COMMON NAMES: Common Large Psilocybe, Magic Mushroom.

MACROSCOPIC FEATURES: **Cap** 2.5–9 cm wide, broadly conical to bell-shaped at first, becoming convex to nearly flat with an umbo at maturity; surface smooth, viscid when moist, white to cream with a yellowish to ochraceous or brownish disc, becoming buff to pale brownish in age; margin often with whitish veil fragments; **flesh** firm, white, bruising blue or greenish blue; odor and taste not distinctive. **Gills** attached, sometimes notched, close to crowded, narrow, gray at first, becoming purple gray to nearly black; edges whitish. **Stalk** 4–16 cm long, 4–12 mm thick, usually tapered upward from a swollen or bulbous base; surface smooth overall or somewhat striate at the apex, whitish, bruising blue or greenish blue; partial veil whitish, usually leaving a superior ring but sometimes only fragments on the cap margin; upper surface of the ring soon blackened from the spore deposit.

SPORE PRINT: Dark purple brown to blackish.

MICROSCOPIC FEATURES: Spores 11–17 × 7–12 μm, broadly elliptic, smooth, purplish brown in water, yellowish in KOH.

OCCURRENCE: Solitary or in groups on herbivore dung, especially cow dung, and on manure-enriched soil in pastures and grasslands; year-round.

EDIBILITY: Hallucinogenic.

REMARKS: It is the largest species of *Psilocybe* in North America and is widely cultivated.

Psilocybe cubensis

Rhodocollybia maculata var. *maculata* (Alb. & Schwein.) Singer

= *Collybia maculata* (Alb. & Schwein.) P. Kumm.

COMMON NAME: Spotted Collybia.

MACROSCOPIC FEATURES: Cap 3.5–10 cm wide, convex when young, becoming broadly convex to nearly flat in age, sometimes with a low, broad umbo; surface smooth, dry or moist, pinkish buff when young, becoming whitish in age, developing reddish-brown to rusty streaks and spots overall, but especially toward the center; **flesh** thin, white; odor mildly unpleasant or not distinctive; taste bitter. **Gills** attached, close to crowded, whitish to buff, developing brown to rusty spots in age. **Stalk** 5–12 cm long, 8–13 mm thick, nearly equal, with a slightly rooting base, hollow; surface dry, longitudinally striate, whitish, developing rusty-brown spots in age.

SPORE PRINT: Pinkish buff to yellowish buff.

MICROSCOPIC FEATURES: Spores 5.5–7 × 5–6 μm, globose to subglobose, smooth, hyaline, typically dextrinoid.

OCCURRENCE: Solitary, scattered, or in groups or fairy rings on humus and buried wood with conifers or in mixed woods; summer–early winter.

EDIBILITY: Edible but usually bitter.

REMARKS: *Rhodocollybia maculata* var. *scorzonerea* (not illustrated) is nearly identical, but it has distinctly yellow gills, and its stalk may be white or yellow. *Rhodocollybia butyracea* (not illustrated) is similar, but its cap and stalk are reddish brown to bay-brown, and its flesh does not taste bitter.

Rhodocollybia maculata var. *maculata*

Ripartitella brasiliensis (Speg.) Singer

MACROSCOPIC FEATURES: **Cap** 1–7 cm wide, hemispheric to convex, becoming broadly convex to nearly plane; surface dry, appressed-wooly, vinaceous reddish brown when young, breaking up and forming small concentric to scattered reddish-brown scales on a whitish to buff ground color, sometimes whitish overall in age or following heavy rains that wash away the scales; margin often with patches of torn partial veil on young specimens; **flesh** thin, whitish to buff; odor and taste not distinctive. **Gills** attached, close, white, not staining when bruised; edges entire. **Stalk** 1.5–5 cm long, 2–6 mm thick, nearly equal, solid; surface dry, silky-fibrillose with scattered tiny brownish scales on a whitish to buff ground color, often with a copious, white, cottony basal mycelium and white mycelial cords; partial veil whitish to brownish, leaving remnants on the cap margin or a faint ring zone.

SPORE PRINT: White.

MICROSCOPIC FEATURES: Spores 4.5–6 × 3.5–4.5 μm, broadly elliptic to subglobose, finely echinulate, hyaline, inamyloid.

OCCURRENCE: In dense groups or clusters on decaying hardwood, especially oak; summer–early winter.

EDIBILITY: Unknown.

REMARKS: *Brasiliensis* refers to Brazil, where this mushroom was first collected and described. It is fairly common in Central and South America and has also been reported from Africa and the Bonin Islands of the western Pacific.

Ripartitella brasiliensis

Russula atropurpurea Peck

MACROSCOPIC FEATURES: Cap 4–10(14)
cm broad, convex, becoming plane with a
depressed disc; surface glabrous to pruinose-
velvety, viscid when wet, dark reddish purple;
disc almost black or olive green, becoming
brownish drab to yellow brown; margin even
to slightly striate; cuticle peels one-third of
the way to the center. **Gills** adnate, subdistant, sometimes forking near the stalk, white,
becoming pale yellow then brownish when
injured or on drying. **Stalk** up to 6 cm long,
1–3 cm broad, spongy to firm; surface glabrous, white or pinkish, and staining brownish
where bruised. **Flesh** brittle, white, changing
from brownish drab to yellow brown where
bruised; odor not distinctive, becoming disagreeable on drying; taste mild.
SPORE PRINT: Whitish to yellow.
MICROSCOPIC FEATURES: Spores 8–11 × 7–8
µm, elliptic to subglobose, ornamented with
warts 0.8–1.2 µm high, hyaline, amyloid.

OCCURRENCE: In mixed pine and hardwood
forests; late summer–early winter.
EDIBILITY: Unknown.
REMARKS: *Atropurpurea* means dark reddish
purple. *Russula subsericeonitens* (p. 411) has a
purplish cap with a cuticle that does not easily peel and a white spore print. The Purple-
bloom Russula, *Russula mariae* (p. 15), has
a 1.5–10 cm broad, wine-red to purple or
violet cap that may have tints of green or yellow and is dusted with a whitish bloom when
fresh. Its cap cuticle peels up to two-thirds of
the distance to the center, and it has a white
stalk that is often flushed pinkish purple. The
application of KOH stains the cap orange. It
has a white to cream spore print and grows
on the ground in hardwoods or mixed woods,
especially near oak. *Russula vinacea* (not illustrated) also has a purplish cap, but it has an
acrid taste.

Russula atropurpurea

Russula ballouii Peck

COMMON NAME: Ballou's Russula.

MACROSCOPIC FEATURES: **Cap** 3–9.5(15) cm broad, convex, becoming plano-convex, depressed at the disc; surface dry, pale brick-red at first and breaking up into small, yellow-brown, areolate patches, becoming yellow-ish ocher to brownish orange as it matures; margin even, not striate; cuticle does not peel. **Gills** adnexed, close, 4–5 mm broad, acute, white to pale buff. **Stalk** 2–6.5 cm long, 0.8–1.8 cm broad, slightly tapered to the apex; surface dry, glabrous, solid, whitish with yellow-brown scales and bands at the base. **Flesh** up to 4 mm thick, brittle, whitish; odor not distinctive; taste acrid.

SPORE PRINT: Creamy white.

MICROSCOPIC FEATURES: Spores 7–9 × 5.5–7.5 µm, oval, with warts 0.2–1 µm high, hyaline, amyloid.

OCCURRENCE: In river and stream bottomland forests; fall–winter.

EDIBILITY: Unknown.

REMARKS: *Ballouii* honors American mycologist W. H. Ballou (1857–1937). *Russula compacta* (p. 403) is similarly colored, but its gills stain reddish brown when rubbed, and its flesh has a fishy odor. The cap colors of *Russula decolorans* (p. 15) are somewhat variable, yellow orange to ocher orange or reddish orange, and the margin is sometimes weakly tuberculate-striate on mature specimens. The cuticle peels one-quarter to two-thirds of the way to the center. The gills are whitish to cream at first, then yellowish, and slowly stain grayish when bruised. The stalk is white and stains gray in age, and the flesh is white and stains grayish and sometimes reddish. It grows on the ground with conifers, especially pines, during summer through early winter.

Russula ballouii

Russula compacta Frost

COMMON NAME: Firm Russula.
MACROSCOPIC FEATURES: **Cap** 7–15 cm wide, broadly convex, sometimes umbilicate and becoming centrally depressed; surface dry to subviscid, glabrous, white to cream, staining rusty ochraceous to cinnamon or orangish brown; margin even, not striate; cuticle peels one-half of the way to the center. **Gills** adnate, close to subdistant, white, staining reddish brown when bruised. **Stalk** 2–12 cm long, 1–4 cm thick, equal, solid, and becoming hollow with age; surface dry, glabrous, white, staining reddish brown when injured. **Flesh** brittle, white, with yellowish tones in age; odor strong, of fish; taste slightly acrid or not distinctive.
SPORE PRINT: White.

MICROSCOPIC FEATURES: Spores 7–10 × 6–8 μm, elliptic to oval, with warts up to 0.7–1.2 μm high, hyaline, amyloid.
OCCURRENCE: Found in mixed pine and hardwood forests; summer–fall.
EDIBILITY: Edible, however, the strong, fishy odor deters many from trying it.
REMARKS: This is one of the larger species of *Russula* and can be recognized by all parts staining reddish brown and its fishy odor. The cap colors of *Russula decolorans* (p. 15) are somewhat variable, yellow orange to ocher orange or reddish orange, and the margin is sometimes weakly tuberculate-striate on mature specimens. The gills, flesh, and stalk slowly stain gray when bruised. Its flesh lacks the fishy odor, and it grows with conifers, especially pines. Also compare with *Russula ballouii* (p. 402), which lacks a fishy odor.

ussula compacta

Russula earlei Peck

COMMON NAME: Beeswax Russula.

MACROSCOPIC FEATURES: **Cap** 3.5–7.5 cm broad, convex-depressed, becoming more depressed in age; surface glabrous or roughened and sometimes pitted, appearing waxy, becoming eroded, pale yellow to yellow, sometimes with yellowish-brown tones; margin even, not striate; cuticle not readily peeling except at the margin. **Gills** adnate to adnexed, distant to subdistant, thick, 3–7 mm broad, with many forking, with few lamellulae, white with some brownish stains. **Stalk** 1–5 cm long, 5–22 mm thick, tapered to the base; surface dry, glabrous, solid but soon cavernous, dingy white to pale yellowish. **Flesh** 4–6 mm thick, brittle, white; odor not distinctive; taste mild to slightly acrid.

SPORE PRINT: White.

MICROSCOPIC FEATURES: Spores 4.5–5.2 × 3–4 μm, subglobose to short ellipsoid, covered with short spines about 0.1 μm high, hyaline, amyloid.

OCCURRENCE: Gregarious in river floodplain forests of hardwoods or in mixed conifer and hardwood forests; summer.

EDIBILITY: Unknown.

REMARKS: At first sight, this species appears to be a species of *Hygrophorus*, however, the amyloid spores quickly eliminate this possibility. *Russula flavida* (not illustrated) has a 2–10 cm broad, obscurely striate, bright yellow to orange-yellow cap and a concolorous stalk. The cap cuticle peels one-fourth to one-half of the way to the center. It has white gills that become pale yellow, a yellow spore print, and grows in hardwoods or mixed woods with oak.

Russula earlei

Russula eccentrica Peck

MACROSCOPIC FEATURES: **Cap** 3–13.5 cm broad, convex, then plane and depressed; surface moist, glabrous, cuticle breaking up into areolate patches at the margin, brownish to grayish brown; cuticle not readily peeling. **Gills** ascending, adnexed, close to subdistant, 7–11 mm broad, acute, thick, waxy, entire, cream to tan or yellowish pink and drying purplish red; lamellulae with 1 or 2 tiers. **Stalk** 1.5–4 cm long, 6–20 mm broad, tapered to the base; surface dry or moist, glabrous, solid to cavernous, dingy pinkish white. **Flesh** up to 10 mm thick, brittle, white to dingy pinkish; odor strong, musty to slightly spermatic; taste varying from mild to bitter.

SPORE PRINT: White.

MICROSCOPIC FEATURES: Spores 7–9 × 5.2–6.8 μm, subglobose to ellipsoid, covered with short spines 0.1–0.2 μm high, hyaline, amyloid.

OCCURRENCE: Gregarious to scattered in mixed pine and hardwood forests; summer–fall.

EDIBILITY: Unknown.

REMARKS: The purplish-red color of the drying gills and the strong odor are distinctive features. *Russula cortinarioides* (not illustrated) has a 3.6–6.5 cm wide, yellowish-brown to reddish-brown or grayish-brown cap that becomes dirty cream to whitish closer to the margin, and the cuticle peels halfway to the center. It has close, whitish gills that become vinaceous to deep brownish red in age, a white stalk that stains grayish when handled, and whitish flesh that weakly reddens when cut and tastes unpleasant and faintly astringent. *Russula polyphylla* (not illustrated) has an 8–13 cm broad, dingy whitish to light brownish-red cap and a cracked cuticle that barely peels. It has crowded, whitish gills that stain reddish brown and are strongly intervenose at the margin and a white stalk that stains reddish when bruised. It has white flesh with a strong farinaceous to nauseating odor, a white spore print, and grows with beech during summer and fall.

ussula eccentrica

Russula grata Britzelm.

= *Russula laurocerasi* Melzer

COMMON NAME: Almond-scented Russula.

MACROSCOPIC FEATURES: **Cap** 4–11.5 cm wide, convex, becoming broadly convex to nearly plane, often depressed at the center, viscid when moist, smooth; margin tuberculate-striate at maturity, pale yellow to brownish yellow; cuticle peels three-quarters of the way to the center. **Gills** attached, close, whitish to creamy white, usually staining brown in age. **Stalk** 2.5–10 cm long, 1–3 cm thick, equal or somewhat enlarged downward or in the middle, smooth or slightly wrinkled, white to pale yellow, usually bruising brown. **Flesh** brittle, white to yellowish; odor like bitter almonds or marzipan; taste acrid or not distinctive.

SPORE PRINT: Creamy white to yellowish.

MICROSCOPIC FEATURES: Spores 7–10.5 × 7–9 µm, subglobose, surface ornamented with warts and ridges up to 2.6 µm high, hyaline, amyloid.

OCCURRENCE: Scattered or in groups, mostly with hardwoods, sometimes in mixed woods; summer–fall.

EDIBILITY: Inedible.

REMARKS: *Russula fragrantissima* (not illustrated) has a larger cap, 7–20 cm wide, a larger stalk, 8–15 cm long and 1.5–6 cm thick, and has a fragrant, then rancid odor. The spores have warts and ridges that are 0.3–1 µm high. *Russula mutabilis* (not illustrated) has a 3.5–8 cm wide, brownish-orange to orange-brown cap with a delicate, yellow pulverulence, especially near the margin. The cap sometimes slowly bruises deep red when young. It has a yellow to orangish-yellow stalk that is often whitish at the apex, and it grows with oaks. *Russula ventricosipes* (not illustrated) is also similar, but it has a tawny-yellow to pale dull brown cap and a white stalk that has a scurfy, reddish, pointed base or is reddish nearly overall. The cap and stalk are usually almost buried in sand.

Russula grata

Russula hixsonii Murrill

MACROSCOPIC FEATURES: **Cap** 15–20 cm broad, convex to depressed; margin even to pectinate, thick; surface dry, dull, smooth at first, becoming strongly pruinose-tomentose, and finally cracking into quilt-like patterns at the center with age, white mottled with pinks and yellows when young, then turning an intense rose pink as it matures, with the center fading to whitish mottled with brown; cuticle peels one-third of the way to the center. **Gills** adnate to almost free, distant, many forked at the base, white to off-white, changing to grayish black in age or when handled. **Stalk** 7–12 cm long, 2–3.5 cm broad, equal, solid; surface glabrous, white, and unchanging. **Flesh** thick, brittle, white, strongly graying with age; odor not distinctive when fresh, very agreeable, like freshly baked cake when dried; taste mild.
SPORE PRINT: Golden yellow.
MICROSCOPIC FEATURES: Spores 9.2–10.9 × 7.6–9 μm, short-ellipsoid, with conical warts 1–1.4 μm high, hyaline, amyloid.

OCCURRENCE: Scattered or in groups on the ground under oak and pine; known only from Florida and southeastern coastal Georgia; summer–fall.
EDIBILITY: Unknown.
REMARKS: The epithet *hixsonii* honors former University of Florida entomology professor Homer R. Hixson (1926–1990), who first collected it. The large caps with intense pink coloration are most distinctive. It was first described from Gainesville, Florida, in 1942 and later rediscovered by Arleen Bessette in southeastern Georgia in 2011. *Russula flavisiccans* (not illustrated) has a 2–11 cm broad, often areolate, pale pink to pale pinkish-red cap with a cuticle that is not separable or just slightly so at the margin. It has white gills that become pale yellow on drying, a white stalk sometimes tinged pinkish, and a bitter or disagreeable taste. It has a white to pale yellow spore print and grows in mixed pine and hardwood forests during summer.

Russula hixsonii

Russula parvovirescens Buyck, D. Mitch. & Parrent

MACROSCOPIC FEATURES: **Cap** 4–8 cm wide, convex, becoming depressed over the center; surface dry, felty to velvety, greenish brown to dark olive green or metallic bluish green, often darker over the disc in age; margin thin, even, weakly striate in age; the cuticle has the appearance of a reticulate pattern and peels one-third to one-half of the way to the center. **Gills** attached to nearly free, close, sometimes forked, white. **Stalk** 3–6 cm long, 8–13 mm thick, nearly equal, solid, glabrous, white. **Flesh** brittle, white; odor and taste not distinctive.
SPORE PRINT: Pale cream.
MICROSCOPIC FEATURES: Spores 6.7–9.1 × 5.7–7.2 μm, subglobose, surface ornamented with warts and ridges up to 1 μm high, hyaline, amyloid.

OCCURRENCE: Solitary, scattered, or in groups on the ground in mixed pine and hardwood forests; summer–fall.
EDIBILITY: Unknown.
REMARKS: The cap of the Quilted Green Russula, *Russula virescens* (not illustrated), is dull green to yellowish green or grayish green over a white ground color and is conspicuously cracked into small crusty patches that do not form a reticulate pattern. The cap cuticle peels about one-half of the way to the center, and its spores measure 6–9 × 5.5–7 μm. It grows on the ground with hardwoods, especially oak and beech, during summer and fall. *Russula aeruginea* (not illustrated) has a smooth, olive-green to yellowish-green cap, white flesh that tastes mild initially and is often acrid after a few minutes, a creamy-white to pale orange-yellow spore print, and grows with oaks during summer.

Russula parvovirescens

Russula perlactea Murrill

MACROSCOPIC FEATURES: **Cap** 4–9 cm broad, convex to plane or slightly depressed; surface glabrous, slightly viscid, white and unchanging; margin even; the cuticle readily peels nearly to center. **Gills** adnate, rather distant, very few forked, white, and unchanging. **Stalk** up to 7 cm long, 1–2 cm broad, equal, glabrous, solid, white, and unchanging. **Flesh** brittle, white, and unchanging; odor not distinctive; taste quickly acrid.

SPORE PRINT: Chalk white.

MICROSCOPIC FEATURES: Spores 10–13.5 × 8.5–10.5 μm, subglobose to broadly ellipsoid, ornamented with warts 0.8–1.7 μm high, hyaline, amyloid.

OCCURRENCE: In hardwoods or mixed woods, especially with oak; fall–winter.

EDIBILITY: Unknown.

REMARKS: The overall white color, very acrid taste, and late fruiting help to distinguish this species. *Russula albida* (not illustrated) is macroscopically nearly identical, but it fruits during summer and has mild, then somewhat bitter but not acrid-tasting flesh. It has a pale creamy-yellow spore print and smaller spores that measure 7–9 × 6–7.5 μm. *Russula ludoviciana* (not illustrated) has a 4–7.5 cm broad, white cap with a pale yellow-brown center, a tuberculate-striate margin, and its cuticle peels most of the way to center. It has close, white gills, a white stalk, and mild-tasting white flesh. It has a creamy-white spore print and grows under oaks in bottomland hardwood forests during summer and fall.

Russula perlactea

Russula subgraminicolor Murrill

MACROSCOPIC FEATURES: **Cap** 3–9 cm wide, convex at first, becoming broadly convex to nearly plane in age, sometimes with a depressed center; surface dry, minutely fibrillose to nearly smooth, uniformly blue green to grass green overall, fading toward the margin in age; margin faintly to distinctly striate; cuticle peels one-quarter to one-half of the way to the center. **Gills** attached, subdistant, broad, forked near the stalk, whitish to cream. **Stalk** 3–10 cm long, 1.6–2.5 cm thick, equal; surface dry, smooth, white. **Flesh** brittle, white, unchanging; odor and taste not distinctive.
SPORE PRINT: Cream to pale ocher.
MICROSCOPIC FEATURES: Spores 7–9.5 × 5.5–8 μm, elliptic, ornamented with warts up to 0.6 μm, hyaline, amyloid.
OCCURRENCE: Solitary, scattered, or in groups on the ground under oaks; fall–early winter.

EDIBILITY: Unknown.
REMARKS: *Russula heterophylla* (not illustrated) has a 5–10 cm wide cap with a slightly striate margin. The cap color varies from yellowish green to brownish yellow, olivaceous, or brown. The cap cuticle peels one-fourth to one-half of the way to the center. It has very close, forked, white to very pale cream gills that are sometimes spotted reddish brown and anastomose near the stalk. It has a white stalk, a white spore print, and grows in hardwoods, especially with oak, from summer through early winter. *Russula crustosa* (p. 15) has a 5–15 cm wide cap that becomes cracked overall into quilt-like patches. It has a striate margin and is variously colored orange yellow to brownish yellow, or sometimes with greenish tints. The cap cuticle peels one-half of the way to the center, it has a cream-colored spore print, and it grows in hardwoods or mixed woods, especially with oak.

Russula subgraminicolor

Russula subsericeonitens Murrill

MACROSCOPIC FEATURES: **Cap** 3.5–8 cm broad, convex to slightly depressed; surface nearly glabrous, slightly viscid, purplish lilac, blackish on the disc; margin even; cuticle does not easily peel. **Gills** almost free, subdistant, not forking, white, and unchanging. **Stalk** up to 5 cm long, 1–1.3 cm broad, slightly tapered upward; surface glabrous and somewhat uneven, white, and unchanging. **Flesh** thin, brittle, white, and unchanging; odor not distinctive; taste mild, then slightly acrid.

SPORE PRINT: Chalk white.

MICROSCOPIC FEATURES: Spores 8–9.5 × 7.5–8 μm, globose to short ellipsoid, covered with warts 0.6–1.0 μm high, hyaline, amyloid.

OCCURRENCE: In mixed pine and hardwood forests; fall–winter.

EDIBILITY: Unknown.

REMARKS: *Russula atropurpure*a (p. 401) is similar but has a yellow spore print. Also similar is *Russula vinacea* (not illustrated), which has a graying stalk.

ussula subsericeonitens

Russula variata Banning

COMMON NAME: Variable Russula.

MACROSCOPIC FEATURES: **Cap** 5–14 cm wide, convex at first, becoming broadly convex to nearly flat, often depressed over the disc in age; surface glabrous, smooth, viscid when moist, sometimes cracked in age, color variable, reddish purple, lavender, green to olive green or yellowish green, or a mixture of these colors; margin weakly striate to tuberculate-striate on older specimens; cuticle peels about one-half of the way to the center. **Gills** attached to slightly decurrent, crowded, repeatedly forked, white to cream. **Stalk** 3–10 cm long, 1–3 cm thick, nearly equal or tapered downward; surface dry, smooth or somewhat wrinkled, white. **Flesh** firm, brittle, white; odor not distinctive; taste slowly peppery to sharply acrid.

SPORE PRINT: White.

MICROSCOPIC FEATURES: Spores 7–11 × 5–8 µm, ovoid to subglobose, with isolated warts and ridges up to 1 µm high, amyloid, hyaline.

OCCURRENCE: Solitary, scattered, or in groups in hardwoods and mixed woods, especially with oak; late spring–fall.

EDIBILITY: Edible.

REMARKS: *Russula vinacea* (not illustrated) has a vinaceous-purple to wine-red cap that is often tinged with ocher-yellow on the disc and peels one-half to two-thirds of the way to the center, creamy-white gills that are often spotted rust color and fork near the stalk, a whitish stalk that often becomes grayish in age, and white flesh that tastes slowly peppery to sharply acrid. The Purple-bloom Russula, *Russula mariae* (p. 15), has a 1.5–10 cm broad, wine-red to purple or violet cap that may have tints of green or yellow and is dusted with a whitish bloom when fresh. Its cap cuticle peels up to two-thirds of the way to the center, and it has a white stalk that is often flushed pinkish purple. The application of KOH stains the cap orange. It has a white to cream spore print and grows on the ground in hardwoods or mixed woods, especially near oak.

Russula variata

Schizophyllum commune Fr.

COMMON NAME: Common Split Gill.

MACROSCOPIC FEATURES: **Cap** 1–4.5 cm wide, fan- to shell-shaped, densely covered with tiny hairs; surface dry, white to grayish white; margin incurved to inrolled when young, often becoming wavy and torn in age; **flesh** thin, flexible, whitish to grayish, sometimes with brownish tinges; odor and taste not distinctive. **Gills** nearly distant, white to pinkish gray, split lengthwise along the free edge, usually serrated or torn. **Stalk** absent or rudimentary.

SPORE PRINT: White.

MICROSCOPIC FEATURES: Spores 5–7.5 × 2–3 µm, cylindric, smooth, hyaline.

OCCURRENCE: Solitary, scattered, or in overlapping clusters on decaying hardwood; year-round.

EDIBILITY: Inedible.

REMARKS: *Schizophyllum commune* means "split gills growing in groups." It can be found on all continents except Antarctica and is a rare cause of fungal sinusitis or lung disease. The Crimped Gill, *Plicaturopsis crispa* (not illustrated), also grows on hardwood but has a fan- to shell-shaped cap, zoned with shades of yellow orange to reddish brown, and gills that are vein-like, crinkled, and often forked.

Schizophyllum commune

Simocybe centunculus (Fr.) P. Karst.

COMMON NAME: American Simocybe.
MACROSCOPIC FEATURES: **Cap** 1–3 cm wide,
convex at first, becoming flat; surface dry,
initially velvety or silky, becoming smooth in
age, olive brown to olive, soon fading, center
remaining darker than the margin; margin
translucent and radially lined; **flesh** brown;
odor and taste not distinctive. **Gills** attached,
close, pale at first, darkening to a yellowish
brown or grayish brown in age; edges white
and appearing fringed or frayed (use a hand
lens). **Stalk** 1–4 cm long, 2–4 mm thick,
equal, hollow; surface initially whitish, then
becoming brown, faintly powdery or scurfy at
the apex when young, basal mycelium white.

SPORE PRINT: Brown.
MICROSCOPIC FEATURES: Spores 6–7.5 × 4–5
μm, elliptic or bean-shaped, smooth, pale
brown.
OCCURRENCE: Scattered on decaying hardwood logs and stumps; spring–fall.
EDIBILITY: Unknown.
REMARKS: The frayed/fringed gill edges are
a distinctive feature of this otherwise easily
overlooked "little brown mushroom." The
cap surface stains red with the application of
KOH.

Simocybe centunculus

Strobilurus conigenoides (Ellis) Singer

COMMON NAME: Magnolia-cone Mushroom.
MACROSCOPIC FEATURES: **Cap** 5–20 mm wide, convex at first, then becoming flat; surface dry, white, covered with a dense layer of minute hairs; margin initially incurved; **flesh** thin, whitish; odor and taste not distinctive. **Gills** attached, close to nearly crowded, white. **Stalk** 2.5–5 cm long, 0.75–2 mm thick, equal, hollow; surface whitish to pinkish brown, finely hairy, with coarse basal hairs attaching it to a Magnolia cone.

SPORE PRINT: White.
MICROSCOPIC FEATURES: Spores 6–7 × 3–3.5 μm, elliptic, smooth, hyaline, inamyloid.
OCCURRENCE: In groups on Magnolia cones or sweetgum balls; summer–winter.
EDIBILITY: Unknown.
REMARKS: *Baeospora myosura* (p. 241) is similar, but it has amyloid spores and grows on conifer cones.

trobilurus conigenoides

Tapinella atrotomentosa (Batsch) Šutara

= *Paxillus atrotomentosus* (Batsch) Fr.

COMMON NAME: Velvet-footed Pax.
MACROSCOPIC FEATURES: **Cap** 4–15 cm wide, convex with an inrolled margin at first, becoming flat or centrally depressed; surface dry, finely hairy, yellowish brown to reddish brown, darkening with age; **flesh** whitish or pale yellow, tough, not staining; odor and taste not distinctive. **Gills** decurrent, close or crowded, forking or crossveined near the stalk, whitish to pale tan, separable as a layer. **Stalk** 2–12 cm long, up to 3 cm thick, equal, off-center to lateral, pale and smooth at the apex, with dark brown velvety or matted hairs below; partial veil lacking.

SPORE PRINT: Pale yellow to yellowish brown.
MICROSCOPIC FEATURES: Spores 5–7 × 3–4 μm, elliptic, smooth, hyaline or pale brown, dextrinoid.
OCCURRENCE: Solitary or in clusters on conifer stumps or logs; summer–early winter.
EDIBILITY: Unknown.
REMARKS: *Tapinella panuoides* (p. 15) also grows on conifer wood, but it lacks a stalk, and the gills are typically crinkled near the point of attachment.

Tapinella atrotomentosa

Tetrapyrgos nigripes (Fr.) E. Horak

= *Marasmiellus nigripes* (Fr.) Singer

COMMON NAME: Black-footed Marasmius.
MACROSCOPIC FEATURES: **Cap** 1–2 cm wide, convex at first, becoming flat, white; surface finely dusted with white powder or bald, often becoming wrinkled in age; **flesh** thin, rubbery, white; odor and taste not distinctive. **Gills** attached or slightly decurrent, sub-distant, crossveined and sometimes forked, white, sometimes staining reddish. **Stalk** 2–5 cm long, 1–1.5 mm thick, equal or tapering downward; surface white at first, becoming blackened in age, tough, dry, coated with minute white hairs.
SPORE PRINT: White.

MICROSCOPIC FEATURES: Spores 8–9 × 8–9 μm, triangular to multipointed, smooth, hyaline.
OCCURRENCE: Solitary or in groups on leaves, twigs, hickory nuts, and other woodland debris; summer–fall.
EDIBILITY: Unknown.
REMARKS: *Nigripes* means "having a black foot," a reference to the stalk that blackens as this mushroom matures. *Marasmius capillaris* (not illustrated) also has a white cap and black stalk, but it grows on oak leaves rather than on woody debris. Its cap is pleated and has a depressed center. The cap of *Marasmius rotula* (p. 370) is also pleated with a depressed center but is less rounded and grows on decaying hardwood.

trapyrgos nigripes

Tricholoma caligatum (Viv.) Ricken

COMMON NAME: Brown Matsutake.

MACROSCOPIC FEATURES: **Cap** 6–12 cm wide, broadly convex; surface dry, with flattened, coarse, pinkish-brown to grayish-brown scales over a paler ground color; margin inrolled and cottony when young, fringed with white remnants of partial veil; **flesh** white to cream; odor farinaceous, unpleasant, or not distinctive; taste bitter or not distinctive. **Gills** attached to nearly free, close, white, usually developing brownish stains. **Stalk** 4–10 cm long, 1.5–3 cm thick, equal, dry, solid, covered with a membranous sheath that first leaves a white, flaring, cottony ring on the upper portion and finally breaks into patches, white above the ring, colored like the cap below.

SPORE PRINT: White.

MICROSCOPIC FEATURES: Spores 6–8 × 4.5–5.5 μm, elliptic, smooth, hyaline, inamyloid.

OCCURRENCE: Scattered or in groups with conifers or hardwoods; fall–winter.

EDIBILITY: Edible if not too bitter.

REMARKS: *Caligatum* means "heavily shod," as in wearing a boot, referring to the prominent sheath on the stalk. The well-known Matsutake, *Tricholoma magnivelare* (not illustrated), is a northern species not known to occur in this region. It is paler, more robust, and smells spicy-sweet.

Tricholoma caligatum

Tricholoma equestre (L.) P. Kumm.

= *Tricholoma flavovirens* (Pers.) S. Lundell

COMMON NAME: Canary Trich.

MACROSCOPIC FEATURES: **Cap** 5–10 cm wide, convex to broadly convex; surface viscid and smooth when fresh, becoming dry, usually developing small central scales, pale to sulfur yellow, often golden brown over the center. **Gills** attached to nearly free, close, pale yellow to bright sulfur yellow. **Stalk** 3–15 cm long, 1–3 cm thick, equal or enlarged at the base, solid, dry, whitish, pale yellow, or sulfur yellow. **Flesh** white; odor farinaceous; taste farinaceous or not distinctive.

SPORE PRINT: White.

MICROSCOPIC FEATURES: Spores 6–7 × 4–5 μm, elliptic, smooth, hyaline.

OCCURRENCE: Scattered or in groups with conifers or in mixed woods; fall–winter.

EDIBILITY: Although listed as edible in many field guides, we cannot recommend it because varieties of this species have caused fatal poisonings in Europe.

REMARKS: *Tricholoma sejunctum* (p. 424) has a golden-yellow to greenish-yellow cap with brownish to blackish radiating fibrils. The cap of *Tricholoma intermedium* (p. 420) has tiny, yellowish-brown or reddish-brown, flat scales and short fibrils over a yellow ground color, lacks yellowish radiating fibrils, and has white gills. *Tricholoma subluteum* (p. 15) has a dull orange to yellow cap with long, radiating, yellowish fibrils, and it has white gills.

Tricholoma equestre

Tricholoma intermedium Peck

= *Melanoleuca intermedia* (Peck) Murrill
= *Tricholoma leucophyllum* Ovrebo & Tylutki

MACROSCOPIC FEATURES: **Cap** 4–10 cm wide, convex to nearly flat, sometimes with a low, broad umbo, glabrous and viscid when fresh, becoming dry, covered with tiny, scattered, yellowish- or reddish-brown flat scales and short fibrils over a yellow ground color; margin inrolled at first and remaining so well into maturity. **Gills** attached, close, white to whitish, with several tiers of lamellulae; edges usually eroded in age. **Stalk** 3–9 cm long, 1–2.5 cm thick, equal, scurfy, solid, becoming hollow in age, white to whitish, bruising brown, especially at the base. **Flesh** white; odor farinaceous; taste farinaceous or not distinctive.

SPORE PRINT: White.
MICROSCOPIC FEATURES: Spores 5–7 × 3.7–4.8 μm, elliptic, smooth, hyaline.
OCCURRENCE: Scattered or in groups on the ground with conifers; fall–winter.
EDIBILITY: Edible.
REMARKS: *Tricholoma equestre* (p. 419) is similar, but it has yellow gills. The cap of *Tricholoma subluteum* (p. 15) is dull orange to yellow with long, yellowish, radiating fibrils. *Tricholoma sulphurescens* (p. 15) has a white to creamy-white cap that quickly stains yellow to brown when handled and white flesh that has a pungent, disagreeable, coal-tar odor. It grows on the ground in woodlands during fall and winter.

Tricholoma intermedium

Tricholoma odorum Peck

= *Melanoleuca odora* (Peck) Murrill

MACROSCOPIC FEATURES: **Cap** 2–9 cm wide, initially convex with a broad umbo and an incurved margin, becoming flat or shallowly depressed in age; surface dry, shiny or dull, smooth, greenish yellow at first, fading in age to yellowish buff or yellowish tan, sometimes brownish over the center; **flesh** somewhat thick, whitish; odor farinaceous or like coal tar or burnt rubber; taste farinaceous or unpleasant. **Gills** emarginate to adnate, close, pale yellow to yellowish buff. **Stalk** 4–12 cm long, 6–12 mm thick, nearly equal or enlarged toward the base, occasionally bulbous, solid; surface dry, smooth, sometimes longitudinally twisted, pale yellow to greenish yellow, especially toward the base.

SPORE PRINT: White.
MICROSCOPIC FEATURES: Spores 7–11 × 5–7 µm, elliptic, spindle- or almond-shaped, smooth, hyaline, inamyloid.
OCCURRENCE: Solitary or in groups or clusters with hardwoods or in mixed woods; fall–winter.
EDIBILITY: Inedible.
REMARKS: *Odorum* means "scented." *Tricholoma inamoenum* (not illustrated), which also smells of coal tar, has a whitish-buff cap and is associated with conifers. *Tricholoma sulphureum* (not illustrated), also similar, differs by having a pale to bright sulfur-yellow cap and stalk and subdistant gills.

Tricholoma odorum

Tricholoma portentosum (Fr.) Quél.

= *Melanoleuca portentosa* (Fr.) Murrill

COMMON NAME: Sticky Gray Trich.
MACROSCOPIC FEATURES: **Cap** 6–12 cm wide, broadly conic, becoming nearly flat in age; surface smooth, viscid to slimy, gray, olive brown to gray brown, or blackish, sometimes with faint yellow or purple tones, often streaky with radial, dark gray fibrils; **flesh** white, sometimes yellowish near the stalk base; odor and taste farinaceous or not distinctive. **Gills** attached to nearly free, close, usually white and yellowing near the margin, sometimes yellowish or gray overall. **Stalk** 5–10 cm long, 1–2 cm thick, equal, covered with tiny fibrils, solid at first, becoming hollow in age, whitish or slightly yellow.

SPORE PRINT: White.
MICROSCOPIC FEATURES: Spores 5.5–7.6 × 3–5 μm, elliptic to oval, smooth, hyaline.
OCCURRENCE: In groups or clusters, often partially buried in pine duff; fall–winter.
EDIBILITY: Edible.
REMARKS: *Tricholoma niveipes* = *Melanoleuca niveipes* (p. 15) is very similar, but its cap lacks yellow tints, its gills are white to gray and do not develop yellow tints even in age, and its spores measure 7–9 × 3–4 μm.

Tricholoma portentosum

Tricholoma saponaceum (Fr.) P. Kumm.

COMMON NAME: Soap-scented Trich.
MACROSCOPIC FEATURES: Cap 2.5–16 cm wide, convex to flat, usually with a broad umbo; surface slippery to moist, smooth, often developing cracks over the center in age, color highly variable, ranging from various shades of dingy greenish yellow to gray green, blue gray, or grayish brown; **flesh** white to pale green; odor like soap, farinaceous, or not distinctive; taste mildly soapy. **Gills** attached or almost free, nearly distant, white to yellowish with a green tinge, sometimes staining pinkish brown or orange. **Stalk** 3.5–11 cm long, 1–4 cm thick, equal to club-shaped or with a slightly bulbous base, solid; surface dry, smooth, white to pale green, often pinkish or orange near the base; flesh white to pale greenish, usually with some pink or orange near the base.
SPORE PRINT: White.

MICROSCOPIC FEATURES: Spores 5–7.6 × 3.5–5 μm, elliptic, smooth, hyaline, inamyloid.
OCCURRENCE: Solitary, scattered, or in groups with conifers or sometimes hardwoods; year-round.
EDIBILITY: Unknown, variously reported as being edible to mildly toxic.
REMARKS: *Saponaceum* means "soapy," a reference to the taste and, sometimes, the odor of this mushroom. It's highly variable appearance can make it difficult to identify. Its key field features are its soap-like odor and the pink to orange-colored flesh at the base of the stalk. *Tricholoma floridanum* (p. 15) has a 4–15 cm wide, pale yellow or pale grayish-yellow cap with a paler margin that remains incurved when mature. It has whitish to pale yellow flesh that lacks a distinctive odor. The gills are close, whitish, and tinged pinkish. Its stalk is pale yellow and often stained dull reddish brown near the base, and it grows in groups with hardwoods, especially oak, during fall and winter.

Tricholoma saponaceum

Tricholoma sejunctum (Sowerby) Quél.

MACROSCOPIC FEATURES: **Cap** 4–9 cm wide, conical, becoming broadly convex with an umbo; surface viscid at first, becoming dry, ground color yellow to golden yellow, with brownish to blackish fibers that radiate from a dark center; **flesh** white to yellowish; odor farinaceous or not distinctive; taste usually bitter or astringent. **Gills** attached, fairly close, white, sometimes tinged yellowish. **Stalk** 5–9 cm long, 1–2 cm thick, equal or enlarged at the base, dry, smooth, solid, white to yellowish.

SPORE PRINT: White.

MICROSCOPIC FEATURES: Spores 5–7 × 3–5 μm, elliptic to subglobose, smooth, hyaline, inamyloid.

OCCURRENCE: Solitary, scattered, or in groups with conifers or in mixed woods; fall–winter.

EDIBILITY: Inedible due to its bitter, unpleasant taste.

REMARKS: *Tricholoma equestre* (p. 419) is similar but has richer brown coloration over its basically yellow cap, lacks the dark radiating fibers, and has gills that are pale to bright yellow. *Tricholoma portentosum* (p. 422) typically has a dark grayish cap, sometimes with faint yellow or purplish tints.

Tricholoma sejunctum

Tricholoma subresplendens (Murrill) Murrill

= *Melanoleuca subresplendens* Murrill

MACROSCOPIC FEATURES: Cap 2–11 cm wide, convex to nearly flat, sometimes with a low umbo; surface viscid when moist, smooth, usually silky, white to cream, developing yellowish to tan or pale pinkish-cinnamon tints or spots, especially over the center, sometimes discoloring blue green; **flesh** white; odor and taste farinaceous or not distinctive. **Gills** attached to nearly free, close or subdistant, with several tiers of lamellulae, white to whitish; edges uneven or finely scalloped. **Stalk** 5–10 cm long, 1–2.5 cm thick, equal or tapered toward the base, dry, silky smooth or slightly scurfy, whitish, usually with yellow to brownish stains overall, sometimes bruising blue green near the base.

SPORE PRINT: White.
MICROSCOPIC FEATURES: Spores 5.6–7 × 4–5 μm, elliptic, smooth, hyaline, inamyloid.
OCCURRENCE: Scattered or in groups with hardwoods or in mixed woods; fall–winter.
EDIBILITY: Unknown.
REMARKS: The occasional blue green bruising reaction in the stalk flesh is distinctive. *Tricholoma inamoenum* (not illustrated) is widely distributed in North America and is similarly colored, but its flesh has a heavily floral or coal-tar odor.

Tricholoma subresplendens

Tricholomopsis formosa (Murrill) Singer

= *Tricholoma formosa* (Murrill) Murrill

MACROSCOPIC FEATURES: **Cap** 3–10 cm wide, convex to broadly convex with an incurved and sometimes wavy margin; surface dry, covered with rusty-brown to tawny fibers and scales over a cinnamon-buff to dull yellow ground color. **Gills** attached, close or crowded, whitish to pinkish cream. **Stalk** 4–8 cm long, 5–10 mm thick, equal or tapered downward, dry, covered with tiny fibers and scales, colored like the cap. **Flesh** whitish; odor and taste disagreeable or not distinctive.

SPORE PRINT: White.
MICROSCOPIC FEATURES: Spores 5–7 × 5–6 μm, ovoid, smooth, hyaline, inamyloid.
OCCURRENCE: Solitary, scattered, or in groups on decaying conifer wood; summer–early winter.
EDIBILITY: Unknown.
REMARKS: *Formosa* means "beautiful or lovely." The cap and stalk of *Tricholomopsis rutilans* (p. 427) have red to purplish-red fibers and tiny scales over a yellowish ground color. *Tricholomopsis decora* (not illustrated) has a yellowish to greenish-yellow cap with blackish fibers and scales.

Tricholomopsis formosa

Tricholomopsis rutilans (Schaeff.) Singer

COMMON NAME: Plums and Custard.

MACROSCOPIC FEATURES: **Cap** 5–12 cm wide, convex to broadly convex with an incurved margin; surface dry, covered with red to purplish-red fibers and tiny scales over a yellowish ground color; **flesh** pale yellow; odor fragrant or not distinctive; taste somewhat radish-like or not distinctive. **Gills** attached, close, with several tiers of lamellulae, yellow. **Stalk** 5–12 cm long, 1–2 cm thick, equal, often curved; surface dry, densely or sparingly coated with red to purplish-red fibers and tiny scales over a yellowish ground color.

SPORE PRINT: White.

MICROSCOPIC FEATURES: Spores 5–7 × 3–5 μm, elliptic, smooth, hyaline, inamyloid.

OCCURRENCE: Solitary, scattered, or in groups on decaying conifer woodchips, sawdust, or the surrounding litter; spring–fall.

EDIBILITY: Edible.

REMARKS: *Rutilans* means "reddish," referring to the color of the fibers and scales. *Tricholomopsis formosa* (p. 426) has a browner cap, whitish gills, and typically has an unpleasant odor.

Tricholomopsis rutilans

Volvariella bombycina (Schaeff.) Singer

COMMON NAME: Silky Rosegill.

MACROSCOPIC FEATURES: **Cap** 5–20 cm wide, oval at first, then expanding and becoming almost flat; surface dry, silky with fine hairs, white when young, becoming yellowish white, then brownish in age; **flesh** white; odor and taste not distinctive. **Gills** free, crowded, white initially, then turning pink. **Stalk** 6–20 cm long, 1–2 cm thick, enlarged downward, white, smooth, arising from a sturdy, sac-like volva that is white to brown; partial veil absent.

SPORE PRINT: Dull pink.

MICROSCOPIC FEATURES: Spores 6.5–10.5 × 4.5–6.5 μm, elliptic, smooth, hyaline.

OCCURRENCE: On hardwood trees, stumps, and logs; summer–fall.

EDIBILITY: Edible.

REMARKS: *Bombycina* means "silky," referring to the surface of the cap. *Volvariella taylori* (not illustrated) has a 2–6 cm wide, distinctly finely hairy, grayish to brownish-gray cap and white flesh that typically has an odor and taste like bleach or radishes. It has free, close to subdistant gills that are whitish at first and become pink at maturity, with finely fringed edges. The stalk tapers upward, is whitish to grayish, and arises from, and is encased by, a thick, gray to brownish, sack-like volva. It grows on the ground in woods, near brush piles and woody debris, or in urban areas in grassy waste places from spring through fall.

Volvariella bombycina

Xeromphalina campanella (Batsch) Kühner & Maire

COMMON NAMES: Fuzzy Foot, Golden Trumpets.

MACROSCOPIC FEATURES: **Cap** 3–25 mm wide, convex to broadly convex with a depressed or dimpled center; surface smooth, moist, yellowish orange to orange brown; margin striate; **flesh** thin, yellowish to brownish yellow; odor and taste not distinctive. **Gills** decurrent, subdistant to distant, pale yellow to pale orange. **Stalk** 1–5 cm long, 0.5–3 mm thick, dry, yellow at the apex and shading downward to a dark reddish brown, with a dense tuft of long, orangish hairs at the base.

SPORE PRINT: Pale buff.

MICROSCOPIC FEATURES: Spores 5–7 × 3–4 μm, elliptic to cylindric, smooth, hyaline, amyloid.

OCCURRENCE: In dense clusters, usually recurved, on well-decayed conifer wood; spring–fall.

EDIBILITY: Unknown.

REMARKS: *Campanella* means "little bells," referring to the shape of the caps and the overall appearance of this little mushroom. *Xeromphalina kauffmanii* (not illustrated) is almost identical but grows on decaying hardwoods.

Xeromphalina campanella

Hypomyces and Other Parasitic Fungi

Members of this group are parasitic species that cover and disfigure many types of fungi, especially gilled mushrooms, boletes, and polypores. They form a thin layer on their host organisms that may be roughened like sandpaper or sometimes powdery or moldy.

Hypomyces chrysospermus Tul. & C. Tul.

MACROSCOPIC FEATURES: **Fruitbody** a parasitic mold that partially or completely covers its host and occurs in three developmental stages; **the first stage** is a white mold that produces elliptical asexual spores called conidia; **the second stage** is powdery, yellow to golden yellow, and produces round, asexual aleuriospores; **the final stage** is the sexual stage that is reddish brown and produces ascospores, which are formed in embedded, globose to flask-shaped perithecia.

MICROSCOPIC FEATURES: Conidia $10–30 \times 5–12$ μm, elliptic, 1-celled, smooth, hyaline; aleuriospores $10–25$ μm, globose, thick-walled, prominently warted, yellow to golden yellow or yellow brown; ascospores $15–30 \times 4–6$ μm, 2-celled, fusiform, hyaline.

OCCURRENCE: On various species of boletes, also reported on some gilled mushrooms and species of *Rhizopogon*.

EDIBILITY: Inedible.

REMARKS: *Chrysospermus* means "having golden spores." *Hypomyces microspermus* (not illustrated) is more commonly encountered and nearly identical, but it has $8–15$ μm globose aleuriospores and smaller ascospores that measure $8–15 \times 2.3–4$ μm. *Hypomyces chlorinigenus* (not illustrated) is very similar, but it has $10–11 \times 4–5$ μm, ovoid to nearly cylindrical conidia, $35–45 \times 15–18$ μm, cylindric and longitudinally ridged aleuriospores, and elliptic-fusiform, 2-celled ascospores that measure $7.5–12 \times 2.5–5$ μm. The Golden Hypomyces, *Hypomyces aurantius* (not illustrated), parasitizes many different types of fungi, especially polypores, and particularly species of *Trametes*. It typically covers the pore surface but may cover the entire host. It forms a thin layer that is initially whitish to buff, then becomes yellowish orange to bright orange or rusty red, and has embedded perithecia. It forms spindle-shaped, acutely apiculate ascospores that measure $20–25 \times 4–6$ μm.

Hypomyces chrysospermus

Hypomyces hyalinus (Schwein.) Tul. & C. Tul.

COMMON NAME: Amanita Mold.

MACROSCOPIC FEATURES: **Fruitbody** and host organism 10–30 cm high, up to 7 cm thick, firm, solid, column- to club-shaped, usually quite phallic, chalky white, yellowish, pale orange, or dull pinkish to pinkish red, roughened like sandpaper; **host organism**'s cap, gills, and other structures rarely discernible; odor and taste not distinctive.

MICROSCOPIC FEATURES: Spores 15–20 × 4.5–6.5 µm, spindle-shaped, 2-celled, prominently warted, hyaline.

OCCURRENCE: On several species of *Amanita*, especially common on *Amanita amerirubescens*; late spring–early winter.

EDIBILITY: Reportedly edible if parasitizing an edible species such as *Amanita amerirubescens*, but not recommended.

REMARKS: If the host organism is dull pinkish to pinkish red, it may also be hosting a second organism, *Mycogone rosea*. The fruitbody of *Mycogone rosea* (p. 16) is a very thin, somewhat uneven and roughened, dull pinkish to pale pinkish-red layer of a parasitic fungus covering the deformed gills, cap, and stalk of its host organism. It may also act as a hyperparasite, growing on another parasitic fungus that has attacked its host. The host organism is often a species of *Amanita*, especially *Amanita amerirubescens*, but numerous other host species may become infected by this mold. *Mycogone rosea* produces 2-celled spores from the ends of vegetative hyphae: a basal cell that measures (7)9–23 × (6)10–20 µm, is globose to subglobose, hyaline, and smooth; and a larger apical cell that measures (15)21–35 × (13)21–23 µm, is globose to subglobose, thick-walled, reddish-pigmented, and warty.

Hypomyces hyalinus

Hypomyces luteovirens (Fr.) Tul. & C. Tul.

COMMON NAME: Russula Mold.

MACROSCOPIC FEATURES: **Fruitbody** a thin, rough layer of a parasitic fungus covering the deformed gills, sometimes the stalk, or rarely the cap of its host organism; parasitic fungus yellowish green to dark green, roughened like sandpaper due to partially embedded perithecia; **host organism** up to 15 cm wide, cap variously colored, flesh white.

MICROSCOPIC FEATURES: Ascospores 28–35 × 4.5–5.5 μm, fusiform, 1-celled, often prominently warted but sometimes nearly smooth, hyaline.

OCCURRENCE: Solitary, scattered, or in groups on various *Russula* species under conifer or hardwoods; summer–fall.

EDIBILITY: Unknown.

REMARKS: It often goes unnoticed because it usually only grows on the underside of its host. The fruitbody of the Lobster Mushroom, or Lobster Fungus, *Hypomyces lactifluorum* (p. 16), is a thin, rough, orange to reddish-orange layer of a parasitic fungus covering the cap, stalk, and gills of its deformed host. It grows on species of *Russula* and *Lactarius* under conifers during summer and fall and is a popular edible species.

ypomyces luteovirens

Jelly Fungi

Members of this group are distinctly gelatinous species that are soft or rubbery or sometimes leathery to fibrous-tough. Most are cushion-shaped to brain-like and a few are erect and spike- to antler-like or irregular. They often grow on wood but sometimes envelop or encrust plant stems, leaves, cones, and other organic debris.

Auricularia angiospermarum
Y. C. Dai, F. Wu & D. W. Li

COMMON NAMES: American Tree Ear, American Wood Ear.

MACROSCOPIC FEATURES: **Fruitbody** 3–15 cm wide, ear-shaped to irregularly cup-shaped, rubbery-gelatinous, stalkless; **inner surface** smooth, yellowish brown to reddish brown or grayish brown to purplish brown; **outer surface** wrinkled, minutely velvety, reddish brown.

MICROSCOPIC FEATURES: Spores 12–15 × 4–6 μm, allantoid, smooth, hyaline, with 1–2 large oil drops; medulla absent.

OCCURRENCE: Solitary but more typically in groups or fused clusters on branches, logs, and stumps of hardwoods; year-round.

EDIBILITY: Edible.

REMARKS: Fruitbodies may shrink during dry periods and expand during rainy weather. *Auricularia americana* (not illustrated) is similar but grows on conifers. The Tree Ear, *Auricularia auricula* (not illustrated), is misidentified in most American mushroom field guides. It is a European species. *Auricularia nigricans* = *Auricularia polytricha* (not illustrated) is similar, but its outer surface is covered by a dense layer of fine grayish hairs that are tufted around the margin, and its spores measure 14.5–17 × 5–7 μm. *Tremella foliacea* (p. 442) is similarly colored, but its fruitbody is a lettuce-like cluster of leaf-like folds, and it has oval to subglobose spores that measure 8–12 × 7–9 μm. *Auricularia scissa* (not illustrated), known only from Florida, is similar but it has a distinctly reticulate inner surface with pit-like depressions and spores that measure 8.7–13 × 3.7–5.7 μm. *Auricularia mesenterica* (not illustrated) has a highly lobed, strongly zonate outer surface with whitish and black bands, a reticulate inner surface, and spores that measure 12.5–15 × 5–6 μm. It grows in overlapping clusters on hardwoods and resembles a Turkey-tail, *Trametes versicolor*. *Auricularia fuscosuccinea* (not illustrated) has a much darker vinaceous-brown to dark reddish-brown outer surface with areas of whitish to grayish hairs, grows on decaying hardwoods, especially Sweetgum, and has spores that measure 11–13.6 × 6.5–8.5 μm.

Auricularia angiospermarum

Calocera cornea (Batsch) Fr.

= *Clavaria cornea* Batsch

COMMON NAME: Horn-like Tuning Fork.

MACROSCOPIC FEATURES: **Fruitbody** up to
2 cm high and 3 mm wide, consisting of
erect, antler-like spikes, simple or sometimes
branched, flexible, rubbery-gelatinous, yellow
to orange yellow.

MICROSCOPIC FEATURES: Spores 7–11 × 3–4.5
μm, cylindric to allantoid, 1-septate at maturity, smooth, hyaline to pale yellow.

OCCURRENCE: Scattered or in groups or clusters on branches and logs of decaying wood,
especially hardwood; summer–fall.

EDIBILITY: Unknown.

REMARKS: *Cornea* means "small horn." *Calocera
viscosa* (not illustrated) has a larger, golden-
yellow to orange-yellow, erect fruitbody that is
antler-like and sometimes repeatedly forked.

Calocera cornea

Dacryopinax elegans (Berk. & M. A. Curtis) G. W. Martin

= *Guepinia elegans* Berk. & M. A. Curtis

MACROSCOPIC FEATURES: **Fruitbody** up to 4 cm high, 5–20 mm wide, somewhat cup- to fan-shaped or spoon-shaped, rubbery-gelatinous; **inner surface** smooth, dark amber brown to blackish brown; **outer surface** smooth to slightly roughened, concolorous with the inner surface; **stalk** round to somewhat flattened, concolorous.

MICROSCOPIC FEATURES: Spores 11–16 × 4.5–6.5 μm, allantoid, 1–3 septate, smooth, yellowish.

OCCURRENCE: Scattered or in groups on decaying hardwood; summer–early winter.

EDIBILITY: Unknown.

REMARKS: *Elegans* means "choice or elegant." *Dacryopinax spathularia* (p. 438) is similar, but its fruitbody is yellow orange with deeply cut lobes, and it has smaller spores that measure 8–12 × 3.5–5 μm.

Dacryopinax elegans

Dacryopinax spathularia (Schwein.) G. W. Martin

= *Guepinia spathularia* (Schwein.) Fr.

MACROSCOPIC FEATURES: **Fruitbody** up to 2.5 cm high, 5–10 mm wide, shoehorn- to spatula-shaped with a wavy margin or fan-shaped with deeply cut lobes, rubbery-gelatinous; **inner surface** smooth, yellow orange to orange; **outer surface** longitudinally ribbed, concolorous; **stalk** round at the base, becoming flattened upward, concolorous, darkening in age.
MICROSCOPIC FEATURES: Spores 8–12 × 3.5–5 μm, allantoid, 1-septate at maturity, smooth, yellowish.
OCCURRENCE: In groups or clusters on decaying wood; summer–fall.
EDIBILITY: Unknown.
REMARKS: *Spathularia* means "spoon-shaped." *Dacryopinax elegans* (p. 437) is similar, but its fruitbody is dark amber brown to blackish brown, lacks deeply cut lobes, and it has larger spores that measure 11–16 × 4.5–6.5 μm.

Dacryopinax spathularia

Exidia glandulosa (Bull.) Fr.

= *Tremella glandulosa* Bull.

COMMON NAMES: Black Witches' Butter, Black Jelly Roll.

MACROSCOPIC FEATURES: **Fruitbody** up to 1.3 cm high, 1–2 cm wide, gland-like to blister-like or brain-like, fused together and forming extensive, irregular, soft, gelatinous masses up to 20 cm or more wide; **surface** smooth or somewhat roughened, shiny, dark reddish brown to blackish brown or black, becoming a black crust when dry.

MICROSCOPIC FEATURES: Spores 10–16 × 4–5 µm, allantoid, smooth, hyaline.

OCCURRENCE: In large clusters on decaying hardwood branches and logs; year-round.

EDIBILITY: Edible.

REMARKS: *Glandulosa* means "resembling glands." *Exidia recisa* (p. 440) forms irregularly lobed to cushion-shaped fruitbodies that are yellowish brown to purplish brown or cinnamon brown.

Exidia glandulosa

Exidia recisa (Ditmar) Fr.

= *Tremella recisa* Ditmar

COMMON NAME: Amber Jelly Roll.
MACROSCOPIC FEATURES: **Fruitbody** up to 2
cm high, 1.5–3.5 cm wide, irregularly lobed
with concave depressions or cushion-shaped,
somewhat erect, with a stalk-like base, forming extensive irregular clusters up to 12 cm or
more wide, rubbery-gelatinous; **surface** shiny,
smooth to somewhat roughened, yellowish
brown to purplish brown or cinnamon brown.
MICROSCOPIC FEATURES: Spores 11–15 × 3–5.5
μm, allantoid, smooth, hyaline.
OCCURRENCE: In groups or clusters on decaying hardwood branches and logs; year-round.
EDIBILITY: Unknown.
REMARKS: *Recisa* means "cut back or cut off,"
a reference to its cushion shape. *Exidia glandulosa* (p. 439) forms gland-like to blister-like
fruitbodies that are dark reddish brown to
blackish brown or black.

Exidia recisa

Helvellosebacina concrescens

(Schwein.) Oberw., Garnica & K. Riess

= *Tremella concrescens* (Schwein.) Burt

MACROSCOPIC FEATURES: **Fruitbody** a soft, rubbery-gelatinous, irregular, whitish to grayish, membrane-like, spreading mass, up to 15 cm or more wide.

MICROSCOPIC FEATURES: Spores 9–14 × 5–8 μm, elliptic to oval or subglobose, smooth, hyaline.

OCCURRENCE: On the ground, clasping and enveloping plant stems and leaves; summer–fall.

EDIBILITY: Unknown.

REMARKS: *Concrescens* means "curdled or congealed." Compare with *Sebacina incrustans* (p. 16), which envelops plant stems, leaves, branches, and cones, but its fruitbody is fibrous-tough, whitish to pale tan, and forms small, lateral projections. Both of these species are mycorrhizal fungi and associate with the roots of hardwoods, particularly oaks.

Helvellosebacina concrescens

Tremella foliacea Pers.

= *Exidia foliacea* (Pers.) P. Karst.

COMMON NAME: Jelly Leaf.
MACROSCOPIC FEATURES: **Fruitbody** up to 10
cm high and 25 cm wide, a lettuce-like cluster
consisting of rubbery-gelatinous, leaf-like
folds; **surface** pale to dark reddish brown or
rarely pale brownish yellow.
MICROSCOPIC FEATURES: Spores 8–12 × 7–9
µm, oval to subglobose, smooth, hyaline.
OCCURRENCE: Solitary or scattered on decaying wood; summer–fall.
EDIBILITY: Edible.
REMARKS: *Foliacea* means "having leaves."
Auricularia angiospermarum (p. 435) is similarly colored, but its fruitbody is ear-shaped
to irregularly cup-shaped, and it has allantoid
spores that measure 12–15 × 4–6 µm.

Tremella foliacea

Tremella fuciformis Berk.

COMMON NAMES: Silver Ear, White Jelly Mushroom.

MACROSCOPIC FEATURES: **Fruitbody** up to 3 cm high and 7 cm wide, a jelly-like mass of delicate, leaf-like, shiny, translucent, silvery-white, complex lobes.

MICROSCOPIC FEATURES: Spores 8–14 × 5–8 μm, elliptic, smooth, hyaline; subglobose, hyaline conidia, up to 4.5 × 3 μm, also sometimes present.

OCCURRENCE: Solitary or scattered on decaying branches and logs of hardwoods, especially oaks; summer–early winter.

EDIBILITY: Edible.

REMARKS: *Fuciformis* means "shaped like seaweed." It is a tropical species with a northern range that extends into the subtropical southeastern United States. This species is a myco-parasite of the wood decay fungus, *Hypoxylon archeri*. It is considered a delicacy in China and Japan.

Tremella fuciformis

Tremella mesenterica Retz.

= *Tremella lutescens* Pers.

COMMON NAME: Witches' Butter.
MACROSCOPIC FEATURES: **Fruitbody** up to 10
cm wide, a spreading, irregularly lobed and
folded mass, often resembling bunched leaves;
surface bald, smooth, shiny, pale yellow to
golden yellow or orange yellow. **Flesh** soft to
rubbery-gelatinous, colored like the exterior
or paler, reduces to liquid during prolonged
wet weather, hard and shriveled when dry.
MICROSCOPIC FEATURES: Spores 10–18 × 8–12
μm, broadly elliptic, smooth, hyaline; subglobose, smooth, hyaline conidia, measuring
3–4.5 × 2.5–3.5 μm, may also be present.

OCCURRENCE: Solitary, in groups, or clusters
on hardwood branches, logs, and stumps,
especially beech and oak; year-round.
EDIBILITY: Edible but flavorless.
REMARKS: *Mesenterica* means "resembling the
middle intestine." The Orange Jelly or Orange
Witches' Butter, *Dacrymyces chrysospermus* =
Dacrymyces palmatus (p. 16), has an edible
fruitbody up to 3 cm high, 1–6 cm wide,
consisting of a spreading, brain-like mass that
is rubbery-gelatinous and softens in age. It is
yellow orange to orange or reddish orange and
whitish near the point of attachment. It grows
in clusters on decaying conifer branches, logs,
and stumps and is often associated with *Stereum* species year-round.

Tremella mesenterica

Morels, False Morels, and Similar Fungi

Members of this group have fruitbodies with a distinct cap or sponge-like head and a conspicuous stalk. Caps or heads may be conic to bell-shaped with pits and ridges, or brain-like, saddle-shaped, or irregularly lobed. Mature stalks are hollow or multichambered. They grow on the ground or on well-decayed wood. They are not found at low elevations or in the far southern range of the Gulf Coast states.

Gyromitra caroliniana (Bosc)
Fr. Eckblad

= *Discina caroliniana* (Bosc) Eckblad
= *Morchella caroliniana* Bosc

COMMON NAMES: Carolina False Morel, Red
False Morel.
MACROSCOPIC FEATURES: **Fruitbody** consisting of a cap and stalk; **cap** 5–18 cm high and
wide, convoluted and brain-like, typically
with several prominent vertical ridges; **outer
surface** moist and lubricous, reddish brown;
undersurface white to whitish; margin
appressed against the stalk, wavy and irregular; **stalk** up to 15.5 cm long, 2.5–8 cm thick,
enlarged at the base, conspicuously ribbed,
white; interior multichambered.
MICROSCOPIC FEATURES: Spores 22–35 ×
10–16 μm, elliptic, reticulate, with one or
more short projections at each end, hyaline.
OCCURRENCE: Solitary or in groups on the
ground in hardwoods or mixed woods; late
winter–spring.

EDIBILITY: Although eaten by some individuals, we do not recommend it because it is
suspected to contain toxins.
REMARKS: This is the largest member of this
group and is most often collected at higher
elevations. The Fluted White Helvella,
Helvella crispa (p. 16), has a fruitbody consisting of a 1–4 cm tall, 2–6 cm wide, saddle-
shaped to irregularly lobed, pale cream to
pale buff cap supported by a stalk. The stalk is
up to 9 cm long, 1–3 cm thick, and enlarged
downward or nearly equal. Its surface is
deeply pitted, ribbed, and whitish to pale
buff or pinkish buff. It grows on the ground
under hardwoods or conifers during summer
through early winter. It is a complex of several
species and more research remains to be done
before species names can be assigned.

Gyromitra caroliniana

Morchella americana Clowez & Matherly

= *Morchella esculentoides* M. Kuo, Dewsbury, Moncalvo & S. L. Stephenson

COMMON NAMES: Common Morel, Yellow Morel.

MACROSCOPIC FEATURES: **Fruitbody** consisting of a sponge-like head and stalk; **head** up to 22 cm high and 13 cm wide, oval to conical or somewhat cylindrical, hollow, divided into pits and ridges of variable color, continuous with the stalk below; **pits** grayish to brown, dark brown when young; **ridges** vertical, horizontal, or oblique, anastomosing, whitish to pale yellow at first, becoming dull yellow to yellow brown at maturity; **stalk** 2–12 cm or more long, 2–9 cm thick, nearly equal or enlarged downward, hollow; surface whitish, granular, often ribbed.

MICROSCOPIC FEATURES: Spores 17–24 × 11–15 μm, elliptic, smooth, hyaline.

OCCURRENCE: Solitary, scattered, or in groups on the ground in various habitats, including mixed hardwoods, burned areas, old railroad beds, or sometimes under conifers; late winter–spring.

EDIBILITY: Edible and choice.

REMARKS: *Americana* means "American." It is the most common yellow morel in North America. *Morchella angusticeps* (p. 448) is similar, but it has a dark brown to brownish-black head with yellow-brown to gray-brown pits. The edible Half-free Morel, *Morchella punctipes* (p. 16), has a fruitbody consisting of a sponge-like head and stalk. The head is up to 4 cm high and 4.5 cm wide, broadly conic with a round to blunt apex, hollow, divided into brown pits and ridges, attached to the stalk about midway and flaring below. It has a slightly granular, typically ribbed, whitish stalk and grows on the ground under hardwoods or in old apple orchards during spring.

Morchella americana

Morchella angusticeps Peck

COMMON NAME: Common Eastern Black Morel.

MACROSCOPIC FEATURES: **Fruitbody** consisting of a sponge-like head and stalk; **head** up to 9 cm high and 6 cm wide, conical to oval or somewhat cylindrical, hollow, divided into pits and ridges of variable color, continuous with the stalk below; **pits** elongated and irregular, yellow brown to gray brown; **ridges** vertical, horizontal, or oblique, anastomosing, dark brown to brownish black; **stalk** 2–10 cm long, 1–4 cm thick, nearly equal or enlarged downward, hollow; surface whitish to dingy yellow, granular, sometimes ribbed.

MICROSCOPIC FEATURES: Spores 22–28 × 11–15 μm, broadly elliptic, smooth, hyaline.

OCCURRENCE: Solitary, scattered, or in groups on the ground in a variety of habitats, including mixed woods, hardwoods with cherry and poplar, burned areas, and conifers, especially pines; spring.

EDIBILITY: Edible and choice, but must be thoroughly cooked. It has caused gastrointestinal distress in some individuals, especially when consumed with alcohol.

REMARKS: It is often the first morel to appear in spring.

Morchella angusticeps

Morchella diminutiva M. Kuo, Dewsbury, Moncalvo & S. L. Stephenson

COMMON NAMES: White Morel, Tulip Morel.

MACROSCOPIC FEATURES: **Fruitbody** consisting of a sponge-like head and stalk; **head** up to 5 cm high and 3 cm wide, conical to oval, hollow, divided into pits and ridges of variable color, continuous with the stalk below; **pits** vertically elongated, smoky to grayish brown when young, becoming tan to yellowish at maturity; **ridges** more or less vertically oriented, with scattered, sunken, horizontal to oblique secondary ridges, irregularly anastomosing, whitish, tan, or yellowish; **stalk** 1–7 cm long, 0.5–2 cm wide, enlarged downward or nearly equal, hollow; surface smooth or granular, whitish to cream or pale tan.

MICROSCOPIC FEATURES: Spores 18–26 × 10–18 μm, elliptic, smooth, hyaline.

OCCURRENCE: Solitary to gregarious among leaves or in grassy areas under a variety of hardwoods, including tulip poplar, ash, and hickory; spring.

EDIBILITY: Edible.

REMARKS: It is sometimes very difficult to spot due to its dried leaf-like colors and small stature.

Morchella diminutiva

Polypores

Members of the Polypores group have hard and woody, tough and leathery, or sometimes firm and flexible fruitbodies with pores on their undersurfaces. They are often kidney-shaped to semicircular or fan-shaped but may be circular, irregular, or, rarely, highly distorted. They vary in size from rather small to very large. Some polypores occur singly while others form large clusters. The tube layer is not easily separated from the cap tissue. Pores are sometimes minute and often require a hand lens to be seen. Species in this group may be stalkless or centrally to laterally stalked. They usually grow on wood but sometimes on the ground. If you are unable to find a match here, try the Carbon, Crust, Cushion, and Parchment group or the Boletes group.

Key to the Polypores

1a. Pores notably elongated to labyrinthine and sometimes appearing gill-like or broken into tooth-like projections, not simply round, angular, or sinuous 2

1b. Pores round, angular, or sinuous, ranging in size from tiny to large 3

2a. Flesh white to cream or tan:
  Abortiporus biennis
  Antrodia albida
  Antrodia juniperina
  Cerrena unicolor
  Daedalea quercina
  Daedaleopsis confragosa
  Daedaleopsis septentrionalis
  Favolus tenuiculus
  Hydnopolyporus fimbriatus
  Irpex lacteus
  Lenzites betulina
  Sarcodontia pachyodon
  Schizopora paradoxa
  Trametes aesculi
  Trametes gibbosa
  Trametopsis cervina
  Trichaptum biforme

2b. Flesh yellow brown to rusty brown or dark brown:
  Gloeophyllum sepiarium
  Gloeophyllum striatum
  Gloeophyllum trabeum
  Inonotus amplectens
  Osmoporus mexicanus
  Porodaedalea pini
  Trichaptum sector

3a. Fruitbody growing on the ground, or appearing to grow on the ground, but may be attached to buried roots 4

3b. Fruitbody growing on wood 6

4a. Fruitbody upper surface with a crusty or varnish-like coating:
  Ganoderma curtisii
  Ganoderma meredithiae
  Ganoderma sessile
  Heterobasidion annosum

4b. Fruitbody upper surface lacking a crusty or varnish-like coating. 5

5a. Flesh white, ivory, cream, buff, or ochraceous:
  Abortiporus biennis
  Albatrellus confluens
  Albatrellus subrubescens
  Bondarzewia berkeleyi
  Heterobasidion annosum
  Hydnopolyporus fimbriatus
  Laetiporus cincinnatus
  Laetiporus persicinus
  Microporellus dealbatus
  Microporellus obovatus
  Pseudofistulina radicata

5b. Flesh yellow brown to rusty brown:
  Onnia tomentosa
  Phaeolus schweinitzii

6a. Fruitbody distinctly stalked. 7

6b. Fruitbody stalkless or with a rudimentary stalk 9

7a. Fruitbody with a white to cream, buff, or ochraceous pore surface that may become brownish in age. 8

7b. Fruitbody with a rusty-brown to dark brown pore surface:
  Onnia tomentosa
  Phaeolus schweinitzii

8a. Fruitbody upper surface with a crusty or varnish-like coating:
  Ganoderma curtisii
  Ganoderma meredithiae

8b. Fruitbody upper surface lacking a crusty
or varnish-like coating:
Abortiporus biennis
Amauroderma sprucei
Bondarzewia berkeleyi
Cerioporus leptocephalus
Favolus tenuiculus
Laetiporus cincinnatus
Laetiporus persicinus
Lentinus arcularius
Lentinus tricholoma
Microporellus dealbatus
Microporellus obovatus
Neofavolus alveolaris
Onnia tomentosa
Panellus pusillus
Picipes badius

9a. Fruitbody with a white to cream, buff,
yellow, orange, ochraceous, rosy-pink,
orange-red, or red pore surface that may
become brownish or grayish in age ... 10

9b. Fruitbody with a violet, brown, purple-
brown to dark brown, gray, or blackish
pore surface 14

10a. Fruitbody with hexagonal pores that are
sometimes radially arranged:
Favolus tenuiculus
Hexagonia cucullata

10b. Fruitbody lacking hexagonal pores ... 11

11a. Fruitbody upper surface with a crusty or
varnish-like coating:
Ganoderma applanatum
Ganoderma sessile
Ganoderma sessiliforme
Ganoderma tuberculosum
Ganoderma zonatum
Tomophagus colossus

11b. Fruitbody upper surface lacking a crusty
or varnish-like coating............. 12

12a. Fruitbody upper or lower surface some
shade of pink, orange, or red:
Fistulina hepatica
Inonotus hispidus
Laetiporus gilbertsonii var. *pallidus*
Laetiporus sulphureus
Pycnoporus sanguineus
Rhodofomes cajanderi
Trametes cinnabarina

12b. Fruitbody upper or lower surface differently colored 13

13a. Flesh white, ivory, cream, buff, or
ochraceous:
Antrodia albida
Antrodia juniperina
Antrodia serialis
Bjerkandera fumosa
Fomitopsis palustris
Gelatoporia dichroa
Heterobasidion annosum
Hydnopolyporus fimbriatus
Ischnoderma resinosum
Leiotrametes lactinea
Niveoporofomes spraguei
Postia caesia
Postia fragilis
Tomophagus colossus
Trametes aesculi
Trametes cubensis
Trametes gibbosa
Trametes hirsuta
Trametes nivosa
Trametes pubescens
Trametes versicolor
Trametes villosa
Trametopsis cervina

13b. Flesh reddish, tawny, ocher, pinkish cinnamon, rusty brown, reddish brown, or
dark brown:
Antrodia serialis
Fuscoporia gilva

       Heterobasidion annosum
       Inonotus amplectens
       Inonotus hispidus
       Inonotus quercustris
       Inonotus rickii
       Pseudoinonotus dryadeus

14a. Fruitbody upper surface with a crusty or
     varnish-like coating:
       Ganoderma sessile
       Ganoderma sessiliforme
       Ganoderma tuberculosum
       Ganoderma zonatum

14b. Fruitbody upper surface lacking a crusty
     or varnish-like coating. 15

15a. Flesh whitish, buff, yellowish, or
     ochraceous:
       Bjerkandera adusta
       Bjerkandera fumosa
       Gelatoporia dichroa
       Hexagonia cucullata
       Trametes nivosa
       Trichaptum abietinum
       Trichaptum biforme

15b. Flesh ocher, tawny, dark chestnut, or
     brown to purplish black:
       Fomes fasciatus
       Fomitiporia apiahyna
       Fuscoporia gilva
       Fuscoporia wahlbergii
       Hexagonia hydnoides
       Inocutis texana
       Inonotus amplectens
       Inonotus hispidus
       Inonotus quercustris
       Nigrofomes melanoporus
       Nigroporus vinosus
       Phylloporia fruticum
       Porodaedalea pini
       Pseudoinonotus dryadeus
       Trichaptum sector

Abortiporus biennis (Bull.) Singer

= *Heteroporus biennis* (Bull.) Lázaro Ibiza
= *Polyporus biennis* (Bull.) Fr.

MACROSCOPIC FEATURES: **Fruitbody** occurring as two morphologically distinct forms: a distorted mass of whitish and brownish tissue covered with pores and a non-distorted form that is almost circular to rosette-like at first, becomes irregularly undulating and lobed in age, and measures 8–16 cm wide; **upper surface** smooth to slightly pitted, finely tomentose, whitish to pale yellow when young, becoming ocher to yellow brown at maturity; margin thin, lobed to crenate, paler than the center, staining reddish brown when bruised. **Pore surface** whitish, bruising reddish brown; **pores** elongate and sinuous, somewhat decurrent, 1–3 per mm. **Stalk** 4–7 cm long, 2–3 cm thick, central or lateral, buff or concolorous with the upper surface, typically with adhering debris. **Flesh** duplex, white to creamy white or tan, soft on the outer portion, firm and corky on the inner portion, staining reddish when cut; odor unpleasant; taste not distinctive.

SPORE PRINT: White.

MICROSCOPIC FEATURES: Spores 4.5–6 × 3.5–4.5 μm, elliptic, smooth, hyaline, with oil drops.

OCCURRENCE: Solitary, in groups, or overlapping clusters on various hardwoods, rarely on conifers, often on the ground attached to buried wood; year-round.

EDIBILITY: Inedible.

REMARKS: *Biennis* means "lasting for two years."

Abortiporus biennis

Albatrellus subrubescens (Murrill) Pouzar

= *Albatrellus ovinus* var. *subrubescens* (Murrill)
   L. G. Krieglst
= *Polyporus subrubescens* (Murrill) Murrill
= *Scutiger subrubescens* Murrill

MACROSCOPIC FEATURES: **Fruitbody** 6–15 cm
wide, convex and circular to kidney-shaped,
sometimes fused and irregular, often slightly
depressed to somewhat funnel-shaped; **upper
surface** dry, glabrous to minutely tomentose,
smooth but becoming wrinkled or cracked
and scaly in age, whitish to pale buff at first,
becoming light yellow to greenish yellow or
brownish yellow at maturity; margin incurved
at first, becoming uplifted, wavy or lobed and
partially eroded in age. **Pore surface** strongly
decurrent, whitish at first, becoming light yellow to pale greenish yellow at maturity, often
developing reddish-orange tints, sometimes
slowly staining brown when bruised; **pores**
angular near the stalk, rounded near the margin, 2–4 per mm. **Stalk** 2–7.5 cm long, 6–30
mm thick, central or eccentric, nearly equal
or tapered in either direction, usually with an
enlarged base, whitish to buff, often with reddish-orange or brownish-orange tints. **Flesh**
thick, firm, brittle to fibrous-tough, white to
creamy yellow, drying yellowish; odor and
taste not distinctive.

SPORE PRINT: White.

MICROSCOPIC FEATURES: Spores 3.5–5 ×
2.5–3.5 μm, ovoid to subglobose, smooth,
hyaline, amyloid.

OCCURRENCE: Solitary, scattered, or in groups
on the ground under pines or with mixed pine
and hardwoods; summer–winter.

EDIBILITY: Unknown.

REMARKS: *Subrubescens* means "somewhat reddish," a reference to the reddish-orange tints
that often develop on the stalk or pore surface.
The addition of FeSO4 to the flesh produces a gray to gray-blue reaction. The Sheep
Polypore, *Albatrellus ovinus* = *Polyporus ovinus*
(not illustrated), is a very similar species with
a more northern distribution. It grows on
the ground with spruce or balsam fir and has
inamyloid spores. *Albatrellus confluens* (p. 17)
has a pinkish-buff to pale orange cap that is
often fused with others, a central or eccentric
white stalk, 3–5 pores per mm, and grows on
the ground under conifers during summer
through early winter.

Albatrellus subrubescens

Antrodia albida (Fr.) Donk

= *Trametes albida* Lév.

MACROSCOPIC FEATURES: **Fruitbody** up to 10 cm or more long, resupinate, often effused-reflexed or forming numerous narrow, overlapping, stalkless caps on a decurrent pore surface. **Cap** up to 3 cm wide, shelf-like, semicircular to fan-shaped, tough to somewhat woody; **upper surface** finely velvety at first, azonate, white to cream, becoming glabrous, sometimes sulcate, and distinctly zonate in age; margin acute. **Pore surface** white to cream; **pores** variable, angular to sinuous and elongated or gill-like, 2–3 per mm. **Flesh** up to 3 mm thick, tough, white; odor and taste not distinctive.

SPORE PRINT: White.

MICROSCOPIC FEATURES: Spores 10–14 × 3.5–5 µm, more or less cylindrical, smooth, hyaline.

OCCURRENCE: Typically forming overlapping caps on various species of hardwoods, rarely on conifers; year-round.

EDIBILITY: Inedible.

REMARKS: *Albida* means "white." *Antrodia juniperina* (not illustrated) grows only on living Juniper species, has much larger daedaleoid to labyrinthine pores that are 1–3 mm wide, and smaller spores that measure 6.5–9 × 2.5–3.5 µm. *Antrodia serialis* (not illustrated) grows in very long sheets, often several feet long, on decaying conifers, has round, thick-walled pores and smaller spores that measure 7–10 × 2.5–4 µm.

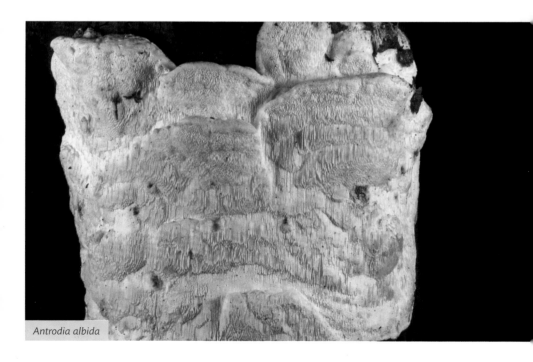

Antrodia albida

Bjerkandera adusta (Willd.) P. Karst.

= *Gloeoporus adustus* (Willd.) Pilát
= *Polyporus adustus* (Willd.) Fr.

COMMON NAME: Smoky Polypore.
MACROSCOPIC FEATURES: **Fruitbody** effused-reflexed or resupinate, spreading, often forming overlapping stalkless caps. **Cap** 2–7.5 cm wide, convex to nearly plane, shelf-like or sometimes forming rosettes, tough to somewhat woody; **upper surface** tomentose at first, becoming nearly glabrous in age, azonate to faintly zonate, whitish to tan, dull ocher, or grayish brown to pale smoky gray; margin acute, whitish when young, darkening when bruised. **Pore surface** pale gray at first, becoming dark smoky gray to blackish at maturity; **pores** angular to irregularly rounded, 4–7 per mm. **Flesh** up to 6 mm thick, tough, pale buff, lacking a dark layer near the tubes; odor not distinctive; taste somewhat sour or not distinctive.

SPORE PRINT: White.
MICROSCOPIC FEATURES: Spores 5–6 × 2.5–3.5 μm, short-cylindric, smooth, hyaline.
OCCURRENCE: Overlapping caps or rosettes on hardwoods or sometimes conifers, sometimes resupinate on the undersurface of decaying logs; summer–early winter.
EDIBILITY: Inedible.
REMARKS: *Adusta* means "scorched," a reference to the smoky-gray colors. *Bjerkandera fumosa* (not illustrated) forms larger fruitbodies, up to 10 cm wide, with a paler pore surface and thicker flesh, up to 1.5 cm thick, with a dark brown line near the tube layer, often with an anise-like odor.

Bjerkandera adusta

Bondarzewia berkeleyi (Fr.)
Bondartsev & Singer

= *Grifola berkeleyi* (Fr.) Murrill
= *Polyporus berkeleyi* Fr.

COMMON NAME: Berkeley's Polypore.
MACROSCOPIC FEATURES: **Fruitbody** 20–75 cm wide, a large overlapping cluster of caps attached to a central stalk. **Cap** 6–25 cm wide, fan-shaped, convex to flattened, sometimes depressed, laterally fused and typically forming a rosette; **upper surface** dry, radially wrinkled and shallowly pitted, obscurely to conspicuously zoned, whitish to grayish, pale yellow, or tan; margin wavy and blunt. **Pore surface** white to creamy white; **pores** angular to irregular, 0.5–2 per mm. **Stalk** 4–12 cm long, 3–5 cm thick, central, solid, roughened, dingy yellow to brownish, arising from an underground sclerotium. **Flesh** up to 3 cm thick, corky to tough, white; odor not distinctive; taste mild when young, bitter in age.

SPORE PRINT: White.
MICROSCOPIC FEATURES: Spores 7–9 × 6–8 μm, globose, ornamented with prominent ridges and spines, hyaline, amyloid.
OCCURRENCE: Solitary or scattered on the ground at the base of hardwood trees and stumps, especially oak; summer–fall.
EDIBILITY: Edible when young and tender, becoming tough and bitter in age.
REMARKS: *Berkeleyi* honors British mycologist Miles Joseph Berkeley (1803–1889). Although the typical fruitbody diameter is 20–75 cm, mature specimens may be more than 100 cm wide. The globose, amyloid spores with spines and ridges are most unusual for polypores. Molecular analysis has confirmed that *Bondarzewia berkeleyi* is related to *Lactarius* and *Russula* species and is classified in the Russulales.

Bondarzewia berkeleyi

Cerioporus leptocephalus (Jacq.) Zmitr.

= *Cerioporus varius* (Pers.) Zmitr. & Kovalenko
= *Polyporus elegans* (Bull.) P. Karst.
= *Polyporus leptocephalus* (Jacq.) Fr.
= *Polyporus varius* (Pers.) Fr.

COMMON NAME: Elegant Black-footed Polypore.

MACROSCOPIC FEATURES: **Fruitbody** consisting of a cap and stalk attached to wood. **Cap** 3–6 cm wide, up to 1 cm thick, circular to kidney-shaped or fan-shaped; **upper surface** glabrous, azonate, tan to yellowish brown or chestnut brown; margin thin, acute. **Pore surface** attached to somewhat decurrent, pale buff; **pores** circular to angular, minute, 5–7 per mm. **Stalk** up to 7 cm long, 2–5 mm thick, central to lateral, glabrous, colored like the cap on the upper portion, black on the lower portion. **Flesh** up to 7 mm thick, corky, azonate, pale buff.

SPORE PRINT: White.

MICROSCOPIC FEATURES: Spores 7.5–10 × 2.5–3 μm, cylindric to slightly allantoid, smooth, hyaline.

OCCURRENCE: Usually solitary or sometimes in groups on decaying hardwoods, occasionally on conifers; late spring–early winter.

EDIBILITY: Inedible.

REMARKS: *Leptocephalus* means "thin head," a reference to the cap of this polypore. *Picipes badius*, formerly *Royoporus badius* (p. 499), has a larger cap, up to 15 cm wide, that is chestnut brown to dark blackish brown with a darker center, has white to buff decurrent pores, and a black stalk.

Cerioporus leptocephalus

Cerrena unicolor (Bull.) Murrill

= *Daedalea unicolor* (Bull.) Fr.

COMMON NAME: Mossy Maze Polypore.
MACROSCOPIC FEATURES: **Fruitbody** 4–10
cm wide, consisting of somewhat flattened,
stalkless caps, sometimes laterally fused and
often forming extensive rows. **Cap** fan-shaped
to semicircular or irregular in outline; **upper
surface** distinctly lobed, often with prominent grooves, covered with a dense layer of
short, stiff hairs arranged in zones, frequently
covered by green algae, whitish, grayish, pale
brown, or green; margin fairly sharp, often
lobed and wavy. **Pore surface** whitish to pale
buff at first, becoming smoky gray to grayish
brown at maturity; **pores** 1–4 per mm, labyrinthine, often splitting and becoming tooth-
like in age. **Flesh** up to 3 mm thick, corky to
fibrous-tough, whitish to pale brown, with a
thin dark zone separating the cap surface from
the flesh.

SPORE PRINT: White.
MICROSCOPIC FEATURES: Spores 5–7 × 2.5–4
µm, cylindric-ellipsoid, smooth, hyaline.
OCCURRENCE: Typically in overlapping clusters, sometimes solitary or scattered on hardwoods, or rarely on conifers; year-round.
EDIBILITY: Inedible.
REMARKS: *Unicolor* means "one color." The
hairy cap surface and labyrinthine pores are
good field identification features.

Cerrena unicolor

Daedalea quercina (L.) Pers.

= *Lenzites quercina* (L.) P. Karst.
= *Trametes quercina* (L.) Pilát

COMMON NAME: Thick-maze Oak Polypore.
MACROSCOPIC FEATURES: **Fruitbody** a stalk-less cap, 5–20 cm wide, attached to wood. **Cap** semicircular to kidney-shaped, convex to nearly flat, leathery to corky or woody; **upper surface** velvety, becoming smooth, then furrowed or cracked in age, often concentrically zoned with shades of brownish yellow, tan, brown, or black; margin blunt and whitish. **Pore surface** whitish to grayish brown; **pores** labyrinthine with tough, thick walls, sometimes elongated near the margin. **Flesh** up to 1 cm thick, tough, dull white to pale brown; odor and taste not distinctive.

SPORE PRINT: White.
MICROSCOPIC FEATURES: Spores 5–6 × 2–3.5 µm, cylindrical, smooth, hyaline.
OCCURRENCE: Solitary or in overlapping groups on decaying hardwoods, especially oak; year-round.
EDIBILITY: Inedible.
REMARKS: *Daedaleopsis confragosa* (p. 462) is similar, but it has thin-walled pores. *Lenzites betulina* (p. 489) is also similar, but it has conspicuously gill-like pores that sometimes fork.

Daedalea quercina

Daedaleopsis confragosa (Bolton) J. Schröt.

= *Daedalea confragosa* (Bolton) Pers.

COMMON NAME: Thin-maze Flat Polypore.
MACROSCOPIC FEATURES: **Fruitbody** a stalk-less cap, 3–16 cm wide, attached to wood. **Cap** slightly convex to nearly flat or semi-circular to kidney-shaped; **upper surface** coarsely wrinkled, rough and scaly at first, becoming finely velvety to nearly smooth in age, with concentric zones, variously colored creamy white, tan, grayish, or pale brown; margin thin and sharp. **Pore surface** tough, whitish to pale brown, bruising pinkish brown; **pores** labyrinthine or sometimes gill-like and elongated. **Flesh** up to 1.2 cm thick, tough, whitish to pale brown.

SPORE PRINT: White.
MICROSCOPIC FEATURES: Spores 7–11 × 2–3 μm, cylindric to allantoid, smooth, hyaline.
OCCURRENCE: Solitary, scattered, or in groups on decaying wood, especially hardwoods; year-round.
EDIBILITY: Inedible.
REMARKS: *Confragosa* means "rough and scaly." *Daedaleopsis septentrionalis* (p. 17) is nearly identical, but it has grayish, distinctly gill-like pores. *Daedalea quercina* (p. 461) has a larger and thicker fruitbody with a conspicuously labyrinthine pore surface that has tough, thick walls and much smaller spores that measure 5–6 × 2–3.5 μm.

Daedaleopsis confragosa

Favolus tenuiculus P. Beauv.

= *Polyporus tenuiculus* (P. Beauv.) Fr.

MACROSCOPIC FEATURES: **Fruitbody** a cluster
of overlapping caps with short stalks attached
to wood. **Cap** 2–10 cm wide, fan-shaped to
semicircular, soft and flexible when fresh,
becoming brittle when dry; **upper surface**
glabrous to slightly roughened, azonate, white,
becoming cream to pale ochraceous; margin
thin, acute. **Pore surface** decurrent, white
at first, becoming cream to pale ochraceous;
pores hexagonal or radially elongated, often
finely incised, typically 1–3 per mm but sometimes up to 2 mm wide. **Stalk** short and lateral
or sometimes rudimentary. **Flesh** up to 3 mm
thick, white to pale ochraceous; odor and
taste not distinctive.

SPORE PRINT: White.

MICROSCOPIC FEATURES: Spores 9–12 × 2–3.5
μm, cylindrical to somewhat boat-shaped with
tapered ends, smooth, hyaline.

OCCURRENCE: Usually in overlapping clusters
but sometimes solitary or in groups on decaying hardwood logs and stumps; summer–early
winter.

EDIBILITY: Unknown.

REMARKS: It is a common species of the tropics that extends northward to the Gulf states
and Georgia. *Neofavolus alveolaris* (p. 492)
has a smaller, scaly, orange-yellow to reddish-
orange cap and a cream to pale yellow pore
surface.

Favolus tenuiculus

Fomes fasciatus (Sw.) Cooke

= *Polyporus fasciatus* (Sw.) Fr.

COMMON NAME: Southern Clam Shell.

MACROSCOPIC FEATURES: **Fruitbody** a woody, stalkless cap with concentric zones. **Cap** 7–18 cm wide, convex, hoof- to fan-shaped or semicircular, stalkless; **upper surface** finely tomentose and slightly roughened when young, becoming hard and nearly smooth at maturity, concentrically sulcate, grayish with concentric zones of reddish brown and grayish brown, often darker brown to blackish brown in age; margin curved and somewhat blunt. **Pore surface** pale brown to dark grayish brown; **pores** circular, 4–5 per mm. **Flesh** up to 4 cm thick at the base, hard and crusty near the upper surface, fibrous to granular and corky below, lustrous golden brown.

SPORE PRINT: White.

MICROSCOPIC FEATURES: Spores 10–14 × 4–5 µm, cylindric, smooth, hyaline.

OCCURRENCE: Solitary, in groups, or sometimes overlapping clusters on hardwood trees, logs, and stumps; year-round.

EDIBILITY: Inedible.

REMARKS: *Fasciatus* means "banded," a reference to the concentric zones of this polypore.

Fomes fasciatus

Fomitiporia apiahyna (Speg.) Robledo, Decock & Rajchenb.

= *Phellinus apiahynus* (Speg.) Rajchenb. & J. E. Wright
= *Phellinus elegans* J. E. Wright & Blumenf.

MACROSCOPIC FEATURES: **Fruitbody** a perennial, stalkless cap attached to wood. **Cap** 2–3(5) cm wide, hoof-shaped to semicircular and shelf-like; **upper surface** glabrous, concentrically zonate and sulcate, dark brown to nearly black, sometimes covered with moss or algae; margin fairly sharp. **Pore surface** grayish brown, sometimes yellowish toward the margin; **pores** circular, very small, 7–9 per mm; tubes up to 2 mm thick per year. **Flesh** up to 2 mm thick, vivid golden brown, woody.

SPORE PRINT: White.

MICROSCOPIC FEATURES: Spores 5–6 × 4.5–5 μm, subglobose to globose, thick-walled, smooth, hyaline, dextrinoid; setae absent.

OCCURRENCE: Solitary, in groups, or clusters on living sabal palms or other woody substrates; year-round.

EDIBILITY: Inedible.

REMARKS: The key identifying features of this polypore include its very small size, dark, concentrically zoned, and sulcate cap, small pores, subglobose to globose dextrinoid spores, and lack of setae.

Fomitiporia apiahyna

Fomitopsis palustris (Berk. & M. A. Curtis) Gilb. & Ryvarden

= *Postia palustris* (Berk. & M. A. Curtis) A. B. De

MACROSCOPIC FEATURES: **Fruitbody** an annual, stalkless cap attached to wood. **Cap** 3–10 cm wide, semicircular, shelf-like; **upper surface** white to creamy white, becoming pale buff in age, smooth to faintly zonate and shallowly sulcate, tomentose to nearly glabrous, with a concolorous, sharp margin. **Pore surface** white to creamy white, becoming pale buff in age; **pores** circular to angular, mostly 2–4 per mm; tubes up to 1.5 cm long. **Flesh** up to 4 cm thick, creamy white, azonate, fibrous to corky.

SPORE PRINT: White.

MICROSCOPIC FEATURES: Spores 6.5–8 × 2.5–3 μm, cylindrical to slightly allantoid, smooth, hyaline.

OCCURRENCE: Solitary or in overlapping clusters on conifers, especially pine, sometimes on hardwoods; late spring–early winter.

EDIBILITY: Inedible.

REMARKS: It causes a brown cubical rot of the host tree. As the illustration shows, it is sometimes a food source for beetles.

Fomitopsis palustris

Fuscoporia gilva (Schwein.) T. Wagner & M. Fisch.

= *Hapalopilus gilvus* (Schwein.) Murrill
= *Phellinus gilvus* (Schwein.) Pat.
= *Polyporus gilvus* (Schwein.) Fr.

COMMON NAME: Mustard Yellow Polypore.
MACROSCOPIC FEATURES: **Fruitbody** a shelf-like, stalkless cap attached to wood. **Cap** 3–12 cm wide, fan- to shell-shaped or sometimes effused-reflexed; **upper surface** subtomentose to nearly glabrous, often wrinkled, sometimes zonate, ocher to bright rusty yellow when young, soon becoming dark yellowish brown to reddish brown, with a conspicuous yellow margin when fresh; margin acute. **Pore surface** bright tawny ocher, darkening in age or when bruised; **pores** variable, round to angular or irregular, 2–5 per mm. **Flesh** up to 5 mm thick, tawny to ocher; odor and taste not distinctive.
SPORE PRINT: White.
MICROSCOPIC FEATURES: Spores 4–5 × 3–3.5 μm, ellipsoid to ovoid, smooth, hyaline; hymenial setae 20–30 × 5–6 μm, sharp, thick-walled.

OCCURRENCE: Solitary, in groups, or overlapping clusters on hardwood trees, logs, and stumps, especially oak; year-round.
EDIBILITY: Inedible.
REMARKS: *Gilvus* means "dull pale yellow," a reference to the cap margin. *Phaeolus schweinitzii* (p. 498) is much larger and usually grows in overlapping clusters or rosettes on buried conifer roots. The Ochre-orange Hoof Polypore, *Porodaedalea pini* = *Phellinus pini* (not illustrated), has a stalkless, up to 20 cm or more wide, hoof-shaped to shelf-like or sometimes effused-reflexed fruitbody. The upper surface is coated with fine, matted hairs toward the margin or nearly overall, is concentrically zoned and furrowed, becomes rough and cracked in age, and is tawny to reddish brown, then dark brown or blackish in age. It has a yellowish to yellow-brown pore surface and circular to angular or maze-like pores, 1–4 per mm. It has a brown spore print and grows on living or dead conifers, especially pines. It is a virulent parasite on the heartwood of mature conifers, causing red ring rot. Red-cockaded Woodpeckers nest in the rot cavities.

Fuscoporia gilva

Fuscoporia wahlbergii (Fr.)
T. Wagner & M. Fisch.

= *Phellinus wahlbergii* (Fr.) D. A. Reid
= *Polyporus wahlbergii* (Fr.) Lloyd

MACROSCOPIC FEATURES: **Fruitbody** perennial, consisting of stalkless caps with distinctive setae. **Cap** 5–20 cm wide, applanate, semicircular to elongated and shelf-like; **upper surface** reddish brown to umber, tomentose, narrowly banded with sulcate to flat zones; margin somewhat blunt and rounded. **Pore surface** grayish brown to brown; **pores** circular, minute, 5–9 per mm. **Flesh** up to 5 mm thick, brown; odor and taste not distinctive.

SPORE PRINT: Whitish to buff.

MICROSCOPIC FEATURES: Spores 4–5 × 3.5–4.5 µm, subglobose, thin-walled, hyaline to very pale yellowish; setae 15–35 × 6–9 µm, mostly hooked, sometimes straight, thick-walled, dark brown, acuminate.

OCCURRENCE: Solitary or in overlapping clusters on decaying hardwood trees; year-round.

EDIBILITY: Inedible.

REMARKS: This is a pantropical species that occurs as far north as South Carolina. Positive identification may require microscopic examination, which demonstrates the conspicuous hooked setae that are most distinctive. Other similar species have non-hooked setae.

Fuscoporia wahlbergii

Ganoderma curtisii (Berk.) Murrill

= *Polyporus curtisii* (Berk.) Cooke

MACROSCOPIC FEATURES: **Fruitbody** consisting of a cap and prominent, or sometimes rudimentary, stalk. **Cap** 3–20 cm wide, fan- to kidney-shaped; **upper surface** roughened and uneven, with concentric zones and shallow furrows, covered with a thin, shiny coat of varnish, glabrous, creamy white when very young, becoming ocher or reddish brown and retaining these colors well into maturity, sometimes becoming partly dull brownish when coated with spores; margin acute or obtuse, yellow to ocher. **Pore surface** whitish to yellowish, becoming brownish in age, staining brown when bruised; **pores** circular or nearly so, 4–6 per mm. **Stalk** 3–12 cm long, 1–3 cm thick, lateral to subcentral, varnished, shiny, dark ocher to dark reddish brown, and darker than the cap. **Flesh** up to 1.5 cm thick, leathery to corky when fresh, becoming tough and rigid when dry, white on the upper portion, brown below.

SPORE PRINT: Brown.

MICROSCOPIC FEATURES: Spores 9–13 × 5–7 µm, ovoid, with a truncate apex and apical germ pore, wall two-layered with interwall pillars, appearing roughened, light brown.

OCCURRENCE: Solitary, in groups, or overlapping clusters on stumps, roots, and trunks of hardwoods, sometimes on the ground attached to buried wood; year-round.

EDIBILITY: Inedible.

REMARKS: *Curtisii* honors American mycologist Moses Ashley Curtis (1808–1872). *Ganoderma meredithiae* (p. 470) is very similar but grows on pine stumps or on the ground at the base of pine trees. Although illustrated in many American field guides, *Ganoderma lucidum* does not occur in North America. Molecular analysis has demonstrated that it is a nearly identical species which occurs in Europe and Asia. *Ganoderma sessile* (p. 471) has a dark red to reddish-brown cap. It is typically stalkless but may have a rudimentary or short stalk that is dark reddish brown.

Ganoderma curtisii

Ganoderma meredithiae Adask. & Gilb.

COMMON NAME: Pine Varnish Conk.

MACROSCOPIC FEATURES: **Fruitbody** an annual, shiny cap with a varnished crust that grows on pines. **Cap** 5–16 cm wide, circular to kidney-shaped; **upper surface** dry, shiny, covered with a thin varnished crust, cream-colored to yellowish buff at first, becoming reddish brown at maturity, concentrically zoned and shallowly sulcate; margin some-what blunt. **Pore surface** creamy white at first, becoming pale pinkish cream at maturity; **pores** circular to angular, 4–6 per mm. **Stalk** 3–10 cm long, 1–2 cm thick, nearly equal or tapered in either direction, central or lateral, colored like the cap, coated with a thin, shiny, varnished crust, sometimes rudimen-tary or absent. **Flesh** up to 2 cm thick, corky to fibrous-tough, buff to pale brown; odor and taste not distinctive.

SPORE PRINT: Brown.

MICROSCOPIC FEATURES: Spores 9.5–11.5 × 5.5–7 μm, ellipsoid, with a truncate apex and apical germ pore, wall two-layered with inter-wall pillars, appearing roughened, pale brown.

OCCURRENCE: Solitary, scattered, or in groups at the base of living pine trees or on dead pines or stumps; year-round.

EDIBILITY: Inedible

REMARKS: This species was named in honor of Dr. Meredith Blackwell of Louisiana State University. All other similar species grow on hardwood trees. Molecular analysis may eventually place this species in synonymy with *Ganoderma curtisii*.

Ganoderma meredithiae

Ganoderma sessile Murrill

MACROSCOPIC FEATURES: Fruitbody consisting of a varnished cap that is typically stalkless. **Cap** 3–25 cm wide, a semicircular or fan- to kidney-shaped or irregular cap, usually stalkless, sometimes with a rudimentary or short stalk; **upper surface** roughened and uneven, often with a few zones or shallow furrows, covered with a thin shiny or dull coat of varnish, glabrous, dark red to reddish brown, becoming ochraceous outward, and with a broad, white margin. **Pore surface** white at first, becoming yellowish then dull brown in age, staining brown when bruised; **pores** more or less circular, 4–6 per mm. **Stalk**, when present, 2–6 cm long, 1–3 cm thick, lateral or subcentral, often twisted, varnished, shiny, reddish brown, and darker than the cap. **Flesh** up to 3 cm thick, leathery to corky when fresh, becoming tough and rigid when dry, often zonate when thick, typically brown but sometimes yellowish.

SPORE PRINT: Brown.

MICROSCOPIC FEATURES: Spores 9–12 × 5.5–8 μm, ellipsoid, with a truncate apex and apical germ pore, wall two-layered with interwall pillars, appearing roughened, brown.

OCCURRENCE: Solitary, in groups, or overlapping clusters on stumps, roots, or on the ground at the base of standing hardwood trees; year-round.

EDIBILITY: Inedible.

REMARKS: *Sessile* means "attached without a stalk." *Ganoderma curtisii* (p. 469) has a bright ocher cap when young that becomes darker as it ages and a lateral to subcentral stalk. *Ganoderma sessiliforme* Murrill (not illustrated) is very similar but much smaller, rarely more than 10 cm wide, and usually grows in overlapping clusters. It has a moderately thin margin, creamy-white to pale brown flesh, and its spores measure 9–11 × 4.5–5 μm.

Ganoderma sessile

Ganoderma tuberculosum Murrill

= *Ganoderma oerstedii* (Fr.) Torrend

MACROSCOPIC FEATURES: **Fruitbody** perennial, consisting of a varnished, stalkless cap attached to decaying wood. **Cap** 7–30 cm wide, up to 4 cm thick, rigid, shelf-like, semicircular to kidney-shaped; **upper surface** glabrous, shiny, shallowly sulcate, typically radially wrinkled, warted and deeply cracked on older specimens, often umbonate near the point of attachment, reddish brown to chestnut-colored, becoming dull dark brown in age; margin blunt, creamy white on immature specimens, becoming reddish brown at maturity. **Pore surface** creamy white at first, becoming brownish in age; **pores** circular, 3–4 per mm. **Flesh** corky when young, becoming tough and woody in age, pale yellowish brown to reddish brown; odor and taste not distinctive.

SPORE PRINT: Brown.

MICROSCOPIC FEATURES: Spores 8 × 6 μm, ovoid, with a truncate apex and apical germ pore, wall two-layered with interwall pillars, appearing roughened to nearly smooth, dark brown.

OCCURRENCE: Solitary or in groups on decaying conifer or hardwood; year-round.

EDIBILITY: Inedible.

REMARKS: This is a pantropical species that also occurs along the Gulf states. *Tuberculosum* means "roughened with wart-like projections," a reference to the cap surface. *Ganoderma lobatoideum* (p. 17) has a fan-shaped cap up to 20 cm wide, which is stalkless or with a rudimentary stalk. The upper cap surface may be dull or somewhat shiny, typically rough and uneven, and often concentrically zoned or sulcate at maturity. The cap color varies from brown to orange brown or reddish brown, with a rounded white margin when actively growing. It has corky-brown flesh, a brown pore surface, 4–7 pores per mm, and grows on decaying hardwood logs and stumps. The spores are obovoid or obpyriform, truncate, smooth, pale brown, and measure 6.5–9 × 4–6.5 μm. *Amauroderma sprucei* = *Ganoderma sprucei* (not illustrated) has a dark reddish-brown, varnished, fan- to kidney-shaped or spoon-shaped cap with concentric zones and shallow furrows, and a prominent stalk. It has creamy-white flesh, globose, thick-walled, distinctly ornamented spores that measure (6–)8–10 μm, and it grows on decaying hardwoods year-round.

Ganoderma tuberculosum

Ganoderma zonatum Murrill

= *Ganoderma sulcatum* Murrill

COMMON NAME: Palm Trunk Conk.

MACROSCOPIC FEATURES: **Fruitbody** a varnished cap attached to palm trees. **Cap** up to 20 cm wide, shelf-like, hard and woody, stalkless or with a rudimentary stalk; **upper surface** soon developing a varnished and shiny crust on young specimens, becoming dull when covered with spores or algae or in age, often variously colored with a mixture of reddish orange, wood brown to dark purplish brown or mahogany, distinctly zonate when mature, smooth or concentrically sulcate; margin thick, rounded or blunt and white when immature, becoming brown in age. **Pore surface** white to cream colored at first, becoming purplish brown in age or when bruised; **pores** circular to angular, 5–6 per mm. **Flesh** up to 4 cm thick, dark purplish brown, concentrically zonate, soft-fibrous.

SPORE PRINT: Brown.

MICROSCOPIC FEATURES: Spores 11–13 × 5–6 μm, narrowly ellipsoid to cylindric-ellipsoid, with a truncate apex and apical germ pore, wall two-layered with interwall pillars, appearing roughened to nearly smooth, brown.

OCCURRENCE: Solitary, in groups, or overlapping clusters on the trunks of palm trees; year-round.

EDIBILITY: Inedible.

REMARKS: *Zonatum* means "having distinct zones." It causes a lethal butt rot of palms. All palms are considered hosts of this fungus. A photograph of an immature specimen is shown in the "Color Key to the Major Groups of Fungi" (p. 17). Other similar species of *Ganoderma* grow on hardwood or conifer species other than palm trees. The Artist's Conk, *Ganoderma applanatum* (p. 17), has a large, stalkless cap with corky to woody flesh. The cap is 5–65 cm wide, shelf-like to somewhat hoof-shaped, thick, and crusty. The cap upper surface is concentrically sulcate, thickened at the attachment point, finely cracked and roughened, and dull brown to blackish brown. It has a white pore surface that stains brown when bruised and small, 4–6 per mm pores. It grows in groups or overlapping clusters on a wide variety of hardwoods year-round.

Ganoderma zonatum

Gelatoporia dichroa (Fr.) Ginns

= *Gloeoporus dichrous* (Fr.) Bres.

MACROSCOPIC FEATURES: **Fruitbody** composed of stalkless, fused caps in rows or shelves. **Cap** up to 10 cm wide, variable from effused-reflexed to resupinate or applanate; **upper surface** finely tomentose to nearly glabrous, somewhat zonate, whitish to ochraceous or grayish ocher; margin acute, undulating. **Pore surface** gelatinous when fresh, separable from the flesh, drying hard and resinous, grayish pink to purplish or reddish brown, with a whitish margin when immature; **pores** round to angular, 4–6 per mm. **Flesh** up to 4 mm thick, soft and fibrous or cottony, white.

SPORE PRINT: White.

MICROSCOPIC FEATURES: Spores 3.5–5.5 × 0.5–1.5 μm, allantoid to cylindrical, smooth, hyaline, inamyloid.

OCCURRENCE: In overlapping, fused groups on decaying hardwood, sometimes on conifers or on old, woody polypores; summer–early winter.

EDIBILITY: Inedible.

REMARKS: *Stereum* species are similar, but they lack pores.

Gelatoporia dichroa

Gloeophyllum sepiarium (Wulfen) P. Karst.

= *Daedalea sepiaria* (Wulfen) Fr.
= *Lenzites sepiaria* (Wulfen) Fr.

COMMON NAME: Yellow-red Gill Polypore.
MACROSCOPIC FEATURES: **Fruitbody** consisting of a stalkless cap with gill-like pores, growing on conifer wood. **Cap** 2.5–10 cm wide, semi-circular to kidney-shaped, slightly convex or flat, tough; **upper surface** covered with short and stiff hairs that become appressed in age, with distinct concentric zones and furrows, bright yellowish red to reddish brown, becoming grayish or blackish in age; margin orange yellow to brownish yellow or whitish, sometimes with tufts of tiny hairs. **Pore surface** tough, golden brown to rusty brown; **pores** thick, elongated and labyrinthine, 1–2 per mm. **Flesh** up to 6 mm thick, tough, yellow brown to rusty brown; odor and taste not distinctive.
SPORE PRINT: White.
MICROSCOPIC FEATURES: Spores 9–13 × 3–5 μm, cylindric, smooth, hyaline.

OCCURRENCE: Solitary, in groups, or overlapping rosette-shaped clusters on decaying wood, usually conifers; year-round.
EDIBILITY: Inedible.
REMARKS: The addition of KOH to the flesh produces a black reaction. *Osmoporus mexicanus* (p. 496) has a shallowly furrowed grayish cap with concentric zones of dull brown to rusty brown, gray, or blackish, a grayish to whitish margin, and distinctly gill-like pores. The fruitbody of the Zoned Gill Polypore, *Gloeophyllum striatum* (p. 17), consists of a cap and rudimentary stalk-like base with a gill-like pore surface. The cap is 1–8 cm wide, semicircular to fan-shaped or fused and rosette-shaped, tough, and flexible. The upper cap surface is distinctly zonate with concentric bands of pale yellowish brown and darker brown. It has conspicuously gill-like pores that sometimes split and form flattened teeth on older specimens. It grows on decaying hardwood from late summer through early winter. *Gloeophyllum trabeum* (not illustrated) has a smooth, weakly zonate to azonate cap, and its pore surface has a combination of small pores, 2–4 per mm, and gill-like pores.

Gloeophyllum sepiarium

Heterobasidion annosum (Fr.) Bref.

= *Fomes annosus* (Fr.) Cooke
= *Fomitopsis annosa* (Fr.) P. Karst.

COMMON NAME: Conifer-base Polypore.
MACROSCOPIC FEATURES: **Fruitbody** a stalk-less cap, 2.5–25 cm wide, attached to wood. **Cap** variable from shelf-like to spreading in rows, semicircular to irregular, sometimes fused; margin rounded, wavy; **upper surface** uneven and roughened with shallow furrows, indistinctly zoned, velvety or glabrous, becoming incrusted, brown, then blackish in age. **Pore surface** ivory to pinkish cream, smooth, glancing; **pores** circular to angular, 4–5 per mm. **Flesh** up to 1 cm thick, corky, azonate, ivory to pinkish cinnamon; odor and taste not distinctive.

SPORE PRINT: White.
MICROSCOPIC FEATURES: Spores 4.5–6.5 × 3.5–4.5 μm, subglobose, finely warted, hyaline, with oil drops.
OCCURRENCE: Solitary or in groups on stumps, roots, or trunks of conifers, especially pine and hemlock, or sometimes on the ground attached to buried roots; year-round.
EDIBILITY: Inedible.
REMARKS: It is a major root rot pathogen of North American conifers. The spores are often difficult to find.

Heterobasidion annosum

Hexagonia cucullata (Mont.) Murrill

= *Favolus cucullatus* Mont.
= *Pseudofavolus cucullatus* (Mont.) Pat.

MACROSCOPIC FEATURES: **Fruitbody** a stalkless cap attached to wood by a small whitish disc. **Cap** 2–8 cm wide, convex to nearly plane, fan- to kidney-shaped; **upper surface** glabrous, smooth, whitish to ochraceous when young, soon becoming ocher to dull ocher, often with a dark reddish tint along the margin. **Pore surface** dark ochraceous to dull reddish or reddish brown; **pores** angular, typically hexagonal, 1–3 per mm. **Flesh** up to 2 mm thick, tough, straw-colored to pale ochraceous; odor and taste not distinctive.
SPORE PRINT: White.
MICROSCOPIC FEATURES: Spores 11–16 × 4–6 μm, cylindric, smooth, hyaline.

OCCURRENCE: Solitary, scattered, or in groups on decaying hardwoods; year-round.
EDIBILITY: Inedible.
REMARKS: *Neofavolus alveolaris* (p. 492) has a reddish-yellow to reddish-orange cap, hexagonal pores, and a short, eccentric to lateral white stalk. *Hexagonia hydnoides* = *Polyporus hydnoides* (p. 17) has a 3–20 cm wide, stalkless, fan-shaped to semicircular cap that is flexible and leathery when fresh and becomes rigid when dry. It has a dark brown to blackish-brown upper surface that is covered with conspicuous erect, stiff hairs that fall off in age. It has a fulvous to dark brown pore surface with a distinct grayish tint and 3–5 round to irregular pores per mm. It grows on decaying hardwood from summer through early winter.

Hexagonia cucullata

Hydnopolyporus fimbriatus (Fr.) D. A. Reid

= *Polyporus fimbriatus* Fr.

MACROSCOPIC FEATURES: **Fruitbody** annual, up to 12 cm wide, consisting of numerous caps with rudimentary stalks growing in rosette-like clusters. **Cap** individual lobes up to 2.5 cm wide, 1.5–3 mm thick, flexible, fibrous to tough, erect; margin undulating, sometimes entire but typically fringed and ragged to incised; **upper surface** slightly velvety, becoming glabrous in age, concentrically zoned or azonate, radially striate or smooth, white to pale tan, darkening as it dries. **Pore surface** variable, nearly smooth to finely warted, reticulate or with flattened teeth or distinctly poroid, white; **pores** angular to sinuous, 2–5 per mm. **Flesh** thin, fibrous, white; odor and taste not distinctive.

SPORE PRINT: White.

MICROSCOPIC FEATURES: Spores 3.5–5 × 2.5–3.5 μm, broadly ellipsoid to subglobose, smooth, hyaline.

OCCURRENCE: In clusters on the ground arising from buried wood or on stumps of hardwoods; summer through early winter.

EDIBILITY: Reported to be edible, but somewhat tough.

REMARKS: *Fimbriatus* means "having a finely torn margin." It has been misidentified and/or misillustrated as *Hydnopolyporus palmatus* in some popular mushroom field guides. The fruitbody of *Sparassis americana* (p. 172) is a rounded, lettuce-like cluster of flattened branches attached to a common, partially buried stalk-like base. The branches are densely arranged with leaf- to fan-like curly, flexible, smooth, azonate lobes that are whitish, cream to pale yellow, or tan.

Hydnopolyporus fimbriatus

Inonotus amplectens Murrill

= *Polyporus amplectens* (Murrill) Sacc. & Trotter

COMMON NAME: Pawpaw Polypore.
MACROSCOPIC FEATURES: **Fruitbody** 1–4 cm wide, 1–2.5 cm thick, hemispherical, clasping, stalkless; **upper surface** soft, velvety, dark yellowish orange; margin obtuse, entire, straw-colored, becoming thin, undulating or toothed, decurved, and concolorous in age. **Pore surface** concave, honey yellow at first, becoming reddish brown at maturity, covered by a yellowish membrane when young; **pores** nearly round, 2–4 per mm, larger when fused, splitting into irregular tooth-like plates in age; tubes 2–4 mm long. **Flesh** soft, spongy-fibrous, rusty brown; odor and taste not distinctive.

SPORE PRINT: White.
MICROSCOPIC FEATURES: Spores 5–6.5 × 3.5–4 μm, ellipsoid, smooth, with 1 or 2 oil drops, hyaline.
OCCURRENCE: Solitary or in groups encircling living twigs of Pawpaw (*Asimina* species).
EDIBILITY: Inedible.
REMARKS: *Amplectens* means "encircling," a reference to its growth habit. *Phylloporia fruticum* = *Inonotus fruticum* (not illustrated) forms 1–5 cm wide, semicircular to round, soft and spongy, golden-yellow to rusty-brown fruitbodies, attached to or encircling twigs or branches of various shrubs and trees, especially oleander and orange. It has a rusty-brown to cinnamon-brown pore surface that becomes very dark brown in age.

Inonotus amplectens

Inonotus hispidus (Bull.) P. Karst.

= *Polyporus hispidus* (Bull.) Fr.

COMMON NAME: Shaggy Polypore.

MACROSCOPIC FEATURES: **Fruitbody** a stalk-less, shelf-like cap with conspicuous, coarse, bright reddish-orange hairs that darken in age. **Cap** 10–30 cm wide, convex, semicircular to fan-shaped, soft or tough; **upper surface** broadly attached, azonate, covered with stiff, bright reddish-orange hairs that become reddish brown to blackish in age; margin rounded and blunt, bright sulphur yellow when young. **Pore surface** uneven, yellow at first, becoming yellow ocher then yellowish brown or blackish in age; **pores** angular to irregularly rounded, 1–3 per mm, sometimes exuding clear droplets. **Flesh** up to 7.5 cm thick, somewhat zonate, soft or tough, yellow to ocher with darker zones, immediately staining brownish when exposed; odor somewhat acidic and pleasant; taste not distinctive.

SPORE PRINT: Brown.

MICROSCOPIC FEATURES: Spores 8–11 × 6–8 μm, subglobose to ovoid, thick-walled, smooth, brown; setal hyphae lacking, setae sometimes present, up to 30 μm long, dark brown.

OCCURRENCE: Solitary or in groups on hardwood trees, especially oak and walnut; summer-early winter.

EDIBILITY: Inedible.

REMARKS: *Hispidus* means "having stiff hairs." The flesh of mature or older specimens is often infested with small, pinkish larvae. *Inonotus quercustris* (p. 481) has a golden-yellow cap that becomes rusty brown in age and has conspicuous setal hyphae in its trama. *Inocutis texana* = *Inonotus texanus* (not illustrated), reported only from Texas and Arizona, has a light brown to buff cap that becomes radially and concentrically cracked into angular scales, a yellow-brown pore surface that becomes dark brown to blackish brown, and grows on living mesquite and acacia. It lacks setae and has spores that measure 7–10 × 4.5–6 μm.

Inonotus hispidus

Inonotus quercustris M. Blackw. & Gilb.

MACROSCOPIC FEATURES: Fruitbody a stalk-less, shelf-like cap growing on living water oaks. **Cap** 12–20 cm wide, convex, shelf-like or sometimes hoof-shaped, soft at first, becoming tough at maturity; **upper surface** moist or dry, azonate, tomentose to appressed-tomentose, golden yellow to orange when young, becoming rusty brown with darker areas in age; margin rounded to acute. **Pore surface** yellow to golden yellow, with a bright golden luster when viewed obliquely, becoming brownish in age; **pores** angular, 3–5 per mm, sometimes exuding clear droplets. **Flesh** moist, soft and spongy at first, becoming dry, firm, and tough at maturity, dark reddish brown with faint concentric zones; odor and taste not distinctive.

SPORE PRINT: Yellowish brown.

MICROSCOPIC FEATURES: Spores 7.5–10 × 5.5–8 μm, ellipsoid, thick-walled, smooth, pale yellow; setal hyphae conspicuous, up to 200 μm long, thick-walled, tapered to a point, dark reddish brown; setae absent.

OCCURRENCE: Solitary or in overlapping clusters on water oak, *Quercus nigra*, sometimes on other oak species; year-round.

EDIBILITY: Inedible.

REMARKS: *Quercustris* means "occurring on oaks." A second illustration of this polypore is shown in the "Color Key to the Major Groups of Fungi" (p. 17). *Inonotus hispidus* (p. 480) lacks setal hyphae. *Inonotus rickii* (not illustrated) is similar and also grows on oak. The upper surface is golden brown at first and becomes dark rusty brown in age. Its pore surface is pale brown, with 2–3 angular pores per mm that sometimes exude clear droplets. It has both setal hyphae and setae and smaller spores that measure 6–8.5 × 4.5–5.5 μm.

Inonotus quercustris

Irpex lacteus (Fr.) Fr.

= *Polyporus tulipiferae* (Schwein.) Overh.

COMMON NAME: Milk-white Toothed
Polypore.

MACROSCOPIC FEATURES: **Fruitbody** a stalkless, spreading, crust-like mass of fused caps on
decaying hardwoods. **Cap** 1–3 cm wide, shell-
shaped to semicircular, convex to nearly plane,
typically laterally fused, stiff; **upper surface**
dry, azonate to faintly zoned, tomentose, white
to creamy white; margin acute. **Pore surface**
white to creamy white; **pores** angular, 2–3 per
mm; tubes and pores splitting and becoming
jagged or tooth-like in age. **Flesh** up to 1.5 mm
thick, tough, white to pale tan.

SPORE PRINT: White.

MICROSCOPIC FEATURES: Spores 5–7 × 2–3
µm, oblong to cylindric, straight or curved,
smooth, hyaline.

OCCURRENCE: In spreading, overlapping clusters on decaying hardwoods; year-round.

EDIBILITY: Inedible.

REMARKS: *Lacteus* means "milk," a reference
to the milk-white color of the fruitbody.
Schizopora paradoxa (p. 505) is similar, but
its fruitbody is a white to cream, spreading
crust that is flat or somewhat projecting and
bracket-like and darkens in age. It usually
has small nodules on the upper surface, tiny
hairs on the margin, and the creamy-white
undersurface is maze-like, with irregular and
angular elongated pores that sometimes form
teeth-like projections. Also compare with *Sarcodontia pachyodon* (p. 504), which has much
larger teeth.

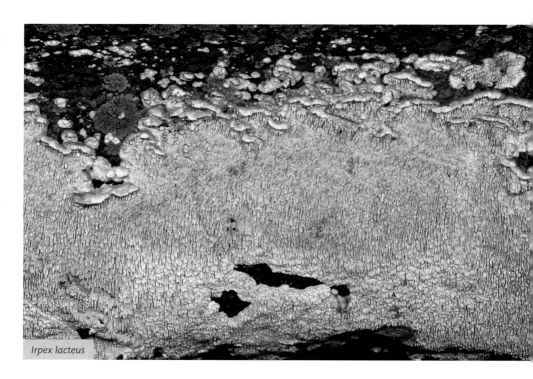

Irpex lacteus

Ischnoderma resinosum (Schrad.) P. Karst.

= *Polyporus resinosus* (Schrad.) Fr.

COMMON NAMES: Resinous Polypore, Steak of the Woods.

MACROSCOPIC FEATURES: **Fruitbody** a stalkless, shelf-like cap, often growing in overlapping clusters. **Cap** 7–26 cm wide, fan-shaped to semicircular, convex to flattened, fleshy and soft when young and fresh, becoming tough or brittle in age; **upper surface** concentrically and radially furrowed, faintly to distinctly zoned, velvety at first, covered with a thin, glossy, resinous crust on mature specimens, dull brownish orange to dark brown; margin thick, rounded, whitish to ocher, frequently exuding drops of amber, resin-like fluid when fresh. **Pore surface** white, staining brown when bruised, becoming pale brown in age; **pores** angular to circular, 4–6 per mm. **Flesh** up to 2.5 cm thick, soft or tough, whitish to pale yellow.

SPORE PRINT: Whitish.

MICROSCOPIC FEATURES: Spores 4.5–7 × 1.5–2.5 µm, cylindric to allantoid, smooth, hyaline.

OCCURRENCE: Solitary, in groups, or overlapping clusters on decaying hardwood; year-round.

EDIBILITY: Edible.

REMARKS: *Resinosum* is a reference to the resin-like, amber-colored droplets exuded by the fruitbody.

Ischnoderma resinosum

Laetiporus gilbertsonii var. *pallidus*
Burds.

COMMON NAME: Southern Chicken.

MACROSCOPIC FEATURES: **Fruitbody** a cluster of overlapping shelf-like caps growing on oak trees. **Cap** up to 20 cm wide, fan- to hoof-shaped or an irregular mass, broadly convex or somewhat flattened, fleshy and soft when young and fresh, becoming tough or brittle in age; margin thick, rounded and blunt at first, becoming acute in age; **upper surface** glabrous, smooth, pale orange to pale pinkish orange, becoming zonate and nearly white in age. **Pore surface** bumpy, uneven and orange to pale orange when young, becoming cream to whitish in age; **pores** circular to angular, 2–4 per mm. **Stalk** lateral and rudimentary, narrowed to the point of attachment. **Flesh** up to 2 cm thick, pale yellow to whitish.

SPORE PRINT: White.

MICROSCOPIC FEATURES: Spores 5–6.5 × 3.5–4.5 μm, broadly ovoid, smooth, hyaline.

OCCURRENCE: In overlapping clusters or sometimes solitary, on standing trunks or logs of oaks, especially Live Oak, *Quercus virginiana*; fall–winter, sometimes year-round.

EDIBILITY: Edible. While not toxic, allergic reactions to this mushroom are more commonly reported than with *Laetiporus sulphureus*. Use caution when eating this for the first time.

REMARKS: *Gilbertsonii* honors American mycologist Robert Lee Gilbertson (1925–2011). *Pallidus* means "pale," a reference to the pale colors of the cap and pore surface.

Laetiporus gilbertsonii var. *pallidus*

Laetiporus persicinus (Berk. & M. A. Curtis) Gilb.

= *Meripilus persicinus* (Berk. & M. A. Curtis) Ryvarden

= *Polyporus persicinus* Berk. & M. A. Curtis

MACROSCOPIC FEATURES: **Fruitbody** a large cap with a central stalk, usually attached to the roots of oak trees. **Cap** 10–26 cm wide, circular to fan-shaped, soft and fleshy when young, becoming tough in age; margin blunt, wavy, sometimes lobed; **upper surface** dry, tomentose, azonate to faintly zoned, smooth at first, becoming uneven with wart-like bumps in age, pinkish brown with a whitish to pinkish cream margin when young, becoming darker brown with a blackish brown margin. **Pore surface** whitish to pinkish cream at first, becoming pale pinkish yellow then pale brown at maturity, quickly staining dark brown when bruised, sometimes exuding amber droplets; **pores** decurrent at least half the length of the stalk, circular, 3–4 per mm. **Stalk** up to 10 cm long, 3–7 cm thick, solid, central, sometimes branched, dry, pinkish brown, often binding leaves and soil at the base. **Flesh** up to 2 cm thick, soft, whitish; odor variously described as resembling ham or bacon or not distinctive; taste unpleasant or not distinctive.

SPORE PRINT: White.

MICROSCOPIC FEATURES: Spores 6.5–8 × 4–5 μm, ovoid to ellipsoid, smooth, hyaline.

OCCURRENCE: Solitary, scattered, or in overlapping clusters, attached to buried or above ground roots at or near the base of living oak or pine trees; year-round.

EDIBILITY: Edible; taste variously described as sour or like fermented ham or delicious.

REMARKS: *Persicinus* means "peach," a reference to the color of the pore surface. Molecular analysis indicates that this species does not belong in the genus *Laetiporus*. Additional research is required to resolve this issue. *Laetiporus cincinnatus* (p. 17) has a pinkish-orange cap and a white pore surface. While not toxic, allergic reactions to this mushroom are commonly reported. Use caution when eating this for the first time. *Laetiporus sulphureus* (p. 486) has an orange cap and a bright sulfur-yellow pore surface.

Laetiporus persicinus

Laetiporus sulphureus (Bull.) Murrill

= *Polyporus sulphureus* (Bull.) Fr.

COMMON NAMES: Chicken Mushroom, Sulphur Shelf.

MACROSCOPIC FEATURES: **Fruitbody** a large, colorful, shelf-like cap often growing in overlapping clusters, usually on hardwoods. **Cap** 5–30 cm wide, fan- to petal-shaped, soft when young, becoming tough in age; margin blunt, wavy, often lobed, pale orange; **upper surface** somewhat velvety, dry, often wrinkled and roughened, bright to dull orange, fading to orange yellow then whitish in age. **Pore surface** bright sulphur yellow; **pores** angular, 3–4 per mm. **Stalk** lateral and rudimentary or absent. **Flesh** up to 2 cm thick, tender to fibrous when fresh, becoming tough and brittle in age; odor nutty or not distinctive; taste not distinctive.

SPORE PRINT: White.

MICROSCOPIC FEATURES: Spores 5–8 × 3.5–5 μm, oval to elliptic, smooth, hyaline.

OCCURRENCE: In overlapping clusters or rosettes, sometimes solitary, on hardwoods, especially oak, rarely on conifers; fall–early winter, sometimes year-round.

EDIBILITY: Edible when young and thoroughly cooked. It has been reported to cause gastrointestinal upset when gathered from conifers or cherry trees, if undercooked, if too old, or when consumed with alcohol. Use caution when eating for the first time.

REMARKS: *Sulphureus* means "sulphur-yellow," a reference to the pore surface. The White-pored Sulphur Shelf, or White-pored Chicken of the Woods, *Laetiporus cincinnatus* (p. 17), forms rosettes of pinkish-orange caps with a pale pinkish-cream margin and a white pore surface. It grows on the ground attached to roots at the base of oak trees or stumps, rarely on other species, from spring through early winter. While not toxic, allergic reactions to this mushroom are more commonly reported than with *Laetiporus sulphureus*. Use caution when eating for the first time.

Laetiporus sulphureus

Leiotrametes lactinea (Berk.) Welti & Courtec.

= *Polyporus lactineus* Berk.
= *Trametes lactinea* (Berk.) Sacc.

MACROSCOPIC FEATURES: **Fruitbody** consisting of solitary or overlapping caps attached to wood. **Cap** 5–25 cm wide, shelf-like, semicircular to fan- or kidney-shaped; margin fairly thick and blunt at first, usually becoming sharper as it ages; **upper surface** typically uneven and conspicuously warted, concentrically zoned or shallowly furrowed, color a variable mixture of whitish to grayish and pale to dark brown. **Pore surface** white to creamy white, becoming dull yellow to brownish in age; **pores** initially round, becoming angular at maturity, 2–3 per mm. **Stalk** absent or rudimentary. **Flesh** up to 2.5 cm thick, corky, white to yellowish; odor and taste not distinctive.

SPORE PRINT: White.

MICROSCOPIC FEATURES: Spores 5–7 × 2.5–3.2 μm, oblong-elliptic to cylindric, smooth, hyaline.

OCCURRENCE: Solitary, in groups, or overlapping clusters on decaying oaks and other hardwood trunks, logs, and stumps, sometimes on the ground, arising from buried wood; year-round.

EDIBILITY: Inedible.

REMARKS: Overlapping and fused clusters of this polypore may be up to 60 cm or more wide. *Trametes cubensis* (not illustrated) is similar, but it has a white to cream or tan cap that becomes reddish to bay from the base outward in age. The cap surface is azonate or irregularly sulcate, and the margin is sharp to slightly rounded. It has very small pores, 5–7 per mm, that are almost invisible to the naked eye (use a hand lens) and larger spores that measure 7–9.5 × 3–3.5 μm. *Leiotrametes lactinea* is often erroneously identified as being *Trametes cubensis*. It is questionable if *Trametes cubensis* even occurs in North America.

Leiotrametes lactinea

Lentinus arcularius (Batsch) Zmitr.

= *Polyporus arcularius* (Batsch) Fr.

COMMON NAME: Spring Polypore.
MACROSCOPIC FEATURES: **Fruitbody** consisting of a cap and prominent stalk attached to wood. **Cap** 1.5–7.5 cm wide, circular or nearly so, broadly convex to shallowly funnel-shaped; **upper surface** dry, covered with small radiating scales, ocher brown to dark yellow brown; margin fringed with short hairs. **Pore surface** white to cream, darkening in age; **pores** angular to hexagonal and radially arranged like a honeycomb, decurrent, 1–2 per mm. **Stalk** up to 4 cm long, 2–5 mm thick, nearly equal or sometimes with an enlarged base, central, solid, scurfy, colored like the cap. **Flesh** up to 1 mm thick, tough to leathery, cream-colored; odor and taste not distinctive.

SPORE PRINT: White.
MICROSCOPIC FEATURES: Spores 7–11 × 2–3 μm, cylindric, smooth, hyaline, inamyloid.
OCCURRENCE: In groups or clusters on fallen branches, logs, and stumps of decaying hardwoods; spring–early summer.
EDIBILITY: Inedible.
REMARKS: *Arcularius* means "having chambers or vaults," a reference to the honeycomb pore surface. *Neofavolus alveolaris* (p. 492) has an orange-yellow to reddish-orange cap and a short lateral stalk. *Lentinus tricholoma* = *Polyporus tricholoma* (not illustrated) also has hairs on the cap margin, but it has a cream to pale tan or pale brown cap and much smaller, round to angular pores, (5)7–9 per mm. It grows on decaying hardwoods from late spring through early winter.

Lentinus arcularius

Lenzites betulina (L.) Fr.

= *Trametes betulina* (L.) Pilát

COMMON NAME: Multicolor Gill Polypore.
MACROSCOPIC FEATURES: **Fruitbody** a stalkless, shelf-like cap growing on decaying hardwood. **Cap** 3–10 cm wide, kidney-shaped to semicircular, nearly plane, tough; **upper surface** velvety to hairy, with distinct multicolored concentric zones of variable color, often white, pink, gray, yellow, orange, or brown, sometimes green when covered with algae; margin acute. **Pore surface** white to creamy white; **pores** thin, conspicuously gill-like, sometimes forking, occasionally with elongated pores near the margin. **Flesh** up to 2 mm thick, tough, white.

SPORE PRINT: White.
MICROSCOPIC FEATURES: Spores 4–6 × 2–3 μm, cylindric to allantoid, smooth, hyaline.
OCCURRENCE: Solitary or in groups on decaying hardwoods, especially birch, oak, and willow, rarely on conifers; summer–early winter.
EDIBILITY: Inedible.
REMARKS: *Betulina* means "birch," a reference to one of the trees on which it grows. *Gloeophyllum* species have brown gill-like pores. *Daedaleopsis confragosa* (p. 462) has whitish to pale brown labyrinthine pores.

enzites betulina

Microporellus dealbatus (Berk. & M. A. Curtis) Murrill = *Polyporus dealbatus* Berk. & M. A. Curtis

MACROSCOPIC FEATURES: **Fruitbody** consisting of a cap and a central to eccentric stalk attached to buried wood. **Cap** 2–10 cm wide, circular to fan- or kidney-shaped, tough at first, becoming hard and woody; **upper surface** dry, somewhat velvety to nearly glabrous, distinctly zonate with a mixture of buff to brown, pale grayish-brown, or pale smoky-gray colors; margin thin, acute, whitish. **Pore surface** white, becoming cream, and finally ochraceous at maturity, sometimes wrinkled; **pores** angular to irregularly rounded, minute, 8–10 per mm. **Stalk** 3–10 cm long, 3–12 mm thick, nearly equal or tapered in either direction, often twisted, dry, rigid, colored like the cap or paler. **Flesh** up to 4 mm thick, tough, white; odor and taste not distinctive.
SPORE PRINT: White.

MICROSCOPIC FEATURES: Spores 4.5–6 × 3.5–4.5 μm, ellipsoid to lacrimoid, smooth, hyaline, weakly dextrinoid.
OCCURRENCE: Solitary, scattered, or in groups on the ground, attached to buried wood or on decaying trunks or stumps in hardwoods or mixed woods; year-round.
EDIBILITY: Inedible.
REMARKS: *Dealbatus* means "off-white." *Microporellus obovatus* (p. 491) has a lateral stalk, a paler spoon-shaped cap, and slightly smaller, subglobose to ellipsoid spores.

Microporellus dealbatus

Microporellus obovatus (Jungh.) Ryvarden

= *Polyporus obovatus* (Jungh.) P. Karst.

MACROSCOPIC FEATURES: Fruitbody a spoon-shaped cap with a lateral stalk attached to wood. **Cap** 2–7 cm wide, spoon- to fan-shaped, sometimes kidney-shaped to nearly circular, tough, becoming hard and brittle; **upper surface** finely velvety, then nearly glabrous in age, white when young, becoming cream to ochraceous, sometimes zonate with darker grayish or brownish zones; margin thin, acute. **Pore surface** white at first, becoming cream to pale straw-colored; **pores** angular, minute, 6–8 per mm. **Stalk** up to 7 cm long, 2–6 mm thick, lateral or sometimes eccentric to nearly central, sometimes rudimentary, typically colored like the cap. **Flesh** up to 3 mm thick, tough, white; odor and taste not distinctive.

SPORE PRINT: White.

MICROSCOPIC FEATURES: Spores 3.5–5 × 2–4.5 μm, subglobose to ellipsoid, smooth, hyaline, inamyloid.

OCCURRENCE: Solitary or in small groups or clusters attached to aboveground or buried wood in hardwoods or mixed woods; year-round.

EDIBILITY: Inedible.

REMARKS: *Obovatus* means "egg-shaped with the broad end up." *Microporellus dealbatus* (p. 490) has a central or sometimes eccentric stalk, a more concentrically zoned, darker cap, and slightly larger, ellipsoid to lacrimoid spores.

Microporellus obovatus

Neofavolus alveolaris (DC.)
Sotome & T. Hatt.

= *Favolus canadensis* Klotzsch
= *Hexagonia alveolaris* (DC.) Murrill
= *Polyporus mori* (Pollini) Fr.

COMMON NAME: Hexagonal-pored Polypore.
MACROSCOPIC FEATURES: **Fruitbody** consisting of a cap and stalk attached to wood. **Cap** 2–6.5 cm wide, convex to depressed or somewhat funnel-like, circular to kidney-shaped; **upper surface** appressed-scaly to fibrillose, orange yellow to reddish orange, fading to pale yellow or tan in age; margin thin, inrolled at first, somewhat fringed. **Pore surface** cream to pale yellow; **pores** angular to hexagonal or multisided and radially arranged like a honeycomb, decurrent. **Stalk** up to 1 cm long, 3–6 mm thick, lateral to nearly central, solid. **Flesh** tough, cream-colored; odor and taste not distinctive.

SPORE PRINT: White.
MICROSCOPIC FEATURES: Spores 9–11 × 3–3.5 μm, cylindric, smooth, hyaline, inamyloid.
OCCURRENCE: Solitary or in groups on fallen branches of hardwoods, especially oak; spring–early summer.
EDIBILITY: Edible but tough.
REMARKS: *Alveolaris* means "pitted like a honeycomb," a reference to the pore surface. Molecular analysis indicates that what is being called *Neofavolus alveoularis* may be two distinct species, and new names will need to be assigned to them. More research needs to be done. *Lentinus arcularius* (p. 488) has a circular, ocher-brown cap with a fringed margin, white to cream, honeycomb-like pores, and a prominent, central, scurfy stalk that is colored like the cap. Also compare with *Hexagonia cucullata* (p. 477).

Neofavolus alveolaris

Nigroporus vinosus (Berk.) Murrill

= *Polyporus vinosus* Berk.

MACROSCOPIC FEATURES: **Fruitbody** a stalk-less, shelf-like cap, broadly attached to decaying wood. **Cap** 2–12 cm wide, leathery or tough, becoming brittle as it dries; **upper surface** slightly velvety to nearly glabrous, sometimes zonate, violaceous to vinaceous brown at first, becoming purplish brown to dark violet at maturity; margin thin, acute. **Pore surface** purplish brown to dark violet or smoky black; **pores** irregularly rounded, minute, 7–8 per mm. **Flesh** up to 6 mm thick, vinaceous brown or paler; odor and taste not distinctive.
SPORE PRINT: White.

MICROSCOPIC FEATURES: Spores 3.5–4.5 × 1–1.5 μm, allantoid to cylindric, smooth, hyaline.
OCCURRENCE: Solitary, in groups, or overlapping clusters on hardwood or conifer trees; year-round.
EDIBILITY: Inedible.
REMARKS: *Vinosus* means "wine red," a reference to colors of the fruitbody. *Nigrofomes melanoporus* (not illustrated), reported from Florida, has a larger, up to 20 cm wide cap that is very hard, sulcate or cracked in age, and dark brown to purplish black. It has a dark brown to blackish pore surface with tiny pores arranged like a honeycomb and broadly ellipsoid spores that measure 4–5 × 3–3.5 μm.

Nigroporus vinosus

Niveoporofomes spraguei (Berk. & M. A. Curtis) B. K. Cui, M. L. Han & Y. C. Dai

= *Fomitopsis spraguei* (Berk. & M. A. Curtis) Gilb. & Ryvarden
= *Tyromyces spraguei* (Berk. & M. A. Curtis) Murrill

MACROSCOPIC FEATURES: Fruitbody a stalk-less, shelf-like or effused-reflexed cap attached to wood. **Cap** 5–9 cm wide, up to 4 cm thick, semicircular to irregular, distinctly corky or tough; **upper surface** azonate, appressed-strigose to nearly glabrous, smooth or roughened, white to ivory or pale ochraceous, sometimes staining greenish blue to grayish blue; margin rounded or acute, concolorous or greenish blue to grayish blue. **Pore surface** white to buff or pale brown; **pores** circular to angular, 3–6 per mm. **Flesh** up to 4 cm thick, corky or tough, azonate, white to ochraceous; odor not distinctive; taste variously described as slightly acidic, bitter, or not distinctive.

SPORE PRINT: White.
MICROSCOPIC FEATURES: Spores 5.5–7 × 4–5 μm, ovoid to broadly ellipsoid, smooth, hyaline.
OCCURRENCE: Solitary, in groups, or clusters on hardwoods; summer–early winter.
EDIBILITY: Inedible.
REMARKS: *Spraguei* honors C. J. Sprague who collected it as an undescribed species. *Postia caesia* (p. 500) is similar, but its fruitbody is soft, white, often with a blue tint, and some-times bruises intensely blue. Its pore surface is white or blue. *Postia fragilis* = *Oligoporus fragilis* (not illustrated) has a whitish to buff cap and pore surface that become reddish brown when bruised or on drying.

Niveoporofomes spraguei

Onnia tomentosa (Fr.) P. Karst.

= *Inonotus tomentosus* (Fr.) Teng
= *Polyporus tomentosus* Fr.

COMMON NAME: Woolly Velvet Polypore.
MACROSCOPIC FEATURES: **Fruitbody** a circular to fan-shaped or irregular cap with a central to lateral stalk that usually grows on the ground. **Cap** 4–17 cm wide, sometimes lobed or fused, tough; **upper surface** dry, velvety or with matted hairs, wrinkled and uneven or sometimes smooth, tan to ochraceous or rusty brown; margin blunt, wavy to irregular when mature, usually paler than the disc. **Pore surface** buff at first, becoming grayish brown to dark brown; **pores** angular, 2–4 per mm. **Stalk** 2–5 cm long, 6–20 mm thick, sometimes rudimentary, velvety, ochraceous to dark rusty brown. **Flesh** up to 6 mm thick, tough, yellowish brown to rusty brown.
SPORE PRINT: Yellowish to pale brown.
MICROSCOPIC FEATURES: Spores 5–6 × 3–4 μm, elliptic, smooth, yellowish; setae present.

OCCURRENCE: Solitary, in groups, or fused clusters on the ground, duff, or decaying wood under conifers; summer–early winter.
EDIBILITY: Inedible.
REMARKS: The flesh stains black in KOH. *Phaeolus schweinitzii* (p. 498) is similar, but it has a larger, dull orange to ocher or rusty-brown cap, up to 26 cm wide, and a yellowish to greenish-yellow pore surface that stains darker brown when bruised or in age. The Shiny Cinnamon Polypore, *Coltricia cinnamomea* (p. 17), has a thin, circular cap, 1.2–5 cm wide, a central stalk, and grows on the ground. The cap is concentrically zoned, silky, shiny, bright reddish cinnamon to amber brown, with dark rusty-brown bands, and a thin, sharp margin. It has a dark reddish-brown to yellow-brown pore surface, small angular pores, and a thin, dark reddish-brown central stalk. It grows in groups, sometimes laterally fused together, on the ground in various habitats from summer through early winter. *Coltricia perennis* (p. 17) is larger, has a dull brownish-orange to pale cinnamon cap, and a brown, decurrent pore surface.

Onnia tomentosa

Osmoporus mexicanus (Mont.) Y. C. Dai & S. H. He

= *Gloeophyllum mexicanum* (Mont.) Ryvarden

MACROSCOPIC FEATURES: **Fruitbody** 3–10 cm wide, consisting of a broadly attached, stalkless cap and gill-like pore surface. **Cap** shelf-like and flattened, tough to woody; **upper surface** finely tomentose when young, especially along the margin, soon becoming glabrous and roughened, often shallowly furrowed, grayish at first, developing concentric zones of dull brown to rusty brown, gray, or blackish; margin acute, often undulating. **Pore surface** ochraceous to reddish brown; **pores** distinctly gill-like and daedaleoid, occasionally rounded near the margin. **Flesh** tough and leathery, rusty brown; odor and taste not distinctive.

SPORE PRINT: White.
MICROSCOPIC FEATURES: Spores 9–12.5 × 3.5–4 μm, cylindrical, slightly curved, smooth, hyaline.
OCCURRENCE: Solitary, in groups, or fused clusters on decaying conifer wood; year-round.
EDIBILITY: Inedible.
REMARKS: *Mexicanum* means "Mexico," a reference to where it was first collected and described. *Gloeophyllum sepiarium* (p. 475) has a bright yellowish-red to reddish-brown cap that becomes grayish or blackish in age, an orange-yellow to brownish-yellow or whitish margin, and thick, elongated, and labyrinthine pores.

Osmoporus mexicanus

Panellus pusillus (Pers. ex Lév.) Burds. & O. K. Mill.

= *Dictyopanus pusillus* (Pers. ex Lév.) Singer
= *Gloeoporus pusillus* Pers. ex Lév.

MACROSCOPIC FEATURES: **Fruitbody** a small cap with a subcentral to lateral stalk, attached to decaying hardwood. **Cap** 3–16 mm wide, convex, semicircular to kidney- or fan-shaped; **upper surface** moist or dry, glabrous or finely pubescent, smooth or finely wrinkled, sometimes with one or two very shallow concentric furrows, white to whitish when young, soon becoming pinkish buff to pale salmon; margin incurved, sometimes sulcate or splitting. **Pore surface** whitish to pale pinkish buff; **pores** angular, somewhat radially aligned, 2–5 per mm. **Stalk** up to 6 mm long, 1–2 mm thick, enlarged downward or nearly equal, finely pubescent, colored like the cap. **Flesh** thin, firm, white; odor and taste not distinctive.

SPORE PRINT: White.
MICROSCOPIC FEATURES: Spores 4.5–6 × 2–3 μm, oblong to ellipsoid, smooth, hyaline, amyloid.
OCCURRENCE: In dense groups and overlapping clusters on decaying hardwood branches, logs, stumps, and trunks; year-round.
EDIBILITY: Unknown.
REMARKS: Like *Panellus stipticus* (p. 385), which has gills on the lower cap surface, it is bioluminescent.

Panellus pusillus

Phaeolus schweinitzii (Fr.) Pat.

= *Polyporus schweinitzii* Fr.

COMMON NAMES: Dye Polypore, Velvet Top Fungus.

MACROSCOPIC FEATURES: **Fruitbody** a large, overlapping cluster of flattened, fused caps attached to the roots of trees. **Cap** 4–26 cm wide, circular to fan-shaped, tough; **upper surface** densely matted and wooly or hairy, faintly to distinctly zoned, dull orange to ocher at first, becoming rusty brown to dark brown in age; margin sharp, wavy, sometimes lobed, yellow orange to brownish orange. **Pore surface** decurrent, yellow to greenish yellow or orange and bruising brown when young, becoming yellowish brown to dark rusty brown in age; **pores** angular, 0.5–3 per mm. **Stalk** 2–7 cm long, up to 5 cm thick, enlarged upward, branched or unbranched, pale to dark brown. **Flesh** up to 3 cm thick, tough, yellowish brown to reddish brown; odor and taste not distinctive.

SPORE PRINT: Whitish.

MICROSCOPIC FEATURES: Spores 5–9 × 3–5 μm, elliptic, smooth, hyaline.

OCCURRENCE: Solitary, in overlapping clusters or rosettes on decaying conifer wood, especially pine, or on the ground attached to buried roots, also reported on cherry; year-round.

EDIBILITY: Inedible.

REMARKS: *Schweinitzii* honors German-American botanist and mycologist Lewis David de Schweinitz (1780–1834), considered by some to be the "Father of North American Mycology." *Onnia tomentosa* (p. 495) has a smaller, tan to ochraceous or rusty-brown cap and a buff to grayish-brown or dark brown pore surface. *Fuscoporia gilva* (p. 467) has a much smaller, dark reddish-brown cap with a yellow margin and usually grows on decaying hardwoods.

Phaeolus schweinitzii

Picipes badius (Pers.) Zmitr. & Kovalenko

= *Polyporus badius* (Pers.) Schwein.
= *Royoporus badius* A. B. De

COMMON NAME: Black-footed Polypore.
MACROSCOPIC FEATURES: **Fruitbody** consisting of a cap and stalk attached to wood. **Cap** 4–20 cm wide, circular to irregular, funnel-shaped or convex to slightly depressed, tough; **upper surface** glabrous, smooth, shiny or dull, pale reddish brown with a darker center when young, becoming reddish brown with a blackish brown center in age; margin incurved at first, thin, acute, wavy or lobed at maturity. **Pore surface** white to pale buff; **pores** circular to angular, 5–7 per mm. **Stalk** 1–3 cm long, 3–16 mm thick, nearly equal or tapered downward, central or eccentric, smooth, reddish brown near the apex, black below. **Flesh** up to 1.5 cm thick, corky, azonate, pale buff; odor and taste not distinctive.

SPORE PRINT: White.
MICROSCOPIC FEATURES: Spores 6–10 × 3–5 μm, cylindric, smooth, hyaline.
OCCURRENCE: Solitary, scattered, or in groups on decaying hardwoods; late spring–early winter.
EDIBILITY: Inedible.
REMARKS: *Badius* means "reddish brown."

Picipes badius

Postia caesia (Schrad.) P. Karst.

= *Oligoporus caesius* (Schrad.) Gilb. & Ryvarden
= *Tyromyces caesius* (Schrad.) Murrill

COMMON NAME: Blue Cheese Polypore.
MACROSCOPIC FEATURES: **Fruitbody** an annual, stalkless cap with soft flesh. **Cap** 2–8 cm wide, shelf-like, semicircular, broadly convex to somewhat flattened; **upper surface** tomentose to strigose, or sometimes glabrous, smooth, whitish, typically with bluish tints, sometimes bruising intensely blue; margin sharp. **Pore surface** whitish to pale gray, usually staining blue; **pores** angular, sometimes split or torn, 3–6 per mm. **Flesh** up to 1 cm thick, soft, spongy, watery when fresh, white, becoming yellowish or grayish in age; odor usually fragrant; taste not distinctive.

SPORE PRINT: Bluish.
MICROSCOPIC FEATURES: Spores 5.5–7.5 × 1–2 μm, cylindric to allantoid, smooth, hyaline.
OCCURRENCE: Solitary or in groups on conifers or hardwoods; summer-early winter.
EDIBILITY: Inedible.
REMARKS: *Niveoporofomes spraguei* (p. 494) has a whitish to ivory cap, usually with greenish-blue stains, and corky to tough flesh. *Postia fragilis* = *Oligoporus fragilis* (not illustrated) has a whitish to buff cap and pore surface that become reddish brown when bruised or on drying.

Postia caesia

Pseudofistulina radicata (Schwein.) Burds.

= *Fistulina radicata* (Schwein.) Schwein.

MACROSCOPIC FEATURES: **Fruitbody** an annual, rounded to kidney-shaped cap, usually with a long, radicating, lateral stalk. **Cap** 3–7.5 cm wide, rounded to kidney-shaped or irregularly lobed; **upper surface** densely tomentose, azonate, yellowish brown, darkening in age; margin acute. **Pore surface** white to cream-colored at first, becoming pinkish buff to ochraceous; **pores** circular, 5–7 per mm. **Stalk** 4–10 cm long, up to 1 cm thick, distinctly lateral, usually tapered downward, typically radicating, colored like the cap or darker, tomentose on the upper portion, sometimes whitish toward the base. **Flesh** up to 7 mm thick, fibrous-tough, white when fresh, becoming pale buff when dry; odor and taste not distinctive.

SPORE PRINT: White.

MICROSCOPIC FEATURES: Spores 3–4 × 2–3 μm, ovoid, smooth, hyaline.

OCCURRENCE: Solitary or scattered on the ground, typically attached to buried wood; late spring-early winter.

EDIBILITY: Inedible.

REMARKS: The Beefsteak Polypore, *Fistulina hepatica* (p. 17), has a much larger, 7–25 cm wide, reddish-orange to pinkish-red or dark red cap, a short lateral stalk, and reddish flesh with red sap. It has a whitish to pinkish-yellow pore surface that becomes reddish brown in age or when bruised and often exudes red sap when fresh. The pores are circular, 1–3 per mm, and the tubes are crowded but distinctly independent and not fused together (use a hand lens). Its flesh is dingy white to pinkish or reddish, marbled with darker and paler areas, and tastes sour to acidic. It grows on trunks and stumps of oaks during summer and fall.

Pseudofistulina radicata

Pseudoinonotus dryadeus (Pers.)
T. Wagner & M. Fisch.

= *Inonotus dryadeus* (Pers.) Murrill

COMMON NAME: Weeping Polypore.
MACROSCOPIC FEATURES: Fruitbody a stalk-less, shelf-like cap growing at the base of oak trees. **Cap** 13–36 cm wide, convex, fan- or top-shaped, sometimes rounded; **upper surface** smooth, azonate, becoming finely rimose in age, whitish when very young, soon buff to brown, typically exuding amber droplets when fresh; margin blunt, concolorous or ivory. **Pore surface** buff, becoming dark brown; **pores** circular to angular, 4–6 per mm. **Flesh** up to 15 cm thick, soft or tough, zonate, bright yellowish brown at first, becoming reddish brown in age, distinctly mottled when cut; odor and taste not distinctive.

SPORE PRINT: White.
MICROSCOPIC FEATURES: Spores 6–8 × 5–7 μm, subglobose, smooth, hyaline, thick-walled, dextrinoid; setae rare or frequent, ventricose, often hooked.
OCCURRENCE: Solitary, in groups, or overlapping clusters, usually at the base of oak trees, on stumps, or on the ground attached to buried roots; year-round.
EDIBILITY: Inedible.
REMARKS: *Dryadeus* refers to oak trees. A second illustration of this polypore is shown in the "Color Key to the Major Groups of Fungi" (p. 17).

Pseudoinonotus dryadeus

Rhodofomes cajanderi (P. Karst.) B. K. Cui, M. L. Han & Y. C. Dai

= *Fomes subroseus* (Weir) Overh.
= *Fomitopsis cajanderi* (P. Karst.) Kotl. & Pouzar

COMMON NAME: Rosy Polypore.
MACROSCOPIC FEATURES: Fruitbody a stalkless, shelf-like cap attached to wood. **Cap** 3–14(-20) cm wide, convex to nearly flat, semicircular to fan-shaped or irregular, tough, becoming corky to brittle when dry; **upper surface** appressed-fibrillose, smooth or somewhat roughened, typically faintly zonate, pinkish brown to reddish brown or grayish brown; margin fairly sharp, typically whitish when young. **Pore surface** rosy pink to pinkish brown; **pores** circular to angular, 3–5 per mm. **Flesh** tough, rosy pink, becoming pinkish brown in age; odor and taste not distinctive.

SPORE PRINT: White.
MICROSCOPIC FEATURES: Spores 4–7 × 1.5–2 μm, allantoid, smooth, hyaline.
OCCURRENCE: Solitary, scattered, or in clusters on decaying conifer wood, rarely on hardwood; year-round.
EDIBILITY: Inedible.
REMARKS: *Cajanderi* honors A. K. Cajander who first submitted a collection as an unknown species.

Rhodofomes cajanderi

Sarcodontia pachyodon (Pers.) Spirin

= *Spongipellis pachyodon* (Pers.) Kotl. &
Pouzar

COMMON NAME: Spongy Toothed Polypore.
MACROSCOPIC FEATURES: **Fruitbody** a leathery
to tough, spreading crust of stalkless, effused-
reflexed overlapping caps on wood. **Cap** 2–5
cm wide, fan-shaped, convex; **upper surface**
white to creamy white, becoming ochraceous
to brownish in age, azonate, nearly glabrous;
margin acute and somewhat incurved. **Pore
surface** white to creamy white, darkening in
age; **pores** gill-like to labyrinthine or poroid
near the margin, breaking up and forming
conspicuous flattened teeth at maturity; teeth
up to 1.5 cm long. **Flesh** 3–8 mm thick, leathery to tough, white to pale cream; odor and
taste not distinctive.
SPORE PRINT: White.
MICROSCOPIC FEATURES: Spores 5–7 × 5–6.5
μm, subglobose, thick-walled, smooth, hyaline.

OCCURRENCE: Solitary, in groups, or overlapping clusters on living hardwood trees, especially oak; year-round.
EDIBILITY: Inedible.
REMARKS: *Pachyodon* means "thick teeth," a reference to the pore surface. *Spongipellis unicolor*
(not illustrated) has whitish to pale buff caps
that become brownish or ochraceous tawny
in age, large circular to angular pores that
become somewhat daedaleoid at maturity but
do not form teeth, and larger, ovoid to ellipsoid spores that measure 7–9 × 6–7 μm. Also
compare with *Irpex lacteus* (p. 482), which has
smaller teeth. *Schizopora paradoxa* (p. 505)
forms a white to cream, spreading crust that
is flat or somewhat projecting and bracket-
like and darkens in age. It usually has small
nodules on the upper surface, tiny hairs on the
margin, and the creamy-white undersurface is
maze-like, with irregular and angular elongated pores that sometimes form teeth-like
projections.

Sarcodontia pachyodon

Schizopora paradoxa (Schrad.) Donk

= *Irpex paradoxus* (Schrad.) Fr.

COMMON NAMES: Split-pore Polypore, Creamy Maze Crust.

MACROSCOPIC FEATURES: **Fruitbody** a spreading crust with small nodules that is somewhat projecting and bracket-like when growing on vertical surfaces, and flat when growing on horizontal surfaces; **upper surface** dry, white to cream at first, darkening to brownish in age, tomentose along the margin; **flesh** thin, leathery, white to cream. **Pore surface** labyrinthine, creamy white at first, darkening to ochraceous yellow in age; **pores** 1–3 per mm, angular to elongated or irregular, often splitting and forming tooth-like projections.

SPORE PRINT: White.

MICROSCOPIC FEATURES: Spores 5–6.5 × 3.5–4 μm, ellipsoid, smooth, hyaline.

OCCURRENCE: Attached to decaying branches of hardwood trees, especially oak, beech, and American hornbeam; year-round.

EDIBILITY: Inedible.

REMARKS: *Irpex lacteus* (p. 482) is similar, but it forms rows of bracket-like caps that are tomentose and white to buff on the upper surface and whitish with tooth-like split pores on the lower surface.

Schizopora paradoxa

Tomophagus colossus (Fr.) Murrill

= *Ganoderma colossus* (Fr.) C. F. Baker

COMMON NAME: Elephant's Foot.
MACROSCOPIC FEATURES: **Fruitbody** a stalkless cap attached to wood. **Cap** up to 30 cm wide and long, up to 10 cm thick, semicircular to elongated or variously irregular, soft when fresh; **upper surface** glabrous, covered with a thin crust that is fairly soft and easily dented, somewhat glossy or dull, yellow to pale brown; margin blunt, whitish to yellow. **Pore surface** white to cream when fresh, ochraceous to pale brown when dry, **pores** angular to rounded, 2–4 per mm, fairly thick-walled; tubes concolorous with pore surface, pale brown, up to 3 cm deep. **Flesh** up to 10 cm thick, creamy white to pale buff, soft, fibrous-spongy, azonate, homogeneous.

SPORE PRINT: Brown.
MICROSCOPIC FEATURES: Spores 14–19 × 8–12 μm, ellipsoid to ovoid, truncate, echinulate, pale brown.
OCCURRENCE: Solitary or in groups on decaying wood or woodchips of various hardwoods, also reported on Southern hackberry and on Australian pine woodchips; late fall–winter.
EDIBILITY: Unknown.
REMARKS: A rare pantropical species that also occurs in Florida. It is easy to recognize because of the pale flesh with a thin, yellow to pale brown crust.

Tomophagus colossus

Trametes cinnabarina (Jacq.) Fr.

= *Hapalopilus cinnabarinus* (Jacq.) P. Karst.
= *Polyporus cinnabarinus* (Jacq.) Fr.
= *Pycnoporus cinnabarinus* (Jacq.) P. Karst.

COMMON NAME: Cinnabar-red Polypore.
MACROSCOPIC FEATURES: **Fruitbody** a stalk-less cap attached to wood. **Cap** 3–14 cm wide, up to 2 cm thick, convex to nearly flat, semicircular to kidney-shaped, tough; **upper surface** dry, azonate, typically uneven and finely roughened or wrinkled but occasionally nearly smooth, bright or dull reddish orange, sometimes mixed with yellow or brownish tints in age; margin acute or rounded. **Pore surface** pale or dark orange red; **pores** circular to angular or sometimes elongated, 2–4 per mm. **Flesh** up to 1.5 cm thick, corky or tough, reddish orange; odor and taste not distinctive.

SPORE PRINT: White.
MICROSCOPIC FEATURES: Spores 4.5–8 × 2.5–4 μm, cylindric to slightly allantoid, smooth, hyaline.
OCCURRENCE: Solitary, in groups, or overlapping clusters on decaying hardwoods, rarely on conifers; year-round.
EDIBILITY: Inedible.
REMARKS: *Cinnabarina* means "reddish orange to bright brick red." The flesh stains black with KOH. The Blood-red Polypore, *Pycnoporus sanguineus* (p. 17), has a smaller and thinner cap, typically less than 5 mm thick, a dark red pore surface, grows exclusively on hardwoods, especially oak, and its spores measure 5–6 × 2–2.5 μm.

Trametes cinnabarina

Trametes gibbosa (Pers.) Fr.

= *Daedalea gibbosa* (Pers.) Pers.

COMMON NAME: Lumpy Bracket.
MACROSCOPIC FEATURES: **Fruitbody** a shelf-like cap attached to wood. **Cap** 5–20 cm wide, up to 3 cm thick, semicircular to fan- or kidney-shaped, corky and flexible when fresh, becoming more rigid when dry; **upper surface** typically bumpy to warted and uneven, distinctly velvety or fuzzy, especially when observed with a hand lens, often concentrically zoned or sulcate, sometimes nearly smooth near the margin, white to cream, buff, or very pale ochraceous, occasionally developing gray tints as it ages, usually green from the base outward due to algae; margin thin, acute, even or lobed, whitish or brownish, usually thickened at the point of attachment. **Pore surface** whitish to cream-colored, becoming grayish ocher in age; **pores** radially elongated and sometimes labyrinthine or nearly gill-like, especially near the margin. **Stalk** typically absent, sometimes short and stubby, up to 3 cm long, concolorous with the cap. **Flesh** up to 1.5 cm thick, tough to woody, white to pale cream.

SPORE PRINT: White.
MICROSCOPIC FEATURES: Spores 4–5.5 × 2–2.5 µm, elliptic-cylindric, smooth, hyaline.
OCCURRENCE: Solitary, scattered, or in groups on decaying hardwoods; year-round.
EDIBILITY: Inedible.
REMARKS: *Trametes aesculi = Trametes elegans* (not illustrated) is very similar, but its upper cap surface is typically finely tomentose to nearly glabrous, its pore surface is highly variable, partly poroid, partly sinuous-daedaleoid, and sometimes partly lamellate, and it has larger spores that measure 5–7 × 2–3 µm. *Leiotrametes lactinea* (p. 487) typically has a thicker margin, at least when young, and smaller pores, 2–3 per mm, that are more uniformly round to angular. *Trametes cubensis* (not illustrated), which may not occur in North America, is similar, but it has a white to cream or tan cap that becomes reddish to bay from the base outward in age. The cap surface is azonate or irregularly sulcate, and the margin is sharp to slightly rounded. It has very small pores, 5–7 per mm, that are almost invisible to the naked eye and larger spores that measure 7–9.5 × 3–3.5 µm.

Trametes gibbosa

Trametes nivosa (Berk.) Murrill

= *Fomitopsis nivosa* (Berk.) Gilb. & Ryvarden
= *Polyporus nivosus* Berk.

MACROSCOPIC FEATURES: **Fruitbody** consisting of a stalkless cap attached to wood. **Cap** 3–16 cm wide, shelf-like, fan-shaped to semicircular, fibrous when moist and fresh, woody when dry; **upper surface** white at first, becoming pale brown, and eventually developing a dark, resinous, cuticular layer that spreads from the base outward in older specimens, glabrous, slightly roughened to nearly smooth, azonate; margin acute. **Pore surface** whitish at first, becoming brownish gray to grayish brown, usually glancing; **pores** circular to angular, 6–8 per mm. **Flesh** up to 2 cm thick, zonate, whitish to cream, tough to woody; odor and taste not distinctive.

SPORE PRINT: White.
MICROSCOPIC FEATURES: Spores 6–9 × 2–3 μm, cylindrical, smooth, hyaline.
OCCURRENCE: Solitary, scattered, or in overlapping clusters on hardwood trees; year-round.
EDIBILITY: Inedible.
REMARKS: The formation of a dark, resinous, cuticular layer in older specimens is a key identifying feature.

Trametes nivosa

Trametes versicolor (L.) Lloyd

= *Polyporus versicolor* (L.) Fr.

COMMON NAME: Turkey-tail.

MACROSCOPIC FEATURES: **Fruitbody** a stalkless cap, typically growing in clusters on decaying wood. **Cap** 2–10 cm wide, fan- to kidney-shaped, thin, tough, flattened, sometimes laterally fused and forming extensive rows; **upper surface** silky to velvety, with conspicuous concentric zones of various colors, often with shades of orange, green, blue, brown, or gray; margin thin, sharp, wavy, sometimes folded or lobed. **Pore surface** white to grayish; **pores** circular to angular, 3–5 per mm. **Flesh** up to 3 mm thick, tough, white to creamy white; odor and taste not distinctive.

SPORE PRINT: White.

MICROSCOPIC FEATURES: Spores 5–6 × 1.5–2 μm, cylindric to allantoid, smooth, hyaline.

OCCURRENCE: Solitary, in groups, overlapping clusters, rows, or rosettes on wood; year-round.

EDIBILITY: Inedible.

REMARKS: *Versicolor* means "of various colors." Molecular studies suggest that this is a massive complex of very similar taxa that are difficult to differentiate. *Trametes hirsuta* (not illustrated) has a conspicuously hairy cap, and its pore surface becomes grayish in age. *Trametes pubescens* (not illustrated) has a finely hairy to smooth, creamy-white to yellowish-buff, azonate or faintly zoned cap. *Stereum* species lack pores on the lower surface.

Trametes versicolor

Trametes villosa (Sw.) Kreisel

= *Polyporus villosus* (Sw.) Fr.

MACROSCOPIC FEATURES: **Fruitbody** a stalk-less, shelf-like or sometimes effused-reflexed cap attached to wood. **Cap** up to 7 cm wide and 1–2 mm thick, semicircular to fan-shaped, often fused laterally, flexible; **upper surface** covered with coarse, elongated, somewhat flattened hairs, distinctly zonate, white to grayish or brown; margin thin, wavy or lobed. **Pore surface** white to cream, becoming brownish in age; **pores** angular, thin-walled, 1–3 per mm, often breaking up and becoming tooth-like. **Flesh** 1.5–3 mm thick, tough, flexible, white; odor and taste not distinctive.

SPORE PRINT: White.

MICROSCOPIC FEATURES: Spores 5.5–8.5 × 2.5–3.5 µm, cylindric to allantoid, smooth, hyaline.

OCCURRENCE: In groups or clusters on decaying conifer or hardwoods; year-round.

EDIBILITY: Inedible.

REMARKS: *Villosa* means "hairy or shaggy." It is usually easy to recognize because of the thin, flexible fruitbody with a hairy cap and large pores that become tooth-like in age. *Trametes hirsuta* (not illustrated) has thicker and larger caps with smaller pores. Compare with *Trametopsis cervina* (p. 512), which is larger, has thicker flesh, and is hard and rigid.

Trametes villosa

Trametopsis cervina (Schwein.) Tomšovský

= *Trametes cervina* (Schwein.) Bres.

MACROSCOPIC FEATURES: **Fruitbody** a stalk-less cap, 3–15 cm wide, attached to wood. **Cap** shell- to fan- or hoof-shaped, often laterally fused, leathery to stiff; margin uneven and wavy; **upper surface** covered with short, coarse hairs, distinctly to faintly zoned or sometimes azonate; zones white to pinkish buff, pinkish cinnamon, and darker cinnamon. **Pore surface** white at first, becoming buff then brownish in age; **pores** angular to irregular when young, becoming conspicuously labyrinthine, then breaking up and becoming tooth-like, 1–3 per mm. **Flesh** up to 1.5 cm thick, fibrous, tough, hard and rigid, white to buff; odor and taste not distinctive.

SPORE PRINT: Whitish.

MICROSCOPIC FEATURES: Spores 7–10 × 2–3 μm, elliptic to slightly allantoid, smooth, hyaline.

OCCURRENCE: Typically in large overlapping clusters on decaying hardwood or, rarely, on conifers; year-round.

EDIBILITY: Inedible.

REMARKS: *Cervina* means "pertaining to deer," a reference to the colors of this polypore. Compare with *Trametes villosa* (p. 511), which is smaller, has thinner flesh, and is flexible.

Trametopsis cervina

Trichaptum biforme (Fr.) Ryvarden

= *Polyporus biformis* Fr.

COMMON NAME: Violet Toothed Polypore.
MACROSCOPIC FEATURES: **Fruitbody** a cluster of stalkless, overlapping, shelf-like caps attached to wood. **Cap** 2–6 cm wide, up to 2 mm thick, semicircular to kidney- or fan-shaped, convex to nearly flat, flexible or stiff; **upper surface** distinctly zonate and variously colored white to grayish, reddish brown, bluish, etc., sometimes green when covered with algae, especially on older specimens; margin thin, wavy, typically violet. **Pore surface** violet to purple brown, sometimes fading to buff; **pores** angular, 2–5 per mm, splitting and becoming tooth-like or jagged in age. **Flesh** up to 1.5 mm thick, tough, white to pale buff.
SPORE PRINT: White.
MICROSCOPIC FEATURES: Spores 5–8 × 2–2.5 μm, cylindric, smooth, hyaline.
OCCURRENCE: In overlapping clusters on decaying hardwood; year-round.

EDIBILITY: Inedible.
REMARKS: The upper surface, especially when colonized by green algae, may be parasitized by Fairy Pins, fruitbodies of *Phaeocalicium polyporaeum* (not illustrated) that resemble dark olive-brown to blackish, miniature matchsticks (use a hand lens). *Trichaptum abietinum* (not illustrated) has a much smaller cap, rarely more than 1.5 cm wide, with whitish hairs, pores that may be split but do not break up to form teeth, and it grows on conifer wood. *Trichaptum sector* (not illustrated) has a semicircular to fan-shaped cap that is often fused laterally. The cap upper surface is white to ochraceous buff. It has a gray or dark purplish-brown to almost black pore surface and angular pores, 3–6 per mm, that often become torn or tooth-like when mature. It grows singly or in overlapping groups on hardwoods year-round.

Trichaptum biforme

Puffballs, Earthballs, Earthstars, and Similar Fungi

Fruitbodies in this group are rounded, oval, pear- to turban-shaped or star-shaped. They are mostly stalkless but sometimes have a short stalk or stalk-like base. The interior spore mass is often white when young and immature but may be orange to reddish or black. The mature spore mass often becomes yellow, purple, brown, or black and powdery. They grow on the ground, underground, or on wood. If you cannot identify your unknown mushroom in this section, try comparing it to the species listed in the Truffles and Other Hypogeous Fungi group.

Astraeus morganii Phosri, Watling & M. P. Martin

COMMON NAME: Barometer Earthstar.
MACROSCOPIC FEATURES: **Fruitbody** up to 9 cm wide and 1–2.5 cm high when fully expanded, consisting of a rounded peridium and star-like rays. **Peridium** nearly round or somewhat flattened, finely roughened, with one, irregular, pore-like mouth, whitish to grayish or grayish brown. **Spore mass** white at first, becoming brown and powdery at maturity. **Rays** 6–12, hygroscopic, up to 5 cm long, yellow brown to reddish brown or grayish to nearly black; inner surface often rimose.

MICROSCOPIC FEATURES: Spores 7.5–10 μm, globose, distinctly tuberculate, brown.
OCCURRENCE: Solitary, scattered, or in groups on sandy soil; year-round.
EDIBILITY: Inedible.
REMARKS: American collections of this taxon have traditionally been called *Astraeus hygrometricus*, which is a European species. *Geastrum arenarium* (p. 523), is similar, but its fruitbody is smaller, the inner surface of the rays is not rimose, and it has much smaller spores that measure 3–4 μm.

Astraeus morganii

Bovista pusilla (Batsch) Pers.

= *Lycoperdon pusillum* Batsch

MACROSCOPIC FEATURES: **Fruitbody** 6–15 mm, rarely up to 20 mm wide, consisting of a peridium with a small, pinched, cord-like rooting base. **Peridium** nearly round or somewhat flattened, forming a small apical pore at maturity, covered with a fine fibrous flocculence that collapses and separates into very small patches or becomes powdery, white at first, becoming dull olivaceous yellow at maturity, and often dark brown in age. **Spore mass** filling the entire peridium, white when young, becoming yellow to greenish yellow, finally brown and powdery at maturity.

MICROSCOPIC FEATURES: Spores 3.2–4.3 µm, globose, smooth or finely tuberculate, with a very short pedicel, often with one large oil drop, brownish.

OCCURRENCE: Scattered or in groups in cemeteries, lawns, fields, yards, and other open grassy areas; year-round.

EDIBILITY: Unknown.

REMARKS: *Pusilla* means "very little," an appropriate name for this easily overlooked puffball. The fruitbody of *Arachnion album* (not illustrated) is 5–15 mm wide, irregularly globose to subglobose, and tapered to a point of attachment where rhizomorphs are present. The peridium is smooth and white at first and becomes areolate and yellowish and breaks into fragments, exposing peridioles at maturity. It has a white spore mass that fills the entire peridium when young and becomes grayish to brownish and powdery at maturity. The spores measure 4.5–6 × 3.5–5 µm, are short-elliptic to subglobose with a short pedicel, thick-walled, and smooth. It grows on soil in grassy areas, in flower beds, on disturbed ground, along paths, or under hardwoods. The Acorn Puffball or Sand Case Puffball, *Disciseda candida* (not illustrated), is similar, but it lacks the distinctive peridioles, and its base is coated with a sand layer, giving it an acorn-like appearance. *Bovista acuminata* (not illustrated) is also similar, but it lacks the distinctive peridioles, and it has a sharply-pointed pore mouth.

Bovista pusilla

Calostoma cinnabarinum Desv.

COMMON NAMES: Hot Lips, Red Slimy-stalked Puffball.

MACROSCOPIC FEATURES: **Fruitbody** with an outer and inner peridium supported by a thick, short stalk. **Peridium** 1–2 cm wide and high, oval to nearly globose, sometimes collapsed; **outer peridium** thick, translucent, gelatinous, with small, orange-red seed-like pieces; **inner peridium** smooth, thin-walled, bright reddish orange, fading to orange or orange yellow in age, with an irregular slit-like mouth surrounded by elevated bright-red ridges. **Spore mass** white at first, becoming buff and powdery at maturity. **Stalk** 1.5–4 cm long, 1–2 cm thick, nearly equal, spongy, coarsely reticulate and pitted, reddish orange to pale reddish brown, covered with a thick gelatinous layer coated with debris.

MICROSCOPIC FEATURES: Spores 14–22 × 6–9 μm, oblong-elliptic, pitted, hyaline.

OCCURRENCE: Solitary, scattered, or in groups on the ground under hardwoods, especially oak, or in mixed woods, often buried up to the peridium; summer–winter.

EDIBILITY: Inedible.

REMARKS: *Cinnabarinum* means "bright red tinted with orange." *Calostoma lutescens* (p. 18) is very similar, but the inner peridium is yellow. *Calostoma ravenelii* (p. 18) is also similar, but it has a scurfy, grayish to straw-colored outer peridium that lacks a gelatinous layer in all stages. These are mycorrhizal species, usually with hardwoods, and while not obvious from their appearance, they are related to *Pisolithus* and *Scleroderma*.

Calostoma cinnabarinum

Calvatia craniiformis (Schwein.) Fr.

COMMON NAME: Skull-shaped Puffball.
MACROSCOPIC FEATURES: **Fruitbody** up to 20 cm high and wide, consisting of a peridium with a conspicuous sterile base, attached to the ground by white rhizomorphs. **Peridium** skull- to pear-shaped or somewhat rounded, typically furrowed or scalloped over the top portion but sometimes nearly smooth, glabrous at first, cracking into irregular patches as it matures, white at first, becoming grayish to pale tan in age. **Spore mass** white and firm when young, becoming yellow to greenish yellow, and finally dingy yellow brown to olivebrown and powdery at maturity. **Sterile base** large, occupying most of the lower third of the fruitbody, chambered, white at first, becoming yellow brown, and finally dark brown in age.

MICROSCOPIC FEATURES: Spores 2.5–3.5 μm, globose, nearly smooth or with minute spines, with a very short pedicel, yellowish.
OCCURRENCE: Solitary, scattered, or in groups in grassy areas or in woodlands; summer–fall.
EDIBILITY: Edible when the spore mass is white. Some individuals have experienced gastrointestinal upset after eating this puffball when the spore mass is yellow or brown.
REMARKS: *Craniiformis* means "skull-shaped." *Calvatia cyathiformis* (p. 519), is similar, but it has a smaller cup-shaped sterile base, its mature spore mass is dull purple to purple brown at maturity, and it has larger spores that measure 4–7 μm.

Calvatia craniiformis

Calvatia cyathiformis (Bosc) Morgan

= *Lycoperdon cyathiforme* Bosc

COMMON NAME: Purple-spored Puffball.

MACROSCOPIC FEATURES: **Fruitbody** up to 20 cm high and wide, consisting of a peridium with a conspicuous sterile base, attached to the ground by white rhizomorphs. **Peridium** round to oval at first, becoming pear- to top-shaped or irregular in age, smooth and glabrous at first, becoming areolate on the upper portion, and breaking into thin, irregular patches that flake off with age, white to pale brown. **Spore mass** white and firm when young, becoming yellowish, and finally dull purple to purple brown and powdery at maturity. **Sterile base** whitish at first, becoming dingy yellow or brownish, and finally dark purple in age, cup-shaped and persisting after the spores have been dispersed.

MICROSCOPIC FEATURES: Spores 4–7 μm, globose, weakly echinulate or tuberculate or nearly smooth, pale lilac.

OCCURRENCE: Solitary, scattered, in groups, or fairy rings on the ground in grassy areas and woodland edges; summer–fall.

EDIBILITY: Edible when the spore mass is white. Some individuals have experienced gastrointestinal upset after eating this puffball when the spore mass is yellow to purple brown.

REMARKS: *Cyathiformis* means "cup-shaped," a reference to its sterile base. *Calvatia craniiformis* (p. 518), is similar, but it has a larger sterile base, its spore mass is yellow brown at maturity, and it has smaller spores that measure 2.5–3.5 μm.

Calvatia cyathiformis

Calvatia rubroflava (Cragin) Lloyd

COMMON NAME: Orange-staining Puffball.

MACROSCOPIC FEATURES: **Fruitbody** 3–12 cm wide, 2–8 cm high, nearly round to pear-shaped, often somewhat flattened at the apex, with a large sterile base, and typically with white rhizomorphs. **Peridium** nearly white with pinkish or lavender tints when young, staining yellow to bright yellow or orange when bruised, cut, or rubbed, becoming ochraceous to bay brown in age, smooth to finely areolate. **Spore mass** white with minute cavities when young, becoming bright yellow orange to dull orange and powdery in age, with a strong and unpleasant odor at maturity.

MICROSCOPIC FEATURES: Spores 3–4 μm, globose, minutely warted, olive-brown.

OCCURRENCE: Scattered or in groups on the ground in gardens, grassy areas, and woodlands; summer–early winter.

EDIBILITY: Edible when the spore mass is white.

REMARKS: The bright yellow to orange staining of the peridium is a diagnostic feature.

Calvatia rubroflava

Chlorophyllum agaricoides (Czern.) Vellinga

= *Endoptychum agaricoides* Czern.

COMMON NAME: Puffball Agaric.
MACROSCOPIC FEATURES: **Fruitbody** a large, oval to turban-shaped mushroom, with a whitish to tan or brownish peridium and distorted, unexposed, white gills that become brown at maturity. **Peridium** 2–7 cm wide, 2.5–10 cm high, oval to turban-shaped or sometimes rounded; surface smooth or finely scaly, whitish at first, becoming tan to brownish at maturity. **Spore mass** fleshy, whitish at first, becoming brown at maturity; odor fragrant or not distinctive when fresh; taste sweet or nutty when fresh. **Stalk** whitish and internal, sometimes extending slightly below the peridium, attached to the ground by a cord.

MICROSCOPIC FEATURES: Spores 6–9 × 5–7 μm, elliptic, smooth, pale brown.
OCCURRENCE: Solitary, scattered, or in groups on the ground or among mosses and grasses in pastures, lawns, gardens, and waste areas; spring–early winter.
EDIBILITY: Edible when young and fresh.
REMARKS: Spores are dispersed when the fruitbody disintegrates or when animals consume them. Compare with *Macowanites arenicola* (p. 365).

Chlorophyllum agaricoides

Chorioactis geaster (Peck) Kupfer ex Eckblad

= *Urnula geaster* Peck

COMMON NAMES: Devil's Cigar, Texas Star.

MACROSCOPIC FEATURES: **Fruitbody** up to 10 cm high and 5 cm wide, elongated, hollow, dark brown, cigar- or spindle-shaped, splitting open at its apex and forming 3–6 earthstar-like rays and a supporting stalk; **outer surface** dry, velvety, covered with a dense coat of appressed dark brownish hairs; **inner surface** moist or dry, smooth, white or whitish at first, becoming yellowish then butterscotch-colored at maturity; **flesh** thick, fibrous-tough to leathery, white.

MICROSCOPIC FEATURES: Asci cylindric or subcylindric, 600–700 × 20–23 μm; spores uniseriate, 50–70 × 12–16 μm, fusoid, often unequal-sided and somewhat allantoid, hyaline or subhyaline; paraphyses strongly thickened above.

OCCURRENCE: Solitary, scattered, or more typically in groups or clusters on the ground, attached to decaying cedar elm (*Ulmus crassifolia*) stumps; fall.

EDIBILITY: Inedible.

REMARKS: The periodic release of spores is often accompanied by a hiss that is audible from several feet away. This rare fungus is only known from Texas and Japan. The Japanese common name for it is Kirinomitake. This taxon is closely related to *Wolfina*.

Chorioactis geaster

Geastrum arenarium Lloyd

= *Geaster arenarius* Lloyd

MACROSCOPIC FEATURES: **Fruitbody** up to 6 cm high and wide when fully expanded, consisting of a rounded peridium and star-like rays. **Peridium** 1.2–2.2 cm high and wide, rounded or somewhat flattened, glabrous, tan to pale grayish or whitish, with a single, apical, conical pore mouth. **Spore mass** firm and whitish at first, becoming brown and powdery at maturity. **Rays** 5–10, hygroscopic, up to 2.5 cm long, acute, pale brown to darker reddish brown or grayish brown, usually coated with a thin layer of sand; inner surface smooth, not rimose.

MICROSCOPIC FEATURES: Spores 3–4 μm, globose, slightly roughened, brownish.
OCCURRENCE: Scattered or in groups in sandy soil in various habitats, usually under hardwoods, especially oaks; year-round.
EDIBILITY: Inedible.
REMARKS: *Arenarium* means "in sandy areas." *Astraeus morganii* (p. 515), is similar, but its fruitbody is larger, the inner surface of the rays is rimose, and it has much larger spores that measure 7–11 μm.

Geastrum arenarium

Geastrum fimbriatum Fr.

= *Geastrum sessile* (Sowerby) Pouzar

COMMON NAME: Fringed Earthstar.
MACROSCOPIC FEATURES: **Fruitbody** up to 4
cm wide when fully expanded, consisting of a
peridium and star-like rays. **Peridium** up to
1.5 cm high and wide, subglobose, glabrous,
dull yellowish to brownish, with a single,
apical, conical pore mouth that is fringed
with tiny hairs, lacking a demarcation zone
or depression. **Spore mass** firm and white at
first, becoming brown to purplish brown and
powdery at maturity. **Rays** 7–11, up to 2 cm
long, bent backward, not hygroscopic, cream-
colored, sometimes with a pinkish tint; inner
surface smooth, not rimose.
MICROSCOPIC FEATURES: Spores 3–4 μm, globose, finely warted, pale brown.
OCCURRENCE: Scattered or in groups on the
ground in conifer or mixed conifer and hardwood forests; summer–early winter.

EDIBILITY: Inedible.
REMARKS: *Fimbriatum* means "fringed with
tiny hairs," a reference to the pore mouth.
Geastrum saccatum (p. 18) is very similar, but
its pore mouth is surrounded by a conspicuous disc-like demarcation zone. The fruitbody of the Collared Earthstar, *Geastrum
triplex* (p. 18), is 1–4.5 cm high and 7–10 cm
wide when fully expanded and consists of
a rounded peridium and star-like rays. The
peridium is 2–3 cm wide, nearly round or
somewhat flattened, and sits in a saucer-
shaped to bowl-like collar. It is whitish at first,
then brownish to grayish as it matures. The
spore mass is firm and white when young and
becomes dark brown and powdery at maturity. It has 4–8 rays that are not hygroscopic
and grows on the ground with hardwoods or
among woodchips during summer through
early winter.

Geastrum fimbriatum

Lycoperdon americanum Demoulin

COMMON NAME: Spiny Puffball.

MACROSCOPIC FEATURES: **Fruitbody** consisting of a peridium and spore mass. **Peridium** 2–5 cm wide and high, nearly round or somewhat flattened, white at first, becoming brownish in age, coated with clusters of long white spines with fused tips that turn brown in age and fall off, leaving a net-like pattern on the surface; pore mouth opens at maturity. **Spore mass** firm, white at first, becoming powdery and purple brown.

MICROSCOPIC FEATURES: Spores 4–6 μm, globose, warted, purple brown.

OCCURRENCE: Scattered or in groups, often among leaves and debris in woodlands; late spring–fall.

EDIBILITY: Edible when the spore mass is white.

REMARKS: The fruitbody of *Lycoperdon pulcherrimum* (not illustrated) is 1.5–3.5 cm high, 2–4 cm wide, and consists of a peridium with a slender base. The white peridium also has spines that are fused at their tips, but they do not darken in age and do not leave marks on the brown inner peridium when they fall away.

Lycoperdon americanum

Lycoperdon marginatum Vittad.

COMMON NAME: Peeling Puffball.

MACROSCOPIC FEATURES: **Fruitbody** 1–5 cm wide, consisting of a peridium and a some-what tapered, sterile, stalk-like base. **Peridium** subglobose at first, becoming slightly flattened to pear-shaped at maturity, white, and covered with short spines or warts that break off in irregular sheets, exposing the nearly smooth, pale to dark olive-brown or reddish-brown inner surface, with a single apical pore mouth. **Spore mass** firm and white at first, becoming olive brown to grayish brown and powdery at maturity.

MICROSCOPIC FEATURES: Spores 3.5–4.5 μm, globose, minutely punctate to nearly smooth, sometimes with a short pedicel, pale brown.

OCCURRENCE: Solitary, scattered, or in groups on the ground, usually in mixed oak and pine woods or on nutrient poor soil; summer–early winter.

EDIBILITY: Unknown.

REMARKS: Other white puffballs may be similar, but their spines or warts do not break off in sheets.

Lycoperdon marginatum

Lycoperdon perlatum Pers.

= *Lycoperdon gemmatum* Batsch

COMMON NAMES: Gem-studded Puffball, Devil's Snuffbox.

MACROSCOPIC FEATURES: **Fruitbody** 2.5–8 cm high, 2–6.5 cm wide, consisting of a peridium with a large, sterile, stalk-like base. **Peridium** pear- to turban-shaped, covered with short spines and granules that easily break off, white at first, becoming pale brown then yellow brown in age, with a rounded, apical pore mouth at maturity. **Spore mass** firm and white when young, becoming yellow to olive, and finally olive brown and powdery at maturity.

MICROSCOPIC FEATURES: Spores 3.5–4.5 μm, globose, weakly echinulate, pale brown.

OCCURRENCE: Solitary, scattered, or in clusters on the ground under conifers or hardwoods, sometimes on mulch or sawdust piles; summer–early winter.

EDIBILITY: Edible when the spore mass is white.

REMARKS: *Perlatum* means "widespread," a reference to the distribution of this common puffball. The fruitbody of *Lycoperdon mole* (not illustrated) is 2.5–7 cm high, 2–6 cm wide, and consists of a peridium and a distinctive, sterile, stalk-like base. The peridium is rounded to pear- or top-shaped, dull white to yellow brown or grayish brown, granular and covered by short, soft, grayish-brown spines at first, and becomes smooth after the spines fall off. It has globose, coarsely warted, light brown spores that measure 4–6 μm, and it grows with conifers or hardwoods from summer through early winter. The Lawn Puffbowl, *Lycoperdon pratense* = *Vascellum pratense* (not illustrated), has a turban- to pear-shaped fruitbody with a rounded to somewhat depressed center and a sterile stalk base. It has a white to pale-yellowish peridium that is covered with granules and fine spines that soon wear away, exposing a shiny brownish inner peridium. A pore mouth is formed at maturity which disintegrates down to a sterile base, causing the fruitbody to appear bowl-like.

Lycoperdon perlatum

Lycoperdon pyriforme Schaeff.

COMMON NAME: Pear-shaped Puffball.
MACROSCOPIC FEATURES: **Fruitbody** 2–5
cm high, 1.5–4.5 cm wide, consisting of a
peridium with a compressed, sterile stalk-like
base. **Peridium** whitish at first, becoming reddish brown to yellow brown with tiny warts
and granules or spines, forming an apical pore
mouth at maturity; lower portion tapered
downward. **Spore mass** firm and white at
first, becoming greenish yellow, and finally
dark olive brown and powdery at maturity.
MICROSCOPIC FEATURES: Spores 3–4.5 μm,
globose, smooth, pale brown.

OCCURRENCE: Scattered or in dense clusters
on decaying wood, sawdust, woodchips, and
organic debris; year-round.
EDIBILITY: Edible when the spore mass is
white.
REMARKS: *Pyriforme* means "pear-shaped." The
Common Stalked Puffball, *Tulostoma brumale*
(p. 18), has a small peridium, up to 2 cm wide,
with a pore-like mouth, supported by a slender stalk up to 5 cm long. It grows on sandy
soil, often in nutrient-poor habitats, from fall
through early winter.

Lycoperdon pyriforme

Lycoperdon radicatum Durieu & Mont.

= *Bovistella radicata* (Durieu & Mont.) Pat.

MACROSCOPIC FEATURES: **Fruitbody** 2.5–9 cm wide, consisting of a peridium with a sterile basal cup, attached to the ground by a rooting base. **Peridium** subglobose to broadly top-shaped, covered overall at first by white granular material and soft, pyramidal warts that are often fused at their tips to form fascicles that wear away irregularly to expose a thin, dull orange-yellow, papery inner layer, which splits open by an apical pore or slit that eventually enlarges, exposing most of the spore mass when mature. **Sterile base** well-developed, cup-like, occupying most of the narrowed basal portion of the fruitbody, white at first, becoming orange yellow at maturity. **Spore mass** white and spongy when young, becoming yellowish to olive, and finally yellow brown and powdery.

MICROSCOPIC FEATURES: Spores 4–5 × 3.5–4.5 µm, oval, smooth, hyaline, with one large oil drop, and a hyaline pedicel 6–12 µm long.

OCCURRENCE: Scattered or in groups on soil in open areas under oaks and pines; year-round.

EDIBILITY: Unknown.

REMARKS: *Radicatum* means "rooting," a reference to the base of the peridium.

Lycoperdon radicatum

Pisolithus arhizus (Scop.) Rauschert

= *Pisolithus tinctorius* Coker & Couch

COMMON NAME: Dye-maker's False Puffball.
MACROSCOPIC FEATURES: **Fruitbody** 5–15(25) cm high, 3.5–12 cm wide, consisting of a peridium, spore mass, and a stalk-like rooting base. **Peridium** tapered downward, pear-shaped to oval or club-shaped, thin, smooth, shiny, dingy yellow to yellow brown, splitting irregularly at maturity and exposing numerous tiny yellowish to brownish peridioles embedded in a black gelatinous matrix. **Spore mass** produced by the disintegrating peridioles, reddish brown to dark brown and powdery at maturity.

MICROSCOPIC FEATURES: Spores 7–12 µm, globose, echinulate, brownish.
OCCURRENCE: Solitary, scattered, or in groups in sandy soil, usually under oak and pine, often with Prickly Pear cacti, typically partially buried; summer–early winter.
EDIBILITY: Inedible.
REMARKS: It is sometimes used to dye silk and wool various shades of brown or black.

Pisolithus arhizus

Rhopalogaster transversarius (Bosc) J. R. Johnst.

= *Lycoperdon transversarium* Bosc

MACROSCOPIC FEATURES: **Fruitbody** 3–9.5 cm high, 1.5–4.5 cm wide, club-shaped to oval, consisting of a peridium, a narrowed stalk with several basal rhizomorphs, and a central columella. **Peridium** granular-roughened to scurfy, with scattered, matted brownish fibers when young, becoming nearly smooth in age, pale reddish brown to yellow brown or olive brown, becoming pale brownish orange as the ground color is exposed, rupturing irregularly and exposing the spore mass at maturity. **Columella** central, extending upward from the base of the stalk throughout most of the peridium, extensively branching crosswise, whitish. **Spore mass** distinctly chambered like a honeycomb, watery-gelatinous, meat-like, conspicuously marbled or veined, dull red to reddish brown at first, slowly staining blackish when exposed, becoming olive brown to darker brown and powdery in age.

MICROSCOPIC FEATURES: Spores 5.5–7.5 × 3–4.5 µm, elliptic, smooth, pale brown.

OCCURRENCE: Solitary, scattered, or in groups on decaying organic matter, including leaf litter, mulch, or woodchips, in oak and pine woods; summer-winter.

EDIBILITY: Unknown.

REMARKS: *Transversarius* means "lying across or crosswise," a reference to the branches of the columella. This species is related to *Suillus* and is mycorrhizal with pines. FeSO4 applied to the surface of the fruitbody produces a green-staining reaction. A photograph of the immature stage of this species is shown in the "Color Key to the Major Groups of Fungi" (p. 18).

hopalogaster transversarius

Scleroderma areolatum Ehrenb.

= *Scleroderma lycoperdoides* Schwein.

COMMON NAME: Puffball-like Scleroderma.

MACROSCOPIC FEATURES: **Fruitbody** 1–4.5 cm wide, consisting of a peridium attached to the ground by a short stalk-like base. **Peridium** oval to broadly rounded or irregular, often somewhat flattened, up to 1 mm thick, firm; surface dry, smooth when young, soon cracking and dividing into small patches, slightly scaly in age, light brown to yellowish brown, becoming darker reddish brown as it matures, splitting irregularly over the top in age. **Spore mass** firm and watery cream when very young, soon becoming purplish, and eventually grayish brown and powdery in age. **Stalk-like base** composed of numerous white rhizomorphs with trapped sand.

MICROSCOPIC FEATURES: Spores (7.5–)11–14(-18.5) μm, excluding spines, globose, not reticulated, brownish; spines 0.2–1.8 μm.

OCCURRENCE: Scattered or in groups, sometimes fused, on the ground or in grassy areas; summer–early winter.

EDIBILITY: Unknown.

REMARKS: *Areolatum* means "cracked," a reference to the peridium. Compare with *Scleroderma texense* (p. 535), which has a thicker peridium.

Scleroderma areolatum

Scleroderma bovista Fr.

COMMON NAME: Potato Earthball.

MACROSCOPIC FEATURES: **Fruitbody** 1.5–4.5 cm wide, consisting of a peridium attached to the ground by a thick stalk-like base. **Peridium** spherical, often somewhat flattened in age, up to 2 mm thick, firm; surface dry, smooth when young, soon cracking and dividing into small patches, slightly to distinctly scaly in age, straw yellow to pale orange yellow when young, becoming reddish brown with olive-gray tints at maturity, splitting irregularly over the top and sides in age. **Spore mass** firm and whitish at first, becoming dark blackish brown and powdery at maturity. **Stalk-like base** composed of a dense mass of rhizomorphs with trapped sand.

MICROSCOPIC FEATURES: Spores 9–16 µm, globose, with a partial to fully developed reticulum, brownish; clamp connections present.

OCCURRENCE: Solitary, scattered, or in groups in oak and pine woods, in waste areas, or on sandy soil in grassy areas; summer–early winter.

EDIBILITY: Poisonous, causing gastrointestinal upset.

REMARKS: *Bovista* means "puffball." The application of KOH to the peridium produces a red reaction. The fruitbody of *Scleroderma meridionale* (p. 18) is 2–6 cm wide, subglobose or irregular in outline, and tapers downward to form a thick, stalk-like, rooting base. The dull ochraceous-orange to brownish peridium is moderately thick, warted, areolate, and slowly splits into irregular lobes, exposing the dark gray, powdery spore mass at maturity. It has globose, echinulate, reticulate, dark brown spores that measure 12–20 µm, and it grows partially buried in sandy habitats, especially dunes, from fall through spring. The fruitbody of *Scleroderma texense* (p. 535) is also similar, but it has a much thicker peridium, smaller spores that measure 8–12 µm, and the spores lack reticulation.

Scleroderma bovista

Scleroderma polyrhizum (J. F. Gmel.) Pers.

= *Scleroderma geaster* Fr.

COMMON NAMES: Earthstar Scleroderma, Dead Man's Hand.

MACROSCOPIC FEATURES: **Fruitbody** 4–12 cm wide when closed, expanding to 16 cm and resembling a giant earthstar when fully open, attached to the ground by a root-like mass of tough fibers. **Peridium** round to oval or irregular, 3–10 mm thick, hard, rind-like, rough, areolate to somewhat scaly, whitish to straw-colored or pale yellow brown, splitting open into rays and exposing the spore mass. **Spore mass** firm and white at first, becoming brown to purplish brown, and finally blackish brown and powdery at maturity. **Rays** 4–8, thick, brown to blackish brown.

MICROSCOPIC FEATURES: Spores 5–10 μm, globose, echinulate, sometimes forming a partial reticulum, purple brown.

OCCURRENCE: Solitary or in groups, often partially buried in sandy soil; summer–early winter.

EDIBILITY: Poisonous, causing gastrointestinal upset.

REMARKS: *Polyrhizum* means "many roots," a reference to the mass of tough fibers that anchor the fruitbody. The application of KOH to the peridium produces a red reaction. *Scleroderma floridanum* (p. 18) is similar but is smaller with a thinner, yellowish-brown peridium and larger spores that measure 9–12 μm.

Scleroderma polyrhizum

Scleroderma texense Berk.

MACROSCOPIC FEATURES: **Fruitbody** 1–7 cm wide, consisting of a peridium attached to the ground by whitish rhizomorphs. **Peridium** rounded to somewhat flattened, 3–7 mm thick, hard, rind-like, coated with small, flat to pyramidal scales, dirty whitish to pale brown at first, becoming yellow brown in age, splitting irregularly at maturity, stalkless. **Spore mass** chambered, firm and white at first, becoming purple black, and finally grayish black and powdery when mature.

MICROSCOPIC FEATURES: Spores 8–12 µm, globose, echinulate, lacking reticulation, brown.

OCCURRENCE: Solitary, scattered, or in groups in sandy soil under conifers or hardwoods, especially pines and oaks; summer–early winter.

EDIBILITY: Poisonous, causing gastrointestinal upset.

REMARKS: *Texense* refers to "Texas," where this earthball was first collected and described. The application of KOH to the peridium produces a yellowish or reddish reaction. *Scleroderma cepa* (not illustrated) is very similar, but its peridium stains darker brown when handled or in age. *Scleroderma bovista* (p. 533) is similar, but it has a much thinner peridium, larger spores that measure 9–16 µm, and the spores are reticulate.

cleroderma texense

Stinkhorns

Species in this group have fruitbodies that are egg-shaped when young. Some become erect and phallic-like with a head and stalk. Others are pear-shaped to nearly round, lattice- or basket-like, or resemble squid with arched and tapered arms. Parts of the fruitbody are usually coated with a foul-smelling, slimy spore mass that often attracts a variety of arthropods. They grow on the ground, mulch, woodchips, or decaying wood.

Aseroe rubra Labill.

COMMON NAMES: Starfish Stinkhorn, Fungus Flower.

MACROSCOPIC FEATURES: **Fruitbody** consisting of an egg-like immature stage that ruptures and gives rise to the mature stage with a central stalk, radiating forked arms, and a volva; **immature stage** 2–4 cm wide, globose to obovate, with basal rhizomorphs, dull white to cream or pale grayish brown, sometimes with grayish spots, with a gelatinous interior; **mature stage** a cylindrical stalk and central disc, with radiating tapered arms and spore mass at the stalk apex, leaving a sac-like volva at the base; **stalk** 4–6.5 cm high, 1.5–3 cm wide, sponge-like, hollow, pinkish to reddish, forming a flattened disc with 5–11 radiating, chambered arms that are often forked near the mid-portion and curled at the tip, with a sac-like volva at the base; **arms** up to 4.5 cm long, bright red; **spore mass** dark olive brown, covering the disk and interior base of the arms, slimy, fetid.

MICROSCOPIC FEATURES: Spores 4.5–7 × 1.7–2.5 μm, elliptic-cylindric with a truncate base, smooth, hyaline to pale brownish.

OCCURRENCE: Solitary or in groups on wood mulch, leaf litter, or on the ground; spring–fall.

EDIBILITY: Inedible.

REMARKS: *Rubra* means "red." It was originally described from Australia and has spread to many parts of the world, including North America.

Aseroe rubra

Clathrus columnatus Bosc

= *Linderia columnata* (Bosc) G. Cunn.

COMMON NAME: Columned Stinkhorn.
MACROSCOPIC FEATURES: **Fruitbody** egg-like at first, up to 7 cm wide, subglobose, whitish, with a gelatinous interior, expanding and giving rise to the stalkless mature stage, which can be up to 16 cm high and consists of a volva and 2–5 spongy, erect, curved, delicate, orange to reddish-orange or rosy-red columns that are fused at their tips; **volva** sac-like, wrinkled and tough, whitish, attached to the ground by one or more whitish rhizomorphs; **spore mass** olive brown, slimy, fetid, deposited on the underside of the columns.
MICROSCOPIC FEATURES: Spores 3.5–5 × 1.5–2.5 µm, smooth, elliptic, yellowish brown.
OCCURRENCE: Solitary, scattered, or in groups on the ground in grassy areas, woodlands, or marginal woodland areas; year-round.

EDIBILITY: Inedible.
REMARKS: This stinkhorn sometimes fruits in very large numbers in woodchips used for landscaping. The fruitbody of *Blumenavia angolensis* (p. 18) is at first egg-like, subglobose, up to 7 cm wide, with a gelatinous interior, and is dark gray to blackish. It cracks into large scales and soon develops longitudinal furrows and splits open at the apex as the fruitbody expands, giving rise to a stalk, terminal columns, and a volva. The stalk is ovoid, white, and terminates in 3–5 unbranched columns that are united at the apex to form a lattice. The volva is wrinkled and whitish but is often darker when remnants of the egg remain attached. The slimy, fetid spore mass is grayish green to grayish olive at first, darkens in age, and is deposited on the underside of the columns. It grows on mulch or fertile soil year-round.

Clathrus columnatus

Clathrus crispus

= *Clathrus americanus* Lloyd

COMMON NAME: Wiffle Ball Stinkhorn.

MACROSCOPIC FEATURES: **Fruitbody** an egg-like **immature stage**, up to 7 cm wide, subglobose, white, with a gelatinous interior, expanding and giving rise to the stalkless or rudimentarily stalked mature stage; **mature stage** round, oval, or irregularly ball-shaped, up to 10 cm wide and 15 cm high, consisting of red or reddish-orange, flattened, interlaced, regularly lined, spongy, roughened branches with a basal volva; **volva** white, sac-like, and anchored to the ground by numerous white rhizomorphs; **spore mass** slimy, fetid, olive to brownish, covering the inner surfaces of the branches.

MICROSCOPIC FEATURES: Spores 3.8–4.2 × 1.8–2.2 µm, oblong-elliptical to cylindrical, smooth, greenish.

OCCURRENCE: Solitary or in groups in gardens, lawns, cultivated soil, or on woodchips used for mulch; year-round.

EDIBILITY: Inedible.

REMARKS: An additional image of this stinkhorn is shown in the "Color Key to the Major Groups of Fungi" (p. 18). Compare with *Clathrus columnatus* (p. 538), which has 2–5 spongy, erect, curved, delicate, orange to reddish-orange or rosy-red columns that are fused at their tips. Also compare with *Lysurus periphragmoides* (p. 540), which has a long, hollow, pinkish-orange stalk.

Clathrus crispus

Lysurus periphragmoides (Klotzsch) Dring

= *Simblum periphragmoides* Klotsch
= *Simblum texense* (G. F. Atk. & Long) Long

COMMON NAME: Stalked Lattice Stinkhorn.

MACROSCOPIC FEATURES: **Fruitbody** an egg-like immature stage that expands and gives rise to the mature stage consisting of a head, stalk, and volva; **immature stage** up to 4.5 cm wide, globose to elongated, with a gelatinous interior, white to buff, attached to the ground by several whitish rhizomorphs; **head** a swollen and rounded terminal network of anastomosing arms that form a lattice; **arms** sharply angled and distinctly corrugated, pinkish to pinkish orange, sometimes yellowish or whitish; **stalk** up to 16 cm high, 1–2 cm wide, hollow, pinkish to pinkish orange, sometimes yellowish or whitish; **volva** oval, membranous, white to buff; **spore mass** slimy, fetid, dark olive green, filling the interior of the head and extending outward from the lattice.

MICROSCOPIC FEATURES: Spores 4–4.5 × 1.5–2 µm, elliptical, smooth, pale brown.

OCCURRENCE: Solitary or in groups on the ground or on mulch; year-round.

EDIBILITY: Inedible.

REMARKS: An additional image of this stinkhorn is shown in the "Color Key to the Major Groups of Fungi" (p. 18). The fruitbody of the Lizard's Claw Stinkhorn, *Lysurus gardneri* (not illustrated), is a white, egg-like immature stage that gives rise to a white head, stalk, and volva. The head consists of 4–6 small, claw-like terminal columns that are bent inward and fused at their tips or are sometimes free on older specimens. It has a slimy, fetid, dark grayish-brown to olive-black spore mass that is deposited between and on the outer portions of the columns. It grows on mulched soil year-round.

Lysurus periphragmoides (B)

Mutinus elegans (Mont.) E. Fisch.

COMMON NAME: Elegant Stinkhorn.
MACROSCOPIC FEATURES: **Fruitbody** an egg-like immature stage that expands and gives rise to the mature stage consisting of a stalk and volva; **immature stage** up to 2.5 cm wide, nearly round to oval or somewhat elongated, with a gelatinous interior, white, attached to the substrate by a white basal rhizomorph; **stalk** up to 18 cm high, 1.2–2.5 cm wide, tapered from the middle in both directions, lacking a clearly defined head, apex with a narrow opening, roughened, spongy, hollow, orange to pinkish orange, rarely pinkish red; **volva** sac-like, wrinkled, tough, whitish; **spore mass** covering the upper third or more of the stalk, olive green to dull greenish, slimy, fetid.

MICROSCOPIC FEATURES: Spores 4–7 × 2–3 μm, elliptic, smooth, pale yellowish green.
OCCURRENCE: Scattered, in groups, or sometimes dense clusters on woodchips, leaf litter, or on the ground; year-round.
EDIBILITY: Inedible.
REMARKS: *Elegans* means "elegant." *Mutinus ravenelii* (p. 542) is similar, but it has a clearly defined head and a conspicuously pitted, pinkish-red to pale purplish-red stalk. *Phallus rubicundus* (not illustrated) has a smooth to slightly roughened, flaring, thimble-like cap that is coated with an olive-brown to dark-brown spore mass. It has an orange to reddish-orange or sometimes pinkish stalk that is coarsely marked with elongated pits.

Mutinus elegans

Mutinus ravenelii (Berk. & M. A. Curtis) E. Fisch.

COMMON NAMES: Ravenel's Mutinus, Little Red Stinkhorn.

MACROSCOPIC FEATURES: **Fruitbody** an egg-like immature stage that expands and gives rise to the mature stage consisting of a head, stalk, and volva; **immature stage** up to 3.5 cm high, 1–2 cm wide, ovoid, with a gelatinous interior, whitish, attached to the substrate by white basal rhizomorphs; **head** clearly differentiated, a somewhat swollen spore mass zone on the upper portion of the stalk, roughened, with a small opening at the apex; **stalk** up to 9 cm high, 1–1.5 cm wide, nearly equal or tapered downward below the head, conspicuously pitted overall, pinkish red to pale purplish red, paler toward the base; **volva** sac-like, membranous, tough, whitish; **spore mass** covering the head or as much as the upper quarter of the stalk, olive green to olive brown, slimy, fetid.

MICROSCOPIC FEATURES: Spores 3.5–5 × 1.5–2.2 μm, elliptic, smooth, pale yellowish green.

OCCURRENCE: Solitary, in groups, or dense clusters on the ground, often around tree stumps, on well-decayed wood, or mulch; year-round.

EDIBILITY: Inedible.

REMARKS: *Ravenelii* honors Henry William Ravenel (1814–1887), a South Carolina mycologist and botanist. *Mutinus elegans* (p. 541) is similar, but it lacks a clearly differentiated head, and it has an orange to pinkish-orange, roughened stalk that is tapered from the middle in both directions. *Phallus rubicundus* (not illustrated) has a smooth to slightly roughened, flaring, thimble-like cap that is coated with an olive-brown to dark-brown spore mass. It has an orange to reddish-orange or sometimes pinkish stalk that is coarsely marked with elongated pits.

Mutinus ravenelii

Phallogaster saccatus Morgan

COMMON NAMES: Club-shaped Stinkhorn, Stink Poke.

MACROSCOPIC FEATURES: **Fruitbody** egg-like, up to 5 cm high, 1–3.5 cm wide, pyriform and narrowed toward the base, or sometimes subglobose, white to pinkish or pinkish lilac on the upper portion, white toward the base, smooth at first, then forming irregular depressions that perforate to expose the spore mass, with a gelatinous interior; **base** attached to the substrate by whitish to pinkish rhizomorphs; **spore mass** slimy, dark green, fetid.

MICROSCOPIC FEATURES: Spores 4–5.5 × 1.5–2 μm, subcylindric, smooth, greenish.

OCCURRENCE: Solitary or in groups on decaying wood or woodchip mulch; year-round.

EDIBILITY: Inedible.

REMARKS: *Saccatus* means "having a sac-like container."

Phallogaster saccatus

Phallus hadriani Vent.

COMMON NAMES: Dune Stinkhorn, Witch's Egg.

MACROSCOPIC FEATURES: **Fruitbody** an egg-like immature stage that expands and gives rise to the mature stage consisting of a head, stalk, and volva; **immature stage** up to 7 cm wide, globose to ovoid, white to violaceus pink, with a gelatinous interior, attached to the substrate by whitish rhizomorphs; **head** up to 5 cm wide, oval to bell-shaped, conspicuously pitted, apex with a white-rimmed opening, sometimes covered by a flap of white volva, usually coated with spore mass; **stalk** up to 26 cm high, 2–3 cm wide, enlarged downward or nearly equal, erect, hollow, spongy, fragile, whitish with pinkish tinges near the base; **volva** membranous, white with pinkish to pinkish-purple tints; **spore mass** slimy, olive green, fetid.

MICROSCOPIC FEATURES: Spores 3–6 × 2–3.5 μm, elongated-ellipsoid, smooth, yellowish.

OCCURRENCE: Solitary, in groups, or clusters in dunes, sandy soil, or cultivated areas; year-round.

EDIBILITY: Inedible.

REMARKS: Ravenel's Stinkhorn, *Phallus ravenelii* (p. 545), is similar, but its head is granular to wrinkled and lacks pits. The Netted Stinkhorn, *Dictyophora duplicata* = *Phallus duplicatus* (not illustrated), is like *Phallus hadriani* and has a deeply pitted head with a white-rimmed opening at the apex, but on the upper portion, its stalk is surrounded by a white, net-like, flaring veil that emerges from underneath the head. It is the largest stinkhorn that occurs in the Gulf States, and it grows on the ground in hardwoods or mixed woods year-round.

Phallus hadriani

Phallus ravenelii Berk. & M. A. Curtis

COMMON NAME: Ravenel's Stinkhorn.

MACROSCOPIC FEATURES: **Fruitbody** an egg-like immature stage that expands and gives rise to the mature stage consisting of a head, stalk, and volva; **immature stage** up to 4.5 cm wide, oval to pear-shaped, whitish to pinkish lilac, with a gelatinous interior, attached to the substrate with pinkish-lilac rhizomorphs; **head** up to 4.5 cm high, 1.5–4 cm wide, conical to ovoid, with a white-rimmed apical opening, granular to wrinkled, lacking pits, covered with spore mass; **stalk** up to 16 cm high, 1.5–3 cm wide, roughened, spongy, hollow, whitish; **volva** tough, wrinkled, whitish to pinkish lilac; **spore mass** slimy, greenish brown to olive brown, fetid.

MICROSCOPIC FEATURES: Spores 3–4 × 1–1.5 μm, cylindric, smooth, hyaline.

OCCURRENCE: Scattered or in groups on or near woody debris, in gardens, and landscape areas; year-round.

EDIBILITY: Inedible.

REMARKS: *Ravenelii* honors Henry William Ravenel (1814–1887), a South Carolina mycologist and botanist. *Phallus hadriani* (p. 544) is similar, but its head is conspicuously pitted. *Dictyophora duplicata* (not illustrated) is larger, has a pitted head, and its stalk is surrounded at the apex by a white, net-like, flaring veil.

Phallus ravenelii

Tooth Fungi

Species in this group are fleshy, leathery, or tough fungi with downward-oriented, uniformly shaped teeth or soft spines. Some species have a cap and stalk; others are fan-shaped to shelf- or icicle-like. They grow on the ground or on wood.

Climacodon pulcherrimus
(Berk. & M. A. Curtis) Nikol.

= *Donkia pulcherrima* (Berk. & M.A. Curtis) Pilát

= *Steccherinum pulcherrimum* (Berk. & M. A. Curtis) Banker

MACROSCOPIC FEATURES: **Cap** 3–10 cm wide, fan-shaped to semicircular, arising from a confluent, spreading base; **upper surface** densely hairy, whitish to pale tan or pinkish tan; **lower surface** covered with crowded short spines, 2.5–5 mm long, whitish at first, becoming pinkish tan in age. **Flesh** fibrous, flexible, white, exuding a sticky, creamy-white fluid when squeezed; odor variously described as woody, resembling preserved figs, or not distinctive; taste not distinctive. **Stalk** a short lateral projection that is sometimes furrowed or absent.

SPORE PRINT: White.

MICROSCOPIC FEATURES: Spores 4–5 × 2–2.5 µm, elliptic, smooth, hyaline.

OCCURRENCE: In overlapping or fused clusters on decaying hardwoods; summer–early winter.

EDIBILITY: Inedible.

REMARKS: *Pulcherrimus* means "beautiful." The flesh and cap surface turn pink to red with the application of KOH.

Climacodon pulcherrimus

Gyrodontium sacchari (Spreng.) Hjortstam

= *Hydnum clavarioides* Berk. & M. A. Curtis

MACROSCOPIC FEATURES: **Fruitbody** annual, effused-reflexed to pileate, often imbricate, soft; **cap** applanate, with many small caps arising and laterally fused to form effused structures, 7–18 cm long and 7–8 cm wide; **upper surface** sticky, wooly to slightly velvety, whitish to orangish yellow, darkening in age; **lower surface** with flattened or conical spines, 5–10 mm long, easily removed from the flesh, olive green to yellow, becoming reddish brown from maturing spores. **Flesh** 3–6 mm thick, soft to spongy, white with yellowish tints; odor not distinctive.

SPORE PRINT: Reddish brown.

MICROSCOPIC FEATURES: Spores 3–6 × 1.9–3.5 μm, ellipsoid to elongated, smooth, thick-walled, dextrinoid.

OCCURRENCE: On decaying hardwood trees; fall.

EDIBILITY: Unknown.

REMARKS: This is the first record of this pantropical species in the United States. It has previously been found in Mexico, Europe, Africa, and Asia.

Gyrodontium sacchari

Hericium erinaceus (Bull.) Pers.

COMMON NAMES: Bearded Tooth, Satyr's Beard.

MACROSCOPIC FEATURES: Fruitbody up to 20 cm high and wide, a whitish to yellowish cushion-shaped mass, giving rise to long spines and resembling a beard. **Spines** up to 9 cm long, white. **Flesh** thick, soft, white; odor and taste not distinctive when young, becoming sour and unpleasant in age.

SPORE PRINT: White.

MICROSCOPIC FEATURES: Spores 5–6.5 × 4–5.6 μm, oval to globose, smooth to slightly roughened, hyaline.

OCCURRENCE: Solitary on trunks, logs, and stumps of decaying hardwood trees; summer–early winter.

EDIBILITY: Edible.

REMARKS: *Erinaceus* means "pertaining to a hedgehog," a reference to having long spines. The edible fruitbody of *Hericium americanum* (p. 19) is 10–25 cm wide and consists of numerous branches with long, delicate spines. The branches arise from a thick stalk-like base, repeatedly fork, and give rise to clusters of white spines at the branch tips. The spines are up to 4 cm long and hang downward. It grows on logs and stumps of conifers or hardwoods during summer through early winter. *Hericium coralloides* (p. 19), also edible, is similar, but it has shorter spines, about 1 cm long, located along the entire length of the branches, not just at the tips.

Hericium erinaceus

Hydnellum aurantiacum (Batsch) P. Karst.

COMMON NAME: Orange Rough-cap Tooth.
MACROSCOPIC FEATURES: **Cap** 5–18 cm wide, convex, becoming broadly convex to nearly plane, occasionally depressed; **upper surface** dry, uneven, breaking up into irregular projections, channels, and cavities, tomentose to appressed-tomentose, sometimes zonate, orange buff to whitish when young, soon becoming orange salmon, then rusty brown with a rusty-orange to whitish margin; **lower surface** covered with spines. **Spines** decurrent, 5–7 mm long, dark brown with grayish-buff tips. **Flesh** fibrous-tough, zonate, buff in the cap, rusty orange in the stalk; odor pungent; taste disagreeable. **Stalk** 2–7 cm long, 5–20 mm thick, enlarged downward to a bulbous base, solid; surface dry, covered with an appressed orange to brownish tomentum, basal mycelium orange.
SPORE PRINT: Brown.
MICROSCOPIC FEATURES: Spores 5–8 × 5–6 µm, subglobose, distinctly tuberculate, pale brown.
OCCURRENCE: Solitary, scattered, or in groups, commonly confluent and forming large rosettes, on the ground under conifers; summer–winter.
EDIBILITY: Inedible.

REMARKS: The cap surface stains black with KOH. It is sometimes used as a dye mushroom. The Red-juice Tooth, *Hydnellum peckii* (not illustrated), has a whitish to pinkish cap that exudes drops of red juice when young and fresh and becomes dark brown in age. It has brownish flesh with a peppery taste, and it grows on the ground under conifers. The *Hydnum rufescens* complex (p. 19), includes 2–12 cm wide, reddish-orange to brownish-orange or pale dull orange fruitbodies with white to creamy-white or orange-yellow spines that usually darken when bruised. The cap surface may be smooth or roughened, wrinkled, pitted, or centrally depressed to umbilicate. All the members of this complex, including the Umbilicate Sweet Tooth, *Hydnum umbilicatum* (not illustrated), are considered edible species. The illustration labeled *Hydnum rufescens* complex, shown in the "Color Key to the Major Groups of Fungi" (p. 19), has appeared in other works, labeled as *Hydnum repandum*, the Hedgehog or Sweet Tooth. Other similar illustrations, also labeled as *Hydnum repandum*, have appeared in numerous other mushroom guides. Recent molecular analysis has demonstrated that *Hydnum repandum* does not occur in North America. Species in the *Hydnum rufescens* complex are currently being formally described.

Hydnellum aurantiacum

Hydnellum caeruleum (Hornem.) P. Karst

COMMON NAME: Bluish Tooth.
MACROSCOPIC FEATURES: **Cap** 3–15 cm wide, convex to top-shaped or nearly plane; **upper surface** dry, azonate, velvety at first, becoming uneven, bumpy and pitted, whitish with bluish tints at first, becoming dark brown when mature; margin soft, velvety and white at first, becoming dark brown at maturity; **lower surface** covered with spines. **Flesh** in cap duplex; upper layer thin, spongy; lower layer tough, typically zoned, blue with areas of orange and brown; in stalk mostly reddish orange with blue areas; odor and taste farinaceous. **Spines** crowded, decurrent, 3–10 mm long, whitish or bluish, becoming brown with white tips in age. **Stalk** 2–6 cm long, 7–20 mm thick, enlarged downward or sometimes tapered downward, brown.

SPORE PRINT: Brown.
MICROSCOPIC FEATURES: Spores 4.5–6 × 3.5–5.5 µm, subglobose to oblong, coarsely warted, pale brown.
OCCURRENCE: Scattered or in groups, often with fused caps, under conifers; summer–early winter.
EDIBILITY: Inedible.
REMARKS: *Hydnellum suaveolens* (p. 554) has a white cap when young that turns tan to brown from the center outward as it matures, is zoned white, has blue to violet flesh, and a fragrant odor.

Hydnellum caeruleum

Hydnellum ferrugineum (Fr.) P. Karst.

= *Hydnellum pineticola* K. A. Harrison

COMMON NAME: Brown Pine Tooth.
MACROSCOPIC FEATURES: **Cap** 3–14 cm wide,
convex, becoming broadly convex to nearly
plane, sometimes irregularly depressed;
upper surface dry, roughened, whitish
pubescent at first, becoming matted and pale
vinaceous cinnamon to reddish brown or dull
brown, occasionally with pink droplets in
humid weather, staining vinaceous cinnamon
then blackish brown when bruised; margin
whitish to pinkish tan; **lower surface** covered
with spines. **Flesh** in two layers, moist, zonate,
dark cinnamon; upper layer thick and spongy;
lower layer fibrous and tough; odor faintly
fragrant to slightly acidic; taste not distinctive

then slowly disagreeable. **Spines** decurrent,
up to 9 mm long, pinkish cinnamon when
young, becoming vinaceous brown. **Stalk**
2–5 cm long, 1–2 cm thick, nearly equal or
slightly enlarged downward, occasionally with
a somewhat bulbous base, solid, dry, felty, pale
to dark cinnamon, sometimes radicating.
SPORE PRINT: Brown.
MICROSCOPIC FEATURES: Spores 4–6 × 4–5 μm,
oblong to subglobose, angular, tuberculate,
pale brown.
OCCURRENCE: Scattered or in groups, sometimes confluent, on the ground under conifers, especially pines; summer–early winter.
EDIBILITY: Inedible.
REMARKS: *Hydnellum spongiosipes* (p. 553) is
very similar but its stalk has a very broad bulbous base, and it grows under hardwoods.

Hydnellum ferrugineum

Hydnellum spongiosipes (Peck) Pouzar

COMMON NAME: Spongy-footed Tooth.
MACROSCOPIC FEATURES: **Cap** 2–10 cm wide, convex, becoming broadly convex to irregularly plane, sometimes depressed; **upper surface** uneven, azonate, dry, finely tomentose, cinnamon brown to reddish brown, sometimes with a grayish bloom, becoming darker when bruised; margin entire or with concentric ridges of secondary growth, often misshapen when fused with other caps; **lower surface** covered with spines. **Flesh** divided into two layers; upper layer thick, spongy, dark brown; lower layer thin, tough, cinnamon brown; odor and taste not distinctive. **Spines** decurrent, up to 6 mm long, brown with slightly paler tips, darkening when bruised. **Stalk** up to 10 cm long, 5–20 mm thick, enlarged downward to a very broad bulbous base, often fused and arising with several others from a thick pad of mycelium, spongy, dark reddish brown to dark brown or grayish brown.
SPORE PRINT: Brown.
MICROSCOPIC FEATURES: Spores 5.5–7 × 5–6 μm, subglobose, moderately to coarsely tuberculate, pale brown.
OCCURRENCE: Solitary, scattered, in groups, or fused clusters on the ground in hardwoods, especially with oak; summer–early winter.

EDIBILITY: Inedible.
REMARKS: *Spongiosipes* means "spongy foot," a reference to the thick, spongy stalk. *Hydnellum ferrugineum* (p. 552) is very similar, but its stalk lacks the very broad, bulbous base, and it grows under conifers. The cap of the Rough Hydnellum, *Hydnellum scrobiculatum* (p. 19), is 3.5–14 cm wide, convex to nearly plane, and often depressed to funnel-shaped. The upper surface is dry, irregularly roughened with pits, horn-like projections, and ridges, usually concentrically zoned, variously colored with dull pink, vinaceous brown, dark rusty cinnamon, and grayish black, and stains purple brown to brown black when bruised. The lower surface is covered with brown spines, up to 3 mm long, with paler tips, and the flesh has a farinaceous odor and taste. It grows on the ground under conifers or hardwoods from summer through early winter. *Hydnellum concrescens* (p. 19) has an irregularly rounded, concentrically zoned, reddish-brown cap with an undulating white marginal zone when growing. The cap surface is dry, somewhat felted, and is sometimes roughened or has irregular projections. It has reddish-brown spines up to 3 mm long and purplish-brown flesh that becomes blackish in the stalk. The caps are often fused, and it grows in conifer or hardwood forests from summer through early winter.

Hydnellum spongiosipes

Hydnellum suaveolens (Scop.) P. Karst.

= *Hydnum boreale* Banker
= *Hydnum suaveolens* Scop.

COMMON NAME: Fragrant Hydnellum.
MACROSCOPIC FEATURES: **Cap** 5–15 cm wide, convex to top-shaped, then broadly convex to nearly flat; **upper surface** dry, tomentose, sometimes with small, rounded or irregular projections, azonate, white when young, becoming tan to brown from the center outward as it matures; margin even, sometimes wavy; **lower surface** covered with 2–5 mm long, decurrent, whitish to brown spines. **Flesh** fibrous, zoned with white and blue to violet hues, darkest near the stalk base; odor fragrant, resembling anise, coumarin, or mint; taste slightly bitter or not distinctive. **Spines** 2–5 mm long, crowded, strongly decurrent, whitish at first, becoming brown. **Stalk** 1.5–5 cm long, 1–2.5 cm thick, hard and woody; surface dry, tomentose, bright blue violet; mycelium dark blue to violet.

SPORE PRINT: Brown.
MICROSCOPIC FEATURES: Spores 4.5–6 × 3–4 μm, subglobose to oblong, tuberculate, angular, pale brown.
OCCURRENCE: Solitary, scattered, or in groups, sometimes fused, on the ground under conifers; summer–early winter.
EDIBILITY: Inedible.
REMARKS: *Suaveolens* means "sweet and agreeable." *Hydnellum caeruleum* (p. 551) has zoned blue flesh with areas of orange and brown, a farinaceous odor and taste, and whitish or bluish spines that become brown with white tips in age.

Hydnellum suaveolens

Mycorrhaphium adustum (Schwein.) Maas Geest.

= *Hydnum adustum* Schwein.

COMMON NAME: Kidney-shaped Tooth.
MACROSCOPIC FEATURES: **Cap** 2.5–7.5 cm wide, kidney- to fan-shaped or nearly circular, broadly convex to nearly plane; **upper surface** finely roughened to somewhat velvety, whitish to tan, staining smoky gray when bruised; margin thin, wavy, faintly zonate, sometimes blackish in age; **lower surface** covered with spines. **Flesh** thin, tough, white; odor and taste not distinctive. **Spines** up to 3 mm long, somewhat flattened, often fused and appearing forked at their tips, white at first, becoming pinkish brown to cinnamon brown at maturity. **Stalk** up to 3 cm long, 1–2 cm thick, lateral to rudimentary or sometimes absent, somewhat velvety, whitish to dull cream.

SPORE PRINT: White.
MICROSCOPIC FEATURES: Spores 2.5–4 × 1–1.5 µm, cylindric, smooth, hyaline.
OCCURRENCE: Solitary, scattered, or in groups, often fused and overlapping, on decaying hardwood branches and logs, especially oak; summer–early winter.
EDIBILITY: Inedible.
REMARKS: *Adustum* means "scorched," a reference to the upper surface staining smoky gray when bruised and sometimes becoming blackish in age. *Loweomyces fractipes* (not illustrated) is a polypore that has similar coloration and grows on wood. Its white lower surface has tiny angular pores.

Mycorrhaphium adustum

Phellodon alboniger (Peck) Banker

MACROSCOPIC FEATURES: **Cap** 3–9 cm wide, convex to broadly convex, becoming nearly plane, sometimes depressed; **upper surface** dry, tomentose or smooth, grayish white with a gray center when young, soon becoming dull brownish to blackish; margin thick, blue gray, becoming thin and paler at maturity, staining blackish when bruised; **lower surface** covered with spines. **Flesh** up to 1 cm thick, duplex; upper layer spongy, black; lower layer firm and black; odor sweetly fragrant; taste slightly acrid or not distinctive. **Spines** up to 4 mm long, decurrent, pale grayish. **Stalk** 4–10 cm long, 1–2 cm thick, tapered downward to a bulbous base, felted, pale to dark brown.
SPORE PRINT: White.

MICROSCOPIC FEATURES: Spores 4.5–5.5 μm, globose to subglobose, coarsely echinulate, prominently apiculate, hyaline.
OCCURRENCE: Solitary, scattered, or in groups on the ground under conifers, especially pines, hardwoods, or mixed woods; summer–late fall.
EDIBILITY: Inedible.
REMARKS: It is sometimes used as a dye mushroom. *Alboniger* means "white and black." *Phellodon niger* (not illustrated) has a dark smoky brown to blackish cap and thinner blackish flesh up to 3 mm thick that is duplex but not obviously so. The cap of *Phellodon melaleucus* (not illustrated) is brownish gray to reddish brown with darker tints, lacks grayish-white coloration overall when young, and its flesh is not duplex.

Phellodon alboniger

Sarcodon imbricatus (L.) P. Karst.

= *Hydnum imbricatum* L.

COMMON NAME: Scaly Tooth.

MACROSCOPIC FEATURES: **Cap** 5–20 cm wide, convex with a depressed center at first, expanding and becoming deeply depressed at maturity, conspicuously scaly; margin incurved and smooth when young, becoming plane and cracked or torn in age; **upper surface** dry, pale brown to dark brown, covered with erect, pointed, brown to dark brown concentrically arranged scales that are less erect toward the margin; **lower surface** covered with decurrent spines. **Flesh** firm, white to pale brown; odor not distinctive; taste slightly bitter or not distinctive. **Spines** 6–10 mm long, pale brown with a grayish tint at first, becoming reddish brown to dark brown in age. **Stalk** 4–10 cm long, 1.5–3.5 cm thick, tapered in either direction or nearly equal, smooth, dry, solid but often hollow in age, pale brown at first, darkening in age.

SPORE PRINT: Brown.

MICROSCOPIC FEATURES: Spores 6–8 × 5–7.5 μm, subglobose, with large irregular warts, pale brown.

OCCURRENCE: Solitary, scattered, or in groups on the ground under conifers or hardwoods; late spring–fall.

EDIBILITY: Edible.

REMARKS: It is sometimes used as a dye mushroom. *Imbricatus* means "covered with scales." *Sarcodon scabrosus* (p. 19) has a rough and scaly cap, but the scales are not erect and concentrically arranged, and it has a blue-green to olive-black stalk base. *Sarcodon underwoodii* (p. 559) also has a scaly cap, but the scales are much smaller, not erect and concentrically arranged, and it has an abruptly pointed, whitish stalk base.

Sarcodon imbricatus

Sarcodon joeides (Pass.) Bataille

= *Hydnum joeides* Pass.

MACROSCOPIC FEATURES: **Cap** 3–11 cm wide, convex, becoming broadly convex to nearly plane, often depressed at maturity, margin incurved when young, becoming uplifted and wavy in age; **upper surface** dry, roughened and irregular, finely fibrillose-scaly, pinkish brown to ocher brown; **lower surface** covered with spines. **Flesh** thick, brittle, pale pinkish lilac on exposure, soon darkening to dark violet; odor farinaceous; taste somewhat acrid to bitter and disagreeable. **Spines** up to 5 mm long, decurrent, pale pinkish brown when young, becoming purplish brown to dull brown in age. **Stalk** 3–7 cm long, 1–2.5 cm thick, nearly equal down to a pointed base, solid; surface dry, longitudinally fibrillose and scurfy, pinkish brown to purple brown, with a blackish-green base.

SPORE PRINT: Brown.

MICROSCOPIC FEATURES: Spores 5–6.5 × 4.5–5 µm, subglobose, coarsely tuberculate, brownish.

OCCURRENCE: Solitary, scattered, in groups, or in fused clusters on the ground under hardwoods, especially oaks; summer–early winter.

EDIBILITY: Inedible.

REMARKS: It is sometimes used as a dye mushroom. The cap stains olive green with NH4OH or FeSO4. The pinkish-lilac flesh that soon darkens to dark violet on exposure is an excellent field identification feature.

Sarcodon joeides

Sarcodon underwoodii Banker

= *Hydnum underwoodii* (Banker) Sacc. &
  Trotter

MACROSCOPIC FEATURES: **Cap** 5–14 cm
wide, convex to nearly plane, often somewhat depressed; **upper surface** pale reddish
brown, dry, cracked when young, and soon
developing small, flattened, pale reddish-
brown scales that darken in age; margin
incurved when young, becoming cracked and
wavy at maturity, typically extending about
2 mm beyond the spines; **lower surface**
covered with spines. **Flesh** in the cap white;
in the stalk pale brown; firm; odor fragrant
or farinaceous, sometimes not distinctive;
taste instantly very bitter. **Spines** 1–3 mm
long, decurrent, white when young, becoming brown with grayish tips at maturity. **Stalk**
3–7 cm long, 8–12 mm thick, tapered downward and usually bent at the ground, with
an abrupt, white, pointed base; surface dry,
scurfy, brown to dark brown.

SPORE PRINT: Brown.

MICROSCOPIC FEATURES: Spores 6–7.5 × 5.5–
6.5 µm, oval to subglobose, coarsely tuberculate, pale brown.

OCCURRENCE: Solitary, scattered, or in groups
on the ground under hardwoods; summer–
early winter.

EDIBILITY: Inedible.

REMARKS: It is sometimes used as a dye mushroom. *Sarcodon scabrosus* (pp. 19, 557) is very
similar, but its stalk base is blue green to olive
black, and it grows under conifers.

Sarcodon underwoodii

Truffles and Other Hypogeous Fungi

Because they are mostly underground fungi, these are not commonly collected. Most of the species in this group must be excavated, although species of *Rhizopogon* are sometimes found partially buried or wholly aboveground. They are nearly round or lobed, and their smooth or roughened to warted outer rind-like surface is often thickened. Although they sometimes resemble puffballs or earthballs, their interior is usually chambered, marbled, or somewhat hollow. If you cannot identify your unknown mushroom in this section, try comparing it to the species listed in the Puffballs, Earthballs, Earthstars, and Similar Fungi group.

Elaphomyces species complex

COMMON NAME: False Truffle.
MACROSCOPIC FEATURES: **Fruitbody** 2–4 cm
wide, subglobose to kidney- or top-shaped;
surface dry, covered with shallow, rounded
to angular warts, yellow brown to blackish,
covering a thick inner rind; **spore mass** firm,
dark brown to dark gray brown or nearly
black, powdery at maturity.
MICROSCOPIC FEATURES: Spores 27–46 μm,
globose to subglobose, densely covered with
spines or irregular warts, sometimes reticulate,
brown to dark red brown or blackish brown.
OCCURRENCE: Hypogeous under oaks, hicko-
ries, other hardwoods, and under conifers,
especially pines; spring–fall.

EDIBILITY: Unknown.
REMARKS: Several species in this complex are
abundant and widespread in North America
but are most diverse in the Gulf Coast region.
Some individual forests in Florida can have
up to six species in a small area. They are
distinct from the true European Deer Truffle,
Elaphomyces granulatus (not illustrated).
They are commonly encountered by spotting the *Tolypocladium* species that parasitize
them. This group is currently being revised by
Michael Castellano.

Elaphomyces species complex

Rhizopogon nigrescens Coker and Couch

MACROSCOPIC FEATURES: **Fruitbody** 1–4 cm wide, rounded to top-shaped or somewhat flattened, lacking a stalk; **surface** a thin peridium of sterile tissue, somewhat sticky when young, becoming tomentose to felty at maturity, yellowish when young, becoming brownish orange to grayish brown, and finally dark brown to blackish in age, staining dull red to reddish brown, then brown when bruised; **interior** composed of minute chambers and bearing spores; **spore mass** firm and whitish when young, becoming grayish yellow to olive brown at maturity.

MICROSCOPIC FEATURES: Spores 6–9 × 2–3.5 μm, subfusoid to oblong, smooth, hyaline to pale yellow.

OCCURRENCE: Scattered or in groups, often partially buried, in sandy soil under pines; summer–early winter.

EDIBILITY: Unknown.

REMARKS: *Nigrescens* means "blackening," a reference to the color of the mature peridium. *Rhizopogon atlanticus* (not illustrated) is similar, but its peridium is whitish when young and becomes pinkish cinnamon to yellowish brown in age or when dried. The spore mass is whitish to buffy brown; its spores measure 7–8.5 × 3–4 μm.

Rhizopogon nigrescens

Rhizopogon roseolus (Corda) Th. Fr.

= *Rhizopogon rubescens* (Tul. & C. Tul.) Tul. & C. Tul.

MACROSCOPIC FEATURES: **Fruitbody** 1.5–6 cm wide, irregularly subglobose to somewhat lobed, lacking a stalk; **surface** a thin peridium of sterile tissue, glabrous, nearly smooth except for a few ridges and depressions, dry or moist but not viscid, white when very young and underground, becoming yellowish with an olive tint, and finally reddish brown or darker brown in age, staining reddish when bruised; **interior** composed of minute chambers and bearing spores; **spore mass** firm and white at first, becoming granular and olive buff at maturity, staining reddish when cut.

MICROSCOPIC FEATURES: Spores 6–10.5 × 2.5–4.5 μm, elliptical, smooth, brownish yellow.
OCCURRENCE: Scattered or in groups under conifers, especially pines, often partially buried, sometimes partially fused; summer–winter.
EDIBILITY: Unknown.
REMARKS: *Roseolus* means "pinkish red," a reference to the color produced when the peridium is bruised or the spore mass is exposed. What has been described as *Rhizopogon roseolus* from North America may not be the same as those found in Europe and may be a new species unique to the Gulf States region.

Rhizopogon roseolus

Tuber lyonii Butters

= *Tuber texense* Heimsch

COMMON NAME: Pecan Truffle.
MACROSCOPIC FEATURES: **Fruitbody** 1–4 cm wide, globular, lobed, stalkless; **surface** smooth, roughened in the furrows, orange brown to reddish brown; **spore mass** firm and white at first, becoming brown with white marbling at maturity, powdery in age; odor a complex mixture of spices, garlic, and cheese.
MICROSCOPIC FEATURES: Spores 30–37 × 22–24 µm, elliptic, with tall spines connected by low lines when mature, hyaline.
OCCURRENCE: Hypogeous under pecan trees; year-round.

EDIBILITY: Edible and choice when mature.
REMARKS: It is often raked up when pecans are harvested. At least three additional *Tuber* species occur in the Gulf States region: *Tuber walkeri* (not illustrated) has been described; the two other species pending publication are *Tuber brennemanii sp. nov.* (not illustrated) and *Tuber floridanum sp. nov.* (not illustrated). For additional information on these last three species, search online.

Tuber lyonii

Zelleromyces cinnabarinus Singer & A. H. Sm.

COMMON NAME: Milky False Truffle.

MACROSCOPIC FEATURES: **Fruitbody** 1–3 cm wide, consisting of a peridium with a small, white basal knob of mycelium at the point of attachment; **exterior** subglobose to irregularly compressed and lobed, often flattened, stalkless; **surface** dry, smooth, brick-red to dull orange brown, sometimes mottled with orange and white; **interior** chambered or marbled with sterile tissue, with a distinct branching columella; **spore mass** firm and orangish white at first, exuding a white latex when fresh specimens are cut, becoming granular and brownish in age; odor pungent like rubber or not distinctive; taste not distinctive.

MICROSCOPIC FEATURES: Spores 12–18 × 11–16 µm, globose to broadly elliptic, thick-walled, ornamented with warts and ridges that form a broken to nearly complete reticulum, hyaline to pale yellow, amyloid.

OCCURRENCE: Scattered, in groups, or clusters on the ground, mycorrhizal with pines; summer–winter.

EDIBILITY: Unknown.

REMARKS: *Cinnabarinus* means "the color of cinnabar," a reference to the outer surface of the peridium. *Rhizopogon* species are similar and are also mycorrhizal with pines, but they lack latex and a columella.

Zelleromyces cinnabarinus

Microscopic Identification of Fungi

When macroscopic characteristics are not enough for positive identification, microscopic examination is commonly used to determine genera and species. Many mycological papers and books, especially technical monographs, use identification keys based on microscopic features, such as spore characteristics, basidia, cystidia, clamp connections, and hyphae. An in-depth discussion of microscopic structures and evaluation techniques is beyond the scope of this book. However, we have included the following information for those interested.

A good quality light microscope is required to do microscopy. It should be equipped with a substage condenser, a built-in light source, and good quality lenses. This includes at least three objective lenses: 10X, 40X, and an oil-immersion 100X, as well as one or two ocular lenses (eyepieces). An ocular micrometer is also required to make accurate measurements of microscopic features. Some ocular lenses have an ocular micrometer already inserted, others do not, and it must be bought separately. Because the magnification of each combination of lenses (ocular plus objective)

is different, the ocular micrometer needs to be calibrated using a tiny glass ruler known as a "stage micrometer." Most microscope dealers, as well as college and university biology departments, have stage micrometers. Usually, folks are more than willing to help with this calibration process.

Spores used in microscopic evaluation can be obtained from three sources: a spore print, from fresh mushrooms, or from dried mushrooms.

- If using a spore print as your source, scrape off a minute sample using a razor or knife blade. Mix it into a small drop of water or another mounting medium, such as KOH. Carefully place a coverslip over the mixture and gently apply pressure on the coverslip using a pencil eraser to distribute the spores and remove air bubbles and excess fluid.
- If using fresh material, remove a small portion of the fertile surface, gills, tubes, etc. Place it in the mounting medium of your choice, add the coverslip, and gently apply pressure as noted above.

- When using dried specimens as your source of spores, allow a small piece of the fertile surface to soak and soften in mounting medium for two or three minutes before adding the coverslip and adding pressure as directed above. Before placing pieces of dried material into a mounting medium, they may be soaked in wetting agents, such as 70-95 percent ethyl alcohol. This helps hyphae and other structures absorb water and regain their original appearance. Also, some microscopic structures, such as cystidia and hyphae, may be easier to see if dyes like phloxine are used (see "Chemical Reagents and Mushroom Identification," p. 569).

When the coverslip is in place, your slide is ready for use. Place a drop of immersion oil on the coverslip and carefully lower the 100X objective lens into the oil. Fine focus the image, adjust the lighting, and examine the spores, cystidia, hyphae, and other structures you wish to observe.

For additional information about microscopic features, refer to *How to Identify Mushrooms to Genus III: Microscopic Features* by Largent, Johnson, and Watling (1977). This valuable reference describes laboratory techniques, equipment and materials, microscope calibration, planes of sectioning, rehydration of dried materials, microscopic structures, and much more.

Chemical Reagents and Mushroom Identification

Although many mushrooms can be identified using only macroscopic features, there are times when the additional use of chemical reagents is most helpful in the identification process. When two macroscopically similar species are difficult to differentiate by visual inspection alone—as are, for example, the fruitbodies of the edible *Boletus partrioticus* and the reportedly poisonous *Boletus miniatoolivaceous*, which appear very much alike—they may be distinguished by chemical means. In the case of *B. partrioticus* versus *B. miniatoolivaceous*, adding a drop of KOH to their cap surfaces will distinguish one from the other. The cap surface of *B. partrioticus* stains olive brown, whereas the cap surface of *B. miniatoolivaceous* stains yellow, rapidly turning to olive green.

Historically, there has not been a consistently accepted procedure for applying reagents to mushroom tissue. People use various applicators, as well as differing quantities of reagent—ranging from scant to copious amounts. We have experimented with many objects for applying macrochemical reagents (toothpicks, paper towels, glass and plastic droppers, and metal probes), and we have tried applying different amounts of reagents. Each applicator and amount of reagent (or combinations of both!) produced accurate results some of the time, but these results were inconsistent. We finally discovered that a cotton-tip swab is easy to use and provides consistently accurate results when used as described here. This is especially important when trying to observe a "flash" or fleeting chemical reaction. The application of too much reagent can obscure this response, sometimes obliterating rapidly changing color sequences. To properly use a cotton-tipped swab, dip it into the reagent and gently apply it to the mushroom tissue using a sweeping motion and minimum pressure. Avoid large drops and puddles of reagent. Use a clean swab every time you are testing tissue to prevent contamination of your reagent.

Reagents should be fresh, not outdated. Although they will keep for several weeks, or sometimes months, we strongly recommend testing them periodically using mushroom tissues with known macrochemical reactions. Store reagents at room temperature, preferably in plastic bottles. Some reagents, especially

KOH, can react with glass to form silicates and may no longer produce accurate macrochemical test results.

Several factors can affect test results. Some of these include color variation on a single specimen, the age of the mushroom, whether the tissue is parasitized or not, moisture content, and if the specimen was refrigerated. Best results are obtained when using recently collected, fresh mushrooms with dry surfaces that have not been refrigerated. If macrochemical testing is done on refrigerated specimens, allow them to warm to room temperature before testing.

Some chemicals are also used for mushroom identification in microscopic work. They are used as rehydrating and mounting media in slide preparations, and for identifying some species based on the appearance and specific staining reactions of spores, hyphae, cystidia, and other microscopic structures.

The following chemical reagents are used for macrochemical testing or microscopic study:

NH_4OH = ammonium hydroxide: 3-14 percent aqueous solution or household ammonia without added soap.

Ammonium hydroxide is also used as a mounting medium for microscopic work. It is ideal for use with dried material that has been rehydrated in a 70–95 percent ethyl alcohol solution.

$FeSO_4$ = iron sulfate: 10 percent aqueous solution.

KOH = potassium hydroxide: 5-14 percent aqueous solution. Potassium hydroxide is also used as a mounting medium for fresh and dried specimens. Unless otherwise stated, spore colors reported in the microscopic features section of each description are based on their appearance when mounted in potassium hydroxide.

Melzer's reagent is a solution of iodine (0.5 g), potassium iodide (1.5 g), chloral hydrate (20 g), and water (20 ml). Since chloral hydrate is a controlled substance, it is difficult to obtain. Searching online for premade Melzer's reagent might be the best option for obtaining this. It is an important chemical used for identifying some mushroom species based on the appearance of their spores, hyphae, cystidia, and other microscopic structures. These structures sometimes stain specific colors when mounted in Melzer's reagent. If they stain bluish gray to bluish black, they are described as amyloid; those that stain reddish brown are dextrinoid; and those structures that stain yellow or remain colorless are inamyloid.

Lactophenol Cotton Blue is a blue dye that is a mixture of lactic acid, phenol, and cotton blue. It is used as a mounting fluid and stain and is useful because it stains cytoplasm pale blue and hyphal wall structures and ornamentation a darker blue.

Phloxine is a red-colored dye used for microscopic examination, especially of hyphae. It is useful because it stains cytoplasm red and makes other contrasting structures, such as cystidia, much easier to differentiate.

Other chemical reagents are useful for microscopic examination of mushroom tissues but are beyond the scope of this work.

Because of striking inconsistencies in the literature, variable results in testing, difficulties due to the subjective nature of color interpretation, and because testing results are simply unknown, macrochemical reactions for many of the species in this book have been omitted. We have provided macrochemical test reactions only when they are reliable, valid, and specifically diagnostic for some species.

Mushrooms for the Table

Do you ever find yourself sheepishly admitting to others that your primary reason for collecting mushrooms is to *eat* them? It happens. Attend enough "formal forays," and you might start hiding your culinary passion under the cloak of wanting to learn more about taxonomy or bioremediation or alternative medicinals or a myriad of other fascinating aspects of mycology. But truth be told, taking up the study of mushrooms, their growth habits, habitats, seasons, and botanical associates is not counterproductive to helping you fill both your basket and your larder with wild fungal delicacies. Expand your mycological knowledge base, and, most likely, you will one day be faced with the tantalizing problem of what to do with an abundance of collected, or homegrown, edibles. In this section, we hope to offer some simple, useful, and safe solutions for this wished-for "difficulty!"

COLLECTING

When gathering mushrooms for the table, it is important not to collect from contaminated habitats, such as chemically treated lawns, golf courses, along major roadways, near railroad tracks, or in orchards where pesticides and fertilizers may have been used in the past, because mushrooms absorb and concentrate heavy metals and other toxic substances.

The most vital rule regarding the consumption of wild mushrooms is, "If in doubt, throw it out!" *Never eat any mushroom unless you are certain of its identification as an edible species.* There are a multitude of "old wives' tales" and "rules" for determining a mushroom's edibility. None of them are true! The only valid "rule of thumb" for safely identifying edible mushrooms, and distinguishing them from poisonous ones, is to learn them one by one, species by species.

Every year there are reports of serious mushroom poisonings, including fatalities. These are usually due to carelessness regarding mushroom identification, consumption of mushrooms by medically compromised or fragile individuals, or the misidentification of species by individuals from different cultures. To minimize the chances of misidentification, we strongly encourage people to join mushroom clubs or mycological societies, connect with local mycologists, take courses and/or workshops, or participate in organized mycological forays and events. These are some of the very best ways to meet and learn from others and to have your mushroom identifications verified.

You cannot be poisoned by handling mushrooms. There are reported cases of some individuals developing contact dermatitis (a poison ivy–like rash) from handling certain species of *Suillus*. This is an allergic reaction and not a poisoning. Most negative reactions associated with eating wild edible mushrooms are caused by eating spoiled or insect-infested fungi, by not cooking mushrooms thoroughly (certain proteins must be denatured by heat to make them digestible), from drinking alcohol forty-eight hours before or after eating some specific mushroom species, and/or by simply eating too many at one sitting! Negative or allergic reactions are usually mild gastrointestinal upset. In the unlikely event of a severe reaction, bring your collection with you when you seek medical attention (see "Testing" section below). If you ever do experience mushroom poisoning, you can help broaden the mycological knowledge base and assist others by reporting your experience to the North American Mycological Association's mushroom poisoning case registry. Their form can be downloaded at http://wwww.namyco .org/toxicology and mailed in or completed and submitted electronically.

STORING AND CLEANING

Most mushrooms, if collected in pristine condition, will keep in the refrigerator for three to five days (*Coprinus* species excluded). The trick is to minimize moisture and eliminate preexisting critters. Toward that end, clean your mushrooms by brushing and/or cutting off excess soil, woody debris, crawlies, and the like (final cleaning will be done just before cooking); wrap them loosely in wax paper, or store them in brown paper lunch bags or in a large, uncovered plastic container lined with paper towels until ready to use. When it's time to cook or preserve your mushrooms, use a brush or damp paper towel to remove all dirt and debris. A knife may be required to cut away stubborn and imbedded bits and occasional larvae and tissue damaged by them. If you must use water, use as little as possible, as mushrooms can act like sponges.

COOKING

Mushrooms can be fried, broiled, sautéed, baked, grilled, and boiled. Generally, cooking quickly over higher heat (2-5 minutes) results in crisper, less intensely flavored mushrooms. Cooking over lower heat for a longer period (5-15 minutes) results in softer mushrooms with a more concentrated flavor. Since there is no single recommended cooking method, experiment and discover what you enjoy most when using your wild mushroom finds.

TESTING

Like various cuts of meat or different types of vegetables, each mushroom species has its own unique flavor, texture, and moisture content— all factors that should be considered when incorporating them into your cooking. You may absolutely love some mushrooms, while finding others to be off-putting or tasteless. It is also extremely important to make certain that you are not allergic to a particular mushroom species. Wheat and peanuts are good and safe edibles for most people, but they can be dangerous for those allergic to them. The same is true for mushroom genera. Each genus should be viewed as a new food group the first time you eat it. If you follow the two simple steps listed below when eating a wild mushroom that is new to you, you'll gain two important pieces of information while ensuring that you will not become severely or violently ill: you will learn whether you are allergic or sensitive to a particular species, and you will become familiar with their unique tastes, textures, and culinary characteristics, enabling you to better incorporate them into your favorite recipes.

- Thoroughly cook a very small amount in a bit of butter with a dash of salt, leaving the rest of your collection in the refrigerator for future consumption (or to take to the emergency room in the rare instance that you become ill).
- Eat a small bite or two (no alcohol, please!), and then wait twenty-four hours to gauge your reaction to it.

PRESERVING

Drying and freezing are the most common ways to preserve mushrooms. However, these methods are not interchangeable for all mushroom species. Some species reconstitute very nicely once dried, others . . . not so good. Certain mushrooms maintain their integrity when frozen, while others are reduced to unappetizing blobs. Below are some of the most commonly used preserving techniques, along with a list of a few species that are either well suited or not recommended for them. We intentionally do not recommend canning as a preservation method. Due to the very real risk of botulism when canning low-acid foods such as mushrooms, we consider it too time and labor intensive, and just too risky. If interested in this method, refer to page 4–13 of the USDA *Complete Guide to Home Canning* (2015), http://nchfp.uga.edu/publications/usda/GUIDE04_HomeCan_rev0715.pdf.

Before preserving mushrooms, regardless of the technique you choose, make sure to start with *thoroughly* cleaned, unspoiled fungi.

DRYING

You can dry mushrooms by stringing them on thread and hanging them in a well-ventilated area; or by placing them in a gas oven, using the heat from the pilot light; or placing them on screens in the sun; or even baking them in the oven. But these methods can result in spoilage due to incomplete or overly slow drying, insect infestation, or, in the case of drying them in the oven, over-drying/cooking (if interested in these methods, you can search the internet). In our opinion, the easiest and the most consistent way to dry mushrooms is to use a home food dryer or dehydrator. They use little energy and can be bought for about thirty-five dollars or more.

Slice large mushrooms into ¼ to ½ inch slices (small mushrooms can be cut in half or kept whole), place on the drying racks, and dry at approximately 90–95°F for a minimum of 24 hours. Larger pieces should be dried for approximately 36 hours. Dried mushrooms should not be soggy or bendable but should be crisp and lightweight. Place into airtight containers (ziplock plastic freezer bags work well), and pop these into your freezer for 2 weeks. This kills any remaining larvae and/or insect eggs. Once removed from the freezer, your dried fungi should keep indefinitely in a cool, dry, dark cupboard.

Drying works best for morels, all boletes, Black Trumpets (flavor will improve over time), and any fungi you plan to grind into mushroom powders. It is not recommended for *Grifola frondosa*, *Laetiporus* species, chanterelles, or oyster mushrooms.

Note: Sun drying, or exposing already dried mushrooms to UV rays or the sun for two days, will boost vitamin D levels. Place mushrooms in the sun, gill-side up. The increased vitamin D levels are held up to a year.

FREEZING

Slice or dice your mushrooms into whatever size you prefer and sauté in a 50:50 mixture of olive oil and butter, with a dash of salt, over medium-high heat (stirring often), for approximately 5 minutes—until almost all the expressed liquid has been cooked off. Allow to cool and place in ziplock freezer bags (express all air out of the bags) or other freezer-safe containers. No need to defrost frozen mushrooms before using, simply add them directly to whatever dish you are preparing (we like to freeze them in small amounts to simplify their use in cooking). Frozen mushrooms should keep well for approximately 6-8 months.

Freezing works best for *Laetiporus* species, *Grifola frondosa*, chanterelles, *Lactarius* species, *Tricholoma* species, *Russula* species, oyster mushrooms, and puffballs. It is not recommended for boletes.

SALTING/BRINING

A traditional preservation technique in Slavic countries, salting mushrooms is a relatively simple process that maintains a texture that is very much like fresh mushrooms. Salted mushrooms keep for several months once refrigerated.
It is *imperative* to *thoroughly* clean your mushrooms (only the caps are used!). Some sources recommend soaking the mushrooms in hot water to loosen dirt and then cleaning them under running water.

Method I

Prepare a brine using 7 ounces (approximately 11 tablespoons) of kosher salt per quart of water by adding salt to boiling water and stirring until dissolved. Allow to cool.
While the brine is cooling, make a 5-percent brine (2½ tablespoons of kosher salt per

quart of water), bring to a boil, and blanch the cleaned mushroom caps for 5 minutes. Drain and allow the mushrooms to cool in a single layer on paper or cotton towels.

Scald an earthenware crock or container, or glass jars or other non-reactive containers; arrange cooled mushroom caps in layers, gill-side down, covering each layer with the cooled brine, until the container is almost filled. Cover with clean cheesecloth or a plate, and place a weight on top. Store for approximately 4 days in a cool, dark place. Check daily to make sure the mushrooms are always covered with brine. Add more brine as needed. After 4 days, move the mushrooms and brine to clean jars and refrigerate.

Method II

Cover each layer of blanched, inverted mushroom caps with a layer of kosher salt mixed with herbs (such as juniper berries, dill, caraway seed, black pepper). Cover, weight, and refrigerate. After twenty-four hours, if they are not submerged in their expressed liquid, add brine to completely cover.

Desalt mushrooms before use by rinsing in cold running water or soaking in multiple changes of cold water, until desired degree of saltiness is reached. Salted mushrooms can be eaten as a traditional appetizer with rye bread and vodka or used as you would fresh mushrooms.

Salting works best for *Lactarius*, *Lactifluus*, oyster mushrooms, *Tricholoma*, and *Russula* species. It is not recommended for morels, boletes, *Laetiporus* species, and puffballs.

INFUSIONS

Infusion is the process of extracting flavors from plant materials in a solvent—in this case, alcohol. This is a creative process where you have the chance to experiment with combinations of fungal and other flavors and spices, very much as in cooking. A nice, mid-price alcohol is all you need. The higher the proof of the liquor used, the greater its ability to extract flavors. A "rectified spirit," either pure or slightly dilute (151–190 proof), will extract more flavor than an 80-proof vodka can and is best saved for medicinal or culinary infusions/extractions. Basically, the longer you allow the mushrooms to steep in the alcohol, the stronger the flavor will be. The more mushrooms and other flavors you add, the stronger the flavor will be. Vodka is the easiest alcohol to begin experimenting with due to its basic flavorlessness. As you progress in your infusion enthusiasm, think about trying fruit brandies or mild bourbons. Experiment with pairings of mushrooms and spices and other flavorings; tinker with vanilla and cinnamon and dried fruit and nuts; play with making sweet liqueur by adding 1-2 tablespoons of sugar (brown or white) per cup of alcohol to your mixture.

The process is a simple one: prepare your mushrooms and other ingredients, combine them in an immaculately clean glass container, and add the alcohol. Cover the container tightly and set it in a cool, dark place. Give it a shake each day to keep the flavors distributed and so, well, it doesn't feel forgotten, and you can keep your impatience at a nice, high pitch. Taste it daily, or every few days, until it reaches the flavor you like (caution: please taste responsibly—over-tasting may leave you with nothing but dregs if you aren't careful!). When the flavor is to your liking, strain the infusion using a coffee filter or several layers of fine cheesecloth to remove the solid bits. Rebottle, label, and store in a cool, dark place.

Here is an easy, basic infusion recipe to start you off.

CHANTERELLE INFUSED VODKA (COURTESY OF JASON BOLIN)

- ½ lb. fresh chanterelles—washed and allowed to sit out overnight to dry somewhat (if they aren't dry when you put them into the vodka, the infusion will be cloudy).
- Approximately 3-3.5 liters of vodka

Combine chanterelles and vodka in a large, clean glass jug or container. Most of the chanterelles will float; a few may sink based on their water content. Set in a cool, dark area for 2-3 days or until most of the chanterelles have sunk to the bottom (taste as you go; if allowed to sit longer, the color gets darker and the flavor stronger).

Once most of the chanterelles sink to the bottom, filter the infusion through coffee filters.

Pour back into the jug.

The infusion will keep for up to 3 months unrefrigerated.

Chanterelle infused vodka

Glossary

acidic: Having a sour or sharp taste.

acrid: Having an unpleasantly sharp and burning taste or smell.

acute: Having a sharp edge.

adnate (gills): Broadly attached to the stalk.

adnate-subdecurrent (gills): Broadly attached and running slightly down the stalk.

Adnexed (gills): Narrowly attached to the stalk and notched.

adnexed-emarginate (gills): Narrowly attached and notched near the stalk.

agglutinate, agglutinated: Becoming glued together.

aleuriospores: Stalkless asexual spores borne laterally.

allantoid: Sausage-shaped.

amygdaloid: Somewhat almond-shaped.

amyloid: Staining grayish to blue black in Melzer's reagent.

anamorph: The asexual stage.

anastomosing: Fusing to form a network.

angular: Having one or more angles.

angular-nodulose: Having one or more angles and tiny knots.

angular-ovoid: Somewhat egg-shaped with one or more angles.

anise-like (odor): Resembling licorice.

annular zone: A partially formed ring composed of partial veil remnants, also called a ring zone.

apex, apices: The uppermost portion.

apical: Pertaining to the uppermost portion.

apical pore: A small opening in the uppermost portion of the wall of a spore.

apiculate: Having a projection at or near the base of a spore.

appendiculate: Hung with fragments of the partial veil.

applanate: Horizontally expanded and shelf-like.

appressed: Flattened onto the surface.

appressed-fibrillose: Having fibrils that are flattened onto the surface.

appressed-strigose: Having long, coarse, stiff hairs that are flattened onto the surface.

appressed-tomentose: Having a thick coating of hairs that are flattened onto the surface.

appressed-wooly: Having a wooly coating of hairs that are flattened onto the surface.

arcuate: Curved like a bow or an arch.

arcuate-decurrent: Curved and extending down on the stalk.

areolate: Marked out into small areas by cracks or crevices.

arms: Extensions of the fruitbody that become coated with gleba.

aromatic: Having an agreeable aroma.

arthropods: Invertebrate organisms with jointed legs, such as beetles and spiders.

asci, ascus: Sac-like structures in which ascospores are produced.

ascospores: Sexual spores formed within an ascus.

aseptate: Lacking cross-walls.

asexual: Produced without the exchange of genetic information.

astringent: Tending to cause the mouth to pucker.

asymmetrical: Not identical on both sides.

attached (gills): Joined to the stalk.

azonate: Lacking zones or bands.

bacilliform: Rod-shaped, resembling a stick.

basal, base: The lowest portion.

basidiospores: Sexual spores formed on a club-shaped cell called a basidium.

basidium, basidia: A club-shaped cell on which basidiospores are formed.

baygall: A low-lying tract of boggy or spongy land that is acidic and commonly populated with trees and shrubs, such as Bay Laurel, Spicebush, Sweetbay Magnolia, and Sassafras.

bay-brown: Reddish brown or chestnut color.

bay-red: Various shades of reddish brown.

beaded: Having a row of exuded droplets.

bearded (margin): Adorned with hairs.

beveled: Obliquely slanted or sloped.

bioluminescent: Having the ability to produce and emit light.

bloom: A dull, thin coating that is typically whitish.

bogs: Acidic wet areas that are surrounded by sphagnum mosses.

brick-red: Rusty red to dull rusty red.

buff: Dull white to very pale yellow.

bulb, bulbed, bulbous: A somewhat rounded swelling.

burgundy: Deep red to reddish purple.

button(s): The immature stage of a mushroom.

caespitose: Occurring in clusters with their stalk bases fused, or nearly so.

calyptriform: Shaped like a lid or candle extinguisher.

campanulate: Somewhat bell-shaped.

canescence: A whitish to grayish dust-like bloom.

cap: The upper part of a mushroom which supports gills, tubes, spines, or a smooth surface on its underside.

carbonaceous: Dark colored, almost black.

carmine: Dark red or purplish red.

cartilaginous: Tough and fibrous, often splitting lengthwise in strands.

caulocystidia: Cystidia found on the stalk.

cavernous: Having hollow spaces.

central: At the middle.

cf.: Used to express a possible identity, or at least a significant resemblance.

chambered: Divided into distinct compartments.

chamois: Grayish yellow.

cheilocystidia: Cystidia that occur on the edge of a gill or the edge of a tube; compare with pleurocystidia.

chicory (odor): Resembling sweet roasted coffee.

chlamydospores: Thick-walled asexual spores.

chlorophyll: A green pigment in plants and some other organisms that absorbs light to provide energy for photosynthesis.

cilia: Slender filaments composed of a bundle of fibers and usually located on the top or margin of a fruitbody.

cinnabar: Vivid reddish orange.

clamp connections: A semicircular bridge-like structure that connects two adjoining cells.

clavate: Club-shaped.

cleft, clefted: A wedge-shaped vertical cut.

close (gills): Spacing that is halfway between crowded and subdistant.

coalesce, coalescing: Running together.

collarium: A collar or ring on the stalk apex into which the inner edges of the gills are inserted.

columella: A persistent sterile column within a spore case.

compressed: Flattened longitudinally.

concave: Having a surface that curves inward.

concentric, concentrically: Having rings or zones within one another in a series.

concolorous: Having the same color(s) as something else.

confluent: Merging and becoming continuous together.

conical: Having the shape of an inverted cone.

conic-umbonate: Having the shape of an inverted cone with a pointed or rounded elevation.

conidia: Asexual spores supported by tiny stalks.

conifer: A cone-bearing tree with needle-like leaves, such as pine.

convex: Curved or rounded like an inverted bowl.

convex-depressed: Curved or rounded and sunken in the middle.

convex-umbilicate: Curved or rounded and having a central funnel-shaped depression.

convoluted: Intricately folded.

copious: Having a large quantity.

corrugated: Coarsely wrinkled or ridged.

cortina: A spiderweb-like partial veil.

cortinate: Having spiderweb-like fibrils.

crenate: Scalloped to round-toothed.

crenulate: Very finely scalloped to round-toothed.

crescent: Resembling a half-moon or sickle-shaped.

crested: Having a showy tuft of projecting teeth.

crimped: Having small, regular folds.

crimson: Deep purplish red.

crinkled: Having small creases or wrinkles on the surface.

crossveined, crossveins: Having tiny wrinkles or raised ridges that connect adjoining gills.

crowded (gills): Having little or no space between gills or pores.

cuboid: Resembling a cube.

culinary: Of or for cooking.

curved-clavate: Club-shaped and curved.

cuticle, cuticular: The outermost tissue layer of the cap or stalk.

cyanophilous: Staining blue in a solution of cotton blue.

cylindric, cylindrical: Having the same diameter throughout its length.

cylindric-allantoid: Having the same diameter throughout and somewhat sausage-shaped.

cylindric-ellipsoid: Nearly having the same diameter throughout its length and resembling an elongated oval with similarly curved ends.

cylindric-oblong: Nearly having the same diameter throughout its length, longer than wide and with somewhat flattened ends.

cylindric-subclavate: Somewhat cylinder-like to somewhat club-shaped.

cystidia: Variously shaped sterile cells that project between, and usually beyond, the basidia, or on the surface of the cap or stalk.

daedaleoid: Resembling a maze.

decurrent: Running down the stalk.

decurrent tooth: A narrow extension of a gill or tube that extends a short distance down the stalk apex.

decurved: Bent downward.

deliquesced, deliquesces: Dissolved into an inky fluid.

depressed: Somewhat sunken.

dextrinoid: Staining orange to orange brown or dark red to reddish brown in Melzer's reagent.

dichotomously: Divided into two portions.

disarticulating: Separating at the cross-walls or joints.

disc: The central area of the surface of a cap.

distal: Farther away from the center.

distant (gills): Widely spaced.

distinctive (odor, taste): Recognizable and comparable to something known.

duplex: Consisting of two distinct layers of different textures.

eccentric: Away from the center but not lateral.

echinulate: Having small spines.

edges (gills): The sharp, free, lower portion most distant from the cap.

effused-reflexed: Spread out over the substrate and turned outward at the margin.

ellipsoid, ellipsoidal: Resembling an elongated oval with curved ends.

ellipsoid-cylindric: Elongated and somewhat cylindric.

ellipsoid-fusoid: Elongated and somewhat spindle-shaped.

ellipsoid-inequilateral: Resembling an elongated oval with unequal sides.

ellipsoid-oblong: Resembling an elongated oval but longer than it is wide and with somewhat flattened ends.

ellipsoid-ovoid: Resembling an elongated oval and somewhat egg-shaped.

elliptic, elliptical: Resembling an elongated oval with similarly curved ends.

elliptic-cylindric: Having nearly the same diameter throughout and slightly oval.

elliptic-fusiform: Somewhat elliptical and somewhat spindle-shaped.

elliptic-oval: Nearly oval and somewhat elongated.

elongate-ellipsoid: Extended and resembling an elongated oval.

emarginate (gills): Notched near the stalk.

embedded: Placed within and surrounded by other matter.

entire: Even, not broken, serrated, or torn.

eroded: Partially worn away and appearing ragged.

erumpent: Breaking through or bursting out.

evanescent: Slightly developed and soon disappearing.

exuded, exuding: Very slowly released.

faces: The sides of a gill.

fairy ring(s): A distribution of mushrooms in a circle which widens from year to year.

farinaceous: An odor variously compared to sliced watermelon rind, cucumber, meal, bread dough, or farina flour.

farinaceous-bitter: Having a mealy to cucumber-like taste with a bitter component.

fascicles: Little bundles.

fasiculate-tomentose: Having tiny hairs in small, scale-like bundles.

felty, felted: Having a texture that resembles a soft, non-woven matted fabric.

fenugreek (odor): A distinctive sweet odor resembling maple syrup.

fertile surface: The spore-bearing portion of the fruitbody.

FeSO4: Iron sulfate, also called iron salt, usually a 10 percent solution.

fetid: Having an offensive odor.

fibrils: Tiny fibers.

fibrillose: Composed of fibrils.

fibrillose-punctate: Having fibrils and tiny points, dots, scales, or spots.

fibrillose-scaly: With tiny scales composed of appressed fibrils.

fibrillose-tomentose: Coated with a thick, matted covering of fibers and hairs.

fibrous: Composed of fibers.

fibrous-cottony: Composed of fibers and resembling cotton balls.

filamentous: Composed of tiny threads.

filiform: Thread-like.

fimbriate: Minutely fringed.

fissured: Split or cracked.

flecked: Marked or dotted with small patches of color or particles.

flesh: The inner tissue of a fruitbody.

flexuous: Bent alternately in opposite directions.

floccose: Tufted like tiny cotton balls.

floccose-scaly: Having scales that are tufted like tiny cotton balls.

floccules, flocculence: Minute scaly tufts resembling cotton balls.

floral: Of or pertaining to flowers.

fluted: Having grooves and ridges.

forceps: Pincers or tweezers used to pick up tissues.

forked, forking: Divided into two or more branches.

fragrant: Having a pleasant scent or aroma.

frayed: Worn at the edge.

free (gills): Not attached to the stalk.

fringed: Decorated with tiny fibrils or hairs.

frondlike: Resembling a leaf, often with many divisions.

fruitbody, fruitbodies: The reproductive stage of a fungus, sometimes called a mushroom.

fulvous: Reddish cinnamon; colored like a red fox.

furfuraceous: Covered with scurfy particles.

furrowed: Marked by grooves.

fuscous: Dark brownish gray to brownish black or purplish brownish black.

fusiform: Spindle-shaped.

fusiform-ellipsoid: Mostly spindle-shaped and somewhat elongated.

fusiform-elliptic: Somewhat spindle-shaped and somewhat elongated.

fusoid: Somewhat spindle-shaped.

fusoid-ampullaceous: Swollen and somewhat spindle-shaped.

fusoid-clavate: Club-shaped and somewhat spindle-shaped.

fusoid-subventricose: Slightly enlarged in the middle and somewhat spindle-shaped.

fusoid-ventricose: Enlarged in the middle and somewhat spindle- shaped.

gelatinous: Having the consistency of jelly.

germination: The first step of spore development and transition to the next stage in its life cycle.

germ pore: A thin portion of the spore wall through which the hypha passes during germination.

germ slit: A fissure or crack in the spore wall that facilitates germination.

gills: Thin or thick, knifeblade-like structures on the undersurface of the cap of some mushrooms.

glabrous: Lacking hairs or scales, bald and smooth.

glancing: Showing shiny highlights when held at a certain angle.

gleba: The spore-bearing tissue of stinkhorns and puffballs, also called a spore mass.

globose: Round, resembling a globe.

gluten: A sticky, glue-like material.

glutinous: Composed of or having gluten.

granulose: Composed of tiny grains.

gregarious: Closely scattered over a small area.

hallucinogenic: Causing profound distortions in a person's perception of reality.

hardwood: Any non-cone bearing tree with broad leaves, such as beech or oak.

hemispherical: Shaped like one-half of a sphere.

herbivore: An animal that feeds on plants.

hexagonal: Having six angles and six sides.

hirsute: Covered with long, stiff fibers or hairs.

homogeneous: Composed of uniform cells or tissue.

honeydew: A sweet, sticky substance excreted by aphids.

host: An organism which supports a parasite or pathogen; also a mycorrhizal partner.

humus: The organic portion of soil formed by the decomposition of leaves and other plant material.

hyaline: Clear and nearly colorless.

hygrophanous: Appearing water-soaked when fresh and fading to a paler color as water is lost.

hygroscopic: Readily absorbing water.

hymenial: Pertaining to the spore-bearing layer of a fungus.

hyperparasite: A parasite that is parasitic on another parasite.

hyphae, hyphal: Thread-like filaments of fungal cells.

hypogeous: Occurring below the ground surface.

imbricate: Overlapping one another like shingles.

inamyloid: Unchanging or staining pale yellow in Melzer's reagent.

incised: Appearing cut into.

incrusted: Covered with a thin, hard crust.

incurved: Bent inward toward the stalk.

infundibuliform: Somewhat funnel-shaped.

inrolled: Bent inward and upward toward the stalk.

intervenose: Having veins on the gill faces that often extend between the gills or from gill to gill.

invertebrate: Lacking a backbone.

involucres: An acorn cupule, a cap.

KOH: Potassium hydroxide, usually a 5–14 percent concentration in water.

labyrinthine: Resembling a maze.

lacerate: Appearing as if torn.

lacrimoid: Shaped like a teardrop.

lamellate: Having gills.

lamellulae: Short gills.

lanceolate: Of much greater length than width and tapering.

larvae, larval: The immature, wingless, feeding stage of an insect.

lateral, laterally: On the side or edge.

latex: A watery or milk-like fluid that exudes from some mushrooms when cut or bruised.

lattice: A grid-like diagonal structure.

lavender: A pale tint of purple.

lilaceous: Pale bluish purple.

lobe(s), lobed: A subdivision with a rounded margin.

longitudinal, longitudinally: Oriented along the vertical axis of the stalk.

lubricous: Smooth and slippery.

macrochemical reactions: Color changes that occur on tissues of the fruitbody when observed with the unaided eye.

macrochemical reagents: Chemical substance added to various portions of the fruitbody to determine color reactions.

macrofungi: Fungi big enough to be seen with the unaided eye.

macroscopic, macroscopically: Able to be seen with an unaided eye.

marbled: Having flecks or streaks of a different color.

margin, marginal: The edge of a mushroom cap.

marginate (basal bulb): Having a circular ridge on a bulb.

marginate (gills): Having edges that are darker than the faces.

marginate-depressed (basal bulb): Having a narrow, circular, horizontal platform on the upper side.

maze: A complex network of interconnected pathways.

median (ring): Situated near the middle of the stalk.

medulla: The most central zone of a fruitbody, composed of parallelly arranged hyphae.

Melzer's reagent: A solution containing iodine, potassium iodide, chloral hydrate, and water, used to test spores and tissues for color reactions.

membranous: Having a membrane.

microscopic: Requiring a microscope to be seen.

mottled, mottling: Having spots or blotches of different shades or colors.

multipointed: Having several or many points.

multiseptate: Having several or many cross-walls.

mycelial, mycelium: Pertaining to a mass of hyphae, typically hidden in a substrate.

mycologists: People who study fungi.

mycophagists: People who eat fungi.

mycorrhizal: Having a mutually beneficial relationship with a tree or other plant.

napiform: Turnip-shaped, bulbous above and tapered below.

NH4OH: Ammonium hydroxide.

non-mycorrhizal: Not forming a relationship with the roots of trees or other plants.

non-striate: Lacking striae.

obclavate: The reverse of clavate, narrowing toward the apex.

obconical: Reversely conical, having the shape of an inverted cone.

oblanceolate: Having a much greater width than length and tapering.

oblique, obliquely: In a slanting direction.

oblong: Longer than wide and with somewhat flattened ends.

oblong-cylindric: Longer than it is wide with somewhat flattened ends and nearly the same diameter.

oblong-ellipsoid: Longer than wide and resembling an elongated oval with curved ends.

oblong-elliptical: Longer than wide and somewhat elliptic.

obovoid: Egg-shaped, with the broader end opposite to the point of attachment.

obpyriform: Reversely pear-shaped.

obtuse: Rounded or blunt.

ocher: Brownish orange yellow.

ochraceous: Pale brownish orange yellow.

olivaceous: Slightly more yellow than olive.

ornamented: Having the surface decorated with warts, spines, reticulation, or other markings.

ostioles: A small, pore-like opening.

oval: Egg-shaped.

ovoid: Somewhat egg-shaped.

pallid: Having an indefinite pale or whitish appearance.

pantropical: Distributed in tropical regions of both hemispheres.

papillate: Having a small, nipple-shaped elevation.

paraphyses: Distinctive sterile cells that keep asci erect.

parasites: Organisms that obtain nutrients from another living organism and cause harm or injury.

parasitic, parasitized, parasitizes: Obtaining nutrients from a living host and causing harm or injury.

partial veil: A layer of tissue that covers the gills or pores of some immature mushrooms.

pathogen: A disease-producing organism.

pectinate: Resembling a comb.

pedicel: A slender stalk.

pendant: Hanging or draping.

perennial: Continuing growth from year to year.

peridiole(s): Tiny egg-like structure that contains spores.

peridium: A rind that surrounds the fertile tissue in a truffle, puffball, or similar fungus.

perithecia: Minute flask-shaped structures containing asci and ascospores.

phallic: Shaped like an erect penis.

phenolic: Pertaining to a class of aromatic compounds that are sometimes used to treat wood or as disinfectants.

photosynthesis: The process by which green plants and some other organisms use sunlight to produce sugar.

pileate: Having a cap or head.

pileipellis: The outermost layer of a mushroom cap, also called a cuticle.

pith: Soft tissue in the interior of a stalk.

plane: Nearly flat.

plano-convex: Shaped like an inverted bowl and nearly flat.

pleated: Repeatedly folded.

pleurocystidia: Sterile cells located between basidia on the faces of gills or on the inner surfaces of tubes.

plicate: Folded like a fan.

pore(s): The open end of a tube, also called the tube mouth.

pore mouth: The opening on a spore case through which spores are expelled.

pore surface: The underside of the cap of a bolete or polypore.

poroid: Resembling pores or composed of pores.

prominences: Extensions projecting from the surface.

pruina: Powdery particles, flakes, or dots.

pruinose: Appearing finely powdered.

pruinose-tomentose: Finely powdered and covered with thick, matted hairs.

pruinose-velvety: Finely powdered with a smooth, soft feel.

pseudoamyloid: Staining deep purplish brown in Melzer's reagent.

pseudoreticulate: Having a false reticulum usually formed by anastomosing ridges.

pseudorhiza: A root-like extension of the stalk.

pubescent: Having short, soft, downy hairs.

pulverulence, pulverulent: Appearing somewhat powdered.

pulverulent-floccose: Powdery and tufted like tiny cotton balls.

pulvinate: Cushion-shaped, slightly convex.

punctae: Tiny points, dots, scales, or spots.

punctate: Marked with tiny points, spots, dots, or scales.

pungent: Having a strong, sharp smell.

pupae: The non-feeding stage of an insect before becoming an adult.

pyramidal: Shaped like a pyramid.

pyriform: Somewhat pear-shaped.

radial, radially, radiate, radiating: Pointed away from a common central point, like the spokes of a wheel.

radicating: Having a root-like basal extension in soil.

rancid: Smelling or tasting unpleasant.

rancid-farinaceous: Smelling or tasting mealy to cucumber-like and unpleasant.

rays: Pointed pieces of a split spore case.

reagents: Chemicals used for making slide mounts for microscopic examination or for observing macroscopic or microscopic color changes.

recurved: Curved backward or downward.

resin, resinous: Composed of a sticky lacquer that may solidify to form a shiny crust.

resinous dots or smears: Small marks or patches of a sticky resin.

resupinate: Reclining on the substrate and facing outward.

reticulate, reticulated, reticulation, reticulum: Raised net- like ridges found on the stalk surface or spores of some mushrooms.

reticulate-shaggy: Having a shaggy, net-like pattern of ridges.

revolute: Rolled back or up.

rhizomorph(s): A thick, cord-like strand of hyphae growing together as a unit.

rimmed (basal bulb): Marked with an encircling outer edge.

rimose: Having distinct cracks or crevices.

rimose-areolate: Cracked and forming tiny patches.

rimulose-areolate: Finely cracked and forming tiny patches.

ring: Remnants of a partial veil that remains attached to the stalk after the veil ruptures, or the uppermost flaring portion of a sheath.

ring zone: Faint remnants of a partial veil, usually composed of tiny fibers, attached to the stalk.

rosette(s): Arranged in the shape of rose petals.

rounded-conic: Having the shape of a rounded inverted cone.

rudimentary: Having a very small stature.

rugose-venose: Coarsely wrinkled and vein-like.

rugulose: Finely wrinkled.

saccate: Sheath-like or cup-shaped.

saprotrophs: Organisms that feed on dead or decaying matter.

scabers: Small, stiff, granular projections on the stalk of some boletes.

scales: Flattened, erect, or recurved projections or torn portions of a cap or stalk surface.

scalloped: Having a wavy outer edge.

scaly-punctate: Marked with tiny dots or points composed of scales.

scarlet: A bright red to slightly orange-tinted red.

sclerotia, sclerotium: Small, rounded to irregular structures composed of dormant hyphae.

scrobiculate: Pitted or smeared, having flat, shiny areas.

scurfy: Roughened by tiny flakes or scales.

seceding (gills): Attached at first and later separating.

semicircular: Shaped like one-half of a circle.

septa, septate: Cross-walls, divided by cross-walls.

serpentine: Having an alternating coil-like pattern that resembles the movement of a snake.

serrate, serrated: Jagged or toothed like a saw blade.

setae: Sharply pointed, microscopic, sterile cells that are usually brown or yellow.

setal hyphae: Thick-walled, pointed, brown hyphae found in the marginal tissue of some polypores.

sexual: Produced with the exchange of genetic information.

sheath, sheathed, sheathing: An outer sock-like tissue layer covering the stalk base upward, at least to the mid-portion.

silicates: Compounds containing the element silicon.

silky-fibrillose: Composed of smooth, soft fibrils.

sinuate: Having a wavy or winding form.

sinuous: Somewhat wavy.

sinuous-daedaleoid: Resembling a maze and somewhat wavy.

sordid: Dingy or dull.

spermatic: Having the odor of semen.

sphagnum moss(es): A type of moss occurring mostly in wet, acidic habitats, especially bogs.

spinulose: Having little spines.

spongy-pliant: Soft, flexible, and tending to be water-soaked.

spore case: A sac-like structure that contains the spore mass.

spore mass: A dense layer of spores produced by puffballs or stinkhorns, also called a gleba.

spore print: A deposit of spores on paper, glass, or some other surface.

spores: Microscopic reproductive cells.

squamules, squamulose: Small scales.

stalk: The erect structure that supports the cap, head, or spore case of a fruitbody.

sterigmata: Tiny, spike-like projections of a basidium on which basidiospores are produced.

sterile (cap margin): Having cuticle tissue that extends beyond the gills, tubes, or other reproductive structures on the underside of the cap.

striae, striate: Small and somewhat parallel lines or furrows.

strigose: Covered with long, coarse, stiff hairs.

stroma: A cushion-like mass of cells in or on which fruitbodies are produced.

stuffed: Containing a soft tissue that usually disappears in age, leaving a hollow space.

subapical: Slightly below the apex.

subcentral: Slightly away from the center.

subcylindric: Having nearly the same diameter throughout the length.

subdecurrent: Extending slightly down the stalk.

subdistant (gills): Halfway between close and distant.

subellipsoid, subellipsoidal: Somewhat like an elongated oval.

subelliptic, subelliptical: Pertaining to a somewhat elongated oval.

subfusiform, subfusoid: Nearly spindle-shaped.

subfusoid: Somewhat spindle-shaped.

subfusoid-ellipsoid: Somewhat spindle-shaped and resembling an elongated oval with curved ends.

subglabrous: Nearly bald.

subglobose: Nearly round.

subhygrophanous: Fading somewhat as the cap dries.

submarginate (basal bulb): Having somewhat of a circular ridge on a bulb.

submembranous: Somewhat resembling a membrane.

subnapiform: Somewhat turnip-shaped.

suboblong: Somewhat longer than wide and with more or less flattened ends.

subovate: More or less egg-shaped.

subovoid: Slightly egg-shaped.

substrate(s): Organic matter that serves as a food source for fungal mycelium, such as soil, leaves, or wood.

subtomentose: More or less woolly.

subumbonate: Slightly and usually broadly raised.

subventricose: Somewhat swollen in the middle and tapered in both directions.

subviscid: Slightly sticky or tacky.

sulcate: Grooved; deeper than striate, less than plicate.

sulcate-striate: Having small and somewhat parallel lines or furrows and slightly deeper grooves.

superior (ring): Located on the upper portion

of the stalk.

swamp: An area of low-lying land that is always wet and often flooded.

symmetrical: Having equal halves facing each other.

synonym(s): An alternate name that has been replaced by a more current one.

taproot: An underground extension of the stalk that tapers downward.

tawny: Dull yellowish brown.

taxa, taxon: A taxonomic group of any rank, such as a species, class, or family.

teliomorph: The sexual stage.

terminal: Situated at the end or extremity.

tiers: A series of rows of different lengths.

tomentose: Coated with a thick, matted covering of hairs.

tomentose-fibrillose: Coated with a thick, matted covering of hairs and fibers.

tomentum: A covering composed of long, soft, hairy filaments that are tangled or matted like wool.

trama: The sterile tissue supporting the spore-bearing layer.

translucent: Allowing light to pass through while causing structures on the other side to not be sharply visible.

translucent-striate: Appearing to have lines or furrows when gill edges are viewed through moist, nearly transparent cap tissue.

transversely: Arranged in a crosswise manner.

trichodermium: A cuticle with the distal portion of the filiform elements of equal length and arranged perpendicularly to the surface.

truncate, truncated: Appearing cut off at the end.

truncate-conic (cap): Having the shape of an inverted cone with a cut-off end.

truncate-ovoid: Somewhat oval with a cut-off end.

tuberculate: Having small warts or bumps.

tuberculate-striate: Having lines or furrows that are roughened by small warts or bumps.

tubes: Narrow, parallel, spore-producing cylinders on the underside of the cap of boletes or polypores.

tufted-erect: With upright, short, compact clusters arising from a common base.

tufts: Short, compact clusters arising from a common base.

twisted-striate: Having parallel lines that spiral.

umbilicate: Having a central, funnel-shaped depression.

umbo, umbonate: A rounded or pointed elevation at the center of some mushroom caps.

undulate, undulating: Somewhat wavy.

uninucleate: Having a single nucleus.

uniseriate: Arranged in a single row.

universal veil: A layer of tissue that completely encloses immature stages of some mushrooms.

vegetative: Non-reproductive hyphae that support or take up nutrients.

ventricose: Swollen in the middle and tapered in both directions.

ventricose-rostrate: Swollen in the middle, tapered in both directions, with a beak-like projection.

verrucose: Covered or marked with small, rounded processes or warts.

vinaceous: Having the colors of red wines.

viscid: Sticky or tacky.

volva, volval: The remains of a universal veil at the stalk base of some gilled mushrooms or the base of the spore case of stinkhorns.

warts, warted: Small patches of tissue on the top of some mushroom caps or blunt projections on the wall of some spores.

whey-like: Watery white.

xeric: Containing little moisture; very dry.

zonate: Marked with concentric bands of color.

zones, zoned: Concentric rings or bands on the cap or stalk of some mushrooms.

References and Resources

PRINT

Arora, D. 1979. *Mushrooms Demystified*. Berkeley, CA: Ten Speed Press. 959 pp.

Babikova, Z., L. Gilbert, T. J. A. Bruce, M. Birkett, J. C. Caulfield, C. Woodcock, J. A. Pickett, and D. Johnson. 2013. "Underground Signals Carried through Common Mycelial Networks Warn Neighboring Plants of Aphid Attack." *Ecology Letters* 16:835–843. Doi:10.1111/ele.12115 [PubMed]

Bessette, A. E., A. R. Bessette, D. P. Lewis, and S. H. Metzler. 1993. "A New Substrate for *Strobilurus conigenoides*." (Ellis) Singer. *Mycotaxon* 68:299–300.

Bessette, A. E., A. R. Bessette, and D. W. Fischer. 1997. *Mushrooms of Northeastern North America*. Syracuse, NY: Syracuse University Press. 584 pp.

Bessette, A. E., A. R. Bessette, and M. W. Hopping. 2018. *A Field Guide to Mushrooms of the Carolinas*. Chapel Hill, NC: University of North Carolina Press. 432 pp.

Bessette, A. E., A. R. Bessette, W. C. Roody, and S. A. Trudell. 2013. *Tricholomas of North America: A Mushroom Field Guide*. Austin, TX: University of Texas Press. 208 pp.

Bessette, A. E., D. B. Harris, and A. R. Bessette. 2009. *Milk Mushrooms of North America: A Field Identification Guide to the Genus Lactarius*. Syracuse, NY: Syracuse University Press. 299 pp.

Bessette, A. E., O. K. Miller, A. R. Bessette, and H. H. Miller. 1995. *Mushrooms of North America in Color: A Field Guide Companion to Seldom Illustrated Fungi*. Syracuse, NY: Syracuse University Press. 188 pp.

Bessette, A. E., W. C. Roody, and A. R. Bessette. 2000. *North American Boletes: A Color Guide to the Fleshy Pored Mushrooms*. Syracuse, NY: Syracuse University Press. 400 pp.

———. 2016. *Boletes of Eastern North America*. Syracuse, NY: Syracuse University Press. 469 pp.

Bessette, A. E., W. C. Roody, A. R. Bessette, and D. L. Dunaway. 2007. *Mushrooms of the Southeastern United States*. Syracuse, NY: Syracuse University Press. 375 pp.

Bessette, A. E., W. C. Roody, W. E. Sturgeon, and A. R. Bessette. 2012. *Waxcap Mushrooms of Eastern North America*. Syracuse, NY: Syracuse University Press. 179 pp.

Bessette, A. R., and A. E. Bessette. 2001. *The Rainbow Beneath My Feet: A Mushroom Dyer's Field Guide*. Syracuse, NY: Syracuse University Press. 176 pp.

Beug, M. W. 2009. "Worldwide Mushroom Poisoning, Diagnosis and Treatment: Comments on Some of the Recent Research." *Fungi* 2(3):11–15.

Beug, M. W., A. E. Bessette, and A. R. Bessette. 2014. *Ascomycete Fungi of North America: A Mushroom Reference Guide*. Austin, TX: University of Texas Press. 488 pp.

Binion, D. E., S. L. Stephenson, W. C. Roody, H. H. Burdsall Jr., L. N. Vasilyeva, and O. K. Miller Jr. 2008. *Macrofungi Associated with Oaks of Eastern North America*. Morgantown, WV: West Virginia University Press. 467 pp.

Both, E. E. 1993. *The Boletes of North America: A Compendium*. Buffalo, NY: Buffalo Museum of Science. 436 pp.

Brundrett, M. C., and B. Kendrick. 1987. "The Relationship Between the Ash-Tree Bolete (*Boletinellus merulioides*) and an Aphid Parasitic on Ash Tree Roots." *Symbiosis* 3:315–320.

Burdsall, H. H. Jr., and M. T. Banik. 2001. "The Genus *Laetiporus* in North America." *Harvard Papers in Botany* 6:3–55.

Buyck, B., C. Cruaua, A. Couloux, and V. Hofstetter. 2011. "*Cantharellus texensis* sp. nov. from Texas, A Southern Lookalike of *C. cinnabarinus* Revealed by Tef-1 Sequence Data." *Mycologia* 103(5):1037–1046.

Buyck, B., I. Olariaga, B. Looney, J. Justice, and V. Hofstetter. 2016. "Wisconsin Chanterelles Revisited and First Indications for Very Wide Distributions of *Cantharellus* Species in the United States East of the Rocky Mountains." *Cryptogamie Mycologie* 37(3):345–366.

Buyck, B., I. Olariaga, J. Justice, D. Lewis, W. Roody, and V. Hofstetter. 2016. "The Dilemma of Species Recognition In the Field When Sequence Data Are Not in Phase with Phenotypic Variability." *Cryptogamie Mycologie* 37(3):367–389.

Buyck, B., and V. Hofstetter. 2011. "The Contribution of Tef-1 Sequences to Species Delimitation in the *Cantharellus cibarius* Complex in the Southeastern USA." *Fungal Diversity* 49:35–46.

Buyck, B., V. Hofstetter, and I. Olariaga. 2016. "Setting the Record Straight on North American *Cantharellus*." *Cryptogamie Mycologie* 37(3):405–417.

Buyck, B., V. Hofstetter, U. Eberhardt, A. Verbeken, and F. Kauff. 2008. "Walking the Thin Line between *Russula* and *Lactarius*: the Dilemma of *Russula* subsect. *Ochricompactae*." *Fungal Diversity* 28:15–40.

Cibula, W. G. 1979. "Fungi of the Gulf Coast I. Two New Species of *Hygrophorus* Section *Hygrocybe*." *Mycotaxon* 10(1):105–115.

Cibula, W. G., and N. S. Weber. 1996. "*Hygrocybe andersonii* A New Psammophilus *Hygrocybe* from Horn Island, A Mississippi Barrier Island." *Mycologia* 88(3):514–516.

Coker, W. C. 1974. *The Club and Coral Mushrooms (Clavarias) of The United States and Canada*. Reprint. New York, NY: Dover. 209 pp.

Coker, W. C., and A. H. Beers. 1970. *The Stipitate Hydnums of the Eastern United States*. Berlin: J. Cramer. 86 pp.

Coker, W. C., and J. N. Couch. 1974. *The Gasteromycetes of the Eastern United States and Canada*. Reprint. New York, NY: Dover. 283 pp.

Elliott, T. F., and S. L. Stephenson. 2018. *Mushrooms of the Southeast*. Portland, OR: Timber Press. 407 pp.

Frank, J. L., A. R. Bessette, and A. E. Bessette. 2017. "*Alessioporus rubriflavus* (Boletaceae), A New Species from the Eastern United States." *North American Fungi* 12(2):1–8.

Freeman, A. E. H. 1979. "*Agaricus* in the Southeastern United States." *Mycotaxon* 8:50–115.

Gilbertson, R. L., and L. Ryvarden. 1986. *North American Polypores. Vol. 1*. Oslo: Fungiflora. 433 pp.

———. 1987. *North American Polypores. Vol. 2*. Oslo: Fungiflora. 451 pp.

Hesler, L. R. 1967. *Entoloma in Southeastern North America*. Berlin: Cramer. 195 pp.

Jenkins, D. T. 1986. *Amanita of North America*. Eureka, CA: Mad River Press. 198 pp.

Kerrigan, R. W. 2016. *Agaricus of North America*. Bronx, NY: New York Botanical Garden Press. 572 pp.

Kimbrough, J. 2000. *Common Florida Mushrooms*. Gainesville, FL: University of Florida. 342 pp.

Largent, D. L., D. Johnson, and R. Watling. 1977. *How to Identify Mushrooms to Genus III: Microscopic Features*. Eureka, CA: Mad River Press. 148 pp.

Lewis, D. P., and C. Ovrebo. 2009. "Mycological Literature on Texas Fleshy Basidiomycota, Two New Combinations, and New Fungal Records for Texas." *J. Bot. Res. Inst. Texas* 3(1):257–271.

Lewis, D. P., and W. G. Cibula. 2000. "Studies on Gulf Coast Agarics (Basidiomycota: Agaricaceae); Notes on Some Interesting and Rare Species." *Texas J. Science* 52(4) Supplement:65–78.

Lincoff, G. H. 1981. *The Audubon Society Field Guide to North American Mushrooms*. Alfred A. Knopf, New York, NY. 926 pp.

Looney, B. P., J. M. Birkebak, and P. B. Matheny. 2013. "Systematics of the Genus *Auricularia* with An Emphasis on Species from the Southeastern United States." *North American Fungi* 8(6):1–25.

Mata, J. L., and R. H. Petersen. 2001. "Type Specimens Studies in New World *Lentinula*." *Mycotaxon* 79:217–229.

Metzler, S., V. Metzler, and O. K. Miller Jr. 1992. *Texas Mushrooms*. Austin, TX: University of Texas Press. 350 pp.

Mueller, G. M. 1992. "Systematics of *Laccaria* (Agaricales) in the Continental United States and Canada, with Discussions on Extralimital Taxa and Descriptions of Extant Types." *Fieldiana*. Series 30. Publication 1435. Field Museum of Natural History, Chicago, IL. 158 pp.

Nguyen, Nhu H., et al. 2016. "Phylogenetic Assessment of Global *Suillus* ITS Sequences Supports Morphologically Defined Species and Reveals Synonymous and Undescribed Taxa." *Mycologia* 108(6):1216–1228.

Nuhn, M. E., M. Binder, A. F. S. Taylor, R. E. Halling, and D. S. Hibbett. 2013. "Phylogenetic Overview of the Boletineae." *Fungal Biol* 117:479–511.

Ortiz-Santana, B., W. C. Roody, and E. E. Both. 2009. "A New Arenicolous *Boletus* from the Gulf Coast of Northern Florida." *Mycotaxon* 107:243–247.

Osmundson, T. W., and R. E. Halling. 2010. "*Tylopilus oradivensis* sp. nov.: A Newly Described Member of the *Tylopilus balloui* Complex from Costa Rica." *Mycotaxon* 113:475–483.

Petersen, R. H., and K. Hughes. 2014. "Cauliflower Tales." *McIlvainea* 23:13–15.

Petersen, R. H., K. W. Hughes, J. Justice, and D. P. Lewis. 2014. "A New Species of *Gomphus* from Southeastern United States." *North American Fungi* 9(9):1–13.

Redhead, S. A., R. Vilgalys, J.-M. Moncalvo, J. Johnson, and J. S. Hopple Jr. 2001. "*Coprinus* Pers. and the Disposition of *Coprinus* Species *sensu lato*." *Taxon* 50:203–241.

Roody, W. C. 2003. *Mushrooms of West Virginia and the Central Appalachians*. Lexington, KY: University Press of Kentucky. 520 pp.

Singer, R., J. Garcia, and L. D. Gomez. 1990. *The Boletineae of Mexico and Central America I and II*. Berlin: J. Cramer. 73 pp.

———. 1991. *The Boletineae of Mexico and Central America III*. Berlin: J. Cramer. 128 pp.

———. 1992. *The Boletineae of Mexico and Central America IV*. Berlin: J Cramer. 62 pp.

Singer, R., and A. H. Smith. 1943. "A Monograph on the Genus *Leucopaxillus* Boursier." *Papers of the Michigan Academy of Sciences, Arts and Letters* 28:85–132.

Singer, R., and R. Williams. 1992. "Some Boletes from Florida." *Mycologia* 84: 724–728.

Smith, M. E., and D. H. Pfister. 2009. "Tuberculate Ectomycorrhizae of Angiosperms: the Interaction between *Boletus rubropunctus* (Boletaceae) and *Quercus* Species (Fagaceae) in the United States and Mexico." *American Journal of Botany* 96(9):1665–1675.

Snell, W. H., and E. A. Dick. 1957. *A Glossary of Mycology*. Cambridge, MA: Harvard University Press. 181 pp.

Tulloss, R. E., and D. P. Lewis. 1994. "*Amanita westii*—Taxonomy and Distribution. A Rare Species from States Bordering the Gulf of Mexico." *Mycotaxon* 50:131–138.

Weber, N. S., and A. H. Smith. 1985. *A Field Guide to Southern Mushrooms*. Ann Arbor, MI: University of Michigan Press. 280 pp.

Woehrel, M. L., and W. H. Light. 2017. *Mushrooms of the Georgia Piedmont and Southern Appalachians*. Athens, GA: University of Georgia Press. 647 pp.

Wolfe, C. B., Jr., and R. E. Halling. 1989. "*Tylopilus griseocarneus*, A New Species from the North American Atlantic and Gulf Coastal Plain." *Mycologia* 81:342–346.

WEBSITES

MushroomExpert.com: www.mushroomexpert.com

Mushroom Observer: www.mushroomobserver.org

Index Fungorum: www.indexfungorum.org

Studies in the Amanitaceae: http://www.amanitaceae.org

A Note on
the Authors

Alan E. Bessette, PhD, is a professional mycologist and distinguished emeritus professor of biology at Utica College of Syracuse University. A member of the North American Mycological Association, the Asheville Mushroom Club, and the Gulf States Mycological Society, he has published numerous papers in the field of mycology and has authored or coauthored more than twenty-five books, including *Edible Wild Mushrooms of North America, Mushrooms of the Southeastern United States, Ascomycete Fungi of North America*, and his most recent book, *A Field Guide to the Mushrooms of the Carolinas*. Alan served as a consultant for the New York State Poison Control Center for more than twenty-five years. During that same time, he also acted as the scientific adviser to the Mid-York Mycological Society. He has been the principal mycologist at national and regional forays and was the recipient of the 1987 Mycological Foray Service Award and the 1992 North American Mycological Association Award for Contributions to Amateur Mycology. In addition to teaching workshops and seminars, Alan volunteers at state parks and reserves providing mycological surveys and educational programs. His current mycological interests include subtropical fungi.

Arleen Bessette, MA, is a retired psychologist, as well as a mycologist and botanical photographer. She has been collecting and studying wild mushrooms for more than forty years. A member of the North American Mycological Association, the Asheville Mushroom Club, and the Gulf States Mycological Society, Arleen has published several papers in the field of mycology and has authored or coauthored eighteen books, including *Mushrooms of the Southeastern United States, Boletes of Eastern North America, The Rainbow Beneath My Feet: A Mushroom Dyer's Field Guide*, and her most recent book, *A Field Guide to the Mushrooms of the Carolinas*. She has won several awards in the North American Mycological Association's annual photography competition, including top honors in both the documentary and pictorial divisions. In addition to volunteering at various state parks and research reserves providing mycological surveys and educational programs, Arleen also teaches national and regional workshops and seminars on varying aspects of mycology. She especially enjoys working with beginning myco-enthusiasts and the newly myco-curious. Her special passions include dyeing with mushrooms, the culinary aspects of mycophagy, and the potential medicinal uses of fungi.

David P. Lewis, MS, is a retired chemist and dedicated mycologist, with a BS and MS from Lamar University, Beaumont, TX, where his master's thesis was based on a study of East Texas mushrooms. David is currently a research associate with the Field Museum of Natural History in Chicago and an honorary staff member of the S. M. Tracy Herbarium at Texas A&M University. As president of the Gulf States Mycological Society since 1998, he has led many mushroom walks, looked for new fungal records from the Gulf Coast and Mexico, and offered his fungal knowledge to many naturalist groups. From 2006 to 2018, he was the Fungal TWIG (coordinator for mycologists) for the Big Thicket National Preserve All Taxa Biodiversity Inventory. David has described many new species and is proud to have had several named for him. In 2009, he received the North American Mycological Association's Award for Contributions to Amateur Mycology, and in 2010, the R. E. Jackson Conservation Award from the Big Thicket Association.

Photo Credits

Except for the following, all the photographs in this book were taken by the authors.

Jason Bolin: *Boletellus ananas, Boletus luridellus, Ganoderma zonatum* (A), *Pulchroboletus rubricitrinus, Tylopilus minor, Tylopilus rhodoconius*

Eric Bush: *Cymatoderma caperatum* (B)

Bill Cibula: *Cantharellus minor, Hygrocybe chamaeleon, Hypholoma ericaceum*

Jim Craine: *Lactarius salmoneus* var. *salmoneus*

Neil Dollinger: *Fomitiporia apiahyna, Ganoderma lobatoideum, Ganoderma tuberculosum, Tomophagus colossus*

Robert Dulaney: frontispiece (Lucas Dulaney with *Amanitas*)

Tim Geho: *Aseroe rubra*

Dan Guravich: *Agaricus rhoadsii, Agrocybe retigera, Amanita flavorubescens, Amanita hesleri, Amanita muscaria* var. *flavivolvata, Amanita thiersii, Amanita volvata* group, *Boletus aurantiosplendens, Calostoma cinnabarinum, Chlorophyllum hortense, Craterellus odoratus, Gymnopilus liquiritiae, Gyromitra caroliniana, Hortiboletus rubellus, Hydnopolyporus palmatus, Lactarius peckii* var. *peckii, Morchella angusticeps, Phallus hadriani, Psilocybe cubensis, Pulveroboletus curtisii, Ramaria conjunctipes, Ramaria fennica, Ramaria murrillii, Ramaria subbotrytis, Russula eccentrica, Tremella foliacea, Tylopilus balloui, Tylopilus indecisus*

Rosanne Healy: *Elaphomyces granulatus* complex

Mike Hopping: *Agaricus pocillator, Clavaria zollingeri, Inonotus hispidus, Pluteus cervinus, Trametes villosa*

Jesús Garcia Jiménez: *Boletinellus rompelii, Clathrus crispus, Lysurus periphragmoides* (A)

Laurel Kaminski: *Inonotus amplectens*

Renée Lebeuf: *Clavariadelphus truncatus, Gymnopus dryophilus* (B), *Ophiocordyceps melolonthae, Tolypocladium ophioglossoides*

Joe Liggio: *Underwoodia columnaris*

Taylor Lockwood: *Glaziella aurantiaca*

Jim Murray: *Chorioactis geaster*

Beatriz Ortiz-Santana: *Boletus aureissimus*

Sarah Prentice: *Parasola plicatilis*

Bill Roody: *Abortiporus biennis, Amanita farinosa, Amanita jacksonii, Amanita onusta, Amanita parcivolvata, Aureoboletus innixus, Aureoboletus russellii, Austroboletus gracilis* var. *gracilis, Baorangia bicolor* complex, *Boletus abruptibulbus, Boletus auripes, Boletus longicurvipes, Boletus pallidus, Boletus roodyi, Boletus variipes, Buchwaldoboletus lignicola, Butyriboletus frostii, Caloboletus inedulis, Cantharellus lateritius, Cantharellus velutinus, Clavariadelphus americanus, Clavulinopsis aurantiocinnabarina, Cyanoboletus pulverulentus, Cyptotrama asprata, Entoloma incanum, Gelatoporia dichroa, Gymnopus dryophilus* (A), *Gyroporus castaneus, Gyroporus cyanescens, Humaria hemi-sphaerica, Hygrocybe andersonii, Hygrophorus sub-sordidus, Hymenopellis furfuracea, Inocybe rimosa, Laccaria amethystina, Lactarius chrysorrheus, Lactarius subpalustris, Lactifluus allardii, Lactifluus petersenii, Lactifluus volemus* var. *volemus, Leccinellum crocipodium, Leccinum rugosiceps, Lentinus arcularius, Limacella illinita, Lycoperdon marginatum, Lysurus periphragmoides* (B), *Macowanites arenicola, Marasmius nigrodiscus, Marasmius rotula, Multifurca furcata, Panaeolina foenisecii, Panus neostrigosus, Phallogaster saccatus, Phylloporus leucomycelinus, Phylloporus rhodoxanthus, Psathyrella delineata, Pulveroboletus auriflammeus, Retiboletus griseus* var. *fuscus, Rhodocollybia maculata, Russula ballouii, Russula earlei, Russula parvovirescens, Russula subsericeonitens, Russula variata, Stereum subtomentosum, Trametes versi-color, Tricholoma niveipes, Tricholoma odorum, Tricholoma portentosum, Tylopilus alboater, Tylopilus badiceps, Tylopilus rubrobrunneus, Tylopilus violatinctus, Wolfina aurantiopsis, Xerocomus hortonii, Xerocomus illudens/Xerocomus tenax* complex (B)

Christian Schwarz: *Clavariadelphus ligula*

Mary Smiley: *Agaricus endoxanthus, Cantharellus cocolobae, Cymatoderma caperatum* (A), *Gymnopilus palmicola, Leucoagaricus meleagris, Russula decolorans, Russula mariae*

Matt Smith: *Tuber lyonii*

Walt Sturgeon: *Calocera cornea, Daldinia concentrica, Entoloma strictius, Xylaria polymorpha*

Tom Taroni: *Blumenavia angolensis*

Robert Williams: *Clavulina floridana*

Rosemary Williams: photograph of Robert S. Williams

Index to Common Names

Index to Scientific Names

Pages on which species descriptions and illustrations appear are indicated by **boldface**.